W9-BGM-535

Promised Lands

David M. Wrobel

PROMISED LANDS

Promotion, Memory, and

the Creation of the American West

 University Press of Kansas

Published by the University Press of Kansas (Lawrence, Kansas 66049), which was organized by the Kansas Board of Regents and is operated and funded by Emporia State University, Fort Hays State University, Kansas State University, Pittsburg State University, the University of Kansas, and Wichita State University

Library of Congress Cataloging-in-Publication Data

Wrobel, David M.

   Promised lands : promotion, memory, and the creation of the American West / David M. Wrobel.

      p.   cm.

   Includes bibliographical references and index.

   ISBN 0-7006-1204-1 (alk. paper)

   1. West (U.S.)—Civilization—19th century.   2. Regionalism—West (U.S.)—History—19th century.   3. West (U.S.)—History, Local. 4. West (U.S.)—Economic conditions—19th century.   5. City promotion—West (U.S.)—History—19th century.   6. National characteristics, American.   7. Pioneers—West (U.S.)—Social conditions—19th century.   8. Pioneers—West (U.S.)—Biography. 9. Frontier and pioneer life—West (U.S.)   10. Memory—Social aspects—West (U.S.)—History—19th century.   I. Title.

F591 .W93 2002

978'.02—dc21   2002007539

British Library Cataloguing in Publication Data is available.

Printed in the United States of America

10 9 8 7 6 5 4 3 2 1

The paper used in this publication meets the minimum requirements of the American National Standard for Permanence of Paper for Printed Library Materials Z39.48-1984.

For Janet, with love

Contents

Acknowledgments

The present study began at the Newberry Library in the summer of 1996, although I did not know it at the time. I had planned to examine three kinds of writing—overland diaries, booster tracts, and pioneer memoirs—all within the framework of a larger study of western regional identity, and I began by reading through a large selection of all three genres in the Newberry's Graff Collection of Western Americana. Yet the boosters and reminiscers kept reemerging in my thinking about western regionalism. The juxtaposition of promoters' imaginative, and not altogether candid, acts of place creation and pioneers' creative and purposeful reimagining of those places gradually emerged as the focus of my study. The overland travel diaries were fascinating, too, but the scholarly ground that accompanied them seemed as well traveled as the migrants' trails themselves. The boosters and reminiscers, by contrast, had received less attention from scholars and were rarely treated together.

Over the next few years I did some traveling of my own, across the country each summer to continue researching the project at the Huntington Library in San Marino, California. These annual trips to the Huntington involved work in a wide range of that institution's rich archival and rare book holdings and secondary works. But whenever the larger study of western regional identity seemed to be growing to unmanageable proportions, the promotional and reminiscence sources kept bringing me back to the fascinating parallels and departures between the visions of promoters and pioneers.

My greatest intellectual debts are to individuals, libraries, and universities. First and foremost, the Huntington Library offered both fellowship support and the fellowship of a community of scholars interested in the West, who discussed the topic with me and led me to new sources. Peter Blodgett, H. Russell Smith Curator of Western History Manuscripts at the Huntington, has been an invaluable guide over the years, leading me through the institution's collections and providing a close reading of some of the chapters. Western history curator Jennifer Martinez has also taken the time to explore the reminiscers with me, while Jennifer Watts, Curator of Western Photographs, has shared her extensive knowledge of California boosterism. All three are exceptionally busy people who take the time to assist other researchers and in doing so help make the Huntington such a wonderful place.

The many members of the Huntington's community of scholars whose insights have sharpened my thinking include Clark Davis, William Deverell, Janet Fireman, Greg Hise, David Igler, the late Wilbur Jacobs, Karen Lystra, Carlos Schwantes, Michael Steiner, David Weber, and Elliott West. Alan Jutzi, Avery Chief Curator of Rare Books, Erin Chase, Library Assistant, and the entire Reader Services staff of the Huntington—Christopher Adde, Romaine Ahlstrom, Jill Cogen, Susi Krasnoo, Anne Mar, and Mona Noureldin—all deserve special mention for their patience, good cheer, and enthusiastic support, which make the Ahmandson Room and the General Reading Room of the Huntington such pleasant places to research, reflect, and write.

While the Huntington became home base for the project, I am also grateful to Chicago's Newberry Library, particularly to its Director, James R. Grossman; Curator, John Aubrey; and former Director, Fred Hoxie. At the University of Wyoming's American Heritage Center (AHC), reference archivist Carol Bowers and historian-editor Phil Roberts kindly guided me to pertinent collections. Both the Newberry and the AHC provided grants and excellent curatorial support. The staff of the Denver Public Library's Western History Collection, especially Philip Panum, and those at Berkeley's Bancroft Library were tremendously helpful during my brief visits. The American Philosophical Society gave funding for the project, as did my former institution, Widener University. I am particularly grateful to Widener for a series of Provost's Grants and Faculty Development Grants that supported the project during my time at that institution.

I spent the spring semester of 1999 at the Center of the American West at the University of Colorado at Boulder and benefited enormously from the Center's interdisciplinary emphasis and the intellectual energy of its Faculty Director, Patricia Nelson Limerick, and core faculty member, William Travis. The Center's breakfast reading group provided invaluable feedback on some of the chapters in their earliest stage, and Patty's comments, as anyone who has learned from her close reading of text would expect, led me to rethink some of my early assumptions. The Center provided an intellectual home and one that I was fortunate to return to in the summer of 2001 to codirect a National Endowment for the Humanities–funded institute for schoolteachers, titled "Perceiving the American West: Expectations and

Outcomes." That experience also sharpened my thinking on western American promotion and memory. I am grateful to all the institute participants and faculty for their spirited discussions, to the Center for inviting me to direct the institute, to the NEH for funding it and providing expert guidance, and to my codirector, Barbara Miller.

Martin Ridge, Walter Nugent, and Charles Alexander all read the final draft of the manuscript and made excellent suggestions for improvement. Charles, my graduate school mentor, encouraged me to complete the manuscript in an expeditious manner. Martin, who has become a mentor to me over the past decade or so, offered similar encouragement. Walter, for the second time in my career, took the time to write extensive commentary on a manuscript. Nancy Scott of the University Press of Kansas offered a series of close readings of the chapters and constant encouragement for the project from the very beginning. I am fortunate to have worked with such an excellent editor, and press, over the years.

The History Department at the University of Nevada Las Vegas has provided the best assistance that a teacher-scholar can ask for—a collegial and supportive environment. My colleagues in western history, Hal Rothman and Andrew Kirk, provided commentary on the book's concluding chapter. The department seminar group, organized by Paul Werth, offered a constructive reading of the introduction and chapter 1. My UNLV graduate students in the historiography course, colloquium, and research seminar, respectively, also offered keen insights on matters related to the project. Mary Wammack, my graduate assistant in spring 2001, provided excellent feedback too.

My greatest debt of all is to my wife, Janet Ward-Wrobel, whose love and support always puts all things into proper perspective; she is my greatest fortune. *Promised Lands* is dedicated to Janet.

Introduction: Imagining and Remembering

In a single statement in 1869, A. G. Brackett summed up two important aspects of white European American thinking about the western United States. He proclaimed:

> The days of isolation for the Far West of the American Continent are rapidly passing away, and the completion of the Pacific Railroad opens a new era in the progress of our Territories. . . . The dull and monotonous mode of traveling by wagon across the Plains is nearly a thing of the past; and he who has accomplished that feat will speak of it years hence as something which reflects great credit upon himself, and is certainly difficult to be realized by those who pass across now in comfortable cars on the Pacific Railroad.[1]

Brackett looked to the future when the West would no longer be a frontier and, at the same time, emphasized that the hardships of the frontier past would be well remembered in that more settled future by participants in the great pioneer adventure. Those two sentiments, the hope for a postfrontier future in the West, followed later by a longing for the frontier past, have played an important part in the formation of western identities. These sentiments are borne out in two genres of western American writing: promotional literature and pioneer reminiscences. This book examines those genres in the late nineteenth and early twentieth centuries. The genres are treated here together, in Janus-like formation, because the ways in which imaginary futures and pasts intersect with and depart from each other illustrate the complicated process by which popular perceptions of the West and white westerners' sense of place in the region were formed and sustained over time. The West treated here is the area from the Pacific Coast to the second tier of trans-Mississippi states (from the Dakotas to Texas), that is, the Plains States and the eleven far western ones that constitute the Census West.[2]

Promotional writings and old-timer recollections have been produced for most places and at various points in time; they are by no means exclusive to the American West in the half century or so from the 1870s to the 1930s. The significance of these particular promotional and reminiscence literatures arises in large part from their production at a particular cultural moment in America: the much-discussed age of anxious transition from the premodern to the modern. In the midst of this shift from the agrarian and small town to the industrial and urban, western promoters hurriedly raced toward the future, often announcing its presence before it had actually arrived, while old settlers lamented that arrival and expressed their reverence for past times.[3]

During this period, boosters literally tried to imagine western places into existence through embellished and effusive descriptions. Sometimes they were successful, and sometimes not. Some western backwaters were transformed into prosperous, heavily populated urban communities; others remained undeveloped and disconnected from networks of trade and transportation. But these boosters were, almost invariably, optimistic fortune-tellers who told present and prospective residents what they wanted and needed to hear about western places. They placed the clear, bright future in the cloudier, less certain present and in doing so tried to brush away the concerns of potential settlers. They often presented desolate frontiers as settled regions, rich in culture and infrastructure, blessed with commercial and agricultural advantages, and devoid of danger and privation. In doing so, the promoters influenced both the sense of place of western residents and the sense that prospective residents and other Americans had of western places.

This study first focuses on the promotional tracts produced for western towns and farmlands in the period from the end of the Civil War into the 1920s. This literature is voluminous; it includes a mass of maps, broadsides, books, posters, pamphlets, cartoons, and magazine and newspaper articles and editorials, all designed to help lure settlers and investors to "new" western places. There were also bodies of promotional writing that sought to draw miners, loggers, migratory farm hands, and other workers into the region's extractive industrial economies and agribusinesses. Since the present analysis emphasizes the relationship between promotion and western sense of place, attention centers on the boosting of permanent settlement rather than on efforts to fill shifting labor needs with transitory workers.[4] Promotional guides were produced by every western state and territory, by multistate regions, such as the Inland Empire of the Northwest, and by many individual counties, in addition to the guides produced by railroad promotional departments for western states, territories, and regions, to induce settlement.[5]

The booster booklets, pamphlets, and maps could be received for the cost of postage or were distributed entirely at the cost of the promoters. They were mostly printed in English, though larger promotional entities, such as railroads, also offered their optimistic wares in the European languages of those countries from which immigrants were being solicited. State- and county-level publications were financed by the railroads or by state immigration societies and chambers of commerce; they were produced in lots of 10,000, 15,000, or even 20,000 or 30,000 per year. Clarence A. Lyman's *Fertile Lands of Colorado and Northern New Mexico,* a publication of the Denver and Rio Grande Railroad, in its ninth edition by 1908, claimed to be the most widely disseminated gratuitously circulated land book ever produced, with over 150,000 copies printed and distributed by that date. The ninth edition added another 15,000 copies to the total.[6] These materials were generally updated every year or two. In any given year there would have been millions of copies of western promotional books and pamphlets in circulation in the United States and Europe.[7] They were such a common sight in people's homes and in public spaces that we can assume most literate Americans and Europeans had some exposure to the promoters' visions of western lands.[8]

Generally within a decade or two after boosters had begun to promote a particular western location, old settlers and pioneers, residing in that now settled region, reminisced about the dangerous and demanding frontier experience of journeying to and settling there. They contrasted those earlier conditions with the ease, comfort, and overcivilization of the new West. Their lamentations over lost or faded frontiers can be found in privately and commercially published books and unpublished manuscripts, articles in regional journals, and the nostalgic annual proceedings of pioneer and old settler societies. These printed reminiscences also appeared in huge numbers—tens of thousands of them adorn the shelves of academic libraries and state historical societies. Pioneer societies began to form all across the West in the decades after the Civil War, and most of them remained active into the Great Depression years.

Western promotional materials and pioneer reminiscences, respectively, constituted visions of western prospects and pasts; they were imaginative efforts to bring places into existence or to hold on to earlier incarnations of places that had since changed. These two bodies of writing are treated here as distinct yet interconnected genres. The booster and reminiscence texts share common qualities, narrative techniques, and purposes.[9] The two genres could be dismissed as, respectively, the lies of unscrupulous salesmen (there were few female booster writers) and the improbable recollections of aging frontiersmen and women—the tall tales of nearly dead white males and females. The promoters could be regarded as the used-car dealers of an earlier age, the reminiscers as the unreliable fisherman chroniclers of yesteryear, whose fish grow ever larger as time recedes and their stories are retold. One's initial impulse in commenting on these writings is to adopt a cynical or ironic tone, to emphasize the vast gulf between rhetoric and reality that characterizes them.

But it is important to treat these sources as reflections of the purpose of their creators rather than as accurate descriptions of past places and events. These acts of imagining and remembering the West may not help us much in reconstructing certain specifics of the western past. Promotional tracts and pioneer reminiscences are thoroughly unreliable as objective gauges of "past reality" (itself a slippery phenomenon) because they were produced for very definite purposes; yet all historical sources are, in some degree, the products of purposeful creation. Those purposes are the focus of this study. The mimetic accuracy of these writings as reconstructions of past places is not the issue here; rather, it is their centrality to the processes by which popular perceptions of the West were constructed, elaborated, disseminated, and sustained. Promoters and reminiscers have generally been placed on the peripheries in scholarly writing about the West. In *Promised Lands,* both groups are placed at the center.

Many boosters were themselves recent pioneers, and they enthusiastically and imaginatively portrayed their western places as promised lands because they desperately wanted their own dreams to be realized. Old settlers' memories of "frontier" adventures and hardships were designed in part to maintain or restore their social status in a new West where some of them felt increasingly irrelevant. The adventures and hardships that they recalled (and may or may not have actually experienced) helped them define their place in changing western cultural environments.

These "western" pioneer remembrances were by no means entirely new, of course. Old settlers of Kentucky, the Midwest, the Arkansas backcountry, upstate New York, and other earlier frontiers also wrote reminiscences. Those previous frontiers of white settlement had their promoters, too, Daniel Boone being among the most memorable.[10] Indeed, we could trace the antecedents of the promotional literature produced for the trans-Mississippi West back to the land advertisements of the late eighteenth century, or even to those produced for the original North American colonies starting in the early to mid–seventeenth century.[11] Furthermore, the settlement of the Midwest, the rush of families into the Oregon Territory starting in the mid-1840s, the California gold rush beginning in 1848, and the Colorado gold rush a decade later were all marked by a voluminous booster literature.[12] Meanwhile, promoters of the city of Chicago, in the middle of the nineteenth century, were taking urban boosterism to new heights.[13] And midwestern promoters continued their efforts to attract settlers in the post–Civil War years, expressing their frustration that the westward migration was only passing through their own promised lands.[14]

Even though those who promoted and those who reminisced about the trans-Mississippi West in the half century or so after the Civil War were just the latest in a long line of imaginers and rememberers on Anglo-American frontiers, it is still true that those lands beyond the Midwest were considered the very last frontiers of settlement. They were the last Wests, the final places where the promise of the white national epic of settlement, with all its varied consequences, would be played out and vividly remembered. This cultural moment derives its significance from the transition going on in America from "island communities" to a more modern, ordered, and integrated nation, from a frontier to a postfrontier society (in the estimation of boosters, old pioneers, and many other Americans).[15] That transition is illuminated by the promoters' denials of the frontier's presence and the reminiscers' lamentations over its passing.

THE STUDY OF western American boosterism is beset with complications that merit discussion. Like all boosters, and like today's advertisers, promoters of the trans-Mississippi West in the late nineteenth and early twentieth centuries were selling promises as well as products. Yet the boosters were more than just earlier versions of contemporary advertising executives.[16] The booster mentality needs some explaining. "The American booster," Daniel Boorstin wrote in 1965, "often was simply speaking in the future tense, asserting what could not yet be disproved." "Especially in the booming West," he further noted, "men acquired a habit of innocent overstatement. . . . As tall talk confused fact and fiction in interestingly uncertain proportions, so booster talk confused present and future."

Boorstin added that "Americans thought they were not exaggerating but only anticipating—describing things which had not yet quite gone through the formal reality of taking place."[17] Historian Gene Gressley, speaking more broadly of a "western character," has noted that "psychologically, he [the westerner] evidenced a freewheeling optimism, a booster enthusiasm that belied his insecurity."[18]

Nonetheless, to explain away the linguistic excesses and factual oversights of western boosters with the claim that they were only anticipating the future, or were just acting out deep-rooted psychological insecurities, is a little too kind. Western American boosting in the late nineteenth and early twentieth centuries was more than just the innocent exaggeration of a few minor details in the cause of bringing the future into being. Supremely optimistic and imaginative accounts of western wonderlands could make even the Garden of Eden seem a little plain. Some boosters were great anticipators, trying to convince themselves as much as others of the promise of western places; others were bold-faced liars selling promises for financial profit and nothing more. But given that boosters of particular western towns and regions were often seeking in their vivid, Arcadian portrayals of western places to counter the often equally exaggerated criticisms of those places penned by boosters of other western locales, some of their excesses become more understandable.[19] Inter- and intrastate rivalries raised the stakes and shaped the heady rhetoric of western boosterism.

So who were these confident image makers? They represented a tremendously varied range of individuals, groups, and entities. Included among them were local newspaper and journal editors (such as California's indomitable Charles Fletcher Lummis and William Allen White of Kansas), local commercial clubs, local and state-level chambers of commerce, along with immigration societies, boards of agriculture, real estate agents, speculators, and landowners, writers for the railroads (such as Robert Edmund Strahorn for the Union Pacific and Benjamin Cummings Truman for the Southern Pacific), and outside colonization societies.[20] It is worth recognizing the presence of both "interior" and "exterior" forces of boosterism, the former composed of those people and organizations within a region, and the latter consisting of outside elements interested less in the character and society of the place itself than in simply profiting from it. However, the lines that separate these two broad categories are far from rigid.

Some of these individuals and organizations resided in and had financial and perhaps psychological attachments to the places they promoted. They had a deep personal investment in lauding the new areas they called home because the very survival of those places, and consequently their own well-being, depended on others viewing their region or town as a promised land and moving to it. There were, in this vein, energetic individuals who wrote hundreds, even thousands, of letters urging potential settlers to relocate to their paradises in the making. Such busy correspondents included Mari Sandoz's father, Jules Sandoz, immortalized in her biography, *Old Jules* (1935). Jules Sandoz (whose promotional efforts are discussed in greater detail in chapter 2) was absolutely relentless in his efforts to draw settlers to western Nebraska and was an exceptionally memorable character. Yet his approach was quite representative of the efforts of thousands of interior boosters across the late-nineteenth-century and early-twentieth-century Wests.[21]

Meanwhile, other promoters and promotional bodies, most generally the outside ones, had only economic interests, not psychological investments, in the western places they described, selling places like they would any other commodities. Yet the goals of interior and exterior boosters often intersected, and they frequently worked together to promote the flow of settlement and capital to western places. Moreover, it seems almost impossible at times to separate the insiders from the outsiders. People who had lived in a town for a mere matter of months, or even weeks or days (newspaper editors are a good example), could become the most committed promoters of that place's fortunes before they had developed any real affinity for the place.[22]

It is difficult to assess the extent to which organized, institutionalized promotional efforts were the determining factor in drawing settlers to western lands.[23] They certainly constitute a treasure trove of information on the ways in which western places were presented to American and European audiences over the course of a half century. Of course, we do not know what percentage of the readers who were exposed to the promotional literature were captivated by the promise of western places and migrated to them. Readers seldom recorded their reactions to the boosters' purple prose. Promotional writings certainly played some part in convincing potential migrants to take a chance, but whether the booster tracts were more influential than letters from friends and relatives already living in the West is hard to determine. And, of course, in weighing the various factors motivating migration, we would do well to remember economic privation and political or religious persecution. "Push factors" sometimes did more to motivate migration than did "pull factors." In some cases, mass-produced promotional materials may have been the deciding factor in an individual's, a family's, or a whole colony's decision to relocate to the West. In many other cases, however, the testimony of people who were known by the potential migrants—friends, acquaintances, and family members—played the primary role in sustaining the process of chain migration. The booster tracts in such cases may have served a supporting but nonetheless significant role in the alleviation of anxieties and the fortification of hearts and minds.[24]

Moreover, the Old Juleses of the West displayed a phenomenal energy level as promotional correspondents, which rendered them institutions in and of themselves. They can be viewed as a bridge between the more typical writers of occasional letters to friends and family members encouraging migration to particular western locations, and the authors of mass-produced promotional tracts for formal institutions such as railroads, states, territories, and chambers of commerce. The lines separating formal, institutionalized western town and land promotion from the informal processes of chain migration are, like the lines between interior and exterior promotional forces, at best faint and permeable. The key issue, then, is not whether formal or informal processes of place promotion were more significant—whether chain migration was more significant than promotional tracts—but how these processes were interconnected and mutually reinforcing.

The optimistic offerings of the boosters often contrasted sharply with the realities faced by new settlers in the West. The boosters' descriptions of fertile, Edenic lands with mild climates certainly did not approximate the grim realities of the early decades of farming in much of the semiarid West. But neither did the encouraging letters of new western residents to friends and family members provide truly objective depictions of western places. In seeking familiar faces to join them, they were trying to bring the promise of their new places to fruition, and such purposes necessitated the employment of no small degree of artistic license. These interior boosters wrote far less often about how places had failed to live up to their promise.[25] Furthermore, such informants were engaging in the most natural and understandable human processes of self-justification. They had taken chances in starting new lives in these locales and wanted to convince those they had left behind of their satisfaction with the momentous decisions they had made. Perhaps these self-conscious correspondents helped alleviate their own doubts and anxieties and bolstered their own commitment to the promise of their new lands through the act of writing optimistic letters to send back to their old homes. The thoughtful observer would surely not view the gap between the actual realities of western places and the expected conditions of those places (as expressed in letters sent back home) as evidence for conscious deceitfulness on the part of settlers.

Nonetheless, western writers and historians—in the tradition of Mark Twain's portrayal, in his novel *The Gilded Age* (1873), of the roguish land speculator Colonel Beriah Sellers—have emphasized the glaring incongruity between promoters' descriptions of western lands and the actual conditions faced by settlers on those lands, and they have been quick to condemn the boosters' excesses.[26] The tendency to weigh up promotional claims against the physical realities of the places being boosted, for the purpose of highlighting the disparity between promise and actual product, between expectations and outcomes, is a common one. However, at times western places indeed developed the kinds of cultural amenities and economic infrastructures that seemed to substantiate the exaggerated rhetoric of the boosters, despite the latter's ardent denials that they engaged in it. These stories of economic success, cultural development—of "progress," to use the language of that time—characterized as they are by consistency between promotional promises and lived realities, are less likely to capture the attention of contemporary scholars and are less well suited to the ironic trope so often employed in scholarship on promotion and in cultural studies of advertising. With all this in mind, we would do well to move beyond irony as the operative trope for writing about boosterism. This approach has the effect of making the boosters seem alien to us, rather than helping us understand them. Boosters of the West were simply too pervasive, too representative an element on the American scene during the late nineteenth and early twentieth centuries (and arguably still today), for us to treat them as anomalous.

Another not uncommon scholarly tendency has been to view western boosters as the human embodiment of the worst excesses of unbridled American capitalism—to demonize them rather than dismiss them. In such dualistic models—of unscrupulous booster villains (in the employ of a corporatist state) and unsuspecting settler victims—the lines connecting intentions and consequences are more clearly drawn than the complexities of their relationship merit.[27] A markedly less ideologically driven approach is taken here. The present study treats the West's promoters and their texts (like the reminiscers and their texts) in a nonteleological manner.[28] The key contours of these writings are outlined, and an attempt is made to trace their influence, rather than to pass judgment on their authors. Instead of searching for direct causal relationships between the assumed malign intent of boosters and the suffering of innocent settlers, I seek to highlight the range of motivating factors involved in this story of western promise and product.

As noted earlier, these promotional descriptions, which constituted a sizable fraction of the fin de siècle reading matter for Americans, must have influenced the way people in the West and the rest of the country thought about the various parts of the region. These books and pamphlets, filled with literary and pictorial images of lands of opportunity, may have served as a psychological safety valve of sorts, providing the possibility of alternative lives for people who nonetheless stayed where they were.[29] The majority of people who perused such sources, perhaps even the majority of those who read them carefully, did not relocate to the West. Still, this mountain of printed promises surely played an important part in shaping people's perceptions of the West.[30]

Explorations of the relationship between this genre of writing and the formation of regional identity are further complicated by the concept of westernness. This concept is largely the intellectual property of white Americans and is very much a product of popular mainstream mythology. Evidently, such a heritage compromises its usefulness in analyses of identity formation in a culturally diverse region. The West's different cultural groups think about westernness in different ways, and some groups may not think about it at all, which diminishes its value as a theoretical construct. Promoters, as we will see, struggled with these related issues of race and westernness.

What is more, as noted earlier, since there is no consensus on the matter of how long one has to reside in a western place to be considered a resident, it is often hard to tell the inside promoters from the outsiders, the westerners from the nonwesterners. It is clear that local and state-level chambers of commerce, immigration societies, and boards of agriculture often worked closely with exterior forces, such as railroad companies, to promote settlement and to develop towns and regions.[31] Understanding this helps undermine notions that western places were simply created, colonized, and generally "acted upon" by outside forces;[32] the relationship between the West's promoters and the growth of American corporate capitalism is more complex than that.[33] Indeed, the study of western promotional imagination and its consequences is characterized by these kinds of complications. Hence, analysis of the subject has to be, in some degree, speculative and suggestive rather than definitive.

SIMILAR COMPLICATIONS MARK the examination of western American reminiscence and the study of memory in general. As white western residents reflected on their roles in the early settlement of their regions, they certainly did not remember havens of culture, climate, and agriculture. Nor were images conjured up of superior schools, mild and equable temperatures, or lands as fertile as those of the Nile Valley. Instead, they remembered the antithesis of the booster's settled, regional West. They recalled harsh frontier Wests of the kind that test and strengthen the human spirit and temper the human constitution. Those residents chose to remember the kinds of places that existed, as the boosters had so fervently claimed, solely in the realm of the imagination. Old settlers did this because their purpose in remembering the past was very different from that of the future-oriented boosters. Nonetheless, pioneer reminiscers, like the boosters before them, still had one textual "eye" focused clearly on the present.

Triumphal tales of white pioneer males (and, to a lesser extent, of white pioneer females) dominated the public consciousness of the West for at least a century and still do, to no small degree, today. Only in recent decades, in fact, has important scholarship on a more racially and ethnically varied and interestingly gendered western past started to have a noticeable effect on that archetypal public consciousness of the region and its past. It is hardly surprising, given this context, that pioneer societies and published pioneer reminiscences have not seemed the most promising of source materials for contemporary scholars of the West. Those pioneer voices (like the voices of the promoters) have been regarded—or discarded—as part of the fabric of the mythic veil that needs only to be lifted for the true face of the western past to be revealed. Nonetheless, in exploring the development of western regional identities, it is wise to keep the tallest of tall tales in our historical frameworks, since mythology and regional consciousness are so fundamentally intertwined. To an important degree, the very endurance of the frontier heritage—with all its implications for race relations—owes its success to the prolific storytelling and organizational efforts of old pioneers. The mythic West is so much easier to deconstruct within scholarly contexts than it is to exorcise from the public consciousness because, in part, of the efforts of older generations in playing up the adventures and glories of the frontier past. The powerful legacy of pioneer reminiscences helps explain why the West's mythic veil is so difficult to remove.[34]

Scholarship on the construction of western mythology, when it is not focusing on amateur and professional historians (most notably, Theodore

Roosevelt and Frederick Jackson Turner, respectively), centers on famous literary figures (including Owen Wister, Zane Grey, and Louis L'Amour), artists (such as Charles Russell and Frederic Remington), filmmakers (including John Ford), and performers (such as Annie Oakley and Buffalo Bill Cody) as the builders of the mythic frontier West.[35] All these memorable individuals certainly played a pivotal role in forging a frontier-western heritage. But the lesser-known participants in the events of that great and often lamentable drama (such as John Burt Colton and Ezra Meeker, whom we will meet in chapter 3), by clinging so steadfastly to their memories of those events, were also vital to that process of frontier heritage preservation. By actively, albeit selectively, remembering their pioneer days, hundreds of thousands of Americans helped forge a meaningful past for themselves, and in lamenting the frontier's passing, they helped ensure its persistence as a theme in the popular consciousness. The centrality of the frontier concept to Anglo-American thought in this period is not diminished by the passing of the model of frontier process as a paradigm for explaining the western past.

In studying these old frontier reminiscers, we need to move beyond any inclination to merely examine the accuracy of people's memories for the purpose of assessing the validity or truthfulness of their accounts. Clearly quantifiable measures of truthfulness are hard to come by when investigating the murky realm of memory and its narrative formations. According to psychologists, "individuals construct memories in response to changing circumstances," and they "reshape their recollections of the past to fit their present needs." We know that on a collective level, "people develop a shared identity by identifying, exploring, and agreeing on memories."[36]

Historian Clyde Milner, in exploring the process by which regional consciousness formed in Montana, has pointed to four "layers" of regional identity: "region as personal locale," "region as national epic," "region as reaction" (i.e., reaction to other peoples, other regions, and even the nation as a whole), and "region as shared memory." Of these categories it is the third and fourth that will occupy this study. Pioneer and first settler organizations, Milner notes, "promoted the informal transmission of shared memories among pioneers."[37] Furthermore, as this book bears out, the two categories of regionally shared memory and reaction-based memory clearly intersect with each other. Regionalism, indeed, can be formed by means of reaction, particularly to other peoples—generally those from later generations—and other places where the process of pioneering was deemed to have been less demanding.

Memories, of course, are not just recollected or reproduced: they are constructed, even invented. The pioneers' purposefully created selective memories were intended to ensure that their authors' roles in history would not be forgotten in the present or the future. Pioneer reminiscers, to borrow the words of Michael Kammen, "arouse[d] and arrange[d] [their] memories to suit [their] psychic needs."[38] The important question in studies of these kinds of memories, David Thelen notes, is "not how accurately a recollection fitted some piece of a past reality, but why historical actors constructed their memories in a particular way at a particular time."[39] Hence, the pioneer reminiscences, like the promotional literature, can be most profitably used as a mirror to reflect the outlook of those doing the reminiscing, rather than as a clear window on the actual events that are described between the covers of their accounts. Older generations of westerners were trying to maintain their status in a changing West by reminding younger generations of the pivotal role they had played in the past.

One suspects, however, that the West's multitudinous pioneer reminiscers were more successful in sustaining the frontier heritage than they were in sustaining their own importance in changing western environments. They helped develop a frontier mythology through their selective memories but hardly maintained any kind of hegemonic control over western social, economic, and political institutions. This latter observation informs our analysis of collective memory. Sociologist John Walton points to two quite distinct theoretical approaches to the production and maintenance of collective memories. The first is the theory of "cultural hegemony," inspired by Antonio Gramsci's political philosophy and Raymond Williams's cultural theory. According to this approach, the same forces that dominate the economic and political machinery of society also control cultural production and create history (through texts and monuments) for the purpose of legitimating their power and preserving the status quo. Collective memories are vital to this purposeful preservation of the established order, and they amount to a kind of "selective tradition." The second is the notion of "social memory," which draws on the ideas of sociologist Maurice Halbwachs and emphasizes the variety of memories produced by different groups within any given society. Explaining this position, Walton notes that it regards collective memory "less [as] a matter of imposed ruling ideas than [as] a plurality of mental worlds that exist in conflict with or insularity from competing ideas." According to this position, collective memories are in flux; they change over time as the needs of different groups change.[40]

Both models, Walton rightly points out, have their shortcomings. Cultural hegemonists tend to overstate the orchestrated nature of power through the organization of memory, while the social memory theorists tend to over-emphasize the plurality of competing memories and to understate the simple fact that some collective memories have been less significant because their articulators were comparatively powerless.[41] The approach undertaken here reflects Walton's sense of the inadequacies of keeping both approaches apart. Western reminiscences constitute a genre because individual authors increasingly played into the established parameters of the form. Their separately produced writings were, in a sense, a collective, self-sustaining effort. Furthermore, in forming pioneer societies to sustain their place in both the past and the present, old western settlers also acted collectively to create memories. It is, however, questionable whether these old pioneers ever exerted any degree of cultural hegemony in western places. Indeed, their constructed memories are a testimony to their sense of declining status rather than to their established power. The memories of older generations of white westerners collided not only with the collective memories of other cultural groups with whom they had previously come into conflict but also with the outlook of younger generations of white westerners who were more concerned with the as yet untold future than with the storied past. Hence, the reminiscences of the pioneers, while certainly organized, and influential on the levels of heritage creation and preservation, failed to preserve the social status of their authors.

PROMISED LANDS examines these visions of western futures and pasts, their roles in shaping a popular consciousness of the West and in shaping the regional outlook of some western residents, and the looming presence of these same kinds of visions in the present. The chapters in part I focus on the genre of promotional writing. Chapter 1 charts the key contours of the booster genre in the late nineteenth century. Special emphasis is placed on the promoters' efforts to present western places as frontiers of opportunity, while at the same time seeking to purge from readers' consciousness the possibility that any of the hardships and dangers, so often associated with the term "frontier," existed in those promised lands. This complicated dance that boosters performed with the frontier concept demonstrates how promotional literature, while it created myths of its own, was antimythic in its response to popular perceptions of the West as a wild frontier. Chapter 2 examines the impact of the depression of the 1890s on the West and on western boosterism, then examines the early-twentieth-century promotional tracts. In this second great age of western boosterism, the contours of the genre shifted a little as promoters became, for the most part, more cautious in their rhetoric.

The chapters in part II focus on the reminiscence genre. Chapter 3 begins with the collectively remembered journey of one particular group of pioneers who crossed Death Valley, the Jayhawkers of '49, and then explores the broader efforts of reminiscers to juxtapose the hardships of their westward journeys with the comfort and ease of travel enjoyed by later generations. The chapter then recounts the efforts of one old pioneer, Ezra Meeker, to memorialize the frontier journey process though transcontinental travel by covered wagon. It closes with the reminiscences of Carrie Strahorn, who recalled the journeys she had taken more than three decades earlier with her husband, Robert, a promoter. Chapter 4 examines the genre of reminiscence as expressed in published recollections and in pioneer society proceedings. Particular emphasis is placed on the reminiscers' attention to the theme of frontier dangers and hardships and how those conditions had shaped the character of the pioneer generations and on their concerns over the decline of manhood and womanhood in a new, postfrontier age.

The two chapters in part III treat the boosters and reminiscers together. Chapter 5 first examines how racial issues complicated promotional efforts, particularly in more culturally diverse parts of the West such as California and the Southwest. The promotional genre both reflected and, because of its pervasiveness, helped shape the racial attitudes of the white majority. However, western boosters were not engaged in any carefully orchestrated effort to justify the oppression of western peoples of color. Instead, they reflected in their books and pamphlets the contradictions and variations that marked European American thinking about race in this period. Similarly, the pioneer reminiscence genre was much more than a mechanism for justifying the American conquest of diverse nonwhite peoples in the West. At times the reminiscers did just that. At other times, however, they expressed great regret over the stereotyped images and misassumptions that had often guided their behavior. Emphasis on these complexities and ambiguities can inform our contemporary discussions of race relations in the West.

Chapter 6 highlights the endurance of the boosters' and reminiscers' approaches in today's struggles for ownership, both literal and figurative, of the American West. This final chapter also places particular emphasis on how contemporary expressions of westernness often parallel the boosterism and reminiscence of the 1870s to 1930s.

The study is intended neither as a comprehensive history of the promotion of western American lands and towns in the late nineteenth and early twentieth centuries nor as a comprehensive history of western reminiscences in those years.[42] Instead, it is an exploration of the contours of the western promotional and reminiscence genres and the ways in which those genres diverged at times and intersected at others.[43] Perhaps the present examination of these intersecting relations between western boosterism and reminiscence will prompt scholars to fill in the multitudinous gaps in coverage by examining how these processes have played out in particular western places. As a reminder of the centrality of promotion and remembrance to the processes of identity formation in the West, both a century ago and today, this book may prompt others to include these genres in their own studies of particular cultural groups. Western boosterism already has a rich historiographical legacy, and the study of western memory, by comparison, is still in its infancy.[44] Still, both offer fertile terrain for scholars of the West and its place in American thought and culture. This work is intended merely as a set of beginnings and not as a series of final words on how western places were imagined into being and then remembered to have been.

Part One:

PROMISES

PROMOTIONAL CONTOURS

AND CLAIMS

The Power of Imagination

> Draw on your imagination, if you can, and picture in the far west a town
> whose rapid progress seems to cause the sun, as it peeps over the morning
> horizon, to stop in astonishment at the improvements of the day before.
> (Yuma, Colorado, promotional poster, 1889; see figure, p. 84)

In 1882 the Passenger Department of the Chicago, Burlington and Quincy
Railroad (CB&Q) published a fascinating little book, *The Heart of the Continent: An Historical and Descriptive Treatise for Business Men, Home Seekers and Tourists, of the Advantages, Resources and Scenery of the Great West.*
The small work covered a large area—Illinois, Missouri, Iowa, Kansas,
Nebraska, and Colorado—and made some very big claims. Those states, the
publication dramatically announced, "form an empire grander in its resources
than any emperor or czar, prince or potentate of the older civilizations ever
swayed sceptre over." Readers learned that this region (1,000 miles long and

300 to 600 miles wide) was "capable of yielding in exhaustless profusion all the products of the temperate zone." It was packed to the brim with "incalculable mineral wealth and pasture-lands on which the cattle of any nation may feed to the full."[1]

As an example of late-nineteenth-century western American boosterism, there is nothing especially unique about the content of *The Heart of the Continent*.[2] In their promotional literature, railroads commonly worked to create regions out of the areas their lines and government land grants traversed. The Union Pacific promoted a "New Northwest," which it commonly referred to as the "Magnificent New Northwest," consisting, in 1880, of Wyoming, Montana, Idaho, and northern Utah. In the mid-1880s the Canadian Pacific presented the lands of Alberta, Saskatchewan, and Manitoba as the "Golden Northwest," and the "Great Northwest." The Northern Pacific was a little less inventive but more possessive, coining the term "Northern Pacific Country" for the lands of eastern Washington and northern Idaho, and later adding Montana to its domain.[3] Furthermore, railroad booster booklets, like other promotional publications, were filled with optimism, grandiose claims, and magical descriptions. But *The Heart of the Continent* was packed with particularly colorful and imaginative prose. The book accomplished quite a feat in covering six states in a mere sixty pages and managing to present each of them in turn as unsurpassable in its riches and unmatchable in its potential. All it took to achieve this seemingly impossible objective was the creative presentation of statistics and a shameless willingness to print some of the more melodramatic prose of the century, no small feat in an optimistic age marked by an abundance of effusive writing.

Prospective settlers who read the book must have faced quite a dilemma when it came to choosing among the cornucopia of riches offered by the CB&Q as potential destinations. How, for example, could Nebraska's brilliant future be questioned after learning that the state's population had "multiplied over a hundred-fold in twenty-five years" (rising from 4,494 to 452,542 between 1855 and 1880)? Since Nebraska's population had grown to an estimated 600,000 by the time of the book's appearance, the publication's inventive demographic calculations must have seemed like logical predictions to some readers.[4] "With a population as dense as that of Ohio— seventy five to the square mile," as those readers learned, Nebraska "would maintain 5,700,000 people." And, "With two hundred and thirty to the square mile, as in Massachusetts, [it] would be an empire of 17,480,000 souls."[5] The little book filled with big claims, it is worth noting, did not address the issue of how all these people would make a living in Nebraska.

With a population of 1,711,263 in 2000, the Nebraska of the new millennium is not living up to the boosters' heady predictions.[6] As the Plains States struggle today to maintain population, contemporary ex-Nebraskans might wonder at the CB&Q's claims that the state's climate "cannot be surpassed for healthfulness and all invigorating qualities." Today's farmers and ranchers would certainly question the railroad's assertion that "the whole state is magnificently watered and dotted with groves of timber." They might be less likely to dispute the claim that the state is situated "in the very belt upon the surface of the globe which has in all ages produced the highest type of men and women, the highest development, physical, intellectual and moral."[7]

Fortunately for would-be settlers in 1882, the CB&Q had a half million acres of "splendid lands" for sale in the eastern and central parts of Nebraska, and even more in the western part of the state. According to *The Heart of the Continent,* the state's soil was "as fertile as the far-famed valley of the Nile" and its climate "as healthful as ever was fanned by the pure airs of primeval paradise."[8] What possible risk could there be for potential settlers if Nebraska land was cheap and fertile and the climate Edenic?

If the reader had not already left for Nebraska on a CB&Q train to settle on railroad land, he or she would surely have wanted first to vacation in Colorado, the state where "rainbows cast their glittering coronets around the mountains, and radiant irises dance in many a romantic gorge." Colorado, the book announced, "is Fairyland, a region where elves and gnomes might sport and make their homes." "Amid these inspiring scenes," the book proclaimed, "the air is pure and dry as that which fanned the cheek of sinlessness in primal Eden." The reader might have wondered whether Eden had been semiarid, or peopled by elves and gnomes, but there seemed no denying that Colorado was indeed "the gold-and-jewel-decked queen of the Rockies."[9] For more than a decade prior to the appearance of *The Heart of the Continent,* Colorado had been presented as a health seekers' paradise, and the prose of its boosters had often reached the same Olympian heights achieved by the CB&Q promotional writers.[10]

Lest cynical readers of *The Heart of the Continent* believe that the CB&Q had published this promotional masterpiece with the merely businesslike and self-interested intention of selling lands and fares, the book reminded them that the actual purpose was purely benevolent. The railroad was interested in promoting this wonderful new region only because it wanted to play a part in the necessary process of western development. The CB&Q reminded readers of its work in bringing "the vast fields and pastures, the rich mines, the boundless opportunities and resources of the great West within reach of the overcrowded human lives of the East." The railroad, for all intents and purposes, was (at least according to its own printed pronouncements) really more a benevolent aid society than a ruthless, profit-driven Gilded Age corporation. It was devoted not to the business of creating wealth but to the more selfless end of bringing "fertile western acres . . . within a few hours' travel of millions of hard-worked and poverty-stricken tillers of eastern flint-hills and sand-barrens." The CB&Q was acting altruistically to ensure the continued functioning of the western safety valve.[11] And if its benevolent efforts, as a side effect, generated a profit, then the rewards were well deserved.

In a similar vein, the Denver, Rio Grande and Western Railway's (DRG&W's) book *The Heart of the Rockies* proudly claimed the same bighearted motives. The booklet's actual purpose was to advertise a newly completed line from Ogden and Salt Lake City, Utah, to Grand Junction, Colorado. (From Grand Junction the line ran through Pueblo and Colorado Springs to Denver.) But the proclaimed purpose was far more memorable. *The Heart of the Rockies* stated that "if the invalid of the east, with hollow eyes and sunken cheeks, finds in these pages hope, and accepts the truth of the salubrious and health giving climate of these mountains and valleys as established facts, 'a life saved' will be an additional reward."[12] The DRG&W was presenting itself as a kind of late-nineteenth-century equivalent of a modern-day consumer advocacy group.

In an age when big businesses were increasingly coming under attack from vocal urban and agrarian reformers, enterprises such as the DRG&W and the CB&Q emphasized that their highest purpose was public service, not the pursuit of private profit.[13] The philosophy of social Darwinism may have been an important element of the business mind-set of the late nineteenth century, but it did not make for good advertising copy. The railroads and their boosters sought to generate trust among readers by claiming that social welfare was their primary mission. Of course, railroad land and passenger departments were hardly as altruistic as they claimed to be, which helps account for why they had to work so hard to earn public confidence in the first place.[14]

Much like the railroad's promotional writers, local town boosters often played hard and fast with the actual realities of the places they described. They presented their infant settlements as metropolises in the making. Often they produced town maps and posters that depicted these places not as they actually were but as they were "projected" to become. A promotional poster for Yuma, Colorado, from 1889 featured not only the actual buildings of the town but also impressive images of the planned ones (some of which Yuma is still waiting for more than a century later). Local boosters claimed that the town's "rapid progress seems to cause the sun, as it peeps over the morning horizon, to stop in astonishment at the improvements of the day before."[15] Yuma boosters may have been especially creative in their emphasis on nature's wonderment over human achievement, but their efforts were typical among late-nineteenth-century and early-twentieth-century town promoters, who commonly mixed and matched existing and future structures in their town legends. In doing this they exhibited their faith in the future, and certainly their understanding that creative visual imagery was necessary to attract new settlers.

Land boosters, as one would expect, also accentuated the positive in memorable ways. By the early 1880s they contended that rain would assuredly "follow the plow." These unbridled optimists insisted that if farmers furrowed the earth, clouds would form, rain would fall, and evaporation from the rain collected in the furrows would, in turn, bring more rain. Given the wet cycle in the semiarid West in those years, it is worth noting that such boundless optimism, while it seems absurd and disingenuous in retrospect (a period of drought in the late 1880s and early 1890s exploded the theory), seems far less illogical when viewed in its precise historical context. Hopeful promoters, farmers, and even U.S. government officials, it must be stressed, were not operating with the benefit of hindsight when they placed faith in what would later prove to be a thoroughly flawed theory.[16]

Meanwhile, by the mid-1870s, in the most semiarid western places (where the natural proclivity of rain for following the plow was deemed less certain, even among the most unrestrained boosters), promoters regularly lauded the effectiveness of irrigation and/or dry farming.[17] Booster pamphlets often argued that irrigation was actually cheaper per acre than providing the artificial fertilizers that were necessary in the East. These publications, as a matter of course, pointed to the long history of irrigation, invariably mentioning its more than 3,000-year tradition in the "valley of the Nile" as a way of emphasizing that the practice was not in any way unusual or unproven.[18] "Cultivation by irrigation," an 1875 promotional map for *Corinne and the Bear River Valley* in Utah Territory (north of the Great Salt Lake), declared, "is the highest form of scientific farming, as it is the most ancient," and the "densest population[s] known . . . have all been cultivated by irrigation."[19] Such claims for the superiority of irrigation over other agricultural methods were common to the promotional writings for the more arid parts of the West. A promotional booklet for New Mexico's Pecos Valley from the early 1890s went so far as to claim that "men who farm by irrigation are the most independent class of people on the earth" because "they never feel a care as to whether it may rain to-morrow, or next week, or next month, or whether it may rain at all." And, to drive home the point that there was nothing anomalous about irrigation as an agricultural practice, the publication noted that easterners would "be surprised to learn that seven tenths of the people of the civilized world live by irrigation, yet such is the fact."[20]

In this way, then, the promotion of western promised lands was built first and foremost upon an instinctual rhetoric of the imagination. For all the differences in specific promotional content that pertain to particular places and periods and to different theories (such as the notion that rain followed the plow) and agricultural approaches (such as irrigation and dry farming), there is a consistent pattern in the contours of western booster literature over time and place. The same characteristics—unrestrained optimism, effusive language, and ostensibly altruistic claims—emerge again and again, from the Great Plains, to the Pacific Coast, to the Great Basin, the Southwest, and the Rockies, all the way from the 1860s and 1870s into the early decades of the twentieth century. The practice of western place promotion was well established by the early post–Civil War years, and there was little need to change the formula drastically just because various western places actually differed radically from one another with respect to their natural environments.

The Qualification of Frontiers

> The Company does not invite its land purchasers to a section the settlement in which imposes upon them the disagreeable and laborious task of reclaiming the land from the dominion of the Savage, the Buffalo and the Cayote. . . . [W]e invite you to a section [that] now presents the aspect of an old civilized country, having advantages inexpressibly superior to many sections of older States from which we invite you to come hither. (Union Pacific Railroad Company map, "Farms and Homes in Kansas," 1879)

Chief among the pervasive themes in the booster writing was the idea that whichever particular western wonders were being promoted, whichever frontiers of opportunity were for sale in the "New West," there were no more actual frontier conditions present. Selling frontiers of opportunity while at the same time denying that settlement of those areas would involve any frontier hardships required the boosters to perform a delicate balancing act.

Late-nineteenth-century Americans of European extraction had a general sense of what a frontier was, since the term was pervasive in the national culture, even if its meaning was rather different from that ascribed to it in Europe. There, "frontier" suggested a largely stationary border, sometimes running along a natural boundary line (a river or mountain range), and sometimes fortified. While European borders sometimes shifted due to wars won and lost (e.g., the Franco-German Alsace border), they were not in a permanent state of flux. For Americans, "frontier" suggested movement, a transitory line, the point of contact between white and Native peoples, the dangerous borderland between a settled homeland and a yet-to-be-tamed new land—a promised land of sorts, but one that would require hardship, sacrifice, and danger for its promise to be realized.

Americans certainly had a sense of the frontier as a "meeting point between savagery and civilization" long before the young Wisconsin historian Frederick Jackson Turner formalized that juxtaposition in his essay "The Significance of the Frontier in American History" in 1893.[21] Americans understood that population density was lower in frontier areas, even if they were unfamiliar with the Census Bureau's precise definition of frontiers as places where the population fell below two persons per square mile. It was generally understood that the American frontier was thin with population and thick with peril; thus, frontier hardship and frontier opportunity went hand in hand. Life on the far western frontier in the late nineteenth and early twentieth centuries was to one degree or another (depending on one's location) a calculated gamble, just as it had been on the Trans-Appalachian frontier a century earlier. That mixture of opportunity and hardship had become entrenched in American folklore by the middle of the nineteenth century. The key for western boosters was to emphasize and reemphasize the opportunity while consistently de-emphasizing the hardship.[22]

While land and town promoters presented western places as Edenic, they never noted that the story of Adam and Eve was a cautionary tale rather than a celebratory one. Promoters essentially characterized western places as Edens before the fall from grace, before the snake had entered the garden, before the forbidden fruit had been tasted. Potential settlers were effectively told that they could venture into paradise without having to worry about the pitfalls, since there were no forbidden fruits in western promised lands.

Establishing this much was the first part of the delicate promotional balancing act. The second part was connected with the growing concern in the late nineteenth and early twentieth centuries that the frontier was closing, that America's western Eden was fast filling up and its promise fast running out. These concerns over the end of the frontier probably served as a catalyst to western settlement by European-Americans. Potential settlers were motivated to stake their claims while there were still some frontier lands left.[23]

Such psychological motivations for western homesteading are difficult to establish definitively, but the theme of the closing frontier certainly found its way into descriptive writing about the West. As early as 1867, a massive, 700-page illustrated volume, *Barber's History of All the Western States and Territories,* warned that the arable areas of the United States were nearly exhausted and that "the turning point in American history" had been reached. This turning point, in author John Barber's estimation, marked "the beginning of that cumulative pressure of population upon the means of subsistence, which is to test the stability of our institutions."[24] Social critic and reformer Henry George would issue the same warning a few years later in *Our Land and Land Policy* (1871), and more famously at the end of the decade in his classic treatise on socioeconomic problems, *Progress and Poverty* (1879).[25]

Booster publications also emphasized that the frontier was closing. A promotional booklet from the mid-1870s advertising the army and navy colony in southern Dakota featured the urgent subtitle *Uncle Sam's Farm Is Growing Smaller Everyday.*[26] Such warnings were common in promotional tracts. But the theme of a closing frontier called for another delicate balancing act by the boosters, in addition to that of selling frontier opportunity without the frontier hardship that presumably ought to accompany it: namely, emphasizing that the frontier wellspring was not drying up so quickly that a potential settler might miss out.

Booster literature frequently contrasted the East's crowded conditions and limited opportunities with the West's invariably greater, though fast-diminishing, ones.[27] Indeed, the closing frontier theme was echoed so often in promotional literature, social theory, and political rhetoric from the 1870s through the 1930s that it became a vital part of the cultural-intellectual milieu of the period.[28] Such concerns probably did help fuel the periodic western land booms of the period. The key, however, was to present western places as "closing frontiers," not "closed frontiers." Promoters accentuated the frontier opportunity by insisting that it was a limited, hence valuable, commodity.

Yet for all their emphasis on diminishing frontier opportunity, western boosters stressed that the remaining lands were absolutely devoid of frontier hardship. Whether in the 1870s or a half century later in the 1920s, booster publications insisted that the places they were lauding were not wild frontiers. In 1876 Fred J. Cross, territorial superintendent of immigration, assured potential immigrants that "Dakota has passed its dark days," and they would not "have to suffer the inconveniences of a pioneer life."[29] Two years later a Pawnee County, Nebraska, publication stressed that "although it partakes of the strong, energetic, cosmopolitan character of all comparatively new sections of the West, [the county] has none of the elements of the frontier."[30] Around the same time, the Union Pacific Railroad emphasized that its lands in western Kansas were no longer in any way the "dominion of the Savage, the Buffalo and the Cayote." Indeed, those lands had "the aspect of an old civilized country," like those from which settlers were being solicited.[31]

The Oregon State Board of Immigration in its plainly titled publication *Oregon As It Is: Solid Facts and Actual Results* (1885), effectively achieved the necessary balance between the presence of frontier opportunity and the absolute absence of physical frontier conditions. The publication stressed that the state was "America's Sunset Land," the "last among the states to be touched by those physical achievements, which have made man so irresistible and invincible in his wrestings and heroisms with the rugged and defiant in nature." Oregon was, the publication asserted, albeit incorrectly, the last frontier of white settlement in the West (portions of the interior West would see waves of white agricultural settlement into the second decade of the twentieth century). But if potential settlers had any concern about the close chronological proximity of the frontier epoch, they were quickly reassured that the "'out west' of the pioneer" had been "obliterated." Oregon was now a settled, cultured place, where people's only burden was the weight of their own agricultural abundance.[32] Another publication from the Oregon State Board of Immigration reiterated the same point a few years later in 1889, noting that the "New Empire" of Idaho and central and eastern Oregon and Washington "offer[ed] all the attractions of a new and rapidly developing field" while also "offer[ing] all the attractions which belong to the long and established community."[33]

While the frontier heritage of western places was commonly discussed in the booster literature of the late nineteenth century, great care was taken to demonstrate that only the positive aspects of that heritage had survived to the present. A promotional pamphlet published by the County Commissioners of Beadle County, Dakota, in 1889 reminded readers of the place's pioneer beginnings. But the author was quick to emphasize that even those "primitive 'shacks,' the sod houses," those early rude dwellings where the first settlers resided, were filled with works of art, books, music, and the various other accoutrements of cultured civilization.[34] Even the frontier past of Beadle County, aside from its primitive architecture, seemed to match the ideal of the Jeffersonian yeoman farmer, a gentleman with plenty of leisure time for enjoying landscaping and literature. What could there be to fear in the Dakota present if the past had been so pleasant? In this way, local boosters in Oregon, Dakota, and other western places joined a long and varied list of great anticipators who reassuringly placed the future in the present by claiming that frontier conditions were a thing of the past.[35]

The same basic theme of the absence of frontier dangers, so evident in the booster literature, also appeared in popular travel literature of the late nineteenth century. One might expect that the potential settler or traveler would be concerned by the title of Winslow Ayer's book *Life in the Wilds of America and Wonders of the West in and Beyond the Bounds of Civilization* (1880), which suggested the presence of wild frontier conditions. But concerned settlers and tourists need not have worried because Ayer painted a romantic dreamscape generous to all parts of the West. As for the "Great American Desert," we find that "the oasis is everywhere—the desert nowhere—but rather Nature's great flower garden where Eden might have been." We learn that in "grandeur and sublimity, the mountains of Wyoming are unsurpassed by any on the continent," that "Nevada is a region of wonders." But the stunning scenery, "the grandeur and achievements of nature," were all just icing on the cake of a civilized western society. "So rapid the advance of civilization," we learn, "that he who would seek the 'wilds of America,' will only find them in Alaska."[36]

Occasionally an unsophisticated booster writer failed to find the right tone in seeking to counter frontier imagery and may have had the unintended effect of discouraging settlement. For example, in *A Land of Sunshine,* a promotional pamphlet for Flagstaff, Arizona, published in 1887, George Tinker inadvertently wrote that readers would be surprised to discover "culture, refinement and elegance" in "a frontier county." The seasoned booster would have insisted that the very presence of such refinement and elegance underscored the inaccuracy, even the absurdity, of perceptions of the place as a frontier county.[37] But such slipups were unusual in western promotional writing, and their rarity is hardly surprising; the frontier theme was so vital to the genre that authors, almost invariably, took great care in articulating it.

Promoting the "New West"

> The doubtful period is past. Others have gone through the days of anxiety, and the thorns of pioneering are removed. (Robert E. Strahorn, *The Resources and Attractions of Washington Territory*, 1888)

Robert Edmund Strahorn was one of the most careful and creative promotional writers of the period. In his first booster publication, *The Hand-Book of Wyoming* (1877), Strahorn devoted a short chapter to undermining notions that the state was an untamed frontier. He chided eastern journalists who came "to the new west with mind[s] literally charged with glaring absurdities" in an effort to provide their "eastern readers [with] experiences from the western plains and mountains which smack of the crude, the rough and the semi-barbarous." For such writers, Strahorn lamented, "to tell of our churches, schools and societies . . . would fall like a chilly drizzle after the glittering rainbow." The real Wyoming, he insisted, bore little resemblance to the frontier imagery that packed the pages of eastern publications about the West. Strahorn admitted that some people in the region adopted the "devil-may-care manner and dress attributed to real frontiersmen," but he noted that most of them were "eccentric immigrants," new arrivals from the East, not sensible, cultured, modern westerners.[38]

Strahorn's approach was wise. While some people were certainly drawn to adventure, one suspects that most settlers preferred assurances to challenges. Certainly there would be little for promoters to gain in the 1870s or 1880s or in later periods by telling settlers to come to the wild frontier and experience savage Indians, semibarbarous frontiersmen, and unfamiliar landscapes. Selling frontier environments, albeit essentially safe and tamed ones, to tourists proved a viable endeavor even at this early date. Visiting and vacationing in the wilderness was one thing, but actually living there was another matter entirely.[39]

Clearly there were certain frontier thrills that could be associated with tourism, yet it would have been an absolute liability to include them in promotional writing designed to attract residents. However, it is important to note that many of the promotional books and pamphlets designed to bring settlers often sought to draw tourists, too, as well as investors; these were multipurpose works. Certainly through the 1880s there is little discernible difference in the descriptions of western places offered to prospective tourists and settlers. While the literature highlights the scenic marvels and geologic wonders of western tourist sites, it also emphasizes, as one would expect, the comforts and conveniences that the tourist can expect to enjoy in the course of visiting these places. It is during the period of the second wave of western promotional writing, in the early twentieth century, that western tourism literature starts to diverge from promotional writing, at least to some degree, with the former more readily emphasizing the primordial, wilderness qualities of western places and presenting them as palliatives for the overcivilization of postfrontier America, and the latter continuing to emphasize the abundance of civilization's comforts and conveniences.

Writing in the 1870s, Strahorn was smart to de-emphasize the wild frontier and stress the presence of social institutions that rendered Wyoming a settled region. While eastern reporters and dime novelists might be seeking "real original westerner[s]—regular frontiersmen—long-haired [men] clad in . . . greasy suit[s] of buckskin," characters who seemed to fit the bill, such as "Buckskin Jack," were not, Strahorn emphasized, a significant part of the "New West." Indeed, Buckskin Jack, it turned out, was far from an authentic frontiersman himself. As one resident explained to a visiting journalist, this ruggedly named character was no "dyed-in-the-wool border genius" but a recent arrival to Cheyenne from Natchez who had been "loafing around, eating free lunches" and manufacturing "sensational yarns" to gullible newcomers impaired by their mythological assumptions about the West.

In this New West (Wyoming), he went on, the loafers were few and far between, and "thrifty western workers" enjoyed an abundance of cultural opportunities. Even the social distinctions that marked the established societies of the East were present in Wyoming, Strahorn assured his readers. There was none of the rough frontier-leveling that easterners might imagine marked the region. He added, "In expecting to find boors and gentlemen upon a common social level the visitor will find himself happily or unhappily disappointed according to his own taste or disposition."[40] Furthermore, Strahorn noted that female suffrage was an important indicator of that cultural advance, adding that male voters were making better decisions about political candidates now that women were present in the electoral arena. Wyoming boosters often emphasized these cultural developments, including women's suffrage, as a strategy to attract white women to the Territory. However, this strategy, ironically enough, was largely driven by the promoters' understanding that places such as Cheyenne were in desperate need of the civilizing influence of female settlement.[41]

Remarkably, Strahorn was only twenty-five years of age when the *Hand-Book of Wyoming* was published, but he was wise and seasoned well beyond his years. By 1877 he had already been working as a newspaperman for over a decade. During the Sioux wars of 1876–1877 he had served as a correspondent for various papers, including the *Rocky Mountain News,* the *Chicago Tribune,* and occasionally the *New York Times.*[42] Strahorn placed such heavy emphasis on the postfrontier character of Wyoming because he understood that the circumstances of the time demanded it. Wyoming had not done a terribly good job of promoting itself in the first half of the 1870s, though not for lack of effort.[43] For one thing, the particularly harsh winters of 1871 and 1872 made prospective settlers wary of Wyoming. Making matters worse, the territory's boosterish newspaper editors, in their eager quest to secure federal support for the removal of all Indians from the region, played up the Indian dangers in exaggerated and fear-inspiring reports. They thereby unintentionally compromised the efforts of other boosters who tried to highlight the safe, settled, and civilized character of the place. Prior to Strahorn, promotional brochure writers, even as they avoided the excessive emphasis of newspaper editors on frontier conditions, had simply failed to develop the right kind of tone in their descriptions. They had too often adopted a defensive manner that underscored outsiders' negative perceptions rather than dissolving them.[44]

In fact, the disappointing lack of progress in Wyoming in the early 1870s led to calls for the territory's dissolution and the annexation of its southeastern part, including the area traversed by the Union Pacific line, by Colorado. It was thought that the augmentation of land and population would assist Colorado's effort to gain statehood. In 1872 President Ulysses S. Grant actually favored abolishing Wyoming and dividing up its lands between Colorado, Idaho, Montana, and Utah.[45] Colorado, of course, became a state in 1876 without the addition of Wyoming lands. Wyoming eventually gained statehood but remains today the least populated state in the Union, with less than half a million residents.

In retrospect it is clear that Strahorn's promotional efforts in the 1877 *Hand-Book* hardly turned the tide for Wyoming; yet his approach—which underscored the modern, settled nature of the place—was clearly the only viable one, and it struck a chord with railroad magnate Jay Gould, who hired him as a publicist for the Union Pacific. Gould wanted Strahorn "to create a

New Northwest of the imagination," and from 1877 to 1883 Strahorn ran the railroad's publicity department and did just that.[46] He produced a number of classics in the promotional booklet genre, including *To the Rockies and Beyond, or a Summer on the Union Pacific Railway and Branches* (1878, and new editions in 1879 and 1881); *The Resources and Attractions of Montana Territory and Attractions of Yellowstone Park* (1879); *Idaho Territory* (1881); *Complete and Comprehensive Description of Oregon* (1888); and *Comprehensive Description of Washington* (1888).[47] Of Idaho, he insisted, echoing the characteristic booster emphasis on the postfrontier character of the New West, "the past has been the roughest pioneering; the future will be full of golden fruition."[48] He assured readers that others had already "gone through the days of anxiety" in Washington and that "the thorns of pioneering" had since been removed.[49]

It is difficult to ascertain the exact role that Strahorn played in attracting settlers to the northwestern states. His own discussions of his significance as a promoter were certainly not restrained. There may have been as many as 50,000 copies printed of each of the first two editions of *To the Rockies and Beyond;* 20,000 copies of *The Resources and Attractions of Idaho;* and, according to Strahorn's claims, a monthly circulation of 50,000 for his promotional magazine, *New West Illustrated,* by 1882 (the publication had begun in 1879). Strahorn was well known as a promoter by western newspaper editors; indeed, the *Helena Herald* described him in 1879 as an "indefatigable searcher after facts," adding that "for the important work he has in hand [he] is probably the cleverest man in the West."[50] Certainly, he was the most important individual promotional voice for the Northwest region in the late 1870s and early 1880s, and his works were still being published, though without recognition of his authorship, by the Union Pacific in the 1890s.

The settled, regional Far West that Strahorn and other boosters created in the 1870s and 1880s was as mythic and imaginative a construct as the wild frontier West that was contemporaneously being created by pulp fiction writers and artists. Scholars have examined in some detail the rhetoric and imagery surrounding the mythic, old, frontier West. However, the American public was also exposed to a New West (or, better, to many New Wests) by the region's promoters as early as the late 1860s—which, incidentally, was when the talk of a "New South" began in the former Confederate states.[51] Samuel Bowles, for one, referred to the "New West" in 1869 in a guidebook for transcontinental railroad travel.[52] And in the 1870s, the New West was designated a new Eden, not just metaphorically but spiritually and practically, when E. P. Tenney outlined the religious possibilities of the nation's newest broad region in his work *The New West: As Related to the Christian College and the Home Missionary.*[53] Beginning in 1879, readers could peruse the possibilities of western settlement in Strahorn's *New West Illustrated,* which promoted Union Pacific lands in the Far West. They could also read other promotional literature for the Plains, Rockies, and Pacific Northwest that was financed by the Union Pacific and published in Omaha, Nebraska, by the New West Publishing Company.[54] By the late 1880s, members of the reading public could behold the "marvels of the New West," from a promotional work on the trans-Missouri region, just as they could wonder at the modernization and ostensible progressivism of the New South.[55] The New West theme was certainly an enduring one: two generations later, in 1909, the Intermountain West was once more being vigorously promoted, this time in a publication titled *New West Magazine.* Indeed, in the Progressive Era of the early twentieth century, the concept of the New West (like the New Democracy, New Nationalism, and New Freedom) was very much in currency as the country experienced one of its periodic waves of "newnessphilia."[56]

Embedding these notions of a new, cultured, postfrontier West (though one still filled with frontier opportunity) took more than just literary prowess. The vivid word pictures of Strahorn and other writers were vital to the cause of western promotion, but so were the visual images that accompanied those descriptions.[57] The railroads vigorously played up the theme of a frontierless New West in their promotional materials and used visual imagery to further this effect. A Santa Fe Railroad picture from 1881, advertising the line's lands on the Kansas plains, illustrates the theme with clarity and humor: a scene labeled "Out of the Woods, into Kansas" (see figure, p. 77), is a beautifully sculpted and ordered landscape featuring a modern house, a church, other farm buildings, and a well-dressed owner leisurely surveying the scene from a horse-drawn carriage. Below this is a second image labeled "In the Woods," featuring a rough, forested, frontier terrain, populated only by a log cabin and an unfortunate farmer trying in vain to plow the tree stump–ridden wilderness.[58] The railroad was presenting Kansas as a state filled with all the postpioneer pleasures of the established, cultured yeoman's farmholding, without the hardships and inconveniences of the frontier phase of development. From the promotional materials, at least, the message was a clear one: the hard work of the frontier phase had long since been completed in Kansas.[59]

In selling opportunities in the western present, the railroads thus manipulated the realities of the conditional future. They worked with publicists such as Strahorn, who had the ability to conjure up pleasant images through their prose, and with illustrators who, as in the Santa Fe Railroad advertisement for Kansas, could effectively ironize such past-future juxtapositions. The railroads also worked with cartographers, such as the Rand McNally firm, which created powerful and effective images of western regions. The Chicago firm began printing railroad schedule and fare books in 1871 and promotional maps in 1872, followed by guidebooks and atlases.[60] Just as the prose in railroad publications presented the West as an accessible, modern region, so, too, did the promotional maps reinforce this notion, and certainly at the expense of cartographic accuracy.[61] The mapmakers engaged in what geographer J. B. Harley has described as "the hierarchicalization of space." That is, they included places central to the purpose of the map and excluded things that would distract viewers' attention.[62] Focusing on towns, parks, and natural wonders, they often conveniently excluded those presences, such as Indian reservations, that might spark uneasiness in the white viewer. However, when Indian lands were about to be opened up to white settlement, they also were featured on the maps.[63]

On the railroad maps the lines demarcating the tracks themselves dominate the topography. Evenly spaced town names fan out from the track lines, which are drawn so thickly that they cover ten to twenty miles in scaled width. The maps were designed to evoke a sense of order and safety for potential settlers considering a purchase, and they drew sharp contrasts between the railroad-dominated areas and the seemingly empty spaces between them. The bolded railroad lines and the printed names of the neatly ordered towns featured on Rand McNally's "Map of the Northern Pacific Railroad and Oregon Railway and Navigation Company, in Vast Areas of the Best Wheat Lands!" (1883; see figure, p. 80) cover half of the Territory of Washington and a quarter of the State of Oregon. Some of the lines shown on the map were still under construction, and most of the towns did not yet exist either. But the map gave the appearance of a thoroughly settled, ordered, risk-free western landscape, one that looks similar to the map's depiction of the eastern half of the country. The map also provided no real evidence of the large-scale presence of Indian peoples in the West.[64] The Northern Pacific map did, however, approximate the reality that was coming to the region being depicted. Between 1883 (when the map was published) and 1893, Oregon and Washington "got three direct transcontinental rail connections," and

Washington gained statehood in 1889.[65] North Dakota, South Dakota, and Montana all gained statehood the same year, as did Idaho and Wyoming in 1890. The creative and futuristic maps produced by and for the railroads played no small part in these transformations.

The railroads worked closely with local promotional groups, such as chambers of commerce, "interior" forces that engaged in similar acts of cartographic creativity and misrepresentation in their efforts to promote regional growth. In a map of "The Inter-Mountain District," produced by the Boise City Board of Trade in the late 1880s, Boise City appears as a metropolis of a very sizable region (comprising four territories and portions of five states). This feat was achieved by presenting the "projected" railroad lines as virtually indistinguishable from those "present" lines already in operation. The Boise City Board of Trade was more honest than some municipal boosters, since its map was subtitled, in part, "the Present and Prospective Railway Connections of Boise City" (see figure, p. 83). Nonetheless, the map certainly made it difficult for the reader to distinguish the present from the future, but that distinction could at least be drawn if the reader had a well-trained eye.[66] Nonetheless, one suspects that such promotional maps and images were created for the purpose of making an initial impression rather than inviting close scrutiny and the skepticism likely to accompany it. One of the goals of western promoters was, however, to nurture skepticism about other western places with which they were competing for the attentions of prospective settlers.

Comparing Promised Lands

> Why go to the Gulf States or to the Pacific Coast in quest of treasures that are hidden at our own doors—that are buried beneath our own feet? Men need not go to Texas or Oregon for homes when thousands of acres of the richest and most productive lands on the continent are lying idle in Missouri and Kansas. (Wilson Nicely, *The Great South-West,* 1867)

Given contemporary American marketing strategies, which so heavily feature direct comparisons of products, it should come as no surprise that from the very earliest beginnings of western boosterism in the late eighteenth century, the promoters of specific places presented their landed wares as superior to other lands. In the early post–Civil War years, the emphasis was often on the fertile lands in the first two tiers of states west of the Mississippi that were often ignored, or passed through without thought to settlement, by land seekers headed to other regions of the West. Wilson Nicely, promoting lands in the "Great South-West" of Missouri and Kansas in 1867, assured eastern and midwestern settlers that they did not need to go to Texas and Oregon to find wonderfully fertile lands when such agrarian treasures lay much closer to home.[67]

Like modern-day marketers, the boosters developed various techniques of comparative analysis to elevate their products over those of their competitors. For example, individual western states contrasted their own (often imagined) cultural advances with the absence of "civilization" in other states and territories with which they were vying for new immigrants. A Nebraska booster publication from 1875 presented the more westerly parts of the country, including neighboring Colorado, as wild, unsettled, and frontierlike, home to conspicuously uncivilized elements such as "adventurers," Indians, and Spaniards. The message to potential western settlers was strikingly clear: if you had any sense, you would head for Nebraska and not venture any farther.[68] Heading too far west, the Nebraska promoters were suggesting, would take you to a frontier of hardship and peril. Meanwhile, the promoters insisted, back in the East the benefits of civilization were accompanied by increases in class conflict, crime, corruption, and congestion. Nebraska, like so many other western places in the half century or so after the Civil War, was presented by its promoters as the perfect mix of advanced culture without its common corollaries, and of frontier opportunity without the attendant dangers and inconveniences.

At other times it made more sense to market certain western regions as being very similar to other more thickly settled western places. A publication entitled *Homes in South-Western Texas: 50,000 Acres, Equal to the Best Valley Land in California* (1881) was written by a former Sonoma Valley, California, farmer who had left the Golden State a decade earlier and now had eight sections of land to sell in an even more promising locality. The book's title and text compared the land, climate, and culture of southwest Texas very favorably with the conditions in California. Furthermore, the author, C. J. Jones, contended that he had no interest in selling to speculators, only to "actual settlers." Perhaps he was, first and foremost, genuinely engaged in a search for good neighbors rather than good profits. Whatever the case, this approach allowed Jones to claim the ethical high ground. He gave the impression that his concern was for the agrarian good fortune and general quality of life of his buyers, rather than for his own profits. Such sentiments paralleled the pretensions to virtue staked out by such railroads as the CB&Q and DRG&W in their promotional literature.

Published in San Francisco and intended to reach California's "surplus population" desperate for "good, cheap land," Jones's thirty-two-page booklet made it clear that the venture involved no risk whatsoever, and in doing so echoed the general contours of the western promotional genre. "Settlements are now fast springing up all over this country," and "it has now ceased to be what it was eight years ago—a frontier country," he declared. California had thus become a closed frontier with "surplus population," while southwest Texas had left behind the stage of frontier peril and hardship but was full of frontier opportunity. "Life and property," Jones insisted, "is now as safe [here] as in the most favored section of the country," and land would soon be worth as much as in more heavily settled areas. A move to southwest Texas, then, would provide the lucky relocator with land in a settled region, and yet at frontier prices.[69]

But California's promoters had problems of their own in the late nineteenth century, besides those that might potentially arise from the efforts of other states' promoters to siphon off the "surplus population" of the Golden State and characterize it as a closed frontier. The most notable of these problems was that California boosters were divided along regional lines. Those lines separated San Francisco from the interior regions up until the early 1880s, and the north from the south from the mid-1880s, when Los Angeles experienced its speculative boom and its first wave of demographic growth (a mere prelude to the enormous growth of the early twentieth century). And, of course, there were intense rivalries between urban boosters within regions, most notably the one between Los Angeles and San Diego in the 1870s.[70]

Throughout the late nineteenth century there were debates in the California legislature over the issue of whether the state should provide funding for promotional efforts. Critics of public funding argued that it would only have the effect of lining the pockets of private interests, such as the railroads, which had already been subsidized by public moneys. During the Southern California boom in the 1880s, San Francisco's Immigrant Association of California actually disbanded after realizing that its efforts to promote the state as a whole were having the unintended effect of nurturing disproportionately high growth in the south.[71] Even the California exhibit at the Chicago World's Fair in 1893, while tremendously successful, was marked by intense rivalry between north and south.[72] Such intrastate rivalries, along with those between business and labor interests, and between farming and mining interests, go a long way toward explaining why California's promotional organizations received so little state funding. Those competing interests also help account for California's failure in the late nineteenth century to attract the numbers of new residents that its resources merited. Finally, those rivalries remind us that current tensions between Northern and Southern California—manifested in periodic movements for formal division of the state—have a long history. Still, for all these interstate and intrastate promotional rivalries, the booster genre's similarities in tone and approach generally overshadowed any differences highlighted in comparative representations of western promised lands.[73]

Havens of Culture, Climate, and Agriculture

> This is the happy Canaan—the holy land; that God, when He made the world, and had gathered the experience of all His efforts, said to himself: "I will now illustrate the crowning glory of My labors with the production of a perfect spot. I will give it wealth of soil and wealth of precious metals; I will enrich it with nature's grandest productions; I will give it splendid mountains, rich and gorgeous valleys, grand and stately forests; I will thread it with magnificent rivers and beautiful brooks; its grasses shall be nutritious; its soil shall produce in generous quantities the best of fruits. I will smile down through cloudless skies upon its beautiful fields; I will fan it with breezes from my broadest sea; I will waft to it the odors of spices and the perfumes of tropic lands; and in the ripeness of time its people shall be great-hearted and generous, liberal and just; and there, in all the perfection of its soil and salubrity of its climate, shall be found the highest social condition of which the creation of My image is capable. (Frank Pixley, editor, *San Francisco Argonaut*, quoting God's description of Riverside, California, c. 1885)

Despite the late-nineteenth-century promotional publications' tremendous detail on terrain, climate, and agricultural and mineral resources, the formulaic nature of the tracts' claims and promises must have given some readers pause. The price paid for such overpromotion was that the obviously different regions of the northern Plains, southwestern deserts, Rocky Mountains, and Pacific Coast all seemed, after a certain point, interchangeable. According to the boosters' words, all these areas were rich in culture and blessed (often quite explicitly so, by God) with mild and invigorating climates, stirring scenery, and fertile lands.

One such area for boosterist exaggeration was education. As a key indicator of cultural advance, education featured prominently in promotional works on the West. One suspects this emphasis was especially valued among prospective immigrants from abroad for whom public schools were generally less readily available (if they existed at all). The inside front covers of town and county promotional publications often featured a picture of the most impressive structure in the vicinity—the public school building. State-level publications often featured a picture of the state university or normal school. Tremendous emphasis was placed on the quality of the educational facilities. An 1870 publication from the State of Oregon, for example, made the very broad, effusive claim that "for its population, there is no state in the Union more liberally provided with educational facilities."[74] The sentiment, expressed in quite general terms, was echoed again and again in the 1870s and 1880s. In 1884 Benjamin Cummings Truman confidently claimed for California that "no State in the Union spends more relatively on its common schools, or has a better educational system or more competent teachers."[75] Robert Strahorn insisted in 1889 that "no state in the Union makes a more generous provision for its public schools, or has a more complete or effective system" than Oregon.[76]

Over time the claims became still more grandiose and specific. In 1887 the Boise City Board of Trade boldly proclaimed that "it is conceded by *all* (italics added) that between the Missouri River and the Pacific Coast there is no school superior to, if any equals, our city school either in discipline, equipment or any other advantages." One would of course have to exclude from the *all* category all those promoters who made essentially the same claim for every other trans-Missouri western town aside from Boise, Idaho. The Boise organization further noted that "citizens always say to strangers, 'You've not seen the city unless you've been to the school house.'"[77]

In 1889 T. E. Farish, Arizona commissioner of immigration, in a publication presenting central and southwestern Arizona as "The Garden of America," emphasized that "no state or territory spends so much per capita in the education of its youth."[78] Probably no more accurate, but similarly intended to both reassure and astound potential settlers, was the claim of Iowa governor Buren R. Sherman, a few years earlier, that his state had "more school teachers . . . than there were soldiers in the American army at the time of the revolution."[79] The preoccupation with schools also suggests that the boosters themselves were attaching great value to the future of the places they promoted by focusing on the education of a younger generation, or at least that the boosters understood, then as now, that those kinds of concerns were important to most potential settlers. Western promised lands could not afford to be educational wastelands.

Such elevated claims about educational facilities also served as further evidence for potential settlers that they would lose nothing in the way of cultural amenities by moving to more westerly places. In addition to educational resources, the boosters stressed the highly developed civic sensibility and heightened moral nature of these fledgling communities. The number of churches and the variety of denominations represented were emphasized, thus assuring prospective settlers that the particularities of their faith would not preclude their smooth incorporation into the wider community.[80] Churches, like schools, became clear symbols of the settled state of civilization, and images of them were regularly included in booster pamphlets and posters.

In addition to schools and churches, hotels figured prominently in the promotional literature. Very often the largest and most impressive of the early structures in new towns, hotels were presented as sure signs that the towns that housed them were bustling centers of commerce. What is more, hotels seemed to provide architectural evidence of the arrival of culture in a particular location, and with those structures in place it seemed only logical that the most cultured people would arrive. Yet, in reality, then, as now, hotels were designed in part to attract commerce and culture to places; they were as much a sign of what a town desired to be as they were evidence of what that place already was.

Beyond the hyping of cultural amenities, boosterist literature's other main focus was the land itself, which was subject to some truly fabulous and fantastic descriptions.[81] Regardless of which western state or territory was presenting its riches, one could generally be assured that the land was at least as fertile as that in the Nile Valley.[82] A Dakota County, Minnesota, booster proclaimed to prospective settlers in 1868: "Perhaps the eye of man never rested on a spot of land better fitted to supply his material wants and meet the necessities of his nature since shut out from the original Eden." He then asked, "Where can a more inviting region be found upon the earth?"[83] An audience at the Philadelphia Centennial Exposition (1876) heard that Oregon is "matchless in all that God and nature could bestow in fitting it as a home for man."[84] Arizona boosters, in typical fashion, contended in 1891 that "with some of the richest and most friable land in the world," their promised land could not "well be disputed to be the Paradise of America."[85] To have offered land any less fertile than that along the Nile would have betrayed a lack of enthusiasm on the boosters' part, and that would have been unwise given the ferocity of the promotional competition. Frank Pixley, editor of the *San Francisco Argonaut,* saw fit to quote, indeed, to create, God's description of Riverside, California. After having made the world, God had, according to the presumptuous editor, decided to create a "perfect spot" to serve as the "crowning glory" of his labors.[86] God, it turns out, made a number of promotional visits to western promised lands in the late nineteenth century. Indeed, such universalizing tendencies backfired somewhat, since they engendered the dilemma of making western wonderlands sound generic.

To offset this danger, one popular approach in booster texts was to meld the mythic and ancient images of Eden and the Nile with discussions of places closer to home and closer in time. Promotional materials directed toward American audiences often drew parallels between western lands and eastern or midwestern lands. The landscape (wherever it happened to be) was always incomparably good, but it was rarely, if ever, presented as being in any way foreign or unusual. A particular western place might parallel the Nile Valley in productivity, but it was compared in more specific terms with places more familiar to potential settlers. In this context, it was not surprising that railroad magnate Jay Gould recognized Robert Strahorn's potential as a publicist for the New Northwest. In *The Hand-Book of Wyoming,* Strahorn had proved himself a master drawer of East-West parallels that facilitated psychological transitions for westward migrants. He noted that "Wyoming's grazing area is greater than the entire state of Kentucky. . . . Her agricultural and fertile soil is greater than that of the States of Massachusetts and Connecticut combined . . . [her] forests [more expansive] than those of the great lumbering State of Michigan."[87] With every comparison the western lands came out on top because they contained more of what was familiar.[88] Booster publications frequently compared western rivers and river valleys to northeastern and mid-Atlantic ones. When it came to landscape presentation (even given the eloquent waxing over striking western vistas), similarities between East and West were notably more common than contrasts.[89]

Still, western promoters could not resist emphasizing that their region's states and territories dwarfed the established eastern and midwestern states in size. For example, an 1879 work on New Mexico as the "New West" noted that the state was "nearly large enough to absorb the whole of New England and New Jersey." Similarly, in the promotional literature produced to attract European immigrants, comparisons were made between the countries of the Old World and western promised lands of the New World, often emphasizing that some individual American states and territories were larger than entire European countries.[90] In an age when national health was crudely measured in terms of demographic and geographic size, such comparisons, between the West and the East and Midwest, and between the West and Europe, would have seemed thoroughly natural.[91]

Regarding the all-important question of the weather in these promised lands, promotional writers played down the notion of climatic extremes by providing tables of figures showing abundant rainfall, limited snowfall, and limited variation in temperature, all in an effort to assure and convince skeptical readers. These statistics served to present the West favorably in relation to eastern and midwestern standards. But there were significant contrasts, too. Boosters sought simultaneously to play up the less humid, more invigorating atmosphere of the West. In the promoters' estimation, Montanans and Dakotans had never had a tough winter, and the occasional cold spells in those places were, at their very worst, merely bracing or invigorating. Indeed, the boosters' winters were surprisingly short all over the West (except when the promoters of one place offered their candid assessments of the weather in rival destinations). Prospective settlers would have found from an 1870 publication that the air in Dakota Territory, even at its very coldest, "is a robe of arctic furs, which holds in and stimulates the resilient fires of vital heat within the body, imparting in their reaction a sense of elastic vigor and redundant animation." The damp air of the East, on the other hand, was a "conductor of heat which it insidiously steals from the softened tissues," thus making mildly cold temperatures virtually unbearable there.[92] Whether the reader then, or today, for that matter, could decipher from the author's pseudoscientific description why the air in Dakota Territory was so healthful is doubtful, but it certainly sounded like good air.

The boosters of hotter, more arid western regions were adept at downplaying climatic extremes, too. Prospective settlers in 1876 would have read that Nevada, far from being, as critics suggested, "a sea of sand—the *Sahara* of America," was the fortunate possessor of a "mild" climate, "not . . . subject to great extremes, either of heat or cold." They would have been pleased to learn, too, that "the days of summer are not warmer than on the east side of the Rocky Mountains, while the nights are uniformly cool and refreshing."[93] Likewise Arizonans, in the mind's eye of the promoters, never had a trying summer. Indeed, Arizona's climatic wonders ensured that "men and women live there to such a ripe old age as less fortunately located people never dream of attaining to."[94]

The theme of longevity, as we shall see, would appear more frequently in the booster literature of the early twentieth century, but it was found occasionally in the promotional tracts of the 1880s and 1890s. Robert Strahorn, for example, after noting in 1881 that Idaho was "in the same latitude as sunny France, Switzerland, and portions of Italy, Spain, and Portugal" and that its climate was quite similar to theirs, soon returned the reader to domestic comparisons. He cited an official report of the surgeon general of the U.S. Army that listed the number of deaths from disease per 1,000 soldiers stationed in the various regions and states. The figure was 17.83 for troops stationed along the Atlantic coast and 12.11 for troops in Arizona, but only 4.77 in Dakota, 4.71 for Wyoming, and 4.66 for Idaho, leaving the reader to conclude that Idaho was the healthiest location in the nation. (Of course, the discerning reader might have concluded that the figures bore some relation to the density of troops stationed in particular areas, which would have been more causally related to the spread of disease than would the presumably Mediterranean or Alpine climate of Idaho, Wyoming, and Dakota.)[95] Interestingly, in an enlarged 1893 edition of Strahorn's promotional booklet on Idaho (one that no longer acknowledged him as author), the military death rate per 1,000 men in Idaho had dropped to a mere 3.74, and the ominous rate of 22.50 was now included for the Gulf States.[96]

If the reader was not convinced by the low military death rate in Idaho, then Strahorn's presentation of the death rates for the whole population in all the states, drawn from the 1870 Census, may have alleviated any doubts about settlement in "the gem of the mountains."[97] Strahorn emphasized that Idaho's minuscule death rate of 0.33 (the percentage of deaths to population annually) was far and away the lowest in the nation. Readers had no need to examine the statistics carefully, since Strahorn explained their meaning definitively: "The mortality of California—the praises of whose climate are caroled in all civilized tongues, is nearly five times greater than that of Idaho; Colorado, a summer-land which is most deservedly the resort of tens of thousands of health-seekers annually, exhibits a mortality nearly three times as great as that of Idaho." Idaho was, undeniably, then, "the healthiest region in America."[98] Strahorn, himself a resident of Idaho, who lived to the age of ninety-two, was living proof.

But Strahorn was far from alone among the boosters when it came to claims on behalf of climate. Indeed, in 1893 the Union Pacific Railroad promotional department—for whom Strahorn had earlier worked—remarked that thousands of people were fleeing the "blizzard-blighting West and icy

North" every year for the recuperative atmosphere of "the El Paso and Panhandle sections," and even "California [could] not excel Texas in this important respect."[99] It turns out that all these western places—from the Plains to the Pacific—had the most enviable climates imaginable. Moreover, just about everywhere in the West one would find consumptives being cured by the climate. The disease-ridden, fume-filled East was, as a matter of course, contrasted with the health-inducing pure air of the West in promotional publications. For example, in 1875 a Utah booster declared that "the entire colonization of the Mississippi Valley, from Pittsburg to middle Kansas, a width of one thousand miles, has been carried on with the almost universal accompaniment of fevers," which was all the more reason to move on to the healthy land of Utah.[100] An Arizona publication from the 1880s presented the testimony of a medical doctor, D. J. Brannon, as incontrovertible evidence of the unhealthly climates of the rest of the country outside of the West. Brannon first noted that "rheumatism, Bright's disease of the kidneys, neuralgia and many conditions of nervous exhaustion are greatly improved or permanently cured by a residence in this country [the Flagstaff, Arizona, area]." Then he proceeded to contend that fully one-half of the residents of the "Atlantic, Middle and Gulf States are carried off by diseases of the respiratory organs." With these kinds of odds—a fifty-fifty chance of death by respiratory organ failure—and in light of the near-total absence of such diseases in Flagstaff and the surrounding area, following the good doctor's advice might well have seemed a wise course to some readers.[101]

Not surprisingly, California's boosters were not to be outdone in the arena of climate promotion in this period. Benjamin Cummings Truman, in his book *Semi-tropical California* (1874), which covered the area from Santa Barbara to San Diego, produced a table of deaths per 1,000 inhabitants to support his argument that the sunny Southland was the safest place to live. With its death rate of only 13 (this figure was, quite conveniently, the same for Santa Barbara, Los Angeles, and San Diego), semitropical California was unmatchable. New Orleans, New York, Baltimore, Philadelphia, Chicago, Boston, St. Louis, and even San Francisco, with their death rates ranging from 37 (New Orleans) to 21 (San Francisco), could not hold a candle to the Southland when it came to the avoidance of death. Truman then provided a classic example of interstate booster rivalry, chiding the "American railroad subsidized land companies" for inducing the poor unfortunates of New England and Europe to seek homes in northwestern states such as

Minnesota, Iowa, Kansas, and Nebraska. To emphasize his point and underscore the wickedness of those states' boosters, he recounted the harrowing results of winter in Minnesota. In January 1873, seventy Minnesotans froze to death in minus-forty-degree temperatures (two of them dying "within a short period of amputation"), and another thirty-one lost limbs or parts of limbs.[102] This juxtaposition of the Southland with the bleak and brutal northwestern tundra was hardly subtle, but it was certainly memorable; as for its effectiveness, we can only guess.

In his best-known work, *Homes and Happiness in the Golden State* (1884), Truman repeatedly emphasized the hollowness of other western states' claims concerning climate and fertility. He warned readers that "fevers and diseases of the malarial character carry off about one-half of mankind, and diseases of the respiratory organs about one-fourth," and comforted them with the knowledge that the southern coast of California was remarkably free of such diseases (Robert Strahorn's claims to the contrary notwithstanding).[103] But most important, Truman established the theme of California as a paradise for small, middle-class landholders, a Jeffersonian arcadia for country gentlemen and women. This was a theme that the Golden State's promoters would pick up on in the next century.[104]

It would have been comforting, one presumes, for potential settlers to learn that there were no climatic dangers and inconveniences to be endured in the West, or at least to be informed that their chosen western promised land was safer and healthier than the others on offer. The late nineteenth century was marked by a proliferation of sanitarium hotels and resorts, especially in California and Arizona. In these healthy places, it was claimed, the wonderful climate would breathe new life into sufferers of respiratory diseases and various other debilitating ailments. Drawing on the testimony of doctors and official government reports to underscore the mildness and general healthfulness of western climates was a common tactic of western promotional writers.[105] This emphasis, of course, is hardly surprising in an earlier era when so many more people depended on climate for their very livelihoods and before modern methods of insulation, heating, and air-conditioning provided relief from climatic extremes. Nonetheless, that earlier approach parallels contemporary promotional approaches in its use of official government statistics and "expert testimony" from doctors. And, of course, climate continues to be used extensively, and quite effectively, in the marketing of western regions today.

Boosterism on Trial

> The book is not written in the interest of any Railroad Corporation, Emigrant Aid Society, or Real Estate Company, nor has any aid been received from these or any other agencies. (Wilson Nicely, *The Great South-West,* 1867)

Perhaps it is inevitable that the path toward creating new settlements in the western United States would have been as marked by boosterist overstatement as it indeed was. Formulaic contours and overreaching claims could, in fact, be a feature of all place creation, city-building, and regional marketing. At the same time, public response and incredulity also affected the process of promotion, occasionally inducing a self-regulatory function in the latter. This process is observable in the skepticism expressed by some of the more astute readers of late-nineteenth-century booster literature. An "anti-boosterist" trend even emerged to counter and moderate the inflated promises of the West. Gazeteer and western traveler J. H. Beadle, for example, provided a decidedly unboosterish account of the whole trans-Mississippi region in his book *The Undeveloped West* (1873). Speaking of the Great Plains, Beadle noted that there were some scattered patches of good land in the region, but he wished to focus on the bad, and to inform readers of what they would not otherwise learn. "The good land," he cynically emphasized, "you will certainly hear of from the magnificent circulars of railroad and emigration companies."[106] A few years later the *Philadelphia Record* warned its readers of the boosters' claims concerning western Kansas, noting that temperatures there ranged from over 100 degrees to as low as minus 40 degrees, and that its moral barometer was no higher than the winter temperatures. Kansans responded angrily—in the form of letters to their local newspapers—to such written assaults on their new Eden.[107] What is more, the abundant rainfall and somewhat milder temperatures of the early and mid-1880s seemed to legitimate their vociferous response to outside criticisms of their climate.[108]

In August 1887, a few months after the previous tragic winter season that had killed many thousands of cattle, not to mention hundreds of people, observers described Nebraska and the Dakotas as "waterless, trackless plains, . . . twin Siberias," and referred to their residents as the unfortunate dupes of railroad boosters.[109] Kansans also suffered during that winter and often presented themselves as victims of unscrupulous land and town promoters, forgetting their earlier defenses of the boosters' visions of paradise.[110]

A few years later, California's boosters were engaged in heated arguments over the propagandistic nature of some of the promotional writing being produced for the state. Sharper-minded (and, perhaps, more honest) boosters feared that the more excessively effusive pronouncements about the state's bright prospects would only nurture the doubts of outsiders, not convince anyone to settle there. Once the boom of the 1880s had gone bust, stories of unscrupulous California boosters and their hapless victims circulated around the country. Charles Dudley Warner, in his California promotional essay "Our Italy," which appeared in *Harper's New Monthly Magazine* in November 1890, tried to restore public faith in the California dream in the wake of the nightmarish bust. In doing so, he was careful to insist that "sensible people" paid no attention to overly exaggerated claims concerning the agricultural possibilities of the state and that "the temporary evils in the train of the 'boom' are fast disappearing." In a classic example of promotional literary resourcefulness, Warner managed to acknowledge the excesses of previous waves of boosterism and then actually repeat them, perhaps leaving at least some readers with an undiminished vision of the state as a promised land "of marvellous beauty."[111]

California's promoters were right to express concerns over the excesses of boosterism, especially given the increasingly skeptical climate of opinion that was developing in this period. In 1896 the publication of a document in England, authored by the British consul general in San Francisco and entitled *Report on the Distress Caused to British Emigrants to California by Fraudulent Land Syndicates and Emigration Agencies,* illuminated these California concerns quite dramatically. Queen Victoria sent the document, which warned potential emigrants against all California real estate propositions, to Parliament.[112] A few years later, local Southern California historian James McGuinn described the boosters as "fellows who had left their consciences (that is, if they had any to leave) on the other side of the Rockies."[113] Indeed, California's promoters seemed to spend much of the late nineteenth century mired in a multitude of conflicting visions of what their state should become, with some of them waging a desperate verbal and written battle against the very expansiveness and effusiveness of those visions.

These various tensions among different promotional organizations and individuals are important to consider. All too commonly, scholars tend to view the forces of boosterism in black-and-white terms as a unified arm of the capitalist state. However, the internecine squabbling that marked California promotional writing as early as the late 1860s set the tone for the rest of

the century. The lack of a united promotional front, along with a combination of other periodic factors—droughts, economic depressions, and negative outside perceptions being chief among them—continued to retard
California's growth throughout the rest of the century.

On occasion, in fact, boosters engaged in acts of self-regulation—eschew-
ing overeffusiveness in their claims and rhetoric—to avoid attracting the barbs
of critics and nurturing the cynicism of potential settlers. Furthermore, as a
kind of reflexive and defensive response to any disbelief over the validity of
their promotional claims, booster writers almost invariably began their tracts
with the statement that they were not exaggerated accounts. Authors even
went so far as to assert that they were not booster publications at all.[114] Ezra
Meeker, in his 1870 promotional pamphlet for Washington Territory (where
he had arrived in 1853), explained that the publication was a response to
interest concerning the region and not an effort to create such interest. "The
great aim," he claimed, "has been to avoid overdrawn statements." And, in
fairness to Meeker, he did avoid the lofty and melodramatic claims and prose
style of most boosters, even admitting that the soil of western Washington
was not as uniformly rich as that of Iowa or Illinois.[115] Meeker proved to be
an effective booster for Washington, despite being far more restrained in his
rhetoric than the average western booster. He subsequently wrote a description of Washington Territory for Horace Greeley's *New York Tribune* and was
commissioned by Jay Cooke of the Northern Pacific Railroad to promote
Washington in the New England states.[116] Meeker's circumstances as a
booster were quite typical—indeed, they were reminiscent of Robert Strahorn's:
both writers were talented young men whose promotional skills were recognized by the railroads.

Nonetheless, Meeker's careful, measured rhetoric was not typical of the
booster genre. Most booster publications heartily denied any exaggeration,
made earnest professions of absolute authenticity, and then proceeded to
make grandiose claims about culture, climate, and agricultural fertility. Arizona boosters in 1891, for example, insisted that their overview was "given
to the public in all candor" and that "nothing [has] been overstated nor has
there been any attempt to boom the Territory beyond what its merits justify"; the same boosters then pronounced that the state had some of the
world's "richest" and "most friable" lands.[117] Similarly, Strahorn, in the preface to his *Hand-Book of Wyoming,* emphasized that "in collecting, sifting
and tabulating these statistics [I have] endeavored to be thoroughly consci-
entious and to accept only that from other hands which has been deemed

thoroughly reliable." But Strahorn also proudly proclaimed in the same preface that he had compiled the book (a sizable, 250-page volume) in sixty days, and he thanked local newspaper editors and other Wyoming officials for their "substantial favors."[118] Strahorn was probably not unaware of these incongruities in his prefatory remarks. Where else was the commissioned (exterior) booster writer on a two-month schedule to go to get his information other than the local (interior) boosters of the state?

The greatest exaggeration in the promotional writings of the period came not in their claims to authenticity but in their presentation of western frontier backwaters as settled, prosperous, regional communities. The boosters' easy transitions from frontier to region were overstated; they claimed, in short, that the future already existed, that the promise of these lands had already come to fruition. Nonetheless, such overstatement was vital to achieving the delicate balance that would eventually attract settlement. The boosters were trying to sell frontiers of opportunity in ostensibly settled, postfrontier regions. Later on, in fact, when agricultural and municipal areas had grown to match the promise of the boosters' claims, the earlier descriptions must have seemed legitimate enough. But in those instances when the frontiers of opportunity turned out to be more limited and frontier hardships prevailed, the boosters' unwavering optimism must have seemed a cruel fiction indeed.

Some of these promoters were clearly forging their own sense of place as they described the kinds of promised lands that they hoped their western residences would become. Furthermore, their writings played an important role in shaping public perceptions of the West. They presented a set of images that ran counter both to the frontier mythology that popular writers and artists were constructing and to the frontier anxieties of intellectuals who bemoaned the closing of the safety valve of free or cheap western lands in the late nineteenth century. Those intellectuals expressed concern over the future of democracy in a frontierless America and worried about the decline of national character in an environment devoid of frontier challenges and dangers. As we shall see, such concerns, while a departure from the rhetoric of western promoters, paralleled the contours of pioneer reminiscences.

THE SECOND BOOSTERIST PHASE

Depression, Catastrophe, and Recovery

Most of the promotional literature of the late nineteenth and early twentieth centuries can be divided into two chronologically distinct phases: one comprising materials generated from the late 1860s into the early 1890s, and the second consisting of tracts written from the end of the 1890s up to around the time of American entry into World War I. Not surprisingly, the production of booster tracts declined during the depression years, from 1893 to 1897.[1] Fewer people had the means to migrate to western towns during that period, and promotional organizations had limited financial resources to produce the literature that might attract settlement.

Climate change also helps explain the decline of boosterism during the depressed midnineties. European Americans had settled in significant numbers on the Pacific Coast, in California and the Oregon Territory, for two decades prior to the late 1860s. But it was not until then that the vast and largely blank space on the map between the ninety-eighth meridian and the West Coast began to fill up with hopeful homesteaders. In the quarter century beginning in the late 1860s, a mass of booster literature accompanied and helped to propel the first great wave of post–Civil War settlement. The passage of the Homestead Act in 1862, which made land available in quarter sections (160 acres) to settlers for the price of a small filing fee and a five-year commitment to improve the property, was of course a tremendously important factor contributing to the rush of settlement into the West. Even if much of the best land passed into the hands of railroads and speculators, a good deal of it still ended up eventually purchased by settlers at prices far lower than those in other, more densely settled parts of the country.[2] But by the late 1880s, a period of unusually high rainfall was coming to an end in the usually semiarid West, and extreme seasonal temperature variations were giving the lie to the promotional insistence on Edenic climates in the new western lands. On the Great Plains, for example, the infamous winters of 1886 and 1887, as well as the drought beginning in the late 1880s and lasting into the mid-1890s, had a negative impact on that region's settlement and promotion even before the depression officially began. When in January 1886 the wind chill factor on the High Plains of western Kansas fell to 100 degrees below zero and the following summer proved unbearably hot, the boosters' insistence on the region's mild and equable temperatures was impossible to sustain.[3]

The contracting economy helps explain why the rate of population growth in much of the West was lower in the 1890s than in the preceding or succeeding decade. Most of the western states and territories gained only limited population during the last decade of the century. California's population increased from 1,213,000 to 1,485,000 in the same decade, but that gain was considerably smaller than the state's population increases in the 1880s or 1900s. (California, and especially Los Angeles County, would experience explosive growth in the early twentieth century.) Nevada actually lost population, shrinking from 47,000 to 42,000 during the 1890s, but its tremendously volatile economy, based largely on mining, was hardly at that time a reliable barometer of western regional trends. Colorado, New Mexico, Arizona, Washington, Oregon, and South Dakota are more indicative of the demographic trend west of the Mississippi in the 1890s. All those states and territories gained population in the 1890s, but the rate of growth was slower than in the 1880s or the 1900s.[4]

The story was the same in Nebraska, where in the peak homesteading years of 1885 and 1886, 11,293 and 10,269 homesteads, respectively, were settled. This flood was reduced to a trickle when the number of entries dropped steadily to 1,301 in 1895 and 1,101 in 1896 (less than 10 percent of the number of 1885 entries).[5] Meanwhile, failed Great Plains homesteaders, ruined by drought and depression, formed an eastward exodus. The population of Kansas dropped from 1,518,788 in 1888 to 1,334,734 in 1895. A little over a century later, in 2000, the population of Kansas was 2,688,418, almost exactly double the 1895 figure, but a paltry growth rate compared with that in most of the rest of the nation. At least half the residents of the Kansas High Plains in 1886 were gone by 1890, and this area of the state has seen little demographic growth in the century since.[6] The settlers' dreams and the promoters' heady assurances of new promised lands where rain would follow the plow must have seemed a cruel set of illusions and hoaxes. Those who remained in the region and continued to struggle with climatic and economic conditions beyond their control in an effort to sustain the promise of the Plains would form the backbone of the radical agrarian movement of the 1890s.[7]

The railroads continued to generate promotional materials in the depression-ridden 1890s, as did state boards and local chambers of commerce, but the volume was lower for much of the decade than it had been previously. There were some important western boosterist efforts in the period. The massive World's Columbian Exposition in Chicago in 1893, with its more than 27.5 million visitors, played a significant role in promoting western lands and resources, as the region's states and territories sponsored lavish displays of their agricultural and mineral products and promise.[8] The Northwest Interstate Fair that opened in mid-August 1894 is another good example: Montana, Idaho, Oregon, Washington, and Alaska came together with the Province of British Columbia to keep the agricultural wonders of those states in the public consciousness.[9] The California Mid-winter International Exposition, also held in 1894, was intended by its host city, San Francisco, to both build on the promotional momentum gained from the world's fair and provide a much needed jolt to a thoroughly depressed urban economy marked by growing levels of unemployment.[10] Such cooperative regional and urban efforts at promotion were prompted in large part by the restricted economic horizons of the period. But these fairs, while they sparked some regional promotional efforts, marked not so much the beginning of a new era of western boosterism as the end of an old one. The impact of the fairs could not outweigh the enormity of the ongoing economic depression.

The Oklahoma Territory was among the exceptions to the general trend of meager western population growth in the 1890s. Because of a series of federally sponsored land rushes into portions of the Indian Territory (between 1889 and 1893),[11] the region experienced meteoric demographic growth in the 1890s, more than tripling from 259,000 to 790,000. North Dakota, Texas, Utah, Idaho, and Wyoming also grew at quite impressive rates that were not much lower than those of the 1880s and 1900s. But aside from Alaska, no western state or territory experienced a growth rate in the 1890s that was considerably higher than those of the preceding or succeeding decades. Alaska doubled in size, from 32,000 to 64,000, but, much like Nevada, it serves as a representative example of the demographic trends in states completely dominated by boom-bust extractive resource economies and thus is not illustrative of trends in those states in search of permanent settlement.

Of course, the generally slow rate of population growth in the West in the 1890s did not result from a decrease in promotional efforts on behalf of western destinations, or from any heightened public consciousness of the exaggerated nature of promotional promises; it was a consequence of the economic downturn and of climatic factors. A depressed national economy simply meant less migration (not more, as frontier safety valve theory advocates expected). In fact, a second era of enhanced promotion of western settlement began with the return of prosperity in the late 1890s and lasted up until around the time of American entry into the Great War, in 1917.[12] An improved economy meant more money for western promotional efforts and a larger pool of prospective migrants.

That second era of intensified promotional efforts, though, has important roots in the depressed 1890s, when western boosters won some important battles over their skeptical and better-informed critics. Irrigation and dryland farming were the issues at the center of these struggles. The reclamation of semiarid lands through irrigation had been promoted cautiously in the late 1870s by the land-use visionary John Wesley Powell, author of the famous government-sponsored *Report on the Lands of the Arid Regions of the United States* (1878). Powell had emphasized the need for small, self-governing, irrigation-based communities in the semiarid West.[13] William E. Smythe, who had grander visions of population growth in the region, was far less cautionary, indeed, in his pro-irrigation rhetoric. Smythe helped create institutional support for such sentiments in the early 1890s in the form of the Irrigation Congress, which he directed, and through the pages of the *Irrigation Age,* the journal he edited.[14]

In the fall of 1893—a year that saw numerous expressions of concern over the perceived closing of the frontier of free or cheap land—the Irrigation

Congress met in Los Angeles and forged its response to the problem.[15] The event was a decidedly booserish affair from the outset. It was held in the city's Grand Opera House, rented by the chamber of commerce for the occasion, and "sixteen-foot cornstalks, grown tall by irrigation, flanked the entryway."[16] The organization's expressed goal was to create a million forty-acre irrigated farms out of the remaining public lands in the West. The apostles of irrigation in attendance seemed to feel that these million new farms would be just a beginning and that there were close to a billion irrigable acres of federally owned land left in the West.[17] Powell, in a dramatic moment in the history of the public domain, told the Irrigation Congress that such claims were wildly optimistic and wrongheaded; he insisted that there were only 100,000 irrigable acres in the region.[18] But bursting the bubble of the boosters with a sharp shot of reality earned Powell their boos, not their thanks.[19] The cold response to Powell's warnings underscores the strength and resilience of the forces of boosterism. In fact, the year before the Irrigation Congress rejected his warnings in 1893, Powell's landmark *Report on the Lands of the Arid Regions of the United States* was actually cited, against his intent, in a Union Pacific Railroad promotional pamphlet in support of the theory that "rain followed the plow."[20]

In the late-nineteenth-century and early-twentieth-century debate over irrigation, Smythe's boosterish optimism won out over Powell's cautious assessment of the limitations of western promised lands. In 1894 Congress passed the Carey Act, which gave public lands to states that would irrigate them. Passed at the height of the depression, it is hardly surprising that the act was not a resounding success. The Newlands Reclamation Act of 1902 was more significant. Drawing on money from government land sales to fund large-scale federal irrigation projects in the West, the Newlands Act became a huge triumph for the supporters of irrigation, and the source of the subsequent Reclamation Service (an organization that developed in 1923 into the Bureau of Reclamation, which would build dams and irrigate larger areas of the West).[21] The beginning of the new century also saw the publication of Smythe's popular book *The Conquest of Arid America* (1899; revised edition, 1905), the intent of which was to laud irrigation as the savior for a frontierless America. Smythe opened the book with the bold declaration that with the application of irrigation technology, "there is room for one hundred million people in the States and Territories between the Missouri River and the Pacific Ocean." A century later his prophecy has been realized, though the region's contemporary population, centered largely in massive metropolitan areas, is distributed in ways that hardly mark the fruition of either Smythe's or Powell's visions for western promised lands.[22]

In the early years of the twentieth century, promoters championed the practice of dryland, or dry, farming with the same supreme assuredness that characterized Smythe and other advocates of irrigation and popularizers of the notion that rain follows the plow. That latter belief, in fact, itself experienced a revival in the early twentieth century, riding the same wave of enthusiasm that accompanied dryland farming.[23] The practice of dry farming (which involved deep plowing to preserve the moisture of the soil) was being popularized by Hardy W. Campbell, a western Nebraska farmer, during the 1890s and was advertised by the railroads after 1902. The new agricultural approach was facilitated by the passage of the Enlarged Homestead Act of 1909, which doubled the size of initial homesteads in semiarid areas to 320 acres. Since dry farming, despite its promoters' heady pronouncements concerning crop yields per acre, was generally marked by significantly lower yields than traditional farming in humid regions, more acreage was required to ensure sizable harvests.[24] Homestead size in some semiarid regions was further increased in 1916 with the passage of the Stock Raising Homestead Act, which allowed for up to 640 acres to enable the implementation of cattle raising as a supplement to farming.[25]

The Progressive Era's combination of irrigation efforts, dry farming, new agricultural machinery, rising crop prices, favorable climatic conditions, a healthy national economy, multiple revisions to the original Homestead Act, and another wave of promotional literature all contributed to a second great homesteading push in the first two decades of the twentieth century. During this time more homesteads were filed than in the nearly four-decade-long period from the original passage of the act in 1862 to the end of the nineteenth century.[26] The "heyday" of homesteading was the period from 1900 to 1913, when 1 million homesteads were filed, whereas in the thirty-eight years from 1862 to 1900, a total of 1,400,000 homesteads were filed—an average yearly rate of less than half that for the 1900–1913 period. In 1913, the peak year for homesteading, nearly 60,000 homesteads covering nearly 11 million acres were "proved up" (i.e., passed into private ownership from the federal government).[27]

Early-twentieth-century regional growth rates could be impressive. The number of farms in the Texas Panhandle and South Plains, for example, rose from 4,131 in 1900 to 14,406 in 1910 and to 19,385 in 1920.[28] Texas, Oklahoma, and California experienced the most significant demographic growth rates in the period, with a combined population increase of 2,715,000 between 1900 and 1917. On a smaller scale, but still clearly reflective of this second great boom in homesteading, Wyoming's population increased at a rate of 58 percent from 1900 to 1910, as over 50,000 new residents moved into the state. Meanwhile, that state's immigration agent complained that Idaho, Oregon, and Washington were receiving the bulk of the settlers.[29] Of course, in addition to the strong levels of homesteading on the public domain, these years were also marked by high rates of purchase of the privately owned lands of railroads and land companies. Not surprisingly, then, this great rush of settlement into the West was also marked by a voluminous booster literature promoting western agricultural regions as the last remaining earthly paradises.

But by late 1919, within a year of the end of World War I, shrinking export markets precipitated the long agricultural depression that brought the second great homesteading boom in the West to an end and lasted through the 1930s. A massive wartime expansion of American agricultural enterprises, combined with the recovery of European agriculture in the immediate postwar years, left American farmers with huge surpluses and limited markets, all of which translated into low prices for crops and livestock. Since many farmers had gone into debt in the previous decades while expanding their holdings and purchasing new machinery, the low food prices left them in a particularly poor state, unable to reduce their debt burdens. In response to these unfortunate circumstances, the Farm Bloc formed in the early 1920s to represent the farmers' needs for debt relief and for higher prices to the federal government, just as the Populist Party had formed during an earlier era of agricultural crisis, the 1890s. In this way, the agricultural depression of the 1920s, like that of the 1890s, marked a watershed in western promotion. Promotional tracts continued to be produced in the 1920s, especially for California. However, aside from the Golden State, the flow of promotional literature for the West was more limited in the 1920s than it had been in the immediately preceding decades, or during the 1870s and 1880s.

Regional Wonderlands

[Dillard County, Texas's] 3,600 foot altitude with . . . attendant glorious ozone, bright sunshine and health-giving air comes near being the *fountain of youth* which men have long sought. (Dillard-Powell Land Company, *Lubbock, Lubbock County, [Texas]*, c. 1908)

Western promotional efforts would continue in the 1920s, but they differed somewhat from the ones that had preceded them. Both the late-nineteenth-century booster literature and that of the early twentieth century promoted lands and towns together. The towns and the agricultural communities surrounding them were presented as symbiotic parts of a whole. This was so because the promoters were constructing miniregions, particularly in the early twentieth century, when most of the booklets focused on several counties together. In some instances, a group of states, such as Oregon, Washington, and Idaho, were presented together. Potential migrants were provided in a single publication with information on available farming lands and town lots in the various counties. A single city, such as Tacoma, "the Electric City of the Pacific Coast," or Spokane, the center of the Inland Empire, might be presented as the emerging metropolis of a region. But even the ostensibly city-centered booster publications placed great emphasis on the available agricultural opportunities and mineral resources in the region.[30] By the 1920s, however, with the second homesteading boom over, much of the western promotional literature was more "town-centered" and placed less emphasis on selling the varied offerings of entire regions.

In this next era of western boosting—from the end of the nineteenth century into the late teens of the twentieth—the same basic themes that had characterized the genre in the late nineteenth century emerged again. Though generally somewhat less effusive than those earlier efforts to promote western promised lands, the early-twentieth-century boosters certainly had their unrestrained poetic moments and could on occasion reach those former Olympian heights in their efforts to sell regions. Southern California's promotional efforts in the early twentieth century—when boosterism became almost a second religion—were an important exception to this trend, as were some of the remarkably unrestrained railroad-sponsored efforts on behalf of eastern and central Montana in the years following the passage of the Enlarged Homestead Act of 1909.[31]

The closing frontier remained an important element in the sales pitches of the later promoters, just as it remained a tenet of American thought and culture. In an article entitled "The Passing of the Promised Land," published in the *Atlantic Monthly* in 1909, Charles Moreau Harger cataloged the increased financial benefits and the absolute lack of pioneer conditions in western agriculture. Not a promoter himself but a respected authority on western lands who contributed a steady stream of articles on the topic to the leading monthly periodicals of the day, Harger offered descriptions that must have delighted boosters.[32] "Not long will the Promised Land beckon the American farmer," he announced, then concluded: "Strange it will seem to have no cheap soil offered as a haven of ease and plenty."[33] While his purposes were not promotional, his observations certainly seemed to support the boosters' contentions, even if his reference to "haven[s] of ease and plenty" was intended as a wry comment on promotional excesses.[34]

In their need to present western frontiers as "closing," not "closed," with the wellspring of opportunity fast running out but not yet dried up, the boosters walked the same frontier tightrope that their promotional predecessors had traversed a generation earlier. For example, in 1906, promoters of Big Horn County, Wyoming, urged the "land-hungry" to "get a foothold before it is too late."[35] Similarly, in a booklet from 1909, the Grants Pass Commercial Club of Josephine County, Oregon, reminded readers that the "great westward movement" would end with the settlement of the "[Pacific] Northwest." "Then," the publication warned, "the homeseeker with small capital will be confronted by the Pacific if he looks to the westward." To drive the point home, the author added: "It is not a pleasant thought that the children of today will have no 'west' to turn to. The present great west with its cheap lands will be closed to them, and while it will still be glorious it will not beckon to the man of slender purse as it does today."[36] Boosters in Douglas County, Oregon, offered the same message, noting that hundreds of thousands of eager settlers, encouraged by the renewed cries of "westward ho!" would head for Oregon in 1909, all the more so because every month was vital, and land prices were sure to increase from 100 to 300 percent. The projected time frame for the meteoric increase in land values was left vague, but a future of plenty was assured for those who moved quickly.[37]

Meanwhile, as boosters utilized the lure of "the final frontier," the post-frontier qualities of western places remained an essential element in their advertising. The end of the phase of frontier opportunity was always placed in the future, but the end of frontier inconvenience and danger was always placed in the past. A. J. Wells, in the "Society" section of his Southern Pacific Railroad publication *The New Nevada* (1906), insisted that the state "is not on 'the frontier'," and further noted that "the railroad and the march of progress have pushed that old line into the Pacific."[38] A few years later, the Tucson, Arizona, Chamber of Commerce reiterated the same sentiment with regard to perceptions of cultural underdevelopment, urging potential home seekers to eschew common misassumptions about the frontier qualities of the region, noting that the Southwest was only "wild and woolly" to the "unsophisticated" observer.[39] In promoting Lubbock County, in the Texas Panhandle, in 1908, a local realty company asked prospective settlers the rather leading question: "Do you want to settle in a country where the hardships of pioneering, as endured by the settlers of a generation and more ago, have been rolled away on the chariot wheels of the modern train, where all the advantages with none of the privations of pioneer life are to be obtained?"[40] The Lubbock County boosters were reconstructing a promotional frontier line: on one side of the line was the earlier pioneering past, when frontier life was dangerous and demanding; and on the other was the postfrontier future, where opportunity will have dried up. In the present there was opportunity without hardship and with all the cultural amenities that accompany the development of civilization, all without the crime and claustrophobia that mark its overdevelopment.

Boosters all over the West took the same basic approach. In 1909 the Chamber of Commerce of the City of Nampa, in "Sunny Southern Idaho," informed potential newcomers that "when one locates in the Nampa Valley it is not necessary to go through the pioneer stages." A few years later, a Southern Pacific Company publication promoting western Oregon declared that the social and industrial development of the state was well under way and that this fact had to be heavily emphasized "lest some would-be settler imagines that this invitation comes from a frontier state still in a raw and undeveloped condition." Such a perception, it was insisted, "would be a radical misconception," and the publication went on to highlight the region's cities, towns, schools, churches, clubs, hotels, transportation facilities, and country homes—its markers of cultural advance. The author concluded that, in light of the incontrovertible evidence presented, "Western Oregon does not suggest pioneer conditions," adding, like the Lubbock promoters, that the inquirer would find "conveniences and privileges of far older States with the opportunities of a new one—that is to say, pioneer advantages without pioneer privations."[41] Another decade later, the same claims were still being made by the Southern Pacific in its advertising: in its brochure *California for the Settler* (1922), the railroad insisted that "these lands virtually constitute a new beginning without pioneer conditions—almost all the advantages of the pioneer are here without his privations." Reemphasizing the point, the author insisted that in California "the new farmer is not forced to take lands that have been picked over; he gets as rich land as if the settlement of the State had just begun."[42]

These kinds of statements echoed through western promotional literature surprisingly late into the twentieth century—certainly through the teens for much of the West and into the 1920s for California. The pervasiveness of such pronouncements concerning the absence of frontier hardships suggests that promoters were seeking, in a quite direct manner, to counter the stereotyped images of western regions that filled the immensely popular pulp fiction of Owen Wister, Zane Grey, and other popular writers of the time. These novelists presented the West as an imaginative place of escape for eastern readers, one where they could experience western adventures vicariously, through the protagonists of the stories. But promoters needed to present western places as the opposite of such imagined locations.

One trick for the promoters was to create the image of a transitory present for a particular place, one in which the grass was greener than it had been in the past or would be in the future of dissipated opportunities. The 1909 Nampa Chamber of Commerce publication began with the statement that "thousands of people in the congested sections of the East" were, "as never before," looking for affordable homes in a good moral and educational climate far removed from the "exhalations of a congested humanity."[43] In selling the economic advantages of the frontier stage without the pioneer privations and inconveniences one would have expected to accompany it, the early-twentieth-century boosters emphasized, as had their late-nineteenth-century counterparts, that these western places were well-developed, culturally advanced regions.[44]

It is important to emphasize, given contemporary western tensions between metropolitan and agricultural areas, that promoters generally presented cities together with the surrounding agricultural lands and mineral resources as a "regional package."[45] And, while they stressed that western lands measured up to or exceeded in productivity those in more humid parts of the country, they also emphasized that western cities compared very well with their more established eastern counterparts. Portland's promoters, for example, claimed in 1903 that the "Rose City" was "in every respect, an Eastern city," intending to imply that it was cultured and sophisticated, not that it was suffering the "exhalations of a congested humanity."[46] The motivation of Twin Falls, Idaho, boosters was similar when they pointed to the "prevailing idea among many Eastern people that the western town consists of shacks and rude, square-built houses with no pretense to beauty or symmetry." They did not hesitate to add that such notions were "quickly dispelled" when people visited their cultured town.[47]

The international expositions staged in Omaha (1898), Portland (the Lewis and Clark Exposition, 1905), Seattle (the Alaska-Yukon-Pacific Exposition, 1909), San Francisco (1915), and San Diego (1915–1917) were partly efforts to demonstrate parity with eastern cities.[48] Regional magazines, directed toward both the residents of western regions and potential newcomers, served the same purpose. *The Coast,* established in Seattle in 1899, mixed traditional booster articles on Pacific Northwestern places with essays and editorials on the richness of culture in the West.[49] When the always indomitable and sometimes irritating Charles Fletcher Lummis took over the editorship of the California booster monthly *Land of Sunshine,* he truly molded a magazine with a regional mission, that of promoting the resources of California and the Southwest.[50]

The quality of schools continued to be a primary emphasis of the boosters' cultural resource promotional pitch in the early twentieth century, just as it had been in the late nineteenth century. A publication issued by the Oregon Railroad and Navigation Company and the Southern Pacific Railroad in 1904 to promote their lines in the Pacific Northwest is reminiscent of the Chicago, Burlington and Quincy's classic *The Heart of the Continent* (1882). The booklet, *Oregon, Washington, Idaho and Their Resources: Mecca of the Homeseeker and Investor,* presented three whole states and dozens of individual cities, towns, and counties, all at the same time and in a single volume, as unmatched, unparalleled, or unsurpassed in the richness of their cultural, agricultural, climatic, scenic, and investment opportunities. The author proclaimed:

> Nowhere in the world has nature been more lavish with her handi-work and scattered more picturesque scenes, encompassing [Portland] with a magnificent and imperishable art gallery of verdure-clad and lofty mountains, whose snow-capped peaks defy the sun's warmest rays and look down upon fertile valleys that fairly groan with the weight of golden grain and fruit. (Rinaldo M. Hall, *Oregon, Washington, Idaho and Their Resources,* 1904)

But for all the dramatic rhetoric and confident claims, the booklet's emphasis on Oregon's schools is particularly memorable. We find that the state's educational efforts have been so thorough "that it is a statistical fact that Oregon stands third from the top in freedom from illiteracy." The statistics were there in the publication for all to see; with 99.58 percent of its population free from illiteracy, Oregon was outpaced only by Nebraska (99.66 percent) and Iowa (99.63 percent).[51] (Iowa had been able to build on its earlier advantage of having "more school teachers . . . than there were soldiers in the [Revolutionary] army"! See chapter 1.) These were the percentages of children from ten to fourteen years of age able to read and write, perhaps not the definitive measure of a region's cultural development and the extent of its cultural amenities; but the figures must have seemed striking to some readers nonetheless.[52]

As a rule, claims concerning the educational advantages of western places, while no less memorable than the statistical evidence supporting Oregonians' high level of emancipation from illiteracy, tended to be more general. "Western Advantages and Opportunities" (1909), an essay in *The Coast,* noted that the schools and educational facilities of the Northwest "put many of the older sections [of the country] to shame when a comparison is made."[53] A few years later, the Wyoming State Board of Immigration claimed that the state employed "a much larger number of teachers . . . in proportion to population than in most of the states." Furthermore, the reader learned, "[a] school is established wherever as many as five pupils can attend." Careful reflection on the claim might have led readers to the conclusion that Wyoming needed to provide so many teachers for so few pupils because the state had a very sparse population spread over a rather large area.[54] Had student-faculty ratios been part of the education-related dialogue of the era, Wyoming's boosters would surely have claimed the most favorable ratios in the nation for their lightly peopled places.

When it came to the wondrously mild, healthful, and invigorating climates of all parts of the West, the boosters' cups overflowed in the early twentieth century, just as they had in the 1870s and 1880s. At the beginning of the new century a Pacific Northwest publication claimed:

> It is a constant source of surprise to the residents of the Pacific Coast that people continue to live in the East and the Middle West, tortured by extremes of heat in the Summer and by as great an extreme of cold during the Winter months, while here they could enjoy the beneficial effects of an equable climate throughout the year, a climate that makes the Coast a Paradise under Summer skies, and the Winter one altogether free from suffering incident to any intensity of cold.[55]

It turns out that this particular claim, when compared with other examples of booster climate advocacy, is actually about as mild as the weather it describes. Often the boosters' claims concerning western climatic benefits were couched in terms that might embarrass even today's most unscrupulous advertising agencies. In 1908, Lubbock County, Texas, boosters warned those with weak lungs and consumptive tendencies who lived in the humid East that their daily experience with "low altitude and damp and poisoned atmosphere" amounted to a "sentence of death . . . already . . . pronounced if they remain where they are."[56] A neighboring land company proclaimed that Lubbock's enormously healthy climate came close to being "the *fountain of youth* which men have long sought."[57] Douglas County, Oregon, boosters were no less subtle when they asked prospective settlers: "WHY FREEZE TO DEATH in the harsh winters of the Eastern States? Why court sickness and even death by exposing yourself to the merciless wintry blasts of the East?" With an average wind velocity of only four miles per hour recorded over thirty-one years, "the lowest record in the United States," who could argue with the promoters of Douglas County, the "Orchard Kingdom"?[58]

Fortunately for would-be settlers, the joys of unparalleled climate and benefits of longevity were also available outside of the West Texas and Oregon wonderlands. They would have learned, for example, that in the "delightful all-the-year-round climate" of Twin Falls, Idaho, "older people forget their aches and pains and regain the free, elastic stride of youth."[59] In Oregon, though, prospective settlers were reminded, the climate was so healthful that official government statistics testified to an annual death rate of only 9.5 per thousand (per annum), "almost two-thirds less than that of New York, Massachusetts and other Eastern states." Furthermore, the state's "Rose City" of Portland, with its "phenomenal death rate" of "about" 9.5, made one only about half as likely to die there as in Denver, with its rate of 18.6, or Portland, Maine, with its rate of 22.[60] The low death rate or longevity card was played so often in the early-twentieth-century booster literature that it became a stock feature of the genre. Still, it was surely a stretch for the infamously polluted mining town of Butte, Montana, to claim in 1928 "a lower death rate than in any other city in the country."[61] Meanwhile, Oregon's boosters confidently asserted that their state's climate was "unsurpassable and unrivalled in the entire world"—except in the summer, that is, a season for which Boulder, Colorado, claimed (probably with some legitimacy) to have the world's most pleasant climate. Boulder, incidentally, also claimed to have "the finest drinking water on this continent," though it offered no statistics about its death rate.[62] Pueblo, Colorado, in 1908, insisted that it had the "finest climate in America" and the "most sunshine of any Colorado city," along with "three big smelters," but (reminiscent of Butte, Montana, and of that era more generally) saw no incongruity between unmatchably healthy climates and smoke billowing from factory chimneys.[63]

Where was the discerning health-seeking settler to go? Boise County claimed to have "more real good, robust health . . . per square foot than in any other section of the globe of the same area."[64] Meanwhile, the boosters of Tacoma, Washington, concluded that their city was the healthiest in the world, with a death rate of only 8.7 per thousand (for the period from mid-1903 to mid-1904), and Nampa Valley, Idaho, also claimed a year-round climate unsurpassed anywhere in the world. The Dalles, Oregon, boosters were more modest, proclaiming only that their climatic conditions were unparalleled anywhere on the continent; and the railroad only claimed "*one of the most* healthful and pleasant [climates] in the world" for Montana. Their Jackson County, Oregon, counterparts eschewed global and continental yardsticks in favor of a more place-specific approach. They presented statistical evidence to demonstrate that their Rogue River Valley region was the climatic clone of Florence, Italy—an approach that California boosters had been using as a matter of course for decades. Boosters of Tucson, Arizona, were more cautious, insisting that their city and surroundings were blessed with "a matchless climate," but warning that "health seekers with insufficient means for proper support should never leave home," and that there was no "light out-door work . . . for semi-invalids" in the region.[65]

Not surprisingly, as had been the case in the late nineteenth century, promotional publications often included direct comparisons with other parts of the West. For example, a Denver promotional magazine from 1905 drew on the expertise of a local medical doctor, Dr. F. E. Prewitt, to drive home the point that those residents suffering from respiratory ailments would feel at ease in the "Queen [City] of the Rocky Mountain Range." Prewitt described Southern California, by contrast, as "invalid-ridden" and marred by a "depressing sameness of climate, excessive humidity or unbearable dust, [and] fleas out of proportion to their food supply." He added that Arizona was malaria-ridden and marked by unbearably intense heat for eight months of the year, while New Mexico and West Texas were plagued by similar conditions. As a consequence of this knowledge, and after having seen the poor progress of the respiratory-challenged in those other western regions, Denver's physicians were keeping their patients at home in paradise, Prewitt declared.[66]

Cautions and Claims in Eden

No one should come to Albany County [Wyoming] expecting to "get rich quick," to achieve success without work and well applied knowledge. . . . Do not build up hopes of fabulous affluence and easy life without work. (Robert W. Innes, *Resources of Albany County, Wyoming,* 1913)

The booster literature of the early-twentieth-century West was, on the whole, more explicit about the need for prospective settlers to bring capital, technical expertise, and a good work ethic than the earlier promotional tracts had been.[67] Late-nineteenth-century boosters had certainly issued occasional cautionary statements about the need for hard work and start-up capital, even in the most productive regions of the West.[68] But these warnings became more common and more pronounced in the second great age of western boosting. Perhaps there was a greater consciousness on the promoters' part of the need to avoid the less restrained style of the earlier boosters, who had deservedly earned a reputation for exaggeration. Certainly, there would have been a greater number of Americans in the early twentieth century familiar with people whose western homesteading efforts had failed. Furthermore, the railroads may have learned some lessons from the tumultuous closing decades of the nineteenth century and decided that a steady stream of commerce, stemming from a less frenzied pace of development, might benefit them more in the long run than had earlier boom and bust cycles. Whatever the reason for the more qualified tone of the later boosters (railroad-sponsored and non-railroad-sponsored alike), their cautionary moments certainly constitute one of the key characteristics of the promotional genre in its second phase.

Typical of such warnings was one contained in a 1914 Northern Pacific Railway tract promoting lands in Montana's Yellowstone region: the booklet noted that the man who goes to the West to engage in dry farming "does not need to be rich, but he must have some capital . . . from $1,000 to $2,000." The publication went on to insist that "failures in the West are due in almost every case, either to lack of capital or laziness. The diligent man with a fair amount of capital should not fail."[69] A 1913 publication from the Laramie, Wyoming, Chamber of Commerce warned prospective settlers not to "build up false hopes of fabulous affluence and easy life without work."[70] Perhaps prospective settlers would have read such statements less as warnings than as challenges: Who likes to think of oneself as lazy, or averse to good, honest labor?

Surely, the letters that potential migrants read in the promotional literature bolstered their confidence. These letters were from successful farmers recording, with great specificity, the details of their agricultural productivity.[71] In a Chicago, Milwaukee and St. Paul Railway booklet from 1907, readers would have found a letter from W. I. Sheets of Sand Creek near Bowman, North Dakota. Sheets noted that he had migrated from Illinois and in his second year in the new location had put in 105 acres of oats, 60 acres of flax, and a few acres of corn and potatoes, in addition to a garden. The list of produce and prices reads like a cornucopia of riches, both agricultural and monetary. Furthermore, he added, his family of eleven "have had excellent health in Dakota," where the summer climate was "perfect," and the winter was mild enough for him to work every day (and during a winter that had been colder than usual). The meaning of all this information could be easily inferred, but Sheets outlined it anyway: "I believe that renters of eastern farms should come to this country. This is the place to get a start and in a few years you can become independent. The country is growing like a young calf, and land values are steadily rising." If unconvinced by the good fortunes of Sheets, who was probably an experienced farmer before he got to North Dakota, prospective settlers would surely have been impressed by the success of another newly arrived North Dakotan, E. D. Jones, of Hettinger County. Jones explained in his letter that he had been a barber for more than twelve years in Indiana, and this was his first experience as a farmer. His record of agricultural productivity had been quite astonishing, and he concluded: "I think this is a pretty good record for a barber, and am proud of it." What is more, his wife, an urban dweller all her life up to that time, had "no desire to go back" to the city.[72]

The legitimacy and trustworthiness of such letters can certainly be called into question. Such skepticism concerning the railroads' representation of ostensibly authentic testimonies of settlers is borne out by a fascinating exchange of actual correspondence that took place in 1909, concerning the far northern plains of the Province of Alberta, Canada. A farmer from the region, Henry Sorensen, had written to the railroad and described the agricultural potential of the place in less than glowing terms. The director of the Canadian Pacific Irrigation Colonization Company, C. W. Peterson, responded: "We have taken the liberty of changing your letter to a certain extent, as, for our purpose, it seems inadvisable to refer to frosts." He had the temerity to add, "We propose making exceptionally good use of your letter in our new Public Opinion pamphlet."[73] The frequency and degree to which farmers' letters were altered beyond their control surely varied from period to period, from railroad to railroad, and from one railroad representative to another. Still, the uniformity of uniquely positive letters, as they were reproduced in the promotional tracts, must have impressed the target group of prospective settlers as testimonies to the ease with which their dreams and aspirations of ownership and independence could be realized.

The West's promised lands would not literally farm themselves, and boosters increasingly admitted as much, but they also presented a flood of statistical evidence to convince the skeptical that risks were minimal. In addition to the letters, there were the climate charts, the rainfall tables, the impressive lists of crops and yields per acre. These tables seemed to lend scientific support to the promoters' promises. The very presence of numbers seemed to provide an inherent credibility to boosterish claims by giving them the appearance of impartiality. Even if the scientific charts did not provide the necessary information to really prove the legitimacy of the common proclamations concerning unparalleled agricultural productivity, the boosters were generally more than able to make a few drops of rainfall go a long, long way. In 1910 the Sherman County (Oregon) Development League, in a railroad-sponsored booklet, admitted that the average rainfall in the region was only ten inches per year. However, low rainfall was not a problem, according to these confident boosters, since "ten inches, coming at the proper season, is as beneficial as many times the amount falling at other than growing seasons."[74] Sherman County was blessed with good timing; it was the beneficiary of climatic coincidence, at least in the estimation of its promoters.

The ostensibly scientific data reproduced in the promotional publications were still often spiced with choice language describing these western lands as agricultural havens. The format of the publications was quite standardized: sections of numeric data and purple prose alternated throughout the text, with the former, "objective" sections lending legitimacy to the effusive claims. Indeed, those claims could on occasion be remarkable. *The Coast* magazine in 1910 presented Island County, Washington,[75] as the "Islands of the Blest," a place where "the fertility of the soil . . . rivals the marvelous valleys of the Mississippi or the Nile." Potential residents of Portland, Oregon, learned they were surrounded by "fertile valleys that fairly groan with the weight of golden grain and fruit"; those of Tucson found there "is no richer soil in the world than that of [the] so-called desert country" around their city.[76] Even with their common qualifications concerning agricultural fertility—qualifications that often took into account the need for dry farming and irrigation—the boosters did not completely lose their penchant for waxing eloquently and, often, unrealistically. Neither did they lose their tendency to provide assurances of their honesty and trustworthiness, a sure sign that a strong undercurrent of cynicism toward the boosters still existed.

These assurances often sounded like those offered during the first phase of western promotional writing. For example, in 1911, Pacific City, Oregon, boosters told readers that their publication "contains no misrepresentations, you can absolutely rely on its contents." What was more, they added, "We make no promises of wonderful things to be done in the future, but leave that to your own foresight." That their hope was to make their promised land "the ATLANTIC CITY of the Pacific Coast" perhaps bears out the need to be careful what one wishes for.[77] But the real point of the claims to legitimacy was that they eschewed wishful thinking (at least in their rhetoric) and purported to present only current realities, and without exaggeration. The Booster Club of Morrow County, Oregon, claimed in its 1911 promotional publication that "the strictest adherence to fact has been the inviolable principle."[78] The following year, Tacoma boosters insisted that "no motive of self-aggrandizement" was behind their publication and, just for good measure, added that "there should be no necessity of assuring the reader that all statements made herein are absolutely authentic."[79] Similarly, in his *Commercial Encyclopedia of the Pacific Southwest* (1911)—a region encompassing California, Nevada, Utah, and Arizona—Ellis A. Davis also insisted that "exaggerated and erroneous reports of the boom literature type have been avoided."[80]

Such claims to rational reliability are so common that they constitute a stock element of the booster genre. Furthermore, these claims seem to have been a vital part of promoters' efforts at disassociation from the exaggerations and manipulations that were increasingly being viewed as the hallmarks of boosterism. It would have been highly inadvisable for promoters to present the climates of western places as merely "not-inhospitable," or their agricultural fertility as just about "acceptable enough to ensure families a living outside of the poorhouse," or their cultural amenities as only "average, but not so limited as to make emigrants wish for their former homes everyday." Such phrases do not appear in the promotional literature, and for good reason. To expect an individual booster or chamber of commerce to have done as much (or as little) for a specific region would have been akin to expecting a farmer to engage in voluntary crop reduction during an age of overproduction without guarantees that neighbors would do the same.

As with the P. T. Barnum origins of the concurrent advertising industry, truth and moderation in booster texts were obviously not intrinsic elements. While it is true that, in hindsight, these qualities should have been the hallmarks of land and town promotion in earlier periods, it is also the case that both exaggerated charlatanism and modest-sounding rationalism worked in promotional literature to convince and sway the readership. Boosters were representing regions that were competing with other places for new popula-

tion. Given this reality, it would have been unwise for any promotional publication to present its subject as anything less than a regional wonderland.
Yet it was vital, given the growing public cynicism concerning the reliability
of promotional literature, for promoters to emphasize the authenticity and
lack of exaggeration of their claims and the accuracy of the statistical data
presented. They were performing a delicate balancing act in trying to present
western places as promised lands and yet remain within the realm of believ-
ability. Their dilemma was similar to that discussed earlier: of presenting
places as frontiers of opportunity and as settled regions bursting at the seams
with cultural amenities, all at the same time. A common approach of promoters was to note that while a particular description or claim might seem
exaggerated to the reader, special efforts had been made to present the place
in the most conservative or reserved terms. Indeed, it would have been far
more surprising for readers not to see assurances of legitimacy in the promotional literature than to see them. Still, it is ironic that one of the surest
marks of booster publications in the early twentieth century continued to be
their attempted disassociation from the genre to which they belonged.

The Consequences of Imagination

> The boosters whipped themselves into a frenzy of enthusiasm. Many hours
> were spent at the barns and about the pigpens discussing the optimistic
> future, while squealing pigs pushed sharp noses through the cracks. (Mari
> Sandoz, *Old Jules* [1935], 213)

What consequences did the imaginative booster mentality have for the formation of regional attachments? Answers can only be speculative, since,
for all the diary, journal, and letter writers of the period, most people were
rarely in the habit of recording formally their thoughts and feelings about
whether their dreams and aspirations concerning new places of habitation
had been realized. Most new migrants have not as a matter of course juxtaposed their expectations of western places (which were shaped, in part
at least, by the promoters' descriptions) with the actual conditions they
eventually faced in those places. People would, one suspects, be more likely
to develop strong attachments to places where the realities of settlement
were not thoroughly incongruous with the boosters' promises. Residents,
surely, are more likely to feel at home in places that turn out to be what
they were promised to be.

However, promises abounded in the unpredictable boom-and-bust western economy of the late nineteenth and early twentieth centuries, and boosterism in that uncertain climate was necessarily a "grow-or-die" philosophy.[81] Unbridled optimism, exaggeration, and imagination were the keys to future kingdoms. The dreams of recently settled individuals and communities could become reality only if members of the community maintained their faith in the future. Those who questioned the feasibility of the dream were labeled "knockers" and were often the objects of social ostracism.[82] Town councils, chambers of commerce, realtors, speculators, newspaper editors, and church societies all jumped on the booster bandwagon, and "information that might deter settlers from coming was rigorously suppressed."[83] An increase in population would ensure the development of more economic and cultural infrastructure, which in turn would raise property values and sustain the cycle of growth.

Questioning a place's promise affected not just those doing the questioning but also all who had put stock, mental and material, in the place. This may help explain why recently arrived settlers in the Plains and other parts of the West reacted so vehemently to more sobering and critical commentaries on their places. Perhaps their attachment to those places, their regional identity, was not even close to being fully formed yet, but their emotional and financial investments in their places were extremely strong. And, through the very process of reacting defensively and forcefully to outsiders' negative assessments of the climatic extremes of western Kansas and other places, new settlers in those regions were forming their attachments to the place. In doing so, they were themselves buying into the booster spirit. Their defensiveness was a manifestation of continued loyalty to the promise of a place.

Not surprisingly, the gap between promised reality and material (physical and economic) reality could become unbridgeable. New settlers cannot live on promises alone. The forces of boosterism and development might coalesce to suppress at least the public expression of individual sentiments that run counter to the optimistic grain. But when times became desperately hard, these confident promotional forces were no longer an unassailable majority. Criticism of the forces of boosterism was sometimes pronounced enough to turn into the majority sentiment. When this was the case, one has to think that the gap between settlers' elevated expectations and the actual conditions they endured played a role in nurturing the spirit of agrarian protest in the West, from the Grange, through the Populist movement, to the Farm Bloc of the 1920s.

Still, western promises had an uncanny way of reconstituting themselves even after they were shattered by the realities of climate or by market conditions outside of farmers' control. Particularly beneficent climatic conditions, such as those that prevailed on the Plains for much of the 1880s, unusually high world prices, such as those of the first two decades of the twentieth century, and the expanded markets of the World War I years sustained old dreams and generated thousands of new ones. Those who had remained in place in the face of adversity, the "stickers," as Wallace Stegner called them, perhaps linked their triumph over economic downturns to their resilience, and in turn viewed that resilience as the backbone of their "westernness."[84]

One of the great unrelenting dreamers and boosters of the Great Plains was Jules Ami Sandoz, father of writer Mari Sandoz. Jules Sandoz was hardly representative of the average settler or booster, but his remarkable effort to create a dreamscape out of the barren Sandhills region of western Nebraska does illuminate some key aspects of the booster mentality. Mari Sandoz's harrowing account of her father's life, *Old Jules* (1935), is, at heart, the story of an incredibly motivated western settler and booster.[85] In trying to ensure the growth of Niobrara County, Jules became a prolific writer of optimistic letters to friends and family back in Switzerland and to people in the eastern United States; he was tireless in his efforts to maintain a post office, which facilitated his mammoth correspondence campaign. He arrived in northeastern Nebraska from the Lake of Neuchâtel area of Switzerland at the beginning of the 1880s. By 1884 he had left one wife behind (his propensity for violence and neglect would later drive a second wife into the asylum, although his fourth and last wife outlived him). Old Jules was, as one scholar has noted, a "mercurial, egotistical, violent visionary."[86] Ultimately, he was an unsuccessful visionary, since his dream of a Sandhills landscape dotted with thriving farms did not become a reality (his own orchard, however, still survives). Today the region, writer Ian Frazier tells us, is "one of the blankest spots on the American map, a big section showing almost no rivers or roads or towns."[87] While there are a number of fairly prosperous large ranches in the region today, contemporary reality in the Sandhills falls far short of the boosters' dreams of dense population.

Frazier says of the Great Plains in general: "We . . . harvest wave after wave of immigrants' dreams and send the wised-up dreamers on their way."[88] He is both right and wrong on this point. Certainly, the experience of real life on the Plains, and in other often-inhospitable regions of the West, must have wised up many of the dreamers. But the immigrants themselves, like

Old Jules, could be creators of dreams as well as victims of them. Jules wrote letters to railroad colonization agents, trying to convince them to induce the railroad companies—such as the Northwestern—to sell his dreams more vigorously.[89] He worked with the railroads to bring more settlers to the region, understanding that more people would bring about an expansion of cultural amenities and transportation networks, as well as raise land values. While Jules himself did not like most people (and surely such sentiments were generally reciprocated), he understood that his dreams for the region depended on their presence. His unwavering confidence caused others to settle and suffer on the Plains, too. The most clearly discernible victims in Mari Sandoz's moving chronicle, however, are not the settlers who took Old Jules Sandoz at his word and migrated to Nebraska but his wives and children (including Mari). The gulf between their expectations (even if they were decidedly minimalist) and the realities of life with Old Jules in the Sandhills was indeed immense. Many of the people to whom he wrote letters did come to the region, but this was no ordinary example of chain migration. Jules Sandoz was a one-man promotional machine whose unrelenting optimism in the face of adversity was astounding. If his daughter's account paints a reliable portrait, then it seems that Jules's intentions as a booster were honest enough—he truly believed that those he attracted to Nebraska would have better lives there than if they remained where they were. But the consequences were tragic for some of those who placed stock in his optimistic imagery. (This gap between expectations and outcomes is certainly a factor in the formation of regional consciousness in general.) Some of those people coaxed into migrating by Jules and other "interior" promoters in turn coaxed others, thereby becoming boosters themselves. As long as a region remained relatively undeveloped, each wave of new arrivals was motivated to encourage a successive wave to come and help the place grow.[90]

The Sandoz case illustrates the incongruities between boosters' inventive presentations of western places and the material conditions that new migrants faced. The promoters' promised lands often turned out to be places where the land was marginal, the climate inhospitable, the cultural amenities scarce, and the population insufficient to attract the infrastructure necessary to sustain or jump-start the cycle of regional growth. Stagnant population growth, or population decline in many parts of the Plains and the Intermountain West, bears out the gulfs between boosters' and settlers' expectations and actual outcomes. The failed Wyoming towns of Eden, Eden Valley, and Jireh (from the biblical "Jehovah jireh," meaning "the Lord will provide") are particularly conspicuous testimony to the fragility of western promised lands.[91] The unsuccessful early-twentieth-century effort to create a haven for homesteaders in central and eastern Montana is another prime example of the distance between expectations and outcomes. Moving beyond the contiguous West, the failed New Deal homesteading efforts in Alaska—the most famous of which was the 200-farm Matanuska colony—are also memorable examples of the incongruity between promotional promises and settler realities.[92] Learning in the late 1920s that "the most striking feature of the climate in and around Juneau" was its "slight variability of temperature," and that it was most comparable to Tahoe, California, and Jacksonville, Florida, must have been striking indeed to prospective homesteaders of the nation's last frontier.[93]

Such examples of hypothetical Edens that never came to fruition lead naturally to cynical assessments of the gap between the advertising and the actual product. Nonetheless, one cannot emphasize strongly enough the benefit of hindsight behind these kinds of responses.[94] Furthermore, as we will see, the exaggerations of western promoters who imagined promised lands in their prose were no more acute than those of pioneer reminiscers who selectively reconstructed equally imaginary places in their writings.

Cover of Chicago, Burlington and Quincy Railroad, The Heart of the
Continent: An Historical and Descriptive Treatise for Business Men,
Home Seekers and Tourists, of the Advantages, Resources and Scenery of
the Great West *(Chicago: Buffalo, Clay and Richmond, printers, for
Chicago, Burlington and Quincy Railroad, 1882). The book centered on
Illinois, Missouri, Iowa, Kansas, Nebraska, and Colorado, describing that
region as "an empire grander in its resources than any emperor or czar,
prince or potentate of the older civilizations ever swayed sceptre over."
(Courtesy of the Western History Collection, Denver Public Library,
C917.8042 D714 HE)*

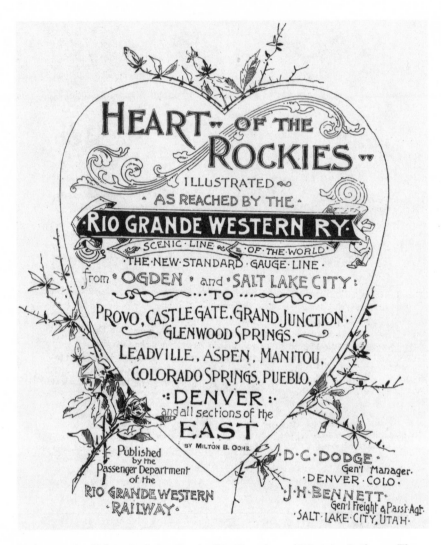

Title page for Milton B. Oohs, for the Rio Grande and Western Railway, *The Heart of the Rockies* (Cincinnati, Ohio: J. H. Bennett, Press of the A. H. Pugh Printing Co., 1890). The author claimed that the Denver, Rio Grande and Western Railway's purpose in advertising this region was purely altruistic, a concerned response to inquiries from potential settlers. He wrote, "If the invalid of the east, with hollow eyes and sunken cheeks, finds in these pages hope, and accepts the truth of the salubrious and health giving climate of these mountains and valleys as established facts, a 'life saved' will be an additional reward." Such claims of benign intentions were common in western promotional literature. (Courtesy of the Huntington Library, ephAPL/Box 1: General West)

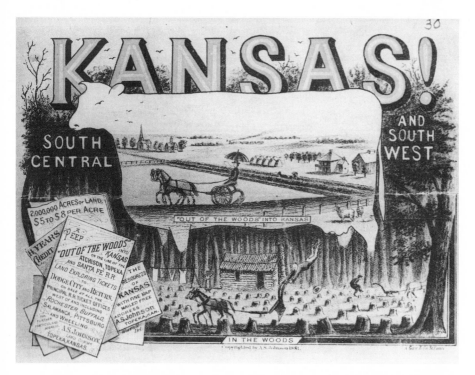

A. S. Johnson, publisher, "Kansas!" Chromolithograph. This advertisement for Santa Fe Railroad lands on the Kansas plains, in a classic juxtaposition of frontier and postfrontier stages, presents Kansas as a tamed and cultured environment where settlers would not experience any of the hardships of pioneering. (Courtesy of the Kansas State Historical Society, HE10ATSF.docpro.1881 #2)

"*Boise City and Valley, from Fort Boise,*" in Robert E. Strahorn, The Resources and Attractions of Idaho Territory: Facts Regarding: Climate, Soil, Minerals, Agricultural and Grazing Lands, Forests, Scenery, Game and Fish, and Reliable Information on All Other Topics Applicable to the Wants of the Homeseeker, Capitalist, and Tourist *(Boise City: Idaho Legislature, 1881), 41. This illustration is typical of town representation by late-nineteenth-century promoters. The four images in the corners of the picture—a typical house, a hotel, the printing office, and a tourist attraction, Boise Hot Springs—offer evidence of the community's cultural development. (Courtesy of the Huntington Library, Rare Book Collection, 78677)*

"Boise City cartoons Pard for starting rival towns." Cartoon image of Robert *Strahorn going about the business of town boosting in Idaho, c. 1880. From Carrie Adell Strahorn,* Fifteen Thousand Miles by Stage: A Woman's Unique Experience During Thirty Years of Path Finding and Pioneering, from the Missouri to the Pacific and from Alaska to Mexico *(New York: G. P. Putnam's Sons, 1911), 506. Described by the Helena Herald in 1879 as "the cleverest man in the West" when it came to the business of place promotion, Robert Strahorn was a prolific writer of booster tracts for the northwestern states. During the Great Depression, Strahorn lost the fortune he had acquired as a promoter. He died in 1944 at the age of ninety-two. (Courtesy of the Huntington Library)*

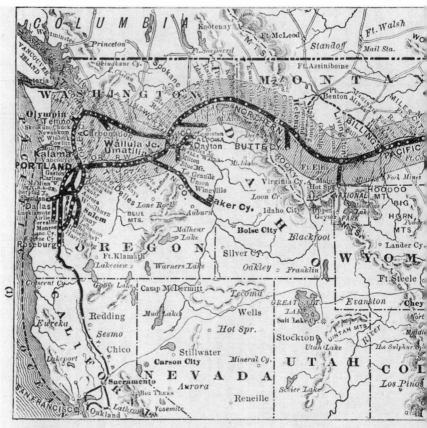

"Map of the Northern Pacific Railroad and Oregon Railway and Navigation Co., in Vast Areas of the Best Wheat Lands! Grazing Lands! Timber Lands! Gold and Silver Districts Along the Line of the Northern Pacific Railroad . . . Through Minnesota, Dakota, Montana, Idaho, Washington, and Oregon in Northern Pacific Country" (*Chicago: Rand McNally, 1883*). *The railroad tracks and accompanying shaded area cover a large portion of Washington, Oregon, Idaho, Montana, and the Dakotas, giving the appearance of a thoroughly settled, ordered, and risk-free western*

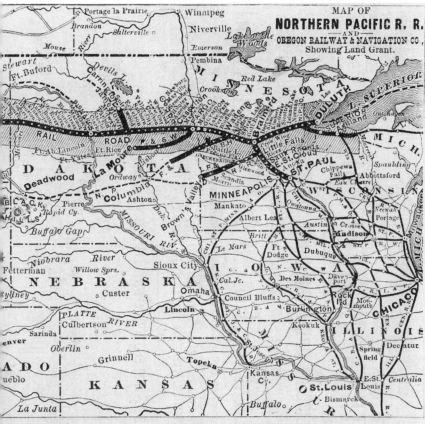

MAP OF
NORTHERN PACIFIC R. R.
—AND—
OREGON RAILWAY & NAVIGATION CO.,
Showing Land Grant.

Shortest Line and Quickest to Montana Points.

mpleted to LIVINGSTON,
aul, and is being rapidly
being pushed eastward,
yet to build to complete
the Pacific Ocean.
rail to the terminal sta-
new four-horse Concord
Helena, connecting at
Iontana.

LIVINGSTON, located on the Northern Pacific, 1030
miles west of St. Paul, at its last crossing of the Yellowstone River going west, is the point of divergence of a
branch to be completed June 1, 1883, running up the
Yellowstone River 62 miles to the YELLOWSTONE NA-
TIONAL PARK. The Clark's Fork Silver Mines; the great
iron and coal deposits; the junction point to National
Park—all contribute to make Livingston an important
and growing city for business and investment.

*landscape. Railroad maps of western regions in the late nineteenth and
early twentieth centuries shrunk the vastness of western space by using
thick bands to represent the tracks and filling much of the image with
the printed names of western towns neatly fanning out on both sides of
the tracks. The fact that many of these towns were projected places
rather than real ones was not emphasized by the cartographers.
(Courtesy of the Western History Collection, Denver Public Library,
C978. O2 V449, n.p.)*

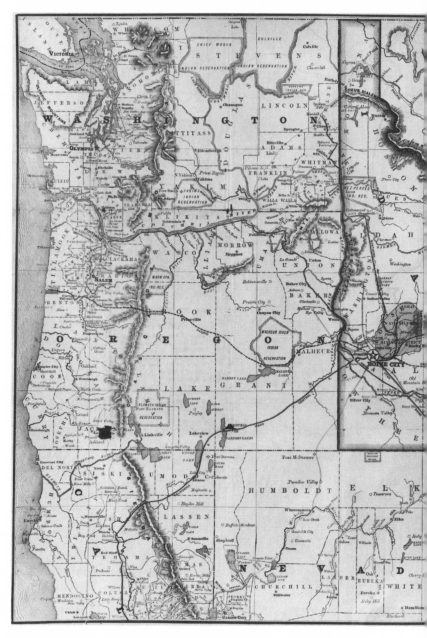

Map of "The Inter-Mountain District: Comprising Idaho, Montana, Wyoming and Washington Territories, the State of Oregon, and Portions of California, Nevada, Utah and Colorado Showing the Present and Prospective Railway Connections of Boise City" (Boise City, Idaho: Boise City Board of Trade, 1887–1888). As this creative map demonstrates,

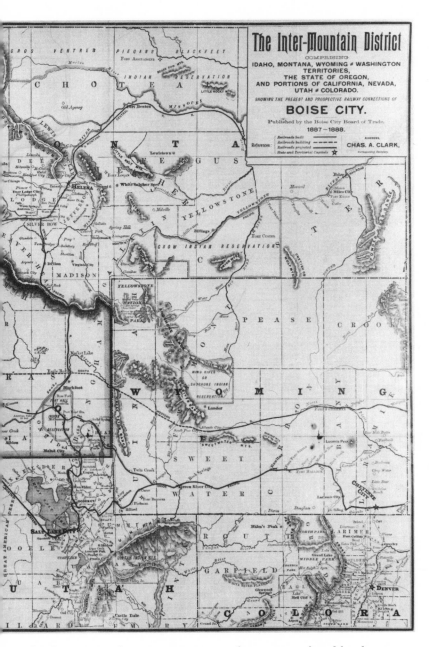

The Inter-Mountain District

COMPRISING

IDAHO, MONTANA, WYOMING & WASHINGTON
TERRITORIES,
THE STATE OF OREGON,
AND PORTIONS OF CALIFORNIA, NEVADA,
UTAH & COLORADO.

SHOWING THE PRESENT AND PROSPECTIVE RAILWAY CONNECTIONS OF

BOISE CITY.

Published by the Boise City Board of Trade.

1887–1888.

References: Railroads built
Railroads building ------
Railroads projected ....
State and Territorial Capitals ☆

ADDRESS:
CHAS. A. CLARK,
Corresponding Secretary

*local promotional organizations were often unencumbered by the
limitations of actual contemporary reality. Boise City appears as a
metropolis of a very sizable region. The map made it difficult for the
reader to distinguish the present from the future. (Courtesy of the
Newberry Library, Everett D. Graff Collection, 338)*

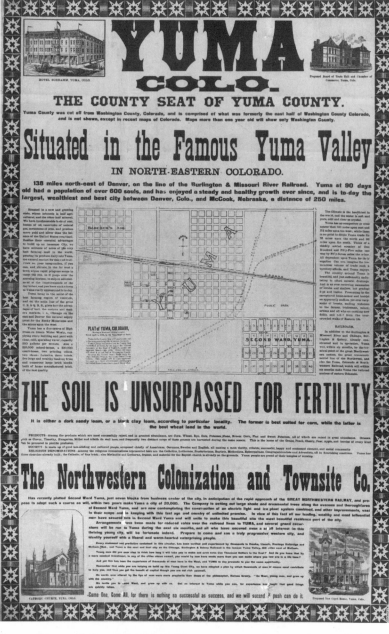

Anon., "Yuma, Colorado" (1889). This promotional poster featured the memorable lines: "Draw on your imagination, if you can, and picture in the far west, a town whose rapid progress seems to cause the sun as it peeps over the morning horizon to stop in astonishment at the improvements of the day before." (Courtesy of the Western History Collection, Denver Public Library, Broadside, DPL, VF Broadside, C978.878 Y91, 1889)

Happy, healthy babies in the "land of sunshine," from Charles Fletcher Lummis's "The Children's Paradise," Land of Sunshine 3 (June 1895): 7–10. Lummis, the editor of the publication, wrote in the piece that "the best legacy you can leave your child is to rear it in a climate which loves children—instead of the old-bachelor surliness of Eastern weather. It is worth more to your baby than all the money you will ever see . . . this chance to form its body and its mind in the Happy Land; to live next to God and Nature; to play in God's sun and air, and suckle at Nature's breast; to be out of doors every day in the year; to be playmate of eternal roses and perennial birds." (Union Eng. Co.; photo by Steckel; courtesy of the Huntington Library)

A year after the appearance of Lummis's first discussion of "The Children's Paradise" (he published a number of subsequent pieces in Land of Sunshine under the same title), Ella S. Hartnell's article "Some Little Heathens" appeared in Lummis's magazine (vol. 5, Sept. 1896, 153–156) and featured this image with the caption "A Coolie Baby." (Mausard Collier Eng. Co.; courtesy of the Huntington Library)

"Idaho, Opportunity," c. 1900, originally published in "Illustrated Idaho," reprinted in The Twin Falls Country, Idaho *(Twin Falls, Idaho: Kingsbury Printing Co., 1913). The cartoon's message is perfectly clear: Idaho is, in every way, the promised land. Cartoon images of this kind commonly appeared in the locally sponsored promotional literature of the late nineteenth and early twentieth centuries. (Courtesy of the Huntington Library, ephAPL: Idaho box)*

"From Idaho" c. 1900, originally published in the Chicago Tribune, also republished in The Twin Falls Country, Idaho *(Twin Falls, Idaho: Kingsbury Printing Co., 1913). While contemporary nutritionists might be appalled at this image's depiction of the healthy causal relationship between physical poundage and financial security, such images are not surprising in the wake of the depression of 1893–1897, the worst economic downturn the nation had yet faced. (Courtesy of the Huntington Library, ephAPL: Idaho)*

Fertile Lands
of Colorado

Front cover of The Fertile Lands of Colorado and Northern New Mexico, *by Clarence A. Lyman (Denver: Passenger Department, Denver and Rio Grande Railroad, 1908). The author claimed that the book was the most widely disseminated gratuitously circulated land book ever produced, with over 150,000 copies printed and distributed by that date. The ninth edition added another 15,000 copies to the total. (Courtesy of the Western History Collection, Denver Public Library, C630.9788D43FE9)*

Front cover of Montana *(n.p.: Chicago, Milwaukee and St. Paul Railway, c. 1910). Images of this kind go a long way toward explaining why railroad promotion is so commonly viewed as one of the era's most unscrupulous business endeavors. In reality, railroad-produced promotional literature was generally no more disingenuous than that produced by state and local immigration societies and chambers of commerce, and was often marked by more cautionary claims. (Courtesy of the Montana Historical Society, PAM.No.3882)*

Cover of California for the Settler *(San Francisco: Southern Pacific Railroad Company, 1922). The image's message is clear: the fertility of the land and healthfulness of the climate make California the perfect place for raising children. The text advised readers that "these lands virtually constitute a new beginning without pioneer conditions—almost all the advantages of the pioneer are here without his privations." (Courtesy of the Huntington Library, Rare Book Collection, 194725)*

"Alaska Summer Contrasts," advertisement in the Criskwell Travel Service's publication Alaska, c. 1930. Even as early as the 1870s, homesteading and tourism were often promoted together in the same publications. Promoters certainly played to the tourist's sense of adventure and de-emphasized that theme when presenting a place's possibilities for settlement, but they also hoped that seasonal tourists might become permanent residents; that was certainly the message of this image of Alaska's homesteading opportunities and natural wonders. (Courtesy of the Huntington Library, ephAPL: Alaska)

Bruce White Advertising and Design and Caribou Springs Ranch, "Caribou Springs Ranch, Build on the Legend," advertisement for "homesteads" in Homes and Land in Boulder County 5/6 (January 1999): 25. "Turn-of-the-century western living" could be offered as a hook at the end of the twentieth century to wealthy buyers seeking solace from metropolitan growth. But emphasizing the value of a place as an escape from civilization would not have been a wise marketing strategy for late-nineteenth-century and early-twentieth-century promoters. (Courtesy of Caribou Springs Ranch and Bruce White Advertising and Design)

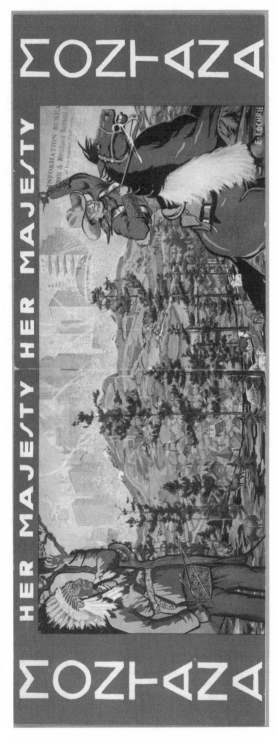

Cover of Charles Wayland Towne, Her Majesty Montana (Butte: Press of the Montana Standard, 1939). These kinds of images of urban-rural, and Native American–cowboy harmony were quite common in western promotional literature of the 1920s and 1930s. Montana, as this image suggests, could be sold to prospective settlers and tourists as a thoroughly modern place, marked by beautiful scenery and a colorful frontier heritage. (Courtesy of the Huntington Library, ephAPL: Idaho Box)

Part Two:
MEMORIES

3

REMEMBERED JOURNEYS

Death Valley Memories

How after weary months of wandering they came suddenly into a beautiful valley, clothed in luxuriant verdure, rich in wild clover and grasses, on which were grazing thousands of fat cattle. It seemed to those weary men as if they were suddenly ushered into paradise. The change was so great; to see everything spread before them in such abundance, and water, pure water, without limit, that every man shed tears, for they were weak as little children. (Jayhawkers' deliverance from Death Valley, newspaper account, 1880)

In early April 1849, a group of thirty-six young men left the towns of Galesburg and Knoxville, Illinois, and joined the California gold rush. The Jayhawkers, as they called themselves, crossed the Plains and Rockies without incident. Upon reaching Salt Lake City, they joined up with a much larger party; the entire group now comprised approximately 200 men, women, and children, more than 100 wagons, and about 500 horses and oxen.[1] The party hired a Mormon guide, Captain Jefferson Hunt, to lead them via the Spanish Trail to Los Angeles, and at the end of September they left Salt Lake. But by early November, the Jayhawkers had become concerned that traveling with Hunt and the larger group would slow them down and prevent them from reaping their fair share of California's precious metals harvest. Another Mormon guide advised the Jayhawkers that they could shave 500 miles off the journey if they took an alternate route. The Jayhawkers and most of the main party separated themselves from Hunt. Then the Jayhawkers and a few others, eager to reach their destination as quickly as possible, split from the main party and tried a shortcut by way of the Walker Pass cutoff.

The shortcut was not fortuitous. The Jayhawker party and various other smaller groups, altogether totaling eighty or so men, women, and children, ended up in what is now known as Death Valley, in southwestern Nevada and eastern California. Nearly 280 feet below sea level at its lowest point, Death Valley is the hottest and driest place on the continent; temperatures of 138 degrees have been recorded there. In that desolate place, albeit not at the height of summer, the Jayhawkers suffered the ravages of hunger, thirst, and physical exhaustion. With their food supply running out, they made it to the western edge of the valley and camped near the 11,000-foot Telescope Peak but could not find a pass to lead them through the Panamint Mountains. On January 13, two Jayhawkers died. One of the two, named Father Fish, had, according to reports, held on to the tail of an ox and literally been dragged up to the top of a summit, where he collapsed. The other, William Isham, had crawled for four miles on his hands and knees, searching for the group, before his body gave out just a few hundred feet from their camp. A third Jayhawker, William Robinson, died two weeks later, after the group had made it out of the valley. The cause of his death seems to have been "drinking too much cold water" at the first spring they found.[2]

On February 4, 1850, three months after separating themselves from the larger group and their Mormon guide, the Jayhawkers emerged from their nightmarish journey, quite literally stumbling onto the San Francisquito ranch in California's Santa Clara Valley. The survivors, by all accounts, looked like walking skeletons, the contours of their teeth clearly visible through the stretched skin and flesh of their gaunt, hollow cheeks. Some had reportedly lost a full 100 pounds in weight. The youngest member of the party, John Burt Colton, a man more than six feet tall and weighing between 150 and 160 pounds, was said to have weighed only 64 pounds at the end of the ordeal. Ironically, the Jayhawkers may have headed south toward Death Valley because of their knowledge of what had happened to the Donner Party farther to the north a few years previously.[3]

The Jayhawkers' journey is a memorable one. It has all the ingredients of grand drama—hope, faith, charity, greed, pain, suffering, endurance, heroism, death, and salvation. Unlike the Donner Party's terrible ordeal, the Jayhawkers' journey was not marked by cannibalism, though one member of the group seems to have suggested it before being run out of the camp by the others.[4] Yet for all the drama, it is hard to find a moral to accompany the story. The young pioneers were driven by a desire to get rich quick, and they chose their ill-fated route in an effort to get rich even more quickky. The Jayhawkers were impatient argonauts, as well as unlucky ones.

But the real story, for our purposes, is not the journey itself but the surviving Jayhawkers' shared memories of it. Even though they did not all stay in Southern California, that place for the Jayhawkers was quite literally "the valley of deliverance." In 1888 Jayhawker Edward Bartholomew wrote to fellow Death Valley argonaut Alonzo Clay about the group's terrifying ordeal and momentous deliverance "from death into life . . . from a state of starvation into a land of plenty." That day, February 4, 1850, Bartholomew wrote, "will be remembered by each survivor until death shall call us one by one from this mundane sphere to meet those gone before us, to join our comrades that fell by our side in that Great American Desert."[5] The notion of a final Jayhawker reunion in the afterlife emerges periodically in the survivors' correspondence. In 1901 Charles Bert Mecum wrote to Lorenzo Dow Stephens that the only place that might come close to matching the beauty of the Santa Clara Valley—"an Eden of flowers, verdure with many streams of pure water, and thousands of cattle grazing"—was Heaven. He added that all the members of the Jayhawker Party would one day be gathered there.[6] As mere mortals we cannot know whether the heavenly reassembly came to pass. But from the letters and speeches left behind, we do know what was on the Jayhawkers' minds when they met together in this world, whether in Illinois, Missouri, Nebraska, or California. They held annual reunions, every February 4 (the date of their deliverance from Death Valley) from 1872 until 1909, when fourteen of the original party, with an average age of 83½, remained. Mini-reunions occurred until 1918, when only two of them, Colton and Stephens, were still alive.

At the reunions and in their correspondence in the late nineteenth and early twentieth centuries, members of the group consistently stressed the theme of deliverance as the party "emerged from the Valley of Death and Starvation to the Sunshine and plenty on the shores of the Pacific."[7] The Jayhawkers spoke of themselves as "true westerners," emphasizing how they had endured hardships in the old frontier West that younger people, ensconced in the myriad modern comforts and conveniences of the safe, tamed new West, simply could not understand. In fact, they reminded each other that their suffering was the very foundation upon which contemporary luxuries rested. For those Jayhawkers who remained in Southern California, a sense of place was molded in part through contrasting that region's agricultural fertility and abundance with the sterility and scarcity of Death Valley, and contrasting the privation-packed pioneer past with the comparative ease and luxury of the present.

The aging Jayhawkers, in their correspondence, commonly equated "westernness" with the trials and tribulations of pioneering, identifying very strongly with a past process, as well as with their present places of residence. They also voiced a deep attachment to the place of their emergence. What connected them in the present was their shared experience in the purgatory of Death Valley and then in the Santa Clara Valley of deliverance, and their collective memories of those events.[8] Those memories also tied them into a wider world of frontier reminiscences, one that included correspondence with Theodore Roosevelt (both prior to and during his presidency), living frontier legend and mythologizer Buffalo Bill, frontier illustrator Frederic Remington, and a host of other rugged pioneer dignitaries and chroniclers.[9]

John Burt Colton, chief organizer of the Jayhawker reunions, also corresponded with the organizers of many other California pioneer societies, including the New England Associated Pioneers of '49 (formed in 1888), Boston's Associated California Pioneers of 1849 (1889), New York's Associated Pioneers of the Territorial Days of California (1875), and the Maryland Society of California Pioneers (1887). The members of these groups did not become permanent Californians or westerners, but they certainly felt a strong attachment to their western past, even as they resided on the East Coast. California gold rushers who had long since returned to Boston, New York, and other eastern cities wrote to Colton about their efforts to "[show] future generations what it has cost to add what was once wild and uninhabited country, to its [the United States'] present grand possibilities."[10] Sensitive to public perceptions of what motivations lay behind their adventures, these past pioneers did not recall a shared desire to strike it rich but instead remembered their role in the more noble and heroic endeavor of taming a wilderness. Gold is not the orbit around which gold rush reminiscences tend to revolve; rather, it is the theme of frontier heroism, the suggestion that participants were part of a great historic moment and movement.[11] Emphasizing, in one's reminiscences, the materialistic ambitions that drove people to the gold fields would have undermined the historical significance of the endeavor and the moral character of the participants.

The Jayhawkers' collective efforts to sustain their shared memory of their journey, along with renewed press coverage of their ordeal, elevated the group's survivors to pioneer hero status. Starting in the 1880s, as expressions of concern over the perceived closing of the American frontier became a part of the national cultural milieu, newspapers and magazines grew eager for stories of past pioneer struggles such as those of the Death Valley emigrants. During the 1890s, expressions of "frontier anxiety" became more acute and even more prevalent as the nation experienced a terrible economic depression, heightened agrarian protest, industrial strife, urban squalor, and continued political corruption.[12] A mountain of accounts of the exploits of old pioneers appeared in books and magazines during the 1890s. In 1893 the *San Francisco Chronicle* published a feature story on the Jayhawkers' ordeal based on information provided by John Burt Colton. In 1894 William Lewis Manly published a memorable account of the events, *Death Valley in '49*. In addition to enduring that horrific ordeal, it was Manly who, with one other man, had set off for the California settlements and returned to rescue some of the families that had been unable to find their way out.[13]

The Jayhawkers continued to receive extensive press coverage into the early twentieth century, and in those articles their courage in the face of adversity was often offered as an object lesson for younger generations that had not experienced the rigors of frontier life. Of course, the message to those younger Americans was not that they should undergo the same hardships as the Jayhawkers and other pioneers to prove themselves worthy successors. Rather, it was emphasized that they should know what had been endured by an older generation of pioneers to lay the foundation for their present comforts. Colton must have felt gratified when an Oregon woman played up this generational contrast in a letter to him in 1914: "These days people do not have any of the hardships that our forefathers had to undergo, and still very often you hear of what a hard time some folks have coming across the continent in Palace Cars."[14]

The previous year, *Land of Sunshine/Out West* editor Charles Fletcher Lummis reminded Colton that the high point of the frontier process was reaching the desired place, "the goal of your marvelous journey." Lummis was no stranger to long and difficult journeys, having himself, in an exhibition of genuine curiosity about the West and of Victorian era manliness, walked all the way from Chillicothe, Ohio, to Los Angeles in 1884. And since the Jayhawkers had, like himself, ended up in Southern California, Lummis thought it only natural and appropriate that Colton deposit the "records of that heroic achievement" in his own Southwest Museum of Art, History, and Science, located just north of Los Angeles. "What the hell has Galesburg or any other Eastern town to do with the Death Valley Party . . . ?" Lummis abrasively asked, adding that "those Eastern points were simply the places you got away from to come to California."[15] Lummis's efforts to acquire the Jayhawkers' papers lasted from 1913 to 1916 and were in the end unsuccessful, although the documents would ultimately end up in the Los Angeles area, just a few miles from the Southwest Museum.

In 1918 the forty-seventh and final Jayhawker reunion and the sixty-ninth anniversary of the party's deliverance took place with the two surviving Jayhawkers, Colton and Stephens, meeting at Stephens's house in San Jose. Colton passed away the following year at the age of eighty-eight.[16] Stephens, the last of the original Jayhawker group, died in 1921, at the age of ninety-five. A decade later, in 1928, the Jayhawkers' offspring (the Sons and Daughters and Grandsons and Granddaughters of the Jayhawkers of '49) began to hold annual reunions in honor of their forebears.[17] In 1930 and 1935, the Jayhawker descendents met, quite appropriately, at the San Francisquito Ranch. In 1938 they gathered on the beautiful grounds of the Huntington Library, Art Gallery, and Botanical Gardens, in San Marino. The Huntington was a fitting host for the event, having acquired the Jayhawker Collection (including diaries of the journey, correspondence, maps, scrapbooks, and photographs) from the Colton family in 1930.[18]

The Jayhawkers' journey was remarkable, but so were the participants' vivid and enduring memories of the experience. They came to view their collective endeavor as an object lesson for younger generations. The Jayhawkers remembered their experience as a group, and they made efforts to ensure that others remembered them, too. Colton, the self-appointed historian of the group, and his companions would surely have been pleased to learn that the archival record of their experience came to be valued by scholars of the West. While the terrible ordeal of the Donner Party has certainly overshadowed that of the Jayhawkers in the national historical consciousness, the Jayhawkers have not been completely forgotten by history, as they feared they might be.[19] Indeed, an elaborate hoax a century and a half after their ill-fated journey put the Jayhawkers back on the historical map. On New Year's Day 1999, the first newspaper account appeared of the discovery of a trunk full of Jayhawker belongings near the Panamint Range. The trunk, as it turned out, was "bunk," which was quite embarrassing for Jerry Freeman, an amateur historian and schoolteacher who had found it. Freeman appeared on the *Good Morning America* television show, and national news programs ran the story, all prior to his learning that the trunk was a fake.[20]

One final and very real element of the Jayhawker saga demands recounting. While Lorenzo Stephens was the oldest surviving member of the party, the Death Valley survivor who lived the most years turned out not to be one of the original group of thirty-six single young men but a married woman, Juliet (sometimes listed as Julia) Wells Brier. Brier, who was one of the first white women to pass through Death Valley, died just a few weeks short of her hundredth birthday. She had traveled with her husband, the Reverend James Welsh Brier, and their three young boys, the memorably named Christopher Columbus, John Wells, and Kirke White.

Even though Juliet Brier and her family were not part of the actual Jayhawker Party (the Briers had tagged along behind the Jayhawkers), the Jayhawkers, in their accounts of the ordeal, spoke of her in laudatory terms. Manly, in *Death Valley in '49,* wrote that the Jayhawkers all agreed that Mrs. Brier was "by far the best man of the [Brier] party."[21] They spoke far less highly of her husband (who is reported to have preached the first Protestant sermon in Los Angeles). James Brier does not seem to have recognized the full magnitude of his wife's bravery and her vital contribution to the family's survival. Furthermore, according to most accounts other than his own, he does not seem to have shown much bravery himself or been of much assistance. Manly describes an incident where Mrs. Brier was stuck in a swamp and her husband remained seated at a safe distance, not offering to help. Lorenzo Stephens helped pull Juliet out and apparently remarked to his Jayhawker companions that if the reverend had been stuck in the swamp, he (Stephens) would happily have left him there.[22] Mrs. Brier, Manly wrote, "did all sorts of work when the father of the family was too tired, which was almost all of the time."[23] The Jayhawkers considered James Brier's "holier than thou" attitude rather irritating but found Juliet Brier inspirational. They thought, Manly added, that the reverend ought to "assert his manliness, take the burden on himself, and not lean upon his delicate and trusting wife."[24]

But Juliet proved not to be so delicate. Each day she loaded and unloaded her family's oxen and sometimes those of the Jayhawkers when they were too tired or weak to perform the task for themselves. She remembered placing her two youngest children "into rawhide bags slung over the back of an ox."[25] Participant accounts note that Juliet "carried" her family (i.e., took primary responsibility for their welfare), and for parts of the journey, it seems, she did literally carry the children, aged four, seven, and nine. At times she cradled one of them in her arms, led a second by the hand, and carried Kirk, the eldest and weakest, on her back. Speaking of Juliet's accomplishments more than a half century later, Charles Lummis described her as "that wonderful little woman . . . [with] magnificent pluck."[26]

It was Juliet who provided her boys and husband with the necessary encouragement to see them through the ordeal; she spurred the Jayhawkers on, too, helping to sustain their spirits.[27] Somehow she managed to preserve her own spirits and her physical health. According to newspaper coverage of the Death Valley crossing a half century later, Mrs. Brier weighed 115 pounds at the beginning of the journey and just 2 to 3 pounds less at the end.[28] According to Lummis, Mrs. Brier began the journey an invalid, weighing only 90 pounds, though his penchant for high drama seems to have led him to stretch truths that needed no stretching.[29] Whatever the case, whether she was an invalid or a waif, both, or neither, the available evidence certainly suggests that she was the hardiest of all the Death Valley pioneers, not just the "best man" of the Brier family.

Juliet Brier did not give her first newspaper interview on the Death Valley crossing until December 1898, almost a half century after the event. The Christmas Day edition of the *San Francisco Call* featured her reminiscences of the journey, "Our Christmas amid the Terrors of Death Valley," a title that effectively illuminated the contrast between the joys of the present holiday season and the privations of previous generations.[30] Notably, the piece appeared less than two months after her husband's death on November 2, 1898. Shortly before he died, James Brier had disassociated himself and his family from the Jayhawker group. The reverend was upset over Manly's recent treatment of him in *Death Valley in '49*. Manly had depicted him as a source of both amusement and frustration to the Jayhawkers during their struggle to make it out of Death Valley. Perhaps the unfavorable contrasting of his efforts to help the larger group and his own family and the heroic sacrifices of his wife particularly embarrassed Reverend Brier. Whatever the case, he wrote to Deacon Richards, who was planning to host the 1899 reunion, demanding that the Briers be struck from the list of members.[31]

Interestingly, a few months later, the 1899 Jayhawker reunion was held in Lodi, near San Francisco, at the home of James Brier's son John Wells Brier and his wife. Juliet Brier was present at the event, as well as at the reunions of 1903, 1908, 1911, and 1913, all held at the same residence. She died on May 26, 1913. Whether her half-century-long silence concerning the events of 1849 resulted from her own deference to patriarchy and respect for her husband or from her own preference for privacy is difficult to determine.[32] The fragmentary evidence that remains certainly suggests that Juliet Brier hardly craved notoriety for her own endeavors. Still, it is surprising that her trials and tribulations in Death Valley are not better known. The haunting pencil sketch of Mrs. Juliet Brier that appeared in the February 24, 1901, edition of the *San Francisco Examiner* has the same kind of visual magnetism as Dorothea Lange's later, much more famous photographic image *Migrant Mother* (1936). But Lange's image illuminated a pressing contemporary problem, while that of Juliet Brier, appearing long after the events had taken place, only called to mind a heritage worth remembering.

Still, the Jayhawkers' memories of their momentous journey lasted for the rest of their lives. And, aside from the accounts of James Brier, which contrasted with those of the rest of the party, those shared memories were generally consistent. It is questionable whether the Jayhawkers ever really considered the reverend to be a true member of their group, though they clearly saw Mrs. Brier as one of their number (see figure, p. 149). In their estimation, she had suffered, endured, and contributed selflessly and bravely to the Jayhawkers' cause; she was a true pioneer whose actions and attitude provided object lessons for younger generations.

Concluding his account *The Jayhawkers of Death Valley* (1938), John G. Ellenbecker wrote that "the passing away of the Jayhawkers took from us a band of men who were typical of the old pioneers—the men and the women who did their work the old hard way." Ellenbecker went on to add of the pioneers, "When we revere them and honor them we pay tribute to a large class that once were common but now are met with no more." And, he wondered in conclusion, "Will we emulate their honesty, their industry, their courage?"[33] That conclusion would have delighted Colton and his fellow Jayhawkers, since garnering the emulation and respect of younger generations was a primary motivation behind their organization and the many other western pioneer societies that began to form in the late nineteenth century.

Pullman Pioneers

> How hard it is to understand the briefness of time that has passed since the great interior country was practically a howling wilderness, inhabited by bands of savages and penetrated only by intrepid trappers and hunters! As we are now whirled along over the Laramie Plains, or through the Echo and Weber Canyons, reclining on luxuriously-cushioned seats, and but a few hours away from the eastern seaboard, we can scarcely realize it. (Alfred Lambourne, *The Old Journey: Reminiscences of Pioneer Days*, 1892–1897)

An interesting though not surprising substrain of the tendency to contrast the demands of the past with the luxuries of the present was the stark juxtaposition of overland journeys with Pullman Palace Car traveling.[34] The heartwarming letter that John Burt Colton received in 1914, emphasizing this contrast between the Jayhawkers and contemporary Pullman pioneers, typified this trend. The Jayhawker papers and other collections of reminiscences are filled with vivid contrasts of the trials and tribulations of overland journeys by foot or wagon in the middle to late nineteenth century and those by train in the late nineteenth and early twentieth centuries. Another old pioneer, Alfred Lambourne (not a Jayhawker), in his published reminiscences that appeared in the 1890s, waxed eloquently about the wonders of modern American civilization. But Lambourne also lamented that in a world of such comforts, including the "luxuriously-cushioned seats" of Pullman cars, "it is well-nigh impossible for the youth of to-day to comprehend the struggles and privations of its pioneer fathers."[35] Historian Francis Parkman sounded much like Lambourne and other pioneer reminiscers when he commented in 1892 on "the effeminate comforts of modern travel."[36]

Such sentiments were frequently voiced at pioneer society meetings. An address to the old pioneers of Los Angeles County in 1909 noted that the audience's "historic memories should be emblazoned on the facade of every worthy enterprise by the late arrivals, who have come here in expensive Pullman cars to make their homes in this new El Dorado."[37] That same year, the Los Angeles County Pioneers used the Pullman allusion (the Pullman maneuver, we might call it) in publicly voicing their dissatisfaction with the local Republican Committee. That committee had refused the old settlers' request to have a pioneer vehicle included in the October automobile welcoming parade for President William Howard Taft. How, the old pioneers asked, could anyone refuse the request of "such men who have lived in this county for the past fifty to sixty years, who made the trail and walked from the Missouri River to this glorious south land"? It was these hardy old settlers, they derisively added, who had made it "possible for the Pullman Pioneer to enjoy the healthiest and most salubrious climate known in the world."[38] In pioneer society proceedings and in published reminiscences, the Pullman Palace Car quickly became a stock symbol of the comfort and ease that made it so difficult for members of the present generation to appreciate their pioneer predecessors.[39]

Rather than settle for just drawing the contrast verbally or in writing, it became common for old pioneers to actually relive, in their imaginations, their earlier journey experiences—ironically enough, from the comfort of Pullman carriages—and juxtapose past privations with contemporary comforts along the way. These were partial reenactments of earlier adventures, experiences that allowed old settlers to draw on the technologies of the present to recapture more vividly a semblance of the past. An early example of this practice of journey reenactment occurred in the fall of 1871. George L. Becker, an old Minnesota pioneer settler, was also a pioneer in the railroad industry and was president of the St. Paul and Pacific Railroad. Becker invited the entire Old Settlers Association of Minnesota to be the first passengers on the railroad across that state. On their trip from St. Paul, over 350 Old Settlers and their families were plied with free food, drink, and cigars. Small surprise that they spoke rather well of the railroad when they reached the terminus, at the Red River of the North. Such journeys helped the Old Settlers emphasize the great gulf (as they envisioned it) between their arduous pioneer experience and the complacency of the present generation.[40] Even though they were the ones riding in luxury in the present, these old pioneers could take pride in the fact that they had experienced the journey under more trying circumstances. Indeed, the Minnesota pioneers boasted that it was their earlier journeys to and transformations of the upper midwestern frontier that had prepared the ground for the great railroad age.

Similar sentiments were voiced by some of the 120 members of the Sacramento Society of California Pioneers, many with their wives and children, who journeyed on a special train of Wodruff's Silver-Palace Cars, from their home city to New York City in 1869. The Sacramento Pioneers departed in mid-September, taking the Central-Pacific Railroad to Promontory Point, Utah, where it had, amid much pomp and circumstance, linked up with the Union Pacific earlier that year. They arrived in New York City a week later.[41] Their journey serves as one of the earliest examples of pioneer journey reconstruction and as a good indicator of early developments in travel tourism.

J. Valerie Fifer notes that by the 1890s, with the western tourist industry quite well established, "Pioneer reconstructions, 'What-it-was-like-in-the-Old Days' trips, were already a feature of that industry." But these were generally reconstructions for a younger, nonpioneer public.[42] Yet the old pioneers themselves represented quite a market for railroad reconstructions of their actual journeys. The California Pioneers of New England left Boston on April 10, 1890, on such a trip. A total of 150 of them, including friends and family members, departed from the Fitchburg Railroad Station, with a crowd estimated at 2,000 there to see them off. In his account of the journey, Nicholas Ball, the director of the organization, wrote that as the train pulled out of the station, "our thoughts and conversation turned to the glorious sunset land to which we were now hastening, surrounded by all the luxuries of modern travel, in such strange contrast with the slow, toilsome, and perilous voyages or marches of but a little more than two score years ago."[43] Those earlier journeys must have been very much in the old pioneers' thoughts during their trip.

At San Bernardino, California, the New England party was met by the San Bernardino Pioneer Society, by the Native Sons and Daughters of the Golden West, and a crowd totaling about 1,500. From there they journeyed to Redlands, Riverside, and Pasadena. On that portion of the trip, Ball records, "we found sleep most welcome, but in dreams we saw again the rugged cañons, the barren hills, the weird Sierras, and the wilderness of '49." Ball may have been presumptuous in recording the content of the dreams of his fellow pioneers, but he certainly captured the general spirit of their reenactive endeavors. From Pasadena the Pullman journeyers went on to San Diego, then Sacramento, then San Francisco, Palo Alto, Monterey, and San Jose, and back home from the Golden State via Truckee, Salt Lake City, Manitou Springs, Denver, and Nebraska, arriving back in Boston in mid-May.[44]

These kinds of reenactments became common enough in the late nineteenth and early twentieth centuries to enter the sphere of popular fiction. A good example of this phenomenon is Margaret Hill McCarter's historical novel *Vanguards of the Plains: A Romance of the Old Santa Fé Trail* (1917). The book's chief characters, Gail Clarenden and her husband, Eloise St. Vrain, whose lifetime love affair had begun on the trail west, celebrate their golden wedding anniversary by following the Santa Fe Trail back "from the raw frontier at Independence . . . clear to the sunny valley of the Holy Faith."[45] The old couple relive the romance of their youth, soaking up the sweet memories on their "golden wedding journey." The whole experience, of course, was possible because they did not have to face the "peril and privation and uncertainty" of earlier days, since "the Pullman has replaced the Conestoga wagon, dainty viands the coarse food smoke-blackened over camp fires, and never fear of Kiowa or Comanche broke our slumber." The "long shriek that cuts the air of dawn was not from wild marauders or a daybreak raid," the old couple remembered, "but from the throats of splendid, steel wrought engines swinging forth upon their solid, certain course." But such modern wonders were made possible by "the deeds of vanguards, who foreran and builded for the softer days of golden-wedding years."[46]

When Gail further elaborated on the theme of the frontier past and the postfrontier present, she illuminated the comparative absence of moral complication in selective memories of the pioneer experience:

> Life is easy for us now, made so by all the splendid, simple forces of those who, in justice, honesty, and broad human sympathy build enduring empire. Not empire gained by bomb and liquid fire . . . but empire builded on the commerce of the land . . . quick transportation on steel-marked trails that girdle harvest fields and fruitful pastures; empire of homes and schools and sacred shrines.[47]

America's frontier story was thus juxtaposed with the horrors of the Great War, which was raging as McCarter wrote her novel.[48] The former was a grand enterprise of settlement and progress, a veritable romance of the prairies, plains, and mountains; the latter was a horrible clash of empires with no such benign visions. The matter of white settler encroachment on the lands of the Kiowa and Comanche and other native peoples seemingly did not register in McCarter's mind as a factor complicating the triumphal narrative of the winning of the West. With such unabashedly progressive pioneering sentiments as this being expressed in the popular literature of the day, the late Progressive Era was hardly dependent on professional historians for the propagation of a heroic frontier theme to provide the nation's majority population with a history it could be proud of. Before embarking on their journey Gail had remarked to her husband, Eloise, that "there is no trail now; only its ghost haunting the way."[49] Such friendly ghosts haunted the postfrontier present, keeping the uncomplicated romance of the frontier squarely in the public imagination.[50]

The Quintessential Journey Reenactor

> We pioneers yearn to have this work begun because of the intense desire to perpetuate the memory of the past and believe it of great importance to

the rising generation in implanting this memory in the breasts of the future rulers of the nation and sowing the seeds of patriotism. (Ezra Meeker's speech to the United States House of Representatives, in *The Busy Life of Eighty-five Years,* 1916)

Of all the creators of the mythic frontier western heritage, Buffalo Bill Cody is surely the most memorable. His "Wild West" (he refused to call the performance a "show," since that label would have compromised the authenticity of his reenactments) toured the United States from 1883 to 1887 and Europe from 1887 to 1893. After 1893, Cody toured both continents and constantly altered the format of his performances in an effort to recapture the glory years. The popularity of the event in the early years was astounding. In five months during 1885, as many as a million people may have seen the performances. During the summer season the following year, the "Wild West" was daily filling a 30,000-person arena in Staten Island. During the Chicago World's Fair in 1893, nearly 6 million people paid to see Cody's reenactments of frontier adventures. But by the first decade of the new century, his "Wild West" extravaganza was becoming a pale reflection of its former self; many reminiscers were saying much the same about the West in general. To drum up public interest, Buffalo Bill embarked on a series of farewell tours starting in 1910. But the public and the press, Cody's latest biographer writes, "became disenchanted with interminable 'Farewell Tours.'"[51] By 1913 the former icon of frontier virility and the horse culture of the cowboy West was being wheeled into arenas in a carriage. Three years later, he joined the Miller Brothers 101 Ranch Wild West Show in a final effort to recapture the old frontier limelight. Yet by this time the seventy-year-old performer's greatest fear, according to a source close to him, was that he would die during a performance. That fear never became a reality; Buffalo Bill died in the Denver, Colorado, home of his daughter on January 10, 1917.[52] He was, despite the pathetic nature of his twilight years, indisputably the greatest frontier showman of them all.

The greatest frontier journey reenactor has hardly garnered the kind of public or scholarly attention paid to Buffalo Bill. Ezra Meeker, though he did, in his twilight years, earn a good deal of press coverage, never was a household name, and certainly is not one today. Yet Meeker's story, if less well known than Cody's, is equally fascinating and reveals a good deal more about the pioneer reminiscence genre. What is more, it has a more memorable ending than that of Cody's slow decline and interminable string of final performances and his fear of the public humiliation that would accompany death in the arena of reenactment.

Back in 1851, as a twenty-one-year-old newlywed, Meeker had journeyed from Indianapolis to the Pacific Northwest, over the Oregon Trail, with his wife, Eliza Jane, and their infant child. In 1870, a generation after arriving in the Puget Sound area, he was proving to be an uncharacteristically trustworthy booster for Washington Territory. His less reliable Washington booster counterparts were claiming, often without qualification, that their region's climate was the best on the globe. Meeker was more forthcoming about the realities of the area. He did not contend that the territory's lands were as fertile as those of the Nile Valley or the Garden of Eden. Indeed, the most he claimed was that the "climate is excelled in no part of the globe for the production of grass, cereals of all kinds, and the *hardier* vegetables." Like other boosters, he had his purple prose moments, but the overall tone of Meeker's promotional tract was restrained.[53]

Meeker, the reliable booster for Washington Territory, became one of the region's most interesting and influential old pioneer reminiscers. The combination of boosting a region and later reminiscing about earlier days in that place, or about the journey to that place, was not that uncommon.[54] A town's boosters were likely to be among its more prominent citizens, and their reminiscences were most likely to be sought after. Forty-six years after the publication of his booster booklet *Washington Territory West of the Cascade Mountains* (1870), Meeker published the fullest version of his reminiscences, *The Busy Life of Eighty-five Years* (1916).[55] The key elements of the pioneer reminiscence genre are all present in Meeker's account. He declared his intent to tell of his experiences in "plain, homely language" so that the later generation "may know how the 'fathers' lived," and "to teach [them] . . . lessons of industry, frugality, upright and altruistic living as exemplified in the lives of the pioneers." These were "not stories of fancy to make exciting reading," Meeker assured his audience. "Truth," he declared, "is stranger than fiction, and the pioneers have no need to borrow from their imagination."[56]

But Meeker, unlike the average pioneer reminiscer, was much more than a mere man of words in his later years. To keep the saga of the region's pioneers alive in the minds of younger generations and ensure that their lessons would not be "lost to the world," Meeker organized the Oregon Trail Monument Expedition to place historical markers along the route they took.[57] He departed from his home in Puyallup, Washington, at the end of January 1906, with a seven-year-old ox and a five-year-old steer pulling an old prairie schooner. Meeker, a remarkably fit seventy-six-year-old (seventeen years senior to Buffalo Bill Cody), with long, flowing white hair and beard, was at the helm, and his equally fit dog Jim, a Scotch collie, ran alongside the outfit. In The Dalles, Oregon, William Mardon joined Meeker's expedition as an assistant and would accompany the old pioneer journeyman for the duration of the trip.

Friends tried to discourage the old man from journeying across the continent and back, but he said he felt as strong as he ever had, and he was motivated by a sense of mission. Meeker had some success in convincing local communities to raise money to erect monuments along the trail in the far western states, but when he reached Kearney, Nebraska, in mid-August, 1,700 miles into the trip, the city's Commercial Club told him it was too busy to call a meeting to consider his request that they honor the pioneers with a marker. As he left the club office, he wondered to himself "if these busy men would ever find the time to die. How did they find time to eat or to sleep?" Then, he asked himself, "Is a business man's life worth the living, if all his wakeful moments are absorbed in grasping for gains?"[58]

Meeker, who entitled his autobiography *The Busy Life of Eighty-five Years,* it should be noted, was not just a busy man but a businessman of sorts himself, a very competent self-promoter, as well as a prolific author. When his book *The Ox-Team; or, The Old Oregon Trail, 1852–1906* was printed in Lincoln, Nebraska, and appeared in October 1906, he sold copies of it (hardcovers for 50 cents, softcovers for 30 cents, along with packets of postcard images of his trip, for 25 cents) to help finance the journey.[59] Sometimes he exchanged a book for a meal and a night's lodging. Meeker's business acumen was not always reliable, however. Earlier in the journey, he had to resort to wiring an old friend to request financial assistance and received a check for $200.[60]

Even though Meeker conducted a little sales business during the course of his travels, his main purpose was clearly not to make a profit but to rouse community interest in what he believed was a very worthy cause. His own sense of the value of the pioneer heritage clashed with the Kearney Commercial Club's sense of what was really important. With their thoughts firmly planted in the present and the future, members of the club seemed to have little time for an old man in a prairie schooner on a mission to memorialize the past. They were boosters, and he was a reminiscer, and there was not much common ground when the purveyors of the future met in the early-twentieth-century present with an advocate for the past, not until a later age when the heritage of places became a more salable commodity.

At the end of August, Meeker reached Grand Island, Nebraska, where he reminisced about the June day in 1852 when he had first passed over the spot, surrounded by "herds of buffalo," "flocks of antelope," and prairie dogs. All those inhabitants, along with the region's human inhabitants, the Indians, he mused (without any sense of remorse), had disappeared, and the "parched . . . barren plain" had been replaced by a "landscape of smiling, fruitful fields, of contented homes, of inviting clumps of trees dotting the landscape."[61] The changes seemed positive to Meeker, who, unlike some other reminiscers, was not one for engaging in spirited tirades against the decadence and degeneracy of the postfrontier age. But he was determined to impress upon the present generation that its "fruitful fields" and "contented homes" were not to be taken for granted; that "parched . . . barren plain" had not transformed itself.

In late April 1907, nearly fifteen months and some 2,800 miles into his journey, as Meeker passed through Columbus, the *Ohio State Journal* highlighted the contrast between the picturesque appearance of Meeker and his prairie schooner outfit and "the busy life of modern civilization" in the city. But, the reporter emphasized, while the old pioneer may have looked unusual in the bustling urban-industrial age, he was by no means irrelevant to it, and a sizable crowd showed up to hear Meeker speak. "His was not 'the voice of one crying in the wilderness,'" the reporter explained, "but the voice of the wilderness and the past calling in the city, with all its modernity, to do its share to pay tribute to those who made modern American cities possible."[62] At the end of November, twenty-two months into his trip, Meeker arrived at the White House and was greeted by President Theodore Roosevelt, another voice of the wilderness and prolific author of frontier adventures designed to serve as object lessons of the strenuous life. He had his picture taken with the president and was "encouraged to believe that my labor had not been lost."[63] Neither was his labor over. Meeker decided to make the return trip to Washington State with his trusty team and his prairie schooner.

While raising funds for the trail markers during the return trip to Washington State, Meeker visited all the public schools in Kansas City. He spoke to more than 11,000 schoolchildren, and he remembered enjoying the "satisfaction of having secured contributions from over 3,000" of them to support the building of a monument in that city. He also donated $25.00 as prize money for the best essay on the Oregon Trail written by a schoolchild. His efforts to raise public consciousness of the pioneering past seemed to be having an effect. In May 1908 he heard that a congressional committee was acting favorably on a bill supported by President Roosevelt to appropriate $50,000 to mark the Oregon Trail. Assured that his mission had been a success, and having been on the road nearly twenty-eight months, Meeker brought his oxteam endeavor to a close and took advantage of the conveniences of the modern age. He shipped his outfit to Portland, Oregon, and arrived there himself, by train, in early June 1908. From Portland he drove the team into Seattle, arriving on July 18. Sales of *The Ox-Team* reached 18,000 copies during the trip and "saved the day" financially, according to Meeker.[64]

Meeker's efforts to memorialize the past, however, were not done in 1908. Two years later he repeated the trip, again with an oxteam, and was on the road for more than twenty-nine months. In June of that year, the City of Kearney, Nebraska, did erect a granite monument to mark the Oregon Trail, and Meeker got to see it when he passed through in July.[65] More important, in February of the following year, his advocacy of the Oregon Trail project was read to the House of Representatives.[66] In 1915 he drove over much of the trail in an automobile. The model, appropriately enough, was a "Path-finder the Great" touring car, manufactured by the Pathfinder Company of Indianapolis. He fitted the vehicle with a special prairie-wagon-style canvas top and called it the "schoonermobile." The following January, Meeker himself addressed the House congressional committee, emphasizing the need to "perpetuate the memory of the [pioneer] past" among the nation's future leaders and thereby nurture their patriotism.[67]

But even after Meeker delivered his message to the nation's political representatives, his work was still not done. In 1924, at ninety-three years of age, he followed the trail for 1,300 miles in an airplane. He founded the Oregon Trail Memorial Association in 1926. Fittingly, on his final journey back over the trail, this time starting from the East Coast in an automobile in 1928, he was taken ill. Meeker was transported back to Seattle by train from Detroit and died a few months later, a few weeks shy of his ninety-eighth birthday. Meeker, born a generation before Buffalo Bill Cody, had outlived him by more than a decade—though it was Cody who outlived Meeker in the American public memory.

Meeker's life spanned the whole period from the first large-scale European-American migration to the "Oregon Country," through the boosting of the region and the efforts to sustain its pioneer heritage; moreover he was a vital participant in all three of those phases.[68] On April 10, 1930, a century after Meeker's birth, the first use of wagons on the Oregon Trail was celebrated on a grand scale, with a proclamation by President Herbert Hoover and a reenactment of the journey of the first wagon train from St. Louis to Oregon, lasting through December of that year. The event was largely a consequence of this one old pioneer's tireless efforts to popularize the cause through his journeys. The degree to which such commemorative events provided some Americans with a mental respite from the worsening depression is anyone's guess. Certainly Hoover saw the courage and forbearance of "the heroic pioneers who won and held the West" as an object lesson for those suffering from the economic ravages of the present.[69]

Meeker's efforts to relive the overland trip illustrate the centrality of the journey process to the formation of sense of place for generations of white western settlers. Meeker's home was Washington, as both territory and state. That was the place he had earnestly and honestly promoted (with an unboosterish lack of exaggeration) and the place where he resided for three-quarters of a century. Meeker was no placeless wanderer who took to the trail on a whim because his attachments to the road were greater than his affinity for his home region. Rather, he was, like John Burt Colton and other Jayhawkers, firmly committed to the notion that understanding the process of getting to places, in more trying times, was essential to the full appreciation of those places in the present.

Furthermore, Meeker's efforts to memorialize pioneer journeys through the construction of monuments were indicative of a larger trend in the early decades of the twentieth century. That trend was also evidenced in the campaign, from 1910 to 1918, of Eliza Poor Donner Houghton, in cooperation with the Native Sons and Native Daughters of the Golden West, to erect a monument to the Donner Party. Eliza, whose parents both perished during that terrible ordeal, was only three when her family began their ill-fated journey.[70] In the course of her correspondence with C. W. Chapman of the Native Sons, he wrote to her in 1910 that "the Donner Party has been selected by us as the most varied and comprehensive in its experiences of all the trains that made these wonderful journeys of thousands of miles, so unique in their daring, so brave, so able, so worthy of the admiration of man."[71] In another letter to Eliza Houghton a few years later, Chapman expressed his hope that the completed monument would "charge the minds of all who behold it with a reverence for those characters who 'gird their armor on; who square their shoulders to the world and who take the brunt of life.'"[72] In the summer of 1918 the monument was unveiled in its location near Truckee, California, with Eliza and the few other remaining survivors of the Donner journey in attendance.

Stories such as the Jayhawkers', Meeker's, and Houghton's merely scratch the surface of the broad phenomenon of remembered journeys and their role in shaping white western identity.[73] The prevalence of such stories has led scholars to view these pioneer reminiscers as a rootless and placeless bunch, so tied to their memories of the frontier past that they failed to develop a meaningful sense of place in the regional present and ended up living in "No Place."[74] Scholars have occasionally illustrated this theme of old pioneer rootlessness within the contemporary society of their twilight years through the fictional character of Grandfather Tifflin in John Steinbeck's classic story "The Leader of the People" (1938).[75] Tifflin is so caught up in the frontier past, the memory of "westering," that he cannot live comfortably in the present. He talks about having led wagon trains across the Plains and mountains to the West Coast, and how he and his old pals would sit on the Pacific shoreline, at the end of the continent, cursing the sea just for being there and thus marking the end of their journey. Grandfather Tifflin is a sad figure, a man out of time and out of place.[76]

But while Grandfather Tifflin may be highly representative of literary depictions of old pioneer placelessness, he is probably less indicative of "real-life" western pioneer reminiscers. He is sad because he is lamenting the passage of time in isolation from his peers. If the story were nonfiction, one suspects that old Tifflin and his pals would have formed a county-level pioneer society and collectively sought solace by engaging in acts of selective remembrance for purposes of mutual admiration, affirmation, and validation, thereby developing and sustaining their sense of place and belonging. While their actual journeys would have been over, their journey down the path of reminiscence would have just begun. For old reminiscers, sense of place in the present was, to no small degree, developed through collective recollections of the processes by which they had journeyed to western places and transformed them. And their efforts to sustain and embellish the legacy of those journeys have played no small part in the construction, elaboration, dissemination, and preservation of the frontier heritage.

Reminiscences of a Booster's Wife

The West of thirty-four years ago is now only a tradition. The picturesque wilderness with its marauding bands of Indians, with its lawless white men . . . and with its vast tenantless reaches of mountains and plains was a reality, with all the vast resources of the domain yet to be developed. (Carrie Adell Strahorn, *Fifteen Thousand Miles by Stage,* 1911)

Women were frequent contributors to the pioneer reminiscence genre, and a good number of women recorded their memories of western journeys. In 1911, while Meeker was in the midst of his second covered wagon trip back across the Oregon Trail, Carrie Adell Strahorn, a resident of Spokane, Washington, published her reminiscences of western travels that had begun some thirty-four years earlier, *Fifteen Thousand Miles by Stage: A Woman's Unique Experience During Thirty Years of Path Finding and Pioneering.*[77] Carrie Strahorn, unlike Meeker, had not herself been a booster, but her reminiscences serve as an interesting companion to the promotional tracts of her husband, Robert Edmund Strahorn (see chapter 1), author of numerous important promotional volumes for the northwestern states, including *The Hand-Book of Wyoming* (1877). Carrie dedicated her 700-page account to her "dear husband."[78] It is interesting to consider together that which Carrie remembered having seen in the West with the things her husband had been paid to see.

Robert had made a career of presenting frontier backwaters as settled regions. *The Hand-Book of Wyoming* had actually concluded with a chapter titled "Reminiscences and Miscellaneous Happenings," which only served to underscore his claims concerning the rapid advance of Wyoming beyond the frontier stage.[79] If old-timers were already reminiscing about the old days, then how could the reader reach any other conclusion than that those old days were long gone and the new, postfrontier West had fully arrived? Yet Carrie recalled a very different set of western conditions from those her husband had described. In dedicating the book to Robert, she noted that he had been her "constant chum and companion," and that it had been her "greatest joy to be [with him] for more than thirty years in the conquering of the wilderness." In the book's preface Carrie further sketched out the contrast between western past and present, emphasizing the region's legacy of "marauding bands of Indians, . . . lawless white men, . . . vast tenantless reaches of mountains and plains."[80]

Robert, in his promotional writings in the late 1870s, had vociferously denied that any wilderness remained to be conquered in the far northwestern regions of the country. He consistently stressed that potential settlers need not be concerned about encountering even the discomforts and inconveniences, let alone the dangers and privations, of the frontier phase of settlement. This message of regional development was a vital one, and he delivered it to great effect and with no small degree of encouragement from the railroad. However, in direct contradiction of the advertised image of a safe and settled Northwest, Carrie noted that the Union Pacific, her husband's employer, had protested vigorously when, in 1877, Robert had demanded to take his new bride along with him on a 15,000-mile promotional trip through the region. She would slow him down, they had insisted. However, Carrie explained that "Mr. Strahorn was firm in his insistence [that she accompany him], and [the railroad officials] were obdurate and arbitrary; they argued and reasoned, then demurred, relented, and finally consented."[81]

It was not just the railroad that raised objections to Carrie's being transported off to the Wild West; family and friends did so as well. Given the historical context, their concerns were perfectly understandable. Pulp magazines and dime novels of the 1870s were filled with stories of lawless gunfighters and savage Indians. General George Armstrong Custer's force had been wiped out at the Battle of the Little Big Horn River just the year before the Strahorns' trip. But while the protests of loved ones were perfectly reasonable, those of the railroad were rather ironic considering that Robert's primary task as a booster was to demonstrate that the New West was no wild frontier but a thoroughly tamed, cultured place where young settlers could take their wives and families without concern for their comfort or safety. Still, Robert, as an advocate of women's suffrage, prevailed in the matter, and Carrie accompanied him for 15,000 miles across the postfrontier western wonderland, even though she did not recollect it as such.

The reader finds in Carrie's recollections everything that was absent from the promoters' descriptions of the New Northwest—including the "broad sage-brush desert," and "real pioneering." She was reflecting back on how conditions had been in various western places during the very time her husband had been penning his promising promotional descriptions of them. In a melodramatic conclusion to the book's final chapter, "The Passing of the Wilderness," Carrie wrote:

> What hardships have been endured and heart-strings crushed and broken; what family ties have been rent by the great movement to the West! [T]hrough an earnest, life-sacrificing ordeal the frontiersman has slowly blazed the way . . . with poverty and suffering. Each has played a part to one great end . . . revealing a land of milk and honey, a land of fruit and flowers, a land of running streams . . . with bread for all the nations, a land of . . . life-giving ozone, where youth holds the charm over years and the ravages of time are lost in eternal bloom.[82]

Carrie noted that "the frontier was a fact and not fiction in the '70s" and that "a woman in the far West was a blessing sent direct from Heaven, or from the East, which was much the same in those days." What is more, she added, "Almost everywhere away from the more favored ox freight lines the modes of living were crude and often far from tempting."[83] "It was," she continued, "a land where eyes often ached with straining from horizon to horizon for the sight of a cabin, and where the heavy rattle of the stage-coach and the howling of coyotes were the only sounds that broke the silence of the vast expanse."[84] Perhaps Carrie was exaggerating a little, selectively remembering the most frontierlike aspects of the past to heighten the dramatic effect of her narrative. Whatever the case, the contrast between the imaginative descriptions of the husband and the colorful recollections of the wife is striking.

In a fascinating chapter titled "Caldwell and Other Frontier Towns," Carrie discussed the depth of emotional investment in parts of the West where promise and actuality were not in alignment. "To plump one's self down in an alkali flat, with railroad survey stakes for company, and expect an Aladdin's lamp to throw pictures of a thriving city," she wrote, "invited feelings of sobbing and laughter so closely allied that one can hardly tell which is which, or which will dominate." Then, she added, "The sobbing must be hidden so deep that one's own sweetheart will not know it is there."[85] Was Carrie speaking in broad generalities about the experience of settlers, or was she recounting her own efforts to hide her feelings of disappointment from her husband? We do know that the young couple lived for a time in Caldwell. Furthermore, Carrie wrote at some length about the gulf between what that place was in the late 1870s and what was expected for it:

> What a desert it was at that point! The ground was as white with alkali as the winter robe of the mountain tops. . . . Not a tree nor a sign of habitation on the townsite, only the white, desolate glare and clouds of choking, biting dust that consumed the very flesh. It seemed like a place deserted by God himself, and not intended for man to meddle with. . . . [T]he vast solitude and desolation held me in a meditative trance. What a forbidding place to build a home; my face was already sore from the poison ash, and my heart sank in a flash of homesickness as I drew out the plans in a great blueprint of the town "to be."

She then described the blueprint, with its streets, residence locations, parks, school and church plots, railroad, depot, hotel, and even the shade trees. "It all looked so complete," she noted, "that I fairly strained my ears to hear the toot of the engine and the ringing of bells. A lift of the eyelids and the dream vanished, leaving a wide chasm between the dream city on paper and the reality."[86]

In addition to this extended commentary on the incongruities between the boosters' visions of promised lands and the starker western realities that prevailed, Carrie's account included coverage of numerous stage holdups and robberies, and various other scenes of wild frontier days. Illustrations by Charles Russell give Carrie's book a very different appearance from her husband's many promotional publications. She even discussed her fear that Robert—who as a promoter had firmly denied the presence of frontier dangers—would be lynched by the residents of nearby Boise City, on account of his boosting of a rival town.

The settled and developed conditions that boosters in the post–Civil War decades claimed already existed all over the West often bore little resemblance to actual circumstances. As noted earlier, however, their descriptions did match quite closely the reminiscers' much later representations of their own settled present, after they had "made the desert bloom like a rose." Carrie, reminiscing about conditions in western places more than three decades after her husband had first presented them, unintentionally contradicted his earlier descriptions. It was only with the passage of time that the postfrontier conditions in the West, so confidently described by the boosters, came to resemble the settled present that pioneer reminiscers so often lamented their own presence in.[87] Indeed, Carrie painted her western present, in 1911, in much the same way that her husband had sketched the Plains and Rocky Mountain West, back in the late 1870s (a time lag of roughly two generations).

The story of the husband's imaginings and the wife's rememberings is replete with irony when read today. Yet one suspects that Robert would have read *Fifteen Thousand Miles by Stage* without being embarrassed by the contradictions between his earlier accounts and those of his wife.[88] Indeed, his unpublished autobiography, "Ninety Years of Boyhood," written in 1942, is filled with language strikingly similar to that in *Fifteen Thousand Miles by Stage,* which suggests that the two of them wrote that book together. Robert perhaps shared in Carrie's published reminiscences as a cathartic exercise— a form of penance for his past actions. We do know from his autobiography that he experienced serious misgivings concerning the effects of his promotional efforts. Robert wrote: "I could not but feel that, for a time at least, many of them would be grievously disappointed in what we could already visualize and enthusiastically paint as a land of plenty." He added that his "worst misgivings arose from thoughts of the hardships to be encountered by the thousands who would now, largely through our early flood of alluring literature, follow in our footsteps."[89]

The marriage of prophecy and memory seems, in the case of the Strahorns, to have been a long and happy one, in spite of the moments of incongruity. Carrie died in 1925. After her death, Robert fared less well. During the Great Depression he lost the significant wealth that he had accumulated as a booster. A reminiscer of sorts, he died in 1944, at the age ninety-two, joining Juliet Brier, Lorenzo Dow Stephens, Ezra Meeker, and a host of other nonagenarian participants in that purposeful endeavor of remembering the frontier past.

ORGANIZING MEMORIES

Forging a Frontier Heritage

You Pioneers of Montana . . . carried the last frontier to the crest of the Rocky Mountains and its receding wave people this valley. . . . You drove the savage red man and bandit from this land and from all lands and dedicated these hills and vales to civilization so that we could come here and build homes for our children. (James U. Sanders, secretary, Society of Montana Pioneers, 1917)

[Westerners] took up regionalism with enthusiasm. They had help from surviving pioneers, some of whom spent their declining years in rituals at Pioneers' Halls spinning tales about themselves, comparing (one of their critics said in 1876) "their achievements to those of Cortez and Pizarro—to the disadvantage of Pizarro and Cortez." (Earl Pomeroy, *The Pacific Slope,* 1965)

Western pioneer societies were the formal organs through which older generations of westerners sought to establish and maintain their status in changing western social environments. These organizations sprang up all over the

West and outside of the West—the Chicago, Maryland, New York, and New England societies of California Pioneers are examples—in the late nineteenth century and generally remained active into the early decades of the next.[1] These societies usually developed within a couple of decades after the first permanent white settlers arrived in a particular western region, and it was generally within the same time frame that individual settlers began to record and publish their reminiscences. These organizations varied in size, from larger ones, such as the Los Angeles County Pioneer Society, with its 1,143 members (682 living and 461 deceased) in 1923, to the Jayhawkers of '49, with its few dozen members at its founding in 1872. Some organizations were formed on the county level (the Los Angeles County Pioneer Society, in 1897, is an example); others on the state level (the Society of Colorado Pioneers in 1872, the Historical Society of Idaho Pioneers in 1881, the Society of Arizona Pioneers, and the Society of Montana Pioneers, in 1884, to name a few); and some, such as the Jayhawkers, bore no relation to units of political organization. Some state historical societies, including Arizona's, evolved from pioneer societies, a point worth considering in accounting for the endurance of the frontier heritage.[2]

Old pioneers understood that the importance of their organizations would be validated by the attention and the involvement of recognized personalities; hence they sent letters to U.S. presidents, and on occasion to famous literary figures, requesting their attendance at annual meetings. In 1887, for example, the Tri-State Old Settlers' Association of Illinois, Missouri, and Iowa invited both President Grover Cleveland and Samuel L. Clemens (Mark Twain) to Keokuk, Iowa. Unfortunately for the hosts, both invitees were unable to attend. Cleveland cited pressing affairs of state as the reason for his absence. Twain, author of perhaps the single most renowned travel narrative of the era, *Roughing It* (1872), wrote back that the one thing he was "particularly and obstinately prejudiced against . . . is travel."[3] Still, the president's tight schedule and Twain's lighthearted commentary on travel phobia probably did not cause the organization too much disappointment. State governors, congressmen, senators, and other political notables were regular attendees at state-level pioneer society meetings, and state-level legislators regularly attended local society meetings.

Membership in these organizations meant a great deal and was eagerly sought. Pioneer societies were often quite restrictive in their admission requirements. The Oregon Pioneer Society limited membership to those who had arrived prior to statehood (January 1, 1853). The Society of California

Pioneers, which reserved admission privileges for those who had arrived before or during the gold rush, actually created two separate categories of members (first class: those who had arrived prior to January 1, 1849; and second class: those who had arrived prior to January 1, 1850). The Society of Colorado Pioneers set December 31, 1860 (i.e., within a year or so of the 1859 gold rush), as the cutoff date. For the Arizona Pioneers, the legitimacy line was set at January 1, 1870; for the first Wyoming pioneer association, the date was July 1, 1884. The admission dates were supposed to mark watershed moments, the defining lines between the unsettled frontier past and the safer, more comfortable modern age.

During the 1890s, members of the Society of Montana Pioneers debated the date set for admission into the association, getting it pushed forward in time from May 26, 1864, to December 31, 1868, thereby allowing more people to lay claim to the title of "pioneer."[4] Most of the pioneer societies renegotiated the original cutoff dates, moving them forward to accommodate the membership wishes of would-be pioneers and, presumably, to sustain the organization's numbers as members began to die off.

One would-be pioneer, Hiram Knowles, had experienced no small degree of frustration over these cutoff dates. Knowles wrote to the Tri-State Old Settlers Association in 1885, thanking it for inviting him to join and gladly accepting. He lamented that he had not been eligible for the Lee County, Iowa, organization because he arrived there in 1844, and the date for eligibility was 1840. Similarly, he missed the California cutoff (1849) by a year, the Nevada cutoff (1860) by two, Idaho (1863) by two, and Montana (1864) also by two years. As a very old and well-traveled settler, he was honored to finally belong to a pioneer society, even though he was unable to make the trip from Butte City, Montana.[5]

One of the benefits of membership in a pioneer society was the opportunity to share formally in the collective memory of the frontier process. The collective and selective memories of the western past played a significant role in forging a sense of place and a sense of belonging among members of these older generations.[6] Sharing their recollected experiences of journeying and adjusting to western places surely provided a degree of self-validation for individuals and for the organizations as a whole. The new, settled West seemed a far cry from the old, pioneer West of their youth. But celebrating their role in building the foundations of contemporary comfort and prosperity probably helped alleviate old reminiscers' sense of disconnection from the modern West, even as they drew striking contrasts between past and present.

These contrasts were a stable feature of speeches delivered to pioneer societies and at times resembled a jeremiad. An early example appeared in a speech delivered to the Old Settlers Association of Johnson County, Iowa, in 1866. The organization was not strictly a "western" pioneer society (at least according to the geographic parameters of this study); however, the group's concerns demonstrate the geographic and chronological continuity in the reminiscence genre from the Midwest to the Far West. Members of the first generation of Johnson County Pioneers were reminded in the speech that they "came to a land sparsely settled, in a state without railroads or telegraphs . . . [and] most of them [had] little besides their strength, their courage, and their will." They were "forced to depend on their own resources for those things which are now so easily attained."[7] The same sentiment was echoed in the constitutions of far western pioneer organizations, such as that of the Society of California Pioneers, which expressed its members' desire to "perpetuate the memory of those whose sagacity, enterprise, and love of independence induced them to settle in the wilderness and become the germ of a new state."[8]

The members of these societies agreed on the broad generalities of the pioneering past—when times were harder, conditions rougher, and the demands greater. As long as the established framework of the morality tale was in place, it did not matter much if individual details varied a little. But when that framework was abandoned, when the glories of the pioneer past were called into question, pioneer organizations reacted. Such was the case in 1893, fittingly, the year when Frederick Jackson Turner was delivering his eulogy in Chicago to the passing of the frontier ("The Significance of the Frontier in American History") and when Buffalo Bill Cody was glorifying the frontier past before millions in the same city. In the winter of that year, the nation entered the worst economic depression in its history up to that time. The Populist Party, with its calls for an increase in the amount of money in circulation and for government control of the railroads and telegraphs, was becoming an increasingly unnerving presence for the eastern establishment. Also in 1893, the Pullman Palace Car Company introduced drastic wage cuts of 25 percent; these cuts sparked the famous Pullman Strike in early 1894, which prompted President Cleveland, on a highly dubious pretense, to send in federal troops and end the strike.

In 1893, with the country in the midst of these crises, the Society of California Pioneers formally struck distinguished historian Hubert Howe Bancroft from its list of honorary members because his seven-volume *His-*

tory of California (1886–1890) had, in the Society's estimation, darkened the proud heritage of the state's early Anglo settlers. Bancroft, with the help of his extensive staff, was a veritable publishing machine. Prior to 1893, he had completed more than fifty large volumes on the Americas that covered more than seven feet of shelf space.[9] He was one of the best-known historians of the late nineteenth century, but certain elements of his version of the California past were at odds with the purposes of the Society of California Pioneers. In retrospect, the Society's condemnation of Bancroft seems rather ironic, since historians have identified him as one of the most significant architects of a positive gold rush heritage for California.[10] As is often the case in historical reconstruction, the process of shaping the key contours of a story can lead to the ironing out of certain wrinkles.

One such wrinkle in the historical record is the report, published in booklet form by the Society, relating to Bancroft's dismissal. Society member and prosecutor Willard B. Farwell wrote in this report that Bancroft had "wantonly and maliciously wrong[ed] the old Argonauts" in his "quasi-history." And, as "living witnesses" to the events that Bancroft described in his work, California's old pioneers had a duty to "correct misstatements and misrepresentations of so-called historians." Bancroft had produced a "monstrous series of libels upon the memories of departed illustrious Pioneers and [a] monstrous perversion of the facts of history." His misreading of the past could not be allowed, Farwell insisted, to stand as the official version of the events, the one that would shape the public consciousness of later generations. The Society was particularly incensed by Bancroft's very critical treatment of John C. Frémont and other key participants in the Bear Flag Revolt, and of General John A. Sutter.[11] Compared with Josiah Royce's damning treatment of Frémont in his *History of California* (1886) and Royce's powerful indictment—in a chapter titled "The Conquerors and Their Consciences"—of the glaring hypocrisy of the nation's efforts to explain away its imperialistic acts in California, Bancroft's treatment seems quite tame.[12] Still, for whatever reasons—perhaps it was just that the sensitivities of the Society's members were more acute in 1893 and that Bancroft's history had simply garnered more public attention than Royce's—it was Bancroft who became the subject of the Society's ire, not Royce.

Farwell's report was sent to Bancroft, and the historian was invited to defend himself in person at Pioneer Hall, in San Francisco, on December 12, 1893. Bancroft did not appear to face the charges, and the Society rescheduled its hearing for December 26, but Bancroft was not present then either. The meeting was rescheduled for January 9 of the next year; again Bancroft did not show. Not surprisingly, the reviled historian was not in attendance at the next rescheduling of the hearing on January 16. The report was finally submitted to the organization's members for action on February 5, with Bancroft absent for the fifth time. The resolution, that the author of the "so-called history" of California be struck from the list of honorary members, was unanimously carried. It was also recommended that the Society's report be distributed to "the Public Libraries of the United States and elsewhere" to serve as a "vindication of the memories of the many early pioneers."[13]

Meanwhile, those memories were being vindicated and preserved in the mass of published pioneer reminiscences that appeared from the Civil War to the Great Depression. Many were commercially published, some were privately printed, and some were simply typed up, or written out in neat script, and handed down to younger generations. A common feature of both the speeches delivered at pioneer society meetings and the recorded reminiscences of old pioneers (like those of the journey rememberers and reenactors) is their authors' tendency to move from the vantage point of the safe, settled, regional present to recount the dangers and hardships of the frontier past. These transitions from region back to frontier are heavily emphasized and often overstated and serve as a kind of converse parallel to the boosters' transitions from frontier to region. Booster literature vigorously denied that frontier conditions existed in the western places being promoted and insisted that only frontier opportunities were present. Pioneer reminiscences, on the other hand, insisted that harsh frontier conditions—requiring the application of great pioneering fortitude—had prevailed.

The two groups of image makers were constructing their pictures of the western present (boosters) and past (reminiscers) at different times. The promotional tracts generally preceded, by a decade or two, the reminiscences centered on a particular place. Yet, the boosters' "present" and the pioneers' "past" were often contemporaneous. Or, to put it another way, boosters and reminiscers were writing at different times but about the same points in time, be they the 1870s and 1880s in western Kansas, Nebraska, and Colorado or the first two decades of the twentieth century in eastern and central Montana or the Texas Panhandle.

One key difference between the two genres is that promotional writers expressed a strong preference for the regional present over the frontier stage, while old pioneers often lauded the simpler, more rugged past.[14] Of course, the boosters' preference for the present was natural, since they were trying to represent western possibilities as actual realities. The old pioneers' fondness for the past is equally understandable: they were reflecting back on the era when they were in their prime and able to endure frontier hardships. Despite these oppositional perspectives, that which the boosters presented, with their great powers of imagination and creative license, as present reality sometimes matched quite closely (at least with regard to basic content) the old pioneers' descriptions of their own present a few decades later. What we see in the published record is a time lag, often about a generation in length, and resulting from both the boosters' overly optimistic projections of the future onto present realities and the reminiscers' melodramatic accentuation of the travails of the past from their present.

The pioneer reminiscences also parallel the booster literature in their earnest claims to authenticity. Promotional pamphlets and booklets, especially by the 1880s, almost invariably began with a claim of legitimacy; likewise for reminiscences. Such insistence upon accuracy and integrity in remembering the pioneer past was—like the boosters' pronouncements of honesty and reliability—vital to the genre. The materials often read something like: "This is not an exaggerated Wild West account, and I am no literary giant; the following are plain words about real events."[15] Not surprisingly, and despite their earnest claims to the contrary, many of the pioneer reminiscences are as fantastic and improbable as the booster booklets. Still, most of the reminiscers (and here again they parallel the boosters), true to their disclaimers, tended not to be literary giants. But their accounts (once more mirroring those of the boosters) tended to be anything but plain, and their prose anything but unrestrained.

It was largely through the power of such memories as these, no matter how colorful, that white Americans constructed a frontier heritage. Indeed, the true significance of the frontier in American history may lie less in any role the frontier actually played in shaping a national character and institutions than in the powerful selective memories of the frontier's influence. The sheer weight of these collective remembrances is astounding. Library shelves are filled with dusty old volumes of reconstructed memories of the West.[16] While the content of these reminiscences focused on the frontier past, their message was directed toward the postfrontier present. As old pioneers recounted bygone ages, they hoped that readers would better comprehend their importance and relevance.

Today we might view the recollectors' literary labors as tall tales, but at the time their creators saw them as parables bearing out the significance of the frontier experience. There were clear morals to these stories. Indeed, older generations of white Americans—including those who had journeyed to the West and stayed, and those who had been involved in historic movements such as the California gold rush and had returned to their eastern and midwestern homes—created a moral universe of their own, rooted in frontier values, and contrasted it with the moral climate of the New West. Their past, itself the product of imaginative re-creation, became their yardstick for measuring the quality of life in the industrial age.

Their reminiscences amount to a kind of "common culture" corollary to the intellectual ruminations of Theodore Roosevelt, Frederick Jackson Turner, William Graham Sumner, and hundreds of other intellectuals over the ominous consequences of the frontier's passing. The grassroots-level concerns expressed in the genre of pioneer remembrance are equally significant in explaining the endurance of the nation's frontier heritage.[17] Turner, in a series of essays from the 1890s—including "The Problem of the West" (1896) and "Dominant Forces in Western Life" (1897), both in the *Atlantic Monthly*—made ideas about the influences of the frontier and the impact of its passing "acceptable within the halls of academia."[18] But tales of the frontier's significance had been echoing around the pioneer halls and adorning the pages of pioneer reminiscences since at least the late 1860s, when Turner was a boy in Portage, Wisconsin. In that town, which was just a generation or so removed from "frontier times," Turner probably heard such tales of frontier hardship and adventure. Indeed, his father, a politician and editor, was a reminiscer of sorts who wrote newspaper columns on the region's history and may have been the principal author of a local county history published in 1880. It certainly would have been the intent of the town's pioneers to ensure that youthful Portagers were informed of the older generation's contributions.[19]

The pioneer society proceedings and reminiscences are filled with discussion of the frontier's role as a shaping force in American and western life. These writings and speeches discussed how the frontier had formed a practically oriented, intuitive character; had molded a new "breed" of hardy, individualistic Americans from the human stock of older sections and nations; had shaped democratic institutions and a heightened spirit of nationalism; and had acted as a safety valve for urban discontent. Furthermore, these sources were also expressions of concern that the frontier, the assumed wellspring of democracy, nationalism, individualism, and rugged self-reliance, was running dry.[20]

Manhood, Femininity, and Memory

> Wherever are found noble characters, for memory's sake, no less than to
> inspire others with a spirit of emulation, we ought to rehearse their
> achievements and tell the stories of their struggles and triumphs. There
> are so many temptations to follow pernicious lives, so few incentives,
> comparatively, toward pure heroism and genuine nobility of character.
> Our part of the world, particularly, is in danger of reclining upon the
> couch of luxury and cultivating the spirit of effeminacy so suicidal to the
> possessor. The sacrifices of ancestral heroes find little appreciation by the
> modern youth, largely from the fact that the perils of early settlement are
> so little known. (E. G. Cattermole, *Famous Frontiersmen, Pioneers and
> Scouts,* 1883)

The perceived passing of the frontier was accompanied by a concern over
the presumed decline of American manhood. E. G. Cattermole expressed
this sentiment in his collection of improbable stories, *Famous Frontiersmen,
Pioneers and Scouts* (1883). He hoped that the remarkable exploits of Boone,
Crockett, Custer, and other frontier legends would inspire the younger generation "with a spirit of emulation." Mimicking Custer's fatally flawed style
of decision making could not have been a sagacious course for younger generations, to be sure. But Cattermole's real emphasis was on the courage,
bravery, independence, and self-reliance of these earlier frontier heroes who
were, in the author's estimation, real men. The present generation of Americans needed to learn from their example, he believed, because its members
were "in danger of reclining upon the couch of luxury, and cultivating . . .
[a] spirit of effeminacy."[21]

Historian Francis Parkman expressed the same fear that the nation's men
were becoming less strenuous, less virile, and less manly in the wake of the
frontier's passing.[22] In his preface to the 1892 edition of *The Oregon Trail,*
Parkman lamented that "the slow cavalcade of horsemen armed to the teeth
has disappeared before parlor cars and the effeminate comforts of modern
travel."[23] Frederic Remington, the quintessential artist of the masculine West
in the 1880s and 1890s, provided the illustrations for Parkman's volume.
Theodore Roosevelt took up the flag of western masculinity around the same
time, worrying about the waning frontier spirit and accompanying decline
in ruggedness. Roosevelt even remarked in 1897 that he would welcome
"almost any war" because it would help reinvigorate national virility.[24] Pioneer
reminiscences reflected the concerns of Cattermole, Parkman, Remington,
Roosevelt, and hundreds of other writers and intellectuals over the impend-

ing effeminization of American manhood. Those earlier frontier times were considered to be, in the commonly uttered language of the late nineteenth century, "times to test men's souls"; and, as Mrs. Brier's example reminds us, it was not just men's souls that were put to the test. The postfrontier present, with its conveniences and luxuries, seemed not to offer the challenges and hardships necessary to sustain manly, frontier traits; indeed, to observers such as Roosevelt and Cattermole, that overly comfortable present seemed antithetical to the spirit and purpose of the frontier past.

In their written reminiscences and at their society meetings, old pioneers, · much like most other Americans, tended not to go quite as far as Roosevelt. They did not, as a matter of course, hanker for war as a restorative for the old frontier spirit. Instead, they hoped that younger generations might somehow learn from and emulate their example. Whether public figures and writers, and the many thousands of lesser-known pioneer reminiscers, worried too much about the waning of American manhood and vigor among the emerging generation of young men is impossible to measure. Their rallying cry of retreating manhood certainly had homophobic undertones. And the mass of frontier adventure stories emphasizing manly virtues—that were published for adolescent males starting in the 1880s—highlights the depth of that concern over the effeminization of youth in the modern era.[25]

While speeches at pioneer gatherings and published pioneer reminiscences tended to present pioneer achievements within a markedly male frame of reference, there was actually a good deal of acknowledgment of the achievements of women pioneers, such as the indomitable Juliet Brier. These old white males were not strident feminists, but neither were they blind to the reality that women had endured great hardships, too, and deserved the accolade "pioneer," even if their involvement with pioneer societies came largely in the form of "auxiliary" organizations. Those organizations included the Native Daughters of the Golden West (formed in California in 1887); the Territorial Daughters of Colorado (1876) and Pioneer Ladies Aid Society of Colorado (1889); and the Ladies Auxiliary of the Society of Arizona Pioneers (1902). These auxiliaries often ended up merging with the main, male organizations, on a full or partial basis. For example, women who met the temporal requirements for admission into the Society of Colorado Pioneers were, after January 31, 1881, declared honorary members of that organization.[26] Women were full members of the Oregon Pioneer Association from the very beginning.[27]

Women were generally present at pioneer society meetings, albeit primarily in their capacity as wives of male members. Most of the annual gatherings featured at least one speech entitled "Pioneer Women" or "Pioneer Mothers," in which male members lauded the contributions of their female counterparts. Just as old pioneers reminisced about the object lessons for contemporary American manhood in the more rugged and demanding frontier past, so the speeches detailing the contributions of women pioneers painted them as a different, hardier, more resilient breed of female than later generations of women. They were described as more capable and self-reliant than contemporary women, who had not experienced the trials and tribulations of the frontier. Pioneer women had endured long journeys and then established homes in largely unsettled places at the journey's end; they had proved resourceful enough to meet their families' needs under the most trying conditions. Modern women had experienced no such baptisms by fire.

Furthermore, while speakers at the old pioneer gatherings lauded the femininity of women pioneers, particularly their purity, wholesomeness, and high moral character, their speeches did not dwell endlessly on those feminine virtues and civilizing tendencies. To be sure, these frontierswomen were regularly honored "for taking up cheerfully the all too neglected burdens which refined society and tamed our wilderness." But they were also honored for "fighting savages, swimming rivers, crossing trackless wastes by night or day."[28] Like their male counterparts, pioneer women were eulogized in reminiscences—many of which they authored and edited—as a superior breed, an example for later generations of white women to emulate.[29] Thus frontierswomen were, in a key sense, deemed to be more "womanly" than their successors precisely because they had proved themselves to be more "manly." Former pioneers thus saw settlement and civilization (like its concomitant fashions) as weakening forces on the spirit of femininity.

Popular late-nineteenth-century works, such as John Frost's *Pioneer Mothers of the West; or, Heroic and Daring Deeds of American Women, Comprising Thrilling Episodes of Courage, Fortitude, Devotedness, and Self-Sacrifice* (1875), played up the theme of the frontierswoman's rugged womanhood. Frost outlined the trying process by which "every inch of their beautiful country had to be won from a cruel and savage foe by unheard-of toils, dangers, and conflicts," and he pointed to the presence of "valor, enterprise, and endurance [on the part] of the men." But he quickly added, "The women rivaled them in all these virtues."[30] Another early example of this veneration of the self-reliant female pioneer type appears in a speech by a Dr. John Bell entitled "The Pioneer Women of Louisa County" (Iowa), delivered in 1860. Dr. Bell noted the importance of "celebrat[ing] the virtues of our pioneer women" because "man has too long monopolized the entire attention of history and the world." He added that "men occupy themselves in celebrating and perpetuating the deeds and heroic actions of men, while those of women are unmentioned and forgotten." Then the doctor declared of these forgotten female heroes, "In those times they were really women; in those days we had no Ladies. They are an institution of a later growth and adapted to a different phase of society." Highlighting the difference made by the hooped petticoats accompanying the more settled era of his present, Bell regretted how back then "a woman could get through the door of her cabin without difficulty, but that would be a feat not so easily accomplished by a modern lady."[31]

The gendered emphasis in so many pioneer speeches and recollections constituted a vital element of the reminiscence genre. The theme of impending cultural decline that surfaced periodically in these writings was designed to underscore the importance of learning from the pioneers' example. Similarly, we can assume that the emphasis on the hardiness of the nation's pioneer mothers—which became a more common feature of the genre in the early twentieth century—was intended to serve as an example to the "new woman" of the Progressive Era and post–World War I era. Harry Noyes Pratt's poem "The Pioneer Mother," which appeared in 1922 as an epigraph in Elisha Brooks's reminiscences of his mother's journey across the Plains seventy years earlier, serves as a good illustration of this purpose:

> She braved the dangers of the West
> And followed on at love's behest.
> The wide, still plains of endless view
> Beneath the deep sky's arching blue;
> The waste of desert lone and dry;
> The mountain ridges, rough and high;
> Cold, hunger, death—she braved them all
> And followed still love's beckoning call.
>
> Love was her strength; devotion, power.
> She grew in fineness with the hour,
> She held of beauty more than face,
> Or form, or body's youthful grace.
> Uncouth of dress or rough of hand,
> And marked by all the miles she spanned,
> She stands above the highest here—
> The Mother of the Pioneer.[32]

Likewise, in 1931, the octogenarian Sarah Camp Galloway offered some words of admonishment for the relatively spoiled "modern housewives who complainingly launder in porcelain sinks and quarrel with their husbands about an electric washing machine." Galloway noted that at fourteen years of age she was doing the family laundry in a creek; on one occasion, when she was attacked by Indians, she fought hand to hand with "a savage" to protect her baby brother. Her account clearly implied that the crises of the modern woman in the New West were at best tempests in teapots.[33] The next year, Grace Erickson (the wife of Montana governor John E. Erickson) echoed Galloway's point when she proclaimed that the real "first ladies" of Montana were the women "who went into the mining camps and the forest and the newly added agricultural areas of this state, braving privation, hardship and often grave peril to erect homes, rear families and help to build a new commonwealth."[34] Some of these reminiscences, in their treatment of gender issues, suggested, then, that the present was decadent in part because the differences between men and women had become unnaturally exaggerated because a later generation of women was less self-reliant, less pioneerlike. Yet, in other reminiscences, this gender gap closed as writers emphasized the growing effeminacy of a new generation of American men who had grown up without the benefit of a frontier to nurture their manhood. Certainly, from the 1880s to the 1930s, issues of manhood and femininity were central features in the creation of western memory.

Object Lessons for New Generations

> It is impossible for rising generations to conceive but a remote idea of the privations and dangers from hostile Indians that the pioneers endured in the early settlement of the West. . . . [The] early settlers . . . endured the hardships and privations that they underwent for the sake of paving the way to our present civilization, where towns, cities and railroads have sprung into existence as if by magic. (Luella Shaw, *True History of Some of the Pioneers of Colorado,* 1909)

The reminiscers' message concerning their generation's hardships, sacrifices, and proud example continued to be delivered often and with urgency in the early twentieth century. An address at the thirty-sixth annual reunion of the Old Settlers Association of Johnson County, Iowa (1902), titled "How

the First Farmers Labored," contrasted past tribulations with the undemanding existence of the present generation, emphasizing that "we did not
live then in an atmosphere of artificial wants and needs."[35] Luella Shaw
made the same point in her 1909 collection of Colorado pioneer reminiscences, proclaiming how it would be impossible for younger Americans to
conceive of the difficulties endured by the state's early settlers in the process of bringing the "present civilization . . . into existence as if by magic."[36]
Her point, of course, was that those modern comforts and accommodations
had not sprung up magically but had been built upon a sturdy foundation
laid by that earlier generation. If culture flowered in the New West, it
was because the blood, sweat, and tears of old settlers had sown their
seeds in the fields of an older West; they had "[made] a garden of prosperity and progress out of the once barren wilderness."[37] Similarly, the
author of a pioneer history of Kansas, published in 1911, remarked that if
his story "should be the means of inculcating a larger measure of respect
and reverence for those who performed so nobly the work of laying out
an empire upon a barren waste," he would be "exceedingly happy over the
outcome."[38]

In 1913 a newspaper obituary for the Arizona pioneer woman Larcena
Pennington Page Scott—who had, according to written accounts, been captured, beaten, and left for dead by Apache Indians sixty years earlier—made
the same point: "Her life demonstrates what pale demographics and statistics fail to make clear, what later generations can otherwise hardly comprehend: the stubborn courage, faith and endurance that enabled Americans
to leave comfort and safety behind, push westward into strange, unsettled
lands, survive with few resources, refuse to surrender, and finally triumph
over the obstacles that beset them."[39] We would not, of course, expect obituary
writers to have placed any emphasis on the issue of whether it was wise for
Page Scott to journey through Apache country in the early 1850s. And certainly we should not expect such writers to have expressed any kind of remorse over the fact that white settlers were encroaching upon occupied lands
and were thus personally responsible for whatever fate befell them; obituar-
ies, as a matter of course, tend to honor the dead, not berate them.[40] Still, it
is interesting that Page Scott's obituary writer deemed her actions not just
admirable but logical; she did what white pioneers had to do to tame wastelands and transform them into promised lands. Her life experience was
turned into an uplifting object lesson.

However, it was not just in the process of honoring the dead that such object lessons were emphasized. There was a central self-referential component to published pioneer reminiscences, which placed the author or, in less egotistical instances, the author's generation at the center of the moral universe from which lessons could be culled. Experience on the frontier became the mark of high moral character and physical constitution. Attaining a healthy perspective on life was deemed next to impossible for those who had not experienced the pioneering past. Eliza Spalding Warren, in her *Memoirs of the West* (1917), emphasized that the changes in the region since the pioneer era were "simply beyond description." She added, "It is only those that have endured all those kinds of hardships and dangers and privations and disadvantages that can in a measure realize the changes."[41] Writing in 1922 about his overland journey as a child from Michigan to California and his subsequent struggles on the West Coast, Elisha Brooks hoped, rather immodestly, that "a sketch of his struggles in his wild pioneer days—thrown as he was entirely on his own resources, and armed only with a resolute will that broke down all barriers—might rouse a spirit of emulation in many a youth now drifting into useless manhood."[42]

The message was clear: a previous generation of pioneers had blazed the trail that led to the land of comfort and ease in which later generations resided, and those beneficiaries ought not to forget the sacrifice of their forebears. Many reminiscers seem to have nurtured their own sense of place and belonging by contrasting the pioneer past with the postfrontier present, much to the detriment of the latter. An early and particularly memorable example of this tendency is a speech by the Honorable John F. Phillips of Kansas City, delivered at the fourth annual reunion of the Tri-State Old Settlers Association of Illinois, Missouri, and Iowa in 1887. The sentiment of "local attachment," Phillips explained (much to the delight of the gathering, one suspects) "was more marked in the earlier settlers than in their offspring." The frontier "perils, hardships, privations and struggles, which wrought out of a dense wilderness and the untamed earth a livelihood," not only forged a pioneer character and constitution "but . . . begot an attachment, akin to devotion, for every cranny and nook where life was so hardly lived." This was a powerful attachment to place, Phillips explained, "a clinging as to one's own creation." The pioneer developed a "love of home," even though his surroundings were simple and austere, and his manners rude. Those were the good old days when "simple faith, . . . unaffected hospitality, . . . honor and moral courage" mattered. "Then look at the world around me," Phillips raged:

> . . . seething with energized craft and duplicity; the people surging, jostling and panting for money-getting, sensuous and sexual gratification—the lustful feat of the eye; with every nerve strung and every faculty strained in the sharp encounter of trade; with shoddyism rampant; our stock exchanges veritable mad houses; commercial centers gambling hells; the newspapers reeking with criminal recitals, social garbage and domestic infelicity; every other man saying: am I my brother's keeper, with our food adulterated and drugs poisoned; our social flunkeyism and cant, our venality and charletanism in politics; I feel, like the old Norseman said, when offered his choice of heaven with the new generation, or hell with the old: "I prefer to be with my ancestors."[43]

Phillips's spirited tirade was not a standard juxtaposition of past and present with the usual firm reminder that the pioneer foundation builders should be honored for their efforts. He was suggesting that those sturdy foundations were crumbling because the pioneers' example was not being followed. It was a grim and sorrowful commentary on a frontier paradise lost, on a later generation's pitiful and reprehensible fall from grace. Such reminiscences suggested the need to return to that simpler, nobler, more honorable, and more moral past. While Phillips's condemnation of the postpioneer present was too angry and bombastic to reflect the general spirit of pioneer reminiscences, those recollections were very often marked by a sense that the present, if not condemnable, was certainly at least lamentable when compared with earlier times.[44]

Pioneer society gatherings in the early twentieth century regularly heard comparative commentaries on the enviable past and the troubled present. In his report "Then and Now: A Retrospective" (1915), Historicus (the appointed historian of the Los Angeles County Pioneers of Southern California) reflected back on the Los Angeles of a half century previous and noted that "then there were no paved streets, no street cars or railroads and no idle men. Now we have plenty of idle men with no work." Historicus further reminisced about the single small, one-story brewery, the mere one dozen saloons, and the sole and small adobe jail ("without anybody in it half the time") of that earlier Los Angeles. "Now," he lamented, "there are half a dozen big breweries, two hundred saloons and immense jails filled up most of the time."[45]

Eva Ogden Putnam, an old Wyoming pioneer, made much the same point in the mid-1920s when she reflected back on her life in the territory in the early 1880s. She questioned whether "hearts today burn with such patriotism" as the old pioneers' hearts did "during simple gatherings and displays." Putnam wondered if, "with auto races and airplane stunts and other exciting happenings," the youth of the present "get one-half the thrills out of a celebration that we did then." Despite the simplicity of that earlier time and the incredible advances of the present, she insisted that "in our few festivities we probably crowded as many thrills as they do today in a whole year of their lives."[46] There was, she insisted, something about those earlier times that elevated the human spirit and the national spirit, that inspired fellowship among people, and that quality had dissipated as the old frontier had disappeared. Putnam's account, while it lacks some of the (melo)drama of Historicus's, better typifies the reminiscence genre.

More than just a matter of taste or preference for the rugged simplicity of the past (and the hardy character it fostered) over the technological innovations of the present, the pioneers' comparative retrospectives often reflected clear political positions. A classic example is Robert Moran's address at the fiftieth annual meeting of the Pioneers Association of the State of Washington in 1939. Moran, a lively eighty-two-year-old president of the organization, spoke of his arrival in Seattle in 1875. "Those were the days," he noted, "when there were no 'New Deal' methods of life to feed the loafer: everybody worked and paid his bills." Life was harder then, Moran explained: "The working day was twelve hours, and common laborers' compensation was two dollars. Man carried on his back his blankets and personal belongings from job to job in logging camp and saw mill. The mattress was provided by nature on the spot." Moran's message was repeated time and again by old settlers who were interviewed in the late 1930s by employees of the Works Progress Administration (WPA), a creation of the New Deal that Moran so abhorred.[47]

Reporting on Moran's election to the presidency of Washington's Pioneers Association, the editor of the *Marine Digest* emphasized how his "strength of character, pioneering courage, stability and sturdiness . . . illustrate the importance of individual achievement." Furthermore, the editor added, "in spite of all the socialized stuff we read about now-a-days, individual achievement remains a mighty factor for progress." Moran's pioneering work in the Seattle shipbuilding industry, the article explained, amounted to an inspirational rags-to-riches saga. "Somewhere in Seattle today," the piece concluded, "there is a youth with only a few cents in his pocket, looking for a job, without 'pull' and alone in a strange town, who by individual achievement will do for this community some day in the future what Mr. Moran did for us in the past."[48]

Moran's strong emphasis on "individual achievement" was far from uncommon during the Great Depression. In fact, the heated debate between
New Deal liberals and conservative Republicans over the relative merits of
cooperation and individualism was on one level an ideological struggle over
what the legacy of the frontier should be in a postfrontier society. Franklin
D. Roosevelt, Henry Wallace, and various other New Dealers argued that in
the current state of economic crisis, it was the responsibility of the government to replace the frontier safety valve with a safety net, namely, a new
federal frontier. Herbert Hoover, Alfred Landon, and other critics of the New
Deal countered with the argument that federal largesse would strangle the
frontier spirit of individualism. They contended that even in the very worst
of times there were frontiers of individual enterprise and effort, and it was
those frontiers, not the frontiers of federal bureaucracy and intervention, that
would save American capitalism.[49]

But Moran and the admiring editor of the *Marine Digest* may have worried too much about a waning emphasis on individual achievement and
enterprise. For all the presumably "socializing" influences of the New Deal,
American youths had already been subjected to a flood of inspirational, individualistic, frontier-western "literature" during the previous decade, indeed,
during the whole of the previous half century. Gauging the impact of these
publications on young Americans may be impossible, but we do know that
they were produced in abundance. Book serials, such as the Young Pioneer
Series, with titles such as *The Pioneer Boys of the Colorado: Braving the Perils
of the Grand Canyon Country* (1926), applied the benign characteristics of
the old nineteenth-century pioneer-frontiersmen type to later generations
of youthful heroes. American boys in the 1920s could follow the whole story
of white frontier advance from the Ohio River Valley across the Plains to the
scenic wonders of the West Coast. Such book series were the invention of
commercial publishing companies, not pioneer societies, but they reflected
the same basic themes, providing a generation of adolescent boys with a sense
of the trials, tribulations, and inconveniences suffered by their counterparts
in earlier times.[50]

The juxtaposition of past and present (much to the detriment of the
present) by older generations is, of course, common in American culture
today and probably in most other cultures, too: such is the ongoing impact
of modernization and postmodernization. Fond memories of times when
youths respected their elders and when moral codes were better honored,
by people of all ages, are pervasive among older generations and parallel the

key contours of the pioneer reminiscence genre. Similarly, the perception that life was lived and appreciated more fully in past times, especially those fraught with danger, is central to most reminiscences, not just those of old western pioneers. Civil War veterans often contended that their experiences provided a frame of reference that nonveterans could never acquire; indeed, some Northern intellectuals who did not experience the war firsthand wrote about a consequent void in their lives.[51] Likewise, British memoirists of the Great War of 1914–1917, historian Paul Fussell has noted, dwelled on the past and found "the present . . . too boring and exhausting to think of, and the future too awful"; in doing this they paralleled the old western pioneer reminiscers to some degree.[52] In much the same way, the generations that lived through the Great Depression in America chided the baby boomer generation's appetite for consumption that had been nurtured by an age of prosperity; the latter group's lack of experience with privation had weakened their moral fiber, according to Depression-hardened Americans.

Western pioneer reminiscers were not unique in drawing these distinctions between past and present, between their moral fortitude and the moral and physical underdevelopment of their successors, between the rich experiences of their lives and the bland, shallow, and superficial experiences of younger generations in the modern world. However, the regularity and purposefulness with which pioneer reminiscers illuminated these differences is notable. Tens of thousands of accounts such as Putnam's were published in state historical society journals, pioneer society proceedings, and "Old West" magazines, all juxtaposing the frontier past and the modern regional present.

While older residents of other broad regions of the country voiced similar sentiments as they nostalgically recalled their own youth, there was a greater sense that western places had been transformed from frontier environments into modern, settled ones. The changes, in all likelihood, were no more acute than in other regions. Areas of the New West were no more different from their "old western" counterparts than parts of the New South were from their "old southern" precursors. Similarly, the transformation of parts of the Northeast precipitated by the rapid industrialization, urbanization, and heavy immigration of the late nineteenth century certainly matched the abruptness of change in parts of the West. Yet it was the West that was wrapped in a mythological cloak, composed partly of notions about a great watershed moment: the perceived closing of the frontier. The folklore that surrounded the West placed special emphasis on the contrasts between past and present. And while white Southerners certainly must have drawn sharp distinctions between the antebellum past and the postwar present, their establishment of a rigid Jim Crow system helped nurture a sense of continuity between past and present. For most pioneer reminiscers, the only real continuity between the frontier past and the postfrontier present was the path leading directly from their perceived hardship in an earlier age to the comforts and conveniences of the modern era, which were made possible by their trailblazing efforts. Past and present appear in the reminiscences like two different worlds, separated by a sharply drawn frontier line that, while it might have disappeared from the maps in 1890, according to the superintendent of the United States Census, did not disappear from their own mental maps; indeed, it dominated them.

Yet pioneer reminiscers, focused as they were on the illumination of their frontier experiences as object lessons for later generations, must have been pleased by the organizational efforts of their offspring. "Young settlers' societies" were formed, in part for the purpose of sustaining community recognition of parents' achievements. The Native Sons of the Golden West, formed in 1875, stated its purpose of "keep[ing] alive the memories of the historic valor of the pioneers, their trials, sufferings and grand achievements, and by teaching to the young men the glory of our past excite them to an enthusiastic effort to advance the prosperity of California."[53] Unfortunately, the Native Sons' professed purpose of advancing present prosperity through the adulation of their past pioneer predecessors was actually manifested in their nativistic rhetoric, which fueled anti-Chinese passions in the state.[54]

Still, whatever the actual activities of these pioneer descendents' organizations, the stated purpose behind their formation was the same across state boundaries and temporal lines. The Sons of Colorado, organized in 1905, began publishing a monthly journal the following year. The publication's purpose, editor Will C. Bishop explained, was to demonstrate how "the younger generation, taking pride in the accomplishments of the pioneers, is resolved to work to perpetuate the memory of the deeds and the efforts of the early settlers, who are passing on to the Great Beyond." "Their reminiscences," Bishop continued, "will be a feature of the work of the Sons of Colorado." And those reminiscences would be published as lessons "for the benefit of those who would emulate the heroism and bravery of the little horde that invaded Colorado when the territory was a vast area in possession of the red man." The journal would serve that purpose for more than a generation, proudly pointing to the pioneers' legacy of conquest.[55] And, in addition to the speeches and personal reminiscences that graced the pages of this and other such publications, *Sons of Colorado* reflected common trends of the genre in publishing numerous lyrical tributes to the old pioneers. While there are few, if any, undiscovered poetic gems among the vast pile of odes to old settlers, they certainly encapsulate the key themes of the genre. In songs and poems such as "S. of C." (Sons of Colorado; 1906) and "The Dust of the Overland Trail" (1907), the Sons of Colorado honored the memory, lauded the physical and moral character, and instructed younger generations to learn from the example of the old pioneers.[56]

Subregional Divides of Western Memory

> Showers of quail and manna fell upon the children of Israel. The Crusaders could feast pon [*sic*] the fruits of prolific valleys, or upon the corn of their defeated enemies. The Pilgrim Fathers satisfied their hunger from the Mayflower, and the maize of friendly Indians. The pioneers of California found a land of sunshine and plenty. But the first settlers of Butte [Montana] met a rigorous climate, an unprolific houseless waste, an obstinate nature, forbidding surroundings and an entire absence of storehouses. Neither quail nor manna, fruits nor corn, milk nor honey, nor provision-laden ships or maize were at their command. They had to "root hog or die," but they "got there all the same," though the road was rough and rocky. (*Butte Bystander,* 1897)

Pioneer reminiscers did more than just draw the contrasts of time and manly virtue when they embedded themselves within a harsh, demanding, yet glorious and memorable frontier heritage. Their recollections not only juxtaposed different eras but also drew contrasts between the severity of the frontier process in particular western places. Earlier, state-level boosters had favorably contrasted conditions in their particular states of residence, which they claimed were fully settled and cultured, with other states where conditions were more "frontier-like." The Nebraska boosters of the mid-1870s, who had warned prospective settlers not to risk the dangerous frontier territory of Colorado, are a good example. Pioneer reminiscers generally drew the contrast in reverse, claiming that they had experienced more demanding and inhospitable frontier conditions than had their pioneer neighbors in other western regions. Old pioneers were sending a message to their regional pioneer counterparts. They stressed that the frontier transformations they had engineered in their particular western places demanded greater endurance and sacrifice than those of their western neighbors. As well as being characterized by an elevated generational pride, the reminiscences are marked by an elevated subregional or state-level pride—the "I'm more western and frontiersman-like than you" syndrome, we might call it.[57]

Pioneer reunions featured numerous speeches emphasizing the particular ruggedness of a region's first white settlers. Oregon pioneers liked to contrast themselves with those in California, noting that the latter had arrived later and entered a landscape and climate too mild and undemanding for them to be considered true frontiersmen and frontierswomen.[58] It is worth emphasizing that Oregon's interior boosters were, in the early twentieth century, simultaneously claiming their state's climate to be the mildest, most equable, most salubrious on the face of the earth. The author of a Southern Pacific publication of 1914 for western Oregon went to great lengths to emphasize that the region was not "a frontier state still in a raw and underdeveloped condition." Indeed, the publication explained, since Oregon's natural conditions were so good, its first (white) settlers did not have their "energy . . . drafted off to conquer difficulties," as would have been the case had the country been "barren and unproductive and its climate harsh."[59] In highlighting the accrual of a whole range of benefits in the present because of the natural advantages of the past, this particular promotional tract directly undercut the subsequent arguments of the state's pioneer reminiscers, who contended that their efforts had conquered Oregon's harsh, inhospitable deserts. Regions, such as the Pacific Northwest, that experienced sustained promotional efforts in both the late nineteenth and early twentieth centuries provide especially interesting examples of the parallels and departures between the booster and reminiscence genres. In these places the first generation of old pioneers and the second generation of boosters were contemporaneously constructing markedly different pictures of the same locales.

When there was no denying the mild climate and agricultural advantages of a place, reminiscers could always stake their claim to quintessential westernness and ruggedness by stressing the particular hardships they had endured in journeying to that place. Thus, California pioneers contended that they had experienced so much danger and privation in the course of their journeys to the Golden State—"separated as it was by such vast wastes of desert lands and pathless mountain heights peopled by hordes of savage Indians"—that they should be considered the greatest pioneers of all. The Jayhawkers, who contrasted the horrors of their journey through the valley of death with their deliverance in the promised land of Southern California, are a part of this tradition.[60]

The hardships of western journeys were often the foundation of claims to elevated pioneer status. Governor R. J. Oglesby of Illinois proclaimed, in a speech to the Tri-State Old Settlers' Association of Illinois, Missouri, and Iowa in 1885, that the audience members were "the last of the pioneers" and that there was "no more pioneer work in the United States." Explaining this bold assertion, he emphasized that these old settlers had arrived in the Mississippi Valley ahead of "the railroads, ahead of navigation, pioneering, civilization." But from that geographic point on, the "railroads went ahead of population," and, Oglesby further noted, "a man can't be a pioneer and travel in a railroad car." In this way, the governor swiftly excluded Kansas, Nebraska, and Colorado from the category of "pioneer states."[61] According to Oglesby's reasoning, the Midwest was the true frontier, the real West where the souls of men and women had been tested; the governor deemed the New West, which stretched from the second tier of trans-Mississippi states to the Pacific, to be just a pale frontier reflection.

In a speech before the same organization two years later, the Honorable John S. Runnells, of Des Moines, Iowa, played up the common theme of the harshness of the Iowa landscape, but he drew his comparisons not with other parts of the West but with other nations. He told the old pioneers assembled that Iowa "was a desolate wilderness before they came . . . [but] at their touch it became as the Garden of Eden." And he contrasted that harsh landscape, "which yielded its richness only to your tireless assaults," with other countries' nonfrontier landscapes. He proclaimed that the "nations of the East opened their eyes to lands flowing with milk and honey. Spices dropped from the leaves; every month furnished its fruit without labor; and all the necessities of life were supplied by the bounty of prodigal nature. And so the people were slothful, self-indulgent, and effeminate. Progress was unknown; invention was unheard of, liberty slept and despotism was law."[62] Runnells was perhaps assuaging his concerns over American manhood when he implied that eastern nations had a cultural monopoly on effeminacy. Certainly, he did not highlight generational differences in American manliness as so many other pioneer reminiscers did; but he did echo the reminiscence genre's common emphasis on the conquering of harsh frontier landscapes as an essential component of character building.

The Old Settlers Association of Johnson County, Iowa, heard a very similar message at its twentieth annual reunion meeting in 1886. The speaker,

C. W. Irish, stated that members of his organization "came here when the county was new, . . . when the unbroken prairie stretched away toward the West, when the mighty oaks along our river had never felt the axe." They had to completely transform an environment. A year later Irish, in another address to the same organization, contrasted the pure motivations of Iowa's settlers, to live on the land honestly and harvest a crop, with the base ambitions of those driven to California by lust for gold, or driven to Kansas and Texas by politics.[63]

California's pioneer reminiscers, particularly those in the north, had been responding to such criticisms of their state's pioneer past ever since the gold rush.[64] Then, from the 1880s into the 1920s, the northern and southern parts of the state constructed divergent and competing pictures of the pioneer past. Northern California drew on the heritage of the gold rush, while Southern California drew on the "Spanish fantasy past," and its spokespeople viewed the gold rush era with the same kind of disdain for crass materialism that C. W. Irish had expressed.[65] The utilization of the "Spanish fantasy past" in Southern California was partly a consequence of the absence of an Anglo pioneer tradition in that region.[66] With no such legacy to draw on, Southern California boosters, such as Charles Lummis, described a romantic, Californio-Hispano past, presenting it as a sophisticated, high-culture alternative to the base money lust that undergirded the society of their neighbors to the north. This kind of intrastate heritage rivalry differed to some degree from the contestations over the pioneer past in other parts of the West.[67]

Claims to the title of quintessential pioneer emanated from every western state and region. These claims generally did not rest on detailed comparative descriptions of western landscapes, or even on extended descriptions of past conditions endured, and certainly not, as was the case in California, on two divergent racial traditions—Anglo and Californio—in different parts of the state. Instead, the claimants of elevated westernness rested their arguments on a set of generalities about the characteristics of their place. These generalities included the place's climate, its landscape, and its nonwhite peoples—that is, the acuteness of the frontier setting—all of which were viewed as elements that had to be subdued for that particular western "desert" to "blossom as the rose."[68] Indeed, as late as 1944, old Wyoming settlers such as C. P. Arnold were trumpeting that same theme. Arnold noted that the pioneers of Wyoming, unlike those of neighboring states, "did not move in social, political, or religious groups, but, rather, "were individualists, the products of an environment never to return."[69] An *Old Timer's Hand Book* for Butte, Montana, claimed that the town's pioneers were the most rugged and frontiersman-like of all pioneers, since they had overcome "a rigorous climate, an unprolific houseless waste."[70] Of course, Butte's boosters, as well as Wyoming's and those of other regions, had, in an earlier age, heartily denied that there was anything even remotely inhospitable about the new Edens they were promoting.

Such incongruities between the promoters' and reminiscers' visions are a testimony to the purposefulness of both these groups of western image makers. Furthermore, the reminiscers' insistence on their elevated westernness has had an enduring legacy that is still evident in contemporary debates in the West. Constructed memories of better times—when people were more virtuous, when western towns were friendlier places, when residents knew the land around them more intimately—are an integral part of today's discourse concerning which groups of westerners best represent the true spirit of a region. Such sentiments, which stand squarely in the tradition of the pioneer reminiscence genre, are, on one level, healthy expressions of regional pride. However, these expressions also often amount to a kind of regional chauvinism that may be less healthy in western environments characterized by cultural and demographic change; indeed, a selectively remembered western heritage is often a reactionary response to these kinds of ostensibly lamentable changes. Some contemporary westerners are squarely within the western pioneer heritage when they effectively wallow in selective memory for the purpose of preserving their cultural and/or class hegemony.

John Burt Colton, 1893, from the Jayhawker Album, Huntington Library. Colton became the organizer of the Jayhawker reunions. He was one of the last remaining members of the group of young adventurers who crossed Death Valley in 1849. He and Lorenzo Dow Stephens were the two attendees at the forty-seventh and final Jayhawker reunion in 1918, the sixty-ninth anniversary of the group's deliverance. Colton died in 1919 at the age of eighty-eight. (Courtesy of the Huntington Library, Photo Collection)

Juliet W. Brier, John W. Brier, and the Reverend James W. Brier, 1893, from the Jayhawker Album, Huntington Library. Juliet Brier was probably the greatest hero of the Death Valley crossing in the fated winter of 1849. While Juliet was lauded as the savior of her family and an inspiration to the Jayhawkers, her husband was remembered less kindly by the Jayhawkers. Responding to these critical accounts, Reverend Brier removed his family from the list of surviving Jayhawkers shortly before he died in 1898. (Courtesy of the Huntington Library, Photo Collection)

"The Brier Family Struggling Across the Arid Wastes of Death Valley,"
pencil sketch of Juliet Brier in 1849, from the San Francisco Call, *December*
25, 1898. Juliet did not offer her reminiscences of the Death Valley ordeal
until a half century later, after her husband, the Reverend James Brier, had
died in 1898. She became a part of the Jayhawker memorial tradition
again in the early twentieth century, hosting four of the group's reunions
at the home of one of her sons. She died in 1913, a few weeks short of her
hundredth birthday. (Courtesy of the Huntington Library, Jayhawker
Collection, Scrapbook #3, p. 100)

Robert Edmund Strahorn and Carrie Adell Strahorn, c. 1879, from Carrie Adell Strahorn, Fifteen Thousand Miles by Stage: A Woman's Unique Experience During Thirty Years of Path Finding and Pioneering, from the Missouri to the Pacific and from Alaska to Mexico *(New York: G. P. Putnam's Sons, 1911), 7. Robert Strahorn always emphasized the postfrontier qualities of western places in his promotional writing in the 1870s and 1880s, commonly noting that "the doubtful period is past," and "the thorns of pioneering are removed." Carrie Strahorn, in her reminiscences, written more than three decades after she accompanied her husband on his northwestern promotional travels, offered a very different picture of the region's state of development in that earlier era. (Courtesy of the Huntington Library)*

Carrie Adell Strahorn, c. 1911, from Carrie Adell Strahorn, Fifteen Thousand Miles by Stage, *n.p. Carrie, who may have cowritten her reminiscences with her husband, Robert, died in 1925. (Courtesy of the Huntington Library)*

From left to right, John Burt Colton with Robert Haslam ("Pony Bob"), Colonel Alex Major, Prentiss Ingraham, and Colonel William F. Cody ("Buffalo Bill"), 1893, from the Jayhawker Album, Huntington Library. Partly as a result of Colton's tireless correspondence on behalf of the Jayhawkers, that group came to be viewed by the media in the late nineteenth and early twentieth centuries as exemplars of the pioneer spirit. (Courtesy of the Huntington Library, Photo Collection)

Ezra Meeker with President Theodore Roosevelt, 1907, from Meeker, The Busy Life of Eighty-five Years of Ezra Meeker: Ventures and Adventures *(Seattle, Wash.: published by the author, 1916; Indianapolis: William B. Burford, 1916). In 1906, Meeker, then aged seventy-six, drove a covered wagon and oxteam across the country from Washington State to Washington, D.C., to memorialize the Oregon Trail. Subsequent trips by covered wagon, automobile, and small plane kept Meeker busy well into his nineties. (Courtesy of the Huntington Library, Rare Book Collection, 94552)*

THE COVERED WAGON

In Miniature for Mantels
Celebrates the Centenary
of the Oregon Trail

ON April 10, 1830, the caravan of "prairie schooners" started its long trek across the plains and over the mountains to Oregon.

And on April 10, 1930, Stern's honors the occasion by introducing to the collectors of Americana a tiny reproduction of the covered wagon driven by Ezra Meeker—a work of art for the mantelpiece or cabinet in the home where traditions of early days in America are cherished.

This model is perfect in every detail from the small front wheels and large hind wheels to the metal-capped tongue. It is 17 inches long, 8¼ inches wide, 9¾ inches high, and the size of the base is 21 x 7¼ inches . . 50.00

STERN BROTHERS
GIFT SHOP—FIFTH FLOOR

Newspaper advertisement for "The Covered Wagon in Miniature for Mantels." (Courtesy of the American Heritage Center, Seymour Collection, box 8, Scrapbook, in commemoration of the centennial of the Oregon Trail and in recognition of Ezra Meeker's efforts to memorialize it)

Cover of Americanism Through Activities, c. 1940, an inspirational pamphlet for American youth. Evidence of Ezra Meeker's continuing influence on America's frontier heritage after his death, this publication urged American youth to continue the work of that relentless pioneer journeyer by preserving historically significant trails. (Courtesy of the American Heritage Center, Seymour Collection, box 6, Folder: "Oregon Trail, Pamphlets")

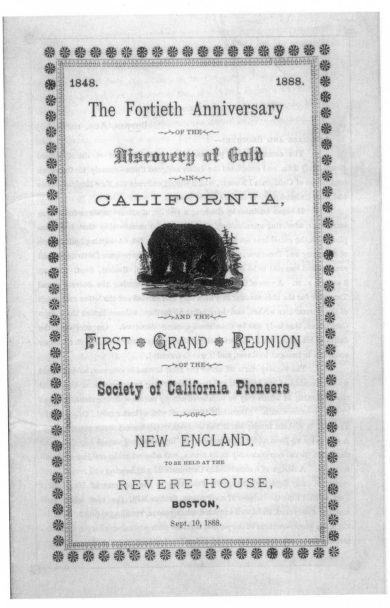

Society of California Pioneers of New England, The Fortieth
Anniversary of the Discovery of Gold in California and the First Grand
Reunion of the Society of California Pioneers (*Boston: Pioneer Card
Co., 1888*). *In the 1870s and 1880s, gold rush pioneers who had
returned to their home states formed associations to commemorate
their role in the pioneering process. Little was said about the pursuit
of profit in the speeches delivered at these meetings. Pioneer qualities,
not gold, were at the center of gold rush reminiscences. (Courtesy of the
Huntington Library, Rare Book Collection, 253334)*

Twenty-First Annual Gathering

OF THE

Western Association of California Pioneers

TO BE HELD

AT THE RESIDENCE OF THE SECRETARY

1015 ELMWOOD AVENUE, EVANSTON, ILLINOIS

THURSDAY, SEPTEMBER 14, 1911

FROM 10 A. M. UNTIL 4:30 P. M.

IN COMMEMORATION OF THE

SIXTY-FIRST ANNIVERSARY

OF THE

ADMISSION OF CALIFORNIA AS A STATE OF THE UNION, AND FOR THE DISBANDMENT OF THE ASSOCIATION

Program cover of the "Twenty-first Annual Gathering of the Western Association of California Pioneers," 1911. Beginning in 1890, this organization, like many other pioneer societies, lasted about a generation. Formed in Chicago, for California pioneers from that region, the WACP disbanded out of necessity—none of its surviving members were younger than eighty-five in 1911. (Courtesy of the Huntington Library, Jayhawker Collection, Scrapbook #6, p. 103)

CALIFORNIA PIONEERS OF '49 HOLD THEIR LAST CAMPFIRE AND DISBAND FOREVER

"'Forty-Niners Recalling Their Pioneer Hardships'," 1911. This photograph accompanied a newspaper report on the disbanding of the Western Association of California Pioneers. Newspapers in this period provided extensive coverage of the activities of pioneer societies. (Courtesy of the Huntington Library, Jayhawker Collection, Scrapbook #6, p. 103)

Part Three:

LEGACIES

PROMOTION, REMINISCENCE,

AND RACE

California as Tainted Eden

> Being white, and of the superior race therefore, you have the privilege of entering any Indian's house, and you will be kindly received, and if you want water out of his oya, or wish to cook your own dinner at his fire, you are welcome. (Charles Nordhoff, *California: A Book for Travellers and Settlers,* 1872)

The powerful legacy of the California gold rush—which had been accompanied by its own wave of colorful promotional writings and images—played a vital role in shaping the wave of booster literature produced a generation later, in the late 1860s and early 1870s.[1] While there was certainly romance, color and comedy in the writings of Mark Twain, Bret Harte, Joaquin Miller, and others, these authors had emphasized the excesses of gold rush life. In so doing, they had burned into the American consciousness an image of California as a lawless, rough-and-tumble place where morals were low and dangers were high.[2]

Some of the state's early promotional writers did little to diffuse such notions of the place as a wild frontier, filled with danger and uncertainty. For example, John Hittell, in the first edition of his popular book *The Resources of California* (1863), drew unnecessary attention to the state's notable natural phenomena, such as earthquakes, when his actual purpose was to diffuse readers' concerns regarding such seemingly unnatural occurrences.[3] Hittell's strong and often controversial views on delicate topics would have been even more unsettling to some readers than his talk of earthquakes. A forty-niner himself, Hittell worked briefly in the mines before deciding that a life of the mind would be more profitable.[4] An unabashed social Darwinist before Herbert Spencer had fully articulated the theory (and a great fan of Spencer afterward), Hittell balked at any kind of restraints, governmental or otherwise, on the accumulation of capital by captains of industry. He advocated attracting financial investment to develop the mining industry and felt that cheap Chinese labor would better facilitate that endeavor than an organized white workforce.[5] White settlement would follow, he insisted, when capitalists created a sturdy economic foundation in the state, but Chinese labor would be vital in the early stages.[6] Hittell presented the Chinese sympathetically, as victims of mobs of white miners and of officers of the law who turned a blind eye when "yellow men [were] beaten or despoiled."[7]

When it came to agriculture, Hittell showed little interest or enthusiasm in the first edition of his promotional tract. What he did have to say about the landed resources of California hardly approximated all the talk of gardens of the world and Nile-like fertility that characterized the promotional writing for the rest of the West and that would become so common in later California boosting. He noted that only about one in ten of the state's acres could be profitably farmed at present and that no more than a quarter of the land would become productive during the remainder of the century (i.e., in nearly four decades). He concluded that with respect to "the proportion of rich land fit for the plough," California was inferior to the Mississippi Valley states and to those of the Atlantic slope. These were hardly the kinds of observations likely to draw throngs of prospective farmers.[8] But Hittell's primary intention, in this particular edition of the book, was to attract capital for the mining industry, not farmers for the land. It was California's mineral potential, not its agricultural promise, that initially attracted Hittell, as a laborer and, later, promoter. Indeed, conflicts between boosters of farming and those who advocated mining as the best area of emphasis for the state would hamper California's promotional efforts for decades to come.[9]

In addition, Hittell drew attention to another set of conflicts within California stemming from the "liberal tone of society" in a state where the white men were "industrious, energetic, brave, . . . ready to avenge an insult, accustomed to carry pistols and knives, quick to use them in quarrel." As for the women, they were "not healthy, as a class." While "the girls are beautiful—beautiful as angels," Hittell wrote, "at twenty-five the women begin to wither, and at thirty-five they lose nearly every trace of physical beauty."[10] This was hardly the kind of language that would attract families. Clearly, Hittell had not yet found his voice as a promotional writer. He was no Robert Strahorn; though he would become a far more effective promoter in later editions of *The Resources of California.*

These were the kinds of images that California's boosters had to work against in the late 1860s and early 1870s, when organizations such as the Industrial Immigration Aid Association and the California Immigrant Union— both privately funded bodies—formed for the purpose of attracting settlers to the state. Indeed, Hittell would himself play a significant role in overcoming those negative images in his more upbeat essay "California as a Home for the Emigrant" (1870), which won a prize from the California Immigrant Union.[11] The essay went through a dozen English editions and was translated into half a dozen European languages. In the piece, Hittell eschewed discussion of cheap Chinese labor as the answer to the Golden State's retarded growth (which most surely was the key to his winning the prize). In doing so, he avoided contradicting the biennial message delivered to the state legislature by Henry H. Haight, governor of California, a few months earlier. Haight had insisted: "We need population—not of races inferior in natural traits, pagan in religion, ignorant of free institutions and incapable of sharing in them without putting [their] very existence in peril—but we need immigrants of kindred races, . . . a farming population from Germany and other European States."[12] But such pronouncements of preference for European labor over Chinese and for farming over mining were not enough for the state to overcome the problem of retarded growth at the beginning of the 1870s.[13]

The image of the state as a failed promised land was being effectively articulated by social commentators such as Henry George as early as 1871 in *Our Land and Land Policy.* In one chapter, "The Lands of California," George offered an alternate image to that of the sturdy, independent, self-sufficient, cultured yeoman farmer who stood at the center of the nation's agrarian mythology. George's California farmers were of two kinds: large estate owners and the renters who "pay such tribute as th[ose] lord[s] of the domain choose to exact."[14] Worse still for prospective settlers, George added, the former class, along with land speculators, "still make a regular business of blackmailing settlers upon the land, or of appropriating their homes."[15] A combination of factors all conspired against hopeful settlers pursuing the homestead ideal. The failed Mexican land-grant system caused uncertainty over ownership and ongoing litigation; and large sections of the state's best lands were granted to the railroads, which in turn were more likely to sell to land companies than directly to settlers. "That," George proclaimed, "is the blight that has fallen upon California, stunting her growth and mocking her golden promise, offsetting to the immigrant the richness of her soil and the beneficence of her climate."[16]

George, in his much better known and more widely distributed work *Progress and Poverty,* also heavily emphasized the problem of land monopoly in California. The book first appeared at the end of the 1870s, and then in numerous editions during the 1880s—much to the chagrin, one must imagine, of the state's promoters.[17] George's writings were a bane to California's business and agribusiness interests in the late nineteenth century, in much the same way that the writings of John Steinbeck and Carey McWilliams were a half century or so later in the late 1930s and early 1940s. All three authors— George, Steinbeck, and McWilliams—offered dystopian narratives, tragic tales of failed promised lands. They all suggested that there was something fundamentally wrong with the socioeconomic system in California and the way in which it governed human relations; and all three, to one degree or another, addressed issues of race.

George's was not a lone voice of doubtfulness in late-nineteenth-century California. Other skeptical observers argued not that California's promise was being withheld from settlers by the forces of monopolism and speculation but that the state's much-touted Edenic climate and agricultural fertility were themselves illusions. Critics could point, for example, to the drought of 1862 to 1865, which had reduced the value of property in Los Angeles County by nearly two-thirds.[18] (The state would experience periodic droughts again throughout the rest of the century.) What is more, the much-heralded arrival of the transcontinental railroad in 1869 did not bring about the massive increase in settlers that California promoters expected. In fact, the reverse occurred: the number of new settlers barely exceeded 10,000 in 1871, only slightly more than a quarter of the number that had arrived two years earlier.[19]

California's boosters, then, had to work against a range of widespread negative images of the state. It was a land already given over to wealthy land barons—a place that had reverted to a state of feudalism. Yet it was an arid wasteland to boot, a place where riches could be no more easily wrought from the land than could blood from a stone. The images often contradicted each other; still, their collective impact on California's reputation was no less significant because of such incongruities. But the most vital issue, the one at the center of so much of the rhetoric and imagery that hampered promotional efforts, was race. California was presented as a wild frontier, and heightened levels of danger, violence, and immoral behavior marked frontiers. But the wildness of frontiers, in the popular perception, also had a great deal to do with the presence of nonwhite peoples.

Since California was a place where Indians, Mexicans, and Chinese mixed with European Americans, it was, in the popular mainstream imagination, no place for white families. Yet, for all the white American fears of California as a racial frontier, it was, after midcentury, a state where peoples of color, not "mainstream" Americans, would most realistically have feared frontier violence. Horrendous episodes of racially motivated violence against nonwhite groups, such as the Los Angeles "Chinese Massacre" of 1871, when 19 Chinese were murdered by a mob of 500 whites who tore through Chinatown, were widely reported in the national newspaper and periodical press. Perhaps the more tolerant among prospective Anglo migrants to California were deterred as much by the intolerance of white Californians as they were by the polyglot nature of the state's population.

Certainly, the pervasiveness of the various dystopic images in the post–gold rush decades constituted a tremendous weight for the state's promoters to lift. Hence, it is not surprising that California experienced such a tiny proportion of western settlement in this period. The state's population in fact grew by only one-third between 1860 and 1900, and most of that growth stemmed from natural increase, not new immigration.[20] A generation after the gold rush, California was proving a tough sell and would for another half century. And, since matters of race were such a vital element of the pictures of California as a dystopia, it should come as no surprise that promoters, in their efforts to undermine and overwhelm those pictures with their own utopian representations, addressed questions of race at great length.

New York Tribune writer Charles Nordhoff was brought to California by the Southern Pacific to help promote the state. He tried to eradicate the wide range of negative images of the Golden State in his tremendously popular and influential work *California: A Book for Travellers and Settlers* (1872).[21] The state, he began, "is to most eastern people still a land of . . . rough miners, of pistols, of bowie-knives, abundant fruit, queer wines, high prices—full of discomforts, and abounding in dangers to the peaceful traveler." However, Nordhoff explained (perhaps to the chagrin of his New York publisher) that New Yorkers were "overridden by a semi-barbarous foreign population; troubled with incapable servants, private as well as public; subject to daily rudeness from car-drivers and others, . . . exposed to inconveniences, to dirty streets, bad gas, beggars, . . . to high taxes, theft, and all kinds of public wrong, year in and year out." Yet, despite all this, the New Yorker "pities the unlucky friend who is 'going to California'" and, Nordhoff exclaimed, provides him "with his parting blessing, a heavy navy revolver." Then Nordhoff proceeded to offer a sparkling image of the real, postfrontier California, where "there are no dangers to travelers on the beaten track, . . . no inconveniences which a child or a tenderly reared woman would not laugh at." After spending half a dozen weeks in this West Coast paradise, Nordhoff offered, "you will perhaps return with a notion that New York is the true frontier land." To reinforce the point, he quoted a California miner who had wryly commented: "We are not saints out here, but I believe we have much less of a frontier population than you in New York."[22]

Writing with very different purposes from Nordhoff, Henry George, in *Our Land and Land Policy,* had offered an even more scathing critique of New York. He described it as a city where "men build stables for their horses, and an army of women crowd the streets at night to sell their souls for the necessities which unremitting toil, such as no human being ought to endure, will not give them." He added that "a hundred thousand men who ought to be at work are looking for employment and a hundred thousand children who ought to be at school are at work."[23] But George did not offer these harrowing images and statistics by way of contrast with the wonders of California. Rather, he suggested that New York was the model that California was following with respect to class relations. As for land policy, he charged that California was following the examples of England and Ireland, where monopolized agriculture was fully entrenched and opportunities for new farmers were nonexistent. But class relations and monopolized agriculture were not the sole issues of concern in George's analysis. Race relations, too, were at the center of his tale of doom and gloom.

California's dire situation was made much worse, George proclaimed, by the "threatening wave of Asiatic immigration whose first ripples are already breaking upon our shores." He stated the racial issue in striking terms: "What the barbarians enslaved in foreign wars were to the great landlords of ancient Italy, what the blacks of the African coast were to the great landlords of the Southern states, the Chinese coolies may be, in fact are already beginning to be, to the great landlords of our Pacific slope."[24] California, once a promised land, had regressed into a feudal state and seemed destined to deteriorate further, as an Asian variant of African-American chattel slavery began to develop. California was, George inferred, the place where the worst of New York's class inequities and the worst of the South's racial inequities came together.

Charles Nordhoff's defense of California and critique of the great metropolis of the East Coast—like Henry George's critique of California as an embryonic New York—also had a racial component. Nordhoff charged that New York "receives a constant supply of the rudest, least civilized European populations" and added that "of the immigrants landed at Castle Garden, the neediest, the least thrifty and energetic, and the most vicious remain in New York." The best of the immigrants left New York for California, Nordhoff insisted, and when they came, it was to stay.[25]

Such critiques of southern and eastern European immigration appeared from time to time in California promotional writings that were seeking to alleviate potential settlers' concerns over the racial diversity of the West Coast. These works suggested that the New Immigration from Europe was threatening to the social order, while the Chinese, Mexicans, and Indians were respectful, faithful, and, ultimately, servile. But these kinds of white racial juggling acts, which sought to place certain nonwhite peoples above white yet non-Nordic Europeans, at least with respect to the issue of their preferred status (read: safety and exploitability) as neighbors, complicated the promotional writing of the period. Furthermore, such purposeful inversions of the prevailing racial hierarchy (as it was commonly perceived by the white majority) probably did not reflect very accurately the actual beliefs of their authors with respect to race. Promoters such as Nordhoff, as they addressed the intricacies of the race issue, were walking a fine line when they claimed that certain nonwhite cultures were preferable to some white cultures as neighbors and as laborers. Their efforts are reminiscent of those of boosters of other western regions who proclaimed frontiers of opportunity while vigorously denying the presence of any attendant frontiers of danger and hardship.

The parallel between the respective promotional balancing acts concerning frontier-related issues and race-related issues is an instructive one, since racial difference was so commonly associated in the Anglo-American mind with frontier settings. There was nothing exceptional about Frederick Jackson Turner's and Theodore Roosevelt's statements in the late nineteenth century concerning the clash between civilization and savagery on western frontiers; they were representative articulators of long-established Anglo-American perceptions.[26] Nordhoff, long before Turner and Roosevelt expressed their thoughts on race and frontiers, was attempting to reorient those established perceptions and downplay the assumed linkage between racial diversity and frontier settings. Nordhoff was trying to convince readers that California's cultural pluralism did not render it a frontier, that the presence of peoples of color did not taint the Pacific Eden.

In his promotional book *California,* Nordhoff gingerly traversed the high wire that crossed the racial divides of his time and place. He provided chapters on the Chinese, old Californios, and Indians. "The three races—the Indians, the old Spaniards, and we 'Americans' [he left out the Chinese in this instance]—live there harmoniously together," he insisted. And such harmony stemmed largely from the fact that all three non-American races (here he included the Chinese) were appropriately subservient and docile. While unable to hide his own personal distaste for Chinese society and culture, and paternalistically labeling all Chinese "John" (a common practice at the time), Nordhoff nonetheless acknowledged that they were hard workers. Furthermore, the Chinese were vital to California's economy, and he chided both major political parties for denouncing them in their campaign platforms when the very "men who make these platforms" had Chinese servants in their homes and Chinese hands on their farms and ranches. Even those leaders, Nordhoff notes, "will tell you that [they] could not get on without Chinese, and that the cry against them is the most abominable demagogism."[27]

Nordhoff certainly, to some degree, damned the Chinese with faint praise. For example, he noted that "John" was "certainly" "teachable" and "a far more civilized being—or, rather, a far less savage creature—than many we get from Christian Great Britain."[28] Still, such statements probably had their intended effect of alleviating rather than exacerbating readers' concerns over the Chinese presence in California. Nordhoff's coverage, while often critical and thoroughly patronizing, nonetheless demonstrates a degree of sensitivity to Chinese culture and a recognition of the senseless hatred directed at the Chinese (the massacre of Chinese in Los Angeles had occurred just the previous year). However, it is also notable that the two chapters on the Chinese that appeared in the first edition of the book were gone from the

1882 edition, which appeared in the same year that the Chinese Exclusion Act became law. The book's publisher seems to have been sensitive to the Chinese issue, too.[29]

Interestingly, Nordhoff's 1872 edition of *California* also included a chapter, "The Indians as Laborers," that was intended to portray the native presence in the state in a more positive light. The Indians in the San Bernardino area were, Nordhoff explained, "a very useful class" who did farm and ranch work and household "chores."[30] Furthermore, he added, they were harmless, as well as servile and compliant. Nordhoff informed his readers that since they were "white, and of the superior race," they were welcome to enter any Indian home, and could even cook their dinner there, if they wished.[31] Perhaps it would have been comforting for potential white settlers and travelers to know that California Indian culture essentially constituted a friendly and complimentary network of service facilities for the privileged race. The Indians, he concluded, were a valuable laboring force and, for all intents and purposes, a good resource to have around. What is more, in an early example of the construction of a "Spanish fantasy past" by white Americans, Nordhoff highlighted the "skill and perseverance" that the "pious priests" of the missions brought to "their task of civilizing the savages." Those efforts, he explained, had been vital to the creation of a compliant Native labor force for later generations of white Americans to utilize.[32] Indeed, the task of the missionary friars had been made easier by virtue of the fact that the Indians were "a race preordained to subjection." "The children of the missions," he concluded, "never grew under [the missionaries'] hands to the stature of men of our century."[33] Nordhoff could hardly have described a less threatening and more useful group than California's Indians.

He further illuminated the prevailing perceptions of racial hierarchy in his discussion of an old Californio who employed Indian labor on his ranch.[34] Nordhoff's treatment of the man is endearing yet patronizing at the same time. The Californio is described as being paternalistic toward the Indian workers; he shows real affection for them, jovially tolerating their regular bouts of drunkenness.[35] But Nordhoff clearly suggested that while the Indians seemed lazy and childlike to the Californio, the Californio, in turn, was a little too relaxed, too enamored of the notion that leisure is the most sacred of all human pursuits, for him or his culture to offer up any serious competition to white Californians. Nordhoff's descriptions underscored prevailing white perceptions of the natural racial hierarchy in the state: the Indians' servility was preordained, and the Californios, in turn, though superior to the Indians, could not resist the force of Manifest Destiny, which carried the advancing tide of an infinitely superior white civilization. While superior to the Indians and Chinese, the Californios, Nordhoff's narrative clearly implied, were no threat to whites, since the Californios accepted the declining influence of their culture in the state. John Hittell had made the same points nearly a decade earlier in *The Resources of California* when he remarked that the Spanish Californians "are a good-natured race, very kind and obliging to their friends, but out of place among Americans, who are too sharp for them in trading."[36]

Writers such as Nordhoff and Hittell were effectively constructing a double-layered declensionist narrative for Indians and Californios—one in which those cultures were rendered as naturally vanishing elements—and offsetting it against a progressive narrative of inevitable white ascendancy and prosperity. This model was pervasive in the promotional writing for the state. Benjamin Cummings Truman provided a less subtle example of the Nordhoff-Hittell approach in his *Semi-tropical California* (1874), which focused on the region from Santa Barbara to San Diego. Truman charted Los Angeles's transition in seven years from a sleepy, backwater Mexican town of "rickety, adobe houses . . . and here and there an indolent native, hugging the inside of a blanket, or burying his head in a gigantic water melon," to a thriving American metropolis.[37] Truman (who would run the Literary Bureau of the Southern Pacific from 1879 to 1890) provided therein an early expression of the common racist sentiment that, for many decades to come, would accompany Anglo commentaries on California's perceived transition from a Hispanic frontier to an American promised land.[38]

However, while California's promotional writers reflected in their works the same conceptions of racial hierarchy that characterized mainstream American thought at the time, they nonetheless expressed a wide range of divergent perspectives. Not surprisingly, individual promoters often exhibited an awkward ambivalence when they adressed the topic of race. Nordhoff, in his *Northern California, Oregon, and the Sandwich Islands* (1875), portrayed the Chinese as clean, hardworking, honest, and reliable. He railed against the mobs of white "Hoodlums" who committed acts of violence against the Chinese. He criticized the authorities for refusing to prosecute such crimes and the newspapers for publishing thoughtless tirades against the Chinese, for pandering to the "vile class" of white "thugs" and "rowdies," and for nurturing a climate of racial intolerance. Nordhoff noted that the Chinese were vital to the economic well-being of Northern California but added that the Chinaman has "grave vices"—such as prostitution—"and it might have been well could we have kept him out." He then concluded that the Chinese as a class were "peaceable, patient, ingenious, and industrious," and that the common claims that their presence denied labor opportunities to white men were "absurd."[39]

Nordhoff's treatment of California's Indian tribes was equally mired in contradictions. He provided a thoroughly uncharitable discussion of his perceptions of the ugliness of Indian women, describing them as "broad-faced, flat-nosed, small-eyed, unkempt, frowzy, undersized, thickset, clumsy"; but he then generated considerable sympathy for California Indians in the course of providing a scathing indictment of the federal policy of placing peaceful people on reservations, and he cataloged examples of white mistreatment of Indians. But he concluded that the only way "to introduce the Indian to civilization" would be "by the only avenue open to savages": "military discipline."[40] Both empathy for and prejudice against minority groups marked Nordhoff's thinking on race matters. And this seeming contradiction places him firmly within the mainstream of promotional writing for the state.

There was no unified "Anglo-Californian-mind" when it came to race; rather, there were varied perspectives, some of which were built upon strong conviction, while others were economically motivated. For example, some promoters pushed the goals of certain industrial interests when they sought to attract Chinese and African-American workers to the state for the purpose of lowering wages and destabilizing the white labor movement; those promoters were certainly not "friends" of the Chinese or of blacks.[41] Others followed the lead of Governor Haight's 1869 address, which shamelessly maligned the Chinese and sought to attract only "kindred races"—immigrants of good European stock.

Such anti-Chinese sentiments appeared with great regularity in the press and in the promotional literature during the next decades. The Reverend S. Goodenough offered a quite typical example in October 1893 (the year after the Chinese Exclusion Act had been renewed) in his essay "The Chinese and Other Foes of American Labor," which appeared in the *California Review*. Echoing a sentiment expressed by scores of writers and thinkers that year, Goodenough declared that the public domain was rapidly being exhausted. He insisted that this new reality ensured that there would be no way for the country to assimilate the Chinese, Russians, Italians, Poles, Slavs, and Bohemians, "mixed races of the Austrian provinces." These groups, the good Christian reverend explained, "are quite divergent ethnologically, from our existing stock." What is more, he added, "they come almost entirely from the lower grades, degenerate, illiterate, filthy, embracing no small percentage of paupers, beggars, criminals, anarchists, nihilists, communists, the lawless and turbulent of all existing types . . . who were more than welcome to leave their native lands."[42] Clearly not yet a convert to the emerging theology of the Social Gospel (which instructed Christians to walk in Jesus' footsteps, treating the weak, poor, and unfortunate as he had), Goodenough had a clear idea of whom the Californian promised land was intended for, and it was not the Chinese, Japanese, Russians, Italians, or any of the other ostensibly unassimilable elements. Because of these peoples, he insisted, "the good digestion of the United States is impaired, and wide-reaching derangement is threatened if a change of diet is not promptly ordered."[43] The editor of the *California Review* responded forcefully to the reverend's racial sermonizing, noting that after the "recent disgraceful scenes" of anti-Chinese rioting in the state, "those willing to engage in such violent measures were not willing to take the places [of the Chinese they had driven out] and do honest work, but preferred free soup and idleness."[44] The debate over the Chinese and over southern and eastern European immigrant labor raged on in California throughout the late nineteenth century and into the twentieth, and much of it played out in the promotional literature that was deemed so vital to the state's interests.

Meanwhile, booster tracts for the Golden State continued to feature extensive discussion of Indian and Hispanic cultures, their utility as laborers, their subservience, and, to a growing degree, their cultural distinctiveness, as expressed through their artisanry—basket weaving, jewelry making, and traditional festivities. This kind of emphasis on the arts and crafts of indigenous cultures would become a stock feature of California promotional writing in the early twentieth century. Still, it is clear that California's Indians, along with the state's Mexican and Chinese residents, were being presented as cultural curiosities by the 1880s, and their status as such was becoming an important element in the racial marketing of the state.

San Francisco's Chinatown was being included in the "Tourist Attractions" sections of guidebooks by this time, and visitors were being instructed to see the place at night "with a policeman or some other functionary." Such adventurous visitors were promised "a perfect piece of China," full of joss houses filled with idols and symbols, and, of course, opium dens "where one comes as near as getting a smell of hell and a sight of the Devil as anywhere else in the world."[45] According to such descriptions, Chinatown was certainly no promised land; yet its attraction was precisely that. With a whole section of the city presented to potential visitors and settlers as a cultural curiosity, another world, its separateness from the mainstream (i.e., the promotional vision of California as a white settler's paradise) was underscored.[46]

Perhaps the most noteworthy characteristic of the California boosterism with respect to race in this period is that the promotional tracts effectively became a forum for discussion of the status of Indians, Hispanics, the Chinese, African-Americans, and southern and eastern European immigrant laborers in the Golden State. Whether the promotional writings merely reflected the various positions and parameters of this dialogue on race or actually played a significant role in shaping them remains uncertain. Yet it seems that the boosters were more proactive than reactive in their treatment of race issues. They were vital voices affecting the present and future cultural composition of the state. It is clear that California's boosters and their critics (such as Henry George), in debating the course that the state should take, could not escape matters of race. It is also evident that the key contours of these debates were visible in the state's promotional literature from the beginning of the 1870s.

Most important, the example of California's boosterism in the 1870s and 1880s illuminates a vital aspect of Anglo-American racial thinking in the period that is too easily overlooked: diversity of opinion. There was no hegemonic majority perspective on matters racial, no unified promotional front; rather, white promoters offered a variety of positions. While none of these positions strayed from popular notions about racial hierarchy and none questioned the position of whites at the apex of the hierarchical structure, promoters provided no consensus on how the rest of that structure should be ordered.[47] California's racial frontier was marked by diverse populations and a diverse range of opinions. Race muddied the waters for Anglo promoters of California, complicating their efforts to present a clear picture of the place.

Promoting the Southwest

> When John C. Frémont passed through the country on his first exploring expedition, he found it necessary to turn loose a howitzer and drop a few shells among the Indians. The Washoes are now but a sore-eyed handful. They are tame enough now, and so is their valley. (William Sutherland, *The Wonders of Nevada,* 1878)

Race was also a problematic factor in the promotion of settlement to the Southwest in the late nineteenth century. Just as some newspaper editors in Wyoming Territory in the 1870s wrote bloodcurdling reports that exaggerated the level of Indian dangers in an effort to secure federal support for the removal of all Indians from the region (and in so doing undercut the efforts of more sophisticated boosters, such as Robert Strahorn, who emphasized postfrontier conditions), some Southwestern boosters made the same kinds of promotional mistakes. This was particularly the case in Arizona, which is hardly surprising given the volatile state of relations between Indians, settlers, and the United States Army in that territory up until 1876. Then, after a short period of calm, terrible conditions on the San Carlos reservation led to Apache resistance under Victorio and Geronimo from 1879 to 1881 and again, under Geronimo, from 1885 to 1886.[48]

Arizona promoters railed against the Apaches and surely played an important role in shaping public perceptions of them. An 1871 publication, *Resources of Arizona Territory,* put out by the Arizona Legislative Assembly, demonized the Apaches by painting a series of shocking images of inhumanity that would become increasingly familiar in the 1870s and 1880s. The Apaches captured Mexican children and later forced them to witness the "murder and torture of their own people"; they were polygamists who made their many wives "do all the hard labor"; and they punished their wives for "any deviation from the paths of virtue" by cutting off their noses. The publication described Apache leader Cochise as a man whose torturous tendencies, "if portrayed, would cause amazement that a just God ever created such a monster"; it then went on to portray those tendencies in graphic detail. "Children are placed on spears and roasted over a slow fire, and writhe in misery until life is extinct," the author insisted. "Men are hanged by the feet and a slow fire kindled at the head, and gashed with knives and pierced with arrows until death gives relief." Women were not killed but were "subjected to a life worse than death." Such barbarism, the author insisted, necessitated federal efforts to subdue the Apaches and make the region safe for white families. But such harrowing descriptions of Apache practices were hardly likely to draw throngs of settlers to the region.[49] Subsequent promotional tracts for the Arizona Territory and works of travel writing in the 1870s and 1880s continued to emphasize the barbarism of the Apaches, even as they insisted that the Indian threat was "rapidly diminishing."[50] The race issue—or, the "Indian problem"—had, from the mid-1860s through the 1880s, made it next to impossible for Arizona promoters to present their territory as a postfrontier paradise.[51]

Boosters made bold statements during the 1880s about the passing of the Apache threat, but their confident language failed to cloak the fact that violent clashes were a part of the territory's immediate past and thus might still be a factor in its immediate future. An 1884 Atchison, Topeka and Santa Fe Railroad promotional tract, for example, insisted that "the savage . . . with the exception of isolated instances . . . has been quiet since 1874, and though he committed atrocities in 1883, his blood-thirsty yell will never again bring sorrow and fear to the Arizona pioneer."[52] This was not the kind of news that would bring a flood of new settlers into the territory. (By 1890, Arizona had only 88,200 residents.)[53] Furthermore, the use of the word "pioneer" as a descriptor for settlers who were in the territory seemed to underscore the frontier condition of the place.

The New Mexico Territory's boosters dealt somewhat more effectively in their writings with the presence of Native peoples. By the end of Lew Wallace's term as governor (1878–1881), the Lincoln County War was over, as were the worst of the Indian troubles. The Atchison, Topeka and Santa Fe joined the Southern Pacific on March 10, 1881, at Deming, completing the first railroad line across the entire territory.[54] New Mexico, it seemed, had left its frontier stage behind and was moving into a new, modern era. In July 1881, the territory's most significant booster, Chief Justice L. Bradford Prince, in an interview in the *New York Tribune*, praised the Native and Hispanic residents of the region. Indeed, Prince insisted that "one of the pleasantest features of life in New Mexico is the society of the cultivated, generous-hearted descendants of the first conquerors of the soil."[55]

Not all of those writing on New Mexico in this period demonstrated the promotional savvy of Prince, who understood that critical discussions of the racial characteristics of nonwhite peoples in the state were not the best strategy for attracting white settlers. For example, Charles R. Bliss, a professor at Colorado College, in a short promotional booklet on the state, described the "great mass" of Mexicans there as "ignorant, superstitious," "rude and primitive."[56] But Bliss, who was not a professional booster, hardly represented the mainstream of New Mexico promotional writing. Most boosters, like Prince, understood that their purpose was to alleviate concerns over the state's racial diversity, not foster them.

An 1884 report from the New Mexico Bureau of Immigration proudly declared that more than 2.5 million pages of promotional material had been produced that year.[57] With 191,000 residents in 1890, New Mexico was hardly experiencing the meteoric growth that some of its boosters had predicted (one of them had estimated a population of 1 million by 1885),[58] though it was doing considerably better than neighboring Arizona.[59] The contribution of promotional efforts to the carving out of New Mexico's comparatively (vis-à-vis Arizona) high rate of population increase in the late nineteenth century is difficult to determine. National newspapers and magazines reported on Arizona's Apache uprisings, and this surely helps explain that territory's retarded demographic growth. But Arizona's boosters could not have helped the situation with their constant references to Indian hostilities and their common descriptions (or, better, constructions) of Apache barbarism. The New Mexico Bureau of Immigration, on the other hand, emphasized that the territory's primary "aboriginal inhabitants" were the Pueblo Indians, "noted for their docility and gentleness of character that demark civilization from barbarism."[60] The bureau further emphasized that the Pueblo Indians, residing in the territory's nineteen pueblos, together numbered 7,681 persons, while the Jicarilla Apaches numbered only 847. No population figure was given for the Mescalero Apaches, but they were described, like the Jicarilla, as thoroughly tamed and contained.[61] Like the Washoe Indians of Nevada who (a booster gleefully noted in 1878) had been blasted into submission by John C. Frémont, New Mexico's Indians, promoters insisted, would present no problem to white settlement and civilization.[62]

However, while New Mexico's Indian and Hispanic peoples were presented as thoroughly nonthreatening in the promotional writings, the state was hardly presented as a migrational haven for other nonwhite migrant groups, and this remained the case for generations. Take, for example, New Mexico Republican senator Albert B. Fall's response to a request from a black promoter, B. M. McKay, in early 1917. McKay wrote to Senator Fall about the emigration of blacks from the South for reasons of personal safety and educational, economic, and political advancement. Surely New Mexico would be a good location for these Republican refugees from Jim Crow, he suggested to the senator. Fall responded at length and with great caution, emphasizing that he was unable to give "very much general encouragement" to the plan. Fall explained that the New Mexico mining industry was staffed by "Italians, Poles and other foreigners"; irrigated lands were occupied by Mexicans and Pueblo Indians; and "in the newer portions of the State where water is available, the lands have long since been acquired in private ownership, and upon such lands either Mexican or white labor is employed."[63]

Fall was offering potential African-American settlers a picture of the state that differed radically from that being presented in the early-twentieth-century promotional tracts, with which he was certainly familiar. In his letter, Fall tried to temper the discouraging tone by noting that his wife had "always preferred colored people around the house," and that he would cheerfully replace his Mexican "labor or tenants" with African-Americans. But he quickly added that "colored people" were generally unfamiliar with irrigated agriculture; furthermore, they were not likely to stay in an area unless they came as a community, and New Mexico would not lend itself to such large-group migration.[64] Fall's evasive letter makes for painful reading today and is surely just one of many hundreds of similar carefully worded but ultimately discouraging responses by promoters and politicians to the hopeful inquiries of African-Americans and other nonwhite groups.

Wonderlands of Whiteness and Color

> It is but fair to suppose that our own highlands, with their clear, elastic atmosphere and bracing, healthful climate, will produce here upon these plains and in these mountains a very superior race of people, noted for great physical endurance and mental power, despising alike all fetters of mind and body. (Robert Strahorn, *The Hand-Book of Wyoming,* 1877)

In western regions that were less racially diverse than California and the Southwest, the comparative absence of discussions of race in booster texts may not seem terribly surprising, but it is quite notable. Indeed, this is one of the most striking aspects of much of the promotional literature of the late nineteenth century. Avoidance of the subject, of course, was a strategy intended to leave the reader with the impression that race was simply *not* an issue in these promised lands. From the immediate post–Civil War years until the beginning of the depression of the 1890s, promotional tracts for the Plains and Rocky Mountain States and for the Pacific Northwest presented wonderlands of whiteness to the public. As noted earlier, Indian reservations were often removed from maps in a cartographic rendering of the "vanishing American" that was contemporaneous with the decline in Native populations and with artists' renderings of a vanishing race.

Claims, such as Robert Strahorn's in 1877, that a "superior race of people" was being produced in the "healthful climate" of the Rockies and the High Plains, appeared often in booster writings. A few years later, in 1882, a promotional publication claimed (as earlier noted) that Nebraska was fortuitously situated in the global belt that had always produced "the highest type of men

and women, the highest development, physical, intellectual and moral."[65]*
In the same vein, California promoters, such as Charles F. Lummis, from
the 1880s on, presented photographic images of healthy and rather hefty
white babies—testaments to the powerful combination of Anglo genes and a
semitropical coastal climate.[66] They, too, were creating wonderlands of whiteness, even as they played up the docility of their state's peoples of color. In
making such claims, Anglo promoters constructed an environmentally de-
terministic model for explaining racial development. They presented regional
wonderlands that shaped moral character, physical constitution, and, more
generally, racial well-being. Long before Frederick Jackson Turner had written about the frontier's role in "promot[ing] the formation of a composite
nationality for the American people," a generation of western promoters were
claiming that white western wonderlands, postfrontier paradises, were the
loci of national racial health and well-being.[67]

But for wonderlands of whiteness to be maintained, promotional writers
had to extend different kinds of welcomes to different racial groups. European-American boosters did more than just seek warm bodies to populate
western regions; they desired the "right kinds" of immigrants to ensure a
healthy body politic. An 1876 broadside for Bell County in central Texas
announced that readers perhaps "will be relieved to know that of the county's
18,000 residents there are less than one thousand blacks" and went on to
add that "the population, both black and white, is as orderly, moral as any
like number in any part of the United States." Such race-centered reassur-
ances from promoters in a former Confederate state, prior to the official end
of the Reconstruction era, should come as no surprise.[68] Historians have
highlighted the exclusionary rhetoric and practice of white promoters of the
Great Plains. The establishment of black communities such as Nicodemus
by Kansas Exodusters is testament both to minority needs to form their own
enclaves and to the conscious efforts of white promoters to steer African-
Americans away from centers of white population. Indeed, even the growth
of all-black towns made white politicians and promoters nervous. In 1878,
Kansas governor John St. John and the Kansas Pacific Railroad were discouraging black migrants from coming to the state. The governor and the railroad offered correctives to the laudatory prose of the promotional tracts,
insisting that the best lands were already gone, the labor market was weak,
and the weather was unpredictable. Writer Ian Frazier exaggerates when,
in recounting these lamentable developments, he remarks: "It was probably
the only time in history that a railroad ever told the truth of a situation to a

prospective settler."[69] Yet black towns such as Nicodemus (established in 1877); Boley, Oklahoma (1904); Allensworth, California (1908); and Deerfield, Colorado (1910), as well as underscoring the important and continuing efforts of black promoters into the early twentieth century, do certainly highlight the West's limitations as a pluralistic promised land.[70] And it should come as no surprise that it was race that gave the lie to promotional claims, in Kansas and other purported western paradises.

African-Americans did migrate to western cities—most notably Denver, Los Angeles, Oakland, Omaha, Portland, San Francisco, Seattle, and Spokane—in the late nineteenth and early twentieth centuries, but not because the mainstream promotional institutions of those places sought to attract them.[71] Black migrants understood that these cities were comparative lands of promise, in spite of the levels of prejudice and segregation that still existed in them. Aspects of the growth of black urban populations in the West highlight the complexities of race-related issues in this period. For example, the size of the black community doubled in Los Angeles in 1903, when the Southern Pacific Railroad brought in nearly 2,000 black workers; but this was hardly an attempt to break down the color lines in the city. Indeed, the railroad had brought in the black laborers for the purpose of breaking a strike by Mexican-American construction workers. Also, beginning in the 1890s, and increasingly in the first three decades of the new century, prospective black migrants to Los Angeles were privy to a stream of promotional writings produced within the city's black community. These tracts emphasized the city's qualities as both a comparative economic promised land and one of social and political equality—"not Paradise," W. E. B. DuBois cautioned readers in 1913, but nonetheless a great improvement over the Jim Crow South, where violence, public segregation, and systematic disenfranchisement prevailed.[72]

In the most racially pluralistic parts of the West, in the early twentieth century, promoters, faced with the demographic reality of diversity, increasingly presented wonderlands of whiteness, tinged with a romantic backdrop of cultural color, to prospective settlers. In Southern California, starting in the 1880s, boosters such as Charles Fletcher Lummis made the "Spanish fantasy past" a feature of their regional promotion and, as a corollary, managed to shift attention away from the racial realities of the present, effectively "privileging the mission over the Mexican," in the words of historian William Deverell.[73] Ignoring the presence of Asians, blacks, and Mexicans, for the most part, in their promotional writings, Los Angeles's mainstream boosters constructed a romantic Hispanic and Native American backdrop for a city that was thoroughly dominated by Anglos. This picture was placed before the public in the form of parades, such as La Fiesta de Los Angeles, first held in the mid-1890s and organized, in part, by Lummis, and through John Steven McGroarty's enormously popular *Mission Play*, which opened in 1912. In addition, from the 1890s into the first years of the new century, Lummis used his journal *Land of Sunshine/Out West* to promote the Landmarks Club, which was devoted to the restoration of missions in Southern California, the Sequoyah League, an organization dedicated to a more benign Indian policy, and his own Southwest Museum, a repository for native artifacts.[74] In this way, Lummis effectively combined place promotion with cultural heritage preservation and myth-building.

Meanwhile, as Mexicans migrated to Los Angeles in huge numbers, particularly between 1910 and 1930, potential white migrants would never have known as much from the mainstream promotional literature. The booster publications featured very few pictures of youthful Mexican laborers but plenty of photographs of the missions and of ancient Indians, sometimes reportedly more than a century old, thereby reinforcing the image of Los Angeles as an Anglo city, with little more than a pleasant tinge of local, and vanishing, color.[75] Thus, while white boosters presented the least racially diverse parts of the West as wonderlands *of* whiteness, the most racially heterogeneous regions, such as Southern California and the Southwest, were marketed to potential Anglo settlers as wonderlands *for* whiteness—regions where cultural diversity was nothing more than an attractive background to the main stage where a narrative of white economic and social opportunity and dominance played out.

Remembering Race Relations

> In speaking of the perpetrators of these wrongs [against the Indians], I cannot spare either age, sex, or former condition in life. Kleptomania prevailed as an epidemic. The desire to take something seized the trader, settler, government employee and even the preachers were not, in all cases, exempt from its attacks. When we had stolen all they had laying around loose, last of all we stole their lands. (William B. Street, of the Tri-State Old Settlers' Association of Illinois, Missouri, and Iowa, 1884)

The efforts of boosters to create a Spanish fantasy past in Southern California speak to the power of constructed memory as a promotional tool. However, it is important to bear in mind that the purposeful reconstruction of the mission past and the Californio heritage were not exclusively Anglo acts. While Lummis, McGroarty, George Wharton James, and other white writers were leading participants in these endeavors, some Californios were involved, too (planning and participating in parades and festivals), understanding that such positive legacy building facilitated their own efforts to maintain social status in the fast-changing California present. Indeed, prominent Californios, most notably General M. G. Vallejo, had been sought out by Hubert Howe Bancroft in the 1870s and were interviewed by Bancroft's assistants. Their personal narratives (more than one hundred of them) served as an important foundation for Bancroft's seven-volume *History of California* (1886–1890)— the work that raised the ire of the Society of California Pioneers in 1893. Bancroft's ethnocentrism ensured that the *History of California* would not be told—despite the abundance of Californio voices he could draw on for his reconstructions—from the Californios' perspective. Yet their testimonials do, nonetheless, bear witness to the efforts of Californios to place themselves at the center of the state's historical record; indeed, we might even view their oral histories as acts of resistance to Anglo domination through the memorialization of the pre-American era.[76]

Anglo pioneer reminiscers, not surprisingly, did not seek out Californio testimonials (as Bancroft did), or those of any other peoples of color, to corroborate or clarify their memories of the frontier past. Yet race was at the center of the Anglo reminiscence tradition. Constructed memories were often used to justify white conquest of the West through emphasis on the savagery of Indian peoples. For example, in his 1884 reminiscences, a former Texas Ranger gloried in the efforts of the "many brave and heroic men [who] lived and died, and did their glorious service upon the frontiers of Texas . . . and drove the wild beast and the red man from the path of civilization"; indeed, the book's lengthy subtitle highlighted the struggles through which *Texas was rescued from the rule of the savage and consecrated to the empire of civilization*.[77] Similarly, Wild West showman Pawnee Bill, in his account *Experience and Adventures on the Western Plains* (1902), focused a good deal of attention on the "long reign of terror, and merciless warfare on the advance guard of civilization" perpetrated by Geronimo.[78]

Such sentiments, concerning Indian acts of savagery and consequent white suffering, were common in pioneer reminiscences and are worth considering in relation to historian Richard White's commentary on Buffalo Bill Cody's "odd story of conquest" (in his Wild West reenactments) in which "everything is inverted." As White notes, in constructing a frontier heritage, "Americans had to transform conquerors into victims." Cody did this by depicting acts of "Indian aggression and white defense . . . Indian killers and white victims . . . in effect, badly abused conquerors."[79] But such purposeful acts of inversion were also deeply embedded in the pioneer reminiscence genre. In the pages of thousands of published pioneer accounts of frontier days and in thousands of impassioned speeches at pioneer society meetings, constructed tales (whether merely embellished or completely invented) of victimized conquerors and victimizing Indians were placed before the public. This was the case both before and after Cody and other performers began to make a visual spectacle of this established contour of the imaginative frontier heritage. Occasional white military defeats in the West, such as the Battle of Little Big Horn—General George Armstrong Custer's famous "last stand" in 1876, which Cody thrillingly re-created for his audiences—did not create the tradition of inversion of conquered and conquerors, victims and victimizers. But such events, including the earlier defeat at the Alamo, did help confirm the veracity of that tradition in the eyes and minds of the American public, just as the reminiscence genre did.

Pioneer reminiscers continued to push the inversion theme into the early twentieth century (and so did Cody). For example, Hilory G. Bedford, in his book of reminiscences, *Texas Indian Troubles: The Most Thrilling Events in the History of Texas* (1905), constructed a story of the tenuous advance of white civilization in the face of seemingly overwhelming Indian opposition. Bedford noted that readers might wonder why these brave settlers did not "give back when they saw they were in great danger," and then proceeded to explain that "to give back at all was equal to surrendering the whole land, for each mile that the Whites would retreat the Indians would at once claim ten more." There was, in his estimation, nothing inevitable about the triumph of white frontier advance in Texas. In light of this, Bedford advocated the organization of efforts to honor those pioneers who had passed on to a place "where the shrieks and groans of those who are being scalped and murdered" would no longer "pierce their ears," a place where their "peaceful repose" would not be disturbed "by the wail of innocent women and children . . . being dragged from their homes as captives by cruel, merciless foes."[80]

There was real purpose behind the book's cataloging of Indian atrocities against innocent white settlers. Bedford was responding to "the idea that the white people have taken the red man's country," and in doing so he proclaimed that "the Indians only occupied this country as the wild beasts did

... they have never done anything to establish their rights to this country
... have never met any of the responsibilities placed upon them by the Creator." Indeed, their "cruel hands [were] dripping with the blood of the best
people of our country," and "the plaintive cries of [their] innocent captives"
still echoed in the pioneers' ears. The progress that Texas had made confirmed, for Bedford, that "the Lord is blessing the works of the white man."[81]
This, seemingly, is as clear a case of absolute good triumphing over absolute
evil as the pioneer imagination could construct. Nonetheless, one is struck
by how Bedford's impassioned tirades against Indian cruelty are generally
offered in response to ideas that the Indians have been mistreated and that
federal policy might be more benign. Was Bedford seeking, on some level,
subconscious or otherwise, to assuage his own personal guilt (as well as that
of his readers) over the victimization of Native peoples by the conquerors,
or did he mean exactly what he said?

Regardless of Bedford's motivations, we can be certain that an undercurrent of remorse over the treatment of Indians did exist in the pioneer
reminiscence genre. As the frontier past became a distant memory and perceived Indian dangers gave way to the precipitous decline of Native peoples,
reminiscers often expressed a tinge of regret over the presumed "pass[ing]
away [of] the luckless red man who yet calls this his home," and in doing so
contributed to the myth of the vanishing American.[82] Some spoke of their
sincere regret at their actions, and at those of their government in a previous era. Perhaps these remorsefulful sentiments were a kind of cathartic
exercise that enabled reminiscers to assuage their guilt and exonerate themselves from blame. For example, William B. Street, an old Nebraska settler,
in a letter that was read to the Tri-State Old Settlers' Association of Illinois,
Missouri, and Iowa, at its meeting in Keokuk, Iowa, in 1884, outlined the
key characteristics of the pioneer type—which he lauded—but then expressed
feelings of sincere guilt over the consequences of the frontier's march westward. The doctrine of "the survival of the fittest," he regretted, "has led our
people into a grievous sin and wrong; done to a people to whom we owe a
greater debt than we shall ever be able to pay; for the time is past." Street
proclaimed his sense of "sorrow and shame" concerning "our treatment of
the 'Red Man.'" To be sure, he explained, the Indians had a "heedless, care-
less, lazy character"; nonetheless, they did not deserve the fate that befell
them. Street insisted that a spirit of "Kloptomania" had motivated both the
United States government and white settlers, and he lamented that after
stealing the Indians' lands, white America did not even have the common

decency to make Indians citizens. Street closed his letter with a call to every member of the association to "use his influence to have some justice, (though tardy,) done to the 'Red Man.'"[83]

Of course, weighed against the oral histories of Native peoples—recounting, from the other side of the frontier line, the story of westward migration—such admonitions of white guilt over past actions appear, at best, a classic case of too little and too late. Yet pioneer declarations of regret, when viewed alongside those recollections that gloried in the conquest of Native peoples and sought to justify them, show at least that the pioneer reminiscence genre was far from monolithic with respect to Indian-white relations. It is not surprising that the old settlers' discussions of race relations—jarring as their terminology is to the modern reader—should indicate a variety of positions on race matters, since diversity of opinion in this area has been a pervasive characteristic of European American thought and culture. But the range of views with respect to race among these reminiscers—which parallels the variety of racial perspectives among the boosters—certainly problematizes common assumptions concerning the contours of the frontier heritage.

6

THE GHOSTS OF WESTERN

FUTURE AND PAST

The Enduring Frontier Heritage

In the context of the pressing concerns facing the contemporary West, it is worth remembering the promoters' and reminiscers' constructions and re-constructions of mythic western places in the late nineteenth and early twentieth centuries. The legacies of these imaginative acts of creation and re-creation are very much in evidence today; indeed, the same kinds of pur-poseful acts are an integral element of today's debates over growth in west-ern communities. The ghosts of western future and past still haunt the western present.

A new generation of boosters continues to develop creative techniques for imagining "new," "better," and no less-western places into being through development. Contemporary land marketers, however, often draw on the frontier heritage in ways that would have been anathema to late-nineteenth-century and early-twentieth-century western promoters. The boosters of that

earlier era were careful to avoid any suggestion that moving to western promised lands might take prospective settlers away from civilization. Quite to the
contrary, they insisted that new western lands offered the full range of cultural amenities that such potential migrants were used to in their home
regions. Today's creative western developers, on the other hand, promise affluent metropolitan refugees the prospect of an escape from the postmodern
angst accompanying overcivilization. Nonetheless, today's western real estate
advertising does echo the promotional past—with its emphasis on frontiers
of opportunity—in presenting these places as the last available frontiers of
landed paradise.

Recent advertising copy for the mini-homestead refuge of Caribou Springs
Ranch, in Boulder County, Colorado, offers a revival of "turn-of-the-century"
(nineteenth century) "western living," yet with no loss of "luxury and design innovation." Here, the promoters announce, is "a unique opportunity
for the sophisticated buyer . . . 726 acres of pastoral paradise." Wealthy home
seekers are informed that "one visit will take you back in time to the Arapaho,
who frequented the Caribou hot springs, to the legendary footsteps of explorer Ceran St. Vrain, and to the remarkable family that worked the land
for multiple generations." Each homestead, the advertisement concludes,
"is a private compound . . . secluded . . . serene . . . yet just 12 minutes north
of downtown Boulder," and at Caribou Springs Ranch (where lot prices, in
2002, range from $449,000 to $1,200,000), "all trails lead to home."[1] In a
similar vein, marketers describe Creek Ranch, in Steamboat Springs, Colorado, as a "ranch preservation community," where for as little as $308,850
per lot, prospective buyers can purchase the promise of a "western lifestyle,"
including access to the "Ranch Headquarters."[2]

Such modern, yet nostalgia-driven, promotional prose might raise skeptical eyebrows among scholars. One perhaps wonders how delighted that
"remarkable family" of homesteaders might be about the development of their
land. Or one might find the notion of a "ranch preservation community"
composed of luxury homesites to be somewhat oxymoronic. Still, it is worth
considering that in many cases—Caribou Springs Ranch, for one—developers
have preserved large areas of open space, a factor that certainly contributes
to the value of homesites but also to the maintenance of wildlife habitats.[3]
Furthermore, scholarly emphasis on the ostensible ironies in the advertising of Caribou Springs Ranch, Creek Ranch, or the hundreds of other similar exclusive frontier getaways in the New West is hardly likely to impact sales.
Any such ironies are clearly no great impediment to either marketers or

purchasers. Frontier associations have made something of a comeback in western land and home advertising in recent years, presumably because they effectively appeal to the needs and desires of contemporary buyers, which are very different from those of prospective homesteaders a century ago.

For those with deeper pockets than the mini-homesteaders of Caribou Springs Ranch and Creek Ranch, mini-ranch properties, such as Harrington Elk Ranch in Steamboat Springs, are advertised in all their old western glory. For $11,500,000, the purchaser of Harrington Elk Ranch will acquire "the Ranch Manager's home . . . [i.e.,] the original homestead built in 1900 . . . [along with] the Saloon [which] is reminiscent of the Wild West . . . and a quaint refurbished log guest cabin." And, of course, the new owner will also acquire the cultural cachet that comes with the knowledge that this "one-of-a-kind property [is] steeped in the rich tradition of the early pioneers."[4]

Meanwhile, as today's marketers draw on the legacies of the Old West, opponents of growth reminisce about how their cherished "old" western communities used to be in purer times, in the "good old days," before the arrival of superaffluent multiple homeowners, mini-homesteads, ranch preservation communities, and metropolitan sprawl. These contemporary reminiscers recall simpler, more civil, and more scenic western places. They often lament what they perceive as the decline of cultural integrity and environmental integrity and the waning of another amorphous quality, "westernness." In expressing such concerns, today's western recollectors offer a classic declensionist narrative that parallels the one constructed by some old pioneer reminiscers who, as early as the late nineteenth century, insisted that the New West could not hold a candle to the old frontier West of their youth. Speaking for the "voices from a forgotten landscape," Verlyn Klinkenborg, writing in the *New York Times* in 2000, states that "for many Coloradans, a kind of geographical fatigue has set in . . . a sense of helplessness." The source of such helplessness, Klinkenborg explains, is found in the "garrison[s] of signature subdivisions closing in on Denver itself."[5] Such longing in the West for open vistas, unblighted by the "scars" and "wounds" of development, and the accompanying assumption that landscapes have become less "pure" and less "authentic" as a consequence of change speak to the enduring legacy of the frontier heritage in the contemporary West.

Drawing on the power of primacy—the notion that length of residence in a place (chronological proximity to an earlier age of authenticity) confers the right to speak for the "spirit" of that place—residents of the Intermountain West and the Pacific Northwest have, in recent decades, expressed their disdain for new arrivals, particularly those coming from California.[6] Their "Caliphobia" (or fear of "Californication") constitutes a good example of the process by which regional identity is nurtured through reaction against other, ostensibly less western, people. However, it is important to consider that the recent demographic growth and accompanying development in some western states (Colorado is a prime example) owes as much to intrastate as to interstate migration.[7] Furthermore, such antimigrant sentiments are as likely to be voiced by urban dwellers as by rural dwellers in states such as Washington, Oregon, Idaho, and Colorado. Such turn-of-the-millennium concerns are not such a great departure from those at the turn of the last century. Perhaps, like the pioneer reminiscers of earlier generations, today's selective western rememberers are really worried about maintaining social status in the New West, even as they present themselves as the protectors of the true spirit of the Old West. One cannot help but be reminded of the restrictive, time-based requirements for pioneer society membership, qualifications that placed a cultural premium on primacy.

Whatever the case, the frontier theme certainly remains important for understanding western identity (or, at least, claims to it) in the past and in the present. In the estimation of many scholars (even those with a sophisticated understanding of the frontier's complex legacy), frontier associations are best dismissed, and memories of the frontier process are best equated with placelessness and immaturity. Yet expressions of identity (literary or otherwise) that grow out of generations of experience in a place are generally viewed as genuine, authentic, and significant expressions of regional identity. This dualistic approach assumes that all those who invoke a frontier heritage are living in the past and in "no place" in particular, while all "regionalist" writers and thinkers are somehow more genuine, more "grounded," and more sophisticated chroniclers of "rootedness" and meaning in actual places.[8] In reality, however, it seems that contemporary western assertions of regional rootedness are often themselves situated within a pioneer heritage, whether real or constructed. The concepts of frontier and region are wrapped up in a complex tangle of claims and counterclaims to western identity that is difficult to unravel.

In considering this complex web of claims, it is important to remember that processes of mobility and adjustment are, in fact, more characteristic of life in the West than in any other American region. The West in the nineteenth and twentieth centuries was marked by greater rates of demographic shifting than the North or the South, and it remains the fastest-growing region of the country—the five fastest-growing states of the 1990s (Nevada, Arizona, Colorado, Utah, and Idaho) are all western.[9] As the writings of Wallace Stegner and Bernard DeVoto illustrate so poignantly, the processes by which people journey to places and then try to adjust to them have been enduring features of western American culture, including literary production.[10] The two processes—movement and adjustment—are closely linked, especially in earlier periods when the journeying was dangerous and demanding. People often got sick on overland journeys to the West from the East, Midwest, and Mexico, on ocean crossings from Asia, and on forced journeys from traditional Indian homelands to reservations. Some people were born along the way; some people died.[11] Overland journeys in the mid–nineteenth century could take half a year, and there is a veritable mass of diaries and, later, reminiscences—including those of the Jayhawkers, Ezra Meeker, Juliet Brier, and thousands of others—chronicling the hardships of those trips. It is hardly surprising that people remembered and embellished their journeys for the rest of their lives. Such journeys—or, at least, recollections thereof—while often highly selective in the white pioneer tradition, were absolutely integral to the process of adjustment to place, the process by which regional identity began to form.[12] It is worth keeping the theme of frontier process (the process of journeying to a region) in the picture as we consider western regional identity and the ways in which an enduring frontier heritage continues to affect it.

Primacy, Authenticity, Promise, and Place

The old pioneer reminiscers of a century ago—expressing the fundamental interrelatedness of notions of frontier and region—did not just remember the hardships of their westward journeys and play up the object lessons that younger generations could learn from their trials on the trails; they also emphasized the fact that they had been "in place" for longer than other white residents. Since, in their estimation, their racial and cultural affiliation generally outweighed completely any claims to primacy that nonwhite groups might have (the remorseful lamenters who emphasized the mistreatment of western peoples of color were in the minority), the fact that Indians and Hispanics had been in place prior to white pioneers rarely factored into the pioneers' ruminations about quintessential westernness. A key contour of the white pioneer reminiscence genre was the conferral of primacy on those white

Americans who had experienced difficult journeys, transformed formerly inhospitable wastelands, and arrived in those places during the frontier period. This contour has its parallel in contemporary western claims to heightened sense of place based upon primacy.

Different people, of course, have widely varying understandings of the places they live in, and it is difficult to determine whether one person's sense of, or attachment to, a place has more validity than another's, whether one person's identification with a place is deeper, richer, or purer than someone else's. Sometimes people exhibit their attachment to a place and its cultural legacies in the most antagonistic, atavistic, nativistic, and violent ways. Neo-Nazi groups in the northern West seeking to "preserve" a "white homeland" serve as instructive cases in point.[13] Drawing direct connections between such lamentable strains of regional expression and the white pioneer heritage would be too simplistic—the reminiscence genre is hardly monolithic with respect to discussions of race. Nonetheless, it is worth considering the dark underside (as well as the positive side) of elevated attachments to place.

Architectural theorist Neil Leach, reflecting on recent developments in central and Eastern Europe, emphasizes the "potential dangers inherent in . . . calls for a regional or national identity." He notes that such "calls . . . for regionalism share something of the nostalgia for a lost tradition—a lost paradise—that is embodied in other contemporary projects to recapture the past." In this way, Leach adds, expressions of regionalism can become "virulent" claims to authenticity.[14] The lessons of ethnic cleansing in the former Yugoslavia, of white militia groups in the West today, and, it might be added, of white citizens' councils in the South in the 1950s and 1960s should be clear: regionalism and sense of place are not always as endearing as 1920s and 1930s literary and artistic depictions of local color and folklife might suggest; they can and do have starker tendencies.[15] Still, it is worth remembering that the foundation of selective remembrance upon which such claims so often rest is a testament to their purposeful construction, not to their authenticity. Sense of place is not an inherently positive or negative phenomenon; rather, it is an expression of attachment that can be manifested in the most positive as well as negative ways, and quite often, one suspects, in more neutral ways that are less evident and less memorable.

In examining space and place in the contemporary West, it is important to recognize the presence of the ghosts of western past—the legacy of the pioneer reminiscence genre. We certainly need to move beyond the simple acceptance of claims to heightened "westernness"—and the authenticity and virtuousness implied in such claims—by some long-term residents of western places. Such selfish claims are, in part, an understandable legacy of pioneer reminiscers' efforts to create and sustain a frontier heritage. But primacy becomes its own self-validation in such expressions of westernness, and it is a value too easily accepted by scholars, which is surprising given the current scholarly skepticism that surrounds the pioneer past. Simply to accept the notion that one group's identification with a place is purer than another's, or more rooted in the landscape, more at one with nature, more authentic, is indicative of a set of unquestioning assumptions about attachment to place.

However, such notions about elevated identification with place are not tied exclusively to the white frontier-western heritage. For example, it is commonly assumed that American Indian peoples have a stronger sense of place, a more profound rootedness in the land, than do other peoples in the West. Indian and white scholars use the phrase "of the place" to distinguish Indians' regional indigenousness from the regional attachments of white westerners who have moved "to the place" and put down roots "in the place."[16] There are, of course, many examples of deep attachment to place among Native American cultures.[17] The West is full of sacred Indian places. Still, it is worth noting that as various Native American peoples were forced onto reservations in the nineteenth century, they came to identify with those places as cultural homelands at the very same time that white homesteaders (of various ethnic stripes) were developing their attachments to other geographic locations, sometimes the former tribal lands themselves.[18]

We know that the surge of white settlement into the West in the second half of the nineteenth century was responsible for the displacement of Native peoples; the policies of containment, or "concentration" (on reservations) and then assimilation, facilitated white settlement in the trans-Mississippi West. It is clear that one set of cultures gained immeasurably at the expense of another. The sense of place that white settlers developed in some parts of the West rested on a foundation of assaults on Indian attachment to place. All of this is clear and incontestable. However, the confident assertions and assumptions about Native sense of place made by both Indian and non-Indian scholars are less incontrovertible. Some American Indian groups and individuals may have a particularly strong sense of place, while others may not. Large Indian populations reside in cities such as Los Angeles, far from their cultural homelands. To simply assume that the condition of "Indianness" alone somehow guarantees a heightened "placefulness," or "rootedness," or authenticity of attachment to place amounts to racial stereotyping of a sort, even if the person doing the assuming has ostensibly "philo-Indian" intentions. We have to ask whether notions of a heightened Native American sense of place are any more uniformly applicable to the varied peoples of Native American descent and affiliation in their contemporary rural, urban, and suburban places of residence than European-American constructs of "westernness" are to the culturally diverse residents of the West.

Claims concerning westerners' elevated attachments to place are tied in part to notions of the West as a land of promise. People of all races and ethnicities have placed great emotional and financial stock in the future promise of western places. Some, looking back to the remembered golden age of their younger days, have reminisced about the loss of western promised lands. This heightened sense of promise may have raised the stakes with respect to identity formation in the West. The human need for self-validation is a vital aspect of gaining a sense of place. In the tradition of the West's boosters and reminiscers, people today still subconsciously try to convince themselves and consciously try to convince others that they did the right thing by coming to, going from, or staying in a particular place. If that place was from the outset imbued with great promise, then the process of self-validation takes on greater urgency. Pronouncements of sense of place may be much like those that follow the making of a major material purchase, such as a house. In the tradition of Jules Sandoz and thousands of other energetic correspondents and place promoters a century ago, we want to convince those around us (and ourselves) that we are eminently satisfied with the decision we made and that the house in question has become a home, a place with meaning.

Such assessments of the self-validating purpose behind assertions about attachment to place may seem cynical; yet they may also serve as a corrective to the easy assumptions we often make about how sense of place is formed. Talking about a heightened sense of place, about an acute affinity for one's surroundings, is a vital part of the process by which sense of place is formed. What is more, highly critical and selective remembrance of one's former place of habitation is often an important part of the process of adjustment to a new locale. An ex-Californian residing in Colorado might draw pointed comparisons between the smog, crime, and congestion of the Southland and the healthy air, friendliness, and wide-open spaces of the Rockies. Such stark juxtapositions of conditions in former and present places are necessary expressions of self-validation that help nurture attachment to new environments; a layer of regional skin has to be shed before a new one can be attached. Additionally, the drawing of such comparisons is a variant of the process by which regional identity forms through reaction.

For some groups and individuals in the West, however, the formation of regional identity may have little to do with perceptions of, or self-validating pronouncements about, positive experience in a new place—as contrasted with the selectively remembered disadvantages of dwelling in a former place. Instead, regional attachments may form through a sense of having experienced a raw deal, yet somehow triumphed over adversity, much like the pioneers of old. The mere fact of survival in a harsh environment may be as profound a shaper of regional consciousness as success in less taxing surroundings.[19] Remember that in the late nineteenth and early twentieth centuries, Anglo pioneers commonly compared the harshness of the particular western environments that they had experienced with those faced by the settlers of other parts of the West. Each regional group of old settlers insisted upon having conquered the most barren and inhospitable environment imaginable. Such needs for regional one-upmanship—fostering an "I'm more western than you" mentality—lead us to ask whether sense of place is really so positive a phenomenon in light of the fact that a group's intense attachment to a place, its heightened regional consciousness, may help explain its unwillingness to share that place with others. The trend in American thought, since the Civil War, has been to view sectionalism as a force for ill and regionalism as benign, but the concepts are not so easily separable, and one group's purported healthy regional identity can seem like sectional intolerance to others.

Californication in the Contemporary West

The impulse of some Intermountain and Pacific Northwesterners in the 1980s and 1990s, and still today, to express their "Caliphobia" and lament the "Californication" of "their" promised lands serves as an instructive example of the bolstering of regional identity through expressions of intolerance—regionalism through reaction. Some westerners express these anti-Californian impulses by sporting "Don't Californicate Oregon," "Washington Is Full. Get Out," "Native Coloradan," and other such bumper stickers and T-shirt slogans.[20] However, any black humor in such printed statements is overshadowed by the fact that they are expressions of regional identity formed through reaction to others. Such expressions of anger or anxiety over the development and destruction of pristine landscapes and the eradication of simple, affordable lifestyles were presumed, in the 1990s, to be a direct consequence of the presence of Californians, whom *Seattle Times* columnist Emmett Watson described as "nitwits," "neurotics," and "sunbleached barbarians."[21] Perhaps the anti-Californian impulse is a natural regional response to the threat of a takeover by a state that now sets the national standard in various areas such as mass entertainment, retail development, hi-tech innovation, and the fast-food industry. But that same impulse can also be viewed more lamentably as evidence of the inability of some western residents to accept, or remember, that the same forces and attractions that drew them to their places are now, in turn, drawing others. Like old immigrants who are often loath to accept newer immigrant groups, some "old" westerners—some of whom are neither particularly old, nor long-term residents of their western regions—evidently fear the heterogenization of their hallowed homes.[22]

The Californication issue, in fact, helps illustrate the problem of "westernness" as a thematic construct.[23] California out-migrants have been motivated by a range of factors, including their perceptions of the Intermountain West and Pacific Northwest as refuges from pollution, congestion, high property values, crime, and racial tension in the Southland; some of the same factors help account for out-migration of white Californians from the Bay Area, too. Their destinations have been a set of quintessentially "western" safe houses, "last best hiding places," exits on the "white flight highway" from the metropolitan monster lying west of "the West."[24] It has been a "back-to-the-land" or "frontier" movement of sorts, displaying a Daniel Boonesque quality as white Californians flee congested places and head into the relatively wide-open spaces of the Intermountain West and coastal Oregon and Washington. But locals draw on the power of primacy (length of residence) to deny the westernness of the newcomers, questioning whether they can ever assimilate and "become western."

The Golden State expatriates are viewed as the great (wealthy) unwashed, people tainted beyond redemption by their former place of residence. If you remember, California's late-nineteenth-century promoters had the burden of countering popular perceptions of the state as a place irredeemably tarnished by aridity, fires, floods, earthquakes, and cultural diversity.[25] Ironically, then, the ex-Californians are deemed to be a danger to the very same western identity and western surroundings they have come in search of.[26] Residents' assessments of former Californians as unwestern are based in part on the perception that these comparatively rich migrants bring all the accoutrements—the technological baggage and luxury automobiles—of their old life with them as they begin their presumably simpler, less harried lives in the wide-open (or, better, less densely peopled) parts of the West.

In addition to serving as an illuminating case study in the power of primacy as a determinant of westernness, the rhetoric surrounding the migration of Californians (and Texans, New Yorkers, New Jerseyites, Illinoisans, and other white Americans) to the rural West also illuminates the power of rural western imagery as a barometer of identity, and the perceived importance of whiteness to the same. California perhaps seems less western than the Intermountain West and the Pacific Northwest to many white Californians because the Golden State has become so racially diverse: Caucasians are now a "minority majority" there.[27] It is less the landscape per se than the mixture of peoples standing against the backdrop of the landscape that nurtures perceptions and misperceptions of westernness. If western mythology does not develop beyond its defining characteristics of white-centeredness and rural-centeredness—if the mythology does not diversify to reflect the region's demographic makeup and its metropolitan character—then how can westernness serve as a thematic construct for a truly inclusive and representative understanding of contemporary sense of place in the region?[28]

The California expatriates and their new "Old Western" communities (in the "New West") also underscore another link between the white western experience and the more racially and ethnically diverse sets of experiences that have marked the region. Sizable fractions of the population within certain parts of the West still crave only the "right kinds of people," if they seek population growth at all. The antimigration sentiment leveled at ex-Californians, while far less severe and marked merely by bumper stickers and barbed comments rather than by violence and oppression, nonetheless brings to mind the attitudes of white westerners and easterners alike toward immigrants from other countries starting in the mid–nineteenth century. Similarly dubious notions concerning the unassimilability of newcomers—and whether they can be fitted or can fit themselves into the existing cultural milieu—have also driven anti-immigration sentiment as successive waves of immigrants have, as part of the process of assimilating, laid claim to the constructs of primacy and authenticity.[29]

In the late nineteenth and early twentieth centuries, demographer Francis A. Walker, historian Frederick Jackson Turner, and a host of other prominent intellectuals expressed concern over the closing of the American frontier. They worried that the New Immigration from southern and eastern

Europe would be less readily Americanized in the frontier's wake. Such arguments were often, in fact, little more than a thinly veiled cover for the ethnic and class-based prejudice that White Anglo-Saxon Protestants felt toward New Immigrants.[30] In a similar vein, the contemporary West's vocal opponents of new migration express frustration that their last frontiers are closing in the wake of new settlement, that their last and best old Wests are disappearing. And it is, of course, true that beautiful valleys and prairies are being cemented over by developers to meet the needs of new western residents. But are not long-term residents' purportedly heartfelt expressions of anxiety over the decline of true westernness, to some degree, at least, a less romantic lament over the influx of outsiders who, while they might show some interest in the locals' dyed-in-the-wool frontier persona, show no deference to them? Such expressions of concern over change do not seem so far removed from those expressed by old pioneer reminiscers a century ago.

The antipathies directed toward new wealthy migrants to the contemporary West are, in no small degree, based on fears of socioeconomic displacement, and hence constitute an inversion of sorts of the class-driven anti-immigrant rhetoric of the 1870s to 1920s. The New Immigrants were lambasted for their peasant origins and out of fear that they would become wards of the state, or would drive down wages by working for a pittance. Indeed, it was labor organizations, such as the Workingmen's Party in California, that were often at the forefront of anti-immigration movements. Big business was generally supportive of unrestricted immigration. Meanwhile, locals today criticize migrants to the Intermountain West and the Pacific Northwest—especially the California expatriates—for driving up property values. Hence, in the case of both earlier anti-immigrant sentiment and contemporary antimigrant sentiment, a combination of economic concerns and perceived cultural differences, along with a broader concern (encompassing economic, cultural, and environmental factors) over the changing nature of place, has characterized local opposition to outsiders. And, of course, the anti-immigrant rhetoric and action of the late nineteenth and early twentieth centuries also find their direct parallel in the contemporary expressions of fear and intolerance directed at Mexican immigrants and other Latinos in the West.[31]

While the casual stereotyping of outsiders is troubling, such expressions of regionalism should not prove surprising. The role of primacy in the formation of regional identity stems in part from a spirit of opposition to outside forces—including migration from other states, immigration from other countries, and the power of the federal government.[32] People often define themselves and their places by reference to what they are not, who they are not, and where they are not. Regional boosters in California, the Pacific Northwest, and other western places in the late nineteenth and early twentieth centuries were constantly emphasizing, even as they imitated eastern political, social, and cultural structures, that they were *not* easterners, that they and their region were superior to what they had left behind.[33] Like the anti-California impulse of today's Intermountain West and Pacific Northwest residents, this antieasternness manifested itself only verbally. But westerners in the same period also defined themselves in part through their opposition to Hispanics, Asians, Native Americans, and African-Americans. This process of self-definition was often far more than mere verbal expression; it could manifest itself through lynching, exclusion, expulsion, deportation (with its gentler official label, "repatriation"), segregation, and race riots.

Incidentally, the construction of the Jim Crow system in the South, while the result of an entirely different set of social circumstances, was contemporaneous with these developments in western race relations in the late nineteenth century. White southerners reforged a regional identity in the wake of military defeat by reestablishing social structures that reflected their sense of or dependence on notions of racial superiority.[34] White westerners forged their identities in a similar way, juxtaposing themselves and their cultural characteristics with those of nonwhite residents of the West.

At other times, however, regionalism has had less to do with opposition to "others" than with community integration and cooperation. Western regionalism has often manifested itself in ways that would make the late-nineteenth-century regionalist, philosopher, and Californian Josiah Royce proud. He advocated a "wise provincialism," an affinity for place devoid of narrow parochialism.[35] The recent efforts of some northern Plains residents to move beyond sectional and sectarian differences to establish interdenominational churches, consolidated school systems, and economic enterprises are a good case in point.[36] Still, it is worth emphasizing that such efforts, while they have bridged sectional and sectarian divides, have rarely sought to bridge the broader cultural divides between races.[37] It is worth considering, too, the possibility that the kinds of healthy attachments to place that naturally lend themselves to interaction and cooperation among and between the different cultural groups residing in that place can form only when residents move beyond the construct of primacy. When residents of western regions stop equating the level of authenticity of their sense of place with their longevity in the place, the kind of wise provincialism that Royce hoped for is more likely to develop.

Change, Mythology, and Regional Identity

Regional identity is not permanent and unchanging; it is not an expression of attachment to place that is fixed in time. Some scholars have stressed movement from process to place, from "relative flux to relative fixity," or even from frontier to region to "postregion," or to a state of "postwesternness" in an increasingly modern, homogenized national culture. It is true that, to some degree, regionalism in the West and in other parts of the country has been an expression of resistance to the forces of homogenization.[38] Nonetheless, regions do not exist in chronological vacuums; they are always affected by social, political, cultural, economic, demographic, and environmental changes—changes that, in turn, precipitate changes in regional identity. We can reminisce fondly—as the old settlers of a century ago were wont to do—about the way things used to be (before the arrival of freeways, fast food, gourmet coffee franchises, and Californians), but regions and cultures will continue to change as they always have.

It is easy to ascribe a simple measure of value to all change—to assert, for example, that western cultures and places are somehow purer and have more integrity when they do not change. But when we do this, we are often remembering the past selectively, recalling those aspects of it that we deem positive and conveniently overlooking other elements. Certainly, for many western residents who lament the changes in the region, their own point of arrival or their younger days in a place are offered up as the watershed moment, the defining line between a golden age and the onset of a lamentable process of decline. However, considering the tremendous rate of change in the West, especially over the last century and a half, it seems illogical that the agents of change are themselves considered unwestern or antiwestern. The boosters, in the long run, have had a more enduring impact on the material reality of the West than the reminiscers, though western reminiscers have always found an audience eager to listen to their lamentations over change. Long-term western residents often assume that harbingers of change are expressing sentiments antithetical to the true spirit of western communities and engaging in inappropriate alliances with alien, exterior forces of change. Scholars, too, sometimes accept that residents who are trying to maintain some mythic notion of a past golden age in their western places are expressing the true spirit of westernness, acting as the region's cultural preservationists. But it is worth remembering that the promoters have been around for longer than the reminiscers—western places were imaginatively created before they were imaginatively re-created.[39]

Half a century of scholarship notwithstanding, as initiated by the publication of Henry Nash Smith's *Virgin Land* in 1950 (which illuminated the processes by which western mythology was created, elaborated, disseminated, and used to simplify the messiness of the western past), there is still a general tendency to play into that very mythology and see the spirit of western places as being under assault from the forces of change. Purported spokespeople of authentic western communities continue to voice their rhetoric of anti-Californication, viewing themselves as "injured innocents" and failing to see their own actions as even mildly nativistic and hypocritical.[40] At least the casual expression of anti-immigrant sentiments is no longer as socially acceptable as it was in the late nineteenth and early twentieth centuries. Perhaps the anti-immigrant, antimigrant, anti-Californication sentiments of residents of the Intermountain West and the Pacific Northwest will become less fashionable, too, as time goes on and people adjust more comfortably to the changes going on around them.

It would be superficially logical to assume that communities and individuals in those places with the longest heritage—rural New England or New Mexico, for example—have a richer, stronger sense of place than those who have resided in western places for only a comparatively short time. According to this rubric, those with the deepest regional roots are most disposed toward protecting their cherished places from change. But such simple logic does not always play out in western regions. There is no shortage of very recently arrived New Jerseyites, Texans, and Chicagoans (even Californians, for that matter) in Colorado and other western states, who express their frustration over the inevitable arrival of the next wave of migrants. The desire to slam shut the proverbial gate or to pull up the proverbial drawbridge behind oneself is common in those parts of the Intermountain West and Pacific Northwest experiencing rapid population growth through migration. In following that common course, are the newly arrived and self-baptized westerners expressing some deep, albeit rapidly acquired, sense of place—a kind of concentrated westernness—to compensate for lack of primacy? It is doubtful.

What is clearer is that a recent change in place—a move from, say, California to Montana—does not seem to diminish the new arrival's attachment to the stock mythic imagery of westernness that is pervasive in that new "old western" location. The migrant, in essence, has made a major life change in moving to a place that he or she perceives, at least to some degree, as somehow frozen in time, unchanging, and is motivated to help preserve that mythic status quo. The new arrival is, in effect, a convert to western mythology—with all the passion of the newly converted—which helps explain the fierceness of her or his attachment to place. Like the settlers drawn by the boosters' promises a century ago, contemporary migrants to the Old/New West are determined to ensure that the place lives up to its promise, and they thus become boosters themselves. If there is any irony in this, perhaps it stems from the fact that such recently arrived westerners have, to some degree surely, been drawn to the region by the latest generation of western promoters. And those promoters, as noted earlier, have developed a penchant for invoking the charms of the old, imagined, western past as they change the material landscape of the western present. But the West's wide-open spaces and its metropolitan spaces have been changing for centuries, even as some of its residents have sought, through selective remembrance of the past, to prevent those changes.

In 1990, over 80 percent of "westerners" resided in metropolitan areas. By 2000, the figure was closer to 90 percent.[41] Yet the prevailing influence of frontier mythology—which emphasizes comparatively empty places, thereby rendering them quintessentially western—ensures that the metropolitan spaces, where most westerners live, seem somehow unwestern. We need to move beyond easy assumptions about rural spaces as "deep places" and think more about the regional identity of all westerners, from ranchers, to reservation residents, to suburbanites, to high-rise condo dwellers. It is worth moving beyond the presumption that sense of place has to be rooted in the land, and at least try to speculate intelligently about nonrural western settings.[42] Cities, like rural dwellings, are built on the land and are often filled with a microcosmic "open space" of municipal parks and private gardens. The experience of nature can be right at one's doorstep, or at least close by, even in the most developed urban settings. After all, as scholars such as Ethan Carr, William Cronon, and Richard White have effectively demonstrated, most seemingly "natural" spaces are "built" environments, just as cities are.[43] Radical though the notion may seem to those engulfed in a haze of romantic rural-centric notions about natural spaces and deep-rooted attachments—or entrenched in equally romantic notions of the modern, high-density city center—there is sense of place in suburbia, too.[44] Scholars need to recognize as much if their explorations of identity in the West are to truly go beyond the realm of myth to represent the full demographic and geographic realities of the region.

However, while acknowledging the limitations of western frontier mythology, we should recognize that the realm of myth nonetheless occupies a deserved place in scholarly explorations of western regionalism. The promoters and reminiscers who imagined and remembered western promised lands from the Civil War to the Great Depression were an influential coterie of honest dreamers and unscrupulous schemers who left their mark on the West itself and on popular assumptions about the place. In addition to emphasizing the dynamism of western regions and the demographic reality of a heavily metropolitanized West, examinations of western sense of place should certainly consider that people have long been drawn to the West as a land of promise. Furthermore, the strength of such promises of the West as a new Eden, regardless of their accuracy, has been a constant factor in the formation of regional identity. Indeed, there is evidence to suggest that the theme of the West as Eden has been attractive to (and may even have played a role in shaping the regional identities of) people of color as well as members of the white, Euro-American majority.[45] Regional identity, it is worth emphasizing, is not just shaped by promises fulfilled; it is affected by broken promises and unfulfilled dreams, too.

To understand regional identity in western places, we have to keep frontier memories and misconceptions—the "West of the Imagination," as historian William Goetzmann calls it—within the frame of analysis.[46] We have to allow that a group's or an individual's sense of place, while it may at times seem to be constructed upon a flimsy foundation of myth and misunderstanding, is deeply meaningful to its possessor/s and continues to influence action. When myth is acted upon, it ends up becoming a very real and tangible force. However, such myth-laden notions of true western identities rooted only in the land and landscapes, in the wide-open spaces, and mired in a strange state of benign cultural stasis, resistant to change and development, do little to help us understand the full range of genius loci in the increasingly diverse, metropolitan, and mobile contemporary West.

To go beyond that mythology, to examine sense of place in the West's many locales, necessitates the opening of a number of scholarly avenues of investigation. There is, for example, a need for broader notions of what constitutes a literary expression of westernness. Such notions need to include urban writing and the writings of peoples of color as "western" writing.[47] Furthermore, we need to explore nonliterary expressions of sense of place in urban spaces as readily as we turn to rural communities for such materials. The letters and diaries of urban westerners, outlining their reactions to and processes of adjustment to places, will require our attention, just as the letters of homesteaders have.

Perhaps scholars will have to abandon "westernness" entirely as a thematic construct, since it so thoroughly mirrors popular notions about a region that apply only to a portion of its residents. If these popular perceptions of the West and its special promise are largely Eurocentric creations, the mythology of a particular group seeking to explain its past actions and justify its present position of dominance, then can other people buy into the myth and "become western"? Has the reality of the West's tremendous racial and ethnic diversity started to alter popular notions of what it is to "be" western? Or have white, mainstream, Eurocentric images of the West prevailed and remained largely unchanged, even as they have become increasingly unreflective of the region's demographic realities? Difficult questions abound. One can only hope that popular perceptions of what it is to be western are broadened to reflect current (and historical) metropolitan and demographic realities—realities that have been more fully illuminated by historical scholarship in the last two decades. If this does not occur, the concept of westernness will have little value for scholars, though it will, unfortunately, retain its usefulness for those westerners seeking to assert their presumed primacy and authenticity in opposition to change.

In the meantime, scholarly investigations of sense of place in the West ought to consider the full weight of the legacies of promotion and memory. Understanding the legacies of the boosters and pioneer recollectors, who helped shape the cultural composition and the heritage of western places, helps us comprehend the enormous task involved either in moving beyond westernness altogether or in restructuring popular perceptions of the West to better represent the cultural complexities of the region. While acknowledging the exaggerations and the omissions inherent in both the promoters' promises and the reminiscers' selective memories, we must also recognize that our postmodern "incredulity toward [such] metanarratives" in search of identity, meaning, and closure (to use Jean-François Lyotard's phrase) should not preclude the repositioning of the value of these discourses within our historiographical frameworks for the West.[48]

Thinking about the ghosts of western future and past, it is not hard to be reminded of Charles Dickens's A Christmas Carol (1843) and how the presence of these specters proved vital to Scrooge's reawakening. There are no easy lessons to be learned from the past—no simple morals of the kind illuminated in Dickens's famous tale—and a fuller understanding of western promotion and memory holds no sure promise for satisfactory resolution of the complex problems facing the West today. Still, there are times when these earlier articulators of western prospects and pasts can serve as mirrors of contemporary trends. Seeing how our actions and attitudes in the present reflect those of the past at least helps us think more carefully about the claims we make on the "true" spirit of western places. We continue to hold onto our own selectively remembered mythic visions of western pasts, just as we continue to construct visions of western futures, and these contemporary creations are often no less fantastic than those of earlier pioneers and promoters. The promotional and reminiscence genres were vital to the actual creation of western places and to the creation of a mythic West. If we are to move beyond, or fully come to terms with, the constricting parameters of that mythic West, we will need to arrive at a fuller understanding of its creators and sustainers and their powerful legacies.

NOTES

Introduction: Imagining and Remembering

1. A. G. Brackett, "Wyoming Territory," *Western Monthly* 2 (September 1869), 169–173, quotation on 173.

2. This is the same area that Walter Nugent focuses on in *Into the West: The Story of Its People* (New York: Knopf, 1999), 7. There is occasional mention of Alaskan boosterism and reminiscences, but no mention of Hawaiian sources. Hawaii may or may not be a part of the West; it is clearly not a part of the processes of promotion and remembrance explored here.

3. The anxieties of this cultural moment have been memorably explored by T. Jackson Lears in his classic study *No Place of Grace: Antimodernism and the Transformation of American Culture, 1880–1920* (New York: Pantheon, 1981). For more on the cultural anxieties of the post–World War I era that accompanied the transition to a modern America, see Roderick Nash, *The Nervous Generation: American Thought, 1917–1930* (New York: Ivan R. Dee, 1990).

4. I do not examine all these kinds of promotional writing, but they certainly warrant further scholarly attention. Gunther Peck's important recent book, *Reinventing Free Labor: Padrones and Immigrant Workers in the North American West, 1880–1930* (New York: Cambridge University Press, 2000), provides coverage of the promotional efforts to attract workers from Greece, Italy, and Mexico to the United States and Canada.

5. Sometimes the railroads sponsored and distributed the state-, territory-, and county-level publications.

6. Clarence A. Lyman, comp., *The Fertile Lands of Colorado and Northern New Mexico: A Concise Description of the Vast Area of Agricultural, Horticultural and Grazing Lands Located on the Line of the Denver and Rio Grande Railroad in the State of Colorado and the Territory of New Mexico. Full Information for Intending Settlers as to Lands Now Open for Entry, or Offered for Sale, and as to the Present Day Opportunities in Fruit Growing, Market Gardening, Stock Raising, Sugar Beets and General Farming*, 9th ed. (Denver: Passenger Department, Denver and Rio Grande Railroad, 1908), Western History Department of the Denver Public Library (hereafter DPL) C630.9788D43FE9.

7. This study focuses largely on the promotional materials intended for distribution in the United States.

8. Jonathan Raban provides good coverage of the distribution of the promotional literature in *Bad Land: An American Romance* (New York: Pantheon, 1996), 26–34,

and in "The Unlamented West," *New Yorker,* May 20, 1996, 60–81, esp. 62–63. See also Patricia Nelson Limerick's critique of Raban's book, "In the Bad Lands: Where the Oats Don't Grow to Perfection," *Times Literary Supplement,* February 28, 1997, 11–12.

9. On occasion, the two separate genres of boosting and reminiscence were joined in a single volume; see, for example, Isaac O. Savage, *A History of Republic County, Kansas* (Beloit, Kans.: Jones and Chubbi, Art Printers, 1901), Rare Book Collection, Henry E. Huntington Library, San Marino, California (hereafter HEH RB), 127727. Savage's book contains both promotional rhetoric and praise for the old pioneers, along with a selection of their recollections. For the most part, though, the genres of promotional writing and reminiscence were quite separate in the late nineteenth and early twentieth centuries.

10. John Mack Faragher provides an excellent discussion of Boone as land surveyor, speculator, and promoter; see *Daniel Boone: The Life and Legend of an American Pioneer* (New York: Henry Holt, 1992). Doyle provides excellent coverage of the promotional efforts for a midwestern town in his chapter "The Booster Ethos," in *The Social Order of a Frontier Community: Jacksonville, Illinois, 1825–1870* (Urbana: University of Illinois Press, 1978), 62–91. For more on early examples of town boosterism on the western frontier, see Richard Lingeman, *Small Town America: A Narrative History, 1620–The Present* (New York: Putnam's, 1980).

11. See, for example, John Farrer, "A Mappe of Virginia," in Gerald A. Danzer, *Discovering American History Through Maps and Views* (New York: HarperCollins, 1991), S5. For more on the land advertisements, see Stephen V. Ward's chapter "Selling the Frontier," in his *Selling Places: The Marketing and Promotion of Towns and Cities, 1850–2000* (New York: Routledge, 1998), 9–28.

12. Peter Boag examines the promotion of Oregon in the mid–nineteenth century in his *Environment and Experience: Settlement Culture in Nineteenth-Century Oregon* (Berkeley and Los Angeles: University of California Press, 1992), especially 146–61; see also William Robbins, *Landscapes of Promise: The Oregon Story, 1800–1940* (Seattle: University of Washington Press, 1997), especially part II, "Settler Occupation and the Advent of Industrialism, 1850–1890," 81–175. The boosterism behind the California gold rush is discussed by J. S. Holliday in *Rush for Riches: Gold Fever and the Making of California* (Berkeley and Los Angeles: Oakland Museum of California and University of California Press, 1999); and by Peter J. Blodgett in *Land of Golden Dreams: California in the Gold Rush Decade, 1848–1858* (San Marino, Calif.: Huntington Library Press, 1999). For the promotional efforts that accompanied the Colorado gold rush, see Elliott West, *The Contested Plains: Indians, Goldseekers, and the Rush to Colorado* (Lawrence: University Press of Kansas, 1998), 122–129.

13. For Chicago boosterism, see William Cronon, "Dreaming the Metropolis," in *Nature's Metropolis: Chicago and the Great West* (New York: Norton, 1991), 23–54. Another useful source on urban boosterism is Carl Abbott, *Boosters and Businessmen: Popular Economic Thought and Urban Growth in the Antebellum Middle West* (Westport, Conn.: Greenwood Press, 1981).

14. See, for example, W. H. Mitchell, *Dakota County [Minnesota]: Its Past and Present, Geographical, Statistical and Historical, Together with a General View of the State* (Minneapolis, Minn.: Tribune Printing Co., 1868).

15. For more on intellectuals' perceptions of the transition from a frontier to a postfrontier America, see David M. Wrobel, *The End of American Exceptionalism: Frontier Anxiety from the Old West to the New Deal* (Lawrence: University Press of Kansas, 1993). For more on the broader transition from a premodern to a modern America, see Robert Wiebe's seminal work *The Search for Order, 1877–1920* (New York: Hill and Wang, 1967); and Alan Trachtenberg's *The Incorporation of America: Culture and Society in the Gilded Age* (New York: Hill and Wang, 1992).

16. Richard White, in his excellent and wide-ranging study *"It's Your Misfortune and None of My Own": A New History of the American West* (Norman: University of Oklahoma Press, 1991), dismisses western boosters a little too easily, noting that they "sought to make towns grow for a simple reason: they wanted to make lots of money" (417).

17. Daniel Boorstin, *The Americans: The National Experience* (New York: Random House, 1965), 296–297.

18. Gene M. Gressley, *West by East: The American West in the Gilded Age*, Charles Redd Monographs in Western History (Provo, Utah: Brigham Young University Press, 1972), 36. In a similar vein, Wallace Stegner said of boosters, "many . . . have been deluded deluders, true believers, wishful thinkers, blindfold prophets"; see his essay "A Geography of Hope," in *A Society to Match the Scenery: Personal Visions of the Future of the American West*, ed. Gary Holthaus, Patricia Nelson Limerick, Charles F. Wilkinson, and Eve Stryker Munson (Niwot: University Press of Colorado, 1991), 218–229, quotation on 223.

19. Richard J. Orsi provides very thorough coverage of California boosters' efforts to counter the criticisms of easterners in "Selling the Golden State: A Study of Boosterism in Nineteenth-Century California" (Ph.D. diss., University of Wisconsin, 1973), 1–38.

20. The list draws on and adds to the categories listed in David M. Emmons, *Garden in the Grasslands: Boomer Literature of the Central Great Plains* (Lincoln: University of Nebraska Press, 1971); and Jan Blodgett, *Land of Bright Promise: Advertising the Texas Panhandle and South Plains, 1870–1917* (Austin: University of Texas Press, 1988).

21. Another instructive example of the booster phenomenon in a literary work that blurs the borders between fiction and nonfiction is O. E. Rolvaag's *Giants in the Earth: A Saga of the Prairie* (New York: Harper and Brothers, 1927), which is closely based on immigrant accounts. For a good discussion of Rolvaag's classic work in this context, see Lingeman, *Small Town America*, 242–245.

22. This study focuses largely on the promotional books, brochures, and maps produced by independent writers, chambers of commerce, and the railroads rather than on the newspaper editors. Those editors, however, are tremendously important, and their articles and editorials surely played a role in shaping the identities of western places. Nonetheless, their newspapers were primarily a vehicle for bringing

news of the outside world to a particular place (and for transmitting local news), rather than one for bringing news of the place to the world outside. The promotional books, brochures, and maps generally had a much wider circulation and were intended primarily for an outside readership rather than a resident readership. For more on the West's early newspaper editors, see David Fridtjof Halaas, *Boom Town Newspapers: Journalism on the Rocky Mountain Mining Frontier, 1859–1881* (Albuquerque: University of New Mexico Press, 1981), esp. chap. 6, "Crusaders for Permanency," 87–99; and Eugene P. Moehring, "'Promoting the Varied Interests of the New and Rising Community': The Booster Press on Nevada's Mining Frontier, 1859–1885," *Nevada Historical Society Quarterly* 42 (summer 1999): 91–118. For a good discussion of the role of a booster-editor in the early twentieth century, see Sally Forman Griffith's chapter "Booster Progressivism," in *Home Town News: William Allen White and the* Emporia Gazette (New York: Oxford University Press, 1989), 113–138.

23. The connection between promotional efforts and rates of settlement is discussed in Ray Allen Billington and Martin Ridge, *Westward Expansion: A History of the American Frontier,* 6th ed., abridged (Albuquerque: University of New Mexico Press, 2001), 358–359.

24. In an old but particularly interesting discussion of these issues, Merle Curti and Kendall Birr pointed to the close relationship between immigration levels from various countries and the amount of money sent to those countries from emigrants working in America; see "The Immigrant and the American Image in Europe, 1860–1914," *Mississippi Valley Historical Review* 37 (September 1950): 203–230, esp. 217–218.

25. For a good discussion of why new western residents stretched the truth in their optimistic representations of their places to friends and family, see Nugent, *Into the West,* 190. He writes: "Migrants . . . trusted their friends and relatives on the scene. The letters did not intend to deceive; the homesteaders who wrote them believed that things were working out, or soon would. . . . They were very often young, optimistic, eager, putting the best face on things, not yet desiccated in both property and personality by lack of rainfall, not yet tempered by failure. . . . Little wonder that they wrote home with enthusiasm. Little wonder that those back home believed them."

26. Emmons's *Garden in the Grasslands* and Blodgett's *Land of Bright Promise* are among the more important works on western boosting. Emmons is more critical of the booster genre than Blodgett, who emphasizes that "the majority of the deceptions that occurred on the [Texas] Plains resulted more from misguided enthusiasm than from malicious intent" (101). Richard O'Connor emphasizes the gap between the rhetoric of the railroad boosters and the realities of farming on the Montana plains in *Iron Wheels and Broken Men: The Railroad Barons and the Plunder of the West* (New York: Putnam's, 1973), 309–335. For a more measured assessment of railroad promotion, see Robert G. Athearn's coverage of Union Pacific promotional endeavors in his *Union Pacific Country* (Lincoln: University of Nebraska Press, 1982), esp. chap. 8, "The Garden of the West," and chap. 9, "Beyond the Magic Meridian," 147–171 and 173–197, respectively; and John C. Hudson's chapter "Townsite Specula-

tors" in his *Plains Country Towns* (Minneapolis: University of Minnesota Press, 1985), 41–50. Hudson notes of the fictional Colonel Sellers that his "weakness . . . was his own inability to distinguish truth from fiction" (47). This was surely the case for many western promoters, who were at times so heavily invested in their own rhetoric as to believe it.

27. For an example of this dualistic approach, see William Robbins, *Colony and Empire: The Capitalist Transformation of the American West* (Lawrence: University Press of Kansas, 1994), esp. chap. 4, "In Pursuit of Private Gain: The West as Investment Arena," 61–82, and his brief discussion of Great Plains promotion on pp. 71–72.

28. This nonteleological approach was attempted by John Steinbeck in his novels *In Dubious Battle* (New York: Covici-Freide, 1936) and *The Grapes of Wrath* (New York: Viking, 1939) and achieved most successfully in *Cannery Row* (New York: Viking, 1945). The approach focuses on what "is," rather than on what could be, should be, or might be. This approach eschews the process of passing judgment, emphasizing instead the complexities of human action and interaction, which underscore the dangers inherent in making assumptions about causal relationships.

29. For more on this theme, see Ellen von Nardroff, "The American Frontier as a Safety Valve: The Life, Death, Reincarnation, and Justification of a Theory," *Agricultural History* 36 (July 1962): 123–142.

30. Raban writes that "the homesteaders who survived the nineteen-twenties found that their attachment to the land had grown beyond reason, as love does." He also suggests that they reproached themselves for their faith in the images of western promised lands, rather than reproaching the railroads for creating the gap between their expectations and the actual outcomes they experienced; see "The Unlamented West," 75.

31. James Blaine Hedges discusses the relationship between the railroads and state boards of immigration in "The Colonization Work of the Northern Pacific Railroad," *Mississippi Valley Historical Review* 13 (December 1926): 311–342, esp. 341, as does John D. Hicks in *The Populist Revolt: A History of the Farmer's Alliance and the People's Party* (Minneapolis: University of Minnesota Press, 1931; reprint, Lincoln: University of Nebraska Press, 1961), 6, 17. For brief, but useful coverage of the relationship between Grand Junction, Colorado, and the Denver and Rio Grande Railway, see Kathleen Underwood, *Town Building on the Colorado Frontier* (Albuquerque: University of New Mexico Press, 1987), 23–27. For a more detailed (and similarly balanced) overview of the role of the railroads in promoting Colorado, see "The Era of the Booster, 1863–1876," in Carl Abbott, Stephen J. Leonard, and David McComb, *Colorado: A History of the Centennial State, rev. ed.* (Boulder: Colorado Associated University Press, 1982), 70–91.

32. Patricia Nelson Limerick uses the phrases "actors" and "acted upon" in her chapter "The Persistence of Natives," in *The Legacy of Conquest: The Unbroken Past of the American West* (New York: Norton, 1987), 180.

33. For more on the theme of the West as a construction of outside forces, see David M. Emmons, "Constructed Province: History and the Making of the Last

American West," *Western Historical Quarterly* 25 (1994): 437–459; see also "A Roundtable of Responses" to Emmons's article in the same volume, 461–486.

34. There is far less scholarly work focused specifically on pioneer reminiscences than there is on boosters. Among the more notable examples are Clyde A. Milner II's "The View from Wisdom: Four Layers of Regional Identity," in *Under an Open Sky: Rethinking America's Western Past*, ed. William Cronon, George Miles, and Jay Gitlin (New York: Norton, 1992), 203–222; the essay appeared earlier under the title "The View from Wisdom: Region and Identity in the Minds of Four Western-ers," *Montana: The Magazine of Western History* 41 (summer 1991): 2–17; and Milner's essay "The Shared Memory of Montana Pioneers," *Montana: The Magazine of Western History* 37 (winter 1987): 2–13. Also useful are Barbara Allen's "Histori-cal Commentary: Landscape, Memory, and the Western Past," *Montana: The Maga-zine of Western History* 39 (winter 1989): 71–75; and William Howarth's "The Okies: Beyond the Dust Bowl," *National Geographic* 166 (September 1984): 327–349.

35. See, for example, Richard Etulain, *Re-imagining the Modern American West: A Century of Fiction, History, and Art* (Tucson: University of Arizona Press, 1996); and David Murdoch, *The American West: The Invention of a Myth* (Reno: Univer-sity of Nevada Press, 2001); Richard White, "Frederick Jackson Turner and Buffalo Bill," in *The Frontier in American Culture: Essays by Richard White and Patricia Nelson Limerick*, ed. James Grossman (Berkeley and Los Angeles: University of California Press, 1994), 7–65. Emmons discusses the role of western mythmakers in "Constructed Province."

36. Quotations are from David Thelen, "Introduction," in his edited collection *Memory and American History* (Bloomington: Indiana University Press, 1990), vii–xix, vii, xi, xiii. Thelen provides a good introduction to the work of psychologists on memory. There is a rich historical literature on memory. Included among the more useful works are Natalie Zemon Davis and Randolph Starn, "Introduction" to the "Forum on Memory," *Representations* 26 (spring 1989): 1–6; Michael Kammen, *Mystic Chords of Memory: The Transformation of Tradition in American Culture* (New York: Knopf, 1991); John Bodnar, *Remaking America: Public Memory, Com-memoration, and Patriotism in the Twentieth Century* (Princeton, N.J.: Princeton University Press, 1992); M. Christine Boyer, *The City of Collective Memory: Its His-torical Imagery and Architectural Entertainments* (Cambridge, Mass.: MIT Press, 1994); and Alan Confino, ed., "Forum: Collective Memory and Cultural History: Problems of Method," *American Historical Review* 102 (December 1997): 1386–1403.

37. Milner, "The View from Wisdom," 213.

38. Kammen, *Mystic Chords of Memory*, 9.

39. Thelen, "Introduction," xv.

40. John Walton, *Storied Land: Community and Memory in Monterey* (Berkeley and Los Angeles: University of California Press, 2001), 289–295, quotation on 291.

41. Ibid., 295–303. Also useful with respect to the theme of memory and identity formation is Benedict Anderson, *Imagined Communities: Reflections on the Origin and Spread of Nationalism*, rev. ed. (London: Verso, 1991).

42. There is, for example, an impressive body of scholarship on the role of boosters in the establishment of social and cultural institutions in midwestern towns—including Doyle's *The Social Order of a Frontier Community;* Timothy R. Mahoney's *Provincial Lives: Middle-Class Experience in the Antebellum Middle West* (New York: Cambridge University Press, 1999); and Griffith's "Booster Progressivism"—but the present study largely avoids the boosters' role in the structuring of western towns, emphasizing instead the nature of their representations of those places.

43. Some parts of the West receive more attention than others in this study, though I have taken care to avoid making generalized claims for the whole West that do not apply equally to its various subregions.

44. The most popular recent work addressing western boosterism is Raban's, *Bad Land,* which deals with the tragedies of settlement in eastern Montana. More grounded in historical research are Barbara Allen's *Homesteading the High Desert* (Salt Lake City: University of Utah Press, 1987); and Paula M. Nelson's *After the West Was Won: Homesteaders and Town-Builders in Western South Dakota, 1900–1917* (Iowa City: University of Iowa Press, 1986). For boosting in western Canada, see David C. Jones, *Feasting on Misfortune: Journeys of the Human Spirit in Alberta's Past* (Edmonton: University of Alberta Press, 1998), esp. 81–116; and John W. Bennett and Seena B. Kohl, *Settling the Canadian-American West, 1890–1915: Pioneer Adaptation and Community Building: An Anthropological History* (Lincoln: University of Nebraska Press, 1995), esp. 159–169. Useful analyses of booster literature include G. Malcolm Lewis, "Rhetoric of the Western Interior: Modes of Environmental Description in American Promotional Literature of the Nineteenth Century," in *The Iconography of Landscape,* ed. Denis Cosgrove and Stephen Daniels (New York: Cambridge University Press, 1988), 179–193; Arthur J. Brown, "The Promotion of Emigration to Washington, 1854–1909," *Pacific Northwest Quarterly* 36 (1945): 3–17; Richard Maxwell Brown, "Rainfall and History: Perspectives on the Pacific Northwest," in *Experiences in a Promised Land: Essays in Pacific Northwest History,* ed. G. Thomas Edwards and Carlos A. Schwantes (Seattle: University of Washington Press, 1986), 13–27; Allan G. Bogue's wide-ranging chapter, "An Agricultural Empire," in *The Oxford History of the American West,* ed. Clyde A. Milner II, Carol A. O'Connor, and Martha A. Sandweiss (New York: Oxford University Press, 1994), 274–313, and Hicks's chapter "The Frontier Background," in *The Populist Revolt,* 1–35. Henry Nash Smith's *Virgin Land: The American West as Symbol and Myth* (Cambridge, Mass.: Harvard University Press, 1970) is also useful for understanding the booster mentality.

1. Promotional Contours and Claims

1. Chicago, Burlington and Quincy Raliroad, *The Heart of the Continent: An Historical and Descriptive Treatise for Business Men, Home Seekers and Tourists, of the Advantages, Resources and Scenery of the Great West* (Chicago: Buffalo, Clay and Richmond, printers, for the Chicago, Burlington and Quincy Railroad, 1882), 9, HEH RB 253034.

2. I use the term "booster" quite broadly to encompass the various individuals, groups, and companies or corporations involved in activities designed to promote western settlement, whether in agricultural regions, towns, or larger urban settings. Occasionally scholars have used the terms "boomer" and "booster" interchangeably. The former term, though, is more often applied to settlers who by the 1880s were camped in the vicinity of Indian Lands in the Oklahoma Territory, waiting for those lands to be opened to homesteading by the federal government.

3. Union Pacific Railroad, "The Union Pacific and Utah and Northern Through Rail Route to Montana and Yellowstone Park," in the Western History Department of the Denver Public Library (hereafter DPL), Broadside (hereafter B), C385.0978 U 57un; Northern Pacific Railroad Company, "Sectional Map Showing the Lands of the Northern Pacific Railroad Co., in Eastern Washington and Northern Idaho, with Condensed Information Relating to the Northern Pacific Country" (1886), DPL, Map (hereafter M), CG4242.G4 1886.N6; "Map Showing the Land Grant of the North- ern Pacific Railroad Company, in Montana, Idaho and in Part of North Dakota and in Part of Eastern Washington" (1890), DPL, M, CG4242.P3 1890.N6; and Cana- dian Pacific Railway, "The Golden Northwest: A Home for All People" (1884), DPL, B, C338.0971 C16go.

4. By 1890 Nebraska's population had passed the 1 million mark, and the con- struction of railroads, most notably the Union Pacific and CB&Q accounted for the bulk of the growth. For more on the topic, see Robert G. Athearn, *High Country Empire: The High Plains and Rockies* (New York: McGraw-Hill, 1960), 170.

5. Chicago, Burlington and Quincy Railroad, *The Heart of the Continent*, 25. This tactic of creating comparative population density figures for states was common among booster writers. See, for example, Robert Edmund Strahorn, for the Union Pacific Railroad, *Oregon: A Complete and Comprehensive Description of the Agri- cultural, Stockraising, and Mineral Resources of Oregon; Also Statistics in Regard to Its Climate, etc., Compiled from the Very Latest Reports of 1888,* 2d ed., revised (Chicago: Rand McNally and Co., Printers, 1889), 7. Strahorn writes that Oregon's population in 1888 was only 300,000, but "were it as closely settled as Switzerland, it would have 12,000,000 people; as France, about 17,000,000; as Holland, about 25,000,000; or, as England, at least 40,000,000." Strahorn was quick to add that in its proportion of "productive to waste land, it will compare well with the average of the foreign countries named."

6. *Census Bureau Statistics,* 2000 Census, www.census.gov. The population of the state as recorded in the 1990 Census was 1,578,385. The estimated population of the state in 1994 was 1,623,000; see James C. Olson and Ronald C. Naugle, *History of Nebraska,* 3d ed. (Lincoln: University of Nebraska Press, 1997), 157. So Nebraska has seen some population growth in the 1990s, though the rate has been very low.

7. Chicago, Burlington and Quincy Railroad, *The Heart of the Continent,* 25. For more on the declining population of Plains farming communities, see Dayton Duncan, *Miles from Nowhere: Tales from America's Contemporary Frontier* (New York: Viking, 1993), particularly the section on rural Nebraska's reaction to Frank and Deborah Popper's "Buffalo Commons" "predictions," 268–278. There were certainly

racial underpinnings to such assertions concerning the impact of environment on human development, and they were made by boosters for all parts of the West (as we will see in chapter 5).

8. Chicago, Burlington and Quincy Railroad, *The Heart of the Continent,* 27.

9. Ibid., 29–30, 32.

10. See Robert G. Athearn, "The Selling of Colorado," in *The Coloradans* (Albuquerque: University of New Mexico Press, 1976), 87–105. For more on "health-seeking," see Billy M. Jones, *Health-Seekers in the Southwest, 1817–1900* (Norman: University of Oklahoma Press, 1967). A good example of health-centered booster literature is Rinaldo M. Hall, *Beautiful Recreation Resorts of the Pacific Northwest: Where They Are and How to Reach Them. A Brief Description of the Trips Up and Down the Columbia River, to the Mountains, Beaches, Inland Resorts, and Fountains of Healing* (Portland, Ore.: General Passenger Department of the Oregon Railroad and Navigation Company, 1905).

11. Chicago, Burlington and Quincy Railroad, *The Heart of the Continent,* 36. It is worth mentioning that the notion of the western lands acting as a safety valve for social discontent in the East had been articulated with great regularity in the decades prior to Frederick Jackson Turner's presentation of the idea in his 1893 essay "The Significance of the Frontier in American History"; for more on this, see David M. Wrobel, *The End of American Exceptionalism: Frontier Anxiety from the Old West to the New Deal* (Lawrence: University Press of Kansas, 1993), 13–25.

12. Milton B. Oohs, for the Denver, Rio Grande and Western Railway, *The Heart of the Rockies* (Cincinnati, Ohio: J. H. Bennett, Press of the A. H. Pugh Printing Co., 1890), n.p. For more on the DRG&W, see Robert Athearn, *Rebel of the Rockies: A History of the Denver, Rio Grande and Western Railroad* (New Haven, Conn.: Yale University Press, 1962). Athearn notes that the DRG&W acronym was used as a negative descriptor for the railroad—"the dangerous and rapidly growing worse."

13. Such claims were present in western promotional literature from an early date. For example, Washington Territory promoter Elwood Evans proclaimed in 1869 that it was "sympathy with humanity crushed to earth in less favored portions of this earth" that prompted him and other boosters to extol the virtues of the region; see Evans, *Puget Sound: Its Past, Present and Future* (Olympia, Washington Territory, 1869), quoted in Arthur J. Brown, "The Promotion of Emigration to Washington, 1854–1900," *Pacific Northwest Quarterly* 36 (January 1945): 3–17, quotation on 5. There is nothing unusual in the professed altruistic intentions of railroad promoters in the late nineteenth century. They differ little from the claims of contemporary car, tire, or brake manufacturers who claim their primary concern is not mere sales but selling public safety.

14. Included among the most notable discussions of railroad booster literature are Carlos Schwantes's categorization of the genre into two broad categories: "The First Railway Age, 1868–1893," and "The Second Railway Age, 1897–1917," in his *Railroad Signatures Across the Pacific Northwest* (Seattle: University of Washington Press, 1993); Schwantes, "Landscapes of Opportunity: Phases of Railroad Promotion of the Pacific Northwest," *Montana: The Magazine of Western History* 43 (spring

1993): 38–51; James Blaine Hedges, "Promotion of Immigration to the Pacific North-
west by the Railroads," *Mississippi Valley Historical Review* 15 (September 1928):
183–203; Hedges, *Henry Villard and the Railways of the Northwest* (New Haven,
Conn.: Yale University Press, 1930); Steven F. Mehls, "Garden in the Grassland
Revisited: Railroad Promotional Efforts and the Settlement of the Texas Plains," *West
Texas Historical Association Yearbook* 55 (1984): 47–66; Richard C. Overton,
Burlington West: A Colonization History of the Burlington Railroad (Cambridge,
Mass.: Harvard University Press, 1941); Robert G. Athearn, *Union Pacific Country*
(Lincoln: University of Nebraska Press, 1982); Richard O'Connor, *Iron Wheels and
Broken Men: The Railroad Barons and the Plunder of the West* (New York: Putnam's,
1973); Merle Curti and Kendall Birr, "The Immigrant and the American Image in
Europe, 1860–1914," *Mississippi Valley Historical Review* 37 (September 1950):
203–230; Edna Monch Parker, "The Southern Pacific Railroad and Settlement in
California," *Pacific Historical Review* 6 (1937): 103–119; Mildred Throne, "Suggested
Research on Railroad Aid to the Farmer, with Particular Reference to Iowa and
Kansas," *Agricultural History* 31 (October 1957): 50–56; Stanley N. Murray, "Rail-
roads and the Agricultural Development of the Red River of the North," *Agricultural
History* 31 (October 1957): 57–66; William S. Greever, *Arid Domain: The Santa Fe
Railway and Its Western Land Grant* (Stanford, Calif.: Stanford University Press,
1954); Greever, "A Comparison of Railroad Land-Grant Policies," *Agricultural His-
tory* 25 (April 1951): 83–90; and David Maldwyn Ellis, "The Forfeiture of Railroad
Land Grants, 1867–1894," *Mississippi Valley Historical Review* 33 (June 1946): 27–
60. Railroad booster magazines include the *Northwest Magazine* (published in Min-
nesota, 1883–1903, under the auspices of the Northern Pacific Railroad) and *Sunset
Magazine* (published in San Francisco, 1898–1912, an organ of the Southern Pacific
Railroad).

15. Anon., "Yuma, Colorado" (1889), DPL, B, C978.878 Y91, 1889; Anon., "Yuma,
Colorado" (1889), DPL , VF B, C978.878 Y91.

16. See, for example, *Report of Rain-Fall in Washington Territory, Oregon, California, Idaho, Nevada, Utah, Arizona, Colorado, Wyoming, New Mexico, Indian
Territory, and Texas for from Two to Forty Years*, 50th Cong., 1st sess., Executive
Documents 91, 282 (Washington, D.C.: Government Printing Office, 1889), HEH
RB 499799. This report from the secretary of war relaying to Congress the findings
of the chief signal officer provides extensive rainfall maps and charts and, in its written
text, reflects the general optimism of the official reporters of rainfall in the semiarid
West. The report was to some degree inconclusive, and it certainly did not deny that
the West, aside from the Pacific Northwest, was semiarid (Montana, Nebraska, and
the Dakotas were not included in the report). However, the report literally seemed
to show the semiarid lands of the West shrinking to an almost insignificant size. The
chief signal officer, A. W. Greely, argued that John Wesley Powell's pronouncements
as director of the Geological Survey concerning the classifiability of western lands
with less than twenty inches of annual rainfall as "arid" had been "unintentionally
overstated." Greely declared that "the point at which a region may be classed as arid
and unfit for successful irrigation should be lowered, it is believed, to 15 inches"

(8). In Greely's report boosters had official backing for their optimistic claims; with a little creativity they could even view the report as evidence that rain was following the plow. Indeed, the report noted that "breaking up the Plains' sod creates moisture." The report could also be used in support of state-controlled irrigation initiatives. A useful summary annotation for the volume accompanies HEH RB 499799.

17. There were earlier examples of irrigation in Anaheim, California, in the 1850s and in Greeley, Colorado, in the 1870s; see Walter Nugent, *Into the West: The Story of Its People* (New York: Knopf, 1999), 108–112, esp. 110.

18. See, for example, Strahorn, *Oregon*, 18; Robert Edmund Strahorn, *The Resources and Attractions of Washington Territory: A Complete and Comprehensive Description of the Agricultural, Stockraising, and Mineral Resources of Washington; Also Statistics in Regard to Its Climate, etc., Compiled from the Very Latest Reports of 1888*, 2d ed., revised and enlarged (Chicago: Rand McNally, and Co., Printers, 1889), 32, HEH RB 78719; Strahorn, *The Resources and Attractions of Idaho Territory: Facts Regarding: Climate, Soil, Minerals, Agricultural and Grazing Lands, Forests, Scenery, Game and Fish, and Reliable Information on All Other Topics Applicable to the Wants of the Homeseeker, Capitalist, and Tourist* (Boise City: Idaho Legislature, 1881), 65, HEH RB 376120; and Colorado Consolidated Land and Water Company, *The Montezuma Valley in Colorado: A Description of Its Location, Scenery, Climate, Antiquities, Irrigating Works, Resources and Advantages* (Cortez, Colo.: Colorado Consolidated Land and Water Company, 1890), 29–35. The quotation concerning the Nile Valley is from *The Resources and Attractions of Idaho Territory*, 65.

19. E. S. Glover, *Corinne and the Bear River Valley, Utah Territory, 1875: Location, Climate, Agricultural and Commercial Advantages, Unsurpassed for Actual Settlers and Colonization Enterprises* (Cincinnati, Ohio: Strobridge and Co., Lithographers, 1875), text on irrigation on back side of foldout map, HEH RB 45811, M. Another useful early text on irrigation is Henry Stewart, *Irrigation for the Farm, Garden, and Orchard* (New York: Orange Judd Company, 1877).

20. *The Pecos Valley: The Fruit Valley of New Mexico* ([Eddy, N.M.], [1892]), HEH RB 382361, 5–6. Interestingly, the publication also drew, as promoters were wont to do on occasion, on an aquatic metaphor to capture the magnitude of this frontier moment, noting that "opportunities like those offered in the Pecos Valley do not present themselves with every new moon; therefore it may be wise to take the tide at its flood and let it lead you on to fortune" (45). Readers may be reminded of Frederick Jackson Turner's rather vague, but memorable notion of the frontier as "the outer edge of the wave"; see "The Significance of the Frontier in American History," in *The Frontier in American History* (New York: Henry Holt and Company, 1920), 1–38.

21. Turner, "The Significance of the Frontier in American History."

22. The frontier-centered rhetoric of western boosters a century ago was the counterpart to the contemporary emphasis among realtors in all regions today on "location, location, location." Yet lines between good locations and poorer locations were not so easy to delineate in a fast-developing western landscape where even deserts could be sold as promised lands.

23. See Barbara Allen, *Homesteading the High Desert* (Salt Lake City: University of Utah Press, 1987), 121–126.

24. John W. Barber and Henry Howe, *Barber's History of All the Western States and Territories: From the Alleghanies to the Pacific and from the Lakes to the Gulf* (Cincinnati, Ohio: Howe's Subscription Book Concern, 1867).

25. Henry George, *Our Land and Land Policy: National and State* (San Francisco: White and Bauer, 1871); George, *Progress and Poverty: An Inquiry into the Cause of Industrial Depressions, and of Increase of Want with Increase of Wealth* (1879; New York: D. Appleton and Co., 1884).

26. H. B. Stevens, *Ho, for Southern Dakota! And the Black Hills: Uncle Sam's Farm Is Growing Smaller Everyday* (Chicago: H. B. Stevens, Agent, 1875).

27. In the late 1880s, Yuma, Colorado, boosters invited "the farmer, tradesman, miner, artisan, all who are seeking new fields and relief from the over-crowded walks of eastern life"; see Anon., "Yuma, Colorado" (1889), DPL, B, C978.878 Y91.

28. For more on the theme of the closing of the frontier, see Wrobel, *The End of American Exceptionalism*.

29. Fred J. Cross, *The Free Lands of Dakota: A Description of the Country; the Climate; the Beautiful Valleys, and Ocean-Like Prairies; the Crops, the Land Laws, and the Inducements Offered to Immigrants* (Yankton, Dakota: Bowen and Kingsbury, 1876), 6. See also Stevens, *Ho, for Southern Dakota!* which makes a point of emphasizing that "the colony is already established" and the work of frontier settlement does not have to be undertaken.

30. A. Besom, *Pawnee County, Nebraska: As It Was, and Is to Be* (Atchison, Kans.: Immigrant Union Publishers, 1878), 72.

31. Central Branch of the Union Pacific Railroad Co., map of "Farms and Homes in Kansas" (1879), DPL, B, C333.336, C333far. The settler in this period perhaps desired a mere semblance of the frontier, while the tourist wanted a genuine frontier or wilderness presence, though shorn of real dangers. The word "frontier" appears very rarely in the nomenclature of western places in this period. An interesting anomaly to this trend is Frontier County, Nebraska, the only county in the entire West (indeed, in the entire United States) that took the name. Frontier County (which, notably, had been established in 1872 by cattlemen, not farmers) had a population of 3,099 in 2000 (a drop of two persons from the 1990 population of 3,101), residing on almost a thousand square miles, giving it a density of 3.2 persons per square mile. While not technically a frontier county (according to census geographer Henry Gannett's 1882 definition of fewer than 2 persons per square mile), and while actually denser than 18 of Nebraska's 93 counties, Frontier County has, by most measures, lived up to its name in the present. Having lost more than 40 percent of its population between 1950 and 1990, the county might well meet the technical requirements for frontier status within the next half century. Frontier County was an anomaly, and if the farmers, rather than the cattlemen, had been doing the naming, it surely would have taken a name more conducive to the solicitation of new immigration. See *Census Bureau Statistics,* 1990 Census and 2000 Census, www.census.gov. For more on Frontier County, see W. H. Miles and

John Bratt, *Early History and Reminiscences of Frontier County* (Maywood, Nebr.: N. H. Bogue, 1894); and Olson and Naugle, *History of Nebraska,* 195.

32. Oregon State Board of Immigration, *Oregon As It Is: Solid Facts and Actual Results* (Portland, Ore.: G. W. McCoy Steam Job Printer, 1885), 63. The text of this publication begins with the claim that "this is in no sense a 'boom' edition, save as easily substantiated facts and truth serve to advance the interests of Oregon." It is worth noting that the phrase "as it is" was common in the booster literature and appeared in numerous titles; it was intended as an additional marker of authenticity and reliability.

33. Oregon State Board of Immigration, *The New Empire: Oregon, Washington, Idaho: Its Resources, Climate, Present Development, and Its Advantages as a Place of Residence and a Field for Investment* (Portland, Ore.: F. W. Baltes and Co., Printers, 1889), 4, HEH RB 34577. This same argument had been made for Oregon as early as 1873 by W. L. Adams in *Oregon As It Is: Its Present and Future, by a Resident of Twenty-five Years: Being a Reply to Inquirers* (Portland, Ore.: Bulletin Steam Book and Job Printing Rooms, 1873). It is worth noting that such self-authenticating titles were common in the promotional literature. Adams's book made much of the fact that frontier days were over, that journeying to this Northwestern promised land now involved "little sacrifice of comfort and money" (61), and that Indian dangers had long since passed. For more on early boosters of the Pacific Northwest, see Sidney Warren's chapter "Builders and Boosters," in *Farthest Frontier: The Pacific Northwest* (New York: Macmillan, 1949), 104–117; William G. Robbins's chapters "Technology and Abundance" and "Nature's Industries and the Rhetoric of Industrialism," in *Landscapes of Promise: The Oregon Story, 1800–1940* (Seattle: University of Washington Press, 1997), 110–141 and 179–204, respectively; and Brown, "The Promotion of Emigration to Washington."

34. Beadle County Commissioners, *History of Beadle County, Dakota: Its Resources, Agricultural and Mineral Wealth* (Beadle County, Dakota: County Commissioners, 1889), 45. For more on the early history of European and European-American settlement in this region, see Howard R. Lamar, *Dakota Territory, 1861–1889: A Study of Frontier Politics* (New Haven, Conn.: Yale University Press, 1956).

35. Adams, *Oregon As It Is.* Adams's booklet is filled with claims of honesty and accuracy; even the motivation behind the publication, as evidenced in its subtitle—*Being a Reply to Inquirers*—suggests the author's altruistic motivations. But there was no denying that the publication was sponsored by and distributed by Ferry, Woodward and Company, Real Estate Agents, and their purpose was selling land and property. Occasionally boosters were too honest, provided too much detail, and effectively undermined their own efforts to present frontier areas as settled regions. Examples of this rare departure from the established contours of the promotional genre in the late nineteenth century include George Alexander Batchelder, *A Sketch of the History and Resources of Dakota Territory* (Yankton, Dakota: Press Steam Power Printing Co., 1870); Thomas McElrath, *The Yellowstone Valley: What It Is, Where It Is, and How to Get to It: A Hand-Book for Tourists and Settlers* (St. Paul, Minn.: Pioneer Press Company, 1880); Northern Pacific Railroad, *The Shortest,*

Quickest and Only Direct Route to All Points in the New Northwest Via the Northern Pacific Railroad (St. Paul, Minn.: James B. Power, Central Agent, 1879). After informing readers of the presence of "Society, Churches, Schools" in the Black Hills region, the publication went on to place great emphasis on the extent of U.S. military protection available in the region—hardly supportive evidence for the promoters' claims that the region was safe and settled. Such examples are memorable because they are so rare in the booster literature of the late nineteenth century.

36. Winslow Ayer, *Life in the Wilds of America and Wonders of the West in and Beyond the Bounds of Civilization* (Grand Rapids, Mich.: Central Publishing Company, 1880), 138, 382, 443, 526, 527. While not a part of the same booster literature genre as the other materials examined in this analysis, Ayer's work does raise the complicated issue of the role of landscape in shaping western identity. Anne F. Hyde, in "Cultural Filters: The Significance of Perception in the History of the American West," *Western Historical Quarterly* 24 (1993): 351–374, argues that "the West has shaping power because of its unique geography and not necessarily because it was or is a frontier" (351). While landscape has indeed been a crucial factor in shaping both western identity and outsiders' perceptions of the West, the booster literature I have examined tends to downplay contrasts between eastern or midwestern and western landscapes and emphasize continuities. Or, when dramatic landscape is emphasized in booster materials of the 1870s and 1880s, care is taken to demonstrate that while the scenery is visually powerful, it serves only as a colorful and inspiring backdrop and not as an impediment to commercial and agricultural progress.

37. George H. Tinker, *A Land of Sunshine: Flagstaff and Its Surroundings* (Flagstaff, Ariz.: Arizona Champion Print, 1887), 7, HEH RB 251989. The careful booster writer, in addressing the frontier theme, would have used language more like the following: "The abundant presence of culture, refinement, and elegance in Flagstaff and its environs illuminates the misinformed nature of conceptions of this place as a frontier county." Another of the rare examples of unsophisticated use of the frontier theme appears in McElrath's *The Yellowstone Valley*. McElrath, though certainly honest, was ineffective as a promoter when he concluded his work with a reminder to readers that "frontier life has its hardships and its vicissitudes wherever it is essayed, and the settler of the Yellowstone should set out prepared to encounter his full share of ups and downs" (132–133).

38. Robert Edmund Strahorn, *The Hand-Book of Wyoming, and Guide to the Black Hills and Big Horn Regions: A Glimpse at the Special Resources of the Territory* (Cheyenne, Wyo.: Knight and Leonard Printers, 1877), HEH RB 32975. The chapter is titled "Manners and Society, with a Few Reflections," 105–109, quotations on 105 and 106. The book is reprinted in installments in *Bits and Pieces: All That's Left of the Old West,* 1 and 2 (1965–1966).

39. Anne F. Hyde, *An American Vision: Far Western Landscape and National Culture, 1820–1920* (New York: New York University Press, 1990). Hyde notes that tourists in this period "wanted . . . [f]rom the safety of the train . . . to view strange animals, as well as miners, desperadoes, Indians, and Mormons. . . . Most tourists, though they did not like the idea of venturing into an entirely alien wilderness, clam-

ored for romantic bits of savagery" (112). For more on western tourism in this pe-riod, see Hal Rothman, *Devil's Bargains: Tourism in the Twentieth-Century American West* (Lawrence: University Press of Kansas, 1998); David M. Wrobel and Patrick T. Long, eds., *Seeing and Being Seen: Tourism in the American West* (Lawrence: University Press of Kansas for the Center of the American West, University of Colorado, Boulder, 2001); and Peter Blodgett's unpublished manuscript, "Vacations at Home: American Tourists in the Rocky Mountain West, 1920–1960,"especially chapters 1 and 2, "Advertising Wonderland: Themes to Entice the Tourist" and "Attracting the Millions: Community Advertising and Tourism in the Rocky Mountain Region." The tour guide booklets put out by the Raymond and Whitcomb Company in the 1880s and 1890s are a useful source for information on how western places were presented to tourists alone, as opposed to how they were presented in the multipurpose publications. For a good sampling of these booklets, see HEH RB 42233, 3 boxes.

40. Strahorn, *The Hand-Book of Wyoming,* 106–107.

41. This observation of Strahorn's concerning the linkage between female suffrage and cultural advance may have been influenced by his wife, Carrie Adell Strahorn, whom we will meet in chapter 3. Robert Strahorn offered a page of quotations from Wyoming officials and residents to support the claim that women's suffrage had played an important role in further civilizing the place. See Virginia Scharff's excellent discussion of how the fact of female suffrage was used to promote Wyoming Territory to potential white women settlers, in *Twenty Thousand Roads: Women, Movement, and the West* (Berkeley and Los Angeles: University of California Press, forthcoming), 110–112, copy in author's possession.

42. Information on Strahorn is drawn from Oliver Knight, "Robert E. Strahorn: Propagandist for the West," *Pacific Northwest Quarterly* 59 (January 1968): 33–45; and Dan L. Thrapp, ed., *Encyclopedia of Frontier Biography,* 3 vols. (Spokane, Wash.: Arthur H. Clark, 1990), 2: 1376.

43. For more on the promotional efforts in Wyoming prior to the publication of Strahorn's *Hand-Book,* see T. A. Larson, *History of Wyoming,* 2d ed., revised (Lincoln: University of Nebraska Press, 1990), 117–119; and Bruce Noble, "The Quest for Settlement in Early Wyoming," *Annals of Wyoming* 55 (fall 1983): 19–24.

44. See, for example, J. H. Triggs, *History of Cheyenne and Northern Wyoming, Embracing the Gold Fields of the Black Hills, Powder River and Big Horn Countries* (Omaha, Nebr.: Herald Steam Book and Job Printing House, 1876), HEH RB 40194.

45. Ibid., 119–120.

46. The "New Northwest of the imagination" quotation is from Schwantes, *Railroad Signatures,* 81. John Findlay also explores the impact of exterior forces in shaping regional identity in "A Fishy Proposition: Regional Consciousness in the Pacific Northwest," in, *Many Wests: Place, Culture, and Regional Identity,* ed. David M. Wrobel and Michael C. Steiner (Lawrence: University Press of Kansas, 1997), 37–70.

47. For a listing of Strahorn's works, see *The National Union Catalogue Pre-1956 Imprints,* vol. 572 (London: Mansell, 1978), 237–238.

48. Strahorn, *The Resources and Attractions of Idaho Territory,* 60.

49. Strahorn, *Washington,* introduction, n.p.

50. Knight, "Robert E. Strahorn," 43–44; quotation is from *Helena Herald,* February 20, 1879, cited in Knight, "Robert E. Strahorn," 42.

51. Southern newspaper editor Henry Grady's famous speech at Delmonico's in 1886 concerning the promise of the New South was the most noteworthy expression of an attitude that had already been evident in the South for two decades. For more on this, see Paul M. Gaston, *The New South Creed: A Study in Southern Mythmaking* (New York: Knopf, 1970), esp. chap. 1, "The Birth of a Creed," 17–42.

52. Samuel Bowles, *The Pacific Railroad-Open. How to Go. What to See. Guide for Travel to and Through Western America* (Boston: Fields, Osgood, and Co., 1869), discussed in D. W. Meinig's section "Delineating the New West," in *The Shaping of America: A Geographical Perspective on 500 Years of History,* vol. 3, *Transcontinental America, 1850–1915* (New Haven, Conn.: Yale University Press, 1998), 31–36.

53. E. P. Tenney, *The New West: As Related to the Christian College and the Home Missionary,* 3d ed. (Cambridge, Mass.: Riverside Press, 1878), 3.

54. The newness label was also applied to states and regions in these years; see, for example, Thomas Dowse's promotional pamphlet *The New Northwest: Montana. Its Past, Present, and Future* (Chicago: Commercial Advertizer Co., Publishers, 1879).

55. *New West Illustrated,* formerly known as *The New West: A Monthly Journal of Immigration,* was published in Omaha. Included among the publications of the New West Publishing Company of Omaha, Nebraska, was Robert E. Strahorn's *To the Rockies and Beyond, or a Summer on the Union Pacific Railway and Branches* (1879). See also William W. Thayer, *Marvels of the New West: A Vivid Portrayal of the Stupendous Marvels in the Vast Wonderland West of the Missouri River* (Norwich, Conn.: Henry Bill Publishing Company, 1888).

56. *New West Magazine* began publication in 1909 and was edited and published by Robert W. Spangler in Salt Lake City, Utah. The magazine focused largely on the Intermountain West, though later issues were devoted to Alaska (in 1919) and Hawaii (in 1920). Walter Weyl's book *A New Democracy* (1912) advocated the development of a democratic system that would be more attuned to the demands of a modern age. Herbert Croly spoke of the New Nationalism in his book *The Promise of American Life* (1909), and Theodore Roosevelt was quite taken with the concept and used it as the basis for his 1912 presidential campaign. Woodrow Wilson responded to the New Nationalism with his New Freedom campaign platform, designed in part by Progressive legal theorist Louis Brandeis. For an example of the linkage between the New West and Progressivism, see James Middleton, "A New West: The Attempts to Open Up the Natural Treasures of the Western States—Utilization and Conservation vs Monopolistic Greed—the Department of the Interior," *World's Work,* 31 (April 1916): 669–680.

Since the Progressive Era, America has experienced Franklin Roosevelt's New Deal and Henry Wallace's supportive book *New Frontiers* (1934), the better-known New Frontier of John F. Kennedy's 1960 campaign, Walter Heller's New Economics, and Dwight D. Eisenhower's New Republicanism and New Look foreign policy, and the phenomenon of the New Left, to name just a few examples. Patricia Limerick uses the phrase "Newest New West" and discusses some of the sources on the New West mentioned here in "The Shadows of Heaven Itself," in *Atlas of the New West,* ed. William Riebsame (New York: Norton, 1997), 151–178, esp. 152.

57. For more on the importance of visual imagery in western promotion, see Jennifer A. Watts, "Nature's Workshop: Photography and the Creation of 'Semi-tropic' California, 1880–1920" (paper presented at the annual meeting of the Western History Association, San Diego, October 2001) and Watts, "Picture Taking in Paradise: Los Angeles and the Creation of Regional Identity, 1880–1920," *History of Photography* 24 (autumn 2000): 243–250.

58. A. S. Johnson, publisher, "Kansas!" chromolithograph, Kansas State Historical Society.

59. Unfortunately for many of those who placed stock in such inventive imagery, the realities of life on the sod-house frontier were far less leisurely and idyllic. See Howard Ruede's harrowing account, *Sod-House Days: Letters from a Kansas Homesteader, 1877–1878,* ed. John Ise (1937; reprint, Lawrence: University Press of Kansas, 1983). For more on the gap between the yeoman ideal and the realities of frontier settlement, see Everett Dick, *The Sod-House Frontier, 1854–1890* (New York: Appleton-Century, 1937); and John Ise, *Sod and Stubble: The Story of a Kansas Homestead* (New York: Wilson-Erickson, Inc., 1936; reprint, Lincoln: University of Nebraska Press, 1987).

60. *Rand McNally and Co's Western Railway Guide,* a monthly periodical established in 1871.

61. For more on this topic, see Jonathon J. Keyes, "Engraved Invitations: Rand McNally and the Representation of the American West in the Nineteenth Century" (seminar paper, University of Chicago, 1995), 14–15.

62. J. B. Harley, "Deconstructing the Map," *Cartographia* 26 (summer 1989): 1–20, discussed in Keyes, "Engraved Invitations," 15–16.

63. Some Rand McNally maps did feature Indian reservations, though the majority seem to exclude them.

64. "Map of the Northern Pacific Railroad and Oregon Railway and Navigation Company," in Northern Pacific Railroad, *Northern Pacific Country* (Chicago: Rand McNally, 1883), DPL C978.02 V449, reprinted in *Rand McNally's Pioneer Atlas* (Chicago: Rand McNally and Company, 1956), 10–11. Similar in its noninclusion of Indian peoples is Rand McNally's "Map of the Atchison, Topeka and Santa Fe Railroad and Its Leased Lines" (1880), reprinted in *Rand McNally's Pioneer Atlas,* 30–31. There is a decided contrast between Rand McNally's railroad maps and its general business maps (which show greater attention to topography, political boundaries, and Indian peoples); see *Rand McNally and Company's Business Atlas, Containing Large-Scale Maps of Each State and Territory of the Great Mississippi Valley and Pacific Slope* (Chicago: Rand McNally and Company, 1876). For more on the railroads' efforts to present western places as decidedly "un-frontier-like," see David M. Emmons, *Garden in the Grasslands: Boomer Literature of the Central Great Plains* (Lincoln: University of Nebraska Press, 1971), 110–111.

It is worth noting that the Rand McNally Company was an equal-opportunity hierarchicalizer of space. A year after producing the "Map of the Northern Pacific Railroad Oregon Railway and Navigation Company," for the Northern Pacific Railroad, the firm produced a very effective map for the Democratic Party's congressional campaign. Titled "How the Public Domain Has Been Squandered," the map depicted the full extent of the lands granted by Republican Congresses to railroad corporations and argued that those lands should be returned to the public domain. See DPL, B, C333.160973 H83.

65. Earl Pomeroy, *The Pacific Slope: A History of California, Oregon, Washington, Idaho, Utah, and Nevada* (New York: Knopf, 1965: reprint, Lincoln: University of Nebraska Press, 1991), 103.

66. Map of "The Inter-Mountain District: Comprising Idaho, Montana, Wyoming and Washington Territories, the State of Oregon, and Portions of California, Nevada, Utah and Colorado Showing the Present and Prospective Railway Connections of Boise City" (Boise City, Idaho: Boise City Board of Trade, 1887–1888), Graff Collection of Western Americana, Newberry Library, Chicago (hereafter NEW GC), 338. As geographer G. Malcolm Lewis puts it, "Focusing on the contemporary, they stressed the future and indicated the nature of the changes by reference to past conditions which had already been modified or even disappeared"; G. Malcolm Lewis, "Rhetoric of the Western Interior: Modes of Environmental Description in American Promotional Literature of the Nineteenth Century," in *The Iconography of Landscape*, ed. Denis Cosgrove and Stephen Daniels (New York: Cambridge University Press, 1988), 179–193.

These cartographic representations of interior boosters are suggestive of a developing regional identity. D. W. Meinig notes that "regions exist in the minds of men, and maps mirror their times"; see Meinig, *The Great Columbia Plain: A Historical Geography, 1805–1910* (Seattle: University of Washington Press, 1968), 3–4, quoted in Katherine G. Morrissey, *Mental Territories: Mapping the Inland Empire* (Ithaca, N.Y.: Cornell University Press, 1997), 140. Morrissey provides excellent coverage of the booster literature of the Inland Empire.

67. Wilson Nicely, *The Great South-West, or Plain Guide for Emigrants and Capitalists, Embracing a Description of the States of Missouri and Kansas* (St. Louis: R. P. Studley and Co., Printers and Binder, 1867), 1, NEW, Case G 884.63.

68. See Emmons, *Garden in the Grasslands,* 53.

69. C. J. Jones, *Homes in South-Western Texas: 50,000 Acres, Equal to the Best Valley Land in California,* 2d ed. (San Francisco: P. E. Daugherty and Company, Printers, 1881). Jan Blodgett, in *Land of Bright Promise: Advertising the Texas Panhandle and South Plains, 1870–1917* (Austin: University of Texas Press, 1988), notes that by 1909, Texas lands were being presented to potential farmers as "the New California," and "the Sunny South" (67).

70. See Robert M. Fogelson, "The Rivalry Between Los Angeles and San Diego," in *The Fragmented Metropolis: Los Angeles, 1850–1930* (1967; reprint, Berkeley and Los Angeles: University of California Press, 1993), 43–62. For the rivalry between Sacramento and Los Angeles from the 1880s to the early 1900s, see Steven M. Avella, "The McClatchy Brothers and the Creation of Superior California" (paper

presented at the annual meeting of the Western History Association, San Diego, October 2001).

71. See Richard J. Orsi, "Selling the Golden State: A Study of Boosterism in Nineteenth-Century California" (Ph.D. diss., University of Wisconsin, 1973), 142–143. Orsi provides detailed coverage of these debates in chap. 2, "Official Boosterism," 114–234.

72. Ibid., 188–206.

73. For more on these rivalries, see Eugene P. Moehring, "'Promoting the Varied Interests of the New and Rising Community': The Booster Press on Nevada's Mining Frontier, 1859–1885," *Nevada Historical Society Quarterly* 42 (summer 1999): 91–118.

74. Board of Statistics, Immigration and Labor Exchange of Portland, Oregon, *Oregon: Its Advantages as an Agricultural and Commercial State* (Portland, Ore.: A. G. Walling Book and Job Printers, 1870), 55.

75. Benjamin Cummings Truman, *Homes and Happiness in the Golden State of California: Being a Description of the Empire State of the Pacific Coast: Its Inducements to Native and Foreign-Born Emigrants; Its Productiveness of Soil and Its Productions; Its Vast Agricultural Resources; Its Healthfulness of Climate and Equability of Temperature; and Many Other Facts for the Information of the Homeseeker and Tourist,* 3d ed. (San Francisco: H. S. Crocker and Co., Printers and Publishers, 1885), 51. For more on education in California boosterism, see "Encouragement for Education," 244–258, in Glenn S. Dumke, *The Boom of the Eighties in Southern California* (San Marino, Calif.: Huntington Library Press, 1944).

76. Strahorn, *Oregon* (1889), 50. It is worth noting that Strahorn was more restrained in his section on "Educational Advantages" in *The Resources and Attractions of Washington Territory* when he wrote merely that "Washington Territory enjoys a good common school system, and is splendidly supplied with higher institutions of learning. An increasing interest is manifested in education, the schools are well attended, and the standard of scholarship is steadily improving" (54). For Idaho he could say only that "the cause of education is keeping pace with the material development of the state," though given his optimistic account of said state's material development, the claim was not overly modest; see Strahorn, *The Resources and Attractions of Idaho Territory,* 117.

77. Map of "The Inter-Mountain District," n.p., italics added. This publication includes an extensive description of the Boise City public schools, including the claim that the city's high schools are superior to those of the East because they prepare students for direct entry into college without a preparatory course of study.

78. T. E. Farish, *Central and Southwestern Arizona: The Garden of America* (Phoenix, Ariz.: n.p., 1889), 29.

79. "Address of Welcome by Iowa Governor Buren R. Sherman," in Tri-State Old Settlers' Association, *Report of the Second Annual Reunion of the Tri-State Old Settlers' Association of Illinois, Missouri, and Iowa, September 30, 1885* (Keokuk, Iowa: R. B. Ogden and Son, Printing and Binding, 1885), 15.

80. The emphasis of the present study, like that of so many works dealing with the West in American thought and culture, is not religion. However, there can be no deny-

ing the importance of religion as a factor in western American settlement and community development. Those interested in the topic would do well to begin with the work of Ferenc Morton Szasz, particularly his *Religion in the Modern American West* (Tucson: University of Arizona Press, 2000); Ferenc M. Szasz and Margaret Connell Szasz, "Religion and Spirituality," in *The Oxford History of the American West*, ed. Clyde A. Milner II, Carol A. O'Connor, and Martha A. Sandweiss (New York: Oxford University Press, 1994), 359–392; Ferenc M. Szasz, ed., *Religion in the West* (Manhattan, Kans.: Sunflower Press, 1984); and Szasz, *The Protestant Clergy in the Great Plains and Mountain West, 1865–1915* (Albuquerque: University of New Mexico Press, 1988).

81. The skepticism with which these booster publications eventually came to be regarded, Carlos Schwantes notes, "forced a new generation of promoters to be more careful about what they asserted, and as a result promotional activity during the second railway age [1897–1917] became more sophisticated"; see Schwantes, *Railroad Signatures,* 92.

82. For a particularly memorable example of the Nile Valley comparison, see James D. Butler, *Nebraska: Its Characteristics and Prospects* ([Burlington, Iowa], 1873), 35.

83. W. H. Mitchell, *Dakota County [Minnesota]: Its Past and Present, Geographical, Statistical and Historical, Together with a General View of the State* (Minneapolis, Minn.: Tribune Printing Co., 1868), quotations on 47 and 39.

84. Henry M. Gilfy, "History and Resources of Oregon" (handwritten manuscript, 1876), 78, in Hubert Howe Bancroft Library (hereafter BANC), PA 37.

85. H. C. Stinson and W. N. Carter, comps., *Arizona: A Comprehensive Review of Its History, Counties, Principal Cities, Resources and Prospects: Together with Notices Of Business Men and Firms Who Have Made the Territory* (Los Angeles: n.p., 1891), preface, unnumbered page, and p. 12.

86. Frank Pixley's quotation from God is itself quoted in Truman, *Homes and Happiness in the Golden State,* 24–26. For another example of the invocation of divine blessing for a California promised land, see the poem "Tustin, the Beautiful":

> Unexcelled in charm and loveliness
> An Earthly Eden Unsurpassed in
> Wealth of Flower and Foliage.
> However, Imagination Cannot Conceive It:
> It must be seen to be realized,
>
> When the Angel of Peace to Earth first descended
> To bless with his presence the children of men,
> 'Mid the fairest of scenes his pathway e'er tended,
> And unto his smile the glad earth smiled again.
> He joyed in the fragrence [*sic*] of orange and roses.
> And loved 'mid their glances to linger or roam,
> And he said: "Here in Tustin, where Beauty reposes,
> I also will linger or build me a home!"

Harris Newmark reproduces the poem in his book *Sixty Years in Southern California, 1853–1913, Containing the Reminiscences of Harris Newmark,* ed. Maurice H. Newmark and Marco R. Newmark (New York: Knickerbocker Press, 1916), 577–578.

87. Strahorn, *The Hand-Book of Wyoming*, 21.

88. George Tinker did not handle the frontier theme effectively in *A Land of Sunshine*, but he did provide a good example of such regional comparative analysis, which underscored the familiarity of the West. He wrote, "This enormous forest, which is the largest in the country outside of Michigan, Wisconsin and Washington Territory, covers an area of over 10,000 square miles, and contains 6,400,000 acres. It is bigger than the State of Massachusetts, is double the size of Connecticut, and covers more ground than the States of Delaware and New Jersey combined" (5).

89. Lewis provides a sophisticated analysis of the "associative" and "dissociative" techniques used in the booster literature. See "Rhetoric of the Western Interior," 183–191. When directed to European immigrants, the booster pamphlets often drew parallels with familiar European landscapes. It is worth noting the parallel here with the tourism industry of the same period, which presented far western landscapes as vacation alternatives to European landscapes; see Hyde, *An American Vision*, esp. chap. 3, "Passage to an American Europe," 107–146, and chap. 4, "European Citadels," 147–190.

Oregon boosters must have been relieved in the early 1880s when an article in *Harper's* magazine noted that the state's landscape, dotted with framed homes, schools, churches, and good farms, was beginning to resemble those of Ohio and New York. See E. Ingersoll, "In the Wahlamet Valley, Oregon," *Harper's*, October 1882, 766; cited in Robert Bunting, *The Pacific Raincoast: Environment and Culture in an American Eden, 1778–1900* (Lawrence: University Press of Kansas, 1997), 100. Late-nineteenth-century western residents and boosters developed a rhetoric of contrast between their culture and that of the East. However, when it came to describing the physical makeup of western places, comparisons with the East and the Midwest were the norm in the booster literature, particularly in the first decades after the Civil War.

90. For a good discussion of this, see "Preparing an Advertising Program" and "Foreign Advertising, 1870–1873," in Overton, *Burlington West*, 158–163, and 359–369, respectively.

91. It is worth noting that outside of references to other parts of the United States and to parts of northern and western Europe, the only other countries and regions mentioned in the western promotional literature of the period appear solely for the purpose of adding an exotic, mythic, or dramatic flavor to the mix—for example, the Nile Valley, ancient Egypt, the Garden of Eden. The reader would search hard, and probably fruitlessly, for comparisons between the West and Asian, African, Middle Eastern, or South and Central American countries. This, of course, was the case because promoters understood that comparisons with familiar places would better serve their purpose of convincing people to move away from their home regions.

92. Batchelder, *A Sketch of the History and Resources of Dakota Territory*, 25–26.

93. John J. Powell, *Nevada: The Land of Silver* (San Francisco: Bacon and Co., 1876), 189, italics in original, HEH RB 1910.

94. Stinson and Carter, *Arizona*, 29.

95. Strahorn, *The Resources and Attractions of Idaho Territory*, 14. Unable to make quite the same elevated claim for Washington's low military death rate, Strahorn

ingeniously linked the state to Oregon and Idaho and noted that "taken as a group, [they] show the smallest rate of [military] mortality of any division of the Union," (15).

96. Union Pacific Railroad, *A Complete and Comprehensive Description of the Agricultural, Stock Raising and Mineral Resources of Idaho: Also Statistics in Regard to Its Climate, etc., etc. Compiled from the Latest Reports of 1892*, 6th ed., presented with the compliments of the Passenger Division of the Union Pacific—the Overland Route (St. Louis, Mo.: Woodward and Tiernan Printing Co., 1893), 11. This is a clear case of gross statistical manipulation. The figures provided in 1893 for virtually all the states and regions listed remain the same as those provided by Strahorn in the 1889 edition, except for the addition of the Gulf States and the even lower figure for Wyoming.

97. Though not the actual title of Strahorn's promotional booklet on Idaho, the title that appears on the front cover of the 1889 edition is "Idaho: The Gem of the Mountains."

98. Strahorn, *The Resources and Attractions of Idaho Territory*, 14–15. It is worth noting that Strahorn drew his figures on mortality from the 1870 Census, since, he said, the 1880 Census was not available to him in 1881, and his claim is almost certainly true. However, in the 1893 edition of the volume, put out by the Union Pacific Railroad, the same statistics from 1870 were used, even though the 1890 Census results were available; see Union Pacific Railroad, *A Complete and Comprehensive Description of . . . Idaho* (1893), 12.

99. Union Pacific Railroad, *The Resources and Attractions of the Texas Panhandle* (St. Louis, Mo.: Woodward and Tiernan Printing Co., 1893), 94, HEH RB 116604.

100. Glover, *Corinne and the Bear River Valley*, section on health on back side of foldout map.

101. Dr. D. J. Brannon, quoted in Tinker, *A Land of Sunshine*, 6.

102. Benjamin Cummings Truman, *Semi-tropical California: Its Climate, Healthfulness, Productiveness, and Scenery; Its Magnificent Stretches of Vineyards and Groves of Semi-tropical Fruits, etc., etc., etc.* (San Francisco: A. L. Bancroft and Co., 1874), 36–39.

103. Ibid., 61.

104. This is the aspect of the book that Kevin Starr emphasizes in his coverage of Truman in *Americans and the California Dream, 1850–1915* (New York: Oxford University Press, 1973), 201.

105. Among the more notable fantastic descriptions of climate, landscape, and agricultural fertility (these factors are often treated together in the booster publications) are A. Besom, *Pawnee County, Nebraska*, 3, 7, and 72; Butler, *Nebraska*, 35; Dowse, *The New Northwest*; Farish, *Central and Southwestern Arizona*, 4, 8; Mitchell, *Dakota County*, 39, 47; Theo C. Camp, *Taos County: Report to the Bureau of Immigration of New Mexico, 1881* (Santa Fe, N.M.: New Mexico Book and Job Printing Department, 1881), 8, 11; William Sutherland, *The Wonders of Nevada: Where They Are and How to Get to Them* (Virginia, Nev.: Enterprise Book and Job Printing House, 1878), 27; Oregon Board of Immigration, *The New Em-*

pire, 3; Las Vegas Hot Springs and Topeka and Santa Fe Railroad Company, *The Climate of New Mexico and Las Vegas Hot Springs* (Chicago: Poole Brothers, Printers, 1883; a publication of the management of the Hot Springs and of the Topeka and Santa Fe Railroad Company); and Stinson and Carter, *Arizona,* inside front cover, unnumbered page.

106. J. H. Beadle, *The Undeveloped West; or, Five Years in the Territories: Being a Complete History of That Vast Region Between the Mississippi and the Pacific* (Philadelphia: National Publishing Company, 1873), 62. Emmons discusses Beadle in his chapter "Dissenters and Defenders," in *Garden in the Grasslands,* 162–198, esp. 162–163. A later and equally cautious account of the West's resources and opportunities for settlement is George W. Romspert, *The Western Echo: A Description of the Western States and Territories of the United States* (Dayton, Ohio: United Brethren Publishing House, 1881). Also interesting in this regard is Louis Adamic's discussion, in his book *Laughing in the Jungle: The Autobiography of an Immigrant in America* (New York: Harper and Brothers, 1932; reprint, New York: Arno Press and the New York Times, 1969), of an anonymous novel sponsored by the Yugoslav Movement in the 1870s, *Obljubljena dezhela (The Land of Promise).* The novel, which traces the harrowing experience of a group of Slovenian peasants who had emigrated to America because of the boosters' enticing descriptions, was designed to counter such promotional promises. Ironically enough, Adamic noted that contrary to the novelist's intentions, *Obljubljena dezhela* actually "stimulated our passion for America." Adamic explained that "we were confident that 'land sharks' . . . could not sell *us* worthless lands in the desert. Indeed we imagined that it would be great sport to guard ourselves against such characters" (26–27).

107. The *Philadelphia Record* criticism was reprinted in the *Hays Sentinel,* September 14, 1877, and is quoted in Craig Miner, *West of Wichita: Settling the High Plains of Kansas, 1865–1890* (Lawrence: University Press of Kansas, 1986), 119.

108. For more on patterns of rainfall in the region, see Gilbert C. Fite, "The Great Plains: Promises, Problems, and Prospects," in *The Great Plains: Environment and Culture,* ed. Brian W. Blouet and Frederick C. Luebke (Lincoln: University of Nebraska Press, 1979), 187–203. Rodman W. Paul provides excellent coverage of late-nineteenth-century farming efforts in the semiarid West in his chapter "Farming in a Land of Little Rain," in *The Far West and the Great Plains in Transition, 1859–1900* (New York: Harper and Row, 1988), 220–251.

109. G. R. Irish, address delivered at the Twenty-first Annual Reunion, August 24, 1887, in Old Settlers' Association, Johnson County, Iowa, *Proceedings of the Johnson County [Iowa] Old Settlers' Association, from 1866–1899* (n.p., n.d.), 48, NEW GC 2132.

110. For more on this theme, see Athearn, *Union Pacific Country,* 174–175.

111. Charles Dudley Warner, "Our Italy," *Harper's New Monthly Magazine,* November 1890, 813–829, quotation on 829. See also Warner's "The Golden Hesperides," *Atlantic Monthly,* January 1888, 48–56, written during the height of the Southern California boom. The latter essay, while it does include a few cynical comments, is generally effusive in tone, which lends a touch of irony to the matter, given Warner's

critique of booster excess in "Our Italy." See also Warner, *Our Italy* (New York: Harper and Brothers, 1891). Andrew Rolle provides useful coverage of California promoters' use of comparisons with Italy and the Mediterranean in his *California: A History,* 2d ed. (New York: Thomas Y. Crowell, 1969), 376–377.

112. Orsi, "Selling the Golden State," 35–36.

113. James McGuinn, *Historical and Biographical Record of Los Angeles and Vicinity* (Chicago: Chapman Publishing Co., 1901), 260, quoted in Dumke, *The Boom of the Eighties in Southern California,* 201. Dumke provides quite extensive coverage of individual boosters, emphasizing that they ran the gamut from the thoroughly unscrupulous to the constructive, decent, even model variety of citizen; see his chapter "Men and Methods," in *The Boom of the Eighties in Southern Califonia,* 200–226. Newmark, in his chapter "The Great Boom, 1887," in his *Sixty Years in Southern California,* 564–587, provides a good sense of the excesses of the boom and reproduces some particularly memorable promotional pronouncements. Concerning the promotional hysteria, he remarks, "I may safely declare that during the height of the infection, two-thirds of our population were, in a sense, more insane than sane" (572).

114. Despite the claims to legitimacy, the discerning reader can generally find the obvious booster giveaways at the end of these publications; for example, when interested individuals are repeatedly reminded that the work in question is *not* a booster publication and then are instructed to apply to Ferry, Woodward and Co., Real Estate Agents; see Adams, *Oregon As It Is,* 63.

115. Ezra Meeker, *Washington Territory West of the Cascade Mountains: Containing a Description of Puget Sound and Waters Emptying into It* (Olympia, Washington Territory: Transcript Office, 1870), preface, unnumbered page, and p. 13, HEH RB 35037. Another quite rare and notable example of booster claims against exaggeration coupled with an actual lack of exaggeration is the inaugural issue of the magazine *Ecce Montezuma: A Monthly Journal Dedicated to the Interests of the Southwest* 1 (January 1884): 1.

116. See Brown, "The Promotion of Emigration to Washington," 5–6.

117. Stinson and Carter, *Arizona,* unnumbered page. Such claims to authenticity had a long tradition in western promotional writing. Nicely, for example, in *The Great South-West,* insisted that "this book is not written in the interest of any Railroad Corporation, Emigrant Aid Society, or Real Estate Company, nor has any aid been received from these or any other agencies. The work has been issued solely at the expense of the author, and for its statements he alone is responsible" (6).

118. Strahorn, *The Hand-Book of Wyoming,* preface, unnumbered page.

2. The Second Boosterist Phase

1. Many of the publications that did appear were reprints of works from the previous decade, or somewhat expanded versions of those earlier works, printed on cheaper paper. See, for example, the 1893 reprints of Robert Strahorn's works:

Idaho: A Complete and Comprehensive Description (Boise City, Idaho: Idaho Legislature, 1881: reprint, St. Louis, Mo.: Woodward and Tiernan Printing Co., 1893); *Oregon: A Complete and Comprehensive Description,* 6th ed. (Omaha, Nebr.: Union Pacific System [1887?]; reprint, Omaha, Nebr.: Union Pacific System, 1893); and *Washington: A Complete and Comprehensive Description,* 6th ed. (Chicago: Rand McNally and Co., [1887?]; reprint, St. Louis, Mo.: Woodward and Tiernan Printing Co., 1893).

2. The literature on the Homestead Act is voluminous. Gilbert Fite provides a useful summary of the historiographical debate surrounding the effectiveness of the act in his essay "The American West of Farmers and Stockmen," in *Historians and the American West,* ed. Michael P. Malone (Lincoln: University of Nebraska Press, 1983), 209–223. Also useful are Robert P. Swierenga, "Land Speculation and Its Impact on American Economic Growth and Welfare: A Historiographical Review," *Western Historical Quarterly* 8 (July 1977): 283–302; and William F. Deverell, "To Loosen the Safety Valve: Eastern Workers and Western Lands," *Western Historical Quarterly* 19 (August 1988): 269–285.

3. Kenneth S. Davis, in *Kansas: A Bicentennial History* (New York: Norton, 1976), 126, provides the information on winter temperatures. Hicks discusses the summer of 1886 in *The Populist Revolt: A History of the Farmer's Alliance and the People's Party* (Minneapolis: University of Minnesota Press, 1931; reprint, Lincoln: University of Nebraska Press, 1961), 31.

4. The figures in the chart are from *Historical Statistics of the United States: Colonial Times to 1970* (Washington, D.C.: U.S. Department of Commerce, Bureau of the Census, 1975), 24–37.

Estimated Population of Western States and Territories, 1870–1910 (in 1,000s)

Region/State	1870	1880	1890	1900	1910	1920
Alaska	—	33	32	64	64	55
Arizona	10	40	88	123	204	334
California	560	865	1,213	1,485	2,378	3,427
Colorado	40	194	413	540	799	940
Hawaii	—	—	—	154	192	256
Idaho	15	3	89	162	326	432
Kansas	364	996	1,428	1,470	1,691	1,769
Montana	21	39	143	243	376	549
Nebraska	123	452	1,063	1,066	1,192	1,296
New Mexico	92	120	160	195	327	360
Nevada	42	62	47	42	82	77
North Dakota	2	37	191	319	577	647
Oklahoma	—	259	790	1,657	2,028	2,028
Oregon	91	175	318	414	673	783
South Dakota	12	98	349	402	584	637
Texas	819	1,592	2,236	3,049	3,897	4,663
Utah	87	144	211	277	373	449
Washington	24	75	337	518	1,142	1,357
Wyoming	9	21	63	93	146	194

5. James C. Olson and Ronald C. Naugle, *History of Nebraska*, 3d ed. (Lincoln: University of Nebraska Press, 1997), 161–162.

6. Population figures are from Davis, *Kansas*, 127, and from *Census Bureau Statistics*, 2000 Census, www.census.gov. Hicks states that half the residents of western Kansas left between 1888 and 1892; see *The Populist Revolt*, 32.

7. Hicks discusses this connection in *The Populist Revolt*, 35.

8. The attendance figure for the Chicago fair is from Robert W. Rydell, *All the World's a Fair: Visions of Empire at American International Expositions, 1876–1916* (Chicago: University of Chicago Press, 1984).

9. Promotional brochure for the Northwest Interstate Fair (n.p., 1894). The publication was directed largely at new "homeseekers." Like other booster literature of the period, it placed special emphasis on agricultural fertility. The booklet also stressed the region's cultural advances, in an effort to "greatly relieve the minds of those who hesitated in coming to the Western country on account of depriving their children of the educational advantages possessed in their Eastern homes" (13). The brochure is in the Henry E. Huntington Library Ephemera Collection, "Washington State" box (hereafter HEH E W).

10. For more on the San Francisco fair, see Barbara Berglund, "Imagining the City: Identity, History, and Memory at the California Midwinter International Exposition, 1894," a chapter in "Ordering the Disorderly City: Power, Culture, and Nation-Making in San Francisco, 1846–1906" (Ph.D. diss., University of Michigan, 2002); and Arthur Chandler and Marvin Nathan, *The Fantastic Fair: The Story of the California Midwinter International Exposition, Golden Gate Park, San Francisco* (n.p., Pogo Press, 1993).

11. For more on the opening of Indian lands in the Oklahoma Territory, see Walter Nugent, *Into the West: The Story of Its People* (New York: Knopf, 1999), 101–105.

12. This chronology corresponds with Schwantes's delineation of railroad promotional material in "The First Railway Age, 1868–1893" and "The Second Railway Age, 1897–1917," in *Railroad Signatures Across the Pacific Northwest* (Seattle: University of Washington Press, 1993); see also Schwantes, "Landscapes of Opportunity: Phases of Railroad Promotion of the Pacific Northwest," *Montana: The Magazine of Western History* 43 (spring 1993): 38–51.

13. For more on Powell and irrigation, see Donald Worster's chapter "Democracy Encounters the Desert," in his excellent biography *A River Running West: The Life of John Wesley Powell* (New York: Oxford University Press, 2001), 337–380.

14. For an informative but uncritical overview of Smythe and the Irrigation Congress, see Martin E. Carlson, "William E. Smythe, Irrigation Crusader," *Journal of the West* 7 (January 1968): 41–47; for a more critical perspective, see Patricia Nelson Limerick, *Desert Passages: Encounters with the American Deserts* (Albuquerque: University of New Mexico Press, 1985), 77–90; and Limerick, *The Legacy of Conquest: The Unbroken Past of the American West* (New York: W. W. Norton, 1987), 135–137.

15. David M. Wrobel, "Crisis in the Nineties," in *The End of American Exceptionalism: Frontier Anxiety from the Old West to the New Deal* (Lawrence: University Press of Kansas, 1993), 29–42.

16. The details surrounding the event and the quotation are drawn from Worster, *A River Running West,* 526–530, quotation on 527.

17. Los Angeles Chamber of Commerce, *Official Report of the Irrigation Congress Held at Los Angeles, California, October 1893* (Los Angeles: Los Angeles Chamber of Commerce, 1893).

18. The debate between Powell and the Irrigation Congress is in ibid., 107–116. Powell's cautionary approach was evident earlier in his article "The Irrigable Lands of the Arid Region," *Century Magazine* 39 (March 1890): 766–776.

19. For discussion of the famous exchange, see Wallace Stegner, *Beyond the Hundredth Meridian: John Wesley Powell and the Second Opening of the American West* (Boston: Houghton Mifflin, 1954), 342–343; Worster, *A River Running West,* 529–530.

20. See David Emmons, *Garden in the Grasslands: Boomer Literature of the Great Plains* (Lincoln: University of Nebraska Press, 1971), 176; the source of this misappropriation of Powell's words was Union Pacific Railroad, *Colorado: A Complete and Comprehensive Description,* 5th ed. (St. Louis, Mo.: Woodward and Tiernan Publishing Co., 1892), 101–102. Emmons (*Garden in the Grasslands,* 90) notes that the same comments appeared in the eighth edition, from 1899.

21. See John Wesley Powell, *Report on the Lands of the Arid Regions of the United States* (Washington, D.C.: Government Printing Office, 1878); William E. Smythe, *The Conquest of Arid America* (New York: Harper and Brothers, 1899; revised edition, New York: Macmillan, 1905; reprinted, Seattle: University of Washington Press, 1969). For more on irrigation, see Donald J. Pisani, *From the Family Farm to Agribusiness: The Irrigation Crusade in California and the West, 1850–1931* (Berkeley and Los Angeles: University of California Press, 1984). Mark Fiege's *Irrigated Eden: The Making of an Agricultural Landscape in the West* (Seattle: University of Washington Press, 1999) is an excellent study of irrigation in Idaho's Snake River watershed in the late nineteenth and early twentieth centuries. Also useful is Richard Lowitt and Judith Fabry, eds., *Henry A. Wallace's Irrigation Frontier: On the Trail of the Corn Belt Farmer, 1909* (Norman: University of Oklahoma Press, 1991).

22. Smythe's most important work on the topic of irrigation was *The Conquest of Arid America.* See also Smythe's *Constructive Democracy: The Economics of a Square Deal* (New York: Macmillan, 1905). Another interesting source for Smythe's thinking on irrigation is *The Colonial Lectures: Delivered in Chicago, November 26, December 3, 10, and 17, 1895, and Subsequently in New York, Massachusetts and Other Eastern States* (n.p., 1896), HEH RB 370462.

23. Nugent, *Into the West,* 110.

24. For more on this topic, see Mary Wilma M. Hargreaves, *Dry Farming in the Northern Great Plains, 1900–1925* (Cambridge, Mass.: Harvard University Press, 1957); and W. Eugene Hollon, *The Great American Desert: Then and Now* (New York: Oxford University Press, 1966), 152–156.

25. For an interesting case study of farming endeavors based on the Enlarged Homestead Act and the Stock Raising Homestead Act, see William P. Fischer, "Homesteading the Thunder Basin: Teckla, Wyoming, 1917–1938," *Annals of Wyoming* 71

(spring 1999): 21–34. Fischer questions the common view of the Teckla homesteaders and, by inference, other dryland homesteaders as naive victims of promotional schemes. A good example of Wyoming's promotional material in this period is Wyoming State Board of Immigration, *Wyoming: The State of Opportunity* (Cheyenne: Wyoming State Board of Immigration, 1920). By the mid-1920s, the promotional literature for Wyoming was beginning to emphasize tourism more heavily than permanent settlement.

26. For a concise and excellent introductory overview of western agriculture in this period, see Michael P. Malone and Richard W. Etulain, *The American West: A Twentieth-Century History* (Lincoln: University of Nebraska Press, 1989), 12–23.

27. Nugent, *Into the West*, 131–132. Of course, the peak homesteading years did vary from state to state. In Wyoming, for example, 1920 and 1921 marked the high point; see Bruce Noble, "The Quest for Settlement in Early Wyoming," *Annals of Wyoming* 55 (fall 1983): 19–24, esp. 23.

28. Jan Blodgett, *Land of Bright Promise: Advertising the Texas Panhandle and South Plains, 1870–1917* (Austin: University of Texas Press, 1988), 102.

29. Nugent, *Into the West*, 133. For the Wyoming increase and the complaint of the state immigration agent, W. T. Judkin, see Noble, "The Quest for Settlement in Early Wyoming," 22.

30. Even the most city-centered of the booster pamphlets provided information on the industrial and agricultural infrastructure of the broader region; see, for example, A. S. Allen, *The City of Seattle, 1900* (Seattle, Wash.: Press of Metropolitan Printing and Binding Co., for the Seattle Chamber of Commerce, 1900), HEH RB 299567.

31. For more on this topic, see Jonathan Raban, *Bad Land: An American Romance* (New York: Pantheon, 1996).

32. Charles Moreau Harger's articles on western agricultural conditions included "The Next Commonwealth: Oklahoma," *Outlook* 67 (February 1901): 273–281; "Today's Chance for the Western Settler," *Outlook* 78 (December 1904): 980–982; and "The Revival in Western Land Values," *American Monthly Review of Reviews* 35 (January 1907): 63–65.

33. Charles Moreau Harger, "The Passing of the Promised Land," *Atlantic Monthly,* October 1909, 461–466, quotations on 465, 466.

34. In ibid., 461–462, Harger discussed the promoters' advertising literature and the railroads' special excursions for prospective settlers—"Homeseekers' Days." Aside from the occasional remark, he was not especially critical of western promoters, since their claims were not incongruent with his assessment of western prospects.

35. A. S. Mercer, *Big Horn County, Wyoming: The Gem of the Rockies* (Chicago: Hammond Press, 1906), 4.

36. Grants Pass Commercial Club and County Organizations, *Grants Pass and Josephine County* (Portland, Ore.: Grants Pass Commercial Club and County Organizations, in conjunction with *Sunset Magazine* Homeseekers Bureau of the Pacific Northwest, 1909), 7, HEH, Promotional Literature, Oregon, box 1 (hereafter HEH E 01). The closed frontier theme was played up in numerous publications. See, for

example, Ellis A. Davis, *Davis' Commercial Encyclopedia of the Pacific Southwest: California, Nevada, Utah, and Arizona* (Oakland, Calif.: Ellis A. Davis, 1911). Davis referred to the Pacific Southwest and the Pacific Northwest as "the last frontier inviting the importation of capital, labor and home-seekers" (unnumbered page).

37. Sutherlin Land and Water Company, *Water Is King in the Orchard Kingdom: The Sutherlin Valley, Douglas County, Oregon* (Roseburg, Ore.: Sutherlin Land and Water Company, 1909), 41, HEH E 01. This colorful, glossy publication would be a contender for the title of least restrained (in its claims) locally produced booster booklet of the early twentieth century, a category in which the competition is exceptionally strong.

38. A. J. Wells, *The New Nevada: What It Is and What It Is to Be: The Era of Irrigation and the Day of Opportunty* (San Francisco: Southern Pacific Company, 1906), HEH RB 2023, 71, 73. See also A. J. Wells, *Nevada* (San Francisco: Passenger Department, Southern Pacific Company, 1911), HEH RB 249846, 59. Such insistence upon the absence of frontier conditions, in various parts of the West and at various times, is characteristic of the promotional literature produced by the Southern Pacific, but no more so than in other promotional literature, including locally produced pamphlets and brochures. One wonders if these essential contours of the promotional genre were simply being reproduced and thus sustained in part through inertia—the unwillingness or simple failure of booster writers to develop new strategies and to rely on stock phrases such as "not wild and wooly," "not a frontier," and "no pioneer privations." On the other hand, the genre was so vast and well developed that one has to conclude that such key themes as climate, the absence of pioneer hardship, agricultural abundance, and cultural advance and such stock phrases as those listed here remained so constant and common because they were so vital and effective. These phrases were thus recycled and were used again and again to great effect.

Interestingly, Wells emphasized that while Nevada had all the cultural institutions common in more established societies, it did not have the rigid social hierarchy that accompanied such institutions elsewhere. Social lineage, the publication declared, was immaterial in Nevada, where "each person stands on his or her own merit according to true worth." In the Silver State, then, at least in Wells's estimation, there were frontiers of social opportunity with no accompanying frontiers of cultural underdevelopment. It is worth noting that Robert Strahorn, writing three decades earlier, in *The Hand-Book of Wyoming, and Guide to the Black Hills and Big Horn Regions: A Glimpse at the Special Resources of the Territory* (Cheyenne, Wyo.: Knight and Leonard Printers, 1877), had emphasized that there were social distinctions in Wyoming, and the presence of such distinctions was a mark of the passing of the frontier of cultural underdevelopment (see Chapter 1). Wells, in *The New Nevada*, on the other hand, emphasized the absence of social hierarchy as evidence that the Silver State was still a frontier of opportunity. Whether the different treatments of social hierarchy in these two works are emblematic of changing attitudes toward class between the late nineteenth century and the Progressive Era, or simply of personal differences in outlook between the two authors is unclear. What is clear is that frontier-centered arguments remained central to western promotional writing long after they were first articulated in the early 1870s.

39. Anon., *Tucson: Chief Commercial City of Arizona* (Tucson, Ariz.: Press of the *Citizen*, [1910?]), 20.

40. Dillard-Powell Land Company, *Lubbock County: The Best Cheap Lands in the Southwest for Diversified Farming* (Lubbock, Tex.: Dillard-Powell, 1908), 27, quoted in Blodgett, *Land of Bright Promise*, 89.

41. Southern Pacific Company, *Oregon for the Settler: A Great Area with Rich Valleys, Mild and Healthful Climate and Wide Range of Products* (San Francisco: Southern Pacific Company, 1914), 7, 60, HEH RB 375527.

42. Southern Pacific Company, *California for the Settler* (San Francisco: Southern Pacific Company, 1922), 7, HEH RB 194725.

43. Nampa Chamber of Commerce, *Nampa Valley and the City of Nampa in Sunny Southern Idaho* (Nampa, Idaho: Nampa Chamber of Commerce, 1909), HEH E, Promotional Literature, Idaho, Wyoming, Montana, Northwest General (hereafter HEH E IWMNG).

44. Historian Carl Abbott notes that on the "metropolitan frontier" of the period 1890–1940, the "dominant concern [of local leaders] was to demonstrate the maturity of their communities," to "prove that their 'instant cities' had become 'regular cities' full of settled and respectable Americans." The western promotional literature of the early twentieth century bears out Abbott's assertion. See Abbott, *The Metropolitan Frontier: Cities in the Modern American West* (Tucson: University of Arizona Press, 1993), xvii. Abbott utilizes Gunther Barth's terms "instant cities" and "regular cities"; see Barth, *Instant Cities: Urbanization and the Rise of San Francisco and Denver* (New York: Oxford University Press, 1975). For more on western urban booster efforts, see John W. Reps, *Cities of the American West* (Princeton, N.J.: Princeton University Press, 1979); and his *Panoramas of Promise: Pacific Northwest Cities and Towns on Nineteenth-Century Lithographs* (Pullman: Washington State University Press, 1984).

45. The railroads commonly advertised portions of lands in adjoining states together as a regional package; see, for example, Northern Pacific Railway, *Eastern Washington and Northern Idaho* (n.p., Northern Pacific Railway, 1910), HEH E IWMNG.

46. The "Rose City" quotation is from Rinaldo M. Hall, *Oregon, Washington, Idaho and Their Resources: Mecca of the Homeseeker and Investor: A Land of Promise and Opportunity, Where the Soil, Climate and All Conditions Are Unsurpassable for the Successful Pursuance of Varied Industry* (Portland, Ore.: Passenger Department of the Oregon Railroad and Navigation Co., and Southern Pacific Co., 1904), 63, HEH E IWMNG; quotations are from this edition, in which the text is essentially the same as in an earlier edition, published in 1903, though the illustrations and the front cover differ.

47. *The Twin Falls Country, Southern Idaho* (Twin Falls, Idaho: Kingsbury Printing Co., [1913?]; published for J. Clyde Lindsey, Real Estate Investments, and for the Union Pacific Railroad System), HEH E IWMNG.

48. Abbott, *The Metropolitan Frontier,* xvii.

49. The editor and manager of *The Coast* was Honor L. Wilhelm. For a good example of the publication's emphasis on the richness of regional culture, see *The Coast* 3 (February 1902): cover page. The magazine is also interesting for its efforts to present the boundaries of the region it promoted. The new map that adorned the cover of the magazine beginning with volume 4 (August 1902), includes Alaska, British Columbia, Washington, and Oregon (all featured on the publication's original cover) along with the new additions, Montana, Idaho, California, Utah, Wyoming, Colorado, and most of Arizona.

50. Lummis's promotional efforts are further explored in chapter 5.

51. Hall, *Oregon, Washington, Idaho and Their Resources,* 11.

52. With the influx of large numbers of southern and eastern European immigrants in the late nineteenth and early twentieth centuries, literacy rates would drop. But large numbers of unassimilated immigrants from non-English-speaking countries were not moving to Iowa, where land prices were relatively high, as much as they were to states and territories in the semiarid West, where homesteading and railroad lands were more readily available. It is worth noting that Iowa, at the turn of the century, was one of the nation's more culturally homogeneous states, and, it should be remembered, this was the tail end of a period of tremendously high literacy in the United States. The state's high rate of "freedom from illiteracy" was not necessarily a measure of the extent of cultural amenities in the state or the quality of its educational system but more likely the consequence of a mix of fortuitous circumstances.

Isaac O. Savage, in *A History of Republic County, Kansas* (Beloit, Kans.: Jones and Chubbi, Art Printers, 1901), 25, HEH RB 127727, claimed that Kansas had the lowest illiteracy rate in the country. The reliability of the claims is less significant in the present context than the fact of the sheer frequency with which they were made. Savage's work is a mixture of boosterism, history, and reminiscence. This mixing of these genres does occur occasionally; see also, for example, Ezra Meeker, *Seventy Years of Progress in Washington* (Seattle: Allstrum Printing Co., 1921). Meeker is discussed in chapter 3.

53. Honor L. Wilhelm, "Western Advantages and Opportunities," *The Coast,* 18 (August 1909): 69–75, quotation on 71.

54. Roy W. Schenck, "Map of Wyoming Resources, Showing at a Glance the Harvest of Gold Which Awaits the Settler and Investor in Wyoming" (Denver, Colo.: Clason Map Co., issued by the Wyoming State Board of Immigration, [1912?]), HEH E IWMNG. For more on the problems of providing educational facilities in the sparsely settled High Plains, see Gilbert C. Fite, "The Great Plains: Promises, Problems, and Prospects," in *The Great Plains: Environment and Culture,* ed. Brian W. Blouet and Frederick C. Luebke (Lincoln: University of Nebraska Press, 1979), 187–203, especially 192–193. This problem has continued to hamper educational efforts in the High Plains down to the present.

55. No author, *Lewis and Clark Centennial Exposition, 1805–1905* (Portland, Ore.: Oregonian Publishing Company, 1901), preface, unnumbered page, HEH E Promotional Literature, Oregon box 2 (hereafter HEH E 02). Interestingly, this booklet

appeared four years before the exposition; and its content is typical of the standard state promotional publications and does not focus extensively on the upcoming exhibit. It is also noteworthy that boosters would utilize the title of the upcoming exposition in a publication that appeared four years before the opening of the event.

56. Dillard-Powell Land Company, *Lubbock, Lubbock County,* 16, quoted in Blodgett, *Land of Bright Promise,* 93.

57. Rawlings-Knapp Realty Company, *Littlefield Lands: The Best Farm Lands* (Kansas City, Mo.: Rawlings-Knapp Reality Co., n.d.), 6, quoted in Blodgett, *Land of Bright Promise,* 93, italics in original.

58. Sutherlin Land and Water Company, *Water Is King in the Orchard Kingdom,* 7.

59. *The Twin Falls Country,* n.p.

60. Hall, *Oregon, Washington, Idaho and Their Resources,* 15. Oregon's claim to the "lowest death rate in the United States" is also made in Grants Pass Commercial Club and County Organizations, *Grants Pass and Josephine County,* 9. The Oregon State Board of Health (OSBH) made much of the state's low death rate. The OSBH's reported annual death rate of 9.47 per 1,000 of population is emphasized in Southern Pacific Company, *Oregon for the Settler,* 59.

61. W. Towne, *Butte, "On Top," and Underground: Its Aspirations, Achievements, History, Industries, and Homes* (Butte, Mont.: Butte Chamber of Commerce, 1928), n.p., HEH E IWNMG.

62. Hall, *Oregon, Washington, Idaho and Their Resources,* 63; Boulder Commercial Association, *Boulder, Colorado* (Boulder, Colo.: Boulder Publishing Co., 1910), 13.

63. Pueblo Business Men's Association, *Pueblo: The City of Sunshine* (Pueblo, Colo.: Pueblo Business Men's Association, [1908?]), HEH E, Promotional, Colorado, box 2. Such matters are of acute concern to contemporary promoters in the smog age; for those of the early twentieth century, smoke billowing from factory chimneys largely signified economic well-being rather than potential impediments to health. Yet on this matter the boosters who were promoting industrial centers had to perform another delicate balancing act. They often pointed to the unhealthy air in the crowded, factory-filled industrial East yet had to illuminate both the superior healthfulness and the industrial productivity of their western wonderlands at the same time.

64. T. C. Egleston, *Boise County, Idaho: Resources, Agricultural and Mineral* (Boise, Idaho: Prepared and published under the direction of T. C. Egleston, Commissioner of Immigration, Labor and Statistics for the State of Idaho, 1903), 8.

65. Louis W. Pratt, *Tacoma, 1904: Electric City of the Pacific Coast* (Tacoma, Wash.: Tacoma Chamber of Commerce and Board of Trade, 1904), 1, HEH E, Promotional Washington State (hereafter HEH E W); Nampa Chamber of Commerce, *Nampa Valley,* n.p.; the Milwaukee Road's claims for Montana's climate are quoted in Raban, *Bad Land,* 186; The Dalles Business Men's Association, *The Dalles, Oregon* (The Dalles, Ore.: Press of the Chronicle Publishing Co., 1906), n.p., italics added, HEH E 01; M. F. Eggleston, *Jackson Co., Oregon* (Jackson Co., Ore.: Honorable Commissioner's Court, 1905), n.p., HEH E 01; Anon., *Tucson,* 20.

66. F. E. Prewitt, M.D., "Denver as a Health Resort: What a Prominent Physician Has to Say About Our Climate," *Colorado: A Monthly Magazine Devoted to Colorado*

in General and Denver in Particular, March 1905, no page numbers, in HEH E, Promotional, Colorado, box 1. For a typical example of the emphasis on Colorado's climate in early-twentieth-century promotional work, see *Colorado* (Chicago and Northwestern Railway, 1914), in HEH E, ibid.

67. Late-nineteenth-century booster publications did on occasion offer warnings and qualifications in connection with their western promises. For example, the "Kansas Pacific Homestead," a broadside from 1876, emphasized that potential Kansas homesteaders had to have *"something to start with"* (italics in original) and were likely to face some "privations"; DPL, B, C330.9781 K1335. See also Thomas McElrath in *The Yellowstone Valley: What It Is, Where It Is, and How to Get to It: A Hand-Book for Tourists and Settlers* (St. Paul, Minn.: Pioneer Press Company, 1880).

68. It is worth pointing out that Robert Edmund Strahorn, for all his confident rhetoric concerning the promise of the northwestern states in the 1880s, did offer words of caution in some of his writings. In *Oregon: A Complete and Comprehensive Description of the Agricultural, Stockraising, and Mineral Resources of Oregon; Also Statistics in Regard to Its Climate, etc., Compiled from the Very Latest Reports of 1888,* 2d ed., revised (Chicago: Rand McNally and Co., Printers, 1889), he wrote that newly arrived farmers "should have at least sufficient capital to be independent for twelve months" and added that "it is often best for the father to go out and pave the way for the little folks" (67). In *The Resources and Attractions of Washington Territory: A Complete and Comprehensive Description of the Agricultural, Stockraising, and Mineral Resources of Washington; Also Statistics in Regard to Its Climate, etc., Compiled from the Very Latest Reports of 1888,* 2d ed., revised and enlarged (Chicago: Rand McNally and Co., Printers, 1889), he wrote: "It is the poorest country in the world for wit-living representatives. It requires health, labor, courage, and persistence to succeed, as elsewhere, and immigrants must expect this" (79). Richard C. Overton provides discussion of the warnings issued to prospective settlers by the railroads as early as the 1870s, in *Burlington West: A Colonization History of the Burlington Railroad* (Cambridge, Mass.: Harvard University Press, 1941), 348–350.

69. Northern Pacific Railway, *What Montana Has to Offer Along the Northern Pacific, Yellowstone Park Line* (St. Paul, Minn.: Northern Pacific Railway, [1914?]) HEH E, IWMNG.

70. Robert W. Innes, *Resources of Albany County, Wyoming, 1913* (Laramie, Wyo.: Laramie Chamber of Commerce, 1913), in American Heritage Center, Special Collections, University of Wyoming (hereafter referred to as AHC SC), W99-c-aL-p.

71. Such letters also appear in great abundance in the literature of the first great booster age. See, for example, "Kansas Pacific Homestead" (1876).

72. "This Is the Place to Get a Start," letter from W. I. Sheets, Sand Creek, North Dakota, to George B. Haynes, Immigration Agent, Chicago, Milwaukee and St. Paul Railway, and "In Fact We Are Well Satisfied," letter from E. D. Jones, Mott, Hettinger County, North Dakota, presumably in response to an inquiry from a prospective settler, in Frederick Jackson Turner Papers, Henry E. Huntington Library (hereafter HEH TU), black box 13, number 257.

73. Letter from Chas. W. Peterson to Henry Sorensen, December 17, 1909, quoted in David C. Jones, *Feasting on Misfortune: Journeys of the Human Spirit in Alberta's Past* (Edmonton: University of Alberta Press, 1998), 89.

74. Sherman County Development League, *Sherman County, Oregon* (Portland, Ore.: *Sunset Magazine* Homeseekers Bureau, [1910?]), 11, 14, HEH E 01.

75. For more on Island County, see Richard White, *Land Use, Environment, and Social Change: The Shaping of Island County, Washington* (Seattle: University of Washington Press, 1980).

76. "Islands of the Blest," advertisement from the Seattle Real Estate Co. for Island County, Washington, in *The Coast* 19 (April 1910): 20; Hall, *Oregon, Washington, Idaho and Their Resources*, 63; Anon., *Tucson*, 6.

77. Pacific City Land Company, *Pacific City, in Tillamook County, Oregon: The Nearest Coast Resort to Portland: The Atlantic City of the West* (Portland, Ore.: Press of Harnden and Co., [1911?]), n.p.

78. Morrow County Booster Club, *Morrow County, Oregon* (Portland, Ore.: *Sunset Magazine* Homeseekers Bureau, [1911?]), 3.

79. Tacoma Commercial Club and Chamber of Commerce, *Tacoma: The City with a Snow-Capped Mountain in Its Dooryard* (Tacoma, Wash.: Tacoma Commercial Club and Chamber of Commerce, 1912), 3, HEH E W.

80. Ellis A. Davis, *Commercial Encyclopedia of the Pacific Southwest*, introduction. In addition to its interesting claim to legitimacy, Ellis's volume is noteworthy for the application of the region label "Pacific Southwest" to the four states that it discusses.

81. Duane A. Smith, *Rocky Mountain Boomtown: A History of Durango, Colorado*, 2d ed. (Niwot: University Press of Colorado, 1992), 10.

82. Nelson, *After the West Was Won*, 84. The "knocker" was periodically referred to in the booster literature. Boosters for the Twin Falls country of southern Idaho contended in 1913 that the wonders of the region had "forever silenced the 'knocker,'" and added, "He is dumbfounded in the presence of the evidence that is before him." See *The Twin Falls Country*, n.p.

83. Hicks, *The Populist Revolt*, 17.

84. See Wallace Stegner, introduction to *Where the Bluebird Sings to the Lemonade Springs: Living and Writing in the American West* (New York: Penguin, 1992), xv–xxiii. Stegner's treatment of "boomers" and "stickers" is discussed in Michael L. Johnson's *New Westers: The West in Contemporary American Culture* (Lawrence: University Press of Kansas, 1996), 111.

85. Mari Sandoz, *Old Jules* (1935; reprint, Lincoln: University of Nebraska Press, 1985). See also the forum on Sandoz in the *Great Plains Quarterly* 16 (winter 1996), especially Betsy Downey's "'She Does Not Write Like a Historian': Mari Sandoz and the New Western History," 9–28.

86. Helen Winter Stauffer, "Afterword," in *Old Jules*, 425–430, quotation on 427.

87. Ian Frazier, *Great Plains* (New York: Farrar, Straus and Giroux, 1989), 157.

88. Ibid., 209.

89. Sandoz, *Old Jules*, 209.

90. These acts of interior promotion have often been addressed in western American literature. A good example is John Steinbeck's 1933 novel *To a God Unknown,* with an introduction and notes by Robert DeMott (New York: Penguin, 1995). The novel's protagonist, Joseph Wayne, leaves Vermont in the early twentieth century and moves to central California, where he successfully establishes a homestead during a period of unusually high rainfall. He writes to invite his brothers to join him: "There's land untaken next to mine. . . . The grass is rich and deep, and the soil wants only turning. No rocks, Thomas, to make your plough turn somersaults, no ledges sticking out" (20). The brothers come and also experience quick success, but the dry years return, and the paradise that Joseph Wayne described loses its promise.

91. For the meaning of Jireh, see Mae Urbank, *Wyoming Place Names* (Missoula, Mont.: Mountain Press, 1988), 108–109. Urbank notes that Jireh was founded in 1908 and became the site of Jireh College, the first junior college in Wyoming. But drought and the post–World War I agrarian depression put an end to the settlement, and the college held its last graduation in 1920. It is interesting to note the boosterish tone of the "Prefatory" section of the Jireh College Bulletin, 1910, W994-t-jir, in SC, AHC, which notes that the college is "in the heart of an excellent agricultural district, and possesses fine natural scenery." The publication goes on to note that "the dry and bracing air is full of tonic and gives vigor to mind and body."

92. For more on this topic, see Orlando W. Miller, *The Frontier in Alaska and the Matanuska Colony* (New Haven, Conn.: Yale University Press, 1975). The promotional publication *Alaska: The Newest Home* (n.p., [1931?]), HEH E, Promotional, Alaska (hereafter HEH E A), includes coverage of Matanuska Valley. The region was described as having a mild climate and a soil of "rich loam underlaid with gravel," which, despite low rainfall, was capable of producing "luxuriant crops without irrigation" (3).

93. Anon., *Juneau Alaska and Vicinity: The Capital of the Northland—A Land of Enormous Natural Resources, of Industry and Homes, of Healthful and Moderate Climatic Conditions—A Wonderland of Alaskan Beauty and Modern Progress. Alaska: Authentic Information* (n.p., [1928?]), 3, HEH E A.

94. One might actually argue, to the contrary, that contemporary cynicism with regard to the promises of modern-day marketers makes us less surprised by the claims of western promoters a century ago.

3. Remembered Journeys

1. The term "Jayhawker" would not be applied to Kansans until the late 1850s.

2. Information on the Jayhawker deaths is drawn from Richard E. Lingenfelter, *Death Valley and the Amargosa: A Land of Illusion* (Berkeley and Los Angeles: University of California Press, 1986), 46.

3. The exact number of people in the Jayhawker Party is difficult to determine, since people periodically joined and abandoned the group during the course of the journey. L. Burr Beldon provides a "census" of all the Jayhawkers in his book *Goodbye Death Valley! The 1849 Jayhawker Escape* (Palm Desert, Calif.: Desert Magazine

Press, 1956). A listing of the Jayhawkers is also available in Jayhawker Photo Album 1, in the Jayhawker Collection, Henry E. Huntington Library, San Marino, California, comprising nine boxes of manuscripts, eight volumes of scrapbooks, and the photo album (hereafter HEH JC).

The brief summary of the Jayhawkers' journey provided here is drawn from various sources, including the entry for the Jayhawker Collection in the *Guide to Historical Manuscripts in the Huntington Library* (San Marino, Calif.: Huntington Library Press, 1979); John G. Ellenbecker, *The Jayhawkers of Death Valley* (Marysville, Kans.: privately printed, 1938); Federal Writers' Project of the Works Progress Administration of Northern California, *Death Valley: A Guide* (Boston: Houghton Mifflin, 1939), 14–19; Margaret Long, *The Shadow of the Arrow* (Caldwell, Idaho: Caxton Printers, 1941); Beldon, *Goodbye Death Valley!;* and L. Burr Beldon, ed., *Death Valley Heroine: And Source Accounts of the 1849 Travelers* (San Bernardino, Calif.: Inland Printing and Engraving Company, 1954); John Walton Caughey, "Southwest from Salt Lake in 1849," *Pacific Historical Review* 6 (1937): 142–164; Frank F. Latta, *Death Valley '49ers* (Santa Cruz, Calif.: Bear State Books, 1979); George Koenig, *Beyond This Place There Be Dragons: The Routes of the Death Valley 1849ers Through Nevada, Death Valley, and on to Southern California* (Glendale, Calif.: Arthur H. Clark, 1984); Lingenfelter, *Death Valley and the Amargosa,* 39–51; and Benjamin Levy, *Death Valley National Monument: Historical Background and Study* (Washington, D.C.: National Park Service, 1969). Leroy Johnson and Jean Johnson, eds., *Escape from Death Valley: As Told by William Manly Lewis and Other '49ers* (Reno: University of Nevada Press, 1987), provides a good overview of research on the Jayhawkers. Genne Nelson has prepared an excellent bibliography of sources related to the Jayhawkers (copy in author's possession).

4. It is possible that one of the other groups traveling across Death Valley around the same time as the Jayhawkers did engage in cannibalism. See Latta, *Death Valley '49ers,* 8.

5. Edward Bartholomew to Alonzo Clay, January 10, 1888, HEH JC, box 1, folder JA 23.

6. Charles Bert Mecum to Lorenzo Dow Stephens, January 16, 1901, HEH JC, box 6, folder JA 712. Mecum had first expressed this theme of deliverance from Death Valley in the letter "To Brother Jayhawkers," dated January 25, 1878, HEH JC, box 1, folder JA 716. It is not surprising that the theme of departed pioneers enjoying the rewards of heaven as spiritual payment for their endeavors is prevalent in the reminiscence genre. A speech delivered at a pioneer society reunion in 1895 serves as a particularly memorable and unsubtle example of the theme: "We firmly believe that these departed pioneers are today somewhere in the measureless beyond, freed from fettering habiliments of clay, on the wings of the spirit, perhaps mounting beyond the sun, passing from system to system—pioneering it may be—and with enraptured, beatific vision drinking in some of the glories of the illimitable universe of God"; address by M. Cavanaugh, in Old Settlers' Association, Johnson County, Iowa, *Proceedings of the Johnson County [Iowa] Old Settlers Association, from 1866 to 1899* (n.p., n.d.), NEW GC 2132, pp. 131–135, quotation on 135.

7. John Burt Colton, annual reunion invitation letter, January 8, 1906, HEH JC, box 4, folder JA 320–330.

8. See, for example, William Lewis Manly, "Climbing in Life" (February 10, 1893), HEH JC, box 3, folder JA 650.

9. HEH JC, Box 3, folder JA 135–138, 1894–1915, "Reunion regrets, etc."; William F. [Buffalo Bill] Cody to John Burt Colton, three letters and one telegram, and John Burt Colton to Theodore Roosevelt, one letter, all in HEH JC, box 5, folder JA 273–278, 1898–1902; and Frederic Remington to John Burt Colton, four letters, HEH JC, box 4, folder No. JA 804–807, 1897–1899. Colton appears in a photograph with Cody, R. H. ("Pony Bob") Haslam, Prentiss Ingraham, and Alexander Majors, in Colonel Prentiss Ingraham, ed., *Seventy Years on the Frontier: Alexander Majors' Memoirs of a Lifetime on the Border, with a Preface by (General W. F. Cody) Buffalo Bill* (Chicago: Rand McNally and Co., 1893), unnumbered page, between pp. 152 and 153.

10. George G. Spurr, Secretary, New England Associated California Pioneers of '49, to John Burt Colton, March 5, 1893, HEH JC, box 3, folder JA 891–892.

11. See, for example, Sharlot M. Hall, "In the Land of the Forty-Niners," *Out West* 29 (December 1908): 397–417.

12. Fuller coverage of the "crisis of the nineties" and the accompanying "frontier anxiety" is provided in David M. Wrobel, *The End of American Exceptionalism: Frontier Anxiety from the Old West to the New Deal* (Lawrence: University Press of Kansas, 1993).

13. William Lewis Manly, *Death Valley in '49* (San Jose, Calif.: Pacific Tree and Vine Co., 1894); reprint, Chicago: Lakeside Press, 1927). The material in the book was originally published as a series of letters in the *Santa Clara Daily* between June 1887 and July 1890. Manly was not an original member of the Jayhawker group, but he and another teamster, John Rogers, traveled with the Illinois party and various other smaller groups, including the Bennett and Arcane families, known respectively as the Bugsmashers and the Mississippians, through Death Valley. It was Manly and Rogers who would travel out of Death Valley to the California settlements and return with food for the Bennett and Arcane families. Manly is included among the Jayhawkers in the Jayhawker Photo Album, HEH, Special Collections, a collection of images taken in 1893. For more on Manly, see Patricia Nelson Limerick, *Desert Passages: Encounters with the American Deserts* (Albuquerque: University of New Mexico Press, 1985), 45–59. *Death Valley in '49* has been republished with foreword by Patricia Nelson Limerick and edited by Leroy Johnson and Jean Johnson (Santa Clara, Calif.: Santa Clara University; Berkeley, Calif.: Heydey Books, 2001).

14. Minnie Moeller to John Burt Colton, January 16, 1914, HEH JC, box 6, folder JA 747–751.

15. Charles Lummis to John Burt Colton, February 12, 1913, HEH JC, box 6, folder JA 591–595. See also Lummis's letters to Colton dated February 14, March 14, and April 6, 1914, and April 18, 1916, HEH JC, box 6, folder JA 596–600. It is worth noting that the two men had recently met, and Lummis's letter of February 12, 1913, followed an apparently quite heated verbal exchange as he sought to acquire important collections, such as the Jayhawkers', for the museum. Incidentally, Colton was

by this time living in Kansas City, Missouri, which in Lummis's estimation was no reason to deposit his party's records there instead of at the Southwest Museum.

16. That same year, 1919, on July 19, the *Saturday Evening Post*, in its "Stories of the Old West" section, featured Frederick R. Bechdolt's essay "How Death Valley Was Named," 30–34, 66, which provided extensive coverage of the Jayhawkers.

17. See Long, "Appendix C: The Jayhawker Reunions," in *The Shadow of the Arrow*, 277–280, 279.

18. The Jayhawker Collection includes correspondence, diaries, newspaper clippings, and a small photograph collection. The Huntington Library also houses the much larger collection of the papers of historian Frederick Jackson Turner. For close to a century, Turner has been at the center of scholarly debates over the significance of the frontier to American and American western history, debates that have paid very little attention to the memories of groups such as the Jayhawkers.

19. Latta, in *Death Valley '49ers*, refers to the efforts of the Jayhawkers and the seven other small parties to cross Death Valley as "the most astounding of all migratory epics to be recorded in the history of the settlement of America" (6–7). If the extent of scholarly coverage and public interest in an event is a yardstick of its importance, then the story of the Death Valley migrants does not live up to Latta's claim. The Jayhawkers and the approximately fifty other migrants have not been forgotten by history, but neither has their epic journey entered the public consciousness to nearly the same extent as that of the Donner Party. Even in late-nineteenth-century works of California history—such as Josiah Royce's *California: From the Conquest in 1846 to the Second Vigilance Committee in San Francisco* (Boston: Houghton Mifflin and Co., 1886)—the Donner Party commonly receives coverage, while the Death Valley migrants do not.

20. See Leroy C. Johnson, "The Trunk is Bunk," in *Proceedings of the Fifth Death Valley Conference on History and Prehistory, March 4–7, 1999*, ed. Jean Johnson (Bishop, Calif.: Community Printing and Publishing, 1999), 252–277.

21. Manly, *Death Valley in '49*, 464.

22. Ibid., 480–481.

23. Ibid. For an interesting account of the Briers' journey, see Rev. John Wells Brier, "The Death Valley Party of 1849," parts 1 and 2, *Out West* 18 (March 1903): 326–335; 18 (April 1903): 456–465. The author of the articles is the son of the Reverend James W. Brier and Juliet Brier. See also Grace Leadingham, "Juliet Wells Brier: Heroine of Death Valley," parts 1 and 2, *Pacific Historian* 8, no. 2 (1964): 61–74; no. 3 (1964): 121–127.

24. Manly, *Death Valley in '49*, 464. A rare exception to the common criticisms of the Reverend Brier in historical accounts is that of L. Burr Beldon in *Death Valley Heroine*, who writes of Manly: "His belittling references to the Rev. Mr. Brier, a sick man who survived despite the loss of one hundred pounds is shameful. The Methodist clergyman rendered a semi-invalid due to an intestinal disorder wasted from 175 to 75 pounds in the ordeal, a deliverance for which he ever gave his Creator credit" (13).

25. The quotation from Mrs. Brier appears in Robert Class Cleland, *From Wilderness to Empire: A History of California* (New York: Knopf, 1969), 132–133.

26. Charles Lummis, editorial note on the 1903 Jayhawker reunion, at the home of Juliet Brier, in Lodi, California, *Out West* 18 (March 1903): 326. For further praise of Juliet Brier and a positive view of her husband, see Charles F. Lummis, *Some Strange Corners of Our Country: The Wonderland of the Southwest* (New York: Century Co., 1891; reprint, Tucson: University of Arizona Press, 1989), 37–42; and the "Death Valley" chapter in Lummis, *Mesa, Cañyon and Pueblo: Our Wonderland of the Southwest—Its Marvels of Nature—Its Pageant of the Earth Building—Its Strange Peoples—Its Centuried Romance* (New York: Century Co., 1925), 63–78; and Thomas Shannon, "With the Jayhawkers in Death Valley Fifty-three Years Ago—A Little Band of Hardy Pioneers," *San Jose Daily Mercury*, November 16, 1903, reprinted in Beldon, *Death Valley Heroine*, 57–60. George Wharton James's chapters "The Generous Heroes of Death Valley, Manly and Rogers," and "The Unknown Heroes of Death Valley," in his *Heroes of California: The Story of the Founders of the Golden State as Narrated by Themselves or Gleaned from Other Sources* (Boston: Little, Brown, 1910), 73–85, 86–93, respectively, make no mention of the Brier family. One suspects that Lummis's extended coverage of the Briers in *Mesa, Cañyon and Pueblo* was partly a response to James's emphasis on Manly and Rogers.

27. In their correspondence the Jayhawkers reflected back on their ordeal and often discussed the bravery of Mrs. Brier. See, for example, Charles Burt Mecum, "To Honored Jayhawkers," February 4, 1872, HEH JC, box 1, folder JA 715. Mecum noted in the letter, "I have always remembered . . . that verry [sic] night after crossing the desert came the cheering words from that good woman Mrs Brier the darkest time is just before the day and other similar expressions of cheer."

28. Latta provides good coverage of Juliet Brier in *Death Valley '49ers*, 1–4.

29. Lummis, *Mesa, Cañyon and Pueblo*, 74.

30. Juliet Brier, "Our Christmas amid the Terrors of Death Valley," *San Francisco Call*, December 25, 1898, 19; reprinted in Belden, *Death Valley Heroine*, 21–28. See also "Mrs. Brier's Last Account," *San Francisco Examiner*, February 24, 1901; reprinted in *The Carson City* (Nev.) *News*, June 8, 1913; this latter reprint is included in Beldon, *Death Valley Heroine*, 31–35.These accounts are also reprinted in Long, *The Shadow of the Arrow*, 195–215. The Reverend John W. Brier died on November 2, 1898.

31. Latta provides some coverage of James Brier's disassociation from the Jayhawkers in *Death Valley '49ers*, 169–186.

32. There certainly seems to have been no lack of media interest in her story.

33. Ellenbecker, *The Jayhawkers of Death Valley*, 130.

34. For a discussion of the luxuries of the Pullman Palace Car and the effect on tourists' perceptions of the West, see Anne F. Hyde, *An American Vision: Far Western Landscape and National Culture, 1820–1920* (New York: New York University Press, 1990), 117–120. The juxtaposition of Pullman Palace Car traveling with more demanding modes of travel in earlier periods also appears often in late-nineteenth-century western guidebooks; however, in these sources the purpose is rather different. Guidebook writers were emphasizing that modern transportation made visiting the West more comfortable; indeed, opulently apportioned train carriages made

western travel a no less cultured experience than visiting Europe. Pioneer reminiscers, on the other hand, stressed that modern transportation, while it made the West more accessible, more comfortable, and perhaps even more cultured, did not necessarily make it a better place. In fact, their true point of emphasis was that one could only really know and understand the West if one had traversed it prior to the Pullman era.

35. Alfred Lambourne, *The Old Journey: Reminiscences of Pioneer Days* (Salt Lake City [?], Utah: George Q. Cannon and Sons Co., 1892–1897), 23. In a similar vein, Robert Vaughn, in his book of reminiscences, *Then and Now; or Thirty-six Years in the Rockies* (Minneapolis, Minn.: Tribune Printing Co., 1900), expressed his hope that "a line here and there will be appreciated by those who ride in palace cars as well as the old pioneers who came West in prairie schooners" (preface, unnumbered page).

36. Francis Parkman, *The Oregon Trail: Sketches of Prairie and Rocky-Mountain Life* (Boston: Little, Brown, 1892), viii.

37. George E. Place, untitled speech in *Annual Report of the Los Angeles County Pioneers of Southern California, 1909–1910* (n.p.: Print of Gazette Publishing Co., 1910), 5; available in Los Angeles County, Pioneer Society Annual Reports, 1908–1915, HEH RB, 106161.

38. In ibid., Appendix, p. 2.

39. The juxtaposition of Pullman Palace Car and prairie schooner appears again and again in the pioneer society proceedings and in published pioneer reminiscences. Among the more notable examples are Emiline L. Fuller, *Left by the Indians: Story of My Life* (Mount Vernon, Iowa: Hawkeye Steam Print, 1892), 7; Vaughn, *Then and Now,* 63; Mrs. William Markland Molson, "Glimpses of Life in Early Oregon," *Quarterly of the Oregon Historical Society* 1 (June 1900): 158–164; 158; Sarah Fell, "Threads of Alaskan Gold" (manuscript, 1904), 35, NEW GC 1303; Arthur L. Stone, *Following Old Trails* (Missoula, Mont.: Morton John Elrod, 1913), 195, 302; Minnie Moeller to John Burt Colton, January 16, 1914; Mrs. Helen B. Ladd, President of the Pioneer Women, address, "Pioneer and Old Settlers' Day," October 16, 1915, at the Panama-Pacific Exposition, in *California Pioneers of Santa Clara County: Pioneer and Old Settlers' Day* (n.p., n.d.), HEH RB 260530, 53–54; George W. Riddle, *History of Early Days in Oregon* (Riddle, Ore.: Riddle Enterprise, 1920), 30. A final example worth mentioning appears in the poem "The Disappointed Tenderfoot," reprinted in Luke Voorhees, *Personal Recollections of Pioneer Life on the Mountains and Plains of the Great West* (Cheyenne, Wyo.: privately published, 1920), in the Ayer Collection, Newberry Library (hereafter NEW AC), 128.5 V8. The poem begins, "He reached the West in a palace car, Where the writers tell us the cowboys are."

40. Old Settlers' Association of Minnesota, *A Sketch of the Organization, Objects, and Membership of the Old Settlers' Association of Minnesota* (Saint Paul, Minn.: Ramaley, Chaney and Co., Printers, 1872), 18–22. In her reminiscence "Pioneering in Crook County," *Annals of Wyoming* 3 (April 1926): 210, Eva Ogden Putnam recounts her chance meeting on a Pullman car with another old-timer from the early days.

41. Sacramento Society of California Pioneers, *Grand Excursion from Sacramento to New York in a Special Train of Pullman Cars via the Great Overland Route* (Sacramento, Calif.: Jefferis Printer, 1869), HEH RB 65323.

42. J. Valerie Fifer, *American Progress: The Growth of Transport, Tourist, and Information Industries in the Nineteenth-Century West* (Chester, Conn.: Globe Pequot Press, 1988), 9.

43. Nicholas Ball, *The Pioneers of '49: A History of the Excursion of the Society of California Pioneers of New England from Boston to the Leading Cities of the Golden State, April 10–May 17, 1890, with Reminiscences and Descriptions* (Boston: Lee and Shepard Publishers, 1891), 5.

44. Ibid., 49.

45. Margaret Hill McCarter, *Vanguards of the Plains: A Romance of the Old Santa Fé Trail* (New York: A. L. Burt Co., 1917), part 4, "Remembering the Trail," 391–398, quotation on 394. The book's dedication page reads: "This story of the old Santa Fé Trail would do honor to the memory of those stalwart men who defied the desert, who walked the prairies boldly, and who died bravely—vanguards in the building of a firm highway for commerce of a westward-moving Empire," unnumbered page. The couple decide to engage in the journey reenactment rather than "have all our children and grandchildren and friends coming to offer us gold coins, gold-headed canes—which I do not use—and gold-rimmed glasses for eyes that see farther and clearer than my spectacled grandsons at the university see to-day" (394).

46. Ibid., 395, 396.

47. Ibid., 397.

48. Whether the United States had entered the war while McCarter was still working on the novel is unclear. The book was published in October 1917; Woodrow Wilson's declaration of war came the previous April.

49. McCarter, *Vanguards of the Plains*, 393.

50. Other novels by Margaret Hill McCarter that helped keep the frontier theme in the public imagination include *The Price of the Prairie* (Chicago: A. C. McClurg and Co., 1911); and *Winning the Wilderness* (Chicago: A. C. McClurg and Co., 1914). Some of McCarter's other novels also have western themes; see *The Reclaimers* (New York: A. L. Burt Co., 1918); and *Homeland: A Present-Day Love Story* (New York: Harper and Brothers, 1922). The old Santa Fe Trail is also featured in *Homeland*.

51. The material on Cody is drawn from the three chapters that Paul Reddin devotes to him in *Wild West Shows* (Urbana: University of Illinois Press, 1999), 53–157, quotation on 155. See also Richard White, "Frederick Jackson Turner and Buffalo Bill," in *The Frontier in American Culture: Essays by Richard White and Patricia Nelson Limerick*, ed. James R. Grossman (Berkeley and Los Angeles: University of California Press, 1994), 7–65.

52. Reddin, *Wild West Shows*, 156.

53. Ezra Meeker, *Washington Territory West of the Cascade Mountains: Containing a Description of Puget Sound and Waters Emptying in to It* (Olympia, Washington Terrritory: Printed at the Transcript Office, 1870), 13, 9–10, italics added, HEH RB, 35037 (and 35036, signed copy of the reprint, also published in 1870).

54. Californian John S. Hittell serves as another good example of the booster-reminiscer combination; see chapter 4. Momentous events, such as world's fairs, also provided the occasion for western places to both sell their future and honor their past within the pages of the same publication; see, for example, Bisbee Daily Review: *World's Fair Edition* (St. Louis: Samuel F. Meyerson Printing Co., 1904), which contains the standard promotional prose and statistical evidence along with a section titled "The Pioneers of Arizona."

55. Ezra Meeker, *The Busy Life of Eighty-five Years of Ezra Meeker: Ventures and Adventures* (Seattle, Wash.: published by the author, 1916; Indianapolis: William B. Burford, 1916). Meeker also authored a number of other works, including *Hop Culture in the United States: Being a Practical Treatise on Hop Growing in Washington Territory, from the Cutting to the Bale* (Puyallup, Washington Territory: E. Meeker and Co., 1883); *Uncle Ezra's Short Stories for Children* (Tacoma, Wash.: D. W. Cooper, Printer, 1910[?]); *Pioneer Reminiscences of Puget Sound: The Tragedy of Leschi* (Seattle, Wash.: Lowman and Hanford Stationery and Printing Co., 1905); *The Ox-Team; or, The Old Oregon Trail, 1852–1906* (Lincoln, Nebr.: Jacob North and Co., 1906), HEH RB 34143, his first published account of the journey; *Ventures and Adventures of Ezra Meeker; or Sixty Years of Frontier Life* (Seattle, Wash.: Rainier Printing Co., 1908); *Personal Experiences on the Oregon Trail Sixty Years Ago* (Seattle, Wash.: published by the author, 1912), a cheap, soft-cover reprint of portions of his previously published books; *Seventy Years of Progress in Washington* (Seattle, Wash.: Allstrum Printing Co., 1921); *Kate Mulhall: A Romance of the Oregon Trail* (New York: published by the author, 1926); and *Ox-Team Days on the Oregon Trail,* in collaboration with Howard R. Driggs, Pioneer Life Series (Yonkers-on-Hudson, N.Y., 1922).

Meeker has been the subject of a few articles, including Gladys Shafer, "Eastward Ho! Ezra Meeker Memorializes the Oregon Trail, 1905–1910," *American West* 5 (November 1968): 42–48; John Clark Hunt, "The Oregon Trail: Then and Now," *American History Illustrated* 3 (May 1968): 24–29; and Bruce J. Noble Jr., "Marking Wyoming's Oregon Trail," *Overland Journal,* 4, no. 3 (1986): 19–31.

56. The phrase "truth is stranger than fiction" appeared quite often in pioneer reminiscences as authors sought to establish the authenticity of their acounts.

57. Meeker, *The Busy Life of Eighty-five Years,* ix, 243–246. Meeker also provided extensive commentary on the grand purpose behind his journey back across the Oregon Trail in "The Lost Oregon Trail" (a lecture that he delivered during his second journey back across the trail in 1910), reprinted in Ezra Meeker, *Story of the Lost Trail to Oregon* (Seattle, Wash., 1915), 22–31, HEH RB 2213. He noted in that speech that "the pioneers of that day were stalwarts—stalwarts in strength, in courage, in integrity, in manly and womanly virtue" (26). He added, "The conquering of the farther West, written in the blood of many martyrs, is a theme not only to fire the imagination, but likewise to bring a sober second thought for the duties of the hour, to preserve the legacy handed down to the present generation, to impel the study of the old-time ways, to compare the present with the past, remembering that all changes are not betterments" (27).

58. Meeker, *The Busy Life of Eighty-five Years,* 303. The Kearney, Nebraska, epidode is also related in *The Ox-Team; or The Old Oregon Trail,* 186–187.

59. Meeker, *The Ox-Team; or, The Old Oregon Trail.*

60. For more on the financing of the trip, see Shafer, "Eastward Ho!" 45–46.

61. Meeker, *The Busy Life of Eighty-five Years,* 305–306.

62. Anon., "Tells the Story of the Oregon Trail: Ezra Meeker, Native Ohioan, Coast Pioneer, Outlines National Road Project. His Ox Team and 'Prairie Schooner' Arouse Much Interest on the Streets," *Ohio State Journal,* April 23, 1907; reprinted in Meeker, *Story of the Lost Trail to Oregon,* 8–14, quotation on 8.

63. Meeker, *The Busy Life of Eighty-five Years,* 306–308.

64. Ibid., 323.

65. See the *Kearney Daily Hub,* June 1, 9, and 11, 1910. For reports on Meeker's second visit to Kearney, see the *Daily Hub,* July 27, 1910.

66. For a full account of the "Trails" issue in Congress, see offprint from the *Congressional Record* (Washington, D.C.: Government Printing Office, 1927), 1–7, in AHC SC.

67. Meeker, *The Busy Life of Eighty-five Years,* 343. An advertisement for the automobile is featured in the volume, which was published in that city. It should be noted that Meeker was not alone in his efforts to memorialize old pioneer trails and other frontier landmarks. Such efforts were commonly undertaken by pioneer societies in the early decades of the twentieth century. See, for example, the Society of Montana Pioneers, *Thirty-third Annual Meeting Report* (Helena, Mont.: Society of Montana Pioneers, 1917), which discusses the construction of monuments for the Mullen Military Road, for cemeteries, and even "historic gulches" (11, 17, 19, 23–24).

68. In addition to his 1906 and 1916 accounts of the journeys back over the trail in the ox-drawn prairie schooner, he also published a book, *Pioneer Reminiscences of Puget Sound,* in 1905. Then, in 1921, during the "down time" between his first Oregon Trail automobile trip and his first plane trip over the old route, his *Seventy Years of Progress in Washington* appeared. Meeker included in the book a chapter titled "Transportation and Travel," 35–47, which chronicled the various changes in conveyances, all of which he had fully experienced. Interestingly, he mused in the chapter about the future possibility of electricity-driven cars (43). The book also contains a full reprint of Meeker's promotional brochure *Washington Territory West of the Cascade Mountains,* discussed in chapter 1.

69. See Dumas Malone, ed., *Dictionary of American Biography,* vol. 6 (New York: Scribner's, 1961), 495–496. For more on the commemoration of the Oregon Trail in 1930, see the folder "The Oregon Trail, Articles," in Edmund Seymour Collection, box 6, AHC SC. Hoover's proclamation is contained in this folder. The same box contains the folder "The Oregon Trail: Reports," which chronicle the work of the Oregon Trail Memorial Association and its successor organization, the American Pioneer Trails Association; miscellaneous flyers and commemorative maps and articles from the 1930 centennial event and a file of newspaper clippings on Meeker are also in the folder.

Those less affected, economically, by the depression could purchase, for fifty dollars, a miniature model (17 inches long, 8¼ inches wide, 9¾ inches high) of Meeker's prairie schooner for their mantelpieces; see newspaper advertisement in Scrapbook, Seymour Collection, box 8, AHC SC 6138; see also the illustration on p. 150, this volume.

70. Biographical information on Eliza Poor Donner Houghton is drawn from the finding aid for the Eliza Poor Donner Houghton Papers in the Huntington Library (hereafter HEH EPDH), which houses the collection.

71. C. W. Chapman to Eliza Poor Donner Houghton, May 22, 1910, HEH EPDH 58138. Houghton's account of the Donner ordeal, *The Expedition of the Donner Party and Its Tragic Fate* (Chicago: A. C. McClurg and Co., 1911), begins with a discussion of Chapman's letter of May 22 and quotes this passage.

72. C. W. Chapman to Eliza Poor Donner Houghton, December 25, 1914, HEH EPDH 58145.

73. For more on this phenomenon in more recent decades, see David Lowenthal, *The Heritage Crusade and the Spoils of History* (New York: Cambridge University Press, 1998); first published as *Possessed by the Past: The Heritage Crusade and the Spoils of History* (New York: Free Press, 1996).

74. Elliott West, "Stories," in *The Way to the West,* Calvin P. Horn Lectures in Western History and Culture (Albuquerque: University of New Mexico Press, 1995), 127–166.

75. See, for example, Richard W. Etulain, *Re-imagining the Modern American West: A Century of Fiction, History, and Art* (Tucson: University of Arizona Press, 1996), 101. Etulain provides a subtle analysis of "The Leader of the People" in relation to issues of regional identity in the West.

76. John Steinbeck, "The Leader of the People," in *The Long Valley* (New York: Viking, 1938), 198–214. While Grandfather Tifflin comes across as a pathetic figure, Steinbeck's story is a fascinating example of generational divides. A gulf separates Grandfather Tifflin from his son, but his grandson loves to listen to the stories of westering and longs for new frontiers.

77. Carrie Adell Strahorn, *Fifteen Thousand Miles by Stage: A Woman's Unique Experience During Thirty Years of Path Finding and Pioneering, from the Missouri to the Pacific and from Alaska to Mexico* (New York: G. P. Putnam's Sons, 1911; republished in two volumes, Lincoln: University of Nebraska Press, 1988); quotations are from the 1911 edition.

78. Robert E. Strahorn's *The Hand-Book of Wyoming, and Guide to the Black Hills and Big Horn Regions: A Glimpse at the Special Resources of the Territory* (Cheyenne, Wyo.: Knight and Leonard Printers, 1877) is discussed in chapter 1.

79. Strahorn, *The Hand-Book of Wyoming,* 243–249.

80. Strahorn, *Fifteen Thousand Miles by Stage,* unnumbered dedication page, and p. 673.

81. Ibid., vi.

82. Ibid., unnumbered dedication page, and p. 673.

83. Ibid., 89.

84. Ibid., vii.

85. "Caldwell and Other Frontier Towns," in ibid., 492–514, quotation on 492–493.

86. Ibid., 494–495.

87. Interesting in this context is Putnam's reminiscence of early days in Wyoming, published in 1926 but reflecting back on the early 1880s, a few years after Strahorn published his *Hand-Book of Wyoming*. In "Pioneering in Crook County," Putnam paints a picture of life in this period as harsh and demanding, just as Carrie Adell Strahorn did. However, Putnam adds, in classic pioneer reminiscence fashion, "What I experienced then seemed as all right and life as good and as worth living as it seems today with all its conveniences and modern inventions" (203). See also Mrs. S. L. Mills's reminiscence, written in 1927, recounting the life of her father, George W. Laney, who came to Wyoming in 1883, "A Wyoming Trail Blazer," *Annals of Wyoming* 6 (July 1929): 216–221.

88. Robert was fifty-nine years old at the time Carrie's book was published. Born in 1852, he would not die until 1944.

89. Oliver Knight discusses Robert Strahorn's autobiography and his possible coauthorship of Carrie Strahorn's *Fifteen Thousand Miles by Stage* in "Robert E. Strahorn: Propagandist for the West," *Pacific Northwest Quarterly* 59 (January 1968): 33–45. The quotations from Strahorn's "Ninety Years of Boyhood" are on p. 259 of the typescript (housed in the library of Albertson College, Idaho), cited in Knight, "Robert E. Strahorn," 45; and in Judith Austin's "Introduction" to Carrie Adell Strahorn, *Fifteen Thousand Miles by Stage,* vol. 1, *1877–1880* (Lincoln: University of Nebraska Press, 1988), vii–xii, x.

4. Organizing Memories

1. Michael Kammen, in *Mystic Chords of Memory: The Transformation of Tradition in American Culture* (New York: Knopf, 1991), 254–282, provides an excellent discussion of the broader national context surrounding the foundation of pioneer societies.

2. Membership figures are from Los Angeles County Pioneer Society, *Historical Record and Souvenir of the Pioneer Society of Los Angeles County* (Los Angeles: Times-Mirror Press, 1923), 18, HEH RB 194183. Interestingly, the Oregon Pioneer and Historical Society was separate from the larger Oregon Pioneer Association. The two groups did attempt to merge in 1874–1875, but the effort failed.

3. The full text of Clemens's response to the Tri-State Old Settlers' invitation reads:

> Dear Sir:—Frankness, candor, truthfulness—these are native to my nature; and so I will not conceal from you the fact that there is one thing which I am particularly and obstinately prejudiced against, it is travel. I should dearly like to see the friends; and would like to *be* there; and *if* there would do my full share, and be as good or as bad, as proper or improper as circumstances might require to make things prosper and go lively—but the journey lies between, and it blocks the way.
> Truly, your friend,
>
> S. L. CLEMENS   Hartford, Conn., June 20, 1887

The letter is in Tri-State Old Settlers' Association, *Report of the Fourth Tri-State Reunion, August 30, 1887* (Keokuk, Iowa: Press of the Gate City, 1887), 67, NEW GC 4197.

4. For more on pioneer society cutoff dates, see Clyde A. Milner II, "The View from Wisdom: Region and Identity in the Minds of Four Westerners," *Montana: The Magazine of Western History* 41 (Summer 1991): 2–17.

5. Hiram Knowles to J. H. Cole, Secretary, Tri-State Old Settlers Association, September 15, 1885, in Tri-State Old Settlers' Association, *Report of the Second Reunion of the Tri-State Old Settlers' Association, September 30, 1885* (Keokuk, Iowa: R. B. Ogden and Son, Printing and Binding, 1885), 73.

6. Milner, "The View from Wisdom," 213.

7. Euclid Sanders, untitled speech, June 2, 1866, in Old Settlers' Association, Johnson County, Iowa, *Proceedings of the Johnson County [Iowa] Old Settlers' Association, from 1866 to 1899* (n.p., n.d.), 22, NEW GC 2132.

8. The statement of purpose was adopted by county-level pioneer societies in California. See, for example, Sacramento Society of California Pioneers, *Constitution and By-Laws* (Sacramento, Calif.: H. A. Weaver, Printer, 1877), 30. For examples of the adoption of the same statement of purpose in other western states, see the Colorado Pioneer Register, containing the "Constitution and By-Laws of the Society of Colorado Pioneers" (1872), in Maria Davies McGrath Collection, DPL; and Arizona Pioneers Historical Society, *Constitution and By-Laws* (1897), HEH RB 425460.

9. For an excellent overview of Bancroft's career, see Charles S. Peterson, "Hubert Howe Bancroft: First Western Regionalist," in *Writing Western History: Essays on Major Western Historians*, ed. Richard W. Etulain (Albuquerque: University of New Mexico Press, 1991), 43–70, esp. 51.

10. For more on Bancroft's role in the construction of a gold rush mythology, see Glen Gendzel, "Pioneers and Padres: Competing Mythologies in Northern and Southern California, 1850–1930," *Western Historical Quarterly* 32 (spring 2001): 56–79, esp. 60–62.

11. Farwell's report "In the Matter of the Society of California Pioneers Vs. Hubert Howe Bancroft, an Honorary Member of Said Society," is in *Proceedings of the Society of California Pioneers in Reference to the Histories of Hubert Howe Bancroft* (San Francisco: Sterett Printing Co., 1894), 4–6. In his report Farwell also highlighted what he saw as numerous errors in Bancroft's *History of Oregon*, 2 vols. (1886–1888).

Josiah Royce, in his earlier work *California: From the Conquest in 1846 to the Second Vigilance Committee in San Francisco* (Boston: Houghton Mifflin and Co., 1886), drew on the documentary sources in Bancroft's library to produce a damning account of Frémont's central role in the Bear Flag Revolt of 1846. Royce wrote: "He brought war into a peaceful department; his operations began an estrangement, insured a memory of bloodshed, excited a furious bitterness of feeling between two peoples that were henceforth to dwell in California, such as all his own subsequent personal generosity and kindness could never again make good." Royce added, "From the Bear Flag affair we can date the beginning of the degradation, the ruin, and the oppression of the Californian people by our own" (111–112). A good portion of Royce's

California, 48–150, is devoted to undermining Frémont's own version of his role in the revolt.

12. Royce, "The Conquerors and Their Consciences," in *California,* pp. 152–156. For excellent coverage of Royce, see Robert V. Hine, *Josiah Royce: From Grass Valley to Harvard* (Norman: University of Oklahoma Press, 1992); Hine, "The Western Intellectual: Josiah Royce," *Montana: The Magazine of Western History* 41 (summer 1991): 70–72; and Hine, "The American West as Metaphysics: A Perspective on Josiah Royce," *Pacific Historical Review* 58 (1989): 267–291.

13. Society of California Pioneers, *Proceedings of the Society of California Pioneers in Reference to the Histories of Hubert Howe Bancroft,* 31–32. The response of the Society to Bancroft's "revisionist" histories serves as an interesting early example of the debate over who owns the past when collective memories collide with historical reconstructions. Notable recent examples of this clash include the controversy surrounding the Smithsonian Institution's 1995 exhibit marking the fiftieth anniversary of the dropping of the atomic bombs, the heated debate over the National History Standards in the middle to late 1990s, and, of course, the storm that accompanied the Smithsonian's *The West as America* exhibit in 1990–1991. Regarding the Smithsonian's Enola Gay exhibit: World War II veterans played a role similar to that of the pioneers as they sought to preserve the sanctity of their memories of past events.

14. The reminiscences, like the booster literature, can be treated as a genre, regardless of the particular subregion that they emerged from or focused on. Promotional writing for different western places is characterized by the same modes of presentation; the same emphasis on mild climate, marvelous fertility, abundant cultural amenities, and frontier opportunities; and an absolute absence of frontier conditions. Similarly, western pioneer reminiscences share certain stylistic features and areas of emphasis. Chief among these features is the reminiscers' emphasis on the hardships of the frontier processes of journeying to, transforming, and adjusting to new western settings.

15. The quotation is a composite constructed by the author. Such remarks can be found in the prefaces of most volumes of pioneer reminiscences.

16. While antiquarians have pored over these sources, professional historians have largely ignored them.

17. An interesting example of this "frontier anxiety" appears in a speech by Illinois governor R. J. Oglesby delivered to the Tri-State Old Settlers' Association of Illinois, Mississippi, and Iowa in 1885. Oglesby noted that "western intellect and vigor" had grown out of the frontier experience, when there had been "a boundless field for the display of our strength, because there seemed no limit to our territory." However, he expressed his concern that with the frontier now closed, the time would come when "we must have room or there will be reaction and decay." He added, ominously, "If this people is to go on swarming and the land not growing an inch, how much of a scholar will it take to tell how long before we have trouble in this precinct?" See Governor R. J. Oglesby, untitled speech, in *Report of the Second Reunion of the Tri-State Old Settlers' Association,* 16–21, NEW GC 4197.

18. Allan G. Bogue, *Frederick Jackson Turner: Strange Roads Going Down* (Norman: University of Oklahoma Press, 1998), 116.

19. For more on Turner's youth in Portage, see ibid., 3–15; see p. 13 for Andrew Jackson Turner's probable authorship of the Columbia County history of 1880.

20. See, for example, Governor R. J. Oglesby, untitled speech, 16–21. Oglesby noted that "this western intellect and vigor all grew out of circumstances"—the circumstances of frontier settlement. In a report to the same Tri-State Old Settlers' Association (of Illinois, Missouri, and Iowa), also in September 1885, Governor E. Carr of Galesburg, Illinois, discussed the emergence of a new American type that had resulted from the intermingling of the "best blood of New England, of the Middle States, of Virginia, and the Carolinas," see pp. 27–30, quotation on 29. These expressions of essential elements of what would later be welded by Turner into a full-fledged frontier thesis were common to the reminiscence genre. These "common culture corollaries" of that thesis demonstrate the pervasiveness of the frontier theme in American thought and culture. For example, a speech by Robert Lucas, delivered at the Thirty-seventh Annual Reunion of the Old Settlers of Johnson County, Iowa in 1903, parallels so closely the key contours of Turner's thesis that scholars would be likely to simply assume that the largely unknown Lucas was deeply indebted intellectually to the now-renowned (among scholars at least) Turner. Like Turner, Lucas used the terms "independence"and "self-reliance" and also discussed the adoption of Indian ways by pioneers. But these terms are so common, and these key contours so well established in the pioneer literature of the period, that we cannot assume direct intellectual debts to Turner. See "Robert Lucas' Address," in Old Settlers' Association, Johnson County, Iowa, *Proceedings of the Johnson County [Iowa] Old Settlers' Association, August 20, 1903* (n.p., n.d.), NEW GC 2135, 4–9. It is worth emphasizing that Turner, unlike some of the later defenders of his theories, did not place great emphasis on the theme of the frontier as a safety valve for urban discontent.

21. E. G. Cattermole, *Famous Frontiersmen, Pioneers and Scouts: The Vanguards of American Civilization. A Thrilling Narrative of the Lives and Marvelous Exploits of the Most Renowned Heroes, Trappers, Explorers, Adventurers, Scouts and Indian Fighters* (Chicago: Donohue, Henneberry and Co., 1890), iii. While not strictly a part of the pioneer reminiscence genre, Cattermole's book certainly reflects the genre's key themes.

22. For more on this theme, see Michael Kimmel, *Manhood in America: A Cultural History* (New York: Free Press, 1996), esp. 60–64, 87–89, 148–155; and Gail Bederman, *Manliness and Civilization: A Cultural History of Gender and Race in the United States, 1880–1917* (Chicago: University of Chicago Press, 1995).

23. Francis Parkman, *The Oregon Trail: Sketches of Prairie and Rocky-Mountain Life* (Boston: Little, Brown, 1892), vii.

24. Roosevelt to Francis V. Greene, September 23, 1897, quoted in Howard K. Beale, *Theodore Roosevelt and the Rise of America to World Power* (Baltimore: Johns Hopkins University Press, 1956), 37.

25. A good example of this increasingly abundant genre is Alice Polk Hill's *Tales of the Colorado Pioneers* (Denver: Pierson and Gardner, 1884), since it typifies the

appearance of numerous state-level collections of pioneer reminiscences by the early 1880s. See also John W. Clampitt, *Echoes from the Rocky Mountains: Reminiscences and Thrilling Incidents of the Romantic and Golden Age of the Great West, with a Graphic Account of Its Discovery, Settlement and Grand Development* (Chicago: Belford, Clarke and Co., 1889), vi.

26. See the *Colorado Pioneer Register,* Maria Davies McGrath Collection, DPL, 27.

27. See Oregon Pioneer Association, "Constitution of the Oregon Pioneer Association," in *Oregon Pioneer Association, Constitution and Transactions, 1st–14th, 1874–1886* (Salem, Ore.: E. M. Waite, Steam Printer and Bookbinder; and Portland, Ore.: Press of Geo. H. Himes, 1875–1887), 1874, p. 4.

28. Colonel Wilbur F. Sanders, "The Pioneers," delivered in Helena, Montana, July 6, 1902, quoted in Mary Ronan and Margaret Ronan, *The Story of Mary Ronan, as Told to Margaret Ronan,* ed. H. G. Merriam (Missoula: University of Montana, 1973), viii.

29. Among the many notable instances of recognition of pioneer women are Jacob Ricord, "Reminiscences of Pioneer Women," speech at the Twenty-seventh Annual Meeting of the Johnson County (Iowa) Old Settlers' Association, August 24, 1893, in *Proceedings;* Charles Prosch, *Reminiscences of Washington Territory: Scenes, Incidents, and Reflections of the Pioneer Period on Puget Sound* (Seattle, Wash., 1904), 122, NEW GC 3367. See also Sarah Fell's autobiography, "Threads of Alaskan Gold" (manuscript, 1904), NEW GC.

30. John Frost, *Pioneer Mothers of the West; or, Heroic and Daring Deeds of American Women, Comprising Thrilling Episodes of Courage, Fortitude, Devotedness, and Self-Sacrifice* (Boston: Lee and Shepard, 1875), 7–8. Many of Frost's stories were from the late-eighteenth- and early-nineteenth-century Trans-Appalachian frontier, but the centerpiece of the book, "Wonderful Fortitude of Female Emigrants," dealt with the terrible privations faced by the Donner Party women in 1846–1847. See also William W. Fowler's *Women on the American Frontier* (Hartford, Conn.: S. S. Scranton and Co., 1876), 3–4. Like Frost, Fowler focused his narrative on the early frontier period.

31. Dr. John Bell, "The Pioneer Women of Louisa County," in Pioneer Settlers' Association of Louisa County, Iowa, *Constitution and By-Laws of the Pioneer Settlers' Association of Louisa County, Iowa, with the Proceedings of the First and Second Annual Festivals* (Wapello, Iowa: John Jenkins, Printer, 1860), 6, NEW GC 3299.

32. Harry Noyes Pratt's "The Pioneer Mother," in Elisha Brooks, *A Pioneer Mother of California* (San Francisco: Harr Wagner Publishing Co., 1922), preface, unnumbered page.

33. "Woman Who Fought Savages Smiles at Troubles," *San Antonio Express,* November 16, 1930, reprinted in *Frontier Times* 8 (January 1931): 179–180.

34. Quoted in Mary Murphy, *Mining Cultures: Men, Women, and Leisure in Butte, 1914–41* (Urbana: University of Illinois Press, 1997), 76. Murphy also points to examples of Montana women in the 1930s who emphasized the importance of such rugged pioneering efforts in settling a new frontier, viewing them as more significant than the pioneering efforts of Montana women in the areas of temperance and suffrage.

35. Mr. Hyde, "How the First Farmers Labored," posthumously delivered paper, Old Settlers of Johnson County, *Thirty-sixth Annual Reunion of the Old Settlers of Johnson County, August 21, 1902* (Iowa City, 1902), 20–24, quotation on 24.

36. Luella Shaw, *True History of Some of the Pioneers of Colorado* (Hotchkiss, Colo.: W. S. Coburn, John Patterson, and A. K. Shaw, 1909), vi.

37. Ibid., 267–268.

38. William A. McKeever, *The Pioneer: A Story of the Making of Kansas,* 2d ed. (Topeka, Kans.: Crane and Co., Publishers, 1912), preface, unnumbered page. The bulk of McKeever's text was composed of an epic poem of about eighty-five pages, 1,700 lines, recounting the harsh conditions that Kansas pioneers had faced and triumphed over. For earlier examples of this sentiment, see N. S. Hurd, "Loyalty of the Pioneers," in Shaw, *True History of Some of the Pioneers of Colorado,* 253–263, quotation on 257; and John S. Hittell, "The Achievements of California," in *Celebration of the Forty-second Anniversary of the Admission of California into the Union, by the Society of California Pioneers,* El Campo, Marin County, September 9, 1892 (San Francisco: B. F. Sterett Book and Job Printer, 1892), 6. Also interesting in this context are Hittell's "Reminiscences of the Plains and Mines in '49 and '50" (the first of the course of Lick [James Lick] Lectures, delivered, before the Society of California Pioneers, San Francisco, January 5, 1887), 17-page typed, numbered pamphlet (offprint), HEH RB 40262.

39. Obituary in *Tucson Star,* quoted in Virginia Culin Roberts, *With Their Own Blood: A Saga of Southwestern Pioneers* (Fort Worth: Texas Christian University Press, 1992), 214.

40. It is, however, worth noting that there was sometimes a tone of remorsefulness in the reminiscences when it came to matters of race, as we will see in chapter 5.

41. Eliza Spalding Warren, *Memoirs of the West: The Spaldings* (Portland, Ore.: Press of the Marsh Printing Company, 1917), 42.

42. Brooks, *A Pioneer Mother of California,* introduction, unnumbered page. Other good examples of emphasis on the frontier and pioneer past as an object lesson for youth are Judge J. H. Metheny, address before the Tri-State Old Settlers' Association of Illinois, Iowa, and Missouri, August 30, 1887, in *Report of the Fourth Tri-State Reunion,* 40; Major William Downie, *Hunting for Gold: Reminiscences of Personal Experience and Research in the Early Days of the Pacific Coast* (San Francisco: California Publishing Co., 1893), which discusses the object lessons learned from the original pioneers by the Native Sons of the Golden West (356–360); Roxana Cheney Foster, "The Foster Family: California Pioneers of 1849," typed manuscript given as a gift to "our children and grandchildren" in 1889, unnumbered page, NEW AC 128.3 F7, 1921.

43. The Honorable John F. Phillips, untitled speech, August 30, 1887, in *Report of the Fourth Tri-State Reunion,* 47–53, quotation on 52.

44. It is worth emphasizing that this juxtaposition of past and present (much to the detriment of the present) by older generations is common in American culture and probably in most other cultures, too. In a general sense, fond memories of times when youths respected their elders and when people could leave their homes unlocked without fear of break-ins are pervasive among older generations and parallel

the key contours of the pioneer reminiscence genre. Pioneer reminiscers were not unique in drawing these distinctions between past and present, though the regularity and purposefulness with which they drew them is notable. For another example of this juxtaposition, similar to Phillips's, though less colorful, see Anon., *Pioneer and Personal Reminiscences* (Marshalltown, Iowa: Marshall Printing Co., 1893), 93.

45. Historicus, "Then and Now: A Retrospective," Los Angeles County Pioneers of Southern California, *Annual Report of the Los Angeles County Pioneers of Southern California for 1914–1915* (n.p., 1915), 118–119. For another example of this kind of juxtaposition of past and present, see William S. E. Justice's poem "Los Angeles in 1867—47 Years Later," in *Annual Report of the Los Angeles County Pioneers of Southern California for 1913–1914* (n.p., 1914), n.p. Justice wrote:

> There were no autos or cars to run you down,
> And our mail came about once a week.
> No gas, no electricity in any part of the town,
> And no newsies crying "Uxtra" on the street.
> . . . .
> But now the town is full of tenderfeet,
> And spread out all over the hills and vales,
> With uniformed policemen on every street,
> And gone are the sheep and cattle trails.
> But it's interesting to listen to the tenderfeet
> Who never saw Indians or crossed the plains,
> Who have lived all their lives on a crowded street,
> And do all their travelling in autos or trains.

46. Eva Ogden Putnam, "Pioneering in Crook County," *Annals of Wyoming* 3 (April 1926): 203–211, quotation on 209.

47. Robert Moran, "An Address by Robert Moran at the Fiftieth Jubilee Meeting of the Pioneers Association of the State of Washington, June 6th, 1939, in Seattle," HEH RB 299566, p. 7. Interestingly, though, many of the Works Progress Administration interviewees, unlike Moran, emphasized cooperation, not individualistic enterprise, as the most important of the old pioneer traits. For example, James Monroe Redd of Utah (born in 1863 and interviewed in 1936) responded to the question "What are some of your impressions of early Utah days?" with the following observations: "A number of hardships and struggles in pioneer days, but we enjoyed life and were more social and cooperatively inclined than today, although we have some splendid highways, a daily mail, radios and electric light (in towns) and many other modern improvements. I feel we were really more happy and contented in pioneer days." The quotation is from the Utah Questionnaires, 1936–1939, pioneer personal histories obtained by the interviewers of the Historical Records Survey, Utah Works Projects Administration (hereafter BANC PF). See particularly the answers to question 314, "What are some of your impressions of early Utah days?" James Monroe Redd's responses are in BANC PF 312, 44. The responses to this question generally contrast the past very favorably with the present and then go on

to emphasize the heightened cooperation and spirit of community of those earlier days. The Utah Questionnaires are available in BANC PF 312–313. The questionnaires, drawing as they did on a large Mormon population influenced by a religious ethic that emphasized cooperation, are probably not reliable indicators of thinking about the relative merits of individualism versus cooperation in the broader West. They may be indicators of a growing concern in Mormon communities over the breakdown of the cooperative spirit.

48. The editorial, titled "Robert Moran: An Inspiration," is from *Marine Digest,* March 4, 1939, and is reprinted at the end of the published version of Moran's speech to the Washington Pioneers, pp. 26–27.

49. For more on the Depression era debates over the frontier's legacy, see Theodore Rosenof, *Dogma, Depression, and the New Deal: The Debate of Political Leaders over Recovery* (Port Washington, N.Y.: Kennikat Press, 1975), especially 20–23, 113–132; Steven Kesselman, "The Frontier Thesis and the Great Depression," *Journal of the History of Ideas* 29 (April 1968): 253–268; Curtis Nettles, "Frederick Jackson Turner and the New Deal," *Wisconsin Magazine of History* 17 (March 1934): 257–65; and Wrobel, "The New Deal Frontier," in *The End of American Exceptionalism: Frontier Anxiety from the Old West to the New Deal* (Lawrence: University Press of Kansas, 1993), 122–142.

50. Harrison Adams, *The Pioneer Boys of the Colorado: Braving the Perils of the Grand Canyon Country* (Boston: L. C. Page and Company, 1926). Adams is the author of the other books in the Young Pioneer Series, which included *The Pioneer Boys of the Ohio, The Pioneer Boys of the Great Lakes,* and similar titles on the Mississippi, the Missouri, Yellowstone, and Columbia, Oregon. And, just in case these stories of white youthful adventure, endurance, and triumph during the nation's frontier advance should leave American boys devoid of knowledge of the nonwhite children of the world, the Page Company also offered the Little Cousin Series, whose sixty or so titles included *Our Little African Cousins, Our Little Alaskan Cousins,* and so on through the cultural alphabet.

The trend of writing pioneer tales for children had begun much earlier. For example, Ezra Meeker included "A Chapter for Children" in his book *The Ox-Team; or, The Old Oregon Trail, 1852–1906* (Lincoln, Nebr.: Jacob North and Co., 1906), 191–197, HEH RB 34143.

51. For more on this, see George Frederickson, *The Inner Civil War: Northern Intellectuals and the Crisis of the Union* (New York: Harper and Row, 1965).

52. Paul Fussell, *The Great War and Modern Memory* (New York: Oxford University Press, 1975), 314.

53. Native Sons of the Golden West, *Grand Parlor Proceedings: Proceedings of the Twentieth Annual Session of the Grand Parlor of the Native Sons of the Golden West,* Redwood City, California, April 26–29, 1897 (San Francisco: Julius Gabriel, 1897), 45.

54. For more on the Native Sons and nativism, see Peter Thomas Conmy, *The Origins and Purposes of the Native Sons of the Golden West* (San Francisco: Dolores Press, 1956), 18–19.

55. Will C. Bishop, "Salutory," *Sons of Colorado* 1, no. 1 (June 1906): 3. The journal lasted for more than twenty years, the last issue appearing in April 1928.

56. Will Chamberlain, "S. of C.," *Sons of Colorado* 1, no. 1 (June 1906): 14; James Barton Adams, "The Dust of the Overland Trail," *Sons of Colorado* 1, no. 10 (March 1907): 21. The latter poem reads:

> And they're with us to-day—many grizzled and gray,
> And their old eyes with pride are aglow
> And they see how the state has grown famously great
> From the wildness they found long ago.
> When the old heroes meet how they love to repeat
> The old story that never grows stale
> Of the brave days of old when the gray schooners rolled
> Through the dust of the Overland Trail.

57. For more on the theme of elevated westernness, see Robert Athearn, *The Mythic West in Twentieth-Century America* (Lawrence: University Press of Kansas, 1989), 233–248. For elevated westernness in Montana, see Joseph Kinsey Howard, *Montana: High, Wide, and Handsome* (1959; reprint Lincoln: University of Nebraska Press, 1983). For the same theme in the Pacific Northwest, see Richard L. Neuberger, *Our Promised Land* (New York: Macmillan, 1938).

58. On the contrast between Oregon and California pioneers, see Frederick George Young, "The Oregon Trail," *Quarterly of the Oregon Historical Society* 1 (December 1900): 339–370, esp. 344–345; and H. S. Lyman, "Reminiscences of William M. Case," *Quarterly of the Oregon Historical Society* 1 (September 1900): 269–295, esp. 277.

59. Southern Pacific Company, *Oregon for the Settler: A Great Area with Rich Valleys, Mild and Healthful Climate and Wide Range of Products* (San Francisco: Southern Pacific Company, 1914), 7, HEH RB 375527.

60. The quotation is from John Hyde Braly, *Memory Pictures: An Autobiography* (Los Angeles: Nuener Company, 1912), 5 NEW GC 390. For additional examples of California reminiscers' claims to pioneer preeminence, see Frank Mattison's address "The Sturdy Pioneers," delivered to the Native Sons of the Golden West during the Admission Day celebrations of 1897, in *Grand Parlor Proceedings*.

61. Governor R. J. Oglesby (Illinois), in *Report of the Second Reunion of the Tri-State Old Settlers' Association,* 16–21, quotation on 18.

62. Honorable John S. Runnells, untitled speech in *Report of the Fourth Tri-State Reunion,* 56–59. (The organization's reports from 1884 to 1887, though published separately, are all bound in one volume.)

63. C. W. Irish, untitled speech at the Twentieth Annual Reunion of the Johnson County, Iowa, Old Settlers' Association (August 18, 1886), in *Proceedings of the Johnson County, [Iowa] Old Settlers' Association, from 1866 to 1899,* 40. Irish's speech to the same group on August 24, 1887, is in Proceedings of the Twenty-first Annual Reunion, August 24, 1887, in *Proceedings, 1866–1899,* 48.

64. For example, John S. Hittell delivered a speech to the Society of California Pioneers on Admission Day (September 9) in 1869 in which he sought to qualify the

common notion that "the passion which drove [California pioneers] to incur the dangers, the privations, and the toils of adventure in our unsettled and almost unknown country, was sordid." Hittell explained that while the pioneers may have "risked their lives and exerted all their energies for gold," they did so "with no miserly feeling." He added that while "they spent their money as fast as they made it," their "extravagance" was not a "base extravagance"; *Nineteenth Anniversary of the Corporate Society of California Pioneers, Oration by Hon. John S. Hittell (A Member of the Society)* (San Francisco: Published by the Order of the Society, 1869), 5–21, HEH RB 36943. The speech is reprinted in John S. Hittell, *The Resources of California: Comprising Agriculture, Mining, Geography, Climate, Commerce, etc, and the Past and Future Development of the State,* 6th ed. (San Francisco: A. Roman and Co., and New York: W. J. Widdleton, 1874). In his "Reminiscences of the Plains and Mines in '49 and '50," Hittell insisted that "of all the long land migrations of large bodies of men recorded in history since the earliest ages, none was more peaceful in the purposes and benefits, none more satisfactory to its participants, and none more beneficial within a lifetime to a large portion of mankind than the march of the goldhunters to California in 1849" (17).

65. Glen Gendzel provides an excellent treatment of this debate between Northern and Southern California over the pioneer heritage and how it played a role in forming the subregional identities of both parts of the state in "Pioneers and Padres," 56–79. William Deverell examines the role of the "Spanish fantasy past" in the formation of regional identity in Southern California in "Privileging the Mission over the Mexican: Regional Identity in Southern California," in *Many Wests: Place, Culture, and Regional Identity,* ed. David M. Wrobel and Michael C. Steiner (Lawrence: University Press of Kansas, 1997), 235–258.

66. The Spanish fantasy past is discussed further in chapter 5.

67. The role of Lummis and other California boosters in drawing on the pioneer past to help shape the identities of regions helps illuminate further the connections between the booster and reminiscence genres, and between those genres and the formation of regional consciousness.

68. As William Deverell shows, even in Southern California, where the Spanish fantasy past was used to elevate Californio culture in the California heritage pantheon, that process paralleled the one wherein Mexican culture was kept separate from the mainstream in the present. On this level, Southern California's utilization of a particular version of the pioneer past reinforced the existing cultural and racial structures of the present, and it thus parallels, rather than diverges from, the general contours of the western pioneer tradition. These issues are explored further in chapter 5.

69. C. P. Arnold, "The Vanished Frontier," pamphlet reprinted in *Annals of Wyoming* 16 (January 1944): 57–60, quotation on 59. Arnold was a past president (1929) of the Wyoming Pioneer Association, an organization that developed in 1925 out of Wyoming's first organization of pioneers, founded in 1884. For more on Wyoming, see Dr. C. G. Countant, *History of Wyoming and the Far West* (Laramie, Wyo.: Chaplin, Spafford, and Mathison, Printers, 1899), 17–19.

70. Guy Piatt, ed., *The Story of Butte: Old Timer's Hand-Book,* special number of the *Butte Bystander,* April 15, 1897 (Butte, Mont.: Press of the Standard Manufacturing and Printing Co., 1897), 19. For more on this theme of elevated westernness in Washington, see Prosch, *Reminiscences of Washington Territory,* 121–122. For South Dakota, see Jesse Brown and A. M. Willard, *The Black Hills Trails: A History of the Struggles of the Pioneers in the Winning of the Black Hills,* ed. by John T. Milek (Rapid City, S.D.: Rapid City Journal Company, 1924), preface, unnumbered page; Brown and Willard described the Black Hills as "the last real frontier border on the continent," a place marked by "the elemental struggle of man with nature." And for the Mormons as the quintessential western pioneers, see Charles W. Carter, *The Exodus of 1847* (Salt Lake City: Utah Lithographing Co., 1897).

5. Promotion, Reminiscence, and Race

1. There is an abundance of work on California boosterism in the late nineteenth and early twentieth centuries. The most detailed of these works is Richard J. Orsi, "Selling the Golden State: A Study of Boosterism in Nineteenth-Century California" (Ph.D. diss., University of Wisconsin, 1973); the present discussion draws heavily on this work. Kevin Starr provides quite detailed coverage of the topic in *Americans and the California Dream, 1850–1915* (New York: Oxford University Press, 1973); *Inventing the Dream: California Through the Progressive Era* (New York: Oxford University Press, 1985); and *Material Dreams: Southern California Through the 1920s* (New York: Oxford University Press, 1990), especially chap. 5, "Boosting Babylon: Planning, Development, and Ballyhoo in Jazz-Age Los Angeles," 90–119. Ralph J. Roske provides a useful overview in his chapter "The Healthseekers, the Real Estate Promoters and the Land Boom," in *Everyman's Eden: A History of California* (New York: Macmillan, 1968). William Deverell and Douglas Flamming provide excellent coverage in their essay "Race, Rhetoric, and Regional Identity: Boosting Los Angeles, 1880–1930," in *Power and Place in the North American West,* ed. Richard White and John M. Findlay (Seattle: University of Washington Press, 1999), 117–143. Other useful recent works include Norman M. Klein, "The Sunshine Strategy: Buying and Selling the Fantasy of Los Angeles," in *Los Angeles: Power, Promotion and Social Conflict,* ed. Norman M. Klein and Martin J. Schiesl (Claremont, Calif.: Regina Books, 1990), 1–38; Mike Davis, *City of Quartz: Excavating the Future in Los Angeles* (London: Verso, 1990), chap. 1, "Sunshine or Noir?" 15–97, and chap. 2, "Power Lines," 99–147; Robert M. Fogelson, *The Fragmented Metropolis: Los Angeles, 1850–1930* (1967; reprint Berkeley and Los Angeles: University of California Press, 1993), chap. 4, "The Great Migration," 63–84; Norman M. Klein, *The History of Forgetting: Los Angeles and the History of Erasure* (New York: Verso, 1997), chap. 1 "Booster Myths, Urban Erasure," 27–72; William Alexander McClurg, *Landscapes of Desire: Anglo Mythologies of Los Angeles* (Berkeley and Los Angeles: University of California Press, 2000); Clark Davis, "From Oasis to Metropolis: Southern California and the Changing Context of American Leisure," *Pacific Historical*

Review 61 (August 1992): 357–386; Jennifer A. Watts, "Picture Taking in Paradise: Los Angeles and the Creation of a Regional Identity, 1880–1920," *History of Photography* 24 (autumn 2000): 243–250; and William Deverell, "Privileging the Mission over the Mexican: The Rise of Regional Identity in Southern California," in *Many Wests: Place, Culture, and Regional Identity,* ed. David M. Wrobel and Michael C. Steiner (Lawrence: University Press of Kansas, 1997), 235–258. Included among the useful works of earlier scholarship on the topic are Glenn S. Dumke, *The Boom of the Eighties in Southern California* (San Marino, Calif.: Huntington Library Press, 1944); and Carey McWilliams, *Southern California Country: An Island on the Land* (New York: Duell, Sloan and Pearce, 1946), especially chap. 8, "The Cultural Landscape," 138–164.

2. It is notable that within a generation after the gold rush, organizations such as the Society of California Pioneers (1869) began to form in the state, and old settlers and prospectors recounted their adventures in embellished form. The weight of these gold rush reminiscences also must have reinforced popular perceptions of the place as still dangerous and unsettled. Even though these old pioneers were writing about an earlier time, the chronological divide, one might conjecture, easily contracted in the minds of readers.

3. John S. Hittell, *The Resources of California, Comprising Agriculture, Mining, Geography, Climate, Commerce, etc, and the Past and Future Development of the State* (San Francisco: A. Roman and Co.; New York: W. J. Widdleton, 1863), 44, HEH RB 32994. Orsi discusses Hittell in "Selling the Golden State," 36.

4. Hittell discusses the general unprofitability of his mining endeavors in "Reminiscences of the Plains and Mines in '49 and '50" (the first of the course of Lick [James Lick] Lectures, delivered before the Society of California Pioneers, San Francisco, January 5, 1887), 17-page typed, numbered pamphlet (offprint), 17, HEH RB 40262.

5. Patronizing, though often quite favorable, treatments of Chinese Americans do appear in the California booster literature of this period; see, for example, Charles B. Turrill, *California Notes* (San Francisco: Edward Bosqui and Co., Printers, 1876), 65.

6. See Richard H. Dillon's excellent "Introduction" to John S. Hittell, *A History of the City of San Francisco and Incidentally of the State of California,* and *A Guidebook to San Francisco,* complete edition of the original works first published in 1878 and 1888 by the Bancroft Company, San Francisco (Berkeley, Calif.: Berkeley Hills Books, 2000), ix–lvii. There is no published biography of Hittell—Dillon's introductory essay is the closest thing available besides Claude Rowland Petty's "Gold Rush Intellectual" (Ph.D. diss., University of California, 1952). Dillon writes of the energetic Hittell, who wrote two dozen books and pamphlets and forty-seven magazine articles, in addition to a mass of newspaper articles: "The frugal German-American was half-packrat, half archivist and (another) half-chamber of commerce" (xli).

7. Hittell, *The Resources of California* (1863), 375. For more on the topic, see Alexander Saxton, *The Indispensable Enemy: Labor and the Anti-Chinese Movement in California* (Berkeley and Los Angeles: University of California Press, 1971).

8. "Agriculture," in Hittell, *The Resources of California,* 151–237, quotation on 151.

9. For more on the conflict between advocates of farming and mining, see Orsi, "Selling the Golden State," 132–134; see pp. 152–156 for coverage of the California State Agricultural Society and its volumes of *Transactions,* which were used to promote farm settlement, but which suffered a cut in funding in the mid-1870s as a result of the pressure of the mining interests.

10. Hittell, *The Resources of California,* 362, 368. Hittell further elaborated on why American men in California were so prone to "Deeds of Blood": "The first and great cause is the high temper of the people. The Americans are an arrogant race. Every man thinks himself as good as his neighbor, if not better. They are a people who will not be insulted. They consider harsh words insulting. They are fond of using harsh words to one another" (375–376). Seeking to explain the withering of American women in California, Hittell wrote: "They are trained up in the dark and in idleness, as though sunshine and work would ruin them. Pastry, pickles, and sweetmeats form a considerable portion of their food, and they are taught to abhor coarse strength and robustness as worse than sins" (368). Hittell further noted, as one would expect, that white American women were comparatively infertile in this environment, though he noted that Irish and "Native Californian" (Hispana) women were quite prolific in the production of offspring.

11. John S. Hittell, "California as a Home for the Emigrant: A Brief Statement of Its Public Lands, Wages, Climate, Agriculture, Manufactures, Attractions, and General Business," in *All About California and Inducements to Settle There* (San Francisco: California Immigrant Union, printed by A. L. Bancroft and Co., 1870), 7–40, HEH RB 116156. The essay was translated into French, German, Danish, Norwegian, Swedish, and Polish; see Dillon, "Introduction," xlvi–xlvii.

12. "His Excellency, the Governor of California, Hon. Henry H. Haight, in His Biennial Message to the Legislature, at the Commencement of Its Session in December, 1869," in *All About California,* 3–4.

13. Chas. S. Capp, manager of the California Immigrant Union, wrote in *All About California,* "It is not a mining, but a *farming* population, that we most desire" (5).

14. Henry George, *Our Land and Land Policy* (1871), reprinted in *Our Land and Land Policy: Speeches, Lectures, and Miscellaneous Writings by Henry George,* ed. Kenneth C. Wenzer (East Lansing: Michigan State University Press, 1999), 1–93, quotation on 25. See also Henry George's earlier essay "What the Railroad Will Bring Us," *Overland Monthly* 1 (October 1868): 297–304.

15. George, *Our Land and Land Policy,* 25.

16. Ibid., 46. Starr provides more extended commentary on *Our Land and Land Policy* and George's *Progress and Poverty* in *Americans and the California Dream,* 134–141.

17. Henry George, *Progress and Poverty: An Inquiry into the Cause of Industrial Depressions, and of Increase of Want with Increase of Wealth* (1879; New York: D. Appleton and Co., 1884). George wrote: "On uncultivated tracts of land in the new State of California may be seen the blackened chimneys of homes from which

settlers have been driven by force of laws which ignore natural right, and great stretches of land which might be populous are desolate, because the recognition of exclusive ownership has put it in the power of one human creature to forbid his fellows from using it" (310).

18. Orsi, "Selling the Golden State," 6.

19. Ibid., 10.

20. Ibid., 11.

21. Charles Nordhoff, *California: A Book for Travellers and Settlers* (New York: Harper and Brothers, 1872). Nordhoff's *California* receives extended commentary here because it was so popular at the time. Harris Newmark, in *Sixty Years in Southern California, 1853–1913, Containing the Reminiscences of Harris Newmark,* ed. Maurice H. Newmark and Marco R. Newmark (New York: Knickerbocker Press, 1916), remarks that Nordhoff's book "did more, I dare say, than any similar work to spread the fame of the Southland throughout the East" (624). Further evidence of Nordhoff's influence is the town named for him in Ventura County, California.

22. Nordhoff, *California* (1872), 18, 19.

23. George, *Our Land and Land Policy,* 88.

24. Ibid., 51. For more on George's views on the topic, see his entry "Chinese Immigration," in *Cyclopedia of Political Science, Political Economy, and of the Political History of the United States, by the Best American and European Writers,* vol. 1, *Abdication-Duty,* ed. John L. Laylor (Chicago: Melbert B. Cary and Co., 1883), 409–414; and Saxton, *The Indispensable Enemy,* 92–103.

25. Nordhoff, *California* (1872), 19.

26. Frederick Jackson Turner, "The Significance of the Frontier in American History," in his *The Frontier in American History* (New York: Henry Holt and Company, 1920), 1–38; Theodore Roosevelt, *The Winning of the West,* 4 vols. (New York: G. P. Putnam's Sons, 1889–1896).

27. Nordhoff, chap. 6, "John," in *California* (1872), 84–92, quotation on 90.

28. Ibid., 91.

29. The other chapter from the 1872 edition devoted partly to the Chinese is chap. 19, "The Chinese as Railroad Builders," 189–194. Charles Nordhoff, *California: For Health, Pleasure, and Residence: A Book for Travellers and Settlers,* new edition, thoroughly revised (New York: Harper and Brothers, 1882). In the months following the massacre, the U.S. government faced vigorous protests from the Chinese government, and the Chinese all across the United States held services for the victims. For a fascinating description of the riot and its aftermath, see Newmark, *Sixty Years in Southern California,* 432–435.

30. Nordhoff, *California* (1872), 155. For more on the theme of Indian wage labor, long neglected by scholars, see Albert Hurtado, *Indian Survival on the California Frontier* (New Haven, Conn.: Yale University Press, 1988); Alice Littlefield and Martha C. Knack, eds., *Native Americans and Wage Labor: Ethnohistorical Perspectives* (Norman: University of Oklahoma Press, 1996); and Patricia Nelson Limerick's discussion of the book in her essay "Going West and Ending Up Global," *Western Historical Quarterly*

32 (spring 2001), 5–23, esp. 12. Nordhoff's chapter "Indians as Laborers," 155–159, in the 1872 edition of *California*, was not included in the 1882 edition.

31. Nordhoff, *California* (1872), 157.

32. Ibid., 155.

33. Ibid., 159.

34. For more on the Spanish fantasy past, see Carey McWilliams, "The Fantasy Heritage," in his *North from Mexico: The Spanish-Speaking People of the United States* (Philadelphia: Lippincott, 1949), 35–47; Mañuel P. Servín, "California's Hispanic Heritage: A View into the Spanish Myth," in *New Spain's Far Northern Frontier: Essays on Spain in the American West, 1540–1821*, ed. David J. Weber (Albuquerque: University of New Mexico Press, 1979), 117–134; Deverell, "Privileging the Mission over the Mexican," 233–258.

35. Nordhoff, "An Old Californio Rancho," in *California* (1872), 148–154, quotation on 149. In this chapter, Nordhoff recounts a conversation with the padrone of an estate about Indian laborers: "'Yes, he had Indians'—seeing me look at several who were skylarking about the place, catching each other with lassos—'they are useful people, not good for much;' he added, 'but quiet;' he paid them fifteen dollars a month; and they bought what they needed at his store" (149). Attention to the topic of Indian drunkenness was a regular feature of the early California promotional literature; see, for example, Hittell's coverage in *The Resources of California* (1863): "The Indians are fond of strong liquor, and when they can get it, frequently become habitual drunkards. The squaws drink as much as the 'bucks.' Among a tribe of drunken men and women, matrimonial constancy is not to be expected; nor is it found among the Indian women in California" (389). In the 1874 edition of the book, though many of Hittell's other stereotyped images of Native Americans remain, the stereotype of Indian drunkenness is no longer included; see "Indians," in Hittell, *The Resources of California: Comprising the Society, Climate, Salubrity, Scenery, Commerce and Industry of the State,* 6th ed. (San Francisco: A. Roman and Co.; New York: W. J. Widdleton, 1874), 48–56.

36. Hittell, *The Resources of California* (1874), 40. The subtitle of the book had changed by the sixth edition; much of the content had been revised, too. In rewriting the work, Hittell had begun to find his voice and to hit his stride as a promotional writer. It is surprising, however, that there is still quite extensive coverage of earthquakes (133–139) in the sixth edition. The coverage of climate, salubrity, scenery, and agriculture is far more positive than in the 1863 edition, though it is worth noting that Hittell is one of California's more restrained and honest promotional writers and thus reminds one of Ezra Meeker; see chaps. 2 and 3. Hittell's claim that the state "can and . . . will sustain a population of twenty millions" (343) has turned out to be quite conservative.

37. Benjamin Cummings Truman, *Semi-tropical California: Its Climate, Healthfulness, Productiveness, and Scenery; Its Magnificent Stretches of Vineyards and Groves of Semi-tropical Fruits, etc., etc., etc.* (San Francisco: A. L. Bancroft and Co., 1874), 21, 27.

38. Interestingly, Truman's very same words concerning "indolent natives" and "gigantic watermelons" appeared a full three decades later in his introduction, "The City of Los Angeles," in Anon., *Los Angeles: The Queen City of the Angels* (Los Angeles: M. Reider, 1904), n.p., HEH RB 372388. Ralph Mann discusses the process by which Hispanic cultural influences were eliminated as white settlers sought to Americanize California in the post–gold rush decades in his *After the Gold Rush: Society in Grass Valley and Nevada City, California, 1849–1870* (Stanford, Calif.: Stanford University Press, 1982), 50.

39. Charles Nordhoff, "The Chinese as Laborers and Producers," in *Northern California, Oregon, and the Sandwich Islands* (New York: Harper and Brothers, 1875), 141–148, quotation on 142.

40. Ibid., 117, 167.

41. Orsi, "Selling the Golden State," 135.

42. Rev. S. Goodenough, "Foes of Labor: The Chinese and Other Foes of American Labor," *California Review* 1 (October 1893): 33–40, quotations on 34, 35.

43. Ibid., 36.

44. Editorial comment, "The Chinese Question," in *California Review* 1 (October 1893), 81.

45. Chas. S. Gleed, ed., *Rand McNally and Company's Overland Guide: From the Missouri River to the Pacific Ocean, Via Kansas, Colorado, New Mexico, Arizona, and California,* rev. ed. (1883; Chicago: Rand McNally and Company, 1885), 181, HEH RB 311922.

46. For more on Chinatown tourism, see Catherine Cocks, *Doing the Town: The Rise of Urban Tourism in the United States, 1850–1915* (Berkeley and Los Angeles: University of California Press, 2001).

47. For more on race and American thought, see Carl Degler, *In Search of Human Nature: The Decline and Revival of Darwinism in American Thought* (New York: Oxford University Press, 1991).

48. See Richard White, "The Federal Government and the Indians," in *"It's Your Misfortune and None of My Own": A New History of the American West* (Norman: University of Oklahoma Press, 1991), 85–118, esp. 107.

49. Legislature of the Territory of Arizona, *Resources of Arizona Territory, with a Description of the Indian Tribes; Ancient Ruins, Cochise, Apache Chief, Antonio, Pima Chief; Stage and Wagon Roads; Trade and Commerce, etc., by Authority of the Legislature* (San Francisco: Francis and Valentine, Steam Printers and Engravers, 1871), 22–23, HEH RB 38225.

50. See, for example, Legislature of the Territory of Arizona, *The Territory of Arizona: A Brief History and Summary of the Territory's Acquisition, Organization, and Mineral, Agricultural and Grazing Resources; Embracing a Review of Its Indian Tribes— Their Depredations and Subjugations; and Showing in Brief the Present Condition and Prospects of the Territory* (Tucson, Ariz.: Citizens Office, 1874), esp. 19, 30–35, HEH RB 40204; E. Conklin, *Picturesque Arizona: Being the Result of Travels and Observations in Arizona During the Fall and Winter of 1877* (New York: Mining Record Printing Establishment, c. 1878), 221–236, HEH RB 601; and Richard J. Hinton, *The Hand-*

Book to Arizona: Its Resources, History, Towns, Mines, Ruins and Scenery (San Francisco: Payot, Upham and Co.; New York: American News Company, 1878), 351–370.

51. For an early example of the awkward efforts of Arizona promoters to address the "Indian problem" as they sought to attract settlers, see *Arizona: Its Resources and Prospects: A Letter to the Editor of the New York Tribune (reprinted from that Journal of June 26th, 1865. By the Hon. Richard C. McCormick, Secretary of the Territory* (New York: Van Nostrand, 1865), 19–20, NEW GC 2583. At the same time that McCormick insists that the complete subjugation of the Apache is imminent, he expresses frustration that the federal government had failed to deal with the Apaches "with the force and pertinacity with which it has handled the Sioux," and thereby retarded the growth of the territory.

52. Atchison, Topeka and Santa Fe Railroad, *Arizona, Her Great Mining, Agricultural, Stock-Raising and Lumber Interests: The Only Direct Route Is via the Atchison, Topeka and Santa Fe* (Topeka, Kans.: Atchison, Topeka and Santa Fe, [1884?]), unnumbered page. The publication's map of Arizona—filled with place-names and topographic detail—serves as a good example of cartographic efforts in this period to make western places appear heavily settled (by white Americans) and perfectly safe. The difficulty of boosting Arizona in this period is further borne out in Gleed, *Rand, McNally and Company's Overland Guide*. The author insists that the territory's Black Range is safe for mining now, even though "it was still unsafe to stay there till less than a year ago" (104–105).

53. Walter Nugent, *Into the West: The Story of Its People* (New York: Knopf, 1999), 126.

54. Calvin Horn provides coverage of these developments in his chapter "Close of an Era: Lew Wallace, 1878–1881," in *New Mexico's Troubled Years: The Story of the Early Territorial Governors* (Albuquerque: Horn and Wallace, 1963), 199–219.

55. "New Mexico: Its Present Condition and Prospects—An Interview with Chief Justice L. Bradford Prince," *New York Tribune*, July 12, 1881, reprinted in *The Resources of New Mexico: Prepared Under the Auspices of the Bureau of Immigration for the Territorial Fair to Be Held at Albuquerque, New Mexico, October 3rd to 8th, 1881* (Santa Fe, N.M.: New Mexican Book and Job Printing Department, 1881), 49–52, quotation on 52, NEW GC 2990.

56. Charles R. Bliss, *New Mexico: The New West* (Boston: Frank Wood Printer, 1879), 9–10, HEH RB 38267. One of Bliss's primary purposes in the publication was to solicit funding for the Santa Fe Academy, which he hoped would serve as a bulwark against the Catholic Church gaining influence in education in the state.

57. New Mexico Territory, Bureau of Immigration, *Territory of New Mexico: Report of the Bureau of Immigration,* February 16, 1884 (Santa Fe, N.M.: New Mexican Printing Company, 1884), 6, HEH RB 78232.

58. A. Daniel Murphy, *New Mexico, Its Attractions and Resources, with Its Rich Deposits of Gold, Silver, Copper, Iron, Coal, and Other Minerals; Its Extensive Grazing Districts, Rich Farming Lands, and Delightful Climate* (St. Louis: Slawson and Pierrot, 1880), 15.

59. Nugent, *Into the West,* 126.

60. New Mexico Territory, Bureau of Immigration, *New Mexico: Its Resources, Climate, Geography, Geology, History, Statistics, Present Conditions and Future Prospects, Official Publication of the Bureau of Immigration, Arranged, Compiled, and Edited by Max Frost, Secretary of the Bureau* (Santa Fe, N.M.: New Mexican Printing Company, 1894), 293, HEH RB 319689.

61. John L. Bullis, Capt. 24th Infy., Actg. Indian Agent, United States Indian Service, Pueblo and Jicarilla Agency, Santa Fe, N.M., November 20, 1893, reprinted in ibid., 293–295.

62. William Sutherland, *The Wonders of Nevada: Where They Are and How to Get to Them* (Virginia, Nev.: Enterprise Book and Job Printing House, 1878), n.p.

63. B. M. McKay to Albert B. Fall, January 19, 1917, in Albert Bacon Fall Collection, Henry E. Huntington Library, box 2, folder 21; and Albert B. Fall to B. M. McKay, January 24, 1917, in ibid.

64. Fall to McKay, January 24, 1917.

65. Chicago, Burlington and Quincy Railroad, *The Heart of the Continent: An Historical and Descriptive Treatise for Business Men, Home Seekers and Tourists, of the Advantages, Resources and Scenery of the Great West* (Chicago: Buffalo, Clay and Richmond, printers, for the Chicago, Burlington and Quincy Railroad, 1882), 25, HEH RB 253034.

66. See Jennifer Watts, "Nature's Workshop: Photography and the Creation of 'Semi-tropic' California, 1880–1920" (paper presented at the annual meeting of the Western History Association, San Diego, 2001).

67. Turner, "The Significance of the Frontier in American History," 22.

68. Anon., "Bell County Texas: A General Invitation to Worthy People" [1876?], NEW GC 247, Broadside box 3.

69. For more on the Exodusters, see Robert Athearn, *In Search of Canaan: Black Migration to Kansas, 1879–1880* (Lawrence: Regents Press of Kansas, 1978); and Nell Irving Painter, *The Exodusters: Black Migration to Kansas After Reconstruction* (1986; New York: Norton, 1992). Ian Frazier discusses Governor St. Johns's and the Kansas Pacific's discouragement of black migration in *Great Plains* (New York: Farrar, Straus and Giroux, 1989), 167–168.

70. Kenneth Marvin Hamilton explores this topic further in *Black Towns and Profit: Promotion and Development in the Trans-Appalachian West, 1877–1915* (Urbana: University of Illinois Press, 1991).

71. Quintard Taylor examines the growth of these towns in "The Black Urban West, 1870–1910" and "The Black Urban West, 1911–1940," in his *In Search of the Racial Frontier: African Americans in the American West, 1528–1990* (New York: Norton, 1998), 192–221 and 222–250, respectively. For discussion of early black migration to cities in the West, see Quintard Taylor, *The Forging of a Black Community: Seattle's Central District from 1870 Through the Civil Rights Era* (Seattle: University of Washington Press, 1994); and Albert S. Broussard, *Black San Francisco: The Struggle for Racial Equality in the West, 1900–1954* (Lawrence: University Press of Kansas, 1993).

72. See Deverell and Flamming, "Race, Rhetoric, and Regional Identity," 124–133. The DuBois quotation is from his article "Colored California," in *The Crisis*, August

1913, 192–193, cited in Deverell and Flamming, "Race, Rhetoric, and Regional Identity," 131.

73. A good example of utilization of the missions in promotional writing is George Wharton James, *In and Out of the Old Missions of California: An Historical and Pictorial Account of the Franciscan Missions* (Boston: Little, Brown, 1905).

74. For more on Lummis's promotion of California's cultural diversity, see Martin Padget, "Travel, Exoticism, and the Writing of Region: Charles Fletcher Lummis and the Creation of the Southwest," *Journal of the Southwest* 37 (autumn 1995): 421–449, esp. 443–445. For more on the *Mission Play,* see Deverell and Flamming, "Race, Rhetoric, and Regional Identity," 123–124; and Deverell, "Privileging the Mission over the Mexican," 248–251.

75. Jennifer Watts discusses these images of ancient Indians in her essays "Nature's Workshop" and "Picture Taking in Paradise," 243–250.

76. For more on the Californio testimonials, see Genaro M. Padilla, *My History, Not Yours: The Formation of Mexican American Autobiography* (Madison: University of Wisconsin Press, 1993); Rosaura Sánchez, *Telling Identities: The Californio Testimonials* (Minneapolis: University of Minnesota Press, 1995); Rosaura Sánchez, Beatrice Pita, and Bárbara Reyes, eds., *Nineteenth-Century Californio Testimonials,* CRÍTICA Monograph Series, (San Diego, Calif.: UCSD Ethnic Studies/Third World Studies, 1994); and Alan Rosenus, *General M. G. Vallejo and the Advent of the Americans: A Biography* (Albuquerque: University of New Mexico Press, 1995).

77. A. J. Sowell, *Rangers and Pioneers of Texas, with a Concise Account of the Early Settlement, Hardships, Massacres, Battles, and Wars by Which Texas Was Rescued from the Rule of the Savage and Consecrated to the Empire of Civilization* (San Antonio, Tex.: Shepard Brothers and Company, Printers and Publishers, 1884), 5, NEW GC 3909.

78. J. H. DeWolff, *Pawnee Bill (Major Gordon W. Lillie), His Experience and Adventures on the Western Plains; or, From the Saddle of a "Cowboy and Ranger" to the Chair of a Bank President* (n.p.: Pawnee Bill's Historica Wild West Company, 1902), 50.

79. Richard White, "Frederick Jackson Turner and Buffalo Bill," in *The Frontier in American Culture: Essays by Richard White and Patricia Nelson Limerick,* ed. James Grossman (Berkeley and Los Angeles: University of California Press, 1994), 7–65, quotation on 27.

80. Hilory G. Bedford, *Texas Indian Troubles: The Most Thrilling Events in the History of Texas* (n.p.: Hargreaves Printing Co., 1905), 7. See also T. A. Babb, *In the Bosom of the Comanche: A Thrilling Tale of Savage Indian Life, Massacre and Captivity Truthfully Told by a Surviving Captive, T. A. Babb, Amarillo Texas, 1912* (Dallas: John F. Worley Printing Co., 1912), HEH RB 35527.

81. Beford, *Texas Indian Troubles,* 13.

82. Charles Prosch, *Reminiscences of Washington Territory: Scenes, Incidents, and Reflections of the Pioneer Period on Puget Sound* (Seattle, Washington, 1904), 125, NEW GC 3367; Brian Dippie, *The Vanishing American: White Attitudes and U.S. Indian Policy* (Lawrence: University Press of Kansas, 1982).

83. William B. Street, Omaha Nebraska, to J. H. Cole, Secretary, Tri-State Old Settlers' Association, Keokuk, Iowa, September 30, 1884, in Tri-State Old Settlers' Association, *Report of the Organization and First Reunion of the Tri-State Old Settlers' Association of Illinois, Missouri, and Iowa* (Keokuk, Iowa: Tri-State Printing Company, 1884), 57–59, NEW GC 4197.

6. The Ghosts of Western Future and Past

1. Bruce White Advertising and Design and Caribou Springs Ranch, advertisement for "Caribou Springs Ranch: Build on the Legend," in *Homes and Land in Boulder County* 5/6 (January 1999): 25. In 1999, lot prices at Caribou Springs Ranch began at $325,000.

2. Prudential Steamboat Realty's Creek Ranch advertisement is in *Homes and Land of Steamboat Springs and NW Colorado* 8 (March–April 2002): 33.

3. At the Caribou Springs Ranch, more than 500 acres of open space has been preserved; see Caribou Springs Ranch, promotional brochure (Bruce White Advertising and Design and Caribou Springs Ranch, 1998), n.p.

4. Prudential Steamboat Realty advertisement for "Harrington Elk Ranch," in *Homes and Land of Steamboat Springs and NW Colorado* 8 (March–April 2002): 8.

5. Verlyn Klinkenborg, "Voices from a Forgotten Landscape," *New York Times,* February 28, 2000, A18.

6. Hal Rothman discusses the theme of primacy, or longevity, at length in *Devil's Bargains: Tourism in the Twentieth-Century American West* (Lawrence: University Press of Kansas, 1999); see esp. 376–377, along with the book's front-matter photograph of Aspen, Colorado, residents lined up in Wagner Park according to their decade of arrival, and its discussions throughout of the tensions between natives and neonatives.

7. See, for example, David Olinger, "Sprawling Colorado—Who's to Blame?" *Denver Post,* February 7, 1999, 1A, 20A, 22A. For more on Colorado's "sprawl," see Michael E. Long, "Colorado's Front Range," *National Geographic* 190 (November 1996): 80–103; and Larry Fish, "Sprawl Spreads Across Colorado, Bringing Concerns with It," *Philadelphia Inquirer,* March 3, 2000, A19.

8. Richard Etulain adopts a very clear model of categorization, featuring the West as frontier, as region, and as postregion, in *Re-imagining the Modern American West: A Century of Fiction, History, and Art* (Tucson: University of Arizona Press, 1996). While Etulain's more recent work *Telling Western Stories: From Buffalo Bill to Larry McMurtry* (Albuquerque: University of New Mexico Press, 1999) places more emphasis on the continuity between the western literary past and present, the basic divisions between frontier and regional literature are still emphasized. Elliott West also distinguishes between process-centered and place-centered accounts in his chapter "Stories," in *The Way to the West: Essays on the Central Plains* (Albuquerque: University of New Mexico Press, 1995), 127–166. Thomas J. Lyon also emphasizes a division between "the 'frontier' level of literature" and a more complex "postfrontier"

outlook in his essay "The Literary West," in *The Oxford History of the American West,* ed. Clyde A. Milner II, Carol A. O'Connor, and Martha A. Sandweiss (New York: Oxford University Press, 1994), 707–741; and in his introductory essay, "The Conquistador, the Lone Ranger, and Beyond," in his edited collection *The Literary West: An Anthology of Western American Literature* (New York: Oxford University Press, 1999), 1–18. Likewise, Wallace Stegner noted that "western literature has been largely a literature of movement, of the road. Now it shows occasional signs of growing out of deeply lived-in places and traditional cultural climates"; see his essay "A Geography of Hope," in *A Society to Match the Scenery: Personal Visions of the Future of the American West,* ed. Gary Holthaus, Patricia Nelson Limerick, Charles F. Wilkinson, and Eve Stryker Munson (Niwot: University Press of Colorado, 1991), 218–229, quotation on 225.

9. The Census Bureau's Mountain West region was the fastest-growing American region of the 1990s, with a rate of 33 percent. See Census Bureau *Statistics,* 2000 Census, www.census.gov.

10. For an excellent study of the impact of place on the writings of Stegner and DeVoto, see John L. Thomas, *A Country in the Mind: Wallace Stegner, Bernard DeVoto, History, and the American Land* (New York: Routledge, 2000). For more on Stegner and western sense of place, see the excellent interviews with the author conducted by Richard W. Etulain, *Stegner: Conversations on History and Literature,* rev. ed. (Reno: University of Nevada Press, 1996).

11. Recent tragic border crossings from Mexico into the United States underscore the continued dangers of migration into the West and the powerful memories that some journeys will generate.

12. For more on the connection between the journey process and regional identity formation, see Clarence Mondale, "Place-on-the-Move: Place and Space for the Migrant," in *Mapping American Culture,* ed. Wayne Franklin and Michael Steiner (Iowa City: University of Iowa Press, 1992), 53–88; G. J. Lewis, *Human Migration* (New York: St. Martin's Press, 1982); Virginia Scharff, *Twenty Thousand Roads: Women, Movement, and the West* (Berkeley and Los Angeles: University of California Press, 2002); and Virginia Sharff, "Mobility, Women, and the West," in *Over the Edge: Remapping the American West,* ed. Valerie J. Matsumoto and Blake Allmendinger (Berkeley and Los Angeles: University of California Press, 1999), 160–171.

13. Richard White provides some discussion of militia groups in his Western History Association presidential address, published as "The Current Weirdness in the West," *Western Historical Quarterly* 28 (spring 1997): 5–16.

14. Neil Leach, "The Dark Side of the *Domus*: The Redomestication of Central and Eastern Europe," in *Architecture and Revolution: Contemporary Perspectives on Central and Eastern Europe,* ed. Neil Leach (New York: Routledge, 1999), 150–162, quotations on 155, 156.

15. The relationship between regionalism and sectionalism is a complex one. During the regional renaissance in the years between World War I and World War II, regional theorists generally viewed regionalism as a positive force that facilitated cooperation and understanding, and sectionalism as a divisive force that fueled ani-

mosities and led to conflict. For more on regionalism in this period, see Robert Dorman, *Revolt of the Provinces: The Regionalist Movement in America, 1920–1945* (Chapel Hill: University of North Carolina Press, 1993); and Michael C. Steiner, "Regionalism in the Great Depression," *Geographical Review* 73 (October 1983): 430–446.

16. Richard Etulain emphasizes the differences between "to the place" and "in the place" in western writing in *Re-imagining the Modern American West.*

17. Anthropologist Keith Basso's work on the Western Apache illuminates deep connections to the land that are maintained through strong oral traditions. See, for example, his *Wisdom Sits in Places: Landscape and Language Among the Western Apache* (Albuquerque: University of New Mexico Press, 1996); *Western Apache Language and Culture: Essays in Linguistic Anthropology* (Tucson: University of Arizona Press, 1990). Basso emphasizes the differences between white westerners' sense of place and Apache attachments to place in "Apache Landscapes and the Oldest Man in Show Low" (lecture presented at the University of Colorado, Boulder, April 26, 1999).

18. Frederick Hoxie examines the theme of the reservation as cultural homeland in "Exploring a Cultural Borderland: Native American Journeys of Discovery in the Early Twentieth Century," in *Discovering America: Essays on the Search for an Identity,* ed. David Thelen and Frederick Hoxie (Urbana: University of Illinois Press, 1994), 135–161; in his essay "The Reservation Period, 1880–1960," in *The Cambridge History of the Native Peoples of the Americas: North America,* ed. Bruce G. Trigger and Wilcomb E. Washburn (New York: Cambridge University Press, 1996), 183–258; and in his study *Parading Through History: The Making of the Crow Nation in America, 1805–1935* (New York: Cambridge University Press, 1995). For a more recent exploration of this theme, see the director Chris Eyre's movie *Smoke Signals* (1998).

19. Barbara Allen's "Historical Commentary: Landscape, Memory, and the Western Past," *Montana: The Magazine of Western History* 39 (winter 1989): 71–75, includes interesting reminiscences concerning the role of harsh landscapes and climates in forging identity.

20. For more on the Washington State bumper sticker, see William Celis III, "California Dreamers Who Move to Seattle Get the Big Chill: Locals Blame the Emigres for Pollution, Congestion, Discos and Tanning Salons," *Wall Street Journal,* October 10, 1989, A1, A9. In Colorado the "Native Coloradoan" bumper sticker is quite popular. Some of the students at the University of Colorado at Boulder sport a bumper sticker that reads "Semi-Native Coloradoan," which serves as an amusing rejoinder to the original.

21. Celis, "California Dreamers," A1, A9.

22. There may be some similarity between the attitude of so many Intermountain westerners to California and the attitude of many upstate New Yorkers toward New York City's residents and urban problems. Similar sectional tensions, of course, exist within the state of California.

23. Incidentally, the pervasiveness of the concept of Californication is evidenced by its entry into popular culture. A notable example is the Red Hot Chili Peppers'

CD *Californication* (WEA/Warner Brothers, 1999), the title track of which explores the theme of the malign influence of California culture on the nation.

24. Mary Murphy utilizes the phrases "last best hiding place" and "white flight highway" in her essay "Searching for an Angle of Repose: Women, Work, and Creativity in Early Montana," in *Many Wests: Place, Culture, and Regional Identity,* ed. David M. Wrobel and Michael C. Steiner (Lawrence: University Press of Kansas, 1997), 156–176, quotations on 172. The original term, "last best place," is drawn from William Kittredge and Annick Smith, eds., *The Last Best Place: A Montana Anthology* (Helena: Montana Historical Society Press, 1988).

25. Mike Davis's *Ecology of Fear: Los Angeles and the Imagination of Disaster* (New York: Metropolitan Books, 1998) tries to reinsert this imagery about Southern California into the popular imagination.

26. For more on the economic reasons for California out-migration in the late twentieth century, see Walter Nugent, *Into the West: The Story of Its People* (New York: Knopf, 1999), 351–379.

27. By September 2000, Caucasians had become a minority in California. See *Census Bureau Statistics,* www.census.gov.

28. This chapter does not explore the theme of the male-centeredness of western imagery. For good coverage of the topic of gender and westernness, see Krista Comer's *Landscapes of the New West: Gender and Geography in Contemporary Women's Writing* (Chapel Hill: University of North Carolina Press, 1999).

29. The scholarly literature on American nativism is enormous and fast growing. Included among these works is John Higham's seminal study *Strangers in the Land: Patterns of American Nativism, 1865–1925* (New Brunswick, N.J.: Rutgers University Press, 1955); and his *Send These to Me: Jews and Other Immigrants in Urban America* (New York: Atheneum, 1975); Ronald Takaki's important edited collection *From Different Shores: Perspectives on Race and Ethnicity in America* (New York: Oxford University Press, 1994); and Dale T. Knobel's *"America for the Americans": The Nativist Movement in the United States* (New York: Twayne, 1996).

30. For more on this topic, see David M. Wrobel, *The End of American Exceptionalism: Frontier Anxiety from the Old West to the New Deal* (Lawrence: University Press of Kansas, 1993), 18–20, 47–52, 118–121.

31. For more on Latino immigration in the contemporary West, see Nugent, *Into the West,* 351–359.

32. Clyde A. Milner II explores how regional identity can form through opposition to outside forces in "The View from Wisdom: Four Layers of Regional Identity," in *Under an Open Sky: Rethinking America's Western Past,* ed. William Cronon, George Miles, and Jay Gitlin (New York: Norton, 1992), 203–222; and in "The Shared Memory of Montana Pioneers," *Montana: The Magazine of Western History* 37 (winter 1987): 2–13.

33. Earl Pomeroy has provided probing discussions of what cultural traits easterners brought west with them; see his seminal essay "Toward a Re-orientation of Western History: Continuity and Environment," *Mississippi Valley Historical Review* 41 (March 1955): 579–600, and book, *The Pacific Slope: A History of California, Oregon,*

Washington, Idaho, Utah, and Nevada (New York: Knopf, 1965; reprint, Lincoln: University of Nebraska Press, 1991). Also interesting in this regard is Louis B. Wright's important work *Culture on the Moving Frontier* (Bloomington: Indiana University Press, 1955). John Findlay notes that westerners' perceptions of the East played an important role in shaping their own identity; see his "Far Western Cityscapes and American Culture Since 1940," *Western Historical Quarterly* 22 (February 1991): 19–43, quotation on 24.

34. See C. Vann Woodward, *Origins of the New South, 1877–1913* (Baton Rouge: Louisiana State University Press, 1951).

35. See Josiah Royce, "Provincialism." This 1902 Phi Beta Kappa Address at the University of Iowa was first printed in the *Boston Evening Transcript;* then reprinted in *Race Questions, Provincialism, and Other American Problems* (New York: Macmillan, 1908; reprint, Arno Press, 1977), 57–108; and more recently published in *The Basic Writings of Josiah Royce,* ed. John J. McDermott (Chicago: University of Chicago Press, 1969), 2: 1067–1088.

36. See James A. Shortridge, "The Expectations of Others: Struggles Toward a Sense of Place on the Northern Plains," in Wrobel and Steiner, *Many Wests,* 114–135.

37. For a good discussion of the range of possibilities—from the most positive to the most negative—associated with regionalism, see Patricia Nelson Limerick, "Region and Reason," in *All Over the Map: Rethinking American Regions,* by Edward L. Ayers, Patricia Nelson Limerick, Stephen Nissenbaum, and Peter S. Onuf (Baltimore: Johns Hopkins University Press, 1996), 83–104, esp. 103.

38. The idea of a dynamic western regionalism is further explored in Steiner and Wrobel, "Many Wests"; and in Edward L. Ayers and Peter S. Onuf's "Introduction" to Ayers, Limerick, Nissenbaum, and Onuf, *All Over the Map,* 1–10. William Cronon, George Miles, and Jay Gitlin discuss the movement from "flux to fixity" in their essay "Becoming West: Toward a New Meaning for Western History," in Cronon, Miles, and Gitlin, *Under an Open Sky,* 3–27. Etulain discusses the theme of movement from frontier to region to postregion in *Re-imagining the Modern American West.* Kerwin Klein discusses the theme of postwesternism in "Reclaiming the 'F' Word: Or Being and Becoming Postwestern," *Pacific Historical Review* 65 (May 1996): 179–215. Virginia Scharff asks whether it is "time . . . for a postwestern history" in "Mobility, Women, and the West," 167. Pertinent to this issue, Roger L. Nichols, in the introduction to his edited collection *American Frontier and Western Issues: A Historiographical Review* (Westport, Conn.: Greenwood Press, 1986), 1–6, asks the question: "If one accepts the idea that the term frontier best fits the pioneering process, then what measurement indicates when the phase of regional development or regional integration marks its completion?" (2).

39. Such matters are further complicated by debates over the preservation of the West's natural environments. Ranchers, for example, often view environmentalists as outsiders who fail to appreciate their need to preserve a way of life. See White, "The Current Weirdness in the West," 13–15.

40. See Patricia Nelson Limerick, "Empire of Innocence," in *The Legacy of Conquest: The Unbroken Past of the American West* (New York: Norton, 1987), 35–54.

41. The statistic on western metropolitanism is from Carl Abbott, *The Metropolitan Frontier: Cities in the Modern American West* (Tucson: University of Arizona Press, 1993), xii. See also Nugent, *Into the West*, 375. Roger Lotchin provides an excellent discussion of the centrality of urban history to understanding the West in "The Impending Western Urban Past: An Essay on the Twentieth-Century West," in *Researching Western History: Topics in the Twentieth Century*, ed. Gerald Nash and Richard Etulain (Albuquerque: University of New Mexico Press, 1997), 53–81; see also Carl Abbott, "The American West and the Three Urban Revolutions," in *Old West/New West: Quo Vadis?* ed. Gene M. Gressley (Worland, Wyo.: High Plains, 1994), 75–99. For further commentary on the need to move beyond rural imagery and deal with western urban arenas, see Patricia Nelson Limerick, "The Realization of the American West," in *The New Regionalism*, ed. Charles Reagan Wilson (Jackson: University Press of Mississippi, 1998), 71–98.

42. A tiny sampling of sources that address the issue of regional identity in metropolitan places includes Edward W. Soja's *Postmodern Geographies: The Reassertion of Space in Critical Social Theory* (New York: Verso, 1989); Allen J. Scott and Edward W. Soja, eds., *The City: Los Angeles and Urban Theory at the End of the Twentieth Century* (Berkeley and Los Angeles: University of California Press, 1996); Michael Sorkin, ed., *Variations on a Theme Park: The New American City and the End of Public Space* (New York: Hill and Wang, 1992); and Edward S. Casey, *Getting Back into Place: Toward a Renewed Understanding of the Place World* (Bloomington: Indiana University Press, 1993). David Goldfield provides an interesting model that western historians might consider in his *Region, Race, and Cities: Interpreting the Urban South* (Baton Rouge: Louisiana State University Press, 1997). Also worth mentioning is Linda Groat, ed., *Giving Places Meaning* (New York: Harcourt, Brace, 1995), a collection of essays on place by environmental psychologists.

43. For more on the at best very fuzzy line separating "natural" environments from built environments, see Ethan Carr, *Wilderness by Design: Landscape Architecture and the National Park Service* (Lincoln: University of Nebraska Press, 1998); William Cronon, "The Trouble with Wilderness; or, Getting Back to the Wrong Nature," in *Uncommon Ground: Rethinking the Human Place in Nature*, ed. William Cronon (New York: Norton, 1995), 69–90; and Richard White, *The Organic Machine: The Remaking of the Columbia River* (New York: Hill and Wang, 1995).

44. For more on sense of place in suburbia, see Lars Lerup, *After the City* (Cambridge, Mass.: MIT Press, 2000); Hal Rothman, "Community from Nothingness," in *Neon Metropolis: The First City of the Twenty-first Century* (New York: Routledge, 2002), 291–316; and Kenneth T. Jackson, *Crabgrass Frontier: The Suburbanization of the United States* (New York: Oxford University Press, 1985).

45. See, for example, Robert Athearn's *In Search of Canaan: Black Migration to Kansas, 1879–1880* (Lawrence: Regents Press of Kansas, 1978); and Nell Irving Painter's *Exodusters: Black Migration to Kansas After Reconstruction* (New York: Norton, 1992).

46. William M. Goetzmann and William N. Goetzmann, *The West of the Imagination* (New York: Norton, 1986).

47. For good coverage of the theme of regional identity in urban settings, see David Fine, ed., *Los Angeles in Fiction: A Collection of Essays,* rev. ed. (Albuquerque: University of New Mexico Press, 1995). For an excellent treatment of a western writer of color, black Los Angeles poet Wanda Coleman, who needs to be considered within the framework of westernness, see Krista Comer, "Revising Western Criticism Through Wanda Coleman," *Western American Literature* 33 (winter 1999): 356–383. See also Comer's coverage of Coleman in *Landscapes of the New West,* 88–103.

48. Jean-François Lyotard, *The Postmodern Condition: A Report on Knowledge,* trans. Geoff Bennington and Brian Massumi, Theory and History of Literature, 10 (Minneapolis: University of Minnesota Press, 1984), xxiv.

Selected Bibliography

Primary Sources

Sources without archive and rare book designations are from the general collections of various libraries, including the Huntington, Newberry, Denver Public, Bancroft, American Heritage Center, and Lied (University of Nevada Las Vegas) libraries.

ARCHIVES AND RARE BOOK COLLECTIONS
American Heritage Center, Special Collections, Laramie, Wyoming (AHC SC)
  Hanesworth Collection (AHC SC)
  Ellen Crago Mueller Papers (AHC SC)
  J. S. Palen Collection (AHC SC)
  Edmund Seymour Collection (AHC SC)
Hubert Howe Bancroft Library, Special Collections, Berkeley, California (BANC SC)
  Utah Questionnaires (BANC PF)
Denver Public Library, Western History Department (DPL)
  Maria Davies McGrath Collection (DPL McG)
Henry E. Huntington Library, San Marino, California (HEH)
  Ephemera Collection (HEH E)
  Eliza Poor Donner Houghton Papers (HEH EPDH)
  Rare Book Collection (HEH RB)
  Frederick Jackson Turner Papers (HEH TU)
Newberry Library, Chicago (NEW)
  Ayer Collection (NEW AC)
  Graff Collection of Western Americana (NEW GC)

PROMOTIONAL JOURNALS
Alaska Monthly Magazine
The Coast
Colorado: A Monthly Magazine Devoted to Colorado in General and Denver in Particular
Ecce Montezuma: A Monthly Journal Dedicated to the Interests of the Southwest
Midwest Review
New West: A Monthly Journal of Immigration
New West Illustrated
New West Magazine
Northwest Magazine
Out West/Land of Sunshine

Rand McNally and Co's Western Railway Guide
Sunset

REMINISCENCE JOURNALS
Annals of Wyoming
Frontier Times
Quarterly of the Oregon Historical Society
Sons of Colorado

PIONEER SOCIETY PROCEEDINGS

Association of Pioneer Women of California. *Constitution, By-Laws and List of Members, 1908.* San Francisco: Press of Van Orden Co., 1908. HEH RB 251642.

Arizona Pioneers Historical Society. *Constitution and By-Laws* (1897). HEH RB 425460.

California Pioneers of Santa Clara County: Pioneer and Old Settlers' Day. N.p., n.d. HEH RB 260530.

Los Angeles County Pioneer Society. Annual Reports, 1908–1915. HEH RB 106161.

———. *Historical Record and Souvenir of the Pioneer Society of Los Angeles County.* Los Angeles: Times-Mirror Press, 1923. HEH RB 194183.

Los Angeles County Pioneers of Southern California. *Annual Report of the Los Angeles County Pioneers of Southern California for 1913–1914, and 1914–1915.* N.p., 1914, 1915.

Native Daughters of the Golden West. *Proceedings of the Seventeenth Annual Session of the Grand Parlor of the Native Daughters of the Golden West, Held at Red Bluff, California, June 9–13, 1903.* San Francisco: Hayden Printing Co., 1903.

Native Sons of the Golden West. *Grand Parlor Proceedings: Proceedings of the Twentieth Annual Session of the Grand Parlor of the Native Sons of the Golden West,* Redwood City, California, April 26–29, 1897. San Francisco: Julius Gabriel, 1897.

Old Settlers' Association, Johnson County, Iowa. *Proceedings of the Johnson County [Iowa] Old Settlers' Association, August 20, 1903.* N.p., n.d. NEW GC 2135, 4–9.

———. *Proceedings of the Johnson County [Iowa] Old Settlers' Association, from 1866 to 1899.* N.p., n.d. NEW GC 2132.

———. *Thirty-sixth Annual Reunion of the Old Settlers Association of Johnson County, Iowa, August 21, 1902.* Iowa City, 1902. NEW GC 2134.

Old Settlers' Association of Minnesota. *A Sketch of the Organization, Objects, and Membership of the Old Settlers' Association of Minnesota.* Saint Paul, Minn.: Ramaley, Chaney and Co., Printers, 1872.

Oregon Pioneer Association. "Constitution of the Oregon Pioneer Association." In *Oregon Pioneer Association, Constitution and Transactions, 1st–14th, 1874–1886.* Salem, Ore.: E. M. Waite, Steam Printer and Bookbinder; Portland, Ore.: Press of Geo. H. Himes, 1875–1887.

———. Constitution, Transactions of the 1st–14th Annual Reunions, 1873–1886. Salem, Ore.: E. M. Waite, Steam Printer and Bookbinder, 1887.

Pioneer Settlers' Association of Louisa County, Iowa. *Constitution and By-Laws of the Pioneer Settlers' Association of Louisa County, Iowa, with the Proceedings of the First and Second Annual Festivals.* Wapello, Iowa: John Jenkins, Printer, 1860. NEW GC 3299.

Pioneers Association of the State of Washington. "Fiftieth Jubilee Meeting of the Pioneers Association of the State of Washington, June 6th, 1939, in Seattle." HEH RB 299566.

Sacramento Society of California Pioneers. *Constitution and By-Laws.* Sacramento, Calif.: H. A. Weaver, Printer, 1877.

———. *Grand Excursion from Sacramento to New York in a Special Train of Pullman Cars via the Great Overland Route.* Sacramento, Calif.: Jefferis Printer, 1869. HEH RB 65323.

Society of California Pioneers. *Proceedings of the Society of California Pioneers in Reference to the Histories of Hubert Howe Bancroft.* San Francisco: Sterett Printing Co., 1894.

Society of Colorado Pioneers. "Constitution and By-Laws of the Society of Colorado Pioneers" (1872). In Colorado Pioneer Register. DPL McG.

Society of Montana Pioneers. *Thirty-third Annual Meeting Report.* Helena, Mont.: Society of Montana Pioneers, 1917.

Tri-State Old Settlers' Association. *Report of the Fourth Tri-State Reunion, August 30, 1887.* Keokuk, Iowa: Press of the Gate City, 1887. NEW GC 4197. (The organization's reports from 1884 through 1887, though published separately, are all bound in one volume.)

———. *Report of the Organization and First Reunion of the Tri-State Old Settlers' Association of Illinois, Missouri, and Iowa.* Keokuk, Iowa: Tri-State Printing Company, 1884. NEW GC 4197.

———. *Report of the Second Annual Reunion of the Tri-State Old Settlers' Association of Illinois, Missouri, and Iowa, September 30, 1885.* Keokuk, Iowa: R. B. Ogden and Son, Printing and Binding, 1885. NEW GC 4197.

DISSERTATIONS AND THESES

Berglund, Barbara, "Ordering the Disorderly City: Power, Culture, and Nation-Making in San Francisco, 1846–1906." Ph.D. diss., University of Michigan, 2002.

Orsi, Richard J. "Selling the Golden State: A Study of Boosterism in Nineteenth-Century California." Ph.D. diss., University of Wisconsin, 1973.

Petty, Claude Rowland. "Gold Rush Intellectual." Ph.D. Diss., University of California, 1952.

Richey, Duke. "Montana Eden: Land Use and Change in the Bitterroot Valley, Pre-History to 1930." Master's thesis, University of Montana, 1999.

GOVERNMENT DOCUMENTS AND PUBLICATIONS

Census Bureau Statistics. 1990. www.census.gov.

Census Bureau Statistics. 2000. www.census.gov.

Historical Records Survey, Utah Works Projects Administration. *Utah Questionnaires, 1936–1939.* BANC SC PF312–313.

Powell, John Wesley. *Report on the Lands of the Arid Regions of the United States.* Washington, D.C.: Government Printing Office, 1878.

Report of Rain-Fall in Washington Territory, Oregon, California, Idaho, Nevada, Utah, Arizona, Colorado, Wyoming, New Mexico, Indian Territory, and Texas for from Two to Forty Years. 50th Cong., 1st sess., Executive Documents 91, 282. Washington, D.C.: Government Printing Office, 1889. HEH RB 499799.

MAPS (M), BROADSIDES (B), AND ATLASES

Anon. "Bell County Texas: A General Invitation to Worthy People" (c. 1876–1877). B, NEW GC 247, Broadside Box 3.

Anon. "Kansas Pacific Homestead." 1876. DPL, B, C330.9781 K1335.

Anon. "Yuma, Colorado" (1889). DPL, B, C978.878 Y91.

Anon. "Yuma, Colorado" (1889). DPL, B, C978.878 Y91, 1889.

Canadian Pacific Railway. "The Golden Northwest: A Home for All People" (1884). DPL, B, C338.0971 C16go.

Central Branch of the Union Pacific Railroad Co. Map of "Farms and Homes in Kansas" (1879). DPL, B, C333.336, C333far.

Farrer, John. "A Mappe of Virginia." In Gerald A. Danzer. *Discovering American History through Maps and Views,* S5. New York: HarperCollins, 1991.

Glover, E. S. *Corinne and the Bear River Valley, Utah Territory, 1875: Location, Climate, Agricultural and Commercial Advantages, Unsurpassed for Actual Settlers and Colonization Enterprises.* Cincinnati, Ohio: Strobridge and Co., Lithographers, 1875. HEH RB 45811, M.

Johnson, A. S., publisher. Kansas! Chromolithograph. Topeka: Kansas State Historical Society, 1881.

Map of "The Inter-Mountain District: Comprising Idaho, Montana, Wyoming and Washington Territories, the State of Oregon, and Portions of California, Nevada, Utah and Colorado Showing the Present and Prospective Railway Connections of Boise City." Boise City, Idaho: Boise City Board of Trade, 1887–1888. NEW GC 338.

Northern Pacific Railroad Company. "Map Showing the Land Grant of the Northern Pacific Railroad Company, in Montana, Idaho and in Part of North Dakota and in Part of Eastern Washington" (1890). DPL, M, CG4242.P3, 1890.N6.

———. "Sectional Map Showing the Lands of the Northern Pacific Railroad Co., in Eastern Washington and Northern Idaho, with Condensed Information Relating to the Northern Pacific Country" (1886). DPL, M, CG4242.G4, 1886.N6.

Rand McNally and Company's Business Atlas, Containing Large-Scale Maps of Each State and Territory of the Great Mississippi Valley and Pacific Slope. Chicago: Rand McNally and Company, 1876.

Rand McNally Company. "How the Public Domain Has Been Squandered." DPL, B, C333.160973 H83.

————. "Map of the Union and Central Pacific Railroads." In *Rand McNally and Co's Western Railway Guide: The Travelers Hand Book to All Western Railway and Steamboat Lines.* Chicago, 1884.

Rand McNally's Pioneer Atlas. Chicago: Rand McNally and Company, 1956.

Schenck, Roy W. "Map of Wyoming Resources, Showing at a Glance the Harvest of Gold Which Awaits the Settler and Investor in Wyoming." Denver, Colo.: Clason Map Co., issued by the Wyoming State Board of Immigration, [1912?]. HEH E IWMNG.

Union Pacific Railroad. "The Union Pacific and Utah and Northern Through Rail Route to Montana and Yellowstone Park." DPL, B, C385.0978, U 57un.

GENERAL

Adamic, Louis. *Laughing in the Jungle: The Autobiography of an Immigrant in America.* New York: Harper and Brothers, 1932; Reprint, New York: Arno Press and the New York Times, 1969.

Adams, Harrison. *The Pioneer Boys of the Colorado: Braving the Perils of the Grand Canyon Country.* Boston: L. C. Page and Company, 1926.

Ayer, Winslow. *Life in the Wilds of America and Wonders of the West in and Beyond the Bounds of Civilization.* Grand Rapids, Mich.: Central Publishing Company, 1880.

Bancroft, Hubert Howe. *The Works of Hubert Howe Bancroft.* 39 vols. San Francisco: A. L. Bancroft and Company, 1882–1890.

Barber, John W., and Henry Howe. *Barber's History of All the Western States and Territories: From the Alleghanies to the Pacific and from the Lakes to the Gulf.* Cincinnati, Ohio: Howe's Subscription Book Concern, 1867.

Beadle, J. H. *The Undeveloped West; or, Five Years in the Territories: Being a Complete History of That Vast Region Between the Mississippi and the Pacific.* Philadelphia: National Publishing Company, 1873.

Bechdolt, Frederick R. "How Death Valley Was Named." *Saturday Evening Post,* July 19, 1919, 30–34, 66.

Carroll, John Alexander. *Pioneering in Arizona: The Reminiscences of Emerson Oliver Stratton and Edith Stratton Kitt.* Tucson, Ariz.: Arizona Pioneers Historical Society, 1964.

Cattermole, E. G. *Famous Frontiersmen, Pioneers and Scouts: The Vanguards of American Civilization. A Thrilling Narrative of the Lives and Marvelous Exploits of the Most Renowned Heroes, Trappers, Explorers, Adventurers, Scouts and Indian Fighters.* Chicago: Coburn and Newman Publishing Co., 1883. Chicago: Donohue, Henneberry and Co., 1890.

Copp, Henry N., ed. *The American Settler's Guide: A Brief Exposition of the Public Land System of the United States of America.* Washington, D.C.: Published by the editor, 1880.

Countant, Dr. C. G. *History of Wyoming and the Far West.* Laramie, Wyo.: Chaplin, Spafford, and Mathison, Printers, 1899.

Fenneman, James N. "Physiographic Boundaries Within the United States." *Annals of the Association of American Geographers* 4 (1914): 84–134.

———. "Physiographic Divisions Within the United States." *Annals of the Association of American Geographers* 6 (1916): 19–98.

Field, Henry M. *Our Western Archipelago.* New York: Scribner's, 1895.

Fowler, William W. *Women on the American Frontier.* Hartford, Conn.: S. S. Scranton and Co., 1876.

Frost, John. *Pioneer Mothers of the West; or, Heroic and Daring Deeds of American Women, Comprising Thrilling Episodes of Courage, Fortitude, Devotedness, and Self-Sacrifice.* Boston: Lee and Shepard, 1875.

George, Henry. "Chinese Immigration." In *Cyclopedia of Political Science, Political Economy, and of the Political History of the United States, by the Best American and European Writers.* Vol. I, *Abdication-Duty,* ed. John L. Laylor, 409–414. Chicago: Melbert B. Cary and Co., 1883.

———. *Our Land and Land Policy: National and State.* San Francisco: White and Bauer, 1871.

———. *Our Land and Land Policy: Speeches, Lectures, and Miscellaneous Writings by Henry George.* Ed. Kenneth C. Wenzer. East Lansing: Michigan State University Press, 1999.

———. *Progress and Poverty: An Inquiry into the Cause of Industrial Depressions, and of Increase of Want with Increase of Wealth.* 1879; New York: D. Appleton and Co., 1884.

———. "What the Railroad Will Bring Us." *Overland Monthly* 1 (October 1868): 297–304.

Gilfy, Henry M. "History and Resources of Oregon." Handwritten manuscript, 1876, 78. BANC, PA 37.

Goodenough, Rev. S. "Foes of Labor: The Chinese and Other Foes of American Labor." *California Review* 1 (October 1893): 33–40.

Hill, Alice Polk. *Tales of the Colorado Pioneers.* Denver: Pierson and Gardner, 1884.

Hobson, Archie. *Remembering America: A Sampler of the WPA American Guide Series.* New York: Collier Books, 1987.

Holmes, Kenneth L., ed. and comp. *Covered Wagon Women: Diaries and Letters from the Western Trails, 1840–1890.* 11 vols. Lincoln: University of Nebraska Press, 2000.

James, George Wharton. *Heroes of California: The Story of the Founders of the Golden State as Narrated by Themselves or Gleaned from Other Sources.* Boston: Little, Brown, and Company, 1910.

Jireh College Bulletin, 1910. W994-t-jir. SC, AHC.

Lummis, Charles F. *A Tramp Across the Continent.* New York: Charles Scribner's Sons, 1982. Reprint, Albuquerque, N.M.: Calvin Horn Publisher, 1969.

Luther, Mark Lee. *The Boosters.* Indianapolis: Bobbs-Merrill Co., 1923.

McCarter, Margaret Hill. *Homeland: A Present-Day Love Story.* New York: Harper and Brothers, 1922.

———. *The Price of the Prairie.* Chicago: A. C. McClurg and Co., 1911.

———. *The Reclaimers.* New York: A. L. Burt Co., 1918.

———. *Vanguards of the Plains: A Romance of the Old Santa Fé Trail.* New York: A. L. Burt Co., 1917.

———. *Winning the Wilderness.* Chicago: A. C. McClurg and Co., 1914.

Meeker, Ezra. *Kate Mulhall: A Romance of the Oregon Trail.* New York: published by the author, 1926.

———. *Uncle Ezra's Short Stories for Children.* Tacoma, Wash.: D. W. Cooper, Printer, 1910[?].

Middleton, James. "A New West: The Attempts to Open Up the Natural Treasures of the Western States—Utilization and Conservation vs Monopolistic Greed—the Department of the Interior." *World's Work* 31 (April 1916): 669–680.

Neuberger, Richard L. *Our Promised Land.* New York: Macmillan, 1938.

Parkman, Francis. *The Oregon Trail: Sketches of Prairie and Rocky-Mountain Life.* Boston: Little, Brown and Co., 1892.

Powell, John Wesley. "The Irrigable Lands of the Arid Region." *Century Magazine* 39 (March 1890): 766–776.

———. "Physiographic Regions of the United States." *National Geographic Monographs* 1 (1895): 66–100.

Richardson, Rupert Norval, and Carl Coke Rister. *The Greater Southwest: The Economic, Social and Cultural Development of Kansas, Oklahoma, Texas, Utah, Colorado, Nevada, New Mexico, Arizona, and California from the Spanish Conquest to the Twentieth Century.* Glendale, Calif.: Arthur H. Clark Co., 1934.

Rister, Carl Coke. *The Southwestern Frontier, 1865–1881: A History of the Coming of the Settlers, Indian Depredations and Massacres, Ranching Activities, Operations of White Desperadoes and Thieves, Government Protection, Building of Railways, and the Disappearance of the Frontier.* Cleveland: Arthur H. Clark Co., 1928.

Rolvaag, O. E. *Giants in the Earth: A Saga of the Prairie.* New York: Harper and Brothers, 1927.

Romspert, George W. *The Western Echo: A Description of the Western States and Territories of the United States.* Dayton, Ohio: United Brethren Publishing House, 1881.

Roosevelt, Theodore. *The Winning of the West.* 4 vols. New York: G. P. Putnam's Sons, 1889–1896.

Royce, Josiah. *The Basic Writings of Josiah Royce.* Ed. John J. McDermott. 2 vols. Chicago: University of Chicago Press, 1969.

———. *California: From the Conquest in 1846 to the Second Vigilance Committee in San Francisco.* Boston: Houghton Mifflin and Co., 1886.

———. "Provincialism." Phi Beta Kappa Address at the University of Iowa, 1902. In *Race Questions, Provincialism, and Other American Problems,* 57–108. New York: Macmillan, 1908. Reprint, Arno Press, 1977.

Ruede, Howard. *Sod-House Days: Letters from a Kansas Homesteader, 1877–1878.* Ed. John Ise. 1937. Reprint, Lawrence: University Press of Kansas, 1983.

Sandoz, Mari. *Old Jules.* 1935. Reprint, Lincoln: University of Nebraska Press, 1985.

Savage, Isaac O. *A History of Republic County, Kansas.* Beloit, Kans.: Jones and Chubbi, Art Printers, 1901, HEH RB, 127727.

Shaw, Luella. *True History of Some of the Pioneers of Colorado.* Hotchkiss, Colo.: W. S. Coburn, John Patterson, and A. K. Shaw, 1909.

Smythe, William E. *The Colonial Lectures: Delivered in Chicago, November 26, December 3, 10, and 17, 1895, and Subsequently in New York, Massachusetts and Other Eastern States.* N.p., 1896. HEH RB 370462.

———. *The Conquest of Arid America.* New York: Harper and Brothers, 1899. Revised edition, New York: Macmillan, 1905. Reprint, Seattle: University of Washington Press, 1969.

———. *Constructive Democracy: The Economics of a Square Deal.* New York: Macmillan, 1905.

Steinbeck, John. *Cannery Row.* New York: Viking, 1945.

———. *The Grapes of Wrath.* New York: Viking, 1939.

———. *In Dubious Battle.* New York: Covici-Friede, 1936.

———. "The Leader of the People." In *The Long Valley,* 198–214. 1938; New York: Viking, 1967.

Stewart, Henry. *Irrigation for the Farm, Garden, and Orchard.* New York: Orange Judd Company, 1877.

Tenney, E. P. *The New West: As Related to the Christian College and the Home Missionary.* 3d ed. Cambridge, Mass.: Riverside Press, 1878.

Thayer, William W. *Marvels of the New West: A Vivid Portrayal of the Stupendous Marvels in the Vast Wonderland West of the Missouri River.* Norwich, Conn.: Henry Bill Publishing Company, 1888.

Turner, Frederick Jackson. "The Significance of the Frontier in American History." In *The Frontier in American History,* 1–38. New York: Henry Holt and Company, 1920.

Warner, Charles Dudley. "Our Italy." *Harper's New Monthly Magazine,* November 1890, 813–829.

Wooten, Mattie Lloyd, comp. and ed. *Women Tell the Story of the Southwest.* San Antonio, Tex.: Naylor Co., 1940).

PROMOTIONAL

Adams, W. L. *Oregon As It Is: Its Present and Future, by a Resident of Twenty-five Years: Being a Reply to Inquirers.* Portland, Ore.: Bulletin Steam Book and Job Printing Rooms, 1873.

Alaska Bureau of Publicity. *General Facts About the Territory of Alaska, in Condensed Form.* Alaska Bureau of Publicity, 1917. HEH E A.

Alaska: The Newest Home. N.p., [1931?]. HEH E A.

Allen, A. S. *The City of Seattle, 1900.* Seattle: Press of Metropolitan Printing and Binding Co., for the Seattle Chamber of Commerce, 1900. HEH RB 299567.

Anon. *Alaska: The Newest Home Land.* N.p., 1931. HEH E A.

Anon. *Juneau Alaska and Vicinity: The Capital of the Northland—A Land of Enormous Natural Resources, of Industry and Homes, of Healthful and Moderate*

Climatic Conditions—A Wonderland of Alaskan Beauty and Modern Progress. Alaska: Authentic Information. N.p., c1928. HEH E A.

Anon. *Los Angeles: The Queen City of the Angels.* Los Angeles: M. Reider, 1904. HEH RB 372388.

Anon. *Tucson: Chief Commercial City of Arizona.* Tucson, Ariz.: Press of the *Citizen*, c. 1910.

Arizona: Its Resources and Prospects: A Letter to the Editor of the New York Tribune (reprinted from that Journal of June 26th, 1865). By the Hon. Richard C. McCormick, Secretary of the Territory. New York: Van Nostrand, 1865. NEW GC 2583.

Atchison, Topeka and Santa Fe. *Arizona, Her Great Mining, Agricultural, Stock-Raising and Lumber Interests: The Only Direct Route Is via the Atchison, Topeka and Santa Fe.* Topeka, Kans.: Atchison, Topeka and Santa Fe, c. 1884.

Batchelder, George Alexander. *A Sketch of the History and Resources of Dakota Territory.* Yankton, Dakota: Press Steam Power Printing Co., 1870.

Beadle County Commissioners. *History of Beadle County, Dakota: Its Resources, Agricultural and Mineral Wealth.* Beadle County, Dakota: County Commissioners, 1889.

Besom, A. *Pawnee County, Nebraska: As It Was, and Is to Be.* Atchison, Kans.: Immigrant Union Publishers, 1878.

Bisbee Daily Review: *World's Fair Edition.* St. Louis: Samuel F. Meyerson Printing Co., 1904.

Bliss, Charles R. *New Mexico: The New West.* Boston: Frank Wood Printer, 1879. HEH RB 38267.

Board of Statistics, Immigration and Labor Exchange of Portland, Oregon. *Oregon: Its Advantages as an Agricultural and Commercial State.* Portland, Ore.: A. G. Walling Book and Job Printers, 1870.

Boulder Commercial Association. *Boulder, Colorado.* Boulder, Colo.: Boulder Publishing Co., 1910.

Bowles, Samuel. *The Pacific Railroad-Open. How to Go. What to See. Guide for Travel to and Through Western America.* Boston: Fields, Osgood, and Co., 1869.

Brackett, A. G. "Wyoming Territory." *Western Monthly* 2 (September 1869): 173.

Butler, James D. *Nebraska: Its Characteristics and Prospects.* [Burlington, Iowa], 1873.

Camp, Theo C. *Taos County: Report to the Bureau of Immigration of New Mexico, 1881.* Santa Fe, N.M.: New Mexico Book and Job Printing Department, 1881.

Chicago and Northwestern Railway. *Colorado.* N.p.: Chicago and Northwestern Railway, 1914. HEH, E, Promotional, Colorado, box 1.

Chicago, Burlington and Quincy Railroad. *The Heart of the Continent: An Historical and Descriptive Treatise for Business Men, Home Seekers and Tourists, of the Advantages, Resources and Scenery of the Great West.* Chicago: Buffalo, Clay and Richmond, printers, for the Chicago, Burlington and Quincy Railroad, 1882. HEH RB 253034.

Colorado Consolidated Land and Water Company. *The Montezuma Valley in Colorado: A Description of Its Location, Scenery, Climate, Antiquities, Irrigating*

Works, Resources and Advantages. Cortez, Colo.: Colorado Consolidated Land and Water Company, 1890.

Conklin, E. *Picturesque Arizona: Being the Result of Travels and Observations in Arizona During the Fall and Winter of 1877.* New York: Mining Record Printing Establishment, c. 1878. HEH RB 601.

Cross, Fred J. *The Free Lands of Dakota: A Description of the Country; the Climate; the Beautiful Valleys, and Ocean-Like Prairies; the Crops, the Land Laws, and the Inducements Offered to Immigrants.* Yankton, Dakota: Bowen and Kingsbury, 1876.

The Dalles Business Men's Association. *The Dalles, Oregon.* The Dalles, Ore.: Press of the Chronicle Publishing Co., 1906. HEH E 01.

Davis, Ellis A. *Davis' Commercial Encyclopedia of the Pacific Southwest: California, Nevada, Utah, and Arizona.* Oakland, Calif.: Ellis A. Davis, 1911.

Dowse, Thomas. *The New Northwest: Montana. Its Past, Present, and Future.* Chicago: Commercial Advertizer Co., Publishers, 1879.

Eggleston, M. F. *Jackson Co., Oregon.* Jackson Co., Ore.: Honorable Commissioner's Court, 1905.

Egleston, T. C. *Boise County, Idaho: Resources, Agricultural and Mineral.* Boise, Idaho: Prepared and published under the direction of T. C. Egleston, Commissioner of Immigration, Labor and Statistics for the State of Idaho, 1903.

Evans, Elwood. *Puget Sound: Its Past, Present and Future.* Olympia, Washington Territory, 1869.

Farish, T. E. *Central and Southwestern Arizona: The Garden of America.* Phoenix, Ariz.: n.p., 1889.

Gleed, Chas. S., ed. *Rand McNally and Company's Overland Guide: From the Missouri River to the Pacific Ocean, Via Kansas, Colorado, New Mexico, Arizona, and California.* Rev. ed. Chicago: Rand McNally and Company, 1885; originally published 1883. HEH RB 311922.

Grants Pass Commercial Club and County Organizations. *Grants Pass and Josephine County.* Portland, Ore.: Grants Pass Commercial Club and County Organizations, in conjunction with *Sunset Magazine* Homeseekers Bureau of the Pacific Northwest, 1909.

Hall, Rinaldo M. *Beautiful Recreation Resorts of the Pacific Northwest: Where They Are and How to Reach Them. A Brief Description of the Trips Up and Down the Columbia River, to the Mountains, Beaches, Inland Resorts, and Fountains of Healing.* Portland, Ore.: General Passenger Department of the Oregon Railroad and Navigation Company, 1905.

———. *Oregon, Washington, Idaho and Their Resources: Mecca of the Homeseeker and Investor: A Land of Promise and Opportunity, Where the Soil, Climate and All Conditions Are Unsurpassable for the Successful Pursuance of Varied Industry.* Portland, Ore.: Passenger Department of the Oregon Railroad and Navigation Co., and Southern Pacific Co., 1904. HEH E IWMNG.

Harger, Charles Moreau. "The Next Commonwealth: Oklahoma." *Outlook* 67 (February 1901): 273–281.

———. "The Passing of the Promised Land." *Atlantic Monthly*, October 1909, 461–466.

———. "The Revival in Western Land Values." *American Monthly Review of Reviews* 35 (January 1907): 63–65.

———. "To-day's Chance for the Western Settler." *Outlook* 78 (December 1904): 980–982.

Hinton, Richard J. *The Hand-Book to Arizona: Its Resources, History, Towns, Mines, Ruins and Scenery.* San Francisco: Payot, Upham and Co.; New York: American News Company, 1878.

Hittell, John S. "California as a Home for the Emigrant: A Brief Statement of Its Public Lands, Wages, Climate, Agriculture, Manufactures, Attractions, and General Business." In *All About California and Inducements to Settle There,* 7–40. San Francisco: California Immigrant Union, printed by A. L. Bancroft and Co., 1870. HEH RB 116156.

———. *A History of the City of San Francisco and Incidentally of the State of California,* and *A Guidebook to San Francisco.* Complete edition of the original works first published in 1878 and 1888 by the Bancroft Company, San Francisco. Berkeley, Calif.: Berkeley Hills Books, 2000.

———. *The Resources of California, Comprising Agriculture, Mining, Geography, Climate, Commerce, etc, and the Past and Future Development of the State.* San Francisco: A. Roman and Co.; New York: W. J. Widdleton, 1863. HEH RB 32994.

———. *The Resources of California, Comprising Agriculture, Mining, Geography, Climate, Commerce, etc, and the Past and Future Development of the State.* 6th ed. San Francisco: A. Roman and Co.; New York: W. J. Widdleton, 1874.

Innes, Robert W. *Resources of Albany County, Wyoming, 1913.* Laramie, Wyo.: Laramie Chamber of Commerce, 1913. AHC SC W99-c-aL-p.

J. Clyde Lindsey, Real Estate Investments, and the Union Pacific Railroad System. *The Twin Falls Country, Southern Idaho.* Twin Falls, Idaho: Kingsbury Printing Co., c. 1913.

James, George Wharton. *Arizona: The Wonderland.* Boston: The Page Co., 1917.

———. *In and Out of the Old Missions of California: An Historical and Pictorial Account of the Franciscan Missions.* Boston: Little, Brown, and Company, 1905.

———. *The Lake of the Sky, Lake Tahoe: In the High Sierras of California and Nevada.* 1915. Chicago: Charles T. Powner Co., 1956.

Jones, C. J. *Homes in South-Western Texas: 50,000 Acres, Equal to the Best Valley Land in California.* 2d ed. San Francisco: P. E. Daugherty and Company, Printers, 1881.

Las Vegas Hot Springs and Topeka and Santa Fe Railroad Company. *The Climate of New Mexico and Las Vegas Hot Springs.* Chicago: Poole Brothers, Printers, 1883.

Legislature of the Territory of Arizona. *Resources of Arizona Territory, with a Description of the Indian Tribes; Ancient Ruins, Cochise, Apache Chief, Antonio, Pima Chief; Stage and Wagon Roads; Trade and Commerce, Etc., by Authority of the Legislature.* San Francisco: Francis and Valentine, Steam Printers and Engravers, 1871. HEH RB 38225.

————. *The Territory of Arizona: A Brief History and Summary of the Territory's Acquisition, Organization, and Mineral, Agricultural and Grazing Resources; Embracing a Review of Its Indian Tribes—Their Depredations and Subjugations; and Showing in Brief the Present Condition and Prospects of the Territory.* Tucson: Citizens Office, 1874. HEH RB 40204.

Lewis and Clark Centennial Exposition, 1805–1905. Portland, Ore.: Oregonian Publishing Company, 1901.

Los Angeles Chamber of Commerce. *Official Report of the Irrigation Congress Held at Los Angeles, California, October 1893.* Los Angeles: Los Angeles Chamber of Commerce, 1893.

Lummis, Charles Fletcher. "The Children's Paradise." *Land of Sunshine* 3 (June 1895): 7–10.

————. *Mesa, Cañyon and Pueblo: Our Wonderland of the Southwest—Its Marvels of Nature—Its Pageant of the Earth Building—Its Strange Peoples—Its Centuried Romance.* New York: The Century Co., 1925.

————. *Some Strange Corners of Our Country: The Wonderland of the Southwest.* New York: The Century Co., 1891. Reprint, Tucson: University of Arizona Press, 1989.

Lyman, Clarence A., comp. *The Fertile Lands of Colorado and Northern New Mexico: A Concise Description of the Vast Area of Agricultural, Horticultural and Grazing Lands Located on the Line of the Denver and Rio Grande Railroad in the State of Colorado and the Territory of New Mexico.* 9th ed. Denver: Passenger Department, Denver and Rio Grande Railroad, 1908. WHC DPL C630.9788D43FE9.

McElrath, Thomas. *The Yellowstone Valley: What It Is, Where It Is, and How to Get to It: A Hand-Book for Tourists and Settlers.* St. Paul, Minn.: Pioneer Press Company, 1880.

Meeker, Ezra. *Hop Culture in the United States: Being a Practical Treatise on Hop Growing in Washington Territory, from the Cutting to the Bale.* Puyallup, Washington Territory: E. Meeker and Co., 1883.

————. *Washington Territory West of the Cascade Mountains: Containing a Description of Puget Sound and Waters Emptying in to It.* Olympia, Washington Territory, Printed at the Transcript Office, 1870. HEH RB 35037. (Also 35036, a signed copy of the reprint, also published in 1870.)

Mercer, A. S. *Big Horn County, Wyoming: The Gem of the Rockies.* Chicago: Hammond Press, 1906.

Mitchell, W. H. *Dakota County [Minnesota]: Its Past and Present, Geographical, Statistical and Historical, Together with a General View of the State.* Minneapolis, Minn.: Tribune Printing Co., 1868.

Morrow County Booster Club. *Morrow County, Oregon.* Portland, Ore.: *Sunset Magazine* Homeseekers Bureau, [1911?].

Murphy, A. Daniel. *New Mexico, Its Attractions and Resources, with Its Rich Deposits of Gold, Silver, Copper, Iron, Coal, and Other Minerals; Its Extensive Grazing Districts, Rich Farming Lands, and Delightful Climate.* St. Louis: Slawson and Pierrot, 1880.

Nampa Chamber of Commerce. *Nampa Valley and the City of Nampa in Sunny Southern Idaho*. Nampa, Idaho: Nampa Chamber of Commerce, c 1910. HEH E IWMNG.

New Mexico Territory, Bureau of Immigration. *New Mexico: Its Resources, Climate, Geography, Geology, History, Statistics, Present Conditions and Future Prospects, Official Publication of the Bureau of Immigration, Arranged, Compiled, and Edited by Max Frost, Secretary of the Bureau*. Santa Fe, N.M.: New Mexican Printing Company, 1894. HEH RB 319689.

———. *Territory of New Mexico: Report of the Bureau of Immigration*, February 16, 1884. Santa Fe, N.M.: New Mexican Printing Company, 1884. HEH RB 78232.

Nicely, Wilson. *The Great South-West, or Plain Guide for Emigrants and Capitalists, Embracing a Description of the States of Missouri and Kansas*, 1. St. Louis: R. P. Studley and Co., Printers and Binder, 1867. NEW Case G 884.63.

Nordhoff, Charles. *California: A Book for Travellers and Settlers*. New York: Harper and Brothers, 1872.

———. *California: For Health, Pleasure, and Residence: A Book for Travellers and Settlers*. New edition, thoroughly revised. New York: Harper and Brothers, 1882.

———. *Northern California, Oregon, and the Sandwich Islands*. New York: Harper and Brothers, 1875.

Northern Pacific Railway. *Eastern Washington and Northern Idaho*. N.p. Northern Pacific Railway, 1910. HEH E IWMNG.

———. *Northern Pacific Country*. (Chicago: Rand McNally, 1883), DPL C972.02 V449.

———. *The Shortest, Quickest and Only Direct Route to All Points in the New Northwest via the Northern Pacific Railroad*. St. Paul, Minn.: James B. Power, Central Agent, 1879.

———. *What Montana Has to Offer Along the Northern Pacific, Yellowstone Park Line*. St. Paul, Minn.: Northern Pacific Railway, [1914?]. HEH E IWMNG.

The Northwest Interstate Fair, 1894. Promotional brochure. N.p., 1894. HEH E W.

Oohs, Milton B., for the Rio Grande and Western Railway. *The Heart of the Rockies*. Cincinnati, Ohio: J. H. Bennett, Press of the A. H. Pugh Printing Co., 1890.

Oregon State Board of Immigration. *The New Empire: Oregon, Washington, Idaho: Its Resources, Climate, Present Development, and Its Advantages as a Place of Residence and a Field for Investment*. Portland, Ore.: F. W. Baltes and Co., Printers, 1889.

———. *Oregon As It Is: Solid Facts and Actual Results*. Portland, Ore.: G. W. McCoy Steam Job Printer, 1885.

Pacific City Land Company. *Pacific City, in Tillamook County, Oregon: The Nearest Coast Resort to Portland: The Atlantic City of the West*. Portland, Ore.: Press of Harnden and Co., [1911?].

The Pecos Valley: The Fruit Valley of New Mexico. Probably [Eddy, N.M.], [1892]. HEH RB 382361.

Portland Directory for the Year 1863: Embracing a General Directory of Citizens, a Business Directory, and Other Statistical Information Relative to the Progress and Present Condition of the City. Portland, Ore.: S. J. McCormick, Compiler and Publisher, 1863.

Powell, John J. *Nevada: The Land of Silver.* San Francisco: Bacon and Co., 1876. HEH RB 1910.

Pratt, Louis W. *Tacoma, 1904: Electric City of the Pacific Coast.* Tacoma, Wash.: Tacoma Chamber of Commerce and Board of Trade, 1904. HEH E W.

Prewitt, F. E., M.D. "Denver as a Health Resort: What a Prominent Physician Has to Say About Our Climate." *Colorado: A Monthly Magazine Devoted to Colorado in General and Denver in Particular* (March 1905), no page numbers. HEH E, Promotional, Colorado, box 1.

Prince, Chief Justice L. Bradford. "New Mexico: Its Present Condition and Prospects"—An Interview with Chief Justice L. Bradford Prince. *New York Tribune,* July 12, 1881. Reprinted in *The Resources of New Mexico: Prepared Under the Auspices of the Bureau of Immigration for the Territorial Fair to Be Held at Albuquerque, New Mexico, October 3rd to 8th, 1881,* 49–52. Santa Fe, N.M.: New Mexican Book and Job Printing Department, 1881. NEW GC 2990.

Prosch, Charles. *Reminiscences of Washington Territory: Scenes, Incidents, and Reflections of the Pioneer Period on Puget Sound.* Seattle, Wash., 1904. NEW GC 3367.

Pueblo Business Men's Association. *Pueblo: The City of Sunshine.* Pueblo, Colo.: Pueblo Business Men's Association, [1908]. HEH E, Promotional, Colorado, box 2.

Raymond and Whitcomb Company guidebooks, c. 1880s–1890s. 3 boxes. HEH RB 42233.

The Resources of Montana and Attractions of Yellowstone Park. Helena, Mont.: Montana Legislature, 1879.

Sherman County Development League. *Sherman County, Oregon.* Portland, Ore.: *Sunset Magazine* Homeseekers Bureau, [1910?].

Southern Pacific Company. *California for the Settler.* San Francisco: Southern Pacific Company, 1922. HEH RB 194725.

———. *Oregon for the Settler: A Great Area with Rich Valleys, Mild and Healthful Climate and Wide Range of Products.* San Francisco: Southern Pacific Co., 1914. HEH RB 375527.

Spaight, A. W. *Resources, Soil and Climate of Texas: Report of A. W. Spaight, Commissioner of Statistics, etc., 1882.* Galveston, Tex.: A. H. Belo and Co., 1882. HEH RB 38005.

Stevens, H. B. *Ho, for Southern Dakota! And the Black Hills: Uncle Sam's Farm Is Growing Smaller Everyday.* Chicago: H. B. Stevens, Agent, 1875.

Stewart, Henry. *Irrigation for the Farm, Garden, and Orchard.* New York: Orange Judd Company, 1883.

Stinson, H. C., and W. N. Carter, comps. *Arizona: A Comprehensive Review of Its History, Counties, Principal Cities, Resources and Prospects: Together with Notices of Business Men and Firms Who Have Made the Territory.* Los Angeles: n.p., 1891.

Strahorn, Robert Edmund. *The Hand-Book of Wyoming, and Guide to the Black Hills and Big Horn Regions: A Glimpse at the Special Resources of the Territory.* Cheyenne, Wyo.: Knight and Leonard Printers, 1877.

———. *Idaho: A Complete and Comprehensive Description.* Boise City, Idaho: Idaho Legislature, 1881. Reprint, St. Louis, Mo.: Woodward and Tiernan Printing Co., 1893.

———. *Oregon: A Complete and Comprehensive Description of the Agricultural, Stockraising, and Mineral Resources of Oregon; Also Statistics in Regard to Its Climate, etc., Compiled from the Very Latest Reports of 1888.* 2d ed., revised. Chicago: Rand McNally and Co., Printers, 1889; [6th ed. Omaha, Nebr.: Union Pacific System, 1893.]

———. *The Resources and Attractions of Idaho Territory: Facts Regarding: Climate, Soil, Minerals, Agricultural and Grazing Lands, Forests, Scenery, Game and Fish, and Reliable Information on All Other Topics Applicable to the Wants of the Homeseeker, Capitalist, and Tourist.* Boise City: Idaho Legislature, 1881.

———. *The Resources and Attractions of Washington Territory: A Complete and Comprehensive Description of the Agricultural, Stockraising, and Mineral Resources of Washington; Also Statistics in Regard to Its Climate, etc., Compiled from the Very Latest Reports of 1888.* 2d ed., revised and enlarged. Chicago: Rand McNally and Co., 1889. HEH RB 78719.

———. *To the Rockies and Beyond, or a Summer on the Union Pacific Railway and Branches.* Omaha: New West Publishing Co., 1879.

———. *Washington: A Complete and Comprehensive Description.* 6th ed. Chicago: Rand McNally and Co. Reprint, St. Louis, Mo.: Woodward and Tiernan Printing Co., 1893.

Sutherland, William. *The Wonders of Nevada: Where They Are and How to Get to Them.* Virginia, Nev.: Enterprise Book and Job Printing House, 1878.

Sutherlin Land and Water Company. *Water Is King in the Orchard Kingdom: The Sutherlin Valley, Douglas County, Oregon.* Roseburg, Ore.: Sutherlin Land and Water Company, 1909. HEH E 01.

Tacoma Commercial Club and Chamber of Commerce. *Tacoma: The City with a Snow-Capped Mountain in Its Dooryard.* Tacoma, Wash.: Tacoma Commercial Club and Chamber of Commerce, 1912.

Tinker, George H. *A Land of Sunshine: Flagstaff and Its Surroundings.* Flagstaff, Ariz.: Arizona Champion Print, 1887. HEH RB 251989.

Towne, W. *Butte, "On Top," and Underground: Its Aspirations, Achievements, History, Industries, and Homes.* Butte, Mont.: Butte Chamber of Commerce, 1928,

Triggs, J. H. *History of Cheyenne and Northern Wyoming, Embracing the Gold Fields of the Black Hills, Powder River and Big Horn Countries.* Omaha, Nebr.: Herald Steam Book and Job Printing House, 1876.

Truman, Benjamin Cummings. *Homes and Happiness in the Golden State of California: Being a Description of the Empire State of the Pacific Coast: Its Inducements to Native and Foreign-Born Emigrants; Its Productiveness of Soil and Its Productions; Its Vast Agricultural Resources; Its Healthfulness of Climate and Equability of Temperature; and Many Other Facts for the Information of the*

Homeseeker and Tourist. 3d ed. San Francisco: H. S. Crocker and Co., Printers and Publishers, 1885.

———. *Semi-tropical California: Its Climate, Healthfulness, Productiveness, and Scenery; Its Magnificent Stretches of Vineyards and Groves of Semi-tropical Fruits, etc., etc., etc.* San Francisco: A. L. Bancroft and Co., 1874.

Turrill, Charles B. *California Notes.* San Francisco: Edward Bosqui and Co., Printers, 1876.

Union Pacific Railroad. *Colorado: A Complete and Comprehensive Description.* 5th ed. St. Louis, Mo.: Woodward and Tiernan Publishing Co., 1892.

———. *A Complete and Comprehensive Description of the Agricultural, Stock Raising and Mineral Resources of Idaho: Also Statistics in Regard to Its Climate, etc., etc. Compiled from the Latest Reports of 1892.* 6th ed. Presented with the compliments of the Passenger Division of the Union Pacific—the Overland Route. St. Louis, Mo.: Woodward and Tiernan Printing Co., 1893.

———. *The Resources and Attractions of the Texas Panhandle.* St. Louis, Mo.: Woodward and Tiernan Printing Co., 1893. HEH RB 116604.

———. *Texas: A Complete and Comprehensive Description of the Agricultural and Stock Raising Resources of the Texas Panhandle Country, Statistics in Regard to Its Climate, etc., Compiled from the Latest Reports [of 1892].* 4th ed. St. Louis, Mo.: Woodward and Tiernan Printing Co., 1893. HEH RB 116604.

Warner, Charles Dudley. "The Golden Hesperides." *Atlantic Monthly,* January 1888, 48–56.

———. "Our Italy." *Harper's New Monthly Magazine,* November 1890, 813–829.

———. *Our Italy.* New York: Harper and Brothers, 1891.

Wells, A. J. *The New Nevada: What It Is and What It Is to Be: The Era of Irrigation and the Day of Opportunity.* San Francisco: Southern Pacific Company, 1906. HEH RB 2023.

———. *Nevada.* San Francisco: Passenger Department Southern Pacific Company, 1911. HEH RB 249846.

Wilhelm, Honor L. "Western Advantages and Opportunities." *The Coast* 18 (August 1909): 69–75.

Wyoming State Board of Immigration. *Wyoming: The State of Opportunity.* Cheyenne: Wyoming State Board of Immigration, 1920.

REMINISCENCES

Anon. *Pioneer and Personal Reminiscences.* Marshalltown, Iowa: Marshall Printing Co., 1893.

Anon. *Pioneer Days in the Southwest from 1850 to 1879: Thrilling Descriptions of Buffalo Hunting, Indian Fighting and Massacres, Cowboy Life and Home Building; Contributions by Charles Goodnight, Emanuel Dubbs, John A. Hart, and others.* 2d ed. Guthrie, Okla.: State Capital Co., 1909. HEH RB 33591.

Anon. *Pioneer Sketches: Nebraska and Texas.* Hico, Tex.: Hico Printing Co., 1915. HEH RB 37438.

Anon. "Woman Who Fought Savages Smiles at Troubles." *San Antonio Express,* November 16, 1930. Reprinted in *Frontier Times* 8 (January 1931): 179–180.

Arnold, C. P. "The Vanished Frontier." Pamphlet. Reprinted in *Annals of Wyoming* 16 (January 1944): 57–60.

Babb, T. A. *In the Bosom of the Comanche: A Thrilling Tale of Savage Indian Life, Massacre and Captivity Truthfully Told by a Surviving Captive, T. A. Babb, Amarillo, Texas, 1912.* Dallas: John F. Worley Printing Co., 1912. HEH RB 35527.

Ball, Nicholas. *The Pioneers of '49: A History of the Excursion of the Society of California Pioneers of New England from Boston to the Leading Cities of the Golden State, April 10–May 17, 1890, with Reminiscences and Descriptions.* Boston: Lee and Shepard Publishers, 1891.

Bath, Frederick C. "Musings of a Pioneer: An Authentic Account of Life in Early Wyoming Taken from the Life of Frederick C. Bath, Laramie, Wyoming." Typed manuscript, 1868. AHC SC 336.

Bedford, Hilory G. *Texas Indian Troubles: The Most Thrilling Events in the History of Texas.* N.p.: Hargreaves Printing Co., 1905.

Bell, Major Horace. *On the Old West Coast: Being Further Reminiscences of a Ranger.* Ed. Lanier Bartlett. New York: Grosset and Dunlap, 1930.

———. *Reminiscences of a Ranger; or Early Times in Southern California.* Santa Barbara, Calif.: Wallace Hebberd, 1927.

Braly, John Hyde. *Memory Pictures: An Autobiography.* Los Angeles: Nuener Company, 1912. NEW GC 390.

Brier, Rev. John Wells. "The Death Valley Party of 1849." Parts 1 and 2. *Out West* 18 (March 1903): 326–335; 19 (April 1903): 456–465.

Brooks, Elisha. *A Pioneer Mother of California.* San Francisco: Harr Wagner Publishing Co., 1922.

Brown, Jesse, and A. M. Willard. *The Black Hills Trails: A History of the Struggles of the Pioneers in the Winning of the Black Hills.* Ed. John T. Milek. Rapid City, S.D.: Rapid City Journal Company, 1924.

Bruce, Robert, Albert H. Baiseley, and Col. George W. Stokes. *Three Old Plainsmen and Three Other Western Stories.* New York: Robert Bruce, 1923. HEH RB 314517.

Carter, Charles W. *The Exodus of 1847.* Salt Lake City: Utah Lithographing Co., 1897.

Cattermole, E. G. *Famous Frontiersmen, Pioneers and Scouts: The Vanguards of American Civilization. A Thrilling Narrative of the Lives and Marvelous Exploits of the Most Renowned Heroes, Trappers, Explorers, Adventurers, Scouts and Indian Fighters.* Chicago: Donohue, Henneberry and Co., 1890.

Clampitt, John W. *Echoes from the Rocky Mountains: Reminiscences and Thrilling Incidents of the Romantic and Golden Age of the Great West, with a Graphic Account of Its Discovery, Settlement and Grand Development.* Chicago: Belford, Clarke and Co., 1889.

Cook, James H. *Fifty Years on the Frontier.* New Haven, Conn.: Yale University Press, 1923.

DeWolff, J. H. *Pawnee Bill (Major Gordon W. Lillie), His Experience and Adventures on the Western Plains; or, From the Saddle of a "Cowboy and Ranger" to the Chair of a Bank President."* N.p.: Pawnee Bill's Historica Wild West Company, 1902.

Dodge, Orvil. *Pioneer History of Coos and Curry Counties: Heroic Deeds and Thrilling Adventures of the Early Settlers.* Published under the auspices of the Pioneer and Historical Association of Coos Co., Oregon. Salem, Ore.: Capital Printing Co., 1898.

Downie, Major William. *Hunting for Gold: Reminiscences of Personal Experience and Research in the Early Days of the Pacific Coast.* San Francisco: California Publishing Co., 1893.

Fell, Sarah. "Threads of Alaskan Gold." Manuscript, 1904. NEW GC 1303.

Foster, Roxana Cheney. "The Foster Family: California Pioneers of 1849." Typed manuscript, 1889. NEW AC 128.3 F7, 1921.

Fuller, Emiline L. *Left by the Indians: Story of My Life.* Mount Vernon, Iowa: Hawkeye Steam Print, 1892.

Gilfy, Henry M. "History and Resources of Oregon." Handwritten manuscript, 1876. In BANC PA 37.

Hall, Sharlot M. "In the Land of the Forty-Niners." *Out West* 29 (December 1908): 397–417.

Hanna, Oliver Perry. "The Old Wild West, Being the Recollections of O. P. Hanna: Pioneer, Indian Fighter, and Frontiersman." Compiled June, 1926, Long Beach, Calif. Typed manuscript. AHC SC 423.

Hittell, John S. "The Achievements of California." In *Celebration of the Forty-second Anniversary of the Admission of California into the Union, by the Society of California Pioneers.* El Campo, Marin County, September 9, 1892. San Francisco: B. F. Sterett, Book and Job Printer, 1892, 5–15. HEH RB 36953.

———. *Nineteenth Anniversary of the Corporate Society of California Pioneers, Oration by Hon. John S. Hittell (A Member of the Society).* San Francisco: Published by the Order of the Society, 1869. HEH RB 36943.

———. "Reminiscences of the Plains and Mines in '49 and '50" (the first of the course of Lick [James Lick] Lectures, delivered before the Society of California Pioneers, San Francisco, January 5, 1887). 17-page typed, numbered pamphlet (offprint). HEH RB 40262.

Hobson, Archie. *Remembering America: A Sampler of the WPA American Guide Series.* New York: Columbia University Press, 1985.

Holman, Frederick V. *Qualities of the Oregon Pioneers.* Address at the unveiling of the statue *The Pioneer* on the campus of the University of Oregon, May 22, 1919. Portland, Ore., 1919. HEH RB 65916.

Houghton, Eliza Poor Donner. *The Expedition of the Donner Party and Its Tragic Fate.* Chicago: A. C. McClurg and Co., 1911.

Ingraham, Colonel Prentiss, ed. *Seventy Years on the Frontier: Alexander Majors' Memoirs of a Lifetime on the Border, with a Preface by (General W. F. Cody) Buffalo Bill.* Chicago and New York: Rand McNally and Co., 1893.

Judson, Katherine Berry. *Early Days in Old Oregon.* Chicago: A C. McClurg and Co., 1916.

Lambourne, Alfred. *The Old Journey: Reminiscences of Pioneer Days.* Salt Lake City [?], Utah: George Q. Cannon and Sons Co., 1892–1897.

Lockley, Fred. *Oregon Yesterdays.* New York: Knickerbocker Press, 1928.

Lyman, H. S. "Reminiscences of William M. Case." *Quarterly of the Oregon Historical Society* 1 (September 1900): 269–295.

Manly, William Lewis. *Death Valley in '49.* San Jose, Calif.: Pacific Tree and Vine Co., 1894. Reprint, Chicago, Lakeside Press, 1927.

———. *Death Valley in '49.* Foreword by Patricia Nelson Limerick. Edited by Leroy Johnson and Jean Johnson. Santa Clara, Calif.: Santa Clara University; Berkeley, Calif.: Heydey Books, 2001.

McIntire, Jim. *Early Days in Texas: A Trip to Hell and Heaven.* Kansas City, Mo., McIntire Publishing Co., 1902. HEH RB 33687.

McKeever, William A. *The Pioneer: A Story of the Making of Kansas.* 2d ed. Topeka, Kans.: Crane and Co., Publishers, 1912.

Meeker, Ezra. *The Busy Life of Eighty-five Years of Ezra Meeker: Ventures and Adventures.* Seattle, Wash.: published by the author, 1916; Indianapolis: William B. Burford, 1916.

———. *Ox-Team Days on the Oregon Trail.* In collaboration with Howard R. Driggs. Pioneer Life Series. Yonkers-on-Hudson, N.Y., 1922.

———. *The Ox-Team; or, The Old Oregon Trail, 1852–1906.* Lincoln, Nebr.: Jacob North and Co., 1906. HEH RB 34143.

———. *Personal Experiences on the Oregon Trail Sixty Years Ago.* Seattle, Wash.: published by the author, 1912.

———. *Pioneer Reminiscences of Puget Sound: The Tragedy of Leschi.* Seattle, Wash.: Lowman and Hanford Stationery and Printing Co., 1905.

———. *Seventy Years of Progress in Washington.* Seattle, Wash.: Allstrum Printing Co., 1921.

———. *Story of the Lost Trail to Oregon.* Seattle, Wash., 1915. HEH RB 2213.

———. *Ventures and Adventures of Ezra Meeker; or Sixty Years of Frontier Life.* Seattle, Wash.: Rainier Printing Co., 1908.

Miles, W. H., and John Bratt. *Early History and Reminiscences of Frontier County.* Maywood, Nebr.: N. H. Bogue, 1894.

Mills, Mrs. S. L. "A Wyoming Trail Blazer." *Annals of Wyoming* 6 (July 1929): 216–221.

Molson, Mrs. William Markland. "Glimpses of Life in Early Oregon." *Quarterly of the Oregon Historical Society* 1 (June 1900): 158–164.

Newmark, Harris. *Sixty Years in Southern California, 1853–1913, Containing the Reminiscences of Harris Newmark.* Ed. Maurice H. Newmark and Marco R. Newmark. New York: Knickerbocker Press, 1916.

Piatt, Guy. *The Story of Butte: Old Timer's Hand-Book.* Special number of the *Butte Bystander,* April 15, 1897. Butte, Mont.: Press of the Standard Manufacturing and Printing Co., 1897.

Pioneer Ladies Club, Pendleton, Oregon. *Reminiscences of Oregon Pioneers.* Pendleton, Ore.: East Oregonian Publishing Co., 1937.

Prosch, Charles. *Reminiscences of Washington Territory: Scenes, Incidents, and Reflections of the Pioneer Period on Puget Sound.* Seattle, Wash., 1904. NEW GC 3367.

Putnam, Eva Ogden. "Pioneering in Crook County." *Annals of Wyoming* 3 (April 1926): 203–211.

Riddle, George W. *History of Early Days in Oregon.* Riddle, Ore.: Riddle Enterprise, 1920.

Ronan, Mary, and Margaret Ronan. *The Story of Mary Ronan, as Told to Margaret Ronan.* Ed. H. G. Merriam. Missoula: University of Montana, 1973.

Royce, Sarah. *A Frontier Lady: Recollections of the Gold Rush and Early California.* Edited by Ralph Henry Gabriel. New Haven, Conn.: Yale University Press, 1932.

Rye, Edgar. *The Quirt and the Spur: Vanishing Shadows of the Texas Frontier.* Chicago: W. B. Conkey Co., 1909. HEH RB 255047.

Savage, Isaac O. *A History of Republic County, Kansas.* Beloit, Kans.: Jones and Chubbi, Art Printers, 1901. HEH RB 127727.

Siringo, Chas. A. *A Lone Star Cowboy.* Santa Fe, N.M., 1919. HEH RB 33774.

Sowell, A. J. *Rangers and Pioneers of Texas, with a Concise Account of the Early Settlement, Hardships, Massacres, Battles, and Wars by Which Texas Was Rescued from the Rule of the Savage and Consecrated to the Empire of Civilization.* San Antonio, Tex.: Shepard Brothers and Company, Printers and Publishers, 1884. NEW GC 3909.

Stone, Arthur L. *Following Old Trails.* Missoula, Mont.: Morton John Elrod, 1913.

Strahorn, Carrie Adell. *Fifteen Thousand Miles by Stage: A Woman's Unique Experience During Thirty Years of Path Finding and Pioneering, from the Missouri to the Pacific and from Alaska to Mexico.* New York: G. P. Putnam's Sons, 1911. Republished in two volumes by the University of Nebraska Press, Lincoln, 1988.

Strahorn, Robert Edmund. "Ninety Years of Boyhood." Unpublished autobiography, typescript in the library of Albertson College, Idaho.

Thompson, Francis M. *Reminiscences of Four-Score Years: Including His Narrative of Three Years in the New West.* Salem, Mass.: Salem Press Co., c. 1912.

Tice, Henry Allen. *Early Railroad Days in New Mexico.* Atchison, Topeka and Santa Fe Railway, 1932. Reprint, Santa Fe, N.M.: Stagecoach Press, 1965.

Vaughn, Robert. *Then and Now; or Thirty-six Years in the Rockies.* Minneapolis, Minn.: Tribune Printing Co., 1900.

Voorhees, Luke. *Personal Recollections of Pioneer Life on the Mountains and Plains of the Great West.* Cheyenne, Wyo.: privately published, 1920. NEW AC 128.5 V8.

Warren, Eliza Spalding. *Memoirs of the West: The Spaldings.* Portland, Ore.: Press of the Marsh Printing Company, 1917.

Williams, James. *Seventy-five Years on the Border.* Kansas City: Press of Standard Printing Co., 1912. HEH RB 88761.

Wooten, Mattie Lloyd, comp. and ed. *Women Tell the Story of the Southwest.* San Antonio, Tex.: Naylor Co., 1940.

Young, Frederick George. "The Oregon Trail." *Quarterly of the Oregon Historical Society* 1 (December 1900): 339–370.

CONTEMPORARY NEWSPAPER ARTICLES

Brown, Patricia Leigh. "It's the New Upstate, Way Out There: North of San Francisco They Want a Whole New Identity." *New York Times,* October 20, 2001, A6.

Celis, William, III. "California Dreamers Who Move to Seattle Get the Big Chill: Locals Blame the Emigres for Pollution, Congestion, Discos and Tanning Salons." *Wall Street Journal,* October 10, 1989, A1, A9.

Klinkenborg, Verlyn. "Voices from a Forgotten Landscape." *New York Times,* February 28, 2000, A18.

Monaghan, Peter. "Lost in Place: Yi-Fu Tuan May Be the Most Influential Scholar You've Never Heard Of." *Chronicle of Higher Education,* March 16, 2001, A14–A18.

Olinger, David. "Sprawling Colorado—Who's to Blame?" *Denver Post,* February 7, 1999, A1, A20–A21.

Simon, Stephanie. "California and the West: California Barely on the Map in Book's New West." *Los Angeles Times,* May 4, 1998, A3, A24, A25.

Weissenstein, Michael. "State Gains Seat in House: Nevada's 66.3 Percent Population Surge in Last Ten Years Paces Nation." *Las Vegas Review Journal,* December 29, 2000, A1, A6.

Winkler, Karen J. "An Atlas of the American West Maps the Region's Boundaries and Attempts to Find Its Heart." *Chronicle of Higher Education,* December 5, 1997, A20–A21.

Secondary Works

Abbott, Carl. "The American West and the Three Urban Revolutions." In *Old West/New West: Quo Vadis?* Edited by Gene M. Gressley, 75–99. Worland, Wyo.: High Plains Publishing, 1994.

———. *Boosters and Businessmen: Popular Economic Thought and Urban Growth in the Antebellum Middle West.* Westport, Conn.: Greenwood Press, 1981.

———. *The Metropolitan Frontier: Cities in the Modern American West.* Tucson: University of Arizona Press, 1993.

Abbott, Carl, Stephen J. Leonard, and David McComb. *Colorado: A History of the Centennial State.* Rev. ed. Boulder: Colorado Associated University Press, 1982.

Allen, Barbara. "Historical Commentary: Landscape, Memory, and the Western Past." *Montana: The Magazine of Western History* 39 (winter 1989): 71–75.

———. *Homesteading the High Desert.* Salt Lake City: University of Utah Press, 1987.

Allen, James Paul, and Eugene James Turner. *We the People: An Atlas of America's Ethnic Diversity.* New York: Macmillan, 1988.

Anaya, Rudolfo, A., and Francisco Lomeli. *Aztlán: Essays on the Chicano Homeland.* Albuquerque, N.M.: Academia/El Norte Publications, 1989.

Anderson, Benedict. *Imagined Communities: Reflections on the Origin and Spread of Nationalism.* Rev. ed. London: Verso, 1991.

Athearn, Robert G. *The Coloradans*. Albuquerque: University of New Mexico Press, 1976.

―――. *High Country Empire: The High Plains and Rockies*. New York: McGraw-Hill, 1960.

―――. *In Search of Canaan: Black Migration to Kansas, 1879–1880*. Lawrence: Regents Press of Kansas, 1978.

―――. *The Mythic West in Twentieth-Century America*. Lawrence: University Press of Kansas, 1989.

―――. *Rebel of the Rockies: A History of the Denver, Rio Grande and Western Railroad*. New Haven, Conn.: Yale University Press, 1962.

―――. *Union Pacific Country*. Lincoln: University of Nebraska Press, 1982.

Austin, Judith. "Introduction" to Carrie Adell Strahorn, *Fifteen Thousand Miles by Stage*. Vol. 1, *1877–1880*, vii–xii. Lincoln: University of Nebraska Press, 1988.

Avella, Steven M. "The McClatchy Brothers and the Creation of Superior California." Paper presented at the annual meeting of the Western History Association, San Diego, October 2001.

Ayers, Edward L., Patricia Nelson Limerick, Stephen Nissenbaum, and Peter S. Onuf. *All Over the Map: Rethinking American Regions*. Baltimore: Johns Hopkins University Press, 1996.

Backes, Clarus, ed. *Growing Up Western: Recollections by Dee Brown, A. B. Guthrie, Jr., David Lavender, Wright Morris, Clyde Rice, Wallace Stegner, Frank Waters*. New York: Harper Perennial, 1989.

Barth, Gunther. *Instant Cities: Urbanization and the Rise of San Francisco and Denver*. New York: Oxford University Press, 1975.

Basso, Keith. *Western Apache Language and Culture: Essays in Linguistic Anthropology*. Tucson: University of Arizona Press, 1990.

―――. *Wisdom Sits in Places: Landscape and Language Among the Western Apache*. Albuquerque: University of New Mexico Press, 1996.

―――. "Wisdom Sits in Places: Notes on a Western Apache Landscape." In *Senses of Place*, edited by Steven Feld and Keith H. Basso. Santa Fe, N.M.: School of American Research Press, 1996.

Beale, Howard K. *Theodore Roosevelt and the Rise of America to World Power*. Baltimore: Johns Hopkins University Press, 1956.

Bederman, Gail. *Manliness and Civilization: A Cultural History of Gender and Race in the United States, 1880–1917*. Chicago: University of Chicago Press, 1995.

Beldon, L. Burr. *Goodbye Death Valley! The 1849 Jayhawker Escape*. Palm Desert, Calif.: Desert Magazine Press, 1956.

―――, ed. *Death Valley Heroine: And Source Accounts of the 1849 Travelers*. San Bernardino, Calif.: Inland Printing and Engraving Company, 1954.

Bennett, John W., and Seena B. Kohl. *Settling the Canadian-American West, 1890–1915: Pioneer Adaptation and Community Building: An Anthropological History*. Lincoln: University of Nebraska Press, 1995.

Billington, Ray Allen. *America's Frontier Heritage*. New York: Holt, Rinehart and Winston, 1966.

Billington, Ray Allen, and Albert Camarillo. *The American Southwest: Image and Reality.* Los Angeles: William Andrews Clark Memorial Library, 1979.

Billington, Ray Allen, and Martin Ridge. *Westward Expansion: A History of the American Frontier.* 6th ed., abridged. Albuquerque: University of New Mexico Press, 2001.

Bingham, Edwin R. *Charles F. Lummis: Editor of the Southwest.* San Marino, Calif.: Huntington Library, 1955.

Blair, Karen J. *The Clubwoman as Feminist: True Womanhood Redefined, 1868–1914.* New York: Holmes and Meier, 1980.

———, ed. *Women in Pacific Northwest History: An Anthology.* Seattle: University of Washington Press, 1988.

Blodgett, Jan. *Land of Bright Promise: Advertising the Texas Panhandle and South Plains, 1870–1917.* Austin: University of Texas Press, 1988.

Blodgett, Peter J. *Land of Golden Dreams: California in the Gold Rush Decade, 1848–1858.* San Marino, Calif.: Huntington Library Press, 1999.

———. "Vacations at Home: American Tourists in the Rocky Mountain West, 1920–1960." Unpublished manuscript, 2002.

Blouet, Brian W., and Frederick C. Luebke, eds. *The Great Plains: Environment and Culture.* Lincoln: University of Nebraska Press, 1979.

Boag, Peter. *Environment and Experience: Settlement Culture in Nineteenth-Century Oregon.* Berkeley and Los Angeles: University of California Press, 1992.

Bodnar, John. *Remaking America: Public Memory, Commemoration, and Patriotism in the Twentieth Century.* Princeton, N.J.: Princeton University Press, 1992.

Bogue, Allan G. *Frederick Jackson Turner: Strange Roads Going Down.* Norman: University of Oklahoma Press, 1998.

Boorstin, Daniel. *The Americans: The National Experience.* New York: Random House, 1965.

Boyer, M. Christine. *The City of Collective Memory: Its Historical Imagery and Architectural Entertainments.* Cambridge, Mass.: MIT Press, 1994.

Bradshaw, Michael. *Regions and Regionalism in the United States.* Jackson: University Press of Mississippi, 1988.

Brechin, Gray. *Imperial San Francisco: Urban Power, Earthly Ruin.* Berkeley: University of California Press, 1999.

Broussard, Albert S. *Black San Francisco: The Struggle for Racial Equality in the West, 1900–1954.* Lawrence: University Press of Kansas, 1993.

Brown, Arthur J. "The Promotion of Emigration to Washington, 1854–1909." *Pacific Northwest Quarterly* 36 (1945): 3–17.

Brown, Richard Maxwell. "The New Regionalism in America, 1971–1981." In *Regionalism in the Pacific Northwest,* edited by William G. Robbins, Robert J. Frank, and Richard E. Ross, 37–96. Corvallis: Oregon State University Press, 1983.

———. "Rainfall and History: Perspectives on the Pacific Northwest." In *Experiences in a Promised Land: Essays in Pacific Northwest History,* edited by G. Thomas Edwards and Carlos A. Schwantes, 13–27. Seattle: University of Washington Press, 1986.

Bryant, Keith L., Jr. *Culture in the American Southwest: The Earth, the Sky, the People.* College Station: Texas A&M University Press, 2001.

Bunting, Robert. *The Pacific Raincoast: Environment and Culture in an American Eden, 1778–1900.* Lawrence: University Press of Kansas, 1997.

Callenbach, Ernest. *Ecotopia: The Notebooks and Reports of William Weston.* New York: Bantam Books, 1990 [orig. published 1975].

Carlson, Martin E. "William E. Smythe, Irrigation Crusader." *Journal of the West* 7 (January 1968): 41–47.

Carr, Ethan. *Wilderness by Design: Landscape Architecture and the National Park Service.* Lincoln: University of Nebraska Press, 1998.

Casey, Edward S. *Getting Back into Place: Toward a Renewed Understanding of the Place World.* Bloomington: Indiana University Press, 1993.

Caughey, John Walton. "Southwest from Salt Lake in 1849." *Pacific Historical Review* 6 (1937): 142–164.

Chan, Sucheng. *Asian Americans: An Interpretive History.* Boston: Twayne, 1991.

Chandler, Arthur, and Marvin Nathan. *The Fantastic Fair: The Story of the California Midwinter International Exposition, Golden Gate Park, San Francisco.* Pogo Press, 1993.

Cherny, Robert W. "Constructing a Radical Identity: History, Memory, and the Seafaring Stories of Harry Bridges." *Pacific Historical Review* 70 (November 2001): 571–599.

Cleland, Robert Class. *From Wilderness to Empire: A History of California.* New York: Knopf, 1969.

Cobb, James C. *The Selling of the South: The Crusade for Industrial Development, 1936–1980.* Baton Rouge: Louisiana State University Press, 1982.

Cocks, Catherine. *Doing the Town: The Rise of Urban Tourism in the United States, 1850–1915.* Berkeley and Los Angeles: University of California Press, 2001.

Comer, Krista. *Landscapes of the New West: Gender and Geography in Contemporary Women's Writing.* Chapel Hill: University of North Carolina Press, 1999.

———. "Revising Western Criticism Through Wanda Coleman." *Western American Literature* 33 (winter 1999): 356–383.

Confino, Alan, ed. "Forum: Collective Memory and Cultural History: Problems of Method." *American Historical Review* 102 (December 1997): 1386–1403.

Conmy, Peter Thomas. *The Origins and Purposes of the Native Sons of the Golden West.* San Francisco: Dolores Press, 1956.

Cook-Lynn, Elizabeth. *Anti-Indianism in Modern America: A Voice from Tatekeya's Earth.* Urbana: University of Illinois Press, 2001.

Cronon, William. *Nature's Metropolis: Chicago and the Great West.* New York: Norton, 1991.

———. "The Trouble with Wilderness; or, Getting Back to the Wrong Nature." In *Uncommon Ground: Rethinking the Human Place in Nature,* edited by William Cronon, 69–90. New York: Norton, 1995.

Cronon, William, George Miles, and Jay Gitlin, eds. *Under an Open Sky: Rethinking America's Western Past.* New York: Norton, 1992.

Curti, Merle, and Kendall Birr. "The Immigrant and the American Image in Europe, 1860–1914." *Mississippi Valley Historical Review* 37 (September 1950): 203–230.

Dary, David. *Entrepreneurs of the Old West.* Lawrence: University Press of Kansas, 1986.

———. *Red Blood and Ink: Journalism in the Old West.* New York: Knopf, 1998.

Davis, Clark. "From Oasis to Metropolis: Southern California and the Changing Context of American Leisure." *Pacific Historical Review* 61 (August 1992): 357–386.

Davis, Kenneth S. *Kansas: A Bicentennial History.* New York: Norton, 1976.

Davis, Mike. *City of Quartz: Excavating the Future in Los Angeles.* London: Verso, 1990.

Davis, Natalie Zemon, and Randolph Starn. "Introduction" to "Forum on Memory." *Representations* 26 (spring 1989): 1–6.

Degler, Carl. *In Search of Human Nature: The Decline and Revival of Darwinism in American Thought.* New York: Oxford University Press, 1991.

Deverell, William. *Railroad Crossings: Californians and the Railroad, 1850–1910.* Berkeley and Los Angeles: University of California Press, 1994.

———. "To Loosen the Safety Valve: Eastern Workers and Western Lands." *Western Historical Quarterly* 19 (August 1988): 269–285.

Deverell, William, and Douglas Flamming. "Race, Rhetoric, and Regional Identity: Boosting Los Angeles, 1880–1930." In *Power and Place in the North American West,* edited by Richard White and John M. Findlay, 117–143. Seattle: University of Washington Press, 1999.

Dick, Everett. *The Sod-House Frontier, 1854–1890.* New York: Appleton-Century, 1937.

Dillon, Richard H. "Introduction" to John S. Hittell, *A History of the City of San Francisco and Incidentally of the State of California,* and *A Guidebook to San Francisco,* ix–lvii. Complete edition of the original works first published in 1878 and 1888 by the Bancroft Company, San Francisco. Berkeley, Calif.: Berkeley Hills Books, 2000.

Dippie, Brian. *The Vanishing American: White Attitudes and U.S. Indian Policy.* Lawrence: University Press of Kansas, 1982.

Dorman, Robert. *Revolt of the Provinces: The Regionalist Movement in America, 1920–1945.* Chapel Hill: University of North Carolina Press, 1993.

Dorst, John M. *Looking West.* Philadelphia: University of Pennsylvania Press, 1999.

Downey, Betsy. "'She Does Not Write Like a Historian': Mari Sandoz and the New Western History." *Great Plains Quarterly* 16 (winter 1996): 9–28.

Doyle, Don Harrison. *The Social Order of a Frontier Community: Jacksonville, Illinois, 1825–1870.* Urbana: University of Illinois Press, 1978.

Dumke, Glenn S. *The Boom of the Eighties in Southern California.* San Marino, Calif.: Huntington Library Press, 1944.

Duncan, Dayton. *Miles from Nowhere: Tales from America's Contemporary Frontier.* New York: Viking, 1993.

Edwards, G. Thomas, and Carlos A. Schwantes, eds. *Experiences in a Promised Land: Essays in Pacific Northwest History*. Seattle: University of Washington Press, 1986.

Ellenbecker, J. G. "The Jayhawkers of Death Valley." Marysville, Kans.: privately printed, 1938.

Ellis, David Maldwyn. "The Forfeiture of Railroad Land Grants, 1867–1894." *Mississippi Valley Historical Review* 33 (June 1946): 27–60.

Emmons, David M. "Constructed Province: History and the Making of the Last American West." *Western Historical Quarterly* 25 (1994), 437–459, and "A Roundtable of Responses," 461–486.

———. *Garden in the Grasslands: Boomer Literature of the Central Great Plains*. Lincoln: University of Nebraska Press, 1971.

Etulain, Richard W. *Re-imagining the Modern American West: A Century of Fiction, History, and Art*. Tucson: University of Arizona Press, 1996.

———. *Stegner: Conversations on History and Literature*. Rev. ed. Reno: University of Nevada Press, 1996.

———. *Telling Western Stories: From Buffalo Bill to Larry McMurtry*. Albuquerque: University of New Mexico Press, 1999.

———. *Writing Western History: Essays on Major Western Historians*. Albuquerque: University of New Mexico Press, 1991.

Faragher, John Mack. *Daniel Boone: The Life and Legend of an American Pioneer*. New York: Henry Holt, 1992.

———. *Women and Men on the Overland Trail*. New Haven, Conn.: Yale University Press, 1979.

Federal Writers' Project of the Works Progress Administration of Northern California. *Death Valley: A Guide*. Boston: Houghton, Mifflin Company, 1939.

Fiege, Mark. *Irrigated Eden: The Making of an Agricultural Landscape in the West*. Seattle: University of Washington Press, 1999.

Fifer, J. Valerie. *American Progress: The Growth of Transport, Tourist, and Information Industries in the Nineteenth-Century West*. Chester, Conn.: Globe Pequot Press, 1988.

Findlay, John. "Far Western Cityscapes and American Culture Since 1940." *Western Historical Quarterly* 22 (February 1991): 19–43.

———. *Magic Lands: Western Cityscapes and American Culture After 1940*. Berkeley and Los Angeles: University of California Press, 1992.

Fine, David, ed. *Los Angeles in Fiction: A Collection of Essays*. Rev. ed. Albuquerque: University of New Mexico Press, 1995.

Fireman, Janet. "The Latitudes of Home: A Particular Place in Western History." *Western Historical Quarterly* 25 (spring 1999): 5–23.

Fischer, William P. "Homesteading the Thunder Basin: Teckla, Wyoming, 1917–1938." *Annals of Wyoming* 71 (spring 1999): 21–34.

Flores, Dan. "Place: An Argument for Bioregional History." *Environmental History Review* 18 (winter 1994): 1–18.

Fogelson, Robert M. *The Fragmented Metropolis: Los Angeles, 1850–1930*. 1967. Reprint, Berkeley and Los Angeles: University of California Press, 1993.

Franklin, Wayne, and Michael Steiner, eds. *Mapping American Culture*. Iowa City: University of Iowa Press, 1992.

Frazier, Ian. *The Great Plains*. New York: Farrar, Straus and Giroux, 1989.

Frederickson, George. *The Inner Civil War: Northern Intellectuals and the Crisis of the Union*. New York: Harper and Row, 1965.

Fussell, Paul. *The Great War and Modern Memory*. New York: Oxford University Press, 1975.

Gastil, Raymond F. *The Cultural Regions of the United States*. Seattle: University of Washington Press, 1975.

Gaston, Paul M. *The New South Creed: A Study in Southern Mythmaking*. New York: Knopf, 1970.

Gendzel, Glen. "Pioneers and Padres: Competing Mythologies in Northern and Southern California, 1850–1930." *Western Historical Quarterly* 32 (spring 2001): 56–79.

Goetzmann, William M., and William N. Goetzmann. *The West of the Imagination*. New York: Norton, 1986.

Goldfield, David. *Region, Race, and Cities: Interpreting the Urban South*. Baton Rouge: Louisiana State University Press, 1997.

González, Deena J. *Refusing the Favor: The Spanish Women of Santa Fe, 1820–1880*. New York: Oxford University Press, 1999.

Gordon, Dudley. *Charles F. Lummis: Crusader in Corduroy*. Los Angeles: Cultural Assets Press, 1972.

Greever, William S. *Arid Domain: The Santa Fe Railway and Its Western Land Grant*. Stanford, Calif.: Stanford University Press, 1954.

———. "A Comparison of Railroad Land-Grant Policies." *Agricultural History* 25 (April 1951): 83–90.

Gressley, Gene M. *West by East: The American West in the Gilded Age*. Charles Redd Monographs in Western History. Provo, Utah: Brigham Young University Press, 1972.

Griffith, Sally Forman. *Home Town News: William Allen White and the* Emporia Gazette. New York: Oxford University Press, 1989.

Groat, Linda, ed. *Giving Places Meaning*. New York: Harcourt, Brace, 1995.

Grossman, James, ed. *The Frontier in American Culture: Essays by Richard White and Patricia Nelson Limerick*. Berkeley and Los Angeles: University of California Press, 1994.

Guide to Historical Manuscripts in the Huntington Library. San Marino, Calif.: Huntington Library Press, 1979.

Gutiérrez, David. *Walls and Mirrors: Mexican Americans, Mexican Immigrants, and the Politics of Ethnicity*. Berkeley and Los Angeles: University of California Press, 1995.

———, ed. *Between Two Worlds: Mexican Immigrants in the United States*. Wilmington, Del.: Scholarly Resources, 1996.

Gutiérrez, Ramón, and Genaro Padilla. *Recovering the U.S. Hispanic Literary Heritage*. Houston, Tex.: Arte Público Press, 1993.

Halaas, David Fridtjof. *Boom Town Newspapers: Journalism on the Rocky Mountain Mining Frontier, 1859–1881.* Albuquerque: University of New Mexico Press, 1981.

Hamer, David. *New Towns in the New World: Images and Perceptions of the Nineteenth-Century Urban Frontier.* New York: Columbia University Press, 1990.

Hamilton, Kenneth Marvin. *Black Towns and Profit: Promotion and Development in the Trans-Appalachian West, 1877–1915.* Urbana: University of Illinois Press, 1991.

Hargreaves, Mary Wilma M. *Dry Farming in the Northern Great Plains, 1900–1925.* Cambridge, Mass.: Harvard University Press, 1957.

Harley, J. B. "Deconstructing the Map." *Cartographia* 26 (summer 1989): 1–20.

Hart, John Fraser, ed. *Regions of the United States.* New York: Harper and Row, 1972.

Hayden, Dolores. *The Power of Place: Urban Landscapes as Public History.* Cambridge, Mass.: MIT Press, 1995.

Hedges, James Blaine. "The Colonization Work of the Northern Pacific Railroad." *Mississippi Valley Historical Review* 13 (December 1926): 311–342.

———. *Henry Villard and the Railways of the Northwest.* New Haven, Conn.: Yale University Press, 1930.

———. "Promotion of Immigration to the Pacific Northwest by the Railroads." *Mississippi Valley Historical Review* 15 (September 1928): 183–203.

Hicks, John D. *The Populist Revolt: A History of the Farmer's Alliance and the People's Party.* Minneapolis: University of Minnesota Press, 1931. Reprint, Lincoln: University of Nebraska Press, 1961.

Higham, John. *Send These to Me: Jews and Other Immigrants in Urban America.* New York: Atheneum, 1975.

———. *Strangers in the Land: Patterns of American Nativism, 1865–1925.* New Brunswick, N.J.: Rutgers University Press, 1955; reprint 1963.

Hine, Robert V. *The American West: An Interpretive History.* 2d ed. Boston: Little, Brown, 1984.

———. "The American West as Metaphysics: A Perspective on Josiah Royce." *Pacific Historical Review* 58 (1989): 267–291.

———. *Josiah Royce: From Grass Valley to Harvard.* Norman: University of Oklahoma Press, 1992.

———. "The Western Intellectual: Josiah Royce." *Montana: The Magazine of Western History* 41 (summer 1991): 70–72.

Hine, Robert V., and John Mack Faragher. *The American West: A New Interpretive History.* New Haven, Conn.: Yale University Press, 2000.

Historical Statistics of the United States: Colonial Times to 1970. Washington, D.C.: U.S. Department of Commerce, Bureau of the Census, 1975.

Hofstadter, Richard. *The Age of Reform: From Bryan to FDR.* New York: Knopf, 1955.

Holliday, J. S. *Rush for Riches: Gold Fever and the Making of California.* Berkeley and Los Angeles: Oakland Museum of California and University of California Press, 1999.

Hollon, W. Eugene. *The Great American Desert: Then and Now.* New York: Oxford University Press, 1966.

————. *The Southwest: Old and New.* New York: Knopf, 1961.

Horn, Calvin. *New Mexico's Troubled Years: The Story of the Early Territorial Governors.* Albuquerque: Horn and Wallace, 1963.

Howard, Joseph Kinsey. *Montana: High, Wide, and Handsome.* 1959; reprint, Lincoln: University of Nebraska Press, 1983.

Howarth, William. "The Okies: Beyond the Dust Bowl." *National Geographic* 166 (September 1984): 327–349.

Hoxie, Fred. "Exploring a Cultural Borderland: Native American Journeys of Discovery in the Early Twentieth Century." In *Discovering America: Essays on the Search for an Identity,* edited by David Thelen and Frederick Hoxie, 135–161. Urbana: University of Illinois Press, 1994.

————. *Parading Through History: The Making of the Crow Nation in America, 1805–1935.* New York: Cambridge University Press, 1995.

————. "The Reservation Period, 1880–1960." In *The Cambridge History of the Native Peoples of the Americas: North America,* edited by Bruce G. Trigger and Wilcomb E. Washburn, 183–258. New York: Cambridge University Press, 1996.

Hudson, John C. *Plains Country Towns.* Minneapolis: University of Minnesota Press, 1985.

Hunt, John Clark. "The Oregon Trail: Then and Now." *American History Illustrated* 3 (May 1968): 24–29.

Hurtado, Albert. *Indian Survival on the California Frontier.* New Haven, Conn.: Yale University Press, 1988.

Hyde, Anne F. *An American Vision: Far Western Landscape and National Culture, 1820–1920.* New York: New York University Press, 1990.

————. "Cultural Filters: The Significance of Perception in the History of the American West." *Western Historical Quarterly* 24 (1993): 351–374.

Hyde, Anne Farrar, Christina Rabe Seger, Sally Southwick, and David M. Wrobel. "Changing Places: Creating State and Regional Identities." Session at meeting of the Western History Association, St. Paul, Minnesota, October 18, 1997.

Ise, John. *Sod and Stubble: The Story of a Kansas Homestead.* New York: Wilson-Erickson, 1936. Reprint, Lincoln: University of Nebraska Press, 1987.

Jackson, Kenneth T. *Crabgrass Frontier: The Suburbanization of the United States.* New York: Oxford University Press, 1985.

Jacobs, Margaret D. *Engendered Encounters: Feminism and Pueblo Cultures, 1879–1934.* Lincoln: University of Nebraska Press, 1999.

Jensen, Merrill, ed. *Regionalism in America.* Madison: University of Wisconsin Press, 1951.

Johnson, Jean, ed. *Proceedings of the Fifth Death Valley Conference on History and Prehistory, March 4–7, 1999.* Bishop, Calif.: Community Printing and Publishing, 1999.

Johnson, Leroy, and Jean Johnson, eds. *Escape from Death Valley: As Told by William Manly Lewis and Other '49ers.* Reno: University of Nevada Press, 1987.

Johnson, Michael L. *New Westers: The West in Contemporary American Culture.* Lawrence: University Press of Kansas, 1996.

Jones, Billy M. *Health-Seekers in the Southwest, 1817–1900.* Norman: University of Oklahoma Press, 1967.

Jones, David C. *Feasting on Misfortune: Journeys of the Human Spirit in Alberta's Past.* Edmonton: University of Alberta Press, 1998.

Jones-Eddy, Julie. *Homesteading Women: An Oral History of Colorado, 1890–1950.* New York: Twayne, 1992.

Kammen, Michael. *Mystic Chords of Memory: The Transformation of Tradition in American Culture.* New York: Knopf, 1991.

Kane, Joseph Nathan. *The American Counties: Origins of Names, Dates of Creation and Organization, Area, Population, Historical Data, and Published Sources.* 3d ed. Metuchen, N.J.: Scarecrow Press, 1972.

Kesselman, Steven. "The Frontier Thesis and the Great Depression." *Journal of the History of Ideas* 29 (April 1968): 253–268.

Keyes, Jonathon J. "Engraved Invitations: Rand McNally and the Representation of the American West in the Nineteenth Century." Unpublished seminar paper, University of Chicago, 1995.

Kimmel, Michael. *Manhood in America: A Cultural History.* New York: Free Press, 1996.

Kittredge, William, and Annick Smith, eds. *The Last Best Place: A Montana Anthology.* Helena: Montana Historical Society Press, 1988.

Klein, Kerwin Lee. *Frontiers of Historical Imagination: Narrating the European Conquest of Native America, 1890–1990.* Berkeley and Los Angeles: University of California Press, 1997.

———. "Reclaiming the 'F' Word: Or Being and Becoming Postwestern." *Pacific Historical Review* 65 (May 1996): 179–215.

Klein, Norman M. *The History of Forgetting: Los Angeles and the History of Erasure.* New York: Verso, 1997.

———. "The Sunshine Strategy: Buying and Selling the Fantasy of Los Angeles." In *Los Angeles: Power, Promotion and Social Conflict,* edited by Norman M. Klein and Martin J. Schiesl, 1–380. Claremont, Calif.: Regina Books, 1990.

Knight, Oliver. "Robert E. Strahorn: Propagandist for the West." *Pacific Northwest Quarterly* 59 (January 1968): 33–45.

Koble, Dale T. *"America for the Americans": The Nativist Movement in the United States.* New York: Twayne, 1996.

Koenig, George. *Beyond This Place There Be Dragons: The Routes of the Death Valley 1849ers Through Nevada, Death Valley, and on to Southern California.* Glendale, Calif.: Arthur H. Clark Company, 1984.

Kurashige, Lon. "Resistance, Collaboration, and Manznar Protest." *Pacific Historical Review* 70 (August 2001): 387–417.

Lamar, Howard R. *Dakota Territory, 1861–1889: A Study of Frontier Politics.* New Haven, Conn.: Yale University Press, 1956.

Larson, T. A. *History of Wyoming.* 2d ed., revised. Lincoln: University of Nebraska Press, 1990.

Latta, Frank F. *Death Valley '49ers.* Santa Cruz, Calif.: Bear State Books, 1979.

Leach, Neil. "The Dark Side of the *Domus:* The Redomestication of Central and Eastern Europe." In *Architecture and Revolution: Contemporary Perspectives on Central and Eastern Europe,* edited by Neil Leach, 150–162. New York: Routledge, 1999.

Leadingham, Grace. "Juliet Wells Brier: Heroine of Death Valley." Parts 1 and 2. *Pacific Historian* 8, no. 2 (1964): 61–74; no. 3 (1964): 121–127.

Lears, T. Jackson. *No Place of Grace: Antimodernism and the Transformation of American Culture, 1880–1920.* New York: Pantheon, 1981.

Lerup, Lars. *After the City.* Cambridge, Mass.: MIT Press, 2000.

Levy, Benjamin. *Death Valley National Monument: Historical Background and Study.* Washington, D.C.: National Park Service, 1969.

Lewis, G. Malcolm. "Rhetoric of the Western Interior: Modes of Environmental Description in American Promotional Literature of the Nineteenth Century." In *The Iconography of Landscape,* edited by Denis Cosgrove and Stephen Daniels. New York: Cambridge University Press, 1988.

Limerick, Patricia Nelson. *Desert Passages: Encounters with the American Deserts.* Albuquerque: University of New Mexico Press, 1985.

———. "Going West and Ending Up Global." *Western Historical Quarterly* 32 (spring 2001): 5–23.

———. "In the Bad Lands: Where the Oats Don't Grow to Perfection." *Times Literary Supplement,* February 28, 1997, 11–12.

———. *The Legacy of Conquest: The Unbroken Past of the American West.* New York: Norton, 1987.

———. "The Realization of the American West." In *The New Regionalism,* edited by Charles Reagan Wilson, 71–98. Jackson: University Press of Mississippi, 1998.

———. *Something in the Soil: Legacies and Reckonings in the New West.* New York: Norton, 2000.

Limerick, Patricia Nelson, Clyde A. Milner II, and Charles E. Rankin, eds. *Trails Toward a New Western History.* Lawrence: University Press of Kansas, 1991.

Lindgren, H. Elaine. *Land in Her Own Name: Women as Homesteaders in North Dakota.* Norman: University of Oklahoma Press, 1996.

Lingeman, Richard. *Small Town America: A Narrative History, 1620–The Present.* New York: Putnam's, 1980.

Lingenfelter, Richard E. *Death Valley and the Amargosa: A Land of Illusion.* Berkeley and Los Angeles: University of California Press, 1986.

Littlefield, Alice, and Martha C. Knack, eds. *Native Americans and Wage Labor: Ethnohistorical Perspectives.* Norman: University of Oklahoma Press, 1996.

Long, Margaret. *The Shadow of the Arrow.* Caldwell, Idaho: Caxton Printers, 1941.

Lotchin, Roger. "The Impending Western Urban Past: An Essay on the Twentieth-Century West." In *Researching Western History: Topics in the Twentieth Century,* edited by Gerald Nash and Richard Etulain, 53–81. Albuquerque: University of New Mexico Press, 1997.

Lowenthal, David. *The Heritage Crusade and the Spoils of History*. New York: Cambridge University Press, 1998. First published as *Possessed by the Past: The Heritage Crusade and the Spoils of History*. New York: Free Press, 1996.

Lowitt, Richard, and Judith Fabry, eds. *Henry A. Wallace's Irrigation Frontier: On the Trail of the Corn Belt Farmer, 1909*. Norman: University of Oklahoma Press, 1991.

Luebke, Frederick, ed. *European Immigrants in the American West: Community Histories*. Albuquerque: University of New Mexico Press, 1998.

Lyon, Thomas J., ed. *The Literary West: An Anthology of Western American Literature*. New York: Oxford University Press, 1999.

Lyotard, Jean-François. *The Postmodern Condition: A Report on Knowledge*. Trans. Geoff Bennington and Brian Massumi. Theory and History of Literature, 10. Minneapolis: University of Minnesota Press, 1984.

Mahoney, Timothy R. *Provincial Lives: Middle-Class Experience in the Antebellum Middle West*. New York: Cambridge University Press, 1999.

Malone, Dumas, ed. *Dictionary of American Biography*. Vol. 6. New York: Scribner's, 1961.

Malone, Michael P., ed. *Historians and the American West*. Lincoln: University of Nebraska Press, 1983.

Malone, Michael P., and Richard W. Etulain. *The American West: A Twentieth-Century History*. Lincoln: University of Nebraska Press, 1989.

Mann, Ralph. *After the Gold Rush: Society in Grass Valley and Nevada City, California, 1849–1870*. Stanford, Calif.: Stanford University Press, 1982.

Matsumoto, Valerie J. *Farming the Home Place: A Japanese American Community in California, 1919–1982*. Ithaca, N.Y.: Cornell University Press, 1993.

McClain, Charles J. *In Search of Equality: The Chinese Struggle Against Discrimination in Nineteenth-Century America*. Berkeley: University of California Press, 1994.

McClurg, William Alexander. *Landscapes of Desire: Anglo Mythologies of Los Angeles*. Berkeley and Los Angeles: University of California Press, 2000.

McWilliams, Carey. *Brothers Under the Skin*. Boston: Little, Brown, 1942.

———. *North from Mexico: The Spanish-Speaking People of the United States*. Philadelphia: Lippincott, 1949.

———. *Southern California Country: An Island on the Land*. New York: Duell, Sloan and Pearce, 1946.

Mehls, Steven F. "Garden in the Grassland Revisited: Railroad Promotional Efforts and the Settlement of the Texas Plains." *West Texas Historical Association Yearbook* 55 (1984): 47–66.

Meinig, Donald. "American Wests: Preface to a Geographical Interpretation." *Annals of the Association of American Geographers* 62 (1972): 159–184.

———. *The Great Columbia Plain: A Historical Geography, 1805–1910*. Seattle: University of Washington Press, 1968.

———. *The Shaping of America: A Geographical Perspective on 500 Years of History*. Vol. 3, *Transcontinental America, 1850–1915*. New Haven, Conn.: Yale University Press, 1998.

———. *Southwest: Three Peoples in Geographic Change, 1600–1970.* New York: Oxford University Press, 1974.

Meyer, M. Judith. *The Spirit of Yellowstone.* Boston: Little, Brown, 1997.

Miller, Orlando W. *The Frontier in Alaska and the Matanuska Colony.* New Haven, Conn.: Yale University Press, 1975.

Miller, Stuart Creighton. *The Unwelcome Immigrant: The American Image of the Chinese, 1785–1882.* Berkeley and Los Angeles: University of California Press, 1969.

Milner, Clyde A., II. "The Shared Memory of Montana Pioneers." *Montana: The Magazine of Western History* 37 (winter 1987): 2–13.

———. "The View from Wisdom: Region and Identity in the Minds of Four Westerners." *Montana: The Magazine of Western History* 41 (summer 1991): 2–17.

———, ed. *A New Significance: Re-envisioning the History of the American West.* New York: Oxford University Press, 1996.

Milner, Clyde A., II, Carol A. O'Connor, and Martha A. Sandweiss, eds. *The Oxford History of the American West.* New York: Oxford University Press, 1994.

Milton, John. *South Dakota: A Bicentennial History.* States and the Nation Series. New York: Norton, 1977.

Miner, Craig. *West of Wichita: Settling the High Plains of Kansas, 1865–1890.* Lawrence: University Press of Kansas, 1986.

Moehring, Eugene P. "'Promoting the Varied Interests of the New and Rising Community': The Booster Press on Nevada's Mining Frontier, 1859–1885." *Nevada Historical Society Quarterly* 42 (summer 1999): 91–118.

Mohl, Raymond A., ed. *Searching for the Sunbelt: Historical Perspectives on a Region.* Knoxville: University of Tennessee Press, 1990.

Mondale, Clarence. "Concepts and Trends in Regional Studies." *American Studies International* 27 (April 1989): 13–37.

Moneta, Daniela, P., ed. *Chas. F. Lummis: The Centennial Exhibition, Commemorating His Tramp Across the Continent.* Los Angeles: Southwest Museum, 1985.

Monroy, Douglas. *Rebirth: Mexican Los Angeles from the Great Depression to the Great Migration.* Berkeley and Los Angeles: University of California Press, 1999.

———. *Thrown Among Strangers: The Making of Mexican Culture in Frontier California.* Berkeley and Los Angeles: University of California Press, 1990.

Morrissey, Katherine G. *Mental Territories: Mapping the Inland Empire.* Ithaca, N.Y.: Cornell University Press, 1997.

Moses, L. G. *Wild West Shows and the Images of American Indians, 1883–1933.* Albuquerque: University of New Mexico Press, 1996.

Mott, Frank Luther. *A History of American Magazines, 1885–1905.* Cambridge, Mass.: Harvard University Press, 1957.

Moynihan, Ruth B., Susan Armitage, and Christiane Fischer Dichamp. *So Much to Be Done: Women Settlers on the Mining and Ranching Frontier.* Lincoln: University of Nebraska Press, 1990.

Murdoch, David. *The American West: The Invention of a Myth.* Reno: University of Nevada Press, 2001.

Murphy, Mary. *Mining Cultures: Men, Women, and Leisure in Butte, 1914–41.* Urbana: University of Illinois Press, 1997.

Murray, Stanley N. "Railroads and the Agricultural Development of the Red River of the North." *Agricultural History* 31 (October 1957): 57–66.

Nardroff, Ellen von. "The American Frontier as a Safety Valve: The Life, Death, Reincarnation, and Justification of a Theory." *Agricultural History* 36 (July 1962): 123–142.

Nash, Gerald D. *Creating the West: Historical Interpretations, 1890–1990.* Albuquerque: University of New Mexico Press, 1991.

Nash, Roderick. *The Nervous Generation: American Thought, 1917–1930.* New York: Ivan R. Dee, 1990; originally published 1970.

Nelson, Genne. "Jayhawker Bibliography." Unpublished manuscript.

Nelson, Paula M. *After the West Was Won: Homesteaders and Town-Builders in Western South Dakota, 1900–1917.* Iowa City: University of Iowa Press, 1986.

Nettles, Curtis. "Frederick Jackson Turner and the New Deal." *Wisconsin Magazine of History* 17 (March 1934): 257–265.

Nichols, Roger L., ed. *American Frontier and Western Issues: A Historiographical Review.* Westport, Conn.: Greenwood Press, 1986.

Noble, Bruce J., Jr. "Marking Wyoming's Oregon Trail." *Overland Journal* 4, no. 3 (1986): 19–31.

———. "The Quest for Settlement in Early Wyoming." *Annals of Wyoming* 55 (fall 1983): 19–24.

Nugent, Walter. *Into the West: The Story of Its People.* New York: Knopf, 1999.

O'Connor, Richard. *Iron Wheels and Broken Men: The Railroad Barons and the Plunder of the West.* New York: Putnam's, 1973.

Odum, Howard W., and Harry Estill Moore. *American Regionalism: A Cultural-Historical Approach to National Integration.* New York: Henry Holt, 1938.

Olson, James C., and Ronald C. Naugle. *History of Nebraska.* 3d ed. Lincoln: University of Nebraska Press, 1997.

Overton, Richard C. *Burlington West: A Colonization History of the Burlington Railroad.* Cambridge, Mass.: Harvard University Press, 1941.

Padget, Martin. "Travel, Exoticism, and the Writing of Region: Charles Fletcher Lummis and the Creation of the Southwest." *Journal of the Southwest* 37 (autumn 1995): 421–449.

Padilla, Genaro M. *My History, Not Yours: The Formation of Mexican American Autobiography.* Madison: University of Wisconsin Press, 1993.

Painter, Nell Irving. *The Exodusters: Black Migration to Kansas After Reconstruction.* New York: Norton, 1992; originally published 1986.

Parker, Edna Monch. "The Southern Pacific Railroad and Settlement in California." *Pacific Historical Review* 6 (1937): 103–119.

Paul, Rodman W. *The Far West and the Great Plains in Transition, 1859–1900.* New York: Harper and Row, 1988.

Peck, Gunther. *Reinventing Free Labor: Padrones and Immigrant Workers in the North American West, 1880–1930.* New York: Cambridge University Press, 2000.

Perdue, R., P. Long, and L. Allen. "Resident Support for Tourism Development." *Annals of Tourism Research* 17 (1990): 586–599.

Peterson, Charles S. "Hubert Howe Bancroft: First Western Regionalist." In *Writing Western History: Essays on Major Western Historians,* edited by Richard W. Etulain, 43–70. Albuquerque: University of New Mexico Press, 1991.

Pisani, Donald J. *From the Family Farm to Agribusiness: The Irrigation Crusade in California and the West, 1850–1931.* Berkeley and Los Angeles: University of California Press, 1984.

Pomeroy, Earl. *In Search of the Golden West: The Tourist in Western America.* 1957. Lincoln: University of Nebraska Press, 1990.

———. *The Pacific Slope: A History of California, Oregon, Washington, Idaho, Utah, and Nevada.* New York: Knopf, 1965. Reprint, Lincoln: University of Nebraska Press, 1991.

———. "Toward a Re-orientation of Western History: Continuity and Environment." *Mississippi Valley Historical Review* 41 (March 1955): 579–600.

Raban, Jonathan. *Bad Land: An American Romance.* New York: Pantheon, 1996.

———. "The Unlamented West." *New Yorker,* May 20, 1996, 60–81.

Rankin, Charles E., ed. *Wallace Stegner: Man and Writer.* Albuquerque: University of New Mexico Press, 1996.

Reddin, Paul. *Wild West Shows.* Urbana: University of Illinois Press, 1999.

Reps, John W. *Cities of the American West.* Princeton, N.J.: Princeton University Press, 1979.

———. *Panoramas of Promise: Pacific Northwest Cities and Towns on Nineteenth-Century Lithographs.* Pullman: Washington State University Press, 1984.

Riebsame, William, ed. *Atlas of the New West.* New York: Norton, 1997.

Ritchie, Robert C., and Paul Andrew Hutton. *Frontier and Region: Essays in Honor of Martin Ridge.* Albuquerque: University of New Mexico Press, 1997.

Robbins, William G. "Capitalism as a Conceptual Tool for Studying the American West." *Western Historical Quarterly* 30 (autumn 1999): 277–293.

———. *Colony and Empire: The Capitalist Transformation of the American West.* Lawrence: University Press of Kansas, 1994.

———. *Landscapes of Promise: The Oregon Story, 1800–1940.* Seattle: University of Washington Press, 1997.

Roberts, Virginia Culin. *With Their Own Blood: A Saga of Southwestern Pioneers.* Fort Worth: Texas Christian University Press, 1992.

Rolle, Andrew. *California: A History.* 2d ed. New York: Thomas Y. Crowell, 1969.

Rosenof, Theodore. *Dogma, Depression, and the New Deal: The Debate of Political Leaders over Recovery.* Port Washington, N.Y.: Kennikat Press, 1975.

Rosenus, Alan. *General M. G. Vallejo and the Advent of the Americans: A Biography.* Albuquerque: University of New Mexico Press, 1995.

Roske, Ralph J. *Everyman's Eden: A History of California.* New York: Macmillan, 1968.

Rothman, Hal. *America's National Monuments: The Politics of Presentation.* Lawrence: University Press of Kansas, 1989.

————. *Devil's Bargains: Tourism in the Twentieth-Century American West.* Lawrence: University Press of Kansas, 1998.

————. *Neon Metropolis: The First City of the Twenty-first Century.* New York: Routledge, 2002.

————. "'Powder Aplenty for Native and Guest Alike': Steamboat Springs, Corporate Control, and the Changing Meaning of Home: Preserving Local Identity amid the Rise of the Modern Ski Industry." *Montana: The Magazine of Western History* 48 (winter 1998): 2–17.

Rothschild, Mary Logan, and Pamela Claire Hronek. *Doing What the Day Brought: An Oral History of Arizona Women.* Tucson: University of Arizona Press, 1992.

Rydell, Robert W. *All the World's a Fair: Visions of Empire at American International Expositions, 1876–1916.* Chicago: University of Chicago Press, 1984.

Sánchez, Rosaura. *Telling Identities: The California Testimonios.* Minneapolis: University of Minnesota Press, 1995.

Saxton, Alexander. *The Indispensable Enemy: Labor and the Anti-Chinese Movement in California.* Berkeley and Los Angeles: University of California Press, 1971.

Scharff, Virginia. "Mobility, Women, and the West." In *Over the Edge: Remapping the American West,* edited by Valerie J. Matsumoto and Blake Allmendinger, 160–171. Berkeley and Los Angeles: University of California Press, 1999.

————. *Twenty Thousand Roads: Women, Movement, and the West.* Berkeley and Los Angeles: University of California Press, forthcoming.

Schlissel, Lillian, Byrd Gibbens, and Elizabeth Hampsten, eds. *Far from Home: Families of the Westward Journey.* New York: Schocken Books, 1989.

Schmitt, Peter J. *Back to Nature: The Arcadian Myth in Urban America.* New York: Oxford University Press, 1969.

Schwantes, Carlos. "Landscapes of Opportunity: Phases of Railroad Promotion of the Pacific Northwest." *Montana: The Magazine of Western History* 43 (spring 1993): 38–51.

————. *Railroad Signatures Across the Pacific Northwest.* Seattle: University of Washington Press, 1993.

Schwartz, Stephen. *From West to East: California and the Making of the American Mind.* New York: Free Press, 1998.

Scott, Allen J., and Edward W. Soja, eds. *The City: Los Angeles and Urban Theory at the End of the Twentieth Century.* Berkeley and Los Angeles: University of California Press, 1996.

Servín, Mañuel P. "California's Hispanic Heritage: A View into the Spanish Myth." In *New Spain's Far Northern Frontier: Essays on Spain in the American West, 1540–1821,* edited by David J. Weber, 117–134. Albuquerque: University of New Mexico Press, 1979.

Shafer, Gladys. "Eastward Ho! Ezra Meeker Memorializes the Oregon Trail, 1905–1910." *American West* 5 (November 1968): 42–48.

Shaffer, Marguerite S. *See America First: Tourism and National Identity, 1880–1940.* Washington, D.C.: Smithsonian Institution Press, 2001.

Sherow, James E., ed. *A Sense of the American West: An Anthology of Environmental History*. Albuquerque: University of New Mexico Press, 1998.

Shortridge, James R. *Peopling the Plains: Who Settled Where in Frontier Kansas*. Lawrence: University Press of Kansas, 1995.

Silverman, Elaine Leslau. *The Last Best West: Women on the Alberta Frontier, 1880–1930*. Montreal: Eden Press, 1984.

Sitton, Tom, and William Deverell, eds. *Metropolis in the Making: Los Angeles in the 1920s*. Berkeley and Los Angeles: University of California Press, 2001.

Smith, Charles W., comp. *Check-List of Books and Pamphlets Relating to the History of the Pacific Northwest, to Be Found in Representative Libraries of That Region*. Olympia, Wash.: Washington State Library, 1909.

Smith, Duane A. *Rocky Mountain Boomtown: A History of Durango, Colorado*. 2d ed. Niwot: University Press of Colorado, 1992.

———. *Rocky Mountain West: Colorado, Wyoming, and Montana, 1859–1915*. Albuquerque: University of New Mexico Press, 1992.

Smith, Henry Nash. *Virgin Land: The American West as Symbol and Myth*. Cambridge, Mass.: Harvard University Press, 1970.

Smith, Sherry L. *Reimagining Indians: Native Americas Through Anglo Eyes, 1880–1940*. New York: Oxford University Press, 2000.

Soja, Edward W. *Postmodern Geographies: The Reassertion of Space in Critical Social Theory*. New York: Verso, 1989.

Sorkin, Michael, ed. *Variations on a Theme Park: The New American City and the End of Public Space*. New York: Hill and Wang, 1992.

Starr, Kevin. *Americans and the California Dream, 1850–1915*. New York: Oxford University Press, 1973.

———. *Inventing the Dream: California Through the Progressive Era*. New York: Oxford University Press, 1985.

———. *Material Dreams: Southern California Through the 1920s*. New York: Oxford University Press, 1990.

Stegner, Page, and Mary Stegner, eds. *The Geography of Hope: A Tribute to Wallace Stegner*. San Francisco: Sierra Club Books, 1996.

Stegner, Wallace. *The American West as Living Space*. Ann Arbor: University of Michigan Press, 1987.

———. *Beyond the Hundredth Meridian: John Wesley Powell and the Second Opening of the American West*. Boston: Houghton Mifflin, 1954.

———. "A Geography of Hope." In *A Society to Match the Scenery: Personal Visions of the Future of the American West,* edited by Gary Holthaus, Patricia Nelson Limerick, Charles F. Wilkinson, and Eve Stryker Munson, 218–229. Niwot: University Press of Colorado, 1991.

———. *Where the Bluebird Sings to the Lemonade Springs: Living and Writing in the American West*. New York: Penguin, 1992.

Steiner, Michael C. "Regionalism in the Great Depression." *Geographical Review,* 73 (October 1983): 430–446.

Swierenga, Robert P. "Land Speculation and Its Impact on American Economic Growth and Welfare: A Historiographical Review." *Western Historical Quarterly* 8 (July 1977): 283–302.

Szasz, Ferenc Morton. *The Protestant Clergy in the Great Plains and Mountain West, 1865–1915.* Albuquerque: University of New Mexico Press, 1988.

———. *Religion in the Modern American West.* Tucson: University of Arizona Press, 2000.

———, ed. *Religion in the West.* Manhattan, Kans.: Sunflower Press, 1984.

Takaki, Ronald. *From Different Shores: Perspectives on Race and Ethnicity in America.* New York: Oxford University Press, 1994.

———. *Iron Cages: Race and Culture in Nineteenth-Century America.* New York: Knopf, 1979.

Taylor, Quintard. *The Forging of a Black Community: Seattle's Central District from 1870 Through the Civil Rights Era.* Seattle: University of Washington Press, 1994.

———. *In Search of the Racial Frontier: African Americans in the American West, 1528–1990.* New York: Norton, 1998.

Thelen, David. *Memory and American History.* Bloomington: Indiana University Press, 1990.

Thomas, John L. *A Country in the Mind: Wallace Stegner, Bernard DeVoto, History, and the American Land.* New York: Routledge, 2000.

Thomson, David. *In Nevada: The Land, the People, God, and Chance.* New York: Knopf, 1999.

Thrapp, Dan L., ed. *Encyclopedia of Frontier Biography.* 3 vols. Spokane, Wash.: Arthur H. Clark Co., 1990.

Throne, Mildred. "Suggested Research on Railroad Aid to the Farmer, with Particular Reference to Iowa and Kansas." *Agricultural History* 31 (October 1957): 50–56.

Trachtenberg, Alan. *The Incorporation of America: Culture and Society in the Gilded Age.* New York: Hill and Wang, 1992.

Tuan, Yi-Fu. "Rootedness Versus Sense of Place." *Landscape* 24 (1980): 3–8.

———. *Space and Place: The Perspective of Experience.* Minneapolis: University of Minnesota Press, 1977.

———. *Topophilia: A Study of Environmental Perception, Attitudes, and Values.* Englewood Cliffs, N.J.: Prentice-Hall, 1974.

Underwood, June O. "Civilizing Kansas: Women's Organizations, 1880–1920." *Kansas History* 7 (winter 1984–1985): 291–306.

Underwood, Kathleen. *Town Building on the Colorado Frontier.* Albuquerque: University of New Mexico Press, 1987.

Urbank, Mae. *Wyoming Place Names.* Missoula, Mont.: Mountain Press, 1988.

Van West, Carroll. *Capitalism on the Frontier: Billings and the Yellowstone Valley in the Nineteenth Century.* Lincoln: University of Nebraska Press, 1993.

Walton, John. *Storied Land: Community and Memory in Monterey.* Berkeley and Los Angeles: University of California Press, 2001.

Ward, Stephen V. *Selling Places: The Marketing and Promotion of Towns and Cities, 1850–2000.* New York: Routledge, 1998.

Warren, Sidney. *Farthest Frontier: The Pacific Northwest.* New York: Macmillan, 1949.

Watts, Jennifer A. "Nature's Workshop: Photography and the Creation of 'Semi-tropic' California, 1880–1920." Paper presented at the annual meeting of the Western History Association, San Diego, October 2001.

———. "Picture Taking in Paradise: Los Angeles and the Creation of Regional Identity, 1880–1920." *History of Photography* 24 (autumn 2000): 243–250.

Webb, Walter Prescott. "The American West: Perpetual Mirage." *Harper's,* May 1957, 25–31.

———. *The Great Plains.* New York: Ginn and Company, 1931.

West, Elliott. *The Contested Plains: Indians, Goldseekers, and the Rush to Colorado.* Lawrence: University Press of Kansas, 1998.

———. *The Way to the West.* Calvin P. Horn Lectures in Western History and Culture. Albuquerque: University of New Mexico Press, 1995.

White, Richard. "The Current Weirdness in the West." *Western Historical Quarterly* 28 (spring 1997): 5–16.

———. *"It's Your Misfortune and None of My Own": A New History of the American West.* Norman: University of Oklahoma Press, 1991.

———. *Land Use, Environment, and Social Change: The Shaping of Island County, Washington.* Seattle: University of Washington Press, 1980.

———. *The Organic Machine: The Remaking of the Columbia River.* New York: Hill and Wang, 1995.

———. "Race Relations in the American West." *American Quarterly* 38 (1986): 396–416.

———. *Remembering Ahanagran: Storytelling in a Family's Past.* New York: Hill and Wang, 1998.

Wiebe, Robert. *The Search for Order, 1877–1920.* New York: Hill and Wang, 1967; republished 1995.

Winks, Robin W. "Regionalism in Comparative Perspective." In *Regionalism in the Pacific Northwest,* edited by William G. Robbins, Robert J. Frank, and Richard E. Ross, 13–36. Corvallis: Oregon State University Press, 1983.

Worster, Donald. *A River Running West: The Life of John Wesley Powell.* New York: Oxford University Press, 2001.

———. *Under Western Skies: Nature and History in the American West.* New York: Oxford University Press, 1992.

———. *An Unsettled Country: Changing Landscapes of the American West.* Calvin P. Horn Lectures in Western History and Culture. Albuquerque: University of New Mexico Press, 1994.

Wright, Louis B. *Culture on the Moving Frontier.* Bloomington: Indiana University Press, 1955.

Wrobel, David M. "Beyond the Frontier-Region Dichotomy." *Pacific Historical Review* 65 (August 1996): 401–429.

————. *The End of American Exceptionalism: Frontier Anxiety from the Old West to the New Deal*. Lawrence: University Press of Kansas, 1993.

————. "The View from Philadelphia." *Pacific Historical Review* 67 (August 1998): 383–392.

Wrobel, David M., and Patrick T. Long, eds. *Seeing and Being Seen: Tourism in the American West*. Lawrence: University Press of Kansas for the Center of the American West, University of Colorado, Boulder, 2001.

Wrobel, David M., and Michael C. Steiner, eds. *Many Wests: Place, Culture, and Regional Identity*. Lawrence: University Press of Kansas, 1997.

Zelinsky, Wilbur. *The Cultural Geography of the United States*. Englewood Cliffs, N.J.: Prentice-Hall, 1973.

Index

Explore the World

NORWAY

Authors:
Gerhard Lemmer, Elke Frey,
Helga Rahe

An Up-to-date travel guide with 141 color photos
and 17 maps

First edition
1999

Dear Reader: Being up-to-date is the main goal of the Nelles series. Our correspondents help keep us abreast of the latest developments in the travel scene, while our cartographers see to it that maps are also kept completely current. However, as the travel world is constantly changing, we cannot guarantee that all the information contained in our books is always valid. Should you come across a discrepancy, please contact us at: Nelles Verlag, Schleissheimer Str. 371 b, 80935 Munich, Germany, tel. (089) 3571940, fax. (089) 35719430, e-mail: Nelles.Verlag@t-online.de

Note: Distances and measurements, including temperatures, used in this guide are metric. For conversion information, please see the *Guidelines* section of this book.

LEGEND

★★ ★★	Main Attraction (on map) (in text)	Flekkefjord Kirken	Place mentioned in Text		National Border
★ ★	Worth Seeing (on map) (in Text)	🌳	National Park,		Expressway
❽	Orientation Number in Text and on Map	✈ ✈	International Airport National Airport		Principal Highway Main Road
▪	Public or Significant Building	\13/	Distance in Kilometers		Other Road
■	Hotel	Glittertinden 2470	Mountain Summit (Height in Meters)		Track Railway
✝	Church	⑤⑤⑤ ⑤⑤ ⑤	Luxury Hotel Category Moderate Hotel Category Budget Hotel Category		Pedestrian Zone
■ ○	Shopping Centre, Market		(for price information see "Accomodation" in Guidelines section)	E6 14	Ferry Route Number
⊷ ●	Bus Station, Underground Station				

NORWAY
© Nelles Verlag GmbH, 80935 München
  All rights reserved

First Edition 1999
ISBN 3-88618-048-4
Printed in Slovenia

Publisher:	Günter Nelles	Photo Editor:	K. Bärmann-Thümmel
Editor in Chief:	Berthold Schwarz	Cartography:	Nelles Verlag GmbH,
Project Editor:	Gerhard Lemmer		München
English Editor:	Anne Midgette	Lithos:	Priegnitz, München
Translation:	Sue Bollans	Printing:	Gorenjski Tisk

TABLE OF CONTENTS

3

GUIDELINES

MAP LIST

Polhavet *Nordkapp*
NORD-
AUSTLANDET
SPITSBERGEN
Longyearbyen
EDGEØYA
Sørkapp **226**

NORWEGIAN

SEA

NORWAY

NORTH
SEA

Nordkapp
Skarsvåg Kåfjord Gamvik Berlevåg
Hammerfest Olderfjord Tanabru Vardø
SØROYA Vadsø
Linahamari
E 6
1139 Lakselv Kirkenes
FINNMARKS- Kasmanen **208**
ALTA
VIDDA **184**
Kautokeino Russia
Oteren
SENJA
E 6
Andenes Kaaresuvanto Palojoensuu Törmänen
718
VESTERÅLEN NARVIK Södankyla
Svolvær **E 10** Kiruna Muonio
LOFOTEN Skarberget Vittangi **E 8** **E 75** Kelloselkä
Leknes Ulsvåg **2123** Svappavaara Kolari Kemijärvi
219 Gällivare Lansjärv Rovaniemi FINLAND
Fauske Jokkmokk Morjärv Karunki
Bodø Töre Keminmaa
Storjord Boden Luleå Pudasjärvi
177 Oulu
Mo i Rana SWEDEN
DØNNA Mosjøen Tärnaby Slagnäs Glommersträsk Jörn Raahe Pulkkila
VEGA Trofors **E 12** Skellefteå
1699 Storuman Bothnia
VIKNA Lycksele Umeå
716 Dorotea Jakobstad
Namsos Grong Vännäsby Pietarsaari
Steinkjer Åsele Örnsköldsvik
FRØYA Strömsund Vaasa (Vasa) **E 75**
SMØLA Stjørdalshalsen Östersund Kurikka Jyväskylä
Kristiansund **E 14** **167** Lunde **249** Jämsä
TRONDHEIM Harnösand Kristinestad
Ålesund Åndalsnes Oppdal Røros **1796** Ånge Sundsvall **E 12**
Nordfjordeid Dombås Tynset Tännäs Pori Nokia TAMPERE
Måløy **2083** Koppang Liusdal Rauma Hämeenlinna Lahti
Flore Lavik **2469** Otta **E 6** Sveg Hudiksvall VANTAA Järvenpää
Lærdalsøyri **E 16** Lillehammer Söderhamn Åland TURKU VANDA
96 BERGEN **144** **E 16** Elverum Mora Gävle ÅBO ESPO HELSINKI
74 Skare Hamar Malung Falun ESBO
OSLO **141** Norra Ny Borlänge Avesta UPPSALA TALLINN
E 134 Hønefoss Torsby **425** Nörrtälje
Haugesund DRAMMEN Väster ås BALTIC
STAVANGER FREDERIKSTAD KARLSTAD ÖREBRO STOCKHOLM ESTONIA
Sandnes **E 18** Larvik **E 6** Eskilstuna HIIUMAA S. Pärnu
Helleland **44** Väner **E 4** SEA
Flekkefjord **E 39** Risør Säffle Norrköping SAAREMAA S. Ainaži
KRISTIANSSAND **58** Mariestad
Mandal Uddevalla Linköping Roja
Skagen GÖTEBORG Vättern Vimmerby Visby Lärbro Ventspils **174** RIGA
Hirtshals Fredriks- Falköping Västervik GOTLAND LATVIA
JÜTLAND havn Varberg Jönköping Oskarshamn Ljugarn Pavilosta LIEPÄJA
Hanstholm Falkenberg **E 4** ÖLAND Burgsvik
Thisted ÅLBORG Växjö Kalmar Borgholm SIAULIAI
Holstebro **E 45** RANDERS Halmstad Ljungby **E 22** Färjestaden
Ringkøbing Grenå **E 6** HELSING- Ronneby Ottenby
Herning ÅRHUS Helsingør BORG Karlskrona
Horsens SJÆLLAND Kristianstad NORWAY
Esbjerg KØBENHAVN MALMÖ Ystad 0 100 200 km

7

THE HISTORY AND CULTURE OF NORWAY

From the First Settlers to the Vikings

For a long time very little was known about the prehistory and early history of Norway, and it is only in the last few years that this period has become the focus of archaeological investigations. Today, it is assumed that it was when the ice covering of the last Ice Age melted (in approx. 10,000 BC) that the west coast of Norway gradually became habitable, from south to north. This process was also facilitated by the Gulf Stream, which warms the Norwegian coast all the way to Spitsbergen.

That settlement of the west coast proceeded at a pretty rapid rate once this had occurred is demonstrated by Stone Age finds on both the Oslofjord and the Altafjord, on the other side of the Arctic Circle. It is not known whether the settlers came across the frozen Kattegat Sea or whether they were already able to come by boats along the coast. It is, however, certain that around 7000 BC, after the ice had melted, the land rose up to create an overland link between Scandinavia and central Europe, which enabled a new Stone Age culture to migrate into the area.

This culture reached its peak in the 5th millenium BC when pottery was introduced; there was probably also a lively trade in greenstone tools along the coast as far north as present-day Trondheim. This culture has been dubbed the "Kitchen Refuse Culture" (*Køkkenmøddinger*) by modern scientists, who

Preceding pages: This view of the Lysefjord is well worth the climb. Oslo schoolchildren parade in celebration of the national holiday. Left: An early specimen of the skills of Viking silversmiths (10th century AD, Vendel style).

deduced that the inhabitants lived primarily from fishing and collecting shellfish from findings from refuse pits from the period, which have since been excavated.

The Neolithic Age, the later Stone Age (approximately 3000-1500 BC), saw the first beginnings of agriculture and livestock cultivation. Pottery continued to be developed ("Funnel-Pot Culture"), but didn't advance beyond a certain still-rudimentary stage. This period also saw the execution of the first simple rock drawings, such as those on Ekeberg near Oslo or the particularly fine examples in the new open-air museum in Alta. Few finds have been made from the Bronze Age (1500-500 BC) in Norway, the reason being that tin, an element of the alloy bronze, is almost nonexistent in Norway, and thus had to be paid for dearly with other goods. There are, however, rock drawings from this period which demonstrate that Norway's Bronze Age inhabitants were familiar with the wheel, the plough and the cart, all objects that could easily be made of wood. Skiing technology was also developed further in this period; this means of transportation would later be taken over by the Vikings. Instead of two boards of equal length, early skiers used one "gliding ski" about three meters long and one pushing ski that was only about one meter long. The religion was probably some form of sun cult, judging on the evidence of sun wheels that appear in many of the rock drawings.

Norway's natural resources were more favorable to the development of technology in the subsequent epoch, the Iron Age (500 BC - AD 300); for there were ample deposits of brown iron ore, known as bog iron, which were easy to exploit once one had mastered the technique of basic smelting. The new metal was used almost exclusively for the production of weapons – evidence that armed conflicts certainly took place in this period between various groups of settlers. In the

13

late stages of the Iron Age, a time of large-scale migration throughout Europe, the first Teutons arrived in Scandinavia. The name "Scandinavia" was coined by Pliny the Elder in the first century AD. In literature on the subject it means something equivalent to Island of Darkness or Island of Destruction.

The area settled by Teutonic tribes soon extended as far as the Arctic Circle. Prime spot for settlement were the bays (*vik*) at the end of the fjords, whose inhabitants became known as "*vik*-dwellers," Vikings. From these hamlets, the men set out on campaigns of conquest and hunting expeditions. Rapid population growth, the paucity of arable land and constant skirmishes between the various tribes spurred the Vikings to pirating expeditions and voyages of discovery. By the 9th century they were already attack-

Above: One of the many stone circles on the ancient road near Fredrikstad. Right: A seaworthy funerary vessel in the Viking ship museum on Bygdøy, Oslo.

ing France, plundering the monasteries at the mouth of the Seine and even besieging Paris, until the French king Charles the Simple, who was not actually so simple at all, made the Viking leader Rollo Duke of Normandy in 911 – after, of course, Rollo's conversion to Christianity. This ended the plundering and privateering of the Vikings, at least in Normandy, where the "Northmen" or Normans, French-speaking Vikings, had soon penetrated into the aristocracy, and were bound by allegiance to the French king. Because of strong residual family ties with their former homelands, a kind of "educational tourism" from Norway to Normandy grew up; many young Viking noblemen had their first tastes of Roman-influenced administration and government, legal codes and military organization in Normandy, and it was here, too, that they were introduced to Christianity.

At the end of the 9th century the Faeroe Islands, Orkney and Iceland were settled by the Vikings, and in 930 they founded

on these islands an autonomous state with its own distinct system of law and government. AD 985 saw the establishment of the first settlements in Greenland, and around the turn of the millennium Leif Erikson discovered Vinland on the Newfoundland coast, in North America; Viking settlements here held on as late as into the 14th century, when they were overrun by Indians and ultimately abandoned.

Much of what is believed known today about the Vikings stems from documents that were recorded at a later period, after Christianity had taken a firmer hold on Norway. It is, however, certain that Vikings attacked the coast of Portugal and, in the Mediterranean, Sicily, Malta, Cyprus and Byzantium. Some of them even made it as far as the Black Sea by way of the Baltic and the rivers of Eastern Europe; on this route of some 2,000 kilometers, they had to portage their boats over the major divides. Such trips required very good nautical and navigational abilities: the Vikings were excel-

lent seamen. Their long, maneuverable dragon boats were among the most seaworthy ships of the time.

Protection and provisions were a concern not only for wives and children, left at home in their absence, but for the voyagers themselves along the way. Bases in Normandy provided back-up for Viking excursions along the Portuguese coast, and not until Sicily had become a base, as well, did they embark on further trips into the eastern Mediterranean. The Viking base of Greenland was a prerequisite for the passage to America, and without the Russian Viking realm of Gardarike, no Viking leader would have dared set his sights on the Black Sea. Necessary to maintain all of this was a well-organized, well-run social infrastructure, which historians were fond of detailing in contemporary chronicles.

It's more than likely that the Vikings' expansionist tendencies were born of the state of hardship in their own country. Anyone who has hardly any land worth cultivating, can only conserve a part of his harvest from the sea, and has no goods worth speaking of to trade is obliged either to turn to aggressive tactics to get his hands on some objects he can barter or to move away altogether. That the Vikings were, in fact, eminently willing to emigrate is demonstrated by the fact that in places where the political situation was favorable, such as Normandy, Sicily and Gardarike, they settled down in permanent communities.

The Middle Ages

The battle of Hafrsfjord (near Stavanger) in AD 872 was the last of a series of battles in which Harald Hårfagra (Fairhair) defeated all the small feudal states one by one, ultimately emerging as the first king of a united realm. This first realm was, however, short-lived. There followed another period characterized by minor kings constantly waging war upon one another, the best-known of them bearing the appropriate name of Eric Bloodaxe. In the end Håkon Jarl, in alliance with the Danish king Harald Blue Tooth, seized power; but he then fell out with his ally, defeated him in the battle of Hjørungavåg and, after a few years of ruling alone, was ultimately deprived of power after a peasant riot.

This was the hour of Olav Tryggvasson (Olav I), a Viking chief from Trøndelag, who in contrast to other pretenders to the throne could prove that he was a true great-grandson of Harald Fairhair. After he had robbed and plundered his way along the North Sea and the Baltic coasts, he had himself baptized by the Bishop of Winchester. He founded Nidaros (Trondheim) and attempted, with the combined assistance of English missionaries and brute force, to establish Chris-

Right: Harald Hårfagra (Fairhair) cuts the bonds of the giant Dofri, who in thanks gave him the strength to unite the empire; Icelandic manuscript illumination, 14th century.

tianity in his realm. These efforts met with stiff resistance from the population, led by the sons of Håkon Jarl, who allied themselves with the Swedish and Danish kings without considering the territorial ambitions of their purported rescuers.

Olav's ally in this civil war was Boleslav, later King of Poland, with whose help he assembled a fleet and sailed to meet his opponents. At Svolder he was challenged, lost the battle, sprang overboard and drowned. This took place in the year 1000, the first definitely established date in Norwegian history.

Part of Norway now came under Danish control, and part under Swedish, while the unoccupied remainder of the country was ruled somewhat haphazardly by the Jarl brothers. The imposed religion of Christianity also lost its supporters; all over the country, people went back to worshipping the old heathen gods.

In 1015 a young man appeared in Nidaros who also declared himself to be a descendant of Harald Fairhair, and successfully advanced his claim to the throne. This Olav had had a chance to prove his mettle in Viking campaigns in the North Sea and the Baltic. For a time he had supported the English king in the struggle against the Danes; later, he had studied government in Normandy and converted to Christianity. As king, he immediately began to implement radical reforms of the Norwegian class system, imposed Christianity with all the brutality of Olav Tryggvasson, created an ecclesiastical administrative body with its own laws and placed the clergy under the control of the Archbishop of Bremen. Since his realm was still under threat from the Danes (Knut the Great, or Canute) and the Swedes, he married the daughter of the Swedish king in order to secure his position abroad.

At home, however, Olav's future was looking considerably less rosy. Even though large sections of the population

were in favor of his reforms, they were by no means in the interests of the aristocracy, whose rights he had considerably curtailed. People therefore conspired openly against Olav, not even scorning the covert assistance of the Danish king – although this later proved to be a grave mistake, as Knut's real aim was the annexation of Norway.

After Olav won the first sea battle with the help of his brother-in-law, who was now the Swedish king, the latter withdrew his aid so that Olav was obliged to abandon his fleet in the Baltic and make his way back to Norway on foot. Here open rebellion broke out against the king; and just when he was up against the wall, Knut made his move, appearing with his fleet on the south coast of Norway. Olav was forced to capitulate and fled to the Viking kingdom of Gardarike in Russia, where his wife's brother-in-law was on the throne.

After his victory, Knut installed a governor in Norway and from then on concentrated exclusively on his other kingdoms, Denmark and England. When this governor died, Olav saw a last chance to win back his kingdom. He assembled a motley army of mercenaries and set out for Nidaros. Just before he reached his goal he was confronted by a peasant army at Stiklestad, lost the battle and died on July 29, 1030. And yet despite this ignominious end – he was hastily buried in a sand bank – this Olav was later revered as the patron saint of Norway.

Knut the Dane, now sure of his Norwegian territory, proceeded to raise taxes considerably, with the result that the peasantry and the aristocracy who had opposed Olav now turned against the Danes. They sent for Olav's son Magnus in Gardarike and in 1035 elected him king of Norway. In the period between Olav's death and the accession of his son, numerous miracles are said to have taken place at Olav's grave, both at the sandbank and at his subsequent resting-place in the Church of St. Clement in Nidaros. This marked the start of an unprecedented campaign of veneration which trans-

stepbrother of St. Olav, whom Magnus had appointed co-regent in his last years of rule. He was not, however, able to retain control of Denmark, and in his attempt to enforce his claim to the English throne, he was killed in the Battle of Stamford Bridge (1066). In this conflict, however, he had so weakened the forces of his opponent Harold that the latter lost the Battle of Hastings three weeks later and the Norman prince William (the Conqueror) became king of England. Harald Hardråda has gone down in Norwegian history as the founder of Oslo, which he also provided with a patron saint, St. Hallvard.

In 1070 his son and successor Olav Kyrre (the Quiet) also founded a town, Bergen, and named Sunniva as its patron saint. She was an Irish princess who fled to Norway to escape marrying a heathen prince and died there. In addition, Olav Kyrre elevated the most important Norwegian towns, Bergen, Oslo and Nidaros, to the rank of dioceses, thus securing their independence from Bremen's ecclesiastical authorities.

formed Olav not only into a saint but also into the eternal king of Norway. In a very short time, Olav's image metamorphosed from that of an ousted and derelict king without a country or people into that of a national saint and symbol of his country's struggle for freedom.

His son Magnus put all his weight behind this veneration, since some of his father's glory was reflected onto himself. On the advice of his *skalden* (counsellors) he abstained from taking revenge on his father's former enemies, and also reduced the severity of the laws, so that even in his lifetime he was known as "Magnus the Good."

After talks with Hardeknut, the son of Knut the Great, Magnus even became his successor, and for five years (1042-47) was King of Denmark, Norway and England. He was succeeded by Harald Hardråda (the Hard Ruler), a younger

The Civil Wars

The peaceful period lasted until 1130, when the last of Olav's grandsons died. As Olav IV (until 1115), Øystein (until 1122) and Sigurd (until 1130), these men had ruled the country jointly and peaceably. Sigurd *Jórsalfari* ("Jerusalemvoyager") had successfully represented the Norwegian kingdom on a crusade to Lisbon, Sicily, the Holy Land, Byzantium and Cyprus, while Øystein succeeded in winning back Jamtland (today part of Sweden).

But on the heels of this period of prosperity came 32 years of virtual civil war. The main reason was the fact that Norway had no binding laws of succession. Kings were supposed to be descended from Harald Hårfagra, but since legitimate and illegitimate sons had equal rights, it was

Above: View of the Romanesque nave of the cathedral at Stavanger. Right: The Birkebeinerne Monument in Lillehammer.

virtually impossible to verify the truth of anyone's claim to the throne by the second generation at the latest, and the number of claimants was legion. Succession to the throne was decided by the Thing, a tribunal. Often there was a compromise and two or even three kings were allowed to reign at the same time. But kings were also allowed to determine their own successors; the practice was to install the designated appointee as a co-regent during the current king's reign, so that he could grow into the office.

After 1150 the number of claimants to the throne grew and, since Harald Hårfagra and his successors had kept no record of their sexual adventures, it was impossible to distinguish genuine successors from bogus ones. Fueling disputes between the rival claimants was the popular belief that true royal blood would in any case triumph in the end. Each party had a group of allies who tried to exploit the competition for their own political ends, and everyone involved kept playing everyone else off against each other until the country was finally in a state of utter chaos. Finally, someone pulled the emergency brake.

Led by the Archbishop of Nidaros, the bishops and aristocracy set up new regulations for the succession, whereby only legitimate sons had a claim to the throne. At the same time, they elected a grandson of Sigurd Jórsalfari king and crowned him as Magnus IV in the cathedral church of Nidaros, construction on which had only just begun. It was the first coronation in the cathedral, which remained the coronation church even after the capital was moved to Oslo.

Self-styled pretenders to the throne did continue to appear, but they were all either defeated or killed. The supporters of the last aspirant, who were called *Birkebeinerne* because they were so poor they wore slippers and gaiters made of birch bark, fled to Sweden. There, they came into contact with Sverre Sigurdson,

a priest from the Faeroe Islands, who promptly declared himself the son of a king and placed himself at the head of the movement. He crowned himself in 1177, a step which was not actually legalized for another seven years. As king, he reinstated hereditary succession to the throne, pushed through judicial and government reforms, and appointed himself head of the church. This displeased the bishops, who formed the so-called "bagler party" (*bargell* = bishop's staff) to confront the *Birkebeinerne*, which had in the meantime grown to become a veritable popular movement.

The conflict escalated into civil war, which continued after Sverre's death in 1202 and culminated in the formation of two separate Norwegian kingdoms, that of the Baglers and that of the *Birkebeinerne*.

Consolidated Royal Power

While Sverre's 13-year-old grandson, Håkon Håkonsson (Håkon IV), was ap-

19

pointed king in 1217, it was another six years before he could be officially named as such. The initial opposition to his appointment was crushed by his guardian and advisor Skule Jarl, who, however, increasingly took the role and responsibilities of a regent upon himself. Even when Håkon IV gave him administrative control over a third of the kingdom, made him a duke, and even married his daughter, Skule was still not satisfied; and he ultimately stirred up open rebellion against the king. Challenged by Håkon in a decisive battle near Nidaros in 1240, Skule Jarl lost his life, and with him the age of civil wars in Norway also came to an end.

Håkon IV was certainly one of the most important kings in the High Middle Ages. Ruling from his court in Bergen, he expanded Norway's territory to greater dimensions than it would ever attain again,

Above: Merchants' banqueting hall in the Schøtstuene, Bergen. Right: Håkon Hall in Bergenshuis Fortress, Bergen.

taking over parts of central Sweden, the islands in the North Atlantic, and later, after peaceful negotiation, Greenland and Iceland. Iceland didn't officially lose its status as a free state until military pressure was applied when Håkon's son Magnus VI was crowned king of Iceland in 1263.

Håkon's trade policy, however, proved to be less successful than his foreign policy was. Although he negotiated a mutually advantageous trade agreement with England in 1223, he also signed a first contract with Lübeck in 1250, on the basis of which the first trading colony of the Hanseatic League was established in Bergen. With this and the following contracts with the Hanseatic League, Norwegian trade passed largely into German hands.

Håkon maintained a closer hold on the government by keeping the highest officials of the realm permanently assembled at his court as the so-called "Council of the Realm." His stone ceremonial hall, which he had built for the wedding of his

son Magnus, still stands today – although it has been frequently destroyed and rebuilt over the years – and is a hallmark of the city of Bergen.

The 12th and 13th centuries also saw the development of Norway's one unique contribution to European church architecture: the stave church. The style grew out of the original trade of its architects and builders: the first stave churches were built by shipwrights (see feature beginning on p. 232).

Håkon's son Magnus VI, known as the "Lawgiver" (*Lagabøtir*) because he introduced a detailed civil law code, also ruled from Bergen; not until 1300 did Håkon V tranfer the royal residence and also the capital to Oslo. Håkon V had no sons, so that a grandson followed him to the throne as Magnus VII; the son of the King of Sweden, he also ruled Sweden until 1355, and resided mainly in that country. The main problem of this period was however the Black Plague, which wiped out fully one-half of Norway's 350,000 inhabitants.

The Age of Unions

The brief union with Sweden was the forerunner of the longest alliance in Scandinavia's history, the Kalmar Union. The son of Håkon VI became king of Denmark at a young age, because his mother Margaret was the daughter of the Danish king; he also ruled Norway until his death at the tender age of 17. His mother assumed the regencies, thus becoming the first Queen of Norway and Denmark; it is she who is considered to be the actual initiator of the Kalmar Union. The first preliminary treaties were signed in 1380, but it was another 17 years before the divergent interests of all parties could be reconciled. Only then was a joint king elected: Eric of Pomerania was crowned in Kalmar in 1397. With this election Margaret had succeeded in getting her great-nephew and preferred candidate onto the throne.

The Union officially lasted until 1523, when the Swedes, led by Gustav Vaasa, regained their independence; however,

Norway remained allied with Denmark until 1814. This alliance was considerably to Norway's disadvantage, as the country was effectively the junior partner, and was sometimes even treated as a colony. With the Reformation, which the Danes pushed through by edict in 1536, Norway even lost its ecclesiastical independence: the overall organization and running of its churches was in the hands of Danish pastors. Official language of the church, public authorities and the schools was Danish; Norwegian survived merely as a regional dialect.

Most of the aristocracy had managed to get itself killed off in years of minor battles, and the economy was firmly in the hands of the German merchants of the Hanseatic League. Thus Christian III met with no opposition whatsoever when he declared in the Danish parliament that Norway had ceased to exist as an inde-

Above: Founded on copper – the mining city of Røros. Right: Poet Henrik Ibsen (1826-1906) in a painting by Erik Werenskiold, 1895.

pendent nation, and had become part of the Danish realm.

Not until the end of the 16th century, in the climate of discovery and adventure that pervaded Europe after the journeys of Columbus, did the demand for the wood, Norway's most important export product, suddenly shoot up. At the same time the Hanseatic League began to lose its privileges.

With Christian IV, a king who was well disposed to Norway had at last ascended the Danish throne. The country's economic situation improved markedly. Christian IV even rebuilt Oslo after it had burned down, rechristening it with his name (Christiania); in 1641, he also founded the city of Kristiansand. He brought in German mining experts to oversee extraction of the silver in Kongsberg and the copper in Røros – measures which were to give Norway a broader economic base. Christian's actions culminated in Norway's finally being recognized as an independent realm in 1660. A Norwegian legal code (*Norske*

Lov) was introduced (although it was in fact no more than a translated edition of Danish law), and the Danish governors, who were often married to Norwegian women, no longer acted solely in the interest of Copenhagen.

A setback came with the great Norwegian War of 1700-1720, when Sweden appropriated several provinces of Denmark and Norway and thus became the dominant power in Scandinavia. By 1740, however, Norway had recovered again. With the growth in international trade, especially overseas, Norwegian shipping companies were also flourishing; at the same time there was a powerful resurgence of Norwegian national consciousness.

In the Napoleonic Wars, Denmark forced Norway onto the side of France; when the English blockaded the Continental ports, therefore, their blockade extended to Norway, as well. Exports and imports came to a complete standstill, and even the country's domestic trade collapsed, since it was primarily conducted by sea. The divergence of Denmark's and Norway's interests came into the open, and even Denmark's attempts at appeasement with such steps as the founding of the university of Christiania were unable to stem the tide of the popular movement "Leave Denmark."

The Modern Age

With the defeat of Napoleon at Waterloo, Norway thought its dreams of independence were on the verge of coming true; instead, however, it had a rude awakening in 1814 when, in the Treaty of Kiel, the Danish king gave the country to anti-Napoleonic Sweden. In Norway, this move met with strong resistance, something even supported by the Danish governor, who was later to reign as King of Denmark as Christian VIII. The Norwegians defiantly held an assembly in Eidsvoll and drew up a Norwegian consti-

tution based on the ideas of Montesquieu (with a separation and balance of powers). This constitution of May 17, 1814 is still valid today in a modified form, and the day it was passed is celebrated as the national holiday. In tough negotiations with Sweden, held in Moss, it was finally agreed that the two states, each with its own distinct laws and parliament, should be united under one crown.

As the death of Charles XIII had marked the end of the Swedish royal line, the Swedes selected as their next king a Napoleonic general, Jean Baptiste Bernadotte, who had represented the Swedish interests very skilfully at the Treaty of Kiel negotiations. This election was approved by the Norwegian parliament (*Storting*) in the same year. Bernadotte's reign saw a period of strong economic growth in Norway. Coastal fishing became deep-sea fishing and industries developed near the coast; at the same time, however, people left rural areas to move to the population centers in increasing numbers.

23

Politically, one consequence of this development was the birth of the "Lawyers' Party," which represented the interests of the civil servants and the upper classes, and the "Peasant Party," the party of the rural populations. The contrast between the parties was even manifested in the language: while the former spoke *Riksmål*, derived from Danish, the peasants' party favored *Landsmål*, which was based on Old Norse.

The 1870s saw the birth of a labor party called the "Left Party," intended as an alternative to the two parties mentioned above; this party brought about reform of the parliamentary system and extensive democratic reforms. Around this time, Norway also began to develop its own cultural identity, something evidenced by such names as Ibsen, Bjørnson, Grieg and Munch.

Above: April, 1940 – the German occupying forces at the train station in Kristiansand. Right: A drilling platform – concrete symbol of the wealth brought by oil exploration.

By the end of the 19th century, however, economic growth could no longer keep pace with the growth of the population, and, with the country's difficulties compounded by the potato blight that traveled over from Ireland, Norway became a classic emigration country. In the last 20 years of the 19th century alone, three-quarters of a million Norwegians sought their fortunes on the other side of the Atlantic. The process continued in the early 20th century; today, there are more than a million Norwegians living in North America. Politically, too, things were in flux: it was around this time that the stage was set for the final conflict with Sweden, since the Norwegians were still treated as a subordinate partner.

The dispute over representation in foreign affairs escalated when Oscar II refused to sign a law the *Storting* had passed dealing with passport and consular matters. The Norwegians held a referendum and voiced their desire to dissolve the union with Sweden. Sweden was obliged to respect their wishes, and since the Treaty of Karlstad of 1905, Norway has once again been independent.

The new nation's first difficulty was that it had no royal family of its own and was therefore forced to appoint a prince from outside Norway as king. This role was assumed by the Danish prince Carl, who was crowned Håkon VII in Trondheim on June 22, 1906. Over the following years, Norway began to lay the foundations of its exemplary social network with such measures as the introduction of the vote for women in 1913. In World War I Norway remained neutral, but lost a large part of its merchant fleet, which had been commissioned by the Allies, to German U-boats.

In 1920, Norway joined the League of Nations and in the same year was given sovereignty over Spitsbergen (Svalbard). The Norwegians annexed the island of Jan Mayen in 1929, but had to relinquish their claims to Greenland in 1933, after a decision handed down by the international court at the Hague.

When World War II broke out and there were fears that Hitler's Germany would attack, Håkon VII, through his English wife, established contact with the British government, hoping to get British troops stationed in Norway to help defend the country. Hitler's army, however, anticipated this and occupied the crucial ports before the British could get there. The sinking of the *Blücher* in the Oslofjord (April 20, 1940) gave the Norwegian government the opportunity to leave the country from Tromsø for England, taking all the important national documents with them; and the Nazi puppet governor Quisling nominally took power. From England, Håkon organized the resistance against Quisling and against the occupying forces, a campaign which involved thousands of Norwegians. In retaliation, Norway was hit hard: its cities were severely bombed, and most of the towns in the north were wiped out altogether. A section of the population did collaborate,

openly or in secret, with the Nazis, including author Knut Hamsun; after the war, only his great age and his obligatory residence in an old age home protected him from prosecution. Officially the Norwegian government in exile in London never capitulated to the Nazis. When Håkon VII finally returned to Norway after the war, it was in Tromsø, the place from which he had left the country, that he first set foot again on Norwegian soil.

After World War II, Norway became one of the founding members of the UN in San Francisco. Until 1965, the Labor Party was in power; since then, the government has moved back and forth between the center-right parties and the Labor Party. Norway was a founding member of EFTA, but since this was dissolved, the country has several times refused to join the European Union. Domestic issues such as the fishing zone, which was extended to 200 nautical miles in 1977, are still Norway's primary concerns. In the same period, a treaty divided European waters into zones for the exploitation of oil and gas, and the largest and most productive of these was assigned to Norway. Because of the oil boom, Norway is now the richest country in Scandinavia; since the first oil crisis in the 1970s, profits have skyrocketed. Norway has even been nicknamed "Sheikh of the North" because it went along with every one of OPEC's price increases without actually being a member.

The present king of Norway is Harald V, who succeeded his very popular father Olav V in 1987. The Norwegian king still nominally has the right to raise a (suspensive) objection to an intended law, is commander of the armed forces, and awards the Nobel Peace Prize every December.

After the end of World War II, the Norwegian Labor Party remained continuously in power until 1965, and it was its leaders who paved the way for the present-day Norwegian social state. The basic principles of this state were never questioned by the center and rightist parties which took power in 1965, 1981 and 1989. Norway's first female Prime Minister, Labor Party member Gro Harlem Brundtland (1981-96), was defeated in one important initiative in 1994 when 52.4% of Norwegians voted against joining the EU. By hosting the winter Olympics in 1994, however, Norway was able to make an excellent impression on the global circuit. After Brundtland's unexpected resignation on October 25, 1996, her more left-wing party colleague Thorbjørn Jagland took over as head of government.

GEOGRAPHY
Why the Fjords are So Deep

Norway's fjords are symbolic both of the beauty of the country's scenery and of the close connection between land and

Right: Thanks to a happy geographical location, apples flourish on Sørfjord.

sea which has played such a dominant part in the lives of Norwegians throughout their history.

The word *fjord* is associated with the word for "travel," expressing the idea that these inlets that cut inland either had to be crossed or used as transportation routes to the sparsely distributed settlements scattered along their shores. Since the Stone Age, the population has remained concentrated in the few areas suitable for settlement in this Scandinavian mountain region and along the Atlantic and the European North Sea coasts.

Life in Norway would be unimaginable without the influence of the Atlantic. Its waters heat up considerably in the subtropical areas of the shallow Caribbean and the Gulf of Mexico. The warm current of the Gulf Stream leaves American coastal waters, continues as the "North Atlantic Drift" past Scotland and Iceland, and then flows all the way along the west and north coasts of Norway.

After such a long journey its temperatures are no longer sub-tropical, but even if at the level of the North Cape, which is at a latitude of 71°N, it can still demonstrate a temperature of 5°C, this is enough to keep all the important Scandinavian harbors on the North Sea and the Barents Sea free of ice throughout the winter. To see how lucky Norway is in this respect, one need only compare regions at the same latitude in Alaska, Siberia or Greenland. Around Cape Farewell in the south of Greenland, at a latitude of 60°N – that is, more than 1,200 kilometers further south than the North Cape – there are blocks of ice floating in the sea even in the summer!

The Svalbard island group also belongs to Norway; the northern tip of this archipelago, at 81°N, is already in the northern Arctic Ocean. Even here, on the west coast of the main island of Spitsbergen, the comparatively "warm" drift from the south softens the arctic influence, but by the time you get to the north of

Spitsbergen, such ameliorating influences have vanished.

Climatically, the North Atlantic is within the moderate zone of the west wind. These winds steer the warm surface waters of the Gulf Stream to the western and northern coasts of Europe. The ocean and the predominant west wind dictate temperture and humidity along Norway's long west coast, keeping the temperature remarkably constant over a distance of more than 1,000 kilometers from north to south.

The city of Bergen, at a latitude of 60°N, has an average January temperature of 2°C, while that of the port of Vardø at 70°N on the Barents Sea is only 7° lower, -5°C. In the summer, the differences are even less, with average July temperatures of 14°C for Bergen and 9°C for Vardø. The differences from east to west, however, are surprisingly pronounced. Oslo, only about 300 kilometers east of Bergen, has average temperatures of -4°C in January (almost like Vardø, 1,200 kilometers further north!), but

18°C in July: a more Continental climate. Here, the North Sea hardly influences the temperatures at all.

The reason for this is the barrier formed by the Caledonian Mountains, more than 2,000 meters high on their western side, and the high plateaus in the west of Norway, which block the Atlantic influence. Instead of warm winters, cool summers and high precipitation (almost 2,000 mm in Bergen, and in several western mountain regions as much as 3,000 mm a year), east of the barrier there are cold winters, hot summers and a rather dry climate (the Gudbrandsdal has only between 300 and 400 mm of rain per year).

Of course, the natural vegetation is also influenced by the temperature, precipitation and groundsoil. In the Oslo area and the narrow strip at the foot of the mountains along the southern coast of Norway, you still find the deciduous trees typical of central Europe: oak, elm, ash, hazelnut and linden. These trees also still thrive in the favorable climate along the west

27

coast, especially in sheltered areas protected from the wind and facing the sun along some of the fjords. Even fruit trees can grow here and thrive, something demonstrated by the cherry orchards on the Sørfjord, the southeastern extension of the Hardangerfjord. Oak trees grow as far north as approximately 64°N, around 80 kilometers north of Trondheim.

The northern Asian-northern European coniferous belt with its pines and firs, the taiga, crosses into Norway from the east and covers around 30% of the country. This is interspersed with birch, mountain ash, aspen, alders and willows which in the autumn results in a magnificent display of color splotched against a background of the dark green conifers. Prominent among the latter is the northern Asian fir (*picea abies obovata*), which, with its slim form and slightly hanging branches, is less likely to be damaged from the weight of the snow in the winter. A certain amount of snow is, however, desirable, since it protects the tree from drying out due to winter frost.

The northernmost natural fir forest in Norway is located in the national park of Saltfjellet-Svartisen, located approximately on the Arctic Circle (66°33'N). Pine trees, more resistant to the cold than some others, are found even further to the west and north, as well as at higher altitudes. Little Stabbursdalen National Park near Porsangerfjord at 70°N has the northernmost pine forest, although this pine-covered island, less than ten square kilometers in area, is already surrounded by a forest of fjell birches.

In places where the conditions are no longer adequate for coniferous forests, the fjell birch (*betula tortuosa*) takes over: toward the Arctic, that is, and at higher altitudes. This is the characteristic tree of the gently undulating Finnmarksvidda plateau in northern Norway.

Right: The stone of the Lofotens is more than a billion years old (Austvågøy).

In this extensive area the taiga gradually gives way to the type of Arctic vegetation known as the tundra, which in Norway is found only on the northern coast of the Nordkinn and Varanger peninsulas on the Barents Sea. The permanently frozen subsoil of the tundra prevents trees from growing: the topsoil thaws only for very short periods, permitting the growth only of low scrub vegetation.

Common plants here include the dwarf birch (*betula nana*), heather-like shrubs, mosses and lichens. The transition zone between the taiga and the tundra is known as wooded tundra, since it has both fjell birches and extensive areas of bare fjell, a treeless heath studded with patches of moorland. In the south of Norway, such landscapes extend across the high mountains where there are no glaciers; in the far north, however, it can reach far down as sea level.

The vegetation zones from south to north, ranging from deciduous forests, firs, pines and fjell birches to the tundra, also occur to a certain extent in the growth at high altitudes in the mountains. Because of the pronounced contrast in climate between eastern and western Norway, the high-altitude vegetation zones are very asymmetrical. Although the mild winters along the North Sea coast are favorable for central European deciduous trees, summers here are too cool for the plants of the taiga, which, although they're not affected by hard winter frosts, tend to thrive best in the heat of a continental summer.

In Jotunheimen, Norway's highest mountain region, which is in the east and therefore has a continental climate, fjell birches grow up to a tree line of nearly 1,200 meters, while pines stop at around 1,000 meters. On the west coast at the same geographical latitude, however, the fjell birch tree line drops below 500 meters, and that of the pines, to 400 meters. Pines are found further west than firs. It has recently been observed that the

areas of coniferous trees are spreading, also to the north, a fact attributed to the gradual warming of the climate, a process which has occurred many times during the Earth's history.

It is not easy to study the geology of Norway, since its rocks have been undergoing a steady process of erosion for more than 400 million years. The country, with an area of 323,878 square kilometers, bordering on Sweden, Finland and Russia, is located on the Baltic Shield; it has existed ever since primeval days, long before any higher life forms had arrived to populate the earth.

By the time life began its rapid development in the Cambrian period around 600 million years ago, numerous mountains had formed on this plate; however, they eroded again over the course of time. Located on the Baltic Shield in northern Norway is the whole area east of the Tanafjord together with the Nordkinn and Varanger peninsulas and the southen part of the Finnmarksvidda. The surface of this ancient land is even and slightly undulating, but also has occasional surprises: at Bigganjarga on the Varangerfjord, geologists have found tillites, prehistoric moraines, which indicate that there must have been ice here even in the pre-Cambrian period.

An even larger area of the Baltic Shield extends from central Sweden into southeast Norway, underlying parts of the Hedmark, the area east and west of the Oslo rift valley formed in the Permian period; most of the Hardangervidda and the Telemark; and all the south part of the country almost as far as Stavanger. The surface here consists mainly of resistant gneiss and granite rocks; it was the fine-grained, light granite from the Iddefjord, east of the Oslofjord, that Gustav Vigeland used for his sculptures in Frogner Park (see p. 50). Silver from Kongsberg, nickel from Evje and many other minerals have come from mines in these old rocks.

Material well over a billion years old forms the core of the Lofoten and Vesterålen islands, which form a separate

Evidence of such movement is to be found in many places in Norway. One of the most prominent mountains of the Hardangervidda, which is for the most part rather regular, is the Hårteigen (1,691 meters) in the western part of this largest mountain plateau in Europe. Beneath the surface, this plateau is composed of the gneiss rock of the Baltic Shield, which was gradually covered with layers of sediment; topmost of these were smooth phyllites, which formed an ideal surface for the Caledonian Mountains to slide onto as they approached from the west. However, 40 million years of wind and weather took their toll on the new surface, and in the east part of the Vidda wore it right away, so that the old bedrock reappeared. This is crowned by a cap of particularly durable gneiss, a leftover from the Caledonian layer of stone; this has served as a shield to protect all of the original layers lying below it, so that at this one relatively limited spot geologists can now measure and count all of the different layers of deposits and stone.

The Saltfjellet-Svartisen National Park presents quite a different picture. The glacial area of the Svartisen and its immediate surroundings are part of the Caledonian covering, and to the east of this the effects of weathering over the years have opened a horizontal window so that it is possible to se through to the Baltic Shield – rather like looking at a bare foot through a hole in a sock.

Given the hundreds of millions of years of erosion in Norway, it is surprising that the country is so mountainous. The highest summits are in Jotunheimen; the Glittertind, measuring 2,462 meters in height, and the Galdhøpiggen, 2,469 meters high. Many other peaks throughout the Caledonian Mountains have a distinctly Alpine look to them. Two events were responsible for this: the land's rising in the Tertiary period and the last Ice Age.

Even in the Cretaceous period (130-170 million years ago) there was consid-

world that still baffles the geologists. *Lofotveggen*, the "Lofoten Wall," which looks from a distance like a uniform whole, proves on closer inspection to be a complex of many groups of rocks from deep down in the earth that have, over the years, been massively eroded away.

Otherwise the whole coastal region from the North Cape to Stavanger, and even extending on in a wide arc from Spitsbergen to Scotland and Ireland was thrust up some 400 to 420 million years ago to form the range that are today known as the Caledonian Mountains, which were connected with the Baltic Shield and in places ran right over it. It is hard to visualize hundreds of yards of massive blocks of stone moving over previously existing hills; bear in mind, however, that the process took several million years.

Above: The Svartisen Glacier near Mo I Rana.
Right: Once glacier valleys, Norway's spectacular fjords are a souvenir of the Ice Age (Geirangerfjord).

erable geological activity. In the northern hemisphere at that period, there was only a single continent. Splitting this from south to north was a deep cleft in the earth's surface which emitted a steady stream of magma, while water gradually flowed in to fill the widening gap: this would expand into the Atlantic Ocean. Europe finally separated altogether from the American continent some 58 million years ago, when the European North Sea was formed.

In the process, the Scandinavian block in Northern Europe rose a little on the west side, while the east side sloped gently downwards. As a result, most of the rivers in Scandinavia in that period began to cut a gentle course descending from the high western part of the block and to the lower eastern side; this can still be observed in many of the rivers in Sweden which flow into the Gulf of Bothnia. Those which flowed in the opposite direction, however, were forced to cut their way through the mountains: the higher these mountains, the more deeply the

rivers had to gouge out their valleys, which came to resemble gorges or have a V-shaped cross-section.

The Tertiary Period (around 70 to 2 million years ago) was initially characterized by a particularly warm, tropical climate, which for reasons as yet unknown cooled down in the course of time. In the most recent geological epoch, the Quarternary, came the Ice Ages which put the finishing touches on the present-day Norwegian landscape. There was a succession of cold and warm periods; in the warm periods, the climate was often warmer than it is today. All over the world, the sea level sank by as much as 100 meters and Scandinavia, like present-day Greenland, was covered by a shield of ice several kilometers thick. Not only did this considerably push down the land mass of northern Europe; the heavy ice also changed the structure of the land's surface. Loose sediment was removed, and the bare stone beneath was either polished or sculpted into crags. On the Atlantic side of the country, tongues of

glaciers followed the course of the narrow river valleys and hollowed them out into U-shapes, some of them well below sea level, before calving over a higher threshhold of rock at the valley mouths into the European North Sea.

The last Ice Age began approximately 100,000 years ago; by about 10,000 years ago, most of the ice, with a few scattered exceptions, had melted. The level of the sea rose, and the deep, steep-sided glacial valleys filled up with water, resulting in elongated lakes and Norway's famous fjords. And there was yet more to the Ice Age's positive legacy: in Jæren, south of Stavanger, the glaciers deposited fertile moraine material, while the water that flowed in to fill the shallow bays around Trondheim and Oslo as the sea level rose contained clay sediment. When, relieved of its burden of ice, the land rose (in the Oslofjord by as much as 200 meters) and dried out, its soil proved particularly fertile and arable. Along the whole coastal strip from Stavanger into the far north the *strandflate*, platforms that look as if they have been deliberately planed, are often located at the foot of steep mountains, are often the only places suitable for a settlement. Geographers are still trying to establish how these platforms came into being. On the Lofoten and Vesterålen islands they form a dramatic contrast to the steep mountain massifs that have been decoratively sculpted by the Ice Age glaciers.

Most of the glacial debris of northern Europe, which is kilometers thick in places, was deposited in northeastern, central and western Europe. What, however, became of the masses of eroded rock and sedimentary deposits which Scandinavia lost in the course of hundreds of millions of years of erosion? These sediments from the various epochs of the earth's geoligical history are deposited at regular intervals along the Norwegian continental shelf as well as on Spitsbergen, where they're spread out as

Above: Alternative to fishing – salmon farming in the fjords (near Reine).

if to form an illustration for a geology textbook. Preserved in a very small area along the east side of the Vesterålen island Andøya are the Råmsa layers from the Jurassic and Cretaceous periods, including some coal seams. Spitsbergen's extensive coal deposits have long been highly prized, and the oil along the North Sea and in the North Atlantic has brought prosperity to Norway.

ECONOMY AND SOCIAL STATE

Central Europeans still think of the Norwegians as earning their money from fishing, agriculture and forestry, on ships and on oil platforms, even though this stereotype has long since ceased to correspond to reality. Since the end of the world economic crisis in the 1920s at the latest, there's been a fundamental structural change: the industrial and service sectors have been steadily developed, while mechanization in agriculture and forestry has led to a sharp decline in the amont of human labor these areas require. Today, only 7% of Norwegians work in these fields, fewer than in the classical industrial countries of England, France or Germany. One consequence has been a large population shift out of rural, agricultural regions. Of the 4.5 million people in Norway today, almost 60% live in towns and more than 70% in "population centers" (*tettsteder*) with more than 200 inhabitants. Considerable effort is invested in preventing the more remote areas from becoming altogether depopulated: subsidies of 260,000 krone per year to support jobs in agriculture are the highest in Europe. Premiums are handed out for foresting farmlands or mowing mountain pastures and the edges of paths as a conservational measure; there are also direct subsidies for the cultivation of potatoes, summer wheat, barley, fruit and other produce.

In the classic fishing areas – around the Lofoten and Vesterålen islands, for exam-

ple – huge sums are being invested to create new jobs in order to compensate for the decline in employment that's resulted from the imposition of more stringent quotas on the catch. People have high hopes for the development of hydrofarms, which receive generous loans. In 1990, 150,000 tons of salmon were already being cultivated, although such abundance also entails a drop in prices. There are also attempts at cultivation of sole and lobster, but to date these have met with rather less success.

Even the forestry industry cannot survive without subsidies, as prices are being forced down by the massive surplus of wood, particularly from the rain forest belts of the world. In this field, the Norwegians are attempting to switch over from simply supplying raw wood to manufacturing ready-made products such as pressboard sheds, wooden houses and furniture, and processing the waste as chipboard.

There are no mineral resources worth mentioning, with the exception of the large oil and gas deposits in the North Atlantic, so that Norway is obliged to import practically all the raw materials required by its indsutry. Long before the oil boom, however, the country had cheap energy in the form of water power. 23% of the useable water power in Europe is in Norway, and 60% of this is exploited. Since it is hard to store electric current, and it can't really be transported over long distances without considerable loss, Norway has tended to concentrate mainly on industries which use a great deal of electricity, such as the smelting of magnesium, aluminium and also iron. In addition, electricity is used as an energy source wherever possible. Thus in Norway almost all the buildings are heated with electricity – it is even used to heat the pavements in Trondheim – and most of the stoves and ovens are also electric.

Current plans to expand the use of hydroelectric power are meeting with in-

creasing opposition. Norway is easily able to meet its own energy needs, and its prices are lower than virtually anywhere else. There is little demand for the surplus power from neighboring countries, and this is hardly likely to change; exporting it to central Europe would require transportation systems costing billions, and only one-quarter of the original electrical current would actually arrive at its destination. Further development of hydroelectric power would also involve the construction of massive buildings: entire waterfalls would disappear, and large stretches of landscape would be disfigured. People against the development are pleading for a moratorium, arguing that there shouldn't be any further discussion of how to extend use of the country's hydroelectric potential until someone has come up with a useful purpose for the sur-

Above: Norway's social state guards over the future of its children. Right: One of many infrastructural improvements – the Tjeldsund Bridge on the Vesterålen Islands.

plus electricity that would result. Those in favor are pinning their hopes on the development of a superconductive cable system, which would make it profitable to export electricity.

In comparison with the service sector, Norway's industry is in decline. Since the 1960s, the number of jobs in trade and industry has declined from 60% to 30%, while the service sector now accounts for almost two-thirds of all jobs. Although a comparable shift from industry to the service sector is taking place all over the world, in Norway this development is still being supported by the social network. Because taxes are extremely high by central European standards, amounting to as much as 80% of an individual's income, there's enough money in the state's coffers to sponsor social services with privately earned money.

Difficult life situations, therefore, such as illness or inability to work, old age and unemployment, are not financed by insurance systems, but rather with money from taxes. Everyone in Norway has a legal

right to medical treatment when ill, to a minimum income known as the "people's pension," to unemployment benefits, and to other similar services. Kindergarten and day-care centers, schools and school meals, teaching materials and school buses, and even the retraining and certification of employees are all financed out of taxes, and the state also provides the personnel to administer such services. The aim of all these endeavors is to make sure that every Norwegian has his or her own income: full employment, that is, for every citizen who is able to work. Norwegians therefore calculate their unemployment rate on a completely different basis than most other European countries: everyone between the ages of 15 and 67, the official retirement age, is held to be employable, apart from students, military conscripts, the sick and invalid, mothers on maternity leave, and prisoners. Everyone elese should have a job, and if one's not available, it should be created.

The unemployment rate therefore reflects the number of people for whom this policy has not worked – temporarily, at any rate – and is currently at 5 percent. If the Federal Republic of Germany used the same criteria, it would have an unemployment rate of more than 30 percent.

There are also state-funded measures to improve living conditions in the more sparsely-populated parts of the country, in order to stem the tide of departure from the rural areas. Cultural centers with comprehensive adult education programs, subsidized music and amateur drama groups, and free community cinemas and libraries are as much a part of this as comprehensive medical facilities. Another series of measures aimed at improving the quality of life is connecting tiny islands, some with populations of barely 100, to the mainland with bridges and tunnels. Both the extensive network of social services and the efforts to implement the country's policy of full employment are extremely expensive. Since both direct taxation (income tax) and indirect taxation (value added tax) have reached the limits of what the people can bear, some of Norway's Scandinavian neighbors have had to start cutting back their social systems. Norway, on the other hand, can still afford its social state, since the profits from the oil and gas production in the North Sea balance out the internal deficit. In 1987 this deficit came to 80 billion krone, around 20,000 krone per capita. Since 1971, when the first oil and gas were found in the Ekofisk Field southwest of Stavanger, the income from these resources has played a crucial part in Norway's economy.

Three principles govern the country's oil and gas policy. One is slow and thorough extraction of the limited supplies; in other words, drilling for oil does not start until a natural gas pipeline is built at the site so that there is no waste of resources. The second is that Norway itself controls the extraction in order to keep the influence of multinational concerns to a minimum; and the third is that profits from the oil and gas are used to pay for investments on the mainland to help prepare the country for the period after the oil resources have been depleted. Since 1995, money has been placed in a so-called "future fund," a foundation for the investments of future generations. Although this had been under discussion for some ten years, it was only then that there was enough surplus oil money to put something into the fund. One reason there hasn't been more money is that in the last few years the road network has been expanded at a cost of billions, and the project is continuing. Rail connections were improved, and new local transportation systems set up in the main population centers.

The fleet of mail boats on the *Hurtigrute*, run by the coastal shipping services, was modernized; today, these vessels are almost like cruise ships. Many ferry links within Norway have been replaced with bridges or tunnels.

These investments are good for tourism, which has increased considerably in recent years. As a result of the improved infrastructure, however, travelers have also tended to cover greater distances in an increasingly short time. Thus, the average stay of tourists in Norway has gone down from 17 to 13 days, a development which has to be compensated for by an increase in their numbers. This could well have a noticable effect on Norway's scenic beauty – at least along the main traffic routes – in the not-so-distant future. Development of further tourist centers is also meeting with resistance. The constant construction of new hotels, which are only used for three to four months a year, is hideously expensive, something which, when reflected in room prices, is more likely to scare tourists away than attract them. A glance at the statistics about average European incomes also indicates that this high-priced country has probably already drained dry the wellsprings of its share of European tourism. Building new hotels, therefore, will only lead to price wars, resulting in a loss of profits that will have to be balanced out by higher turnover – a process that Norway really wanted to avoid. Critics of this development thus favor a less concentrated form of tourism, with fewer guests spread out over a longer season.

A further problem for Norway's economy is its relationship with the EU. The Norwegians last rejected entry in 1994, although all their Scandinavian neighbors are now members. In spite of the free trade agreement, Norway's borders have recently become the outer borders of the EU, and this involves the payment of duties and taxes. Norway's entrepreneurs, therefore, are loudly demanding export subsidies in order not to lose their regular customers in Scandinavia and the rest of Europe. Backing up their protests is the threat of transfering jobs in export-

Right: Fishermen's concerns about their fishing grounds is one obstacle to Norway's joining the EU.

oriented fields to other EU countries. Norway's refusal to enter the EU will certainly create considerable problems for the country. Its decision to remain apart is the consequence of a strange coalition of agricultural and fishing interests and the oil sector, which was able to stir up and exploit ancient Norwegian cultural Angst with great skill. The population was presented with a nightmare vision of the decline of Norwegian agriculture, of fishermen from southern Europe exhausting Norway's already depleted fish stock, and, playing on what was probably the greatest fear, the specter of Brussels distributing Norway's oil revenues to poor European states such as Portugal, Greece or Ireland. Still, Norway continues in its customs and passport union with Sweden, Finland and Denmark, and so far, no one has suggested that this be dissolved. Norway will therefore have to receive some kind of special status, probably something along the lines of quasi-membership in spite of nominal non-membership.

The intention to extend oil and gas exploration into the far north is also a highly controversial domestic issue. After trial drilling off Tromsø proved successful, it is now suspected that there are rich fields on the far side of the 65th parallel, which would be able to pick up where the gradually dwindling supply in southern Norway is leaving off. However, this move is being fiercely resisted by northern Norway's fishermen, who fear the pollution of their fishing grounds.

The end of the Cold War has also brought its problems to the country. Norway is the only member of NATO that actually borders on Russia; northern Norway, therefore, boasts a concentration of military installations. Now that the Warsaw Pact has dissolved, however, these installations have become obsolete, and they are in the process of being dismantled. Finding or creating adequate employment for the specialized personnel who used to work in these bases will prove to be a major – not to say an expensive – undertaking.

OSLO – THE CITY AND ITS FJORD

Oslo

SVINESUND

HALDEN

MOSS

OSLO

SVINESUND, HALDEN AND MOSS

The **Oslofjord** extends more than 130 kilometers from the Skagerrak north to the capital. Its wooded shores are not particularly steep, and have seen human settlement ever since the last Ice Age glacier melted. Today, the Oslofjord is one of the most densely-populated areas in Norway; Oslo residents, especially, keep up weekend and holiday homes around its outer, more rural extremities.

Anyone coming overland from central Europe into Norway crosses from the south over the **Svinesund ❶**. Arching over this sound, which is a good 60 meters deep, is a bridge that at the time of its construction in 1946 was the highest in Scandinavia; the sound itself is a popular mooring-place for a veritable fleet of pleasure boats. Drivers can park their cars on either the Swedish or the Norwegian side and take a stroll across the bridge on foot.

Two kilometers further on, in **Løkkeberg**, the *Riksveien* (R21) branches off

Preceding pages: Zooming toward the future – skateboarders in front of Oslo's Town Hall. On a sunny day, there's not a seat to be had here – the Aker Brygge on Oslo's harbor. Left: You've got to start young if you want to be a real Norwegian.

toward **Halden ❷**. This town, called **Fredrikshalden** until 1927, is today the center of eastern Norway's wood processing industry and lumber trade. It grew up below **Fredriksten Fortress**, which the Danes and Norwegians built as a defense against the Swedes after having lost Schonen to them in the Peace of Roskilde of 1658. Over the years, this fortress was to see frequent military conflict between the erstwhile partners in the Kalmar Union alliance. It commands a splendid view of the surrounding countryside; within it, an iron **pyramid** commemorates the death of the Swedish king Charles XII, who was struck by a ricocheting bullet in 1718. The building also houses the **Municipal Museum** with memorabilia from this period. Also worth a look is the municipal theater in **Rød Herregård**, with its Baroque stage which dates from 1830.

Returning to the main road (E6) to continue on to Oslo, travelers can turn off onto the R110 at Skjeberg for another pleasant detour over to **Fredrikstad ❸**, the old fortress town on the estuary of the **Glåma**, at the mouth of the Oslofjord. This marks the start of the so-called **"Highway of the Ancients"** (*Oltidsveien*) with relics from the earliest periods of settlement: rock drawings from the Bronze Age at **Solberg**, **Begby** and

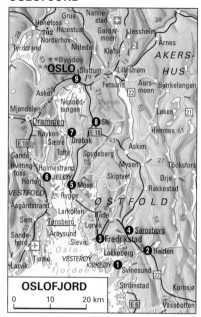

OSLOFJORD

```
0        10        20 km
```

Against it. On the **Island of Jeløy** ❻ across from Moss, connected by a bridge to the mainland, is **Alby Manor**, which today houses a gallery of modern art.

Ten kilometers west of the E6 is the beach resort of **Drøbak** ❼, which has a fine wooden church from the 18th century and is also the location of the fortress of **Oscarsborg**. It was from here, at the narrowest point of the fjord, that a Norwegian soldier fired the gun "Moses" on the day of the German invasion and sank the *Blücher*. This bought time for the king and enabled him and the government to flee Oslo, taking the most important documents with them, and go into exile by way of Tromsø.

Continuing along the E6, you come, after a few more kilometers, to **Ski** ❽, which in fact gave its name to what is now a popular sport, since it was in this area that the oldest rock drawings of people with these boards on their feet were found. The area around Ski is very popular with Oslo-dwellers seeking to get away from the pressure of the city. If you're coming from out of town, however, this region also effectively marks the periphery of Norway's capital, which, like Bergen and Trondheim, imposes a toll on every driver entering the city.

**OSLO

Extending over 450 square kilometers, **Oslo** is one of the largest capitals of the world in terms of area, although only 90 square kilometers are actually built up. There are more farms with cows, horses, pigs and chickens here than in all the other capitals of Europe put together. Today, Oslo has a population of half a million; greater Oslo numbers more than a million. Founded in 1050 by Harald Hardråda, "the hard ruler," it is also the oldest capital in Scandinavia. Apart from his battles against the Danes, this king is said to have known no worldly pleasures – a characteristic which Norway's Scan-

Hornes, or, from the Iron Age, the 200 burial mounds at **Storedal Field**, by Storedal. **Sarpsborg** ❹ at the end of this route, is said to have been founded by St. Olav. Here, at the edge of the present town, is the **St. Olav Rampart**, the only extant Viking fortification in Norway. **St. Nicholas Church**, which King Øystein built in the 12th century, marks the transition from the heathen to the Christian period: it incorporates stones carved with runes, sculpted heads, and a Romanesque baptismal font.

Forty kilometers farther north is **Moss** ❺. After the Eidsvoll constitution was completed in 1814 it was here, in the **Konventionsgården**, that the Treaty of Kiel was drawn up, forcing Norway into union with Sweden. Norway's enthusiasm for this arrangement is clearly reflected in the referendum about whether or not to continue it that was held 90 years later: 368,000 voters were in favor of separating from Sweden; all of 184 were

Right: Akershus Fortress, Oslo.

dinavian neighbors rather unkindly aver the city still reflects.

Hardråda named the monk Hallvard as the city's patron saint. This saint, in an attempt to protect a pregnant woman accused of theft, fled with her; he was caught and, pierced by four arrows, thrown into the **Drammensfjord** with a millstone round his neck. Since, however, his body did not sink, he was given a proper burial and his grave immediately became the site of many miracles. He still features on the city's coat of arms, seated on a throne with arrows and millstone in his hands and the woman he protected crouched thankfully at his feet. His first shrine was in St. Mary's Church, which Hardråda built for his city, but after Oslo had become the seat of a bishop under Olav Kyrre, his sacred relics were transferred to the city's first cathedral church, St. Hallvard's. This was pulled down in the 17th century and its stones used to strengthen the walls of *Akershus ❶. This fortress ranks as one of the most important medieval buildings in Norway. Its

site, on the **peninsula of Akernes**, was probably Hardråda's stronghold, as well, which Håkon V later expanded and turned into a residence when he transferred the seat of government from Bergen and the capital from Trondheim to here. It was at this time that the Hanseatic League also established itself in Oslo. After the Black Plague of 1349 and the Kalmar Union in 1397, Oslo declined in importance, and it was completely destroyed in the great fire of 1624. Christian IV of Denmark had it rebuilt and renamed it Christiania, after himself. After 1877 it was called Kristiania; in 1925, it finally reclaimed its original name of Oslo. It also regained its role as capital and residence when Norway separated from Denmark in 1814, although it has only "really" been a proper capital again since the dissolution of the union with Sweden in the year 1905.

Apart from the castle, little has remained or been excavated of medieval Oslo, the center of which was east of Akershus at the foot of **Ekeberg**. This is hardly surprising, since today the area of medieval Oslo is occupied by the station and major throughway junctions. Therefore all that's left today are the remains of the foundation walls of **St. Hallvard's Cathedral** (Oslogate 13) and the **Ladegård**, built over what was left of the **Bishops Palace**, which was in turn built on top of the foundations of an earlier St. Olavs Church. There are also ruins of an old **Cistercian monastery** on the island of Hovedøya in the fjord. The part of Oslo known as "Old Town" today is the rectangle between the main train station (*Sentralstasjon*), Karl Johansgate, City Hall (Rådhus) and the fjord. The buildings in this quarter are no longer those put up by Christian IV, but the street layout still follows his original plan.

The City Center

Oslo's hallmark is its monumental ***Rådhus ❷**, or City Hall. Begun in 1931 and not inaugurated until 1950, this brick edifice consists of a main building and two 60-meter-high towers, the eastern one of which contains a carillon. Based on plans by A. Arneberg and M. Poulsen, the building sports a façade adorned with sculptures and reliefs depicting scenes from historical and present-day Norway; among the artists who contributed to the interior are Sørensen, Krohg and Edvard Munch. Some of the city's administrative departments are here, as is the city council's assembly room and an interesting collection of state gifts that have been received over the years. The main hall, the "living room" of the people of Oslo, has excellent acoustics and is thus also used as a concert hall. At the back of City Hall, where the entrance for normal public business and tours is located, is horseshoe-shaped **Fridjof Nansen Square**, designed to complement the building.

A few paces away, at the end of **H. Heyerdahlsgate** with its souvenir shops, is **Karl Johansgate**, the main drag of the

city of Oslo, filled with strollers and shoppers, especially in summer. This boulevard, laid out under Charles XIV John (the eponymous Karl Johan), runs past the central train station and the Stortinget – or parliament building – with the palace, and is the focus of city life in the summer. If you're coming from City Hall, you hit this avenue near the neoclassical edifice of the **National Theater ❸**, which dates from the 19th century; part of its interior is in the Art Nouveau style.

In front of the theater are statues of the national poets Henrik Ibsen and Bjørnstjerne Bjørnson. To the right of the National Theater is the so-called **Studenterlunden**, once a small city park with a music pavilion, now popular with

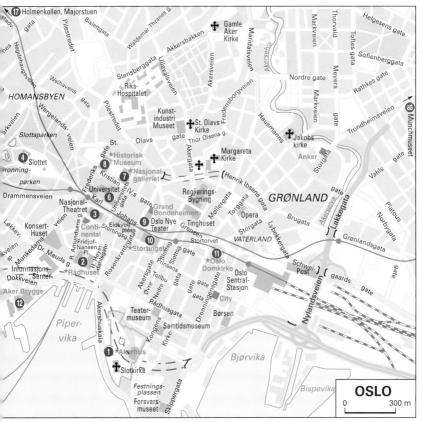

Map labels: Holmenkollen, Majorstuen · Bislettgata · Waldemar Thranes g. · Gamle Aker Kirke · Maridalsveien · Akerselva · Helgesens gate · Toftes gata · Sofienberggata · Thorvald Markveien · Meyers · Rathkes gate · Pilestredet · Akersbakken · Stensbergata · Ullevålsveien · Akersveien · Fredensborgveien · Nordre gate · Markveien · gate · Trondheimsveien · 18 Munchmuseet · HOMANSBYEN · Welhavens gate · Wergelandsveien · Riks-Hospitalet · Pilestredet · Kunst-industri Museet · St. Olavs Kirke · Thor Olsens g. · St. Olavs gate · Hausmanns · Jakobs kirke · Anker · Vahls · Slottsparken · Margareta Kirke · Storgata · Slottet · Historisk Museum · Nasjonal-galleriet · Henrik Ibsens gate · GRØNLAND · Platous · Norbygata · Dronning-parken · Frederiks gate · Kristian IV.s gate · Universitets gate · Karl Johans · Universitetet · Regjerings-Bygning · Mollergata · Torggata · Lakkegata · Grønlandsgata · Drammensveien · Nasjonal-Theatret · Grand Bondeheimen · Eidsvolls plass · Stortingsgata · Oslo Nye Teater · Grensen · Tinghuset · Opera · Brugata · Storgata · Lybakkergata · Konsert-Huset · Continental · Fridtjof-Nansens Pl. · R. Amundsens g. · Stortinget · Stortorvet · VATERLAND · Grønlandsgata · Løkkev. · Munkedams veien · Dr. Mauds g. · H. Heyer-dahlsgate · Rosenkrantzgata · Øvre Slottsgate · Prinsens gate · Oslo Domkirke · Schwei-Post · gaards gate · Informasjons-Senter · Dokkveien · Rådhuset · Akersgate · Nedre Slottsgate · Tollbu gata · Dronningensgate · Oslo Sentral-Stasjon · City · Nylandsveien · Aker Brygge · Piper-vika · Akershuskaia · Teater-museum · Kongens gate · Rådhusgata · Kirkegata · Børsen · Samtidsmuseum · Akerhus · Bjørvika · Bispevika · Slotkirke · Festnings-plassen · Skippergata · Forsvars-museet

OSLO
0   300 m

street musicians, and with a beer garden to boot. If you turn left you can see, among the new concrete blocks of downtown, a single more venerable building, the former Hotel Majestic. However, this edifice holds no fond memories for older Oslo residents, as during the German occupation it was the headquarters of the Gestapo.

At the western end of Karl Johansgate is the driveway to the **Palace** ❹. Built between 1825 and 1848, this stately edifice has, since Olav V, been used only for administrative and representational purposes. The old king lived on his farm on the island of Bygdøy, while the present one lives on Holmenkollen. In front of the palace is an equestrian statue of its

builder, Charles XIV John, dating from 1875. By the driveway is a statue of the mathematician Abel by Gustav Vigeland, who also created the statue of poet Camilla Collett behind the palace. Although the palace itself is not open to the public, its park is always open, and during the day, if the king isn't there, people can also go into the palace's inner courtyard. The small yellow house at the end of the park is the **Nobel Institute** ❺. Alfred Nobel stipulat[...]
peace prize award[...]
should be presented[...]
not changed even af[...]
from Sweden.

Strolling back al[...]
Karl Johansgate, th[...]

come to is the **University** ❻, which Frederick VI founded in 1811; today, this building contains the university law school. It's here, in the **Aula** or Great Hall, which is decorated with remarkable murals by Edvard Munch, that the Nobel Peace Prize is presented every year on December 10.

Behind the university is the ***National Gallery** ❼ (entrance at Universitetsgate 13) with an important collection of works by Norwegian artists including Munch (*The Scream* is here); old masters such as Rubens, El Greco and Rembrandt; and more recent French artists such as Cezanne, Degas and Gauguin.

The neighboring building contains the ***Historical Museum** ❽ (entrance at Fredriksgate 2): highlight of its displays is a comprehensive collection of objects from the Viking period, between the 9th and 11th centuries.

: Seeing and being seen – summertime in Karl Johansgate. Right: Real stay-sentry in front of Oslo's castle.

At the corner of Karl Johansgate and Rosenkrantzgate is the **New Theater** ❾, the largest theater in Oslo, which generally hosts revues and musical productions. Oslo's showcase boulevard seems to end at the **Storting** ❿, or parliament building. Adorning the **assembly room** here is a monumental painting by Wegeland depicting the *Constitutional Assembly of Eidsvoll*; this event also gave the name to the square in front of the building, **Eidsvoll Square**. Diagonally opposite, at the entrance to **Akersgate**, is the remarkable **Masons' Lodge**. A couple of hundred yards further east is the **Stortorvet**, the large marketplace, with a statue of the Danish king Christian IV. Dominating the south side of this square is Oslo's ***Cathedral** ⓫, which was consecrated in 1697. In the mid-19th century, the Hamburg architect Chateauneuf rebuilt its tower, and the interior of the cathedral was completely restored after World War II. Of particular interest here are the **ceiling painting** by Lous Mohr (*Holy Trinity*, 1938), the Baroque altar,

City Map pp. 46-47, Info pp. 52-53

the pulpit (1700) and Arrigo Minerbi's silver sculpture of *The Last Supper* in the **Savior's Chapel**, added on in 1950.

Behind the cathedral are the **bazaar halls** which were built along the old walls around the church, today a center for artisan work. This marks the end of the busy part of Karl Johansgate. Turn south and follow **Kirkegate**, with its fine houses from the 17th to 19th centuries; a short walk brings you to the fortress of ★**Akershus** ❶. Christian IV had a Renaissance palace built in this medieval fortress. A few years ago there was talk of pulling this down because it spoiled the character of the complex as a whole, but the idea was abandoned, and today the palace is used for state occasions. Visitors can inspect the **Christian IV Hall** and the **Palace Church** with its **crypt**, the burial place of the family of Håkon VII; as well as an Armed Forces Museum and the **Norwegian Resistance Museum** (*Norges Hjemmefrontmuseum*). A memorial commemorates the 42 resistance fighters who were executed here in 1945.

A few years ago, the quay area opposite the castle on the **Piperivika** harbor basin underwent a striking process of tranformation and revitalization. By day, the new ★**Aker Brygge** ❷, in the elaborately reconstructed sheds of the former Aker shipyard, is a popular shopping center, while in the evening it attracts gourmets and pub-goers, who flock to the restaurant ships tied up along the quay.

★★Bygdøy Museum Island

In front of the Rådhus, you can board a boat for a tour of the harbor and the offshore islands, or go directly over to the "museum island" – actually a peninsula – of **Bygdøy** ❸ (which you can also reach by car or by the 30 bus). The boat ties up in front of the **Fram Museum**, where is also moored the *Gjøa*, the ship in which Amundsen negotiated the Northwest Passage in 1903-06. Within the museum's

huge hall is the *Fram* itself, the ship which Nansen first used for his venture into the Arctic Ocean, and was then deployed by his former first officer Amundsen on his race to the South Pole, which, as is well-known, he won. Next to this building is the **Kon-Tiki Museum**, displaying the raft on which Thor Heyerdahl sailed from South America to Polynesia in 1947. Unfortunately, his theory of migration and settlement which he set out to prove with this journey turned out to be wrong; his achievement as a sailor, however, remains indisputable.

Follow **Bygdøynesvei** to get to the **Viking Ship Museum**, which displays three ships, each 20 meters long and named after the places where they were found. Such vessels served the Vikings in pre-Christian times both as transportation for their raids and expeditions and as tombs for their chiefs. The ships in the museum were used for burial, as demonstrated by the funerary objects found inside them, which are also on display. Behind this building is the **Norsk Folke-**

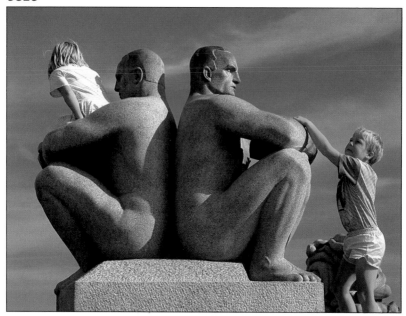

museum, an open-air museum with houses and farms arranged according to their area of origin. There are also old apothecaries, village shops and artisan workshops. In the main building there is an exhibition of household items from Sami territory (Lappland), and the original study of Henrik Ibsen. Other highlights of the museum are the stave church of Gol, dating from the 13th century, which has been rebuilt here, and the Raulandstue (14th century) from the Numedal. If you follow Huk Aveny, a bridge leads over to the island of **Dronningen**, where you can dine at the Najaden, one of the best fish restaurants in Norway. From here, you can also catch the boat back to the Rådhus.

The Vigeland Grounds

To get to ★**Frogner Park** ⑭ and the **Vigeland Grounds** that lie within it, you

Above: It's child's play to grasp Vigeland's statues – literally – in Frogner Park.

can either walk or take public transport. Allow about 25 minutes for the walk from the palace drive through the **Palace Park** and along **Wergelandsveien**, **Hegdehaugsveien** and **Bogstadveien** to the station of **Majorstuen**, which leads you along busy, lively streets lined with many old restored residences and diplomats' houses. If you opt to take the *Tunnelbana* (subway train), which leaves from behind the National Theater, get out at Majorstuen station; bus no. 11 also goes here from the square in front of the Rådhus.

Walk a little way along **Kirkevei** and you are soon at the gate which Vigeland designed as an entrance to his park. In the 1920s, the city of Oslo put this space at the artist's disposal for his life's work, which he in turn created and presented as a gift to the people of Oslo.

Vigeland was born Gustav Thomsen in southern Norway in 1869. His father, both pietistic and an alcoholic, used to beat his children on Good Friday for the simple reason that on the day when Our

Lord suffered, people on earth should suffer too. Understandably, the son ran away from home and spent the rest of his life trying to come to terms with this childhood through his sculpture, only finally to establish that it was impossible to obliterate the traces of the past and that despite all his efforts he would forever remain a stranger to such emotions as love and tenderness. Nor did periods he spent in Trondheim or Paris bring him any closer to resolving his problems.

Back in Oslo he plunged into his life's work, the park that was intended to symbolize every aspect of life. For this he personally created or designed 650 sculptures and reliefs in granite and bronze. These are presented as the **Bridge Group**, the **Fountain Group**, the **Pillar of Life**, a 17-meter monolith comprised of 121 intertwined figures, and the **Wheel of Life**. Vigeland's skill as an artist and breadth of vision are breathtaking. And his somber interpretation gives an underlying poignancy to his depictions, especially those of women and children. Thomas Hobbes' observation that man preys on man has here been captured in stone.

To the left of the entrance is the **Municipal Museum** ⑮ with documentation about the city's history; close by, the **Vigeland Museum** ⑯ preserves Vigeland's studio. Its tower preserves the urn containing the artist's ashes.

Oslo's Local Hill

Visitors to Oslo can ascend the hill of **Holmenkollen** ⑰ in true period style. The Holmenkollen train departs from behind the National Theater, and takes half an hour. On fine weekends, you have to get up very early to avoid a long wait times at the station.

More than 1,000 kilometers of cross-country ski trails extend over and around this 370-meter hill. In summer, they are used as hiking trails; in winter, most of

them are illuminated. The **Holmenkollen Ski Jump** is famous as the largest ski jump in Norway, although it is used only once a year, during the Holmenkollen Ski Festival in March. In the summer the outrun is used as an open-air swimming pool, with a floating **concert and theater stage**.

A lift runs up to the top of the jump, where there's also a restaurant. Below this is the **Ski Museum**, which illustrates the development of skis and ski equipment with a variety of exhibits. Some of Nansen's polar equipment is also on display, and there is a statue of him at the entrance to the museum.

On the way up to the jump is a monument to King Olav V, depicted on skis with his poodle, Troll. This was a present to him from the inhabitants of Oslo on his 80th birthday, as the king was an enthusiastic skier and paid regular Sunday visits to Holmenkollen.

The main road leads on uphill to Oslo's **Television Tower** *(Tryvannstårnet)* on top of the hill. From the observation deck here there's a splendid panoramic view of the city and the fjord. The same view may be obtained free of charge from the **monument to the road-building director Kråg** on Voksenkollveien.

The Artist and the Ice Princess

Of Oslo's many other museums, two are especially worth a mention. The **★Munch Museum** ⑱ at Tøyengate 53, in the east part of the city, contains the legacy of Expressionist painter Edvard Munch, including paintings, sculptures, drawings and watercolors.

West of town, reached on the E18 toward Drammen or by taking the Drammen railway to Blommenholm, is the **Henie-Onstad Center** ⑲, an important collection of international art which the figure skater and Olympic medalist Sonja Henie assembled together with her fourth husband.

SVINESUND

i Right on the E6 on the Norwegian side, tel. 69195152, open Jan 1-April 30, Mon-Sat 9 am-4 pm, May 1-31 Mon-Sat 9 am-6 pm. June 1-30 daily 9 am-6 pm, July 1-Aug 31 daily 9 am-8 pm, Sept 1-30 Mon-Sat 9 am-6 pm, Oct 1-Dec 31 Mon-Wed 9 am-4 pm.

S **Grødahls Kro & Motell**, right on the E6, tel. 69195198.

HALDEN

i Storgt. 6, tel. 69181478, opening hours as in Svinesund.

SS **Grand Hotel**, Jernbanetorget 1, tel. 69187200 (with its own golf course). **Park Hotel**, Marcus Thranesgt. 30, tel. 69184044 (good Norwegian restaurant). **S** **Fredrikahald Småhotel**, Ohmes Plass, tel. 69188222.

Fredriksten Fortress, **City Museum**: Open June 15-Aug 15 10 am-6 pm, other times 11 am-5 pm, **Rød Manor** and **Theater**, same opening hours.

FREDRIKSTAD

i In the fortress, tel. 69320330, same opening times as Svinesund.

SSS **Hotel Fontenen**, Nygaardsgt. 9/11, tel. 69300500.

CAMPING: **Fredrikstad Motel og Camping**, Torsnesvn. 16, 1630 Gamle Fredrikstad, tel. 6932-0315, cabins and rooms.

MOSS

i Tel. 69253295, same opening times as Svinesund.

SS **Hotel Refsnes Gods**, Godset 5, tel. 69270411 (tennis courts, bike rental). **S** **Mossesla Kro & Motell**, Strandgt. 27, tel. 69253131 (typical motel). *CAMPING:* **Nes-Camp**, tel. 69270176.

DRØBAK

i Tel. 64935087, same opening hours as Svinesund.

SSS **Reenskaug Hotel**, Storgt. 32, tel. 64933360 (magnificent hotel right on the fjord, excellent restaurant, golf, tennis and sailing).

Oscarsborg Fortress, open to visitors from sunrise to sunset.

JELØY ISLAND

Alby Manor (gallery), open 11am-7 pm.

OSLO

i Vestbaneplassen 1, tel. 82060100 or, from abroad, +47-22830050. Same hours as Svinesund.

Accommodation Service, at the Main Train Station, personal appointments necessary, as a fee is charged.

SSS **Grand Hotel**, Karl-Johan-Gt. 31, tel. 22429390 (old-style luxury in the heart of the city, with indoor pool). **Holmenkollen Park Hotel**, Kongesvn. 26, tel. 22922000 (great view of the city and the fjord). **Continental**, Stortingsgt. 24/26, tel. 22824000. **Scandic Crown Hotel**, Parkvn. 68, tel. 22446970 (very quiet location, great buffet).

SS **Anker Hotel**, Storgate 55, tel. 22997500 (good Norwegian restaurant). **Ambassadeur Best Western**, Camilla Collett Vn. 15, tel. 22441835 (quiet location, indoor pool). **Carlton Hotel**, Parkvn. 78, tel. 22430430 (pleasant atmosphere, comfortable rooms). **City Hotel**, Skippergt. 19, tel. 22413610. **Hotel Karl Johan**, Karl Johan Gt. 33, tel. 22427480. **Hotel Bondeheimen**, Rosenkrantzgt. 8, tel. 22429530 (central, lots of groups). **Rainbow Hotel Europa**, St. Olavsgt. 31, tel. 22209990 (at the park, a hotel for tour groups).

S **Ambiose Bed 'n' Breakfast**, Østbyfaret 9D, tel. 22278509. **Bella Vista**, Åmundvn. 11 B, tel. 22654588 (small, quiet hotel at the edge of town). **Cochs Pensjonat**, Parkvn. 25, tel. 22604836 (typical pension).

HOSTEL: **Oslo Vanderhjem Haraldsheim**, Haraldsheimvn. 4, Grefsen, tel. 22222965. *CAMPING:* **Bogstad Camp & Turistcenter**, tel. 22198565. **Ekeberg Camping**, tel. 22198568.

Bagatelle, Bygdøy Allee 3, tel. 22410052, the best, and most expensive, fish restaurant in town. **Blom**, Karl Johan Gt. 41 B, tel. 22427300, artists' hangout with great interior. **Louise**, Stranden 3, in the shopping center Aker Brygge, with interior decoration taken from an old ferry, tel. 22375450. **Najaden**, on the island of Bygdøy, tel. 22438180, nice fish restaurant with views of downtown. **King George Steakhouse**, Støget Torggt. 11, tel. 22421195, good steakhouse.

RESTAURANTS WITH VIEW/OBSERVATION DECK: **Frognerseteren**, Holmenkollenvn. 200, tel. 22143736 and **Holmenkollen**, Holmenkollenvn. 199, tel. 2214-6226, both with great Norwegian buffets.

CAFÉS: **Teatercafeen**, in the Hotel Continental, boasts a typical coffee house atmosphere. **Grand Café**, in the Grand Hotel, Ibsen's regular hangout.

Aker Brygge, shopping arcade with a number of shops under one roof. Other possibilities are around **Stortorvet** and between the **Town Hall** and **K. Johan Gate**.

Specializing in artisan work are **Norway Design**, Stortingsgate 28, Forum, Rosenkrantzgate 7 and the **Association of Applied Artists**, Møllergt. 4. All open Mon-Fri 9 am-5 pm, Sat 9 am-2 pm.

Basarhallene, behind the cathedral, open weekdays 10 am-5 pm, Sat 10 am-2 pm, ideal for fans of good arts and crafts work, but not cheap.

📷 *CENTER:* **City Hall**, open May-August Mon-Sat 9 am-5 pm, Sun noon-5 pm; September-April Mon-Sat 9 am-4 pm, Sun noon-6 pm, entrance fee charged in summer. **University Aula**, Karl Johan Gt. 47, open in July, noon-2 pm. **National Gallery**, Universitetsgt. 13, tel. 22200404, open Mon, Wed, Fri 10 am-6 pm, Sun 11 am-4 pm. **Historical Museum**, Frederiksgt. 2, open mid-May to mid-September daily except Mon 11 am-3 pm, other times noon-3 pm. **Storting**, July/August, guided tours at 10 am, 11:30 am and 1 pm. **Cathedral**, Karl Johan Gt. 11, tel. 22415374, open daily 10 am-4 pm, services Sun 11 am and 7:30 pm.

AKERSHUS: The grounds of **Akersus Fortress** are accessable from 6 am to 9 pm daily; interior open May to mid-September 10 am-4 pm, guided tours at 11 am, 1 and 3 pm. Closed May 2 & Sept 15. **Museum of Norwegian Resistance**, open Sun 11 am-4 pm and Mon-Sat 10 am-3 pm (until 4 pm in summer).

BYGDØY MUSEUM ISLAND: **Frammuseum**, tel. 22123550, open April-October 11 am-3 pm, longer in summer. **Kon-Tiki Museum**, tel. 22438050, open June-August 9:30 am-5:45 pm, other times 10:30 am-4 pm. **Viking Ship Museum**, open daily 11 am-3 pm, May-August 9 am-6 pm. **Norsk Folkemuseum**, open May 15-September 14 daily 10 am-5 pm, other times 11 am-3 pm.

OTHER AREAS: **Vigeland Grounds**, open between sunrise and sunset. **Vigelandmuseum**, west of Halvdan Svartes Gt., open May 1-October 31 daily 10 am-6 pm, other times noon-4 pm, Sun until 6 pm, closed Mon. **Ski Museum**, on Holmenkollenschantze, open May through September 10 am-5 pm, other times until 3 pm. **Tryvannstårnet Television Tower**, open May through September 10 am-5 pm, other times until 3 pm. **Munch Museum**, Tøyengt. 53. (bus 29), open June 1-September 15 daily 10 am-8 pm, other times 11 am-4 pm, Sun noon-4 pm, closed Mon. **Henie-Onstad Center**, Høvikodden (bus 151, 153 or 162) tel. 6754- 3050, open Sat and Mon 11 am-5 pm, other times 9 am-9 pm.

📷 In Oslo there are a number of golf courses; you can get details from the tourist information offices. In summer, there's a free open-air swimming pool open next to the Vigeland Grounds; in winter, the tennis courts there become skating rinks. Around Oslo, there are more than 300 kilometers of cross-country ski trails. Oslofjord is perennially popular with sailors. North of Oslo, by Ås, there are a number of marked hiking trails, with information about both nature and local culture along the way; for information, call 64940260.

📷 Late March: Oslo Holmenkollen Ski Week. Mid-June: Norwegian folk dancing Mon and Thu in the Oslo Concert House. Early August: Oslo Jazz Festival. Mid-August: Oslo Mariendalen, historic open-air theater.

🍸 Oslo's nightlife is somewhat limited in quantity. In summer, you can go out around the **Studenterlunden** and in the bars in the Aker Brygge area; in winter, you're stuck with the bars in the larger hotels along Karl Johan Gt.

➕ **Pharmacy with first-aid service,** Jernbanetorget 4B, tel. 22412482.

☎ **Post Office**, Dronnings Gt. 15, open Mon-Fri 8 am-8 pm.

Telegraph Office, Kongens Gt. 21, entrance on Prinsengt, open 24 hours.

✈ *AIR:* The new airport at Gardermoen, 47 kilometers north of downown Oslo, has replaced the old Fornebu Airport. The high-speed train "NSB Gerdermo" takes 19 minutes to get from the airport to town.

SAS Reservations Office, Oslo, tel. 64816050, **Braathens** SAFE, tel. 64826000, **Widerøe**, tel. 64817229, **Air Stord**, tel. 53403742.

TRAIN: Daily service to Trondheim, Bergen, Stavanger, Åndalsnes and Narvik (via Stockholm); for information, call NSB Personentrafikdivisjonen, Prinsengt. 7-9, tel. 81500888.

BUS: From the bus station on Schweigaardsgt. 8-10, north of the train station, there are daily buses to destinations all over the country. For information, contact NOR-WAY-Bussekspress, Schweigaardsgt. 8-10, tel. 23002440.

CIRCUMVENTING OSLO: If your are coming from the south of Sweden and want to travel on to southern Norway, you can avoid traveling through the city of Oslo by crossing the Oslofjord by ferry.

The shortest crossings are: **Moss-Horten**, departures often, trip takes only about 25 minutes; **Strömstad** (Sweden)-**Sandelfjord** (Norway), trip takes about two and a half hours. The harbor of **Larvik** is serviced directly by ferries from the Danish harbor of **Fredrikshavn**; this is a recommendable port of entry to southern Norway.

LARVIK

ℹ️ Storgate 32, tel. 33139100, June 1-August 30, 9 am-8 pm, otherwise Mon-Fri 9 am-4 pm.

🛏 ⓢⓢⓢ **Quality Grand Hotel Farris**, Storgate 38/40, tel. 33187800, private yacht harbor.

ⓢ **Holms Motell & Cafetria**, E18 Amundrød, tel. 33192480, good place to make an interim stopover.

📷 **Herrgården** with the **Larvik Museum**, open May 26-September 1, 11 am-4 pm, June 30-August 17 until 5 pm. **Navigation Museum**, open June 15-August 31, 11 am-2 pm, Sun noon-3 pm. **Tanum Church**, 7 kilometers southwest, open June 20-August 15, Mon-Fri 11 am-3 pm. **Tjølling Church**, 7 kilometers east, open in summer.

SOUTHERN NORWAY

THE COAST FROM TELEMARK TO KRISTIANSAND
NORDSJØVEGEN/STAVANGER
RYFYLKE, SULESKAR AND SETESDAL ROADS
THE TELEMARK CANAL

THE COAST FROM TELEMARK TO KRISTIANSAND

West of **Larvik ❶**, the E18 winds its way through the forested hills of the province of **Telemark**. The landscape here is dominated by pine and fir forests nestled between eroded, yet nonetheless steep, fingers of rock; the few farms here have to make do with the scanty patches of arable land in the narrow valleys. In this part of southern Norway, mining the area's wealth of mineral resources and forestry have been the main sources of revenue, and activity, for the population.

Brevik ❷ may even be proud of the massive silo of the *Norcem* cement works that looms up out of the trees beside the E18. Its limestone galleries, as much as 200 meters below sea level, are a tourist attraction in the summer. Locals, however, probably prefer it when visitors turn their attention to the wooden houses of this 150-year-old harbor town on the Eidangerfjord, particularly under the guidance of the "historic" night watchman.

When the Brevik Bridge, 40 meters high, was completed in 1962, bearing the

Preceding pages: Reflections – rock formations at Elkeland. Left: Dizzying view of Tysefjord from the Preikestolen.

E18 across the Frierfjord, the ferry landing of **Stathelle** more or less sank into oblivion. The town has become even sleepier ever since the new Grenland Bridge and adjoining tunnel were completed in 1996, which has shifted the main flow of traffic still farther to the north. Vacationers, however, are aware of the attractions and variety of the Skagerrak Riviera, and are happy to take the small coast roads, if they are not already traveling by boat.

Langesund ❸, which was known throughout Europe for its shipyard as early as the Middle Ages, and later became an equally important export harbor for lumber for construction, now offers its extensive harborage to pleasure craft. It isn't only the coast that offers inviting routes for boat trips; skippers can also turn their craft up the 105-kilometer Telemark Canal into the interior.

Less than 30 kilometers further on is **Kragerø ❹**, Langesund's lovely rival, which painter Edvard Munch described in 1909 as "the pearl of the coastal resorts." Its tourist office has adopted this quote as the town's slogan, and all six of the antique shops – in a place with a population of 10,000 – are doing very well out of it. Fanning out from the protected harbor, excursion boats distribute crowds of visitors across the offshore skerries.

Particularly attractive is the island of **Jomfruland** ❺, 7.5 kilometers long and no more than 1 kilometer wide, and covered with the debris of a terminal moraine: highlights include nature reserves, bird sanctuaries, and a lighthouse dating from 1839. Agricultural methods of two centuries ago are documented at the museum in the old estate of **Berg Kragerø**, while the German fortifications from World War II in **Trolldal** ❻ are a reminder of more recent history. In the interior, in the old parish of **Bamble** ❼ near the E18, there are a number of abandoned open mines such as **Ødergårdens Verk**, where until the beginning of the 20th century as many as 800 laborers mined the apatite deposits.

In the neighboring *fylke* of Aust-Agder the little white-painted town of **Risør** ❽ is particularly proud of the fact that all of its houses are still made of wood. The current city watchman regales visitors with eloquent descriptions of this picturesque town's heydays, in the 16th century, when the timber trade with the Netherlands brought prosperity, or in the 19th century, the era of the sailing ships. Another 20 kilometers southwest is **Tvedestrand** ❾, another contender for the unofficial title of most attractive coastal resort. Today boasting 2,000 residents, it once served as the harbor for three communities in the hinterland, and until the early 18th century iron was still also being shipped from the **Næs Iron and Steel Works** here (Næs Jernverk, 2 kilometers west of the E18). In operation until 1880, these works are now a museum. Even smaller, and only accessible by boat, is **Lingør** ❿. Spread out over four islands, this car-free settlement of little wooden houses won the award of "Best-Kept Village in Europe" in 1990, and ever since, thousands of tourists have been coming here every summer to verify this for themselves.

Arendal ⓫, the region's capital, boasts shopping streets, hospitals, schools and

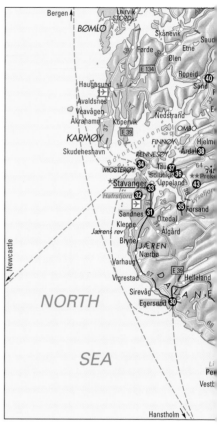

the only *vinmonopolet* for miles around. Almost all the old houses were destroyed in fires, although the district of **Tyholmen** on the waterfront is being rather laboriously cultivated as a historic wooden house district. On its south side, overlooking one of the two tourist harbors, stands a plain, nearly unadorned wooden building dating from 1812, impressive by virtue of its size, which became the **Town Hall** in 1844. The picturesque narrow bay of **Pollen** is more popular, but Arendalers take the precaution of warning visiting seafarers who are sensitive to noise that on warm summer nights the place can be lively until the wee hours, as there are numerous restaurants and bars along the quay. The **Aust Agder Museum** in the

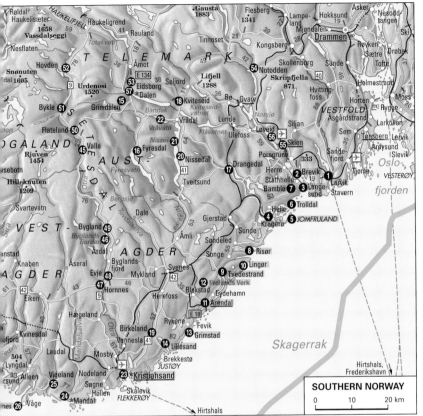

north part of town gives a detailed picture of the eventful past of the town and the surrounding area. The era of the sailing ships, iron ore mining and processing, and in particular the production of iron stoves, brought the area renown. In **Stallen** (on the R42 toward Evje), **Frolands Verk ⑫**, an iron and steelworks built in 1765 with a Rococo administrative building, is now a museum.

Grimstad ⑬ is attractive not only for fans of the playwright Henrik Ibsen, who began an apprenticeship here as a chemist in 1844 when he was 15. Against the backdrop of the red boatsheds by the harbor and the white wooden houses of the town center rises the picturesque hill topped with Norway's second-largest

wooden church (1881). Little appears to have changed since Ibsen's day, and the atmosphere of the period is also very successfully recreated in the **museum** dedicated to him.

Continuing west, the E18 runs along the coast for short stretches between Grimstad and **Lillesand**, thus offering even passing visitors a glimpse of the region's bewildering scenic variety: wooded bays, green, stony islands and bare skerries. This is summer vacationland for countless holiday-makers, with a coastline so indented that everyone can find a secluded spot. Foreign visitors should remember that Norwegians value their privacy and follow the unwritten rules which dictate that people maintain a

certain distance, even in the great out-doors. The beauty of the interior, where the forests and lakes are populated by elks, red deer and beavers, is best explored on foot or by canoe. Tourism in the area around the R41 (*Telemarksvegen*) between the coast at Kristiansand and the Telemark Canal at Kviteseid is still in its infancy, much to the satisfaction of anyone who loves solitude and nature; the only real visitor attractions are small museums created out of historic farms (**Grimdalen** ⑮, **Fyresdal** ⑯, **Drangedal** ⑰ and **Kviteseid Bygdetun** ⑱) or local industries, such as peat litter production near **Birkeland** ⑲ and stone products in **Nessedal** ⑳.

Visitors can embark on a boat to explore the lakes of **Nisser** ㉑ and **Vråvatn** ㉒, or you can enjoy the scenery and locks from the excursion boat *Fram*. Knowledgeable locals lead visitors on walking "beaver safaris" or offer courses in how to

Above and right: The island world of the skerry coast, a yachting paradise in the summer.

use traditional tools to build a real Norwegian log cabin. Hiking trails in the hills west of the lakes are another attractive option.

*Kristiansand

Although he founded this town by the place where the Otro flows into the Skagerrak in 1641, the Danish king Christian IV did not live to see **Kristiansand** ㉓ flourish. Not even its designation as a garrison town in 1666, when **Christiansholm Fortress** was built, nor the Bishop of Stavanger's moving here in 1682, which meant the town acquired its **cathedral**, ushered in true prosperity. For this, Kristiansand had to wait until the age of industrialization 300 years later, when it was brought into the national traffic network.

Today, Kristiansand is the undisputed economic center of southern Norway. Ferries from Denmark (Hirthals) provide a direct link with central Europe, and the rail connection, the E18 and 39 and the

Southern Norway

good route north via the Setesdal on the R9 make this a good location for trade and industry.

But don't assume that this means that there's little here for tourists. Within the geometric grid of streets that comprises the old town center of **Kvadraturen**, the eastern district, **Posebyen**, consists almost entirely of original wooden houses that still evoke a 17th-century look, even if most of them are actually of more recent vintage. The fortress has been rebuilt and is picturesquely located between two yacht harbors. Anglers enthuse about the Otra with its abundant fish. The **Botanical Gardens**, the **Natural History Museum**, medieval **Oddernes Kirke** and the **Vest-Agder Fylkesmuseum** are all on the east bank of the Otra and are easy to reach with one of the free bikes which the tourist office loans out. **Dyreparken**, the zoo, located on the E18, is known for its real pack of wolves; also well known **Kardemomme By**, a play town for children. One of the main motors of industrial development, the **Setesdal railway**,

which from 1895 on transported ore from the nickel mines of Evje to Falconbridge Nikkelverk in Kristiansand, is already a museum piece: in summer, fans of historic railways can board it for the 5-kilometer stretch it still operates (Grovane - Beihølen, north of Vennesla).

ON THE NORDSJØVEG AND THE E39 THROUGH THE FAR SOUTH

On its way from Kristiansand to Stavanger (about 250 kilometers) the "fast" E39 meets up several times with the "slow" variation along the coast: the **Nordsjøveg** tourist route.

*Mandal ㉔ is one of the best of the many attractive towns along the south coast. The **Mandalselva** separates the harbor and industrial districts on the east side from the town of white wooden houses nestling under the steep cliffs on the west side. The large Empire Church (1821) and some important business houses dating from the 18th century, when the business of exporting salmon

and wood to England was flourishing, still grace this southernmost town of Norway. The rest of the houses sport the traditional exterior covering of white-painted wooden paneling.

Immediately to the south is the 800-meter sandy beach of **Sjøsanden**, perfect for swimming and a rarity on this rocky skerry coast. The main attraction here is the annual shellfish festival in August, when the largest crab buffet in the world is set out in the streets of the town.

In **Vigeland** ㉕, where the sculptor Gustav Vigeland grew up, the R460 branches off from the E39 to **Kap Lindesnes** ㉖, the southernmost point of Norway and the border between the Skagerrak and the North Sea. There's been a navigational light on this rocky tongue of land since 1656. Some 50,000 visitors flock here every year, to be informed by a sign that the distance from

Above: Not a bad life – a picnic on the beach. Right: The old harbor of Stavanger, guarded by the cathedral tower.

here to the North Cape by road is still 2,518 kilometers.

The neighboring peninsula of **Lista** ㉗, which is blessed with a little more topsoil, was already densely populated in the Stone Age. During the Bronze Age the main route along which bronze was imported ran through this area. Rock drawings with depictions of ships in **Penne** ㉘, as well as burial mounds with significant funerary objects, are testimony to the wealth that flowed in as a result of sea trade with the rest of Europe. The **Fedafjord** runs so far inland that at its end, at **Kvinesdal**, the coast road meets up with the E39. Along this whole stretch there are splendid views of the water and the steep slopes around it; here, newcomers to Norway get their first sight of a "real" fjord.

In the protected harbor of **Flekkefjord** ㉙, the wooden houses in the small neighborhood of **Hollenderbyen** are a reminder of the importance of trade with the Netherlands in the 16th and 17th centuries. Here, the Nordsjøvegen and E39 once again go their separate ways. The Nordsjøvegen passes through the magnificent rocky landscape of **★Dalane** on the way to the centuries-old harbor of **Egersund** ㉚ (with a ferry connection to Hanstholm, Denmark), then continues on through the lush green pastureland of **Jæren**. The moraine soil of this area was already being intensively cultivated in the Bronze and Iron Ages, as well as in the days of the Vikings; its sandy subsoil is responsible for the gravel and white dune beaches that extend for miles along the coast.

Gently rolling, predominantly agricultural, this countryside is ideal for bike tours; small wonder, indeed, that bicycles have been produced in **Sandnes** ㉛ since 1880. Visitors can also rent a *sykkel* in order to explore, for example, the **Kongepark** leisure center, the large **Rogaland Arboretum** and the site of the battle at **Hafrsfjord** ㉜, where Harald Fairhair es-

tablished his sovreignty over the Norwegian provinces in 872. From Jæren, there are also numerous small museums, galleries, prehistoric sites and beaches that can be reached by bike.

*STAVANGER

At the center of an area where human settlement extends back for thousands of years, **Stavanger** ❸❸ was an excellent location for the bishopric that was established in 1125; 120 years later, this town on the **Vågen**, a harbor bay narrowing to a point, received its official town charter. From 1682 to 1686, however, both of these honors were temporarily lost to Kristiansand. The town's Anglo-Norman style **cathedral** is dedicated to St. Swithin, a Bishop of Winchester. The three-aisled Romanesque nave dates from the 12th century; the long, High Gothic choir with two flanking towers was added at the end of the 13th century. The narrow gray building overlooks the lively marketplace and the Vågan, whose waters teem with excursion boats, supply ships and visiting pleasure craft. On the north side of this harbor are the oldest parts of town, which were often ravaged by fire through its history.

Around the hill of **Valberg**, crowned with a fire tower, are grouped numerous bars, restaurants, hotels, modern shops and offices. On the south side of the harbor, by contrast, some 150 cozy and very well-kept little wooden houses from the mid-19th century line the narrow streets of **Gamle (Old) Stavanger**. The only **Canning Museum** in the world (*Hermetikkmuseet*) is very appropriate in this nostalgic setting.

It was, in fact, the abundant supplies of fish, and the business of canning it, that were responsible for Stavanger's growth from the 19th century into the 20th. Since 1971, however, more of its wealth has stemmed from the oil platforms 170 kilometers away in the North Sea. Oil revenues have enabled Stavanger to devote generous sums to preserving its past and to finance new building projects.

With 100,000 inhabitants, including a large population of foreigners, the town has excellent art galleries and museums devoted to archaeology, book printing, road building and telecommunications. For a long time there have been plans to build a super-modern oil museum, but future tourists may well take helicopters out to on-site drilling rig museums in the Ekofisk Field, instead.

As the prosperous capital of the *fylke* of **Rogaland**, Stavanger can afford excellent traffic connections around the **Boknafjord**. Hydrofoils and ferries cross the waters, but are rendered partly superfluous by kilometers-long tunnels as much as 230 meters below sea level (the **Rennfast** stretch of the E39 to Bergen has provided a fast road link to 13th-century **Utstein Monastery** on the island of **Mosterøy ㉞** and high bridges.

Above: The old wooden church of Årdal, Rogaland, features decoratively painted walls.
Right: A route with a difference – the Telemark Canal between Skien and Dalen.

THE NEW ROADS: RYFYLKE, SULESKAR AND SETESDAL

First opened in 1965, the **Ryfylke Road** (R13) bills itself as a tourist route with many sights between the Lysefjord in the south and the point where it joins the E134 at Røldal. From Stavanger, you reach it by taking the car ferry to Tau. Near the road here are well-preserved ruins from the Bronze and Iron Ages: a prehistoric village has been excavated at **Forsand ㉟**; between Jøpeland and Tau are the rock drawings of **Solbakk ㊱**; in **Tau ㊲**, a *kultursti* forms a path to prehistoric excavations; finds at **Årdal ㊳** include Viking boathouses; and the largest Iron-Age cemetery is in **Ritland ㊴** (near Suldal). Farms dating from the 16th century, some growing fruit (such as **Vigatunet**, in the area near **Sand ㊵**) document historic agricultural practices.

In the 19th century, the famous salmon river of **Suldalslågen** was flanked by exclusive hotels for the English "salmon lords." In the **Salmon Studio**, a salmon ladder at **Sand** 🐾, visitors can watch through a glass wall as the popular fish travel on their journey upriver.

In **Suldal** 🐾, on the guided tour of **Kvilldal** 🐾, Norway's largest power station, visitors learn about the control of the vast masses of water on the Ryflkeheiene in the reservoir of **Blåsjø** and about the massive **Ulla-Førre** hydroelectric project. This project is dubious from an economic point of view, and definitely harmful from an ecological one.

Access roads to the power station buildings did, however, help to open up the fjell areas between the Ryfylke region and the Setesdal to hikers and skiers. In these uplands alone, crisscrossed with marked walking trails, there are 70 huts belonging to hiking associations.

Steep-sided *****Lysefjord**, 40 kilometers long, can only be properly explored by boat. For a more immediate experience of the precipitous cliffs, however, take the marked trail from the parking lot at the Prekestolhytta up to the ****Prekestolen** 🐾 or "pulpit" (a 20-kilometer drive from Tau via Jørpeland; allow 3-4 hours for the hike there and back). From the viewing platform here, which has no safety railings, there is a sheer drop of some 600 meters.

Past **Lysebotn** 🐾, at the inner end of the fjord, a car ferry (reservation advised) runs twice a day over to the start of a breathtaking mountain road with 27 hairpin bends climbing up into the beautiful highland landscape; from here you can continue east into the Setesdal. The **Suleskar Road** cut the route from Oslo to Stavanger down to 489 kilometers, enabling hikers to easier access, especially since there is also an express bus service in summer, the *Suleskarekspressen.*

In **Valle** 🐾, this bus line enters the Setesdal. In 1939, a through road, the R9, was completed between Haukeligrend in the north and Kristiansand on the south coast; this mainly follows the Otra valley. Some of the infamous, arduous trade

Southern Norway

routes of days gone by through the Setesdal, as well as east and west over the fjell heights into the adjacent valleys between **Fyresdal** (see p. 60) and **Sirdalen**, are today used as hiking trails.

Present-day Setesdal dwellers are trying to entice tourists to stop off here instead of just passing through. Scenic highlights of the Setesdal include the long resevoir, **Byglandsfjorden** 🐾; the impressive cliffs between **Valle** and **Bykle**; and the bare fjell heights of the *****Setesdalheiene** with their panoramic views of mountains, flecked with snow even in summer, and the breathtaking descent to the Haukeli Road. In **Hornnes** 🐾, the **Setesdal Mineral Park** in the former copper and nickel mines is worth a visit, and the **Mineralsti** trail from **Evje** 🐾 leads past disused mines.

Bygland 🐾, **Flateland** 🐾 (**Rygnestad**) and **Bykle** 🐾 (**Huldreheimen**) have museums documenting the rural culture of past ages. Tiny **Bykle Kirke** dates from the 17th century, although the painted roses that adorn it are from the

19th century. **Hovden ⑫**, in the north, is a popular base for hikers and skiers.

THE TELEMARK CANAL

Norway's first export, going back to the Vikings, was stone from **Eidsborg ㊱** in the Telemark. From this secluded mountain village with its tiny stave church, it was transported to the sea over water: 500 meters down from the village and 72 meters above sea level is **Bandak Lake**, 25 kilometers long, which continues as the **Kviteseidvatnet** and **Flåvatnet** to a point only 20 kilometers from the **Norsjø**. The southern end of this joins up with the Friersfjord and is thus also linked to the Skagerrak.

This water route, however, has only been fully navigable since 1892. 1861 saw the construction of locks at **Skien ㊿** and **Løveid ㊱** in order to create a transportation route between the sea and the northern end of the Norsjø, where the paper factory at **Notodden ㊴** was built in 1872. However, another 14 locks were necessary in order to get boats up to a height of 72 meters; this allowed early tourists, who were just starting to come into the area, to travel by steamship to **Dalen ㊼** to stay in that town's magnificent, exclusive, Swiss-style **hotel**. From there, horse-drawn carriages bore them along the Haukeli Road to Bergen.

Today a nostalgic boat trip along the **★Telemark Canal** has again become an attractive way of seeing the splendid landscape of the Telemark region; private boats are also allowed on the canal. The Telemark Canal, in fact, is one of the few interior waterways in Scandinavia which can be explored by boat – the Göta Canal in Sweden is another – since none of Norway's rivers is completely navigable. Although the canal is only open in the summer, the area offers plenty of other attractions, including several skiing centers, which can be enjoyed all year round from the Hotel Dalen.

SOUTHERN NORWAY

BREVIK / STATHELLE / LANGESUND

ℹ Brevik, at the Korvetten Hotel, tel. 35570200, June 1-August 30, 9 am-8 pm, other times Mon-Fri 9 am-4 pm. **Langesund**, tel. 35965320.

▬ $$ **Korvetten Hotel**, Brevik, tel. 35571166. **Quality Skægården Hotell og Badepark**, Stathelleveien 35, 3970 Langesund, tel. 35973011, with luxurious indoor and outdoor pools. **Langesund Bad Gjestegård**, Badeveien 5, 3970 Langesund, tel. 35973529, on the sea, also cabins and camping.

$ **Fjellstad Gård**, Hyttesenter Fjellstad, 3960 Stathelle, tel. 35972618, open May-September, cabins. **Rognstranda Camping**, 3960 Stathelle, tel. 35973911, directly on Rognfjord, sand beach, cabins. **Langesund Bad**, Badeveien 5, 3970 Langesund, tel. 35793529.

KRAGERØ / RISØR

ℹ Kragerø: tel. 35982388. Risør: 37152270, 37150855.

▬ $$ **Victoria Hotel**, P.A. Heuchsgt. 31, 3770 Kragerø tel. 35981066. **Villa Bergland**, Kragerøveien 73, tel. 35980000, located 300 meters from the sea, apartments. **Det Lille Hotel**, 4950 Risør, tel. 37151495, this small place only has two rooms. **Jegertunet Hotell**, Øysang, 4990 Søndeland, tel. 37154690. **Risør Hotell**, Tangengt. 16, 4950 Risør, tel. 37150700.

$ **Furumo Gjesthus**, Sirisvei 13, 4950 Risør, tel. 37153234. **Ferieleiligheter Øya, Aud og Reidar Risøy**, Galeioddveien 19, 3770 Kragerø, tel. 35980939, apartments, charter boats for trips. **Kragerø Sportell, Konferanssenter, Vandrerhjem**, Lovisenbergvn. 20, 3770 Kragerø, tel. 35983333, open February-November.

ARENDAL

ℹ Postboks, tel. 37022193, June 1-August 30, 9 am-8 pm, other times Mon-Fri 9 am-4 pm.

▬ $$$ **Clarion Tyholmen Hotel**, Teaterplassen, tel. 37026800, golf course and bike rentals. Scandic **Hotel Phønix Arendal**, Friergangen 1, 4800 Arendal, tel. 37025160, economical summer prices.

$$ **Arendal Hotell**, Vestregate 11, 4800 Arendal, tel. 37025300. **E18 Hotellet**, Harebakken, on the E18, tel. 37036200.

$ **Breidablikk Gjestegård**, Tromsøya, 4818 Fœrvik, tel. 37085127.

🏛 **Town Hall**, visitors allowed during office hours. **Aust-Adgar Museum**, open Mon-Fri 9 am-3 pm, Sat 9 am-1 pm, Sun noon-3 pm.

GRIMSTAD

📇 Postboks, 4890 Grimstad, tel. 37044041, June 1-August 30, 9 am-8 pm, other times Mon-Fri 9 am-4 pm.

🛏 💲💲 **Helmeshus Hotel**, Vesterled 23, 4890 Grimstad, tel. 37041022. **Strand Hotel Fevik**, Fevik, tel. 37047322. **Grimstad Hotell**, Kirkegt. 3, 4890 Grimstad, tel. 37258566, historical building in the center of town. **Sørlandet Hotell og Kurssenter**, Televn. 5, 4890 Grimstad, tel. 37090500, apartments.

💲 **Ekely Gjestgivergård**, Fevik, tel. 37047149. **Skotevig Maritime Senter**, 4770 Høvåg, tel. 37274600, cabins, apartments, beach, fishing and diving center, boat trips. **Moysand Camping**, Grefstad, 4890 Grimstad, tel. 37040978, on the beach, cabins. **Marivold Camping**, Postboks 297, 4891 Grimstad, tel. 37044623, open mid-May to late August, cabins. **Bagatell Camping**, 4870 Fevik, tel. 37047467, on the sea, cabins. **Morvigsanden Camping**, Stølevn. 25, 4890 Grimstad, tel. 37043636, open July-August, 5 kilometers from Grimstad, sand beach good for kids, cabins.

🏛 **Ibsen House**, open May 15-September 15, 10 am-3 pm.

KRISTIANSAND

📇 Gyldenløvesgt. 31, tel. 38026065, June 1-August 30, 9 am-8 pm, other times Mon-Fri 9 am-4 pm.

🛏 💲💲💲 **Hotel Caledonien**, Vestre Strandgt. 7, tel. 38029100, right on the beach. 💲💲 **Ernst Park Hotel**, Rådhusgt. 2, tel. 38028600, quiet downtown hotel. **Hotel Bondeheimen**, Kirkegt. 15, 4611 Kristiansand, tel. 38024440, small hotel located in the town center. 💲 **Ansgar Sommerhotell**, Fr. Franssons Vn. 4, tel. 38043900, open early June to early August.

YOUTH HOSTEL: **Tangen**, Skansen 8, 4610 Kristiansand, tel. 38028310, open January 15-December 15, east of town center.

🏛 **Cathedral Church**, open July and August, Mon-Fri 9 am-2 pm. **Oddums Church** open Mon-Fri 9 am-noon, **Vest Agder Museum**, **Natural History Museum**, open June 20-August 20, weekdays 10 am-6 pm, May 19-September 8, Sun noon-6 pm. **Zoo, Botanical Gardens**, May-October 9 am-7 pm, other times 10 am-3 pm. Free bicycles are available to visitors at the Tourist Information Office.

MANDAL

📇 Adolf Tidemandsgt. 2, 4500 Mandal, tel. 38278300.

🛏 💲💲 **First Hotel Solborg**, Nesevn. 1, 4500 Mandal, tel. 38266666, low summer prices, lovely setting somewhat above the town. 💲 **Tregde Feriesenter**, Tregde, 4500 Mandal, tel. 38268800, 8 kilometers from Mandal, apartments. **Kløbmandsgaarden Vandrerhjem**, Store Elvegate 57, 4500 Mandal, tel. 38261276, cozy wooden house in the center of town. **Sjøsanden Feriesenter**, Postboks 471, 4501 Mandal, tel. 38261419, long sand beach near the woods, cabins.

STAVANGER

📇 Postboks 11, tel. 51859200, June 1-August 30, 9 am-8 pm, other times Mon-Fri 9 am-4 pm.

🛏 💲💲💲 **Radisson SAS Hotel**, Løkkevn. 26, tel. 51567000. **Victoria Hotel**, Skansegt. 1, tel. 51867000. 💲💲 **Grand Hotel**, Klubbgt. 3, tel. 51895800. **Radisson SAS Globetrotter Hotel**, Lagårdvn. 61, tel. 51528500.

HOSTEL: **Stavanger Vandrerhjem Mosvangen**, Henrik Ibsen Gt. 21, tel. 51872900.

🍴 **Jans Mats & Vinhus**, Breitorget, tel. 51524502, best place in town. **Galeien Bistro**, Hundvågvn. 27, tel. 51549144, good fish restaurant.

🏛 **Cathedral Church**, open May 15-September 15, weekdays 9 am-7 pm, Sun 1-6 pm, other times daily except Sun, 10 am-3 pm. **Canning Museum**, Østre Strandgt. 88, open June 15-August 15, Tue, Thu 11 am-4 pm, other times the first Sun in the month. **Utstein Monastery**, on the R1 toward Bergen, open May 1-October 31, daily 1-4 pm. **Stavanger Museum**, Musegt. 16, and **Stavanger Maritime Museum**, Nedre Strandgt. 17/19, both open June 15-August 15, daily 11 am-3 pm, other times Sun 11 am-4 pm.

🚢 There are several rapid ships a day that travel to Bergen by way of Haugesund; for information, contact Partederiet Flaggruten ANS, Postboks 2005, 5024 Bergen, tel. 55238780.

HORNNES / EVJE

📇 Evje, Postboks, Evje, tel. 37931400, June 1-August 30, 9 am-8 pm.

🛏 💲💲 **Dolen Hotell**, Evje, tel. 37930200, only hotel in town. CAMPING: **Hornnes Camping**, Hornnes, tel. 37930305. **Odden Camping**, Evje, tel. 37930603.

🏛 **Setesdal Mineral Park** and **Mineral Museum**.

🎫 Early July sees Evje's large mineral congress and trade fair.

DALEN / VINJE

📇 Postboks, Dalen, tel. 35077065.

🛏 **Dalen Hotell**, 3880 Dalen, tel. 35077000. **Vinje Hotel Park**, 3890 Ytre Vinje, tel. 35071300. **Groven Camping og Hyttergrend**, Ytre Vinje, tel. 35071421.

🚶 Telemark Canal Tours: May 11-September 15, service between Skien and Dalen, Wed, Fri and Sat from Skien to Dalen, Thu, Sat and Sun in the opposite direction. For information, contact Turisttrafik, Postboks 2813, 3702 Skien, tel. 35530300.

FROM OSLO VIA THE HARDANGERVIDDA TO BERGEN

SOUTHERN ROUTE:
OSLO – HAUGESUND – BERGEN

NORTHERN ROUTE:
HØNEFOSS – GOL – EIDFJORD – BERGEN

From Oslo to Bergen

Vidda means plateau or large area of highland, and the ***Hardangervidda** is the largest plateau in Europe. It extends over some 7,500 square kilometers, at an average altitude of 1,300 meters, and centers around the national park of the same name, which, measuring more than 3,400 square kilometers, is the largest in Scandinavia. The glaciers of the Ice Age made their mark here in the undulating surface of the land, cleft with bare rocks, countless lakes, stony areas of moraine. In the northern part of the region, the Hardangerjøkel (*jøkel* means glacier) exists to commemorate the area's glacial past. It's often foggy and rainy up on the barren plateau; even summer is no guarantee against occasional snowfall. Inhabiting this wilderness of moss and lichen are some 40,000 reindeer.

In the Neolithic period, when the climate was warmer than it is today, early settlers probably cultivated land and livestock in these highlands. In recent centuries, however, the land has presented a hostile aspect to both settlers and travelers. Still, some hardy hunters, herdsmen and traders braved privations and discomfort to fight their way across

Preceding pages: Summer night over Bergen's Bryggen. Left: A young fisherman proudly displays the day's catch.

this mountainous barrier between eastern and western Norway.

Even today, the main transportation arteries avoid, or skirt, the Hardangervidda: the E134 runs south of it, the R13 west, and the R40 east. Only in the north did stubborn 19th-century Norwegians start construction of the railway line that linked Oslo with Bergen in 1909. Today, the R7 also crosses the *vidda*; unlike the train, this road makes a southern arc around the Hardangerjøkul in the western fjord region.

Today, these routes give some 25,000 nature-lovers and hikers seeking to get away from civilization access to the bleak and challenging beauties of the Hardangervidda's 1,700 kilometers of hiking trails and 50 huts. Thanks to gravel roads and boats operating on some of the lakes, people can now travel into isolated regions in relative comfort.

Still, allow 5 to 8 days to cross the *vidda*'s vast expanse; the journey requires considerable staying power, but doesn't present many steep ascents, apart from the peaks of ***Hårteigen** ❶ (1,690 meters) or the ***Hardangerjøkul** ❷ (1,600 meters). The western edge of the *vidda*, where steep, overgrown slopes drop sharply toward the Hardangerfjord, are best taken as descents at the end of the trip.

Map pp. 74-75, Info pp. 90-91
71

THE SOUTHERN ROUTE:
OSLO – HAUGESUND – BERGEN

Kongsberg

From Oslo, the E18 and E134 run to the old mining area of **Kongsberg ❸**, at the southern edge of the Hardangervidda. Christian IV of Denmark founded this town after he had opened up silver mining here in 1624, bringing in German mining experts to advise him. Early prosperity brought the town's population up to 10,000 in the 18th century, which made it, at that time, the second-largest city in Norway. Kongsberg's Baroque church, designed by mining foreman J.A. Stuckenbrock and built between 1740 and 1761, is one of the largest in the country, seating 2,400 people. The former smelting works by the Lågen has today been converted into a **Mining and Coin Museum**. There has been no active mining in Kongsberg since 1959, but in **Saggrenda ❹**, 7 kilometers further west on the E134, tourists can enter one of the old shafts, the **Kongens Gruve**, 2,300 meters across and 350 meters deep.

The R40 follows the eastern edge of the Hardangervidda from Kongsberg in the south to Geilo in the north. Following the abandoned railway line and the flow of the Lågen, which rises on the *vidda*, it runs through the magnificent landscape of **Numedal**. **Rollag ❺** boasts a stave church dating from the 13th century; in the 15th and 16th centuries it was rebuilt and fitted with windows. The stave church at **Nore ❻** dates back to the 12th century, although its cruciform plan was a later, 18th-century addition. **Uvdal's ❼** stave church also dates from the 12th century, but the west portal is all that remains today of the original old building.

The northern extension of this valley was one of the poorest regions of Norway

Right: Storehouses on stilts (stabbur) like these go back a long way.

well into the 20th century. Here dwelt the cattle dealers and peddlers Knut Hamsun described in one of his novels; with hard-earned funds gained from peddling, they built up small herds of cattle which grazed on the Hardangervidda in the summer and were sold again in the autumn. Today, at a height of more than 1,000 meters, a few skiing centers have been developed, bringing the inhabitants noticeable prosperity. At the end of the R40, in **Ustedal**, you reach Geilo (see p. 81).

Through the Valleys of the Telemark to Heddal

Taking the E134 after Kongsberg, you pass through Notodden, a town dominated by heavy electrical industry, to ***Heddal ❽**, which boasts the largest **stave church** in the world. Begun in the 12th century, dedicated to the Virgin Mary in the mid-13th century, it had, by the 14th century, already been rebuilt. Originally, stave churches were built with a small ambulatory and were windowless apart from small ventilation slits. In these ambulatories, where the congregation gathered during the intervals in services that could last for as long as ten hours, the townspeople negotiated business deals, conducted local politics, or sealed marriage contracts. A small hole in the wall of the choir in the inner part of the church enabled lepers, who were excluded from the service, to participate indirectly from the ambulatory. To create more space, almost all the ambulatories were incorporated into the interior of the churches between the 14th and 17th centuries; in Heddal as in many other churches, you can still clearly see where they were from the shorter distance between the staves of the outer walls. A special feature at Heddal, however, is the 13th-century **door frame** adorned with a wealth of woodcarvings of animal and plant motifs. Inside the church, impressive features in-

From Oslo to Bergen

clude 14th-century **frescoes** and a carved **bishop's chair** from the same period. The windows were not added until restoration work in the 19th century, when the church was practically rebuilt. Across the road from the church is a reconstruction of its **bell tower**, while nearby there is a small **district museum**.

Fifteen kilometers away is **Sauland ⑨**, a pretty little village at the point where the **Tuddalsdal** joins intersects with Heddal. From here, a narrow dirt road leads to **Tuddal ⑩** (25 kilometers). Six kilometers away, the **Høyfjellhotell** is the starting point for tours into the **Gausta Region**. The ***Gaustatoppen ⑪**, the highest peak south of the Hardangervidda (1,881 meters), commands remarkable views over southern Norway. The ski season here lasts into July; there are also numerous marked hiking trails. From Rjukan, hikers can take the R37 and continue by boat over the Møsvatn to reach the center of the Hardangervidda.

Seljord ⑫ on the E134, at the northwest end of the lake of the same name, is a starting point for expeditions to the **Lifjell**, where the highest peak is the **Gyrannat** (1,550 meters), popular with skiers. In Seljord itself, **St. Olav's Church** is worth a visit: it dates from 1180 and contains the oldest altar in Norway, which goes back to the period before the Reformation and was probably made in Germany.

Detour to Dalen

Little **Morgedal ⑬**, also on the E134, was home to the inventor of ankle bindings for skis. In **Høydalsmo**, the R45 branches off toward Dalen. Before you get to **Dalen** itself you pass the **stave church of Eidsborg ⑭**, which is dedicated to St. Nicholas of Bari. By the 17th century this church was already in such a state of disrepair that carved planks from the stave church of Lårdal (which no longer exists) had to be used to rebuild it; the wall paintings were added in this period as well. A few hundred yards north of the stave church is the start of a walking trail to the rockfall of **Ravnejuvet**, an hour away. The road serpentines at a perilous angle down to Dalen: it has 7 bends with a 12 meter radius, and a gradient of 15 percent. The best view is to be had 250 meters or so before the first bend. ***Dalen **, on the picturesque **Bandaksvatn**, marks one end of the **Telemark Canal**, which runs from Skien to Dalen. Until the Bergen railway was opened the journey to Dalen formed a substantial part of the route from Oslo to Bergen; after Dalen this continued via Røldal, Odda and the Hardangerfjord. Today the trip through the Telemark Canal is a popular excursion which takes around 10 hours one way by motorboat (see p. 66).

On the Southern Edge of the Hardangervidda

Today **Åmot ⑯**, on the E134, is the capital of the largest district of Telemark, **Ytre Vinje ⑰**. In around 1200, at the time of King Sverre, Vinje was the region's ecclesiastical and hence the administrative center. The church of 1796 is still standing on the foundation beams of an old stave church; excavations beneath this unearthed the oldest church book in Norway. From **Haukeligrend** the E134 continues as the Haukeli Road toward Haugesund, while the R9 branches off to run down through the Setesdal to Kristiansand.

The **Haukeli Road**, opened in 1866, is one of the finest roads through the mountains of southern Norway. Unfortunately, several lay-bys with spectacular views have been sacrificed to recent road improvements, but the safety of the road has increased as a result. From Haukeligrend it winds its way up onto the **Haukelifjell**, which starts at **Botn**. The road then continues through numerous tunnels to **Haukelisæter ⑱**, a tourist resort at the end of the Ståvatnet. Not only a winter sports center, this town is also a starting point for hikes into Hardangervidda National Park. At **Mannevatn**, you can leave your car for several days at a time if you want to go off on a hike; the parking lot is signposted. The old road reaches its highest point at the old **Dyrskar Pass** (1,148 meters), the watershed between the Atlantic and the Skagerrak, which command an overwhelming panoramic view. Unfortunately, the old road is not always open and you may be obliged to negotiate the pass through the new 6-kilometer tunnel instead.

From here, the E134 descends a good 700 meters through a desert of stone and scree to the town and lake of **Røldal ⑲**. Located here is an Iron Age cemetery with 34 burial mounds; there's also an interesting stave church. Mentioned for the

first time in a document from the 15th century, the church itself probably dates from the 13th century, although the decorations remaining in the choir and nave were added at least 300 years later. The altarpiece was painted by Gottfried Hendtzschel, one of the many German artists who traveled through Norway in the 17th century looking for commissions and hoping to find more jobs through the recommendations of satisfied clients.

From **Breifonn** the route is truly spectacular. It first mounts up to **Røldalsfjell** and continues, through several tunnels, to the **Seljedal Gorge**. Here, too, there is an old, very steep stretch with a great many hairpin turns, which is, unfortunately, often closed. In the parking lot past the

Seljestad Tunnel there's a monument commemorating the miraculous rescue of a mail coach driver: the man was buried by an avalanche, and no one could find him until he started to blow his horn to attract the attention of rescuers. From here, on a clear day, you can see the **Folgefonn** snowfields 20 kilometers away. Branching off here, the R13 leads past the **Låtefoss**, 164 meters high, to **Odda** and the **Sørfjord**, an arm of the Hardangerfjord system about 19 kilometers away. Another branch of this fjord system is the **Åkrafjord**, which the E134 follows. At **Rullestad ⑳** an old winding road leading down to the fjord has become the most famous mountain road in Norway thanks to Hertevig's painting *Rullestadjuvet*,

which hangs in the National Gallery in Oslo. **Etne ㉑** is already on the fjord, located at the mouth of the **Etneelva**, an acknowledged fishermen's paradise. Etne's wooden church was probably built over the remains of a former stave church. At Våg the E134 meets the E39, which runs from Stavanger to Bergen. Here, as in many other places along the western coast of Norway, there are a number of *bauta* stones, memorial stones from pre-Christian times.

The Capital of the Little Kingdoms: Haugesund

Thirteen kilometers further on is **Haugesund ㉒**, situated on the Haugesund peninsula and the island of **Karmøy**, which the **Karmsund** separates from the mainland. From Skre, signs indicate the route to the **Steinsfjell** (226

Above: The barren Hardangervidda is Europe's largest plateau. Right: A delicacy – young herring fresh from the grill.

meters), Haugesund's local hill, which has a fine view of the town and the offshore islands.

By 8000 BC, the Gulf Stream had already freed the coast of ice and the first settlements were established. The small kingdoms which developed later on were also concentrated in southwest Norway, as we know from the five recorded royal residences in Vestland. The most important is said to have been that of Harald Hårfagra.

According to the 13th-century saga of Snorri Sturluson, this first ruler to unify the Norwegian kingdoms took up residence on the island of Karmøy and died there in 930. He was buried in **Haraldshaugen**, about 2 kilometers north of the present town. Today, his grave is adorned with a 17-meter granite obelisk, surrounded by 29 small menhirs symbolizing the 29 small kingdoms that Harald unified. This memorial was, however, erected at a much later date, commemorating the thousandth anniversary of his death.

Today, a bridge connects the island of Karmøy to the mainland; found by the eastern pier of the bridge were a group of *bauta* stones dubbed "The Five Foolish Virgins." South of the bridge is the old settlement of **Avaldsnes** ㉓ with a **stone church** of St. Olav dating from 1250. The church stands on land once occupied by a **royal residence** attributed to Harald Hårfagra. A slender *bauta* stone 6.5 meters high, "Virgin Mary's Needle," stands near the church, leaning slightly toward it. Three kilometers north of this are the **Rehaugene**, massive burial mounds from the Bronze Age.

Present-day Haugesund (population 28,000) owes its existence to the development of deep-sea fishing in the mid-19th century, when large catches of herring were here brought to land. When these began to diminish, the growing merchant marine fleet and attendant shipbuilding industry were able to compensate fully for the loss of jobs. Today, Haugesund is reaping the profits of the oil boom; because of its depth, the fjord system of the **Boknafjord** ㉔ is an ideal place for the construction of drilling rigs and oil platforms. Another major employer is the aluminum works on Karmøy, and Haugesund is also the administrative and service center for a large area of the surrounding countryside. At the southern tip of Karmøy is **Skudeneshavn** ㉕ with an attractive old town center dating from the 19th century; it has, however, lost its role as a ferry harbor since the completion of the new route via Bokn to Rennesøy.

The Island Route to Bergen

From Haugesund, high-speed boats run to Stavanger (1 hour 20 minutes) and Bergen (2 hours 50 minutes). The most attractive overland route to Bergen is the northern route thought the world of western Norway's islands. Buses, for example, take about 5 hours to get from Haugesund to Bergen, staying mainly on

From Oslo to Bergen

the E39 as well as the ferries from Valevåg to Skjersholmane (20 minutes) and Sandvikvåg to Halhjem (50 minutes). If you have the time, there are scenic alternatives that lead you off the main road.

Leaving Haugesund to the north on the R47, you go through an area of prehistoric settlement. The coastal village of **Bleivik**, just 8 kilometers west of the R47, was the original home of the so-called *Bleivikmann*, the oldest depiction of a human being ever found in Norway; this sculpture, an impressive 8,000 years old, is now in the Bryggen Museum in Bergen.

The R47 runs into the E39, which leads, after another 32 kilometers, to the Valevåg-Skjersholmane ferry. This runs 31 times a day, round the clock, and also docks at the island of **Stord**, where Bronze Age funerary stele have been found near the capital, **Leirvik** ㉖. At the northern end of the island is Sandvikvåg, where ferries depart for Halhjem, on the mainland, 26 times a day. The E39 runs along the east coast of Stord; at approximately the halfway point, **Jektevik**, there's a ferry over the **Langenuen** to **Hodnanes** and the neighboring island of **Tysnesøy**. Here, the R49 leads to the ferry at **Våge**, which makes the 35-minute trip over to the E39 and **Halhjem** 9 times a day.

From Halhjem, you pass through **Nesttun** on the 40-kilometer drive into the old city of **Bergen ③** (see p. 84).

THE NORTHERN ROUTE:
HØNEFOSS – GOL – EIDFJORD – BERGEN

Between Oslo and Bergen, the Bergen Railway, the R7 and the E16 all bypass Hardangervidda National Park to the north. All three meet up in **Hønefoss ㉗**, some 60 kilometers north of Oslo. which is also on the Bergen railway and long distance bus route. At the confluence of the Randselv and the **Begna** (**Ådalselv**), the town is divided in two by the latter river. In the middle of town it forms a double waterfall, although this is only really impressive when there is high water. The water's power was harnessed early on: by the 17th century there were already more than 20 water-powered sawmills. There are several interesting excursions to be made from Hønefoss, both by car and by bicycle.

At **Steinsfjord**, shortly before Hønefoss, a narrow road leads off from the E16 and runs around the fjord. Almost at the same point, a steep path leads up to the **Krokskogen ㉘** with the **Kings' and Queens' View** (*Kongens Utsikt*). Near these turnings, at the bridge over the Krokesund, is the **Sundøya Restaurant**; commanding a magnificent view of the sound and **Tyrifjord**, this is a popular place with day-trippers, and accordingly busy.

Right: In the autumn the reindeer for which there is not enough winter feed are slaughtered.

Four kilometers before Hønefoss is the old church and parish house of **Norderhov ㉙**. Buried in the church is the minister's wife who in 1716 tricked the Swedish army into an ambush resulting in the capture of the "Lion" – not the animal, of course, but rather a notorious colonel in the Swedish army who went by that epithet. Also recommended is an excursion along the **Randsfjord ㉚**, the fourth-largest lake in Norway with an area of 136 square kilometers.

There are two ways to get from Hønefoss to Gol: one leads along the Ådalselv, Lake Sperillen and the Begna and through the Valdres Valley, the other along Lake Krøderen and through the Hallingdal. Both routes are very scenic, with an equal amount of traffic on each, but only the first one is accessible year-round.

Excursion to the Valdres Valley

Fertile and forested is the countryside around the rivers and lakes and up into the **Valdres Valley**. Meadows and fields extend over the hillsides, dotted with small farmhouses. The E16 runs along the eastern shore of Lake Sperillen, with the summits of the fjell, between 1,000 and 1,200 meters high, visible in the distance.

At the end of the lake is the small village of **Nes ㉛**; from here, you can detour over to **Hedalen ㉜** (25 kilometers away), where there's a 12th-century stave church, although it was completely rebuilt in the 18th century. However, the nave, the decorated **portal**, **reliquary**, **crucifix** and the **Madonna** on the altar all date from the Middle Ages; while the paintings, in the delightful naive style typical of many Norwegian churches, are from the 16th century. From Hedalen you can either return to Nes or take the small toll road to **Begndal**, which brings you back to the E16.

At **Bagn ㉝** there is an interesting cruciform **church**, with an interior consid-

ered to be a typical example of *bonder-barokk* (rural Baroque). Not far from here, in **Reinli ㉞**, is another 12th-century stave church.

Passing through the tourist resorts of **Aurdal** and **Leira**, the road continues on to **Fagernes ㉟**. Here, in the ski region of the upper Valdres, there's even a small airfield for skiers who are in a hurry. Fagernes itself lies at the mouth of the river **Neselv**, which cascades in waterfalls into the Strandefjord, famous for its wealth of fish. An open-air museum displays old farmhouses and wooden household goods, examples of a kind of rural woodworking that has almost disappeared. From Fagernes, the E16 contines on to Sognefjord; to the northeast, the R51 leads to the **Jotunheimen**, Norway's high mountain massif.

Halfway to Sognefjord, drivers on the E16 can stop off at the stave church of **Vang ㊱**. In 1300, Norway had around 1,300 churches, of which two-thirds were stave churches. Over the ensuing centuries some of these windowless and nearly

lightless buildings were rebuilt, several burned down and many others were replaced by more practical – that is, easier to heat – stone buildings. The treasures of the old churches found their way into the new buildings, while the old support beams and rafters of the old edifices were irreverently used as firewood. This was common practice until the mid-19th century, when the Norwegian painter C.C. Dahl in Dresden sounded the alarm. His book *Examples of Sophisticated Wooden Architecture from Early Centuries in the Interior of Norway* was meant as a cry for help – but it went unheeded. In order to save some remnants of a tradition that was almost past saving, he bought the condemned stave church of Vang and, when he couldn't find anywhere where he could set it up in Norway, offered it for sale to the king of Prussia, Friedrich Wilhelm IV. The latter made a present of the church to the Countess of Redern, who had it rebuilt in Brückenberg in the Sudetenland (present-day Czech Republic) where it still stands today.

A little to the south of Fagernes, in Leira, the R51 branches off to Gol and into the **Hallingdal**. The 47 kilometers over the **Storefjell** are now lined with one tourist resort after the other. New hotels, restaurants, ski lifts and cross-country ski runs are springing up everwhere; the number of tourists has been steadily increasing for years and has long since overtaken the number of inhabitants of the barren fjell. This has created a new problem: the landscape is being spoiled by the proliferation of holiday homes. At **Gol** ⓷, the R52 joins the R7 at the point where the Hallingdal, coming from the west, veers southeast.

The Hallingdal Route

After leaving Hønefoss, the R7 runs through **Sokna**, on the *elv* of the same name, to **Lake Krøderen** ⓸. Averaging only about 1 kilometer wide but 100 meters deep and 40 kilometers long, this is

Above: Rural scene between Gol and Leira

one of the largest lakes in Norway. At its northern end is **Gulsvik**, also known as the "Gateway to the Hallingdal." Here the road crosses over to the west side of the **Hallingdalelv**, while the Bergen railway continues on the east side. The river, which goes on to form several lakes, is relatively slow here, and is fed by numerous tributaries, most of them in the form of waterfalls tumbling from the fjell. Many of these falls are used to produce hydroelectric power. From **Flå** ⓷, with its attractive 19th-century church, you can see across the river to **Vassfarnet** ⓸, a nature park. As a mark of gratitude for Sweden's help during World War II, King Olav V donated 15 tons of the local granite, which lies around here in massive chunks, to the zoo in Stockholm. At **Nesbyen** ⓸, located on a rise of scree, is the **Hallingdal Folkemuseum**, with traditional buildings and household goods. In the first week of July a large market is held here, which today draws large numbers of tourists. Nesbyen, at an altitude of 167 meters, has such favorable climatic conditions that the highest temperature ever recorded in Norway, 35.6°C, was measured here. Two toll paths lead up onto the fjell, where there is overnight accommodation in Alpine huts.

Twenty kilometers north is **Gol** ⑰, which together with Geilo, Hol and Ål is one of the Hallingdal's best-known winter sports resorts. Among the amenities here are numerous hotels, 200 kilometers of cross-country ski trails, and a chair lift that goes up a further 450 meters with a panoramic view at the top. The town's old stave church, however, is now in the Norsk Folkemuseum in Oslo.

From here, travelers can detour over to **Hemsedal**. The R52 passes the **Hemsila** waterfall and continues through a narrow, attractive valley to the **Eikre Dam** ㊷, 550 meters long; the reservoir empties into a tunnel to supply the Gol power plant with water. At the **Hjelmen** power plant there is a good view of the **Hydnefoss**, which plunges 140 meters at **Veslehorn**. The R52 continues to **Hemsedal** ㊸, which used to be the largest skiing center in Scandinavia before Lillehammer's Olympic Games; the road intersects with the E19 at **Borlaug**.

From Gol, the R7 runs upstream beside the now increasingly torrential Hallingdalselv, which forms numerous waterfalls. The valley itself widens; here the farmhouses are halfway up the slopes. Agriculture, however, takes something of a back seat to tourism in the area's economy.

Twenty kilometers past Gol is **Torpo** ㊹, which has the oldest building in the valley, a 12th-century stave church. This, too, was scheduled to be pulled down at the end of the 19th century, and while ways of saving it were still being discussed, the farmers took matters into their own hands and destroyed the choir. Fortunately, the nave has been preserved. Consecrated to St. Margaret of Antioch, the church has delightful ceiling paintings with scenes from the life of the saint, as

well as fine ornamental carving on the doorframe.

The stave churches of **Ål** ㊺ and **Hol** ㊻ did not escape the wave of demolition; some of the wonderful carvings and ceiling paintings from Ål's are displayed in the Historical Museum in Oslo. Today, however, each of these places has its own **open-air museum**. The so-called **Aurlandsvei** branches off (R50, 97 kilometers) at **Hagafoss** and leads through numerous tunnels to the Aurland, a side arm of Sognefjord.

Past Hagefoss, the R7 follows the narrow wooded Ustedal, in which the Ustaelva has cut a deep gorge. The Bergen railway also follows this route to **Geilo** ㊼. This community, at a height of 800 to 1,000 meters and with a population of 2,700, has everything a winter sports enthusiast could wish for: accommodation in 40 buildings ranging from hotels to huts, 16 ski lifts, 19 downhill runs and more than 200 kilometers of cross-country ski trails. But Geilo is also very popular in summer as a good base for hikes in the nearby Hardangervidda. A few kilometers away, in **Fekjo**, there are 17 burial mounds from the Viking era, discovered in 1923, which have still to be properly investigated.

To reach **Ustaoset** on the Ustevatn, the road ascends to a height of 1,000 meters. At the end of the lake it then veers away from the Bergen railway, which begins its journey through the high fjell and goes up to a height of almost 1,300 meters. Riding the **Bergen Railway** is one of the highlights of a vacation in Norway; the 470-kilometer trip, now completely electrified, takes you through 200 tunnels and over 300 bridges, as well as some stunning landscape. The journey takes 8 hours.

A particularly interesting segment of this trip is the 100-kilometer stretch from **Haugastøl** to **Myrdal**, where passengers can transfer to the **★Flåm railway**. This 20-kilometer branch line to the **Aur-**

From Oslo to Bergen

landsfjord is one of the most spectacular rail routes in Europe, dropping in a series of narrow curves and tunnels from 1,000 meters to sea level, which corresponds to a gradient of 5 percent.

A must for mountain bikers is the *Rallarveg, an unpaved, bumpy, and extremely beautiful walking and cycling trail through the stunning mountain landscape parallel to the railway from Geilo to Flåm ⓭. The most interesting section, from Haugastøl to Flåm, takes two days by bike. Accommodation is available at the highest point, in Finse (1,212 meters); from here it is all downhill, around exciting hairpin curves between Myrdal and Flåm (you can rent sturdy *Rallar* bikes at the train stations).

From Haugastøl, the R7 climbs gradually westwards, past many well-stocked fishing lakes, to reach its highest point at

Above: Mountain biking on the Rallerveg – a laborious but rewarding undertaking. Right: The wait will soon be over – the Flåm train departs hourly from Myrdal.

Dyranut (1,246 meters), from where it slowly descends into the Bjoreia Valley. The Dyranut district has accommodation of various categories and is ideal as a base for excursions in the Hardangervidda and guided walks in the glacier area of the *Hardangerjøkulen ❷. These walks are also offered from **Finse Station**, the highest station to be found on the Bergen railway.

Not far from **Dyranut** is the **Sysenvatn**, a reservoir which has a maximum capacity of up to half a million cubic meters of water, which can thus keep the power plants at the edge of the fjell going even in summer. Here, the modern road follows the so-called *Nordmannsslepa*, the old trade route over the Hardangervidda.

At **Fossli** ⓭, a side road leads to the **Fossli Hotell**, where you have the best view of the *Vøringfoss ⓭, one of the biggest waterfalls in Norway, where the Bjoreia drops almost 200 meters into a deep valley, the **Måbødal**. Unfortunately, the reservoirs on the *vidda* have noticeably lessened the quantity of water in it.

The Fossli Hotell is the starting point for one of the most beautiful, although rather strenuous, hikes in the Hardangervidda area, which goes via the **Demmevasshytta** (where you can stay overnight) east of the Hardangerjøkulen to the train station of Finse, and takes 14 to 18 hours.

Fossli marks the start of the most attractive part of the R7: the road winds down from an altitude of 800 meters to sea level through tunnels, along the sides of cliffs and round hairpin turns. From **Eidfjord** ⓭, at the inner end of the Hardangerfjord, there's a path leading through a 2-kilometer-long tunnel that represents the sole access to the isolated mountain farmstead of **Kjeåsen**. This detour is worth the effort for the splendid view at the end of it over the mountains and fjords.

The Hardangerfjord

Between Odda and Husnes, the **Hard-angerfjord** 52 is 120 kilometers long; its longest point. This fjord system has a sheltered climate, and the slopes are covered with large fruit plantations. Fruit cultivation here goes back to monks in the Middle Ages, who not only introduced apples, pears, cherries, plums and various berries, but also experimented with apricots, peaches and grapes. In spring, the flowering trees are still a major tourist attraction. The fruit can only be grown at low levels, as in many places the banks are very steep; in places, the fjell rises as much as 1,000 meters above the fjord's waters.

There are several different ways to get from Eidfjord to Bergen. One is to take the R7 along the south bank of the Eidfjord to **Brimnes**. Here, a ferry provides shuttle service across the fjord, and the road continues on through the new tunnel to **Granvin**. From here, the R572 leads over to Ulvik, where the first potatoes were cultivated in Norway in 1765. Past Granvin, the R7 continues to **Kvanndal**, whence ferries depart for **Utne** and **Kinsarvik** on either side of the Sørfjord. Today there's no sign of the Bjølvefoss waterfall that used to cascade at **Ålvik**; the water has been harnessed to drive a power plant with an artificial fall of 800 meters. After the bridge over the **Fykse-sund** comes **Norheimsund**: before the last bend in the road, there's a good view of the snowfield of **Folgefonn** opposite.

Also appealing are detours around the **Sørfjord** 53. At Kinsarvik, the river **Kinso** has created a veritable landscape of waterfalls. At **Lofthus** 54 is the so-called "monks' track," a path made by the monks of the Lyse Monastery of Bergen to get to the *søre Norddmannsslepa* and on to Oslo. In order to enjoy the view, however, you have yourself to climb the 900 meters to the top of the track; small wonder that experienced Hardangervidda hikers generally choose this route for their descent. **Ullensvang** 55, just southeast of here, was the summer home of the

Griegs; the town also has a small 13th-century church, which was restored in the 18th century. The southern end of the Sørfjord, around **Odda**, has unfortunately become far less attractive since 1906, when the first iron and steel works were built. Before the advent of industry, this was one of the first areas to attract tourists from abroad and it has been trying to regain its reputation since the smelting works closed down. **Sandvin** ㊷ is the starting point for expeditions to and onto the Folgefonn. The R550 leads back along the Sørfjord's west bank. **Aga** ㊹ has a small museum in a former courthouse; **Utne** ㊸, a 19th-century cruciform church with a medieval interior and the **Hardanger Folkemuseum**.

From Utne, you can either return by ferry to the R7 (20 minutes, 25 departures a day) or follow the R550 to **Jondal** and

Above: Låtefossen, one of the few large, untamed waterfalls in the south of Norway. Right: Inscription over the treasury of the Hansa merchants of Bergen.

cross to **Tørvikbygd** (20 minutes, 15 departures). Here, after 3 kilometers along the R49, is the **Berge Farmstead** ㊾, unusual in its large concentration of oaks, a tree that is otherwise rather rare in Norway; 20 kilometers further on is the R7. A few kilometers further toward Bergen is **Steindalsfoss** ㉍, a popular tourist attraction where visitors can walk under a 40-meter waterfall. In **Trengereid**, the R7 meets up again with the E16, giving travelers the option of entering Bergen via either Indre Arna or Nesttun. On weekdays, the toll required to enter the city is levied on both stretches. Bergen was the first city in Norway to introduce a toll for every car that enters its perimeters.

BERGEN

Bergen ㉑ – the name may derive from *Bergvin* (mountain meadow) – is situated on the inner bays of the **Byfjord** on a peninsula connected to the mainland only by a narrow bridge of land at Trengereid. On the land side, Bergen is protected by a semicircle of 7 fjell hills, and on the sea side, by a chain of offshore islands: it is an ideal location for a settlement and trading post, and probably already long settled by the time Olav Kyrre transferred the bishopric to Bergen in 1070 and granted it a town charter. After Håkon IV was proclaimed king in 1217, he made Bergen his seat of government in 1223, a function the city was to retain for the next 77 years. Dating from this time are the Håkonshallen (Håkon's Hall) and Bergenhus Fortress. At this time, the city was already an important trading center for everything from wine to wheat and fish to furs; it could be described as an early form of free trade zone.

When widespread famine broke out in the mid-13th century, Håkon IV appealed to the city council of Lübeck for supplies of grain, flour and malt. Because these supplies were naturally delivered on credit, the council of Lübeck, the leading city of the Hanseatic League, was in a position to demand certain privileges, which were put in writing in 1278 and formed the basis of the subsequent trade colony.

This colony's development was also influenced by a second important factor: because the only way to preserve fish was to dry or salt it, the production of the food consumed all over Europe on Friday, the day of fasting in the Catholic Church, required enormous amounts of salt. The Hanseatic League, however, had the salt monopoly, which meant that it was deeply involved in the fish monopoly. Soon all the fish designated for export had to be transported to Bergen, salted or dried, and then shipped out under the Hanseatic flag. The boats returned to Bergen laden with salt, weapons, cloth, wine, malt and even eggs and nuts: a shipowner's dream of perpetually loaded ships come true.

In its role of shipping company, the Hanseatic League took over the east side of Vågen Bay, which from then on was known as the *Tyskebryggen* (German

Wharf). Bergen thus became one of the Hanseatic League's most important trade centers together with London, Bruges and Novgorod. It was, in fact, even busier than any of these other places: in 1400 the Germans owned 300 firms and in 1408 even acquired St. Mary's Church, the town's finest piece of architecture, which was not returned to the Norwegians until 1766.

The Reformation, which the Hanseatic League of course supported, marked the beginning of its decline. Once Luther named Good Friday as the only day of fasting, the demand for fish in Europe dropped dramatically. Furthermore, the power-hungry League finally provoked resistance on the part of the Norwegians. In 1688 there were only 88 firms left; a Norwegian shipping company was officially founded in 1754; and in 1766 the last Hansa firm was sold to the Norwegians. The end of the Hanseatic League ushered in a new age of prosperity for the town, which became an even more cosmopolitan place.

In the 19th century, Bergen's harbor lost pride of place to that of Oslo, which had access to a more advantageous interior. It wasn't until 1908 that Bergen acquired a better overland connection in the form of the Bergen Railway; modern roads followed later. Today Bergen is the provincial capital of Hordaland and seat of the Protestant bishopric of Bjørgvin. It is also the starting point or terminus of numerous ferries operating to England, Scotland, Denmark, and the Faeroe and Shetland Islands. There are fast shipping links to Stavanger and the Sognefjord and Nordfjord, and Bergen is also the southernmost port of the coastal shipping line (*Hurtigrute*). There are daily flights from Bergen to every other part of the country.

The City Center

Old Bergen was built mainly of wood. Fires destroyed the town time and again,

Above: A visit to the morning market is a must for fish and seafood fans.

most recently in 1916; finally, after World War II, the houses were built only of stone. The oldest still existing or restored houses are on *Tyskebryggen*, which for understandable reasons lost the "Tyske" or "German" part of its name and has been known as Bryggen since the end of World War II; it is one of the four sites in Norway on UNESCO'S World Cultural Heritage list.

The center of Bergen is the ★**Torget** ❶ (marketplace) at the south end of the **Vågen**, the old harbor; here the picturesque **fish market** (*Fisketorget*) still takes place every day. On the southern side of the market there is a statue of the comic playwright Ludvik Holberg, who was born in Bergen; behind this is the old **stock exchange** ❷, which today houses the Bergen Bank. The ★★**Bryggen** extends along the northeastern edge of the Vågen basin. Built by German tradesmen, the old Hanseatic houses, long narrow wooden buildings with sharply pointed roofs, were divided into *stuer* (rooms for the individual establish-

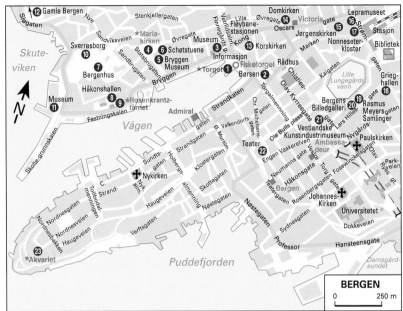

ments). Only the first of these buildings, the 18th-century **Finnegård**, was restored at an early date; in 1872 it became the **Hanseatic Museum ❸**. Here, visitors can see how these houses were originally set up and used: the first floor was used exclusively as a warehouse, while on the second floor were the bedrooms, dining room and offices; and the top floor provided sleeping quarters for the employees and apprentices.

Strolling through the Bryggen, taking time to look in at the houses, some restored, some newly built, many housing galleries and crafts shops, you eventually come to Statsbrugaten. A few yards along this road is ***St. Mary's Church ❹** (*Mariakirken*), a Romanesque-Gothic structure from the 12th/13th centuries which is probably the oldest building in Bergen. The Romanesque nave was built at the beginning of the 12th century and the choir was rebuilt and extended in the 13th century in the Gothic style. The 1676 pulpit was donated by Hanseatic merchants, something indicated by

plaques bearing their names; it is the finest Baroque pulpit in Norway. The 15 statues of saints in the church are also labeled with the names of their donors; created by a 17th-century Danish artist, they have been painted over several times since their execution. The most splendid feature of the church is the Late Gothic altar, which dates from the end of the 15th century and was probably crafted in Lübeck. The many German graves in the cemetery around the church are also a reminder of the Hanseatic age. St. Mary's was so "German" that even after the church was given back to the Norwegians, sermons here were still given in German until 1868.

Opposite the church is the **Bryggen Museum ❺** (Øvregate 50), displaying all the finds unearthed in excavations along the Bryggen between 1955 and 1968. Organized by subject, they ___ ___ light on old practices of cr___ churches and monasterie___ sure pursuits in the Mi___ museum also has the lar___

runes in the world. Almost right next to the Bryggen Museum is the **Schøtstuene** ➏ (Øvregate 54), the assembly rooms of the Hanseatic merchants, with their original interiors. In front of the Schøtstuene is the **monument to Snorri Sturluson**, the Icelandic writer who was responsible for recording most of what is now known of old Norwegian history, and who was murdered, probably by order of Håkon IV. There is also a copy of this monument, a work of the sculptor Vigeland, on Snorri's old farm in Iceland. Only a few yards away is the Svednesgård with the **Treasury of Bergen** (*Tracteursted*), a small, solid stone house where the merchants locked away their business records and valuables during their absence or at night because of the danger of fire.

Not far from St. Mary's Church on the **Festningskai** (fortress quay) is the old

Above: Street in the museum village of Gamle Bergen (Old Bergen). Right: A highlight of the ~~ r for music- and theater-lovers – the ~~ Festival

Bergenhus Fortress ➐, which once guarded the harbor entrance. The most important part of the fortress is the **Håkonshallen** ➑, which Håkon IV built between 1247 and 1261 for the wedding of his son Magnus. The hall is in the English Gothic style, evidence of the origin of its architects, who may have been sent as a gesture of friendship on the part of the English king Henry III. After a mere five years, the hall burned down; it was rebuilt in 1280, only to fall into ruin after Håkon V moved his residence to Oslo. Until 1840, it was used as a granary, but was then restored, thanks to a local initiative, from 1880 to 1895. In 1944, an ammunition ship exploded next to it and once again it was destroyed. It has never been proved whether or not this explosion was intentional, but the fact that it happened to occur on Hitler's birthday is seen by some as indicative. The Håkonshallen was rebuilt between 1957 and 1961; preserving its old-fashioned appearance, but fitted out with such modern conveniences as electricity and heating, it is used for ceremonial occasions such as royal or state visits.

On the quay is the ***Rosenkrantz-tårnet** ➒, a medieval tower which was built from older structures in the 16th century by Erik Rosenkrantz. Visitors can examine and disassemble an architectural model of the tower which fully demonstrates the complexity of its design; this edifice, too, was rebuilt in the 1960s. Above the sheds and stalls of Bergenhus are the remains of the **Sverresborg** ➓, an earlier fortress which dates from the time of King Sverre. Right at the end of the pier, behind Bergenhus, is the **Fishing Museum** ⓫, stocked with information about coastal and deep-sea fishing in Norway.

North of the town center are the districts of **Skuteviken** and **Sandviken** with the open-air museum of **Gamle Bergen** ⓬ (Old Bergen). This consists of 30 original wooden houses; together, the ensem-

ble forms a museum, but the buildings are still used and inhabited.

Back on the market follow Kong Oscar gate to the **Korskirken** ⓭, a 12th-century church which was rebuilt in the 17th century in the Renaissance style. By the church door is a relief commemorating the "Greenland apostle" Egede, who embarked from here on his missionizing expedition in 1721.

Two hundred yards further on is the **cathedral** ⓮, which was built on the foundations of an earlier church dedicated to St. Olav. A bit further on is a second church, the **Jørgenskirken** ⓯, and a hospital of the same name which today houses the **Leprosy Museum** ⓰. The ruins of the **Nonneseter Monastery** ⓱, a Cistercian monastery from the 12th century, are also located here. Kong Oscar Gate ends east of the station at a **city gate** from the 17th century.

Passing the train station, the library and the bus station, you come to **Grieg Hall** ⓲ on Strømgate, the city's new concert hall. This wooden building, which was opened in 1978, is famous all over the world for its acoustics. On the west side of the Lille Lungegård lake are two museums: the **Rasmus Meyer Collection** ⓳, a museum of modern art based on the extensive collection donated by its namesake, and the **Municipal Art Museum** ⓴, which also exhibits modern art. At the end of the Lille Lungegård lake is the **Museum of Arts and Crafts** ㉑, next to the little municipal park, with ceramics and goldsmith work; between the park and the **theater** ㉒ lies **Ole Bull Square**, with statues of the violin virtuoso Ole Bull, the composer Grieg and the poet Bjørnstjerne Bjørnson, the latter of which is also a work of Vigeland.

Sights Around Bergen

Definitely worth a visit is the ***Aquarium** ㉓ on the tongue of land between Vågebecken and Puddefjord, in **Nordnespark**: one of the largest in Europe, it is stocked solely with fish from the North Sea and North Atlantic. The only non-native element here are the penguins, whose daily promenade is a great attraction for visitors.

One sight in Bergen than no visitor should miss is sunset from the top of the *Fløyen. To get to the valley station of the **Fløy funicular** ⓐ, walk a hundred meters or so east from the Torget along the Vetrlidsalmennig; the funicular runs almost to the top of Bergen's local hill, 319 meters high. When the sun sets in the evening behind the chain of mountains opposite, there is a fascinating play of light and shadow which changes from minute to minute as the sun gradually lowers behind the clouds.

Twenty-six kilometers south of Bergen, in **Fana** ⓑ, is the **Fana Church**. This is the last survivor of a circle of 14 small medieval pilgrimage chapels; and its silver candelabra is said to have been responsible for many miracles. Close by are the ruins of **Lyse Monastery**, the biggest Cistercian monastery in Norway, which was abandoned after the Reformation; its stones were later used in the construction of the Rosenkrantztårnet. On the offshore island of **Lysøen** is the extremely unusual **villa of the violinist Ole Bull**, built in a mixture of just about every conceivable architectural style, with an adjoining concert hall.

Also south of the town and well signposted is **Troldhaugen**, the villa belonging to Edvard and Nina Grieg, who are both buried here. The house now contains Grieg memorabilia collected by the composer's wife, and in the garden is Grieg's "composing hut," where he withdrew to find the quiet and the inspiration he needed to compose.

A new concert hall has also been built which is in constant use during the International Bergen Festival (end of May/beginning of June). This festival is the cultural highlight of the year: it offers something for everyone, from folklore through theater and music performances to art exhibitions.

KONGSBERG

ℹ️ Storgate 35, tel. 32735000, June 1-Aug 31, 9 am-8 pm, other times Mon-Sat 9 am-4 pm.
🏨 ●●● **Quality Grand Hotel**, Christian Augustsgt. 2, tel. 32732029. ●● **Gyldenløve Hotel**, Hermann Foss Gt. 1, tel. 32731744, only hotels in town. *HOSTEL:* **Kongsberg Vanderhjem**, Vinjes Gt. 1, tel. 32732024.
🏛️ All near Lågenbrücke. **Church**, open May 18-Aug 31, 10 am-5 pm, except during services. **Silver Smelting House** and **Museum of Norwegian Coins**, May 18-September 30, 10 am-4 pm. **Lågendal Museum**, May 18-Aug 31, 11 am-4 pm. **Saggrenda Silver Mine**, 7 km toward Notodden, guided tours from May 18 to 31 and from Aug 16 to 31 at 12:30 pm; from June 1 to Aug 15 at 11 am, 12:30 and 2 pm.
🎫 July 1: Folk dancing at the Lågendal Museum at 7 pm.

HEDDAL / NOTODDEN

ℹ️ Postboks, Notodden, tel. 35013520, June 1-August 31, 9 am-8 pm, otherwise Mon-Sat 9 am-4 pm.
🏨 ●●● **Bolkesjø Hotell**, Bolkesjø, 3670 Notodden, tel. 35018600. ●● **Norlandia Telemark Hotel**, Torget 8, 3670 Notodden, tel. 35012088.
🏛️ **Stave Church**, June-August weekdays after 10 am, Sun after 1 pm. **Open-Air Museum**, same hours.

TUDDAL / RJUKAN

ℹ️ Postboks, Rjukan, tel. 35091290, open June 1-Aug 31, 9 am-8 pm.
🏨 ●● **Gaustablikk Høyfjellshotel**, 3660 Rjukan, tel. 35091422, comfortable high-fjell hotel, ideal base for hikers and winter sports fans. **Euro Park Hotel**, Sam Eydec g. 67, 3660 Rjukan, tel. 35090288. **Skinnarbu Høyfjellshotel**, Møsvatn, tel. 35095461. ● **Rjukan Gjestehus**, Såheimsvn. 11, 3660 Rjukan, tel. 35092161. **Rjukan Hytte- og Caravanpark**, Postboks 100, 3660 Rjukan, tel. 35096353, cabins. **Bøen Camping**, 3697 Tuddal, tel. 35024016, cabins. **Hogstul Hytter**, 3697 Tuddal, tel. 35024092, cabins. *CAMPING:* **Øystul Camping**, Øystul, 3697 Tuddal, tel. 35024088.

HAUGESUND

ℹ️ Postboks, Haugesund, on the harbor, tel. 52725055, open June 1-Aug 31, 9 am-8 pm.
🏨 ●●● **Rica Maritim Hotel**, Haugesund, Åsbygt. 3, tel. 52711100, very attractive establishment with large rooms. ●● **Rica Saga Hotel**, Haugesund, Skippergt.11, tel. 52711100, harbor views. *HOSTEL:* **Røvær Vandrerhjem**, Røvær Island, tel. 52718035, June 15-Aug 15.

Haralds Haugen, always open. **Avaldsnes Church**, Mon-Fri 9:30 am-11 am. **Karmsund Open-Air Museum**, 10:30 am-2 pm, Thu until 6 pm, Sun 12:30-3 pm.

 You can book **fishing tours** at the tourist information center by the harbor.

 There are a number of flights every day to Bergen and Oslo. There are four rapid boats a day to Bergen and seven to Stavanger; call 72511444 for info.

HØNEFOSS

 Storgate 4, tel. 32117723, open June 1-August 31, 9 am-8 pm, other times Mon-Sat 9 am-4 pm.

 Quality Ringerike Hotel, Kongensgt. 3, tel. 32127200. **Grand Hotel**, Stabellsgt. 8, tel. 32122722. **Euro Bergland Hotell**, 3534 Sokna, tel. 32145144, cheap summer rates. **Onsakervika Camping**, 3530 Røyse, tel. 32157333, nice sand beach, cabins. **Vik Camping**, 3530 Røyse, tel. 32159240, 10 km from Hønefoss, on the lake, cabins. **Utvika Camping**, 3531 Krokkleiva, tel. 32160670, cabins.

 Sundøya, Krokkleiva, tel. 32159140, located between the lakes, with great views out over them; spectacular in the evening.

HEDALEN

 Stave Church, open June 20-Aug 12, 11 am-4 pm.

GOL

 Postboks, Gol, at the train station, tel. 32075115.

 Storefjell Høyfjells Hotel, Golsfjell, tel. 32073930, *the* hotel for winter sports: in a beautiful setting, but very expensive. **Eidsgaard Turist Hotel**, Gol, Sentrumsvn. 130, tel. 32075644. **Torvstua Appartement** and **Restaurant**, reasonably priced, with large portions of Norwegian food, Gol, Sentrumsvn. 85, tel. 32075195. *CAMPING:* **Tubbehaugen Camping**, Gol, tel. 32073916, lovely setting.

BERGEN

 Bryggen 7, tel. 55321480, May 2-Sept 30 weekdays 8:30 am-9 pm, other times Mon-Sat 9 am-4 pm.

 Inter Nor Hotel Neptun, Valkendorfsgt. 8, tel. 55901000, very good restaurant. **Hotel Admiral**, Sundsgt. 9, tel. 55236400, be sure to reserve a room on the water; extremely expensive, however. **Ambassadeur Hotel**, V. Torggt. 9, tel. 55900890, beautifully renovated old hotel. **Hotel Bergen**, Håkonsgt. 2, tel. 55233962, almost a luxury-class hotel, but more reasonably priced. **Hotel Victoria**, Kong Oscarsgt. 29, tel. 55315030, well-tended older building. **Rosenberg Gjestehus**, Rosenberggt. 13, tel. 55901660. **Strandhotel**, Strandkaien 2B, tel. 55310815, also with a lovely

view of the harbor. *HOSTEL:* **Bergen Vandrerhjem**, Montana, J. Blytts vei, Landås, tel. 55292900. *CAMPING:* **Bergen Camping Park**, Breistein, tel. 55248808.

 Bellevue, at the Fløyen look-out point, tel. 55310240. **Bryggen Tracteursted**, Bryggestredet, tel. 55314046, Norway's oldest inn, still serving mead in horns. **Fiskekrogen**, on the fish market, tel. 55317566, excellent fish restaurant. **Kjøttbøsen**, Vaskerelven 6, tel. 55231459, meat dishes. *CAFÉS:* **Bergenhus**, Strandkaien 4. **Bettinas Café**, Vaskerelven 39. **Lido**, Torgalmenningen 1, also serves light snacks, beer and wine.

 Galleriet, Torgalmenningen, 60 shops under one roof.

 Fish Market weekdays 7 am-4 pm. **Hanseatic Museum**, in Finnegård at the edge of Bryggen, June 1-September 1, 9 am-5 pm. **Mariakirken**, May 1-August 31 weekdays 11 am-4 pm, other times Tue-Fri noon-1:30 pm. **Bryggen Museum**, opposite the Mariakirken, May-August, daily 10 am-5 pm, other times weekdays 11 am-3 pm, Sat and Sun noon-3 pm. **Schøtstuene**, Øvregt. 50, June-August 9 am-5 pm, otherwise 11 am-2 pm, October-April Sundays only. **Bergenhus Fortress**, at the end of the Festningskeien, May 15-September 14, 10 am-4 pm, other times Sun noon-3 pm. **Rasmus Meyer Collection**, Rasmus Meyer Alle 7, May 15-September 15, 11 am-4 pm, other times noon-3 pm. **Aquarium**, May 1-September 30, 9 am-8 pm, other times 10 am-6 pm. **Troldhaugen**, 6 km south of the city, May 2-October 1, 9:30 am-1:30 pm and 2:30-5:30 pm. **Gamle Bergen**, open-air museum in the park, park always open, houses open for tours from late May to late August, 9:30 am-4:30 pm.

 End of May-early June, **Bergen Festival**, tickets available at Grieg Hall, tel. 55312170; you can also buy tickets there for concerts in **Troldhaugen**.

 Daily **flights** to Oslo, Stavanger, Haugesund, Trondheim and Skien. There are at least 5 trains a day on the Bergen train route, year-round; contact NSB Travel Center, Postboks 673, Bergen, tel. 55966900. **Rapid buses** run daily to Oslo (*Haukeliekspressen*), to Kristiansund (*Kystbussen*) and to Trondheim (*Trondheimekspressen*); local service departs from the bus station on Strongate, south of the train station. Contact Bergens Nordhordaland Rutelag, tel. 55548700 (regional) or 22175290 (*Ekspressbusse*). **Hurtigrute** boats dock every day at 10:30 pm by Puddefjord Bridge (reserve well in advance), tel. 040/376930. There are daily **passenger ships** to the Nordfjord and Årdalstangen on the Sognefjord; contact Fylkesbaatane i Sogn og Fjordane, Strandkai Terminals, 5013 Bergen, tel. 55324015.

From Oslo to Bergen

FROM BERGEN TO TRONDHEIM

FROM FJORD TO FJORD
THE E39 COASTAL ROUTE
THE INNER FJORD ROUTE

FROM FJORD TO FJORD

Old harbor towns are best approached or left by sea. There's a way to do this in Bergen. The best-known route is the shipping route of the mail boats, the ****Hurtigrute**, which has been in continuous operation since 1893, run by four shipping companies for the royal mail. Combined freight and passenger ships, these vessels once measured between 2,000 and 3,000 G.R.T.; but today, they have taken on the dimensions of medium-sized cruise liners, and nearly all of them can even take vehicles. The 11 ships of the *Hurtigrute* run all year-round according to a fixed timetable which takes eleven days for the round trip from Bergen to Kirkenes, on the Russian border, and back. The route is so designed that harbors which the boat calls in at during the night or not at all on the outward journey are visited by day on the return trip. Passengers can embark or disembark at any point along the way, but anyone who stays on the boat for longer than 24 hours has to book a cabin. The route runs from Bergen (Puddefjordsbroen) via Måløy, Ålesund, Molde, Kristiansund,

Previous pages: Midsummer night on the Sognefjord. Left: The shimmering blue ice caves of the Jostedalsbreen.

Trondheim, Brønnøysund, Sandnessjøen, Bodø, Svolvær, Harstad, Tromsø, Hammerfest and Honningsvåg to Kirkenes. Apart from the main harbors, where the ships stop for a longer period and passengers can get out and explore town, there are a number of smaller loading harbors where people can embark or disembark. You can also get off at one harbor and travel on with another boat one or more days later. Make sure to reserve places before you get to Norway for whatever stretches you want to do, and a place for your car; you'll need to book at least three months in advance if you're going in the tourist season (June to August).

On the south side of the Puddefjordsbroen, small boats depart for the Sognefjord. Stopping off at Balestrand and Leikanger, they take five hours to reach Flåm at the end of the Aurlandsfjord, the southeastern point of the Sognefjord; after a stay of two hours, they run back to Bergen. The whole excursion takes around 13 hours, but you can get on or off at any stop and continue the journey by bus or the Flåm railway.

There are two main land routes from Bergen to the north. The first one is the **Fjord Road** (E39) from Bergen via Ålesund and on to Trondheim. This includes all the highlights of Norwegian coastal scenery, but takes a long time, since drivers have to use no fewer than 12 ferries within a distance of approximately 700 kilometers. Considerably longer, in terms of milage, is the **Inner Fjord Route**, but this is also very scenic, and since the roads it involves are in better condition, you can in fact travel faster. It also takes you past a few tourist highlights, such as the Geirangerfjord and the Trollstig, although you can also reach these from the coastal route by following signposted side roads. At these points it is also possible to change from one route to the other. Scandinavians have an American rather than a central European relationship to distances – weekend excursions of 500 kilometers are normal – but this isn't something every visitor need emulate: in order to do justice to the magnificent scenery and the many points of interest on the way, you could easily take a week to cover either route.

THE E39 COASTAL ROUTE TO TRONDHEIM

After leaving **Bergen ❶**, the E39 comes, at **Breistein**, to the Sørfjord. On the other side of the fjord is **Osterøy ❷**, the largest inland island in Europe with an area of 324 square kilometers. In 1992, the ferry that used to dock at **Steinstø** was replaced with a bridge. One disadvantage with Norway's many new bridges is that they generally require a toll for vehicles and passengers; only on public buses is the toll included in the ticket. However, this toll is to only be exacted for a maximum of 20 years; after that, the bridge will be held to be paid off.

Water and Ice: Sognefjord and Josedalsbreen

An interesting detour leads to **Seim ❸**, the royal residence of Håkon I the Good, who is said to be buried here. **Håkon's Court** had already been used by Harald Fairhair, and was restored in the 1950s.

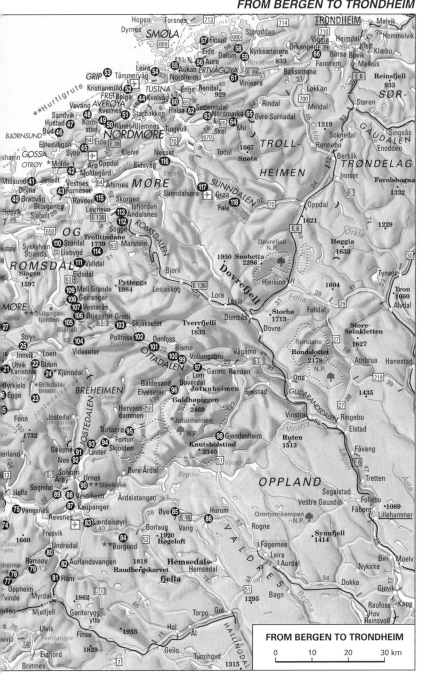

From here there is a splendid view over the **Seimsfjord**. The E39 continues through **Eikanger** and **Bjørsvik** along the coast of the **Osterfjord**, with countless vistas to tempt photographers. From **Vikanes**, the road climbs through the **Romarheimsdal** to an altitude of almost 500 meters, and then drops again to sea level at **Matre ❹**. From here, a summer road leads over the fjell to **Svartemyr** and **Oppedal**. From Svartemyr, a small ferry runs to **Nordeide** on the Sognefjord's opposite shore (a 40-minute crossing; departs 3 times a day).

Traveling through the **Hope Tunnel**, the E39 comes to **Fjordsdal**, then Oppedal, by which time it's in the province of **Sogn og Fjordane**. Here, the regular ferry runs across the Sognefjord to **Lavik** (a 20-minute trip, 18 times a day). The ferry journey has been shortened, since there is an increasing tendency in Norway to move the ferry stops from the ends of the side fjords to the main fjord, even when this necessitates dynamiting operations or the construction of tunnels.

Norway's largest fjord, the ****Sognefjord ❺**, extends a total of some 180 kilometers from **Rutledal** at the coastal end to the northeastern tip of the **Lustrafjord**. Never more than 5 kilometers wide, it reaches depths of more than 1,300 meters. In the side fjords at the eastern end of the system the cliffs rise almost vertically out of the water to tower as much as 1,200 meters over the fjord's surface. In contrast to the fjord's northern shore, its southern side has hardly been developed at all and only has summer paths. This is because of the fjord's east-west alignment: its northern shore gets more sun, and is therefore a more popular place to live.

The E39 follows the Sognefjord's coast for a short distance east, passing the bay

Right: The glorious late summer colors of the fjell are all too brief: here, summer passes directly into winter.

near **Breivik ❻** where the fjord is at its deepest (1,308 meters), and veers north at **Vadheimsfjord** to the town of the same name. Here, a small path leads to the **Gamla Steinbru ❼** (Old Stone Bridge), an arched bridge of uncut stone built entirely without mortar.

In the **Ytredal**, which the road now follows, there are further examples of this type of bridge, which the farmers built in order to be able to drive their herds of cattle up to the summer pastures while the snow was still melting and the water level still high, thereby prolonging the summer farming season.

The road continues via **Sande** to **Førde ❽** at the end of the **Førdefjord**, which is also sometimes called the Sunnfjord. The administrative and service center of this fjord system, it also has an airport which is an important link in the domestic air network. Seventy kilometers to the west is the town of **Florø ❾**, the only place in the whole province with a city charter. Once centering around deep-sea fishing, its economy now revolves around offshore drilling technology and supplies for the the oil platforms.

The area was settled a very long time ago, as demonstrated by the Bronze Age rock drawings at **Ausevik ❿**. On the offshore island of **Kinn ⓫** is the **Kinnkirke**, a Romanesque stone church dating from the 12th century. The island of **Svanøy ⓬**, to the south, originally belonged to the bishops of Bergen, who established here the manor house and estate of **Svanøygård**. After the Reformation, this became royal property; it now serves as a conference center. In the park there is still a St. Olav's cross, a stone cross with runic inscriptions. There are ferry links from both islands to Florø.

From Førde, the E39 continues to climb. After 20 kilometers it reaches **Jølstravatn**, a lake 30 kilometers long. 17 funeral steles and 25 stone burial mounds have been found in this area; most are from the Bronze and Iron Ages,

and there are also three from the more recent Neolithic period. The most important finds are exhibited in the Bryggen Museum in Bergen. In **Ålhus** ⓭ is the old vicarage in which the painter Nikolei Astrup spent his youth (1880-1928). **Årdal** ⓮ has a lovely picnic site with grilling facilities splendidly located on a lake full of fish; you can get your lunch out of the lake and cook it on the spot.

From the eastern shore, the R5 leads up through a tunnel under the **★★Jostedalsbreen**. This *breen* (glacier), extending over an area of some 1,000 square kilometers, is the largest plateau glacier in continental Europe. Its central peak is the **Høgste Breakulen**, 1,953 meters in height. The glacier measures more than 100 kilometers from southwest to northeast; its ice is up to 500 meters thick; and it extends a number of arms into the valleys. Like many other European glaciers, the Jostedalsbreen is gradually melting. Past **Skei**, you can go up to **Klakegg** ⓯, where there are two summer roads up to the glacier. From **Fonn**, at the end of one

of these paths, there are guided glacier walks; it is not advisable to venture onto the glacier on your own.

Where Herring Meets Cod: The Nordfjord

After Kalkegg the road leads down through the **Våtedal** between steep, narrow rock cliffs. By **Egge** ⓰, the **Nonsfoss** waterfall tumbles from a dizzying height. The road continues through **Byrkjelo** to **Reed** ⓱, which has the largest Neo-Gothic church in Norway. In Vassenden, a side road leads to the **Eidsfoss** ⓲, Europe's largest salmon ladder. This term denotes a natural cascade which the salmon leap up on the way to the spawning grounds where they themselves originally hatched. The Eidsfoss is 300 meters long and 33 meters high, and has 74 steps which the salmon must gradually mount, going against the current.

Sandane ⓳ on the **Gloppefjord**, marks the start of the **Nordfjord** system. This fifth-largest Norwegian fjord ex-

tends from **Måløy** to **Loen**, a distance of 90 kilometers, and runs parallel to the Sognefjord almost exactly along the 62nd parallel of latitude.

Sandane has an open-air museum, and in nearby **Gjemmestad** ㉒ there are more burial mounds from the Ice Age. The largest of these, 50 meters long and 7 meters high, is known as *Tinghogjen*: this mound is illuminated by the last of the evening sun on Midsummer's Day. From Sandane, you can either continue to **Anda** and take the ferry across the Nordfjord to Lote (a 10-minute crossing, 27 times a day) or go back to Byrkjelo and make the very rewarding circumnavigation of the whole end of the Nordfjord, for which you should allow an extra day.

If you do go back to Byrkjelo, take the R60 over the 640-meter fjell; before and at **Karistova** ㉑ are two places with a good view of the Jostdalsbreen to the

Above: Horse-drawn carriage on the way to the Briksdalsbreen. Right: Fjord horses, once indispensable to agriculture.

south. From here the road, which is less than 6 meters wide at this point, serpentines down to **Utvik** around six double bends, within each of which there is a place for drivers to pull over and admire the view of Utvik. Driving along the fjord, the next stop is **Innvik**; there are views here of the **Storlaugpik** (1,556 meters) and the **Ceciliekruna** (1,775 meters), which can be climbed from here. **Olden** ㉒ has an octagonal church built in 1756; the original edifice, however, burned down only ten years later and was promptly rebuilt. Among its treasures is the Bible belonging to Christian II.

From Olden, a summer road leads along the lake of Oldevatn, 15 kilometers long, to the ***Briksdalsbreen** ㉓, northern arm of the big Jostedalsbreen glacier, popular with visitors. A half-hour hiking trail leads right to the edge of the glacier; most of the route is also serviced by carriages drawn by fjord horses. Caution is essential: in summer, large chunks of ice, some as big as houses, break off the glacier and fall into the lake below. However, you can take guided ice tours. The shimmering blue ice – glaciers absorb the red components of light – spreads picturesquely over an end moraine, rising high above the scrubby vegetation.

From **Loen**, a side road follows the Lovatn, a lake that reaches a depth of 200 meters, up to ***Kjenndal** ㉔ at the foot of the **Noresnibba** (1,823 meters), from where you can climb up to the **Kjenndalsbreen**. To the west there is a splendid view of the 2,000-meter **Ramnefjell**; to the east are the highest peaks of the Jostedalsbreen, the 2,018-meter **Brensnibba** and the 2,083-meter **Lodalskåpa**. Guided tours to both these mountains depart from Kjenndal. Another classic hike from Loen is the ascent to **Skålatårnet** (1,843 meters); the round trip takes about 9 hours.

Continue along the **Innvikfjord** to reach **Stryn** ㉕, a transportation hub of sorts – the R15 leads east from here to the

From Bergen to Trondheim

Geirangerfjord – which, like Olden and Loen, is a good place to stop off for the night. Points of interest are an old merchant house, the *Walhalla Gjestveri*, and King Oscar Hall, built in the Viking style, with dragons. On the **Strynfjell**, at an altitude of some 1,000 meters, there's skiing in the summer. Just west of Stryn is the turnoff to the R613, the panoramic route along the Nordfjord. The best view comes 22 kilometers further on, near **Nos**. From **Randabygd ㉖** there's a footpath for the 15-minute walk to **Tvinnfoss**, a double waterfall which you can walk under without getting wet.

The R15/60 continues across the Strynfjell; the two roads split again at Kjøs. From here, the R60 leads to Hellesylt on the Geirangerfjord, and the R15 goes to the **Hornindalsvatn ㉗**, the clearest lake in Norway. 22 kilometers long and up to 514 meters deep, it is the deepest lake in Europe; its water level is 55 meters above that of the Nordfjord. The R15 continues along its southern bank to **Nordfjordeid ㉘**, an important

business and service center on the Nordfjord (population 2,300) which was once also the center of fjord horse breeding. These placid horses were once essential to thousands of farms, but as agriculture has been increasingly mechanized, their numbers have dropped drastically. Here you can either continue north on the E39 or make another detour to the Vestkapp (West Cape).

If you opt for the Vestkapp, drive along the Eidsfjord to **Stårheim**, where there is a splendid view south across the water to the Blånibba, 1,670 meters high. By **Almenningen ㉙** is the highest cliff in Europe, the **Hornelen**, rising vertically out of the sea to a height of 860 meters. Witches and trolls are said to dance on top of it on bright summer nights; less imaginative souls explain away this phenomenon as a product of mist and fog. Boats to the Hornelen which also call at **Vingen ㉚** on the opposite shore, where there are more than 2,000 prehistoric rock drawings, surprisingly mainly representations of deer.

The island of **Vågsøy** is connected with the mainland by a bridge 1,200 meters long. Its main settlement, **Måløy ③**, is one of Norway's leading exporters of fresh fish. The Nordfjord marks the boundary between the cod supplies of the northern and the herring of the southern waters, and fishermen here can therefore switch from one species to the other as necessary. In the past, western Norway's farmers used seasonal fishing as a way to earn a little supplementary income; today, however, they generally fish only for themselves.

Recent years have seen the development of salmon farms which supply Europe with fresh and smoked salmon all year round. This salmon improved noticeably in quality after the introduction of new feeding methods. In the early days the fish were simply fed fish meal, with extra carotin added before they were slaughtered to give the fish the desired red color; today, however, farmers use computerized feeding programs which perfectly reproduce natural feeding behavior. Salmon reared in this way are almost indistinguishable from wild salmon in terms of appearance and taste. Large quantities of chemicals do have to be used, however, because of the confined space in which the fish are bred. For fear of bacteria, which could destroy whole stocks, no visitors are allowed on any of the salmon farms.

Around **Hendanes** are bizarre cliff formations, including the **Kannestein ③**, a rock which the wind has sculpted into the form of an hourglass. Preserved in the old merchant town of **Vågsberget ③** are seven buildings of historic interest.

From **Maurstad** the R61 and R620 cross the **Stadlandet** peninsula to the **Vestkapp ③**. Legend has it that Kjerringa, a creature similar to the Loreley, lived on this bare, windswept rock; she is

Right: The attractive houses around Ålesund's harbor were rebuilt after the fire of 1904.

said to have had the same fatal consequences for local fishermen and seafarers as her counterpart on the Rhine. From the Vestkapp there's a magnificent view; the small cafeteria here also issues a Vestkapp certificate. On **Selje ③**, the island opposite the cape, are the remains of a Benedictine monastery dating from the 12th century, with the restored **St. Albans' Tower**.

From Nordfjordeid the E39 crosses a high spur of the **Kyrkefjell** (300 meters) to **Bjørkedal** and continues to **Folkestad** on the **Voldafjord**, where there is a ferry to **Volda ③** (15 minutes, 25 times a day).

On the Volda peninsula you pass the house where Ivar Aasen, the linguist and founder of *Nynorsk*, was born. You then come to **Ørsta** on the fjord of the same name. This fjord is already part of the Storfjord system, the largest and most complex of all the fjord systems, which extends across a large portion of the northern Vestland province, **Møre og Romsdal**.

From Ørsta, a little town with a population of 6,000, the E39 continues along the **Ørstafjord** and **Vartdalsfjord** to **Festøy**. Here the ferry crosses the Storfjord (a 20-minute crossing, 36 times a day) and hence also the cruise ship route going to and from the Geirangerfjord.

Passing **Spjelkavik** the road continues to Ålesund, which is situated on three skerry islands and is the center of the district of **Sunnmøre**.

*★Ålesund: The Emperor and Art Nouveau

Ålesund **③** takes its name from the sound which separates the town's two main islands, **Nørrøya** and **Aspøya**. A "young" town, founded as recently as 1848, it owes its existence to the fish its fleet brought in from all of the northern waters. Most of the catch is either frozen or turned into preserves, but dried, salted cod is also still produced and continues to

find a market in the Catholic countries of southern Europe. Ålesund experienced the worst catastrophe in its history in 1904, when the town was almost entirely destroyed by fire. When the German emperor Wilhelm II heard the news he immediately dispatched ships with food, doctors and medicine. As a great fan of Scandinavia, he also donated large sums of money for the reconstruction of the town, which was completed in only three years.

As Art Nouveau was the style of the day throughout Europe, a Norwegian variant of this was created in Ålesund. Gestures of the town's gratitude to Wilhelm II include a street that still bears his name, as well as a huge monument in **By Park** below the cliff of **Aksla**. This rock, which you can either drive up (the access road turns off the main road into Ålesund) or ascend by climbing more than 400 steps up from By Park, has a fantastic view over the fjord system and the skerries, which can be especially lovely in the evening.

Ålesund's predecessor was the old Viking settlement of **Borgund**, some 5 kilometers to the west. Parts of this have been excavated and this complex today belongs to the **Borgundkaupanger Museum** (Sunnmøre Museum), although located separately from it. Excavated here were two Viking houses with their storehouses, together with the household articles they contained; the harbor complex; and the foundations of an old church from the period immediately after the arrival of Christianity.

The church was probably dedicated to Mary and corresponded to the nearby **Borgund Church**, which was originally dedicated to St. Peter. This stone church, of which the present transept is the oldest part and dates from the 13th century, was later enlarged by turning the former nave into the transept and adding a nave running north to south. The altar was thus moved from the east to the north side, but the remains of the original altar on the east side can still be seen. Very little has remained of the original furnishings, but

the modern wooden decoration suits the little old church very well.

Located immediately behind the church are more than 40 old houses and farmsteads belonging to the Borgund-kaupanger Museum. There is also an exhibition of 30 boats that were used to travel the fjords and the open sea.

The old harbor basin, the **Indre Haven** in Ålesund itself, is very attractive with its painstakingly restored houses, numerous restaurants and bars. A startling feature of **Ålesund Church** are the large-scale mosaics and stained-glass windows in the interior, the work of Enevold Thømt.

The offshore islands of Valderøy, Vigra, Giske and Godøy are linked to the mainland by toll bridges and tunnels. On **Valderøy** 38 is **Skonghellen**, a cave more than 100 meters deep containing draw-

Above: Art Nouveau was the predominant architectural style when Ålesund was rebuilt.
Right: In the summer the island of Runde is a mass of breeding birds.

ings that are said to have been made 25,000 years ago, before the end of the last Ice Age. However, visiting the cave is not advisable, as the entrance, at a height of 57 meters, is a tricky scree slope which requires considerable skill to climb.

At the southern end of Valderøy is **Kongshaugen**, an old royal residence which a bishop by the name of Neumann had excavated. A most unexpected find in the heap of stones were nails of Roman make. North of this, on the island of **Vigra**, is Ålesund's new airport, completed in 1990.

The nearby island of **Giske** has rather more historic associations, as the seat of the famous Giske family which once owned more than 200 farms in Norway and also made a fortune out of fishing, trade and privateering. The Giskes reached the height of their power in 1030, when Harald Hardråda married a woman from this familly, Tora.

Two Norwegian kings were born of this union: Magnus II and Olav Kyrre. It is open to question whether Rollo, the first Duke of Normandy, was also a Giske, since the Danes also claim him. The French, however, believe the Norwegians: the town of Rouen has presented the town of Ålesund with a statue of Rollo, *Gange Rolv*, which stands in Ålesund's By Park.

In the Giske family chapel there is also a genealogical tree of the English royal family, which of course goes back to Rollo, as well. This family chapel demonstrates the Giskes' international connections, although it has never been discovered where the white marble for the chapel came from. The marble is hard to recognize as such, as it had to be painted with lime to protect it against the aggressive sea air. Today the Giske chapel is popular for weddings in Ålesund and the surrounding area.

For the convenience of the 200 residents of **Godøy**, a pleasant island for a

walk in the brisk ocean air, a 3.4-kilometer tunnel was dug to connect it with the mainland.

Naturalists and bird-watchers should flock to the island of ***Runde** ㉟, 20 kilometers away. Resident here is the largest bird colony in southern Norway, with hundreds of thousands of breeding birds, including gannets and kittiwakes. Visits to this wildlife preserve are most rewarding during breeding season, which falls in June and July. A toll bridge links Runde to the island of Hareid.

From Ålesund to Molde, Town of Poets and Roses

To continue on from Ålesund along the coast and across its islands, there is again a choice of two routes. The western of these, by way of Midsund, is much more time-consuming, albeit more scenic than the faster eastern variation. In both cases, you have to take the E136/39 back to **Skødjebru**, northern Europe's largest stone bridge. Here, the R661 branches off

to **Eidsvik** at the end of the **Grytefjord**; follow the R659 along the shores of small lakes and side fjords to **Brattvåg** ㊵. This fishing harbor is the central town in the **Haram** district because it's the main ferry dock for boats to all the offshore islands. A 20-minute ferry ride (7 times a day) brings you to **Dryna** on the island of **Midøy**. Shortly before **Bjørnerem**, a strange stone fence marks the border between Sunnmøre and Romsdal. It was put up when this was the border between Danish Norway and Sweden, from 1658 to 1660.

As the islands are all linked by bridges, it doesn't take long to reach **Midsund** ㊶, on the island of **Otrøy**. Midsund lives from fishing and processing of the catch; it's also a veritable paradise for recreational deep-sea fishermen, who can try their luck either from the mainland or from a boat. The R668 leads past attractive **Otrøy Church** dating from 1878 to the ferry harbor of **Jenset**.

Since there are no offshore islands here, there is a fine view of the open sea, although observers may have to contend with the strong northwest wind. On the little road that runs south across Otrøy, also leading to Jenset, there are, at **Sør-Heggdal**, **Opstad** and **Nord-Heggdal**, rock drawings of a kind otherwise only found on the other side of the Arctic Circle. The ferry crossing from Jenset to Julneset takes 15 minutes; there are 25 ferries a day.

After 8 kilometers the road comes to the "rose town" of **★Molde ⑫**, which has earned this epithet because of its mild climate. Maple, lime and horse chestnut trees and several types of roses grow here on the far side of the 62nd parallel, farther north than anywhere else in the world. Molde, with a population of 20,000, is one of the most important tourist resorts on the coast of western Norway. In the 14th century it was already an important harbor for the flourishing wood trade with England and Holland; later on, wood was replaced with other goods.

Growing slowly but steadily, Molde had a town charter by 1742. But the city's centuries of development were cruelly interrupted when Molde was bombed by the Germans in 1940 and completely destroyed. Also wiped out in the bombardment were the royal birches (*kronbjørkja*) which Håkon VII and Crown Prince Olav had planted on a visit here. After the war, King Olav V planted new ones as a symbol of a new beginning.

As might be expected, the town's reconstruction only adhered in part to the original city plan; in many places, developers opted for more generous, larger-scale solutions. The best view of the town is from the observation point of **Varden**, where from 400 meters up you can look out over the 80 snowcapped peaks of the Romsdalfjell opposite.

Right: Roses are the hallmark of Molde; here, at a latitude farther north than they're found anywhere else in the world, they not only grow, but flourish.

Further points of interest are the **Romsdal Museum** at the upper end of the town park, which preserves at least 60 houses from Møre and Romsdal, and the open-air museum on the island of **Moldeholmene**.

Moldegård is the name of a collection of patricians' houses on the **Fannestrandvei**, the oldest of which dates from the 16th century. Among them is the **Amtmannsgård**, which the Møller family has owned for generations. The poet Bjørnstjerne Bjørnson (who won the Nobel Prize in 1903), who went to school in Molde, often came here as a guest of his schoolfriend This Møller, and Ibsen wrote his *Rosmersholm* in the house's blue drawing-room.

The second alternative route from Ålesund to Molde is the E136/39 over **Sjøholt**, the high part of the Romsdalfjell, and the **Skorgedal** to the **Tresfjord,** a side arm of the Romsdalfjord (you can also drive from Sjøholt through Stordal to the Geirangerfjord, and thus change over to the inner fjord route). The E136/39 climbs steeply, reaching its highest point at Fjellstuva. Between the many snow-capped peaks of the **Romsdalfjell** there are numerous summer roads leading to signposted hiking trails. Many of these begin at so-called *seter*, summer farms where you can eat, drink, and leave your car.

At **Skorgenes**, the E39 bears due north and passes through the ecclesiatical town of **Vestnes Furneset ⑬** to reach the dock from which the ferry leaves for the 35-minute crossing to Molde (making the trip 26 times a day).

The E136 circumnavigates the Tresfjord on the eastern shore; from there, ferries cross the Romnsdalsfjord to Molde. From this point on, the E136 unfortunately has relatively little to offer, apart from a number of new tunnels and a broad and newly paved surface. However, it is useful for a detour via Åndalsnes to Trollstig.

Dried Cod, Cliffs and Churches: From Molde to Kristiansund

1992 saw the completion of the expressway between Molde and Kristiansund, an immense project that involved connecting the three islands of Kristiansund not only to one another but also, by means of bridges and tunnels, with the mainland to the north and south. This route (E39) first follows the **Fannefjord** to **Oppdøl** and then ascends to the Fursefjell, which reaches altitudes of up to 1,000 meters. From here it goes down to the **Batnfjord** and follows it past **Gjemnes**. The E39 then continues over an imposing suspension bridge to the island of **Bergsøya**; while the R1 branches off and runs through a tunnel to the island of **Frei** and towards Kristiansund.

Near the tunnel's mouth, on the island, is the church settlement of Frei, surrounded by old sailors' graves and several burial mounds. In 1951, Håkon VII unveiled a monument commemorating the battle that took place 1,000 years ago between Håkon III and the minor king Erik Ullserk. Håkon was the victor in this conflict and Ullserk lost his life; he is also honored with a memorial stone. Not far from **Kvalvåg ㊹**, where the ferry used to dock, are the ruins of **Bjøkerstad**, a former residence built for Håkon III; a summer road runs past it. Shortly before the bridge to Kristiansund, at **Bolga**, there is a splendid view of the islands of Kirklandet, Nordlandet and Innlandet, on which Kristiansund is located.

Much more beautiful than this route, the most interesting part of which in any case comes after Kristiansund, is the one that runs directly along the Atlantic. To reach this, turn off from the E39 a few kilometers east of Molde, at **Arø**, and continuing on the R64 to **Sylte ㊺**, where the actual Atlantic stretch begins (R664).

Near Sylte is one of the strangest "churches" in Norway: ***Trollkyrka**, the church of the trolls. This is actually a limestone cave 70 meters long and as much as 7 meters high, which contains a waterfall. The hike up to the mouth of this

cave isn't all that easy, and takes about an hour and a half; sturdy shoes and a flashlight are essential for a visit. This eerie cave was veritably predestined to be mythologized as the trolls' shrine. These fabulous beings who populate Norwegian fairy tales shun the light, and therefore retreat into caves and holes in the ground. And with good reason: if the sun does catch them, they turn into stones. They have tails like cows, which the female trolls hide under long skirts, and they sing in spine-tingling tones. In other respects, they demonstrate fully human characteristics and behavior, ranging from the friendliness of an elf to the maliciousness of Rumpelstiltskin. It's only natural that creatures around whom so many popular beliefs have grown up would have their own place of worship: the troll church.

The R664 passes through **Elnesvågen** on the **Julsund**, which is traversed by the

Above: Fairy tales and legends aplenty have grown up around the subject of trolls. Right: In the Troll church.

shipping route from Molde to Kristiansund. At **Bud** ㊻, a small fishing village on a point of land jutting out into the ocean, all the ships are obliged to make a detour out into the open sea, as there are no more offshore islands along this stretch of coast. This passage, known as the *Hustadvika*, has been notorious for centuries. More than 3,000 miniature islands and cliffs stick out of the sea or lurk just beneath the water's surface, and ships have to make a wide arc around them. Fishermen, however, are obliged to venture in among these dangerous rocks, as it is here that the most fish are to be found.

Bud itself played an important part in Norwegian history: in 1533 the last Archbishop of Trondheim, Olav Engelbrektson, assembled here the remaining members of the national council and representatives of the middle classes in order to push through the separation of Norway from Denmark through the election of a Norwegian king. It was a desperate attempt to stem the tide of the Reformation, which had already taken in Sweden and was steadily gaining ground in Denmark. The attempt failed and Norway remained with the Danes, who introduced the Reformation here four years later and thus drove Englbrektson out of the country and into exile in Rome.

The whole stretch of coast that follows is dominated by the fishing industry. Although there was a slump in business when the shoals of herring failed to materialize at the end of the 16th century, things soon recovered after the Dutchman Jappe Ippe settled in Kristiansund in 1692. Known as the "father of *klippfisk*," it was he who introduced the method of splitting cod in half, soaking it in brine and then drying it on the rocks, creating a durable, and exportable, product. The Hustadvika coast, where there are so many bare cliffs and rock surfaces, offers ideal terrain for this type of conservation. An alternate method was to implement wooden frames with poles on which the drying fish could be hung. This saved on labor, since it meant the fish didn't have to be turned over by hand to dry on both sides.

Southwest of Bud is the rocky island of **Bjørnsund**, once an important fishing center, but finally abandoned by its last inhabitants in 1960. The houses have remained standing; since then, they've only seen use in the summer, by their owners or by tourists. In the warmer months there is also a ferry connection over the mainland.

Near **Hustad 47** there's another royal residence, the legendary **Hustadir**, where King Øystein died in 1123. It is located at the end of a small fjord, the only one of note on the Hustadvika coast.

Tiny **Sandvik** has one famous son: Anders Sandvig, founder of the best-known Norwegian open-air museum in Lillehammer, was born here. In **Vevang 48** the R664 rejoins the R64; this is the beginning of *Atlanterhavsveien, a bridge road some 8 kilometers long which connects the small islands at the entrance to the **Kornstadfjord**. Today, this route, a toll road, is the biggest tourist attraction between Molde and Kristiansund. Not only has it improved the local infrastructure, but it's also one of the few places on the mainland from which people can get a taste of the skerries and the open sea. There are also a number of lay-bys and parking lots where drivers can pull over to enjoy the views. In good weather, when the sea is calm, you can even see down into the fascinating world underwater; diving is also becoming increasingly popular here. When the weather is fine the anglers stand practically shoulder to shoulder, and even if a strong northwest wind is blowing the raging of the elements makes a fascinating spectacle.

Kårvåg is on the island of **Avarøya**; here, you can (and should) leave the R64 and turn onto the 11-kilometer inner fjord route that runs through Hestad to

Kvernes. At **Kornstad 49**, which has a 19th-century church, you come to the fjord of the same name. At **Rånes 50** (*Rånestangen*) are the **Håkorv**, huge Bronze Age burial mounds up to 21 meters in diameter. The road follows the Kvernesfjord to **Rugse**, where there is a magnificent look-out point several hundred yards from the road.

On the spit of land occupied by **Kvernes 51** there are two churches. From the parking lot, the old **stave church** is almost completely hidden by the new church. The former is hard to recognize as such, as it has been rebuilt several times over the centuries. It probably dates from the 13th century, but lost its ambulatory as early as 1432; and in 1633 the choir was renovated and enlarged. Beautiful 16th-century paintings have been preserved in the interior, as have parts of the old retable. In the northern transept are coffins which were found under the church floor.

Kvernes also has a small **open-air museum** with ten buildings, including *rorbuer*, wooden huts that were used for storing boats and also for sleeping in during the fishing season. Today many *rorbuer* are being modernized and rented out to tourists. At **Bruhagen**, the road rejoins the R64, which continues on to **Bremsnes** and the ferry to Kristiansund.

*Kristiansund – Wood, Fish and Oil

The history of the town of **Kristiansund** ⑫ also began with the wood trade. Wood from the interior of the country, tied into rafts and floated downriver to the coast, was shipped from here to Scotland and England by merchants from Fosna in Trøndelag. They called their settlement *Litte Fosna*, a name that the main island of Kirkelandet kept until 1742. When King Christian VI granted the town its own charter, however, the place was renamed.

By this point, the herring trade had already risen to replace the wood trade; and herring was later replaced, in its turn, by dried cod; the town even had its own fleet that exported the fish as far afield as Brazil and Cuba. Although fish still plays an important part in the town's economic life today, the focus has noticeably shifted to the building of special ships and repairs for the offshore oil industry.

Kristiansund is a new town, as the bombardment of 1940 destroyed all of its historic buildings with the sole exception of the **Lossiusgård**, an old patrician farmstead dating from the 18th century. This is located on the northern tip of the island of Innlandet, with a splendid view of the old harbor, **Vågen**. The best panoramic view is from **Varden**, a hill on the **Vuggavei** near the old fresh-water reservoir of **Vanndammen**. On Varden there is now a small lookout tower in place of the former watchtower that once guarded the entrance to the harbor.

Right: In spite of diminishing stocks, fishing is an important branch of the economy.

Located on the **Langvei**, the road into Kristiansund, is **Kristiansund Church**, indubitably one of the most unusual churches in all Norway. The creation of O. Østbye in the 1960s, it has huge colored windows so designed that the interior of the church reflects every change in the light outside.

The **Nordmøre Museum** is an interesting fishing museum with exhibits illustrating the various methods of catching and processing all manner of fish. More direct experience of the water is possible in the busy **harbor**, a hive of activity with passenger ferries (which run back and forth in a grid pattern to connect the three islands), passenger ships, oil suppliers and fishing boats which sell their catch right on the quay. In front of the modern town hall boats leave for a highly recommended tour to the island of **Grip** ⑬, 14 kilometers to the northwest. Surrounded by 80 tiny islands, it is only inhabited in the summer and has the smallest stave church in Norway.

Between Kristiansund
and Trondheim

There are three routes from Kristiansund to Trondheim, ranging from 190 kilometers to 250 kilometers in length and including one to three ferries. The first route (R680) runs along the coast and the outer fjords, while the second (R71) follows the inner fjords; the two meet up halfway to Trondheim. The third alternative, through the Surnadal (R65), runs past the hiking area of Trollheimen.

Running east from Kristiansund, the R680 passes the airfield on its way to **Seivika**. The ferry across the Årsundfjord to **Tømmervåg** on the island of **Tustna** takes 25 minutes and runs 16 times a day. From Tømmervåg, the road follows Tustna's northwest coast; with mountains of up to 900 meters high and an inland lake, this island is today a popular weekend destination for Kristiansund's resi-

dents. The sunsets here are particularly spectacular: seen from the look-out point by **Leira** 🞄, the sun sinks into the sea right behind the island of Grip. From here a small path leads up onto the fjell in the interior of the island.

Leaving Tustna, drivers cross the new bridge at **Gullstein** and come to **Nordheim** on the island of **Stabben**. Here, in the 10th century, there was a sea battle between Harald Hårfagra (Fairhair) and a minor king from Nordmøre; Fairhair won, and consequently added this area to his growing realm. **Aukan** 🞄 is a busy ferry port; ferries leave from here for **Smøla**, **Hitra** and **Vinsternes** on **Ertvågøy** (a 15 minute crossing, 20 times a day). There are also numerous fishing huts on the island and along the coast and the fjords.

A bridge across the **Foldfjord** leads to **Ånes** on the **Auresund**. Located in this sound is the island of Rotøya with the ruins of the old trade settlement of **Lurvik**. The ferry to **Aure** 🞄, back on the mainland, takes 15 minutes and runs 25 times a day. Aure's church, which itself dates from the 1920s, contains a 15th-century retable depicting Apollonia, patron saint of dentistry. The clergyman's house dates from the early 19th century. Aure is also a center for sport fishermen, as well as hunters out to bag a few of the area's large deer population.

Near **Eide**, the road comes to the **Drommesund**, which it now follows. At **Torset** there is a small bridge to the offshore island of **Skarsøy**; on this island, at **Finset** 🞄, is one of the largest stalactite caves in all of Norway. **Arvåg** marks the end of the sound, and **Brekka**, the border between the provinces of **Møre og Romsdal** and **Sør-Trøndelag**.

On the **Heimsfjell** the road makes a sharp turn to the south. This area, with its abundance of game, is a good place to buy products made of deer and elk leather. **Dalum** 🞄 is a downhill skiing center, and **Kyrksæterøra** 🞄 is well-known for its salmon and trout farms. It is also a source of silicon, the material vital to the computer industry: 50,000 tons of it are ex-

tracted here annually. The road follows the **Rovatn**, a lake with an ample stock of fish, and at Vinjeøra joins the E39, which continues in the direction of Trondheim.

Another route from Kristiansund to Trondheim starts on the R1 out of Kristiansund and over the island of Frei to the island of Bergsøya, then continues on the E39 across another bridge to **Aspøya**, part of the **Tingvoll** peninsula. On the other side of Tingvoll a ferry runs from **Kanestraum** to **Halsanaustan** (a 20-minute crossing, 20 times a day). In **Halsa** ⑥⓪ at the end of the **Skålvik** is **Halsa Church**, one of Norway's finest rural churches, which dates from the 18th century. Out in the sea west of **Hendset** lie the offshore islands of Stabben and Ertvågøy. Continuing on around the **Valsøyfjord**, the road passes through three tunnels on its way to **Rendal**, but you can save 22 kilometers by using the new bridge. From here, you go along the

Above: Elk are by no means rare, but they are unfortunately rather camera-shy.

Vinjefjord, where there are plenty of lay-bys with panoramic views and several attractive picnic spots, complete with grills. In **Vinjeøra** ⑥① at the end of the fjord is an octagonal church dating from 1820, with a crucifix that probably dates from the 11th century and is therefore the oldest in Norway. Here, the E39 joins up again with the R680. **Baksetrene**, at 350 meters, marks the highest point on the route; it also commands views of the **Gråorfjell** (800 meters) and the 1,000-meter **Ruten** to the south.

At **Fannrem**, the R65 joins the E39, which continues on to Trondheim. This is the shortest route between Kristiansund and Trondheim.

The third variation starts out in the same way as the one above; but in **Betna**, east of Halsa, the E39 and the R65 branch apart. By **Settemsdal** ⑥② a commemorative stone pays tribute to the courageous huntsmen who in 1756 freed the 12 inhabitants of a house that was being besieged by a bear. At **Nordmarka** ⑥③, between **Bæverfjord** and **Skei**, there's another panoramic outlook, as well as a limestone cave with stalactites, the **Linåskirka**. At Skei, the road leaves the fjord system and climbs up into the Surnadal.

Mo ❻ has a Y-shaped church unique in Norway which dates from 1728. A plaque in the church commemorates a visit by King Christian V and states that the king is "always welcome" and "can eat and drink" at any time.

Extending south of the R65 is ***Trollheimen**, one of the loveliest hiking regions in Norway. Along the roads that surround this area there are a range of campgrounds, private huts and youth hostels; wihtin the area itself are three large, full-service huts managed by the Trondheim Hiking Association, as well as a number of simpler, or private, accommodations. The highest peaks here measure more than 1,800 meters; one attraction for climbers is the striking Dalatårnet, "the Matterhorn of Norway." Hikers especially appreciate the varied valley and mountain landscapes with a wide range of plant and bird life, as well as a large population of red deer.

From **Øvre Surnadal ❻**, on the R65, a summer road leads to Gråsjøen, a mountain lake and the start of a five-hour hiking trail to the **Trollheimshytta**. The **Rindal**, which branches off at **Bolme**, is also a good hiking and fishing area and has camping facilities.

At **Storås** the R65 reaches the **Orkla**, one of the best salmon-fishing rivers in Norway. To the south, an especially beautiful road leads along the Orkladal to the E6; while to the north, the road continues to **Orkanger ❻** on the **Orkdalsfjord**, a side arm of the Trondheimfjord. This village, with a population of 6,000, is the terminus of the **Thamshaven railway**, which used to connect the harbors on the Trondheimfjord; today, the train operates as a railway museum, making summer runs to **Løkken Verk** in the upper **Orkla Valley**.

THE INNER FJORD ROUTE FROM BERGEN TO TRONDHEIM

This route primarily involves using the E16 as far as Sogndal and also follows the Bergen railway as far as Voss. Although once a route of spectacular scenic beauty, it has lost a great deal of its original charm due to the tunnels that have replaced the hairpin bends, leveled, widened roads and stretches of straight expressway. Today the E16 is doubtless one of the most frequented roads in western Norway, and not just because of road improvements but also because, in spite of everything, it is still a scenic route. It is also the most important connection between Oslo and Bergen. Parts of the old road are, however, still open and there are several points at which drivers can switch from the new E16 to the old R13.

Leave **Bergen** along Ytre Arna, Indre Arna and the new toll tunnel at **Garnes**, and continue to Trengereid where the E16 and R7 fork. The former follows the **Veafjord**, which forms the eastern border of the island of Osterøy, until past **Vaksdal ❻**. This town is the unofficial "mill" of Norway, producing thousands of tons of fish meal and concentrated feed as well as flour and noodles. The history of this industry is illustrated by the 250-year-old wood mill, which, still in working order, now functions as a museum.

The **Dalevågen Tunnel** leads to **Dale ❻**, main village of the Vaksdal district with a population of 5,000. From here there is a summer road past the **Hamlagrøvatn** to **Bulken**, a place of great scenic beauty which is rather enigmatically advertised in the informational brochure the town has, but advertized rather ambiguously in the local brochure with the slogan "fasten your seat belts" – open to a variety of interpretations.

The **Bolstadfjord** which now follows is the final inland arm of the Bergen fjord system; from here, you can still reach the town by boat. **Bolstadøyri** was the home of the poet Knut Horvei, who lived in the building known as the "palace," a 16th-century manor with a magnificent library which is, unfortunately, not open to the public. The river **Vosso**, which flows into the **Evangervatn** at this point, rates as the best salmon river in the area. On the market square of **Evanger** 69 (population 250) is the statue of a local son who became a senator in America.

Bulken also marks the beginning of the Voss skiing area. From here, there is a good view of the 1,305-meter peak of **Gråsida** to the southeast. A small side road leads to the three-house village of **Bergslien**, birthplace of the dynasty of painters and sculptors of the same name. The E16 follows the northern shore of the **Vangsvatn**, which ends at Voss; on the south side a summer road has been built soley to give anglers better access to the water in the salmon season.

⋆Voss

Voss 70 is a new old town with a population of 14,000 –"old" because it is known to have existed more than 2,000 years ago, "new" because it had to be rebuilt after World War II. About 1 kilometer before the town center as you approach it from Bergen on the **Gullfjordsvei**, which runs parallel to the E16, are the **Finneloft** and the **Lydvaloft**. The former is probably the oldest wooden secular building in Norway: once part of an aristocratic farm, it dates from the 13th century. The second farm, built at least 200 years later, has been restored; within it, there are still fragments of the wall painting from the late Middle Ages with which it was originally decorated. Also outside the town center is the valley end of the **Hangursbanen**, a cable car which ascends to a height of 660 meters; at the top is a restaurant with a magnificent view over the town and lake. The **Hangursnolten** is also the location of Voss's ski center, which has a number of lifts and 40 kilometers of cross-country ski trails.

Right: Ski purists and aficionados swear by Telemark bindings.

A little north of the town center, at the end of the Mølsterveien, is the Mølstertunet complex, the **Voss Folkemuseum**. In contrast to many other open-air museums, these houses are still in their original location; a 400-year-old settlement was simply converted into a museum. South of town, on the Randalselv, the **Magnus Dagestad Museum** displays a range of Norwegian folk art and crafts.

The main feature of interest in the town, however, is **Voss Church** (*Vangskyrkja*). It was built between 1271 and 1277 on the site of a wooden church that St. Olav had put up in 1023. The octagonal tower is constructed of massive wooden beams joined only by wooden nails. The church itself is a Romanesque stone building made of local slate, with walls up to 150 centimeters thick. Dominating the impressive interior is an altar painted by Elias Fiigenschoug, a Bergen-born student of the great artist Peter Paul Rubens. Further features of interest are the Renaissance pulpit, the paintings of prophets and saints in the choir, and the wooden decoration in the nave.

Southeast of the church, on the lake side of the post office, there's a **St. Olav's Cross**, one of the oldest such crosses in existence; the citizens of Voss are said to have put it up immediately after their conversion to Christianity in 1023. Close by is the Bergslien Stone, which commemorates a local dynasty of painters and sculptors. Last of this line, the sculptor Nils Bergslien created a bronze relief of a bridal procession, complete with horses, which adorns the assembly house by the station; a wooden copy of this work is on display in Mølstertunet. Little **St. Olav's Chapel** is now used by the nuns of the congregation of St. Francis Xavier as a meditation center; members of the public

can also apply to attend. In the summer, the adult education center here also offers very popular painting courses.

At Skulestadmoen there is a turnoff to the skiing center of **Bavallen** ❼; its slalom and downhill slopes are up to the standards of international competitions. At **Tvinde** ❼, at the end of the Løvatn, there's another open-air museum, the **Nesheimtunet**, which includes an interesting salmon smokehouse with one of its smoking chambers in working order. Passing **Taulen** and **Hole Bru**, the road continues to **Vinje** ❼, where the village church, dating from 1868, contains an altarpiece by the above-mentioned Nils Bergslien.

En Route to Fridtjof the Giant: Detour to *Vik and Vangsnes

Just under 20 kilometers north of Vinje, shortly before the R13 disappears into the tunnel under the border between the provinces of Hordaland and Sogn og Fjordane, the most spectacular stretch of this road begins. After four hairpin turns with a gradient of up to 15 percent, the road reaches the top of the **Halsebakken**, which has the best view of the Sendefoss waterfall to the west. The **Målsetvatn** is a paradise for trout fishermen, and at Svingen there is a splendid view of **Vik** ❼ on the Sognefjord. From the village center, a side road leads to the **Hopperstad stave church**, which dates from the mid-12th century. Ornamenting its interior is a Gothic altar baldachin, beautifully carved with heads and fine ornamentation; it is painted with illustrations of scenes from the childhood of Christ. Built before St. Andrew's crosses were used to stabilize this type of construction, the church still demonstrates certain features of stone architecture such as the cubiform capitals of the nave, which were structurally not necessary at all. There are a number of St. Andrew's crosses present as structural elements, but these all date from later renovations.

Having completely restored the Hopperstad stave church at the end of the 19th

century, the architect Blix also bought the nearby Romanesque **stone church of Hove** and restored that, too. The Hove Church is an architectural oddity: its builders borrowed the kind of zigzag ornamentation that's a feature of Norman English buildings to adorn the tower portal. Dating from the 12th century, this is probably the oldest stone building in the province of Sogn; Blix himself is also buried here. *Olsok* services are still held in the church; this is the service held on *Olsok* day, July 30, the anniversary of St. Olav's death.

There were probably one or two other churches in the vicinity, but these have long since disappeared. The high proportion of churches even in sparsely-populated areas is due to the fact that most of the churches were privately owned, and were only open to the members of the families that owned them.

Above: The stave church of Hopperstad at Vik.
Right: The deep Sognefjord is also suitable for cruise ships.

Other members of the community who were not so privileged as to have their own place of worship had to make their way to the nearest parish church.

The R13 continues to **Vangsnes** ⓫. Approaching it, you can see the **colossal statue of Fridtjof**, a 13-meter figure atop a 14.5-meter granite pedestal, from a long way off.

Fridtjof is the hero of the Icelandic legend who entered the god Baldur's sacred grove in order to look for his lover, Baldur's daughter Ingeborg. Since she was already married to someone else, Fridtjof had to atone for his offence; but on his deathbed, Ingeborg's aged and noble husband bequeathed him both wife and realm. The statue itself was made by Max Unger for the German emperor Wilhelm II, who then presented it to the Norwegians. This was just one of many gifts and bequests which this potentate made to the country, which he loved; in fact, even today he is more popular in Norway than in his home country, and not even the German occupation in World War II sig-

nificantly changed this fact. In the southeast corner of the park where the statue stands is the **Fridtjofshaug**, and on the east side the **Ingeborgshaug**; these Bronze Age burial mounds are popularly held to be the graves of the famous lovers. This, however, remains a matter of speculation, and just as there is little historical proof to demonstrate that Ingeborg and Fridtjof ever actually existed, so, too, the identities of those who are buried in these mounds remain unknown.

From Vangsnes, a ferry makes the 15-minute crossing (19 times a day) via **Dragsvik** to **Balestrand** **⑦⑥** (Baldurstrand) where there is also a statue of the divinity Baldur. Balestrand is one of the most important tourist resorts on the Sognefjord; from here, boats depart to practically every other town on the fjord. You can also take the ferry that shuttles the 15 minutes over to **Hella**, from where you can continue on to Sogndal. Since the new R5 from Sogndal to Bøyum opened in 1995, ferry service to the end of the **Fjærlandsfjord** has been discontinued.

Waterfalls, Winding Roads and Ferries: Stalheim - Gudvangen - Flåm

If you omit the above detour or return to Vinje, the main E16 continues on to **Oppheim** **⑦** on the lake **Oppheimsvatn**. In the church here, the altar painting is yet another work by the prolific Nils Bergslien. Oppheim is a tourist center with hiking and winter sports facilities; the chair lift to **Bergshovden** enjoys especially heavy use. The local open-air museum has unusual "row houses" as much as 300 years old; this form of construction may represent an early attempt to save energy.

After Haugsvik, the road climbs steeply to **Stalheim**, where the rock cliffs fall almost vertically to the **Nærøydal** below. Today, visitors can enjoy one of the most magnificent views in Norway in comfort from the armchairs of the **Stalheim Hotell**, a view that was already attracting painters in the 19th century. One of the first to warm to its beauty was the "romantic realist" C. Dahl (1788-1857), a

native of Bergen, whose famous picture *View of Stalheim* now hangs in Oslo's National Gallery. Although it made the view famous, this image can't really be blamed for the transformation of the foyer of the Stalheim Hotel into an international souvenir shop purveying a full range of cheap mementos and kitsch, from knick-knacks of Far East manufacture to landscapes by bad Dahl imitators.

From the upper end of the ***Stalheimskleiva** ⑦, a road built in the 19th century from the valley up onto the fjell, you have the best view of the **Stalheimfoss**, a waterfall that plunges some 126 meters in a gorge 550 meters deep. The *kleiva* is the steepest road in Europe: with a gradient of as much as 20%, it winds down into the valley in turns with as little as an 8 to 10 meter radius. Now that a tunnel has been built for

Above: The Aurlandsfjord forms the southern end of the Sognefjord system. Right: Flåm station marks the start of one of the most spectacular railway trips in Europe.

the E16, this is only used as a summer road. From the third bend, there is a good view of the Silvefoss, another waterfall which drops an impressive 240 meters.

Visible above the waterfall is the farmhouse where the poet Per Silve (1857-1904) grew up. Silve was the first Norwegian "working-class writer"; he portrayed the problems of the early Industrial Age from a worker's point of view in books such as his greatest masterpiece, *The Strike*. In front of the small **museum**, which displays 2,000 exhibits in 20 buildings, there is a **memorial stone** to this author. Stalheim was also popular with Kaiser Wilhelm II, who enjoyed the view from here of the Sognefjell and the Nærøydal, and often met up with the Norwegian king.

At its lower end, the Stalheimskleiva rejoins the E16, which now follows the Nærøyelv to **Gudvangen**, where the *elv* flows into the fjord. The ****Nærøyfjord** flows into the Aurlandsfjord, which is the southern end of the Sognefjord system. Until 1992, the only way to continue on

from this point was by boat. The car ferry between Gudvangen and Revsnes (Lærdalsøyri) or Kaupanger (Sogndal) takes more than 2 hours. After the completion of the tunnel between Gudvangen and Aurland, ferry service between those two towns was suspended, but the other car ferries still run, as the road between Aurland and the Lærdal is closed in winter and hence does not meet the requirements of a European road. The ferry between Gudvangen and **Lærdalsøyri** thus counts as part of the E16, while the overland connection is the R50. In the 19th century, after the Stalheimskleiva was built, the ferry was part of the postal route between Oslo and Bergen, and in summer as many as 500 horses and carriages at a time are supposed to have waited to get across.

It is almost impossible to say which route onwards from Gudvangen is most attractive. The fjord trip toward Revsnes/Kaupanger through the Nærøyfjord, which is only 500 meters wide, and the ★★**Aurlandsfjord**, which is nearly as nar-

row, with near-vertical walls and many waterfalls, is certainly one of the most beautiful mini-cruises in Norway. However, the land route is also very attractive. In any case, make sure to detour over to **Ramsøy** ⑦, which has the best view over the end of the Nærøyfjord, with the waterfall **Kjelsfoss**, also called *Brudesløret* (Bridal Veil), plunging down into it from above the lookout point. The Viking king Karl (Kalv) is supposed to be buried here.

Ferries, however, are relatively small, only run five times a day, and cannot be booked in advance. If you therefore opt for the land route from Gudvangen, you'll pass through two tunnels, 5 and 11 kilometers, on your way to Flåm. At **Langhuso**, where there is a brief interruption in the long tunnel drive, there is a turnoff to **Undredal** ⑧, approximately 7 kilometers away. The stave church of Undredal is unrecognizable as such from the outside; this miniature church is the smallest of its type on the Norwegian mainland, only 3.7 meters wide and seating just 40 worshippers.

Flåm 🐼, at the end of the Aurlands-fjord, is a typical tourist resort, with a fine country hotel, the **Fretheim Hotel**, dating from the late 19th century. The **train station** and the harbor form the center of the town. In the peak season, as many as seven trains a day on the famous **Flåm Railway**, Europe's steepest and Scandinavia's most spectacular railway line, operate from here to Myrdal, where it is possible to change to the Bergen line.

From Flåm, you can embark on a very attractive excursion called "Norway in a Nutshell," which takes approximately 5 hours round trip. The combination ticket, sold in the town, covers a boat ride through the Nærøyfjord to Gudvangen, followed by a bus to Voss, a train to Myrdal on the Bergen line and the Flåm train back to Flåm. From Flåm's **harbor** there are passenger boats available to

Above: Even in well-preserved stave churches – like this one in Borgund – the wood has to be regularly treated. Right: The west portal with the "Norn inscription."

Balestrand, Gudvangen and Utredal, as well as a fast boat to Bergen, which takes three hours.

Flåm Church, dating from the 17th century, stands above the town next to the **Flåmelv**. This river, 44 kilometers long, tumbles from the fjell, at an altitude of 1,500 meters, to the fjord; it is famous for salmon and salmon trout.

The R50 follows the fjord to **Aurlandsvangen 🐼**, which, with a population of 1,000, is the trading and service center, as well as the ecclesiastical center, for the whole area. The **Vangen stone church**, a Gothic building dating from the 13th century, is one of the oldest in the whole province.

Steep Road to an Old Church: From Aurland to Borgund

From **Aurland** the R50, also called the "Summer E16," climbs steeply along the wall of the fjord up onto the fjell, commanding spectacular views from each of its hairpin turns to tempt photographers.

The road then follows the **Hørnadal** and descends again through the **Erdal** to the fjord at Lærdal. This road – narrow but completely paved – is sometimes still closed into early June after particularly heavy winters, since it goes up to a height of 1,300 meters. Around the glacier area of the **Blåskavlen** there are marked hiking trails, and there are a few isolated farmsteads scattered along the road; apart from these, the area is almost entirely uninhabited.

On the south side of the **Lærdalsfjord** the R50 joins the E16. Here the roads have been rebuilt, and on the northbound R5 there is now a new ferry service that shuttles between Fodnes and Mannheller (about a 15-minute crossing), which can only be reached via **Lærdalsøyri ⑬**. This town, which is also known as the "green town" because of the fertility of the soil here, still has a few fine old wooden houses, including the so-called Hanseatic Farm.

From here, 27 kilometers on the E16 toward Oslo brings you to ****Borgund ⑭**, where Norway's best-preserved **stave church** stands, an absolute must on a tour of this area. It is still in its original location, and apart from the windows, which were set in later, has kept its original 12th-century form. Today it is a model for the restoration of other stave churches, since it demonstrates all the elements of architecture and decoration typical of this building type.

The "staves" (*stavre* means "mast" or "column") which make up the frame of the church were dried in the forest, a technique that was also used for making ships' masts: after the branches were cut off and the bark peeled away, the bare trunks were exposed to the wind and weather for 10 to 15 years to take all the inner tension out of the wood. These staves, erected on ground plates, support the saddle roof; they are joined to one another by means of St. Andrew's crosses, framing timber and cleats, with-

out the use of a single nail. It's no coincidence that these buildings resemble ships; their construction is at once extremely stable and so elastic that, rather than resisting the wind, the church is able to move with it.

Surrounding the building's core is a low gallery, protected by a penthouse roof which, like the main roof, is covered with wooden shingles. The ridgepole is adorned with dragon's heads and other mythical creatures; although these are heathen symbols, in the early days of Christianity in Norway they probably represented a kind of insurance against the spirits and demons the worshippers had officially given up. This thesis is also supported by the runic inscription on the west portal, which reads: "I rode past on St. Olav's Day. The Norns did me great harm as I rode past."

Paintings in the originally windowless churches were initially rare and of modest proportions; they only gradually became more common as the interior lighting advanced from pine torches to oil

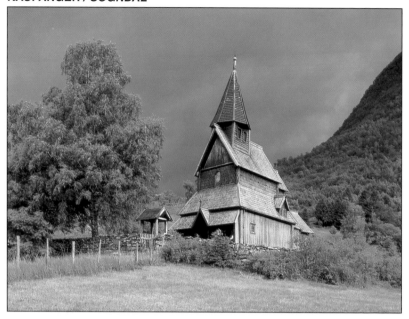

lamps and candles. The stave church of Borgund is consecrated to St. Andrew. It has probably only survived in such good condition because the area's farmers were affluent enough to keep two churches going after the new one was built. Even an empty church must be varnished regularly – hence the dark resin color of the older stave churches – and other repairs are also necessary. The best time to visit is at midday.

Borgund is frequently overrun with tourists; an alternative might be to visit the little-known stave churches of **Øye ㊄** and **Hurum ㊅** (54 and 84 kilometers toward Fagernes, respectively).

Back in Lærdalsøyri, follow the new E16/R4 and cross the **Årdalsfjord** to Mannheller to come, after a few miiles, to **Kaupanger ㊇** on the peninsula between the Lustra- and Sogndalsfjords. This former ferry town, which will soon just be a

Above: On an old thingstead in Urnes is the oldest stave church in Norway. Right: Detail from the north portal.

place on the road, also boasts a stave church from the 12th century. Rebuilt in the 19th century and subsequently restored, it now parades itself the style of a **Renaissance church**; and the original church treasure, which had dispersed to other locations over the years, has now been returned. Excavation work revealed two previous churches under the present building, which, judging from the coins that were found, originated in the early 11th century.

Kaupanger also has a **Boat Museum**, with fjord boats from previous centuries. Halfway to Sogndal, in **Vestrheim ㊈**, is the **Sogn Folkemuseum**, which has 32 original buildings and a new main hall with more than 25,000 exhibits. **Sogndal ㊉**, which has a population of 4,500, is the trade and administrative center of the region. It is known for a famous **runic stone** some 1.5 meters high dating from the 11th century, with an inscription attributing it to St. Olav. This town is also a center for hobby fishermen, and has a number of hotels.

A World of Ice:
Over Jotunheimen to Lom

Sogndal is at the intersection of two major roads, the R5 and the R55. The R5 comes from the Jostedalsbreen in the north and ends in the south at Lærdalsøyri on the E16. The R55 follows the Sognefjord until it meets the E39 at Vadheim; it's more interesting, however, to follow this road northeast across the Jotunheimen to Lom.

At **Solvorn** it is worth taking a small detour over to the **Lustrafjord**, for across the fjord stands the ****stave church of Urnes** ⑨, one of the four buildings in Norway which is on UNESCO's World Cultural Heritage list. Although the car ferry only runs once or twice a day, passenger boats cross the fjord regularly, so that you can leave your car in Solvorn and make the journey. A ten-minute boat ride and a ten-minute walk will bring you to the church of Urnes, which sits in a beautiful, secluded spot on a natural plateau more than 50 meters above the fjord, right next to a farm. There has been a place of worship here ever since prehistoric times; in the early days of the Vikings it was the site of a thingstead. The church was also itself once the center of a huge farm. It was built in the mid-12th century, and the north wall and the northern portal are at least 100 years older, making Urnes the oldest remaining stave church.

If the carving at Urnes is compared with that of the Viking ships in the museum in Oslo, especially the Oseberg ship, there are striking similarities. Accordingly, the style known as the "Urnes style" corresponds to 9th-century Viking tradition, whatever its original source may actually have been. The church itself is a simple wooden building with no high staves or St. Andrew's crosses; the construction is supported by simple wooden pillars one story high, their capitals ornately carved with mythical creatures. In the 17th century the choir was extended,

while the roof turret was added in the 18th century. The enamel inlays on the altar candelabra indicate connections with the town of Limoges in the south of France. In the choir is a crucifixion group which dates from the 13th century. The seated Madonna, one of the oldest statues of the Virgin Mary in Norway, has been transferred from the church to the collection of the University of Bergen. A unique seven-armed candelabra in the form of a Viking ship, which also dates from the 13th century, is a further indication of the seafaring tradition with which the early church architects, and parishioners, identified.

A few kilometers north of Urnes, the **Krokendal** and the **Feigedal** branch off from the district road to **Skjolden**. In the 17th century, gold was found in both of these valleys. Located in the Krokedal is **Kroken Manor**, which belonged to influential Norwegian families from the 14th century on, but is now deserted and falling into ruin. The Feigedal, meanwhile, boasts the **Feigefoss**, one of the largest

southeast (between here and the R55) is a high-altitude, rather challenging hiking area with a number of huts and countless other accommodation options along the roads that run around this glacier territory: the E39, R15, and R55. For most tourists, this area appears rather difficult of access; but information centers such as **Jostedalen Nasionalparksenter** (on the R15), **Fjærland** (off the R5) and **Jostedal** (R55/R604) try to make it a bit more appealing. Here, people less familiar with mountain regions can turn for advice and tips. There are also a number of ways to penetrate into the world of the glaciers from the surrounding valleys in relative comfort: on access roads, by boat, or even in horse-drawn carriages.

From **Nes** ㉑, there is a good view of the Feigefoss on the other side of the fjord. Here, too, is the **Walaks Hotell og Motell**, one of Norway's attractive country hotels, which also organizes boat trips to Urnes. The **Flahamar Gård**, an old farmhouse, is under preservation order; and Ludvig Holberg (1684-1754), regarded as the father of Danish literature, once served as tutor to the family here.

The village of **Luster** ㉓ (pop. 500) has a beautiful stone church, **Dale Church**. Beneath its 16th-century frescoes of Bible scenes, restorers have found traces of paintings some 300 years older. Thanks to its mild climate, Luster is a health resort, and the best view of the surroundings is actually from the sanatorium, reached by means of a cable car. At the end of the Lustrafjord is the vacation resort of **Skjolden** ㉔, sandwiched between water and mountains, where you can hike, take boat trips, sail or catch salmon. A summer road leads up to **Åsetvatn**, where there are three waterfalls which plunge between 260 and 320 meters.

waterfalls in the country, which cascades 218 meters to the valley floor.

Back at Solvorn, the R55 continues to Lustrafjord. **Gaupne** ㉑, center of the district of Luster, has a 17th-century wooden church which incorporates a portal from an older stave church. It has an interesting Renaissance-style interior, and is painted with colorful ranks of intertwined flowers. From Gaupne, the **Jostedalsvei** (R604) leads up to the ㉘**Nigardsbreen**, a much-visited tongue of a glacier on the southern edge of the Jostedalsbreen. From the parking lot, the end of the glacier is 40 minutes away on foot or by boat across the glacier lake; and guided ice tours are available.

To hike across a plateau glacier and the surrounding glacier-covered heights you need experience and/or a knowledgeable guide. **Breheimen**, the region to the

The rest of the 83-kilometer stretch to Lom is dominated by the ***Jotunheimen**, a highland area rather like the Alps which is bordered by the Gudbrandsdal and Valdesdal in the east and the Sognefjord

Above: Guided glacier walks to the Nigardsbreen. Right: A rewarding climb – the view from Galdhøpiggen, at an altitude of 2,469 meters.

in the south. The name Jotunheimen (Home of the Giants) was coined by students who, on hiking trips through the area, were reminded of the frost and ice giants of the Edda saga. Extending over 3,500 square kilometers, 1,140 square kilometers of which are a national park, this is Northern Europe's highest fjell. The ★**Galdhøpiggen** (2,469 meters) and the ★**Glittertind** (2,464 meters) are also Norway's highest mountains.

In total, the fjell has more than 250 summits higher than 1,800 meters. Most of Jotunheimen is above the tree line, which here runs at a rather high 1,100 meters and must have been even higher after the last Ice Age, something indicated by the pine roots that have been found in the high moors. Studding the area are countless lakes which, together with pretty valleys, alpine pastures and picturesque farmhouses, combine to give the landscape its particular charm.

If the Jotunheimen is a paradise for hikers and mountaineers in the summer, it becomes, in winter, an agglomeration of one ski resort after another. Snow is guaranteed from December to April; in fact, it usually lasts into June, until the summer roads are also open again, while the first snow can fall as early as September. Lining the larger roads are private hotels and pensions; on the hiking trails the *Norske Turistforening* (DNT) has six serviced and 15 unserviced huts, which can accommodate up to 600 people. On its way to the watershed on the border between the provinces of Sogn og Fjordane and Oppland, the R55 ascends, in a series of twists and turns, from sea level to a height of 1,440 meters.

The road climbs evenly as far as **Fortun**, which once sported a stave church that was later transferred to Fantoft, near Bergen. From here, it continues as a *slyngvei*, a serpentining road; at each of its bends is a lay-by where drivers can pull over to take in the different, even-widening views of Fortun and the Lustrafjord. At Berge, the Dutch queen Wilhelmine and the crown princess Juliane probably enjoyed the view when

they were traveling with 16 horses across Jotunheimen, then called Sognefjell, in 1924. They didn't take this road, however, since it was not opened until 1938; the highest serpentine road in Norway, it continues to ascend until it reaches Turtagrø (1,000 meters). Before it was opened, the only routes across the fjell were medieval trade roads, which were only suitable for horse-drawn sleighs or packhorses.

In **Turtagrø** 95 is the famous, comfortable **Turtgarø Hotell**, starting point for mountain hikes and climbing tours. One popular destination is **Skagastølstinda**, the third-highest mountain in the area at 2,405 meters. The first, easier section of this hike takes four hours and ends at the Skagstølsbotn, at a serviced *baude* (hut) offering overnight accommodation. From here, the path runs up to the summit, a

Above: There is no shortage of white water here – rafting in Jotunheimen. Right: Jute carpets with Old Norwegian motifs are popular souvenirs from Lom.

walk which takes another four hours, and rates as difficult. For **Fanavåk** (2,075 meters, 4-5 hours) and **Klypenåser** (1,145 meters, 2-3 hours) it is essential to take a guide; this can be organized through the hotel.

From the Turtagrø Hotell there is also a private road to **Øvre Årdal**; however, it would probably be quicker to cover the 30 kilometers on foot than with a normal vehicle along this route. The best view from this road is from the menhir at **Oscarshaugen**, where the Swedish-Norwegian crown princes Carl XV and Oscar II stayed overnight on their hikes in the 19th century.

The R55 then continues past glaciers and peaks to the **Hervassdammen**. On the old **Hervassbru** is the hut in which Henrik Ibsen was forced to spend three days and nights with his mountain guide in 1862 due to a storm. One result of this enforced sojourn is that he got to know his companion so well that he incorporated some of his traits into the figure of Peer Gynt. Ibsen was not the only poet who hiked in this area: Holberg, Asbjørnsen and H. A. Wergeland also spent holidays here and used some of their experiences in subsequent works. At the highest point of this stretch is the **Sognefjell Turisthytta**, a base for hikers as well as for cross-country skiers interested in using the nearby summer ski trails.

From here, the R55 drops steeply through the Breiseterdal and the Leirdal and passes through the tourist resorts of **Krossbu** and **Bøvertun**. In **Elveseter** there is a big old farm which has been converted into a hotel, the Fjellro Turistheim; and in **Galdesand** 96 is one of the few churches in Jotunheimen, the octagonal Bøverdal church dating from 1864.

A summer road leads to the **Juvasshytta**, starting point of the path to the top of Galdhøpiggen, a climb of three to four hours. In good weather, you can see for almost 100 kilometers, a view that takes in the peak of Glittertind, the height of which can never be given absolutely correctly because of its permanent covering of snow. Don't attempt this ascent in bad weather. From the picturesque **Roisheim Hotell** there is a private road to the **Spiterstulen Turisthytta** (12 kilometers), starting point for hikes to the **Svellnosbreen**.

The road winds down through the **Bøverdal** to Lom, where it meets the R15. With a population of 700, **Lom** 97 is an up-and-coming tourist resort with the infrastructure of a medium-sized service center (doctor, post office, bank, supermarket and garage).

One-hundred-and-fifty-thousand tourists a year already come to visit the town's **stave church**, which is certainly older than the date it was first mentioned in a document, 1240. It is dedicated to the Virgin Mary, as well as John the Baptist and St. Olav. The staves are connected with St. Andrew's crosses; 20 staves support the semicircular balcony.

In the 17th century, the church was extended to the west, windows were cut in the walls and it was redesigned as a cruciform church. The choir and pulpit are from the 18th century and decorated with acanthus leaves, symbol of the growth of faith; the roof is covered with wooden shingles, and impressive dragons' heads crown the ridgepole. The pillars and archivolt (molding round the arch) of the north portal are decorated with carved tendrils and animals, which, although of later vintage, were influenced by the Urnes style.

The **Lom Bygdemuseum** (Museum of Local History) includes the **St. Olavstugga**, a house in which the saint is said to have stayed overnight. Also worth a look is the **Storstabbur**, a three-story corn granary. Today, the old **Gaustadstuggu** is part of the **Fossheim Hotell**, the interior of which could compete with many a local history museum with its wealth of objects.

The R15 continues eastward from Lom towards Otta in the Gudbrandsdal. Any-

one who wants to take the ★**Sensengrat Day Tour** to the top of **Besseggen** (1,743 meters), the mountain made famous by Ibsen's *Peer Gynt*, turn off south at Randen onto road 51 and continue on to **Gjendesheim** (98).

From there, you can travel 30 minutes by boat or four hours on foot to the **Memurubu hut**; from here, the path continues via the dramatic knife-edge Sensengrat ridge of the Besseggen to Gjendesheim (six hours, rated difficult).

To the Geirangerfjord

West of Lom, the R15 follows the Ottadal for 60 kilometers to Grotli. The area has a low rainfall but abundant water, as the snow on the fjell continues to melt into the autumn and feeds the river in the process. Along the river are cataracts, small waterfalls and sizeable lakes, all of them teeming with fish. The Ottadal has more farms and settlements than the valleys of Jotunheimen. Most of the churches are either cruciform churches from the 17th century or octagonal ones from the 18th century; and all have carved pulpits and altarpieces.

Above: In winter, the boat traffic on Lake Gjende comes to a standstill. Right: Even in summer, there's still ice on the Djupvatn.

Vollungsbru (99) is known for its *gråstain* (gray stone), a type of fine granite which is used, among other things, to make small carvings and souvenirs. **Bismo** (100) is called the "accordeon town," as this musical instrument is not only produced here, but also enthusiastically played by many of the townspeople. In **Dønfoss** (101), the Otta forms a waterfall 14 meters high, which is easily accessible; the path to the 281-meter **Pollfoss** (102), by contrast, is harder going. **Skjåkseter** marks the start of the ski area of Grotli, which is used well into the summer. If you're in a hurry, you can take the R15 from Grotli to Langvatn and then down to Geiranger on the R63.

If time is not an issue, take the R258 route from **Grotli** (103); this route starts off

Map pp. 96-97, Info pp. 134-135

in wintry conditions and ends after three hours (27 kilometers) in spring. Narrow and winding, this gravel road through the snow is only single-track in places, but as there are a number of passing places it isn't difficult driving.

Large chunks of ice dot the surface of the Langvatn even in summer, and the **Strynfjell** is a scree desert bleak as a lunar landscape. Glaciers, waterfalls and mountains up to 2,000 meters high are to be seen from what is one of the oldest roads in Norway. Shortly before **Videseter** 104 are the first ski lifts, which even operate in the summer: in fact, summer is the peak ski season here, and people come from miles around in order to ski in August.

From Videseter, the R258 descends around numerous double bends into springtime. By the **Gjøl bru** it rejoins the R15; if you take the new tunnel you are back at the turnoff to Geiranger in 15 minutes, and, at an altitude of 930 meters, back in winter again. The first few miles of the R63 take in another 100 meters of

vertical ascent, and the road reaches its highest point at the **Djupvatn**, which is also where the Otta has its source.

By this lake, where the covering of ice never completely thaws, is a restaurant which is open in summer. A toll road runs from here to the top of the ***Dalsnibba**; from the observation platform at its summit, 1,495 meters up, you have a fantastic view of the fjell, the winding road down to Geiranger and the fjord itself. From this height the cruise ships in the fjord and the cars crawling up and down the road look like toys.

The Dalsnibba is particularly beautiful at sunset, when the last rays of the sun in the west light up the fjord and the peaks turn golden. The road down to Geiranger drops almost 1,500 meters within 24 kilometers of winding but well-kept road; in fact, the fjord is only 6 kilometers away as the crow flies. This downhill trip is spectacular; the road, originally opened in 1895, has 20 narrow curves, some of them hairpin turns. Here, too, you pass directly from the rough highland climate to the mild, protected environment of the fjord.

After about 2 kilometers, a small footpath leads to the **Blåfjell** ⑩ with the *Jyttergryte* (giant pan), a glacier pan 2.2 meters wide and almost 10 meters deep. Shortly before the **Øvre Blåfjellbro** there is a splendid view of the **Flydalshorn** in the west and the **Vindåshorn**, **Såthorn** and **Grindalshorn** in the east. From here you can also make out the so-called "Eagle Road" that climbs the fjell on the other side of the Geirangerford.

At **Ørjaseter** ⑩, *Knuten*, a junction of the old route that dates from before 1895, has been put under a preservation order as an example of road construction of that period. The R63 continues across a small plateau and down through the **Flydal**. On the **Flydalsjuvet** there is a parking lot where you can stop and admire the view; at least half of all the photographs on the postcards of Geirangerfjord were probably taken here.

At **Hole**, a short road turns off to **Vesterås** ⑩, which is nothing but a farmhouse with a large number of goats and a cafeteria. The "walk" to the Storsetfoss, a waterfall which you can walk beneath, takes a good hour and should be regarded more as a training route for strenuous mountain hikes.

At the **Utsiken Bellevue Hotel**, a memorial stone commemorates the coronation of Håkon VII. Above Geiranger is the beautiful, completely renovated **Union Hotel**, a 19th-century establishment with a terrace where, over a cup of coffee, guests can admire the fjord in peace, away from the crowds in the center of town. However, the cemetery wall, by the 19th-century parish church, is an equally quiet place from which to enjoy the view, and costs nothing at all.

Geiranger ⑩ itself today consists almost solely of hotels, pensions and sou-

Right: Seekers of solitude are unlikely to find it on the Geirangerfjord in the summer.

venir shops. This is not surprising considering that the normal quota in high season is 2-3 cruise liners and 20 busloads of tourists a day. ****Geirangerfjord**, also called the "appendix" of the Sunnylvsfjord, is part of the Storfjord system. Some 15 kilometers long, this fjord arm is surrounded by steep cliffs up to 800 meters high.

On the few steep mountain pastures are small farmhouses, but farming here is no longer viable and they have now been abandoned. These farmhouses did have one advantage in days gone by: since the only way to climb the steep cliffs was with the aid of safety ropes, the royal tax collectors had great difficulty carrying out their job: residents simply removed the ropes before they got there. Children who wanted to play outside also had to be secured to prevent them from tumbling into the fjord below.

There are various round trips on the fjord from Geiranger, with departures several times a day. The best is the trip on the car ferry to **Hellesylt** (a one-hour ride 4-13 times a day, depending on the season). Because the ferries are relatively high, there is a better view from the deck than the little fjord boats can offer. A recorded guide that runs during the trip describes all the sights in several languages; these include the famous waterfalls "Suitor," "Bridal Veil" and "Seven Sisters," all of which are only visible during the spring thaw.

To return to Geiranger from Hellesylt, you can go back on the ferry or, more precisely, a combination of ferry and bus, such as the route through **Stranda**, then by ferry from Stranda to **Liabygda** (a 15-minute crossing, 20 times a day) and from **Linge** to **Eidsdal** (a 10-minute crossing with frequent service) around the Sunnylvsfjord and **Norddalsfjord** back to Geiranger. You can of course also do this with your own car. Also attractive are evening seaplane rides, which offer panoramic views of fjord and fjell.

For a long time, Geiranger was only accessible by water or on the Djupvass Road. But 1954 saw the completion of the **Ørnesvingen** (Eagle's Wings), a *slyngvei* which ascends at least 620 meters in 6 kilometers; it starts at **Møll-Grande** , a small village with attractive 200-year-old houses. At each curve the view expands, and at the top of the road there's a parking lot from where drivers can take in the whole panorama. **Korsmyra** marks this road's highest point; from here, it follows the Eidsdal to the town of the same name on the Norddalsfjord, where a 10-minute ferry ride brings you to Linge on the northern shore.

From Linge, a worthwhile detour leads to **Stordal** , 20 kilometers away. Just outside the village is **Stordal Church**, a building from the 18th century. This is less interesting for its architecture than for the wall and ceiling paintings inside the church, which were created early on in its history.

A journeyman who urgently needed money offered his services to the local community as a church painter and was taken on. It was probably the first and last commission of his life. There is no question that his oeuvre is absolutely unique. The figures of the saints with their hair on end look more like Slovenly Peter, while the symbols of the evangelists – angel, bull, lion and eagle – are fantasy creatures pure and simple, and the artist's use of perspective anticipated the developments of Cubism by several centuries.

A few kilometers past Linge, **Valldal** lies at the mouth of the **Tafjord**. Along this fjord's northern shore runs an ancient path that is said to have been used by St. Olav on his flight to Gardarike. On this path there is also a memorial stone for the 40 victims of the landslide of 1934 when 2 million cubic meters of rock slid from the cliff into the fjord.

The Valldal, protected from the wind by its north-south alignment, is the strawberry center of central Norway; strawberry fields line the road, and in season the farmers sell their produce by the roadside.

*The Trollstig

After 22 kilometers the road reaches the bridge called **Gudbrandsbru**, which crosses the deep canyon, only 5 meters wide, cut by the **Gudbrandselv**. From here, it continues past small lakes and waterfalls up to **Skærsura**, where legend has it that St. Olav and his followers had to clear a path through the mighty boulders: the 20 men are supposed to have rolled away more than 100 boulders as big as houses.

Stigrøra marks the highest point of this stretch, and is followed shortly afterwards by the large parking lot of **Troll-stigheimen**. In addition to a restaurant, a cafeteria and various souvenir shops, there is a path to the observation platform some 500 meters away. This has the best view of the Trollstig, a road built in 1936 into the almost vertical mountainside, and of the Isterdal some 300 meters below.

There is also an impressive Alpine panorama: to the west are mountains around 1,500 meters high, including the **Bispen** (Bishop), **Kongen** (King), **Drottningen** (Queen) and **Karitind**; while to the east is the jagged horizon formed by the **Trolltindane**, or "Witches Peaks," some 1,760 meters in height. There are hiking trails up all these mountains, but they should only be attempted with an experienced guide; for this is a summer skiing area, and winter conditions prevail all year round.

Caravans and campers are not allowed on the eleven hairpin turns of the **Troll-stig Road** (*Trollstigvei*). A short stop on the Stigfossbru is recommended: the waterfall is so close to the road that if you aren't careful to stand on the side protected from the wind, you may be the recipient of an unwanted shower.

Right: Trollstigen, the troll road, consists of eleven hairpin turns zigzagging up the steep mountainside.

Once at the bottom, in the Isterdal, look back up at the Trollstig and the impressive mountains towering above it. In **Sogge** ⑫, there is a path to **Grytten Church**, an attractive peasant church dating from the 19th century.

After a few kilometers the road enters the picturesque village of **Åndalsnes** ⑬ (population 3,000) at the end of the Romsdalsfjord, at the mouth of the river Rauma. This is also the terminus of the Rauma railway, a branch line of the Nordland railway which comes from Dombås; the town is also a port of call for cruise liners, and various firms here keep in business supplying the oil platforms in the Atlantic. At the beginning of this century, it became a base for climbing tours in the Trollstig area; its **Tinden** (Peaks) **Museum** documents the development of climbing.

Between Åndalsnes and Trondheim

From Åndalsnes, there are two possible routes drivers can take to Trondheim: you can either take the E136 through the Romsdal to Dombås and continue on the E6 to Trondheim, or take the R64/660/62 to Sunndalsøra and go through the Sunndal to hook up with the E6 at Oppdal.

The E136 through the Romsdal is the fastest connection; the well-made road following the foaming Rauma and the railway line is almost all on the level. The most striking sight along this stretch is the **Trollveggen**, the 1,000-meter west wall of the Trolltindane, which was not climbed until 1967.

Ten kilometers further on is a turnoff into the **valley of Marstein** ⑭, one of the narrowest valleys in Norway, which gets no sunlight for fully 5 months of the year. For the next 80 kilometers there are no particular highlights.

The road continues through the sparsely-populated Romsdal and **Lågen-**

dal, and in Dombås joins the E6, the King's Way between Oslo and Trondheim.

The alternative route to Trondheim around the Romsdalsfjord is some 40 kilometers longer than the E136 route. From Åndalsnes, take the R64 along the **Is-** and **Rødvenfjords** to **Åfarnes**, then the R660 along the **Langfjord** and **Eresfjord** to **Eidsvåg** and **Eidsøra**, and then follow the R62 to Sunndalsøra, the inner end of this fjord system.

The road isn't as good as the E136, but involves only a few, moderate ascents and hardly any tight curves. It's also a beautiful fjord-seeing drive, and there are any number of spots where drivers can pull over to stretch their legs or go for a picnic, such as the segment of road between **Hen** and **Skorgen** on the R64 by the Rødvenfjord, which has the best panoramic views.

From **Leirheim**, a road runs west to **Rødven** ⑮, which has one of the most northerly stave churches in Norway; its nave, portal and crucifix date from the Middle Ages. At the north end of the Langfjord is the **Nesset Parish House** ⑯, where poet Bjørnstjerne Bjørnson grew up.

Sunndalsøra ⑰ is an industrial town (population 5,000) with Norway's second-largest power station and two aluminum smelting works. Not far from here in the **Lilledal** is **Store Kalken** (1,880 meters), a mountain with a 1,600 meter precipice on its west side and a 200 meter stone "hat" on top.

The R70 from Sunndalsøra continues 70 kilometers in an easterly direction to join up with the E6 in Oppdal. On the way you pass the narrow **Sunndal** with the river **Driva** down below; this valley is very prone to avalanches in the winter and the houses are built close together on the slopes, so that the snow passes over the top of them.

Near **Fale** ⑱ is the **Storfale Gård**, an old farmhouse typical of the area. The last 116 kilometers on the E6 from Oppdal to Trondheim (see p. 153) have no particular highlights.

FLORØ

i Postboks, 6900 Florø, tel. 57747505, open June 1-Aug 31, 9 am-8 pm, other times Mon-Sat 9 am-4 pm.

= **SS** **Victoria Hotel** AS, Markegt. 43, tel. 57741000. *CAMPING:* **Krokane Camping**, on the R5 2 km before Florø, tel. 57742220.

i In summer, daily passenger ferry service to **Kinn Island**; call 57747505 for information. Hurtigrute ships land daily at Florø at 4:45 am (northbound) and 8 am (southbound); there are also several boats a day on the Bergen-Nordfjord line.

SKEI I JØLSTER

i Skei i Jølster, tel. 57728588.

= **SS** **Skei Hotel**, 6850 Skei i Jølster, open end of January to mid-December, cheap summer rates. **S** **Jølstraholmen Camping**, 6840 Vassenden, tel. 57727135, family vacation center, on the south end of the Jølstravatnet.

BYRKJELO

i Tel. 57867301 and 57866100. Reservations of campsites and huts in the Jostedalsbreen area; can arrange guided tours of the glacier region.

= **SS** **Karistua Hotell**, 6867 Ultvik, tel. 57876513, 91396220, open May to September. **Reed Camping**, Reed, 6865 Breim, tel. 57868133, open May to mid-September, cabins. **Vandrerhjem**, tel. 57867321, open May 15-September 15.

OLDEN

i Tel. 57873126; offers bike and boat rentals, fishing permits. Open June 1-Aug 31, 9 am-8 pm, other times Mon-Sat 9 am-4 pm.

= **SS** **Olden Fjordhotel**, tel. 57873400. **Yris Hotel**, tel. 57873240. **S** **Olden Krotell**, tel. 57873455, April-September. **Briksdalsbre Fjellstove**, 6877 Briksdalsbre, tel. 57873811, mid-April to end of September, cabins. *CAMPING* (with cabins): **Gytri Camping**, 6870 Olden, tel. 57875934, 13 km from Olden on the way to Briksdalsbreen. **Løken Camping**, 6870 Olden, tel. 57873268, 2 km from Olden town center. **Melkevoll Bretun**, 6876 Oldedalen, tel. 57873864, on the edge of the national park, glacier tours. **Oldevatn Camping**, 6870 Olden, tel. 57875915, between Olden and Briksdalsbreen on the lake, boat rentals.

≡ **Olden Church**; pick up the key next door. **Briksdal Glacier**, horseback and hiking tours to the Briksdal Glacier, glacier tours, Briksdalsbre Fjellstove, tel. 57873811.

LOEN

i Just east of Alexandra Hotel. Fishing permits. June 1-Aug 31, 9 am-8 pm, otherwise Mon-Sat 9 am-4 pm.

= **SS** **Hotel Alexandra**, tel. 57875050. **Hotel Loen** **AS**, tel. 57877800, lovely building with large buffet. **S** **Gjestehuset Loen**, tel. 57877663.

i **Kjenndal Glacier**, boat trips from Sande Camping across the Lovatnet, tel. 57877659.

STRYN

i Tel. 57872323. Bike rentals, fishing permits. June 1-Aug 31, 9 am-8 pm, other times Mon-Sat 9 am-4 pm.

= **SS** **King Oscar's Hall**, tel. 57871953, unusual edifice, dragon style. **Stryn Hotel**, tel. 57871166. **S** **Vesla Pensjonat**, Myrane 20, tel. 57871006.

⚑ Summer skiing on the Strynfjell, tel. 57872323.

ÅLESUND

i Rådhuset, 6025 Ålesund, tel. 70121202, open June 1-Aug 31, 9 am-8 pm, other times Mon-Sat 9 am-4 pm.

= **SSS** **Rica Parken Hotell**, Storgt. 16, tel. 70125050, lovely location near By Park. **Scandic Hotel**, Molovn. 6, tel. 70128100. **SS** **Hotel Noreg**, Kongensgt. 27, tel. 70122938. **Bryggen Home Hotel**, Apotekegt. 1/3, tel. 70126400. *HOSTEL:* **Ålesund Vandrerhjem**, 6003 Ålesund, Parkgt. 14, tel. 70120425.

≡ **Borgundkaupanger Museum**, May 20-Sept 15, 11 am-4 pm; during summer, until 6 pm. **Borgund Church**, open June-Aug, Tue-Sat 10 am-2 pm. **Ålesund Church**, weekdays May-September, 10 am-4 pm. **Giske Church**, Giske Island, occasionally open during the summer; if not, inquire next door.

i Bus or car trips to **Giske Island** and the **bird island of Runde**, overland from Hareid Island.

🚢 Ferries depart every hour for Hareid from 6:30 am-4 pm. There are several ships every day to Langevåg and Molde; tel. 71219500.

MOLDE

i Postboks 484, 6401 Molde, tel. 71257133, June 1-Aug 31, 9 am-8 pm, other times Mon-Sat 9 am-4 pm.

= **SSS** **First Hotel Alexandra**, tel. 71251133. **SS** **Hotel Nobel**, Amtman Kroghsgt. 5, tel. 71251555. **Hotel Molde**, Storgt. 19, tel. 71215888.

≡ **Romsdalmuseum**, open June-Aug 10 am-6 pm, Sun noon-6 pm. **Moldegård**, privately owned; can only be visited from outside.

KRISTIANSUND

i Rådhuset, at the harbor, tel. 71586380, open June 1-Aug 31, 9 am-8 pm, other times Mon-Sat 9 am-4 pm.

= **SS** **Hotel Rica**, Storgate 41/43, tel. 71676411. **Inter Nor Grand Hotel**, Bernstorfstr. 1, tel. 71673011.

≡ **Kvernes Stave Church**, on the way from Molde, by arrangement, tel. 71511587 or 71513232. **Lossius-**

gård; only from outside. **Kristiansund Church**, week-days 10 am-7:30 pm; in winter 10 am-2 pm. **Nordmøre Museum**, Sun noon-3 pm, Tue-Fri 10 am-2 pm and 5-7 pm, closed Thu.

VOSS

i Postboks 57, 5701 Voss, tel. 56510051. Fishing permits. June 1-Aug 31, 9 am-8 pm, other times Mon-Sat 9 am-4 pm.

SSS Parkhotel Vossevangen, tel. 56511322. **Fleischers Hotel**, Evangervn. 13, tel. 56511155, classic 19th-century country hotel. **Stalheim Hotel**, 20 km on the Gudvangen road, 5715 Stalheim, tel. 56520122. **SS Oppheim Hotel**, tel. 56522500. **Hotel Jarl**, tel. 56511933. **S Voss Hotel & Appartement**, Bulken, tel. 56514500. **Voss Turistheim**, tel. 56511577.

Mølstertunet, May 1-Oct 1, 10 am-5 pm. **Magnus Dagestad Museum**, Tue-Sun 11 am-3 pm. **Voss Church**, summer 9 am-7 pm, services in English Sun 9 am and 9 pm, June-Aug; in Norwegian 11 am. **Nesheimtunet**, open to groups by arrangement through the tourist office. **Hopperstad Stave Church**, 20 km north, near Vik, open May 15-Sept 15, 10 am-6 pm.

FLÅM

i Postboks, 5743 Flåm, at station, June 1-Aug 31, 9 am-8 pm, otherwise Mon-Sat 9 am-4 pm, tel. 57632106

SS Fretheim Hotel, tel. 57632200. **S Heimli Pensjonat**, 5743 Flåm, tel. 57632300. **Furukroa**, Flåm Turistsenter, tel. 57632325. **Flåm Camping og Vandrerhjem**, 5743 Flåm, tel. 57632121, hostel, cabins, camping, bike rentals. **Lunde Gard & Camping**, 5745 Aurland, tel. 57633412, cabins.

Undredal Church, 10 km towards Gudvangen; get key in the house next door (on the right). **Flåm Church**, open in summer with the arrival of trains or boats.

Flåm train to Myrdal, boat excursions to Bergen. For information on *Norway in a Nutshell* tours, call 55966900 / 57633313 or ask at the Flåm train station.

SOGNDAL

i Postboks, 5800 Sogndal, tel. 57673083, open June 1-Aug 31, 9 am-8 pm, other times Mon-Sat 9 am-4 pm.

SSS Quality Sogndal Hotel, tel. 57672311, bikes, boat moorings. **SS Hofslund Fjordhotel**, tel. 57671022. **S Loftesnes Pensjonat**, Fjørevn. 17, tel. 57671577.

Borgund Stave Church, 30 km south on E16, daily in summer 9 am-8 pm. **Sogndal Folkemuseum**, May 15-Aug 30, 10 am-1 pm. **Kaupanger Stave Church**, 8 km south, May 20-Aug 31, reserve by phone at tourist office in Sogndal. **Urnes Stave Churche**, 10 km north, on Lustrafjord, June 20-Aug 20, 10:30 am-4:30 pm.

JOTUNHEIMEN

SS Walaker Hotell, 5815 Solvorn, tel. 57684207, first hotel in town, attractively restored, open mid-April to mid-Oct. **S Bygdin Høyfjellshotell**, 2953 Beitostolen, tel. 61341400. **Jotunheimen Fjellstue**, 2087 Bøverdalen, tel. 61212918. **Juvasshytta**, 2087 Bøverdalen, tel. 61211550, daily glacier tours.

LOM

i Postboks, 2686 Lom, next to the stave church, tel. 61211286, open June 1-Aug 31, 9 am-8 pm, other times Mon-Sat 9 am-4 pm.

SS Fossheim Turisthotell, tel. 61211205, furnished like a museum. **Fossberg Hotell, Motell, Hytter og Kafeteria**, 2686 Lom, tel. 61211073, motel, cabins. **S Brimi Fjellstugu**, 2683 Tessanden, tel. 61239812, open Feb-April, June-Oct. **Nordal Turistsenter**, 2686 Lom, tel. 61211010, cabins. **Lom Motell og Camping**, 2686 Lom, tel. 61211220, free fishing permits for guests. **Gjeilo Camping**, 2690 Skjåk, tel. 61213032, 7 km west of Lom, cabins. **Furulund**, 2686 Lom, tel. 61211057, cabins, open May-Sept.

Stave church, open June 15-Aug 15, 9 am-9 pm.

GEIRANGER

i Postboks, 6216 Geiranger, by the ferry dock, tel. 70263099, June 1-Aug 31, 9 am-8 pm, other times Mon-Sat 9 am-4 pm.

SSS Union Hotel, old building, with fjord views, tel. 70263000. **SS Union Hotel**, new building. **Hotel Utsikten Bellevue**, tel. 70263003. **S Grande Fjordhotel & Hytter**, tel. 70263090.

Stordal church, 35 km north on the Valldal-Ålesund road, open daily during July and August 11 am-4 pm.

Fjord trips: for information, call 84660502. Ferries to Hellesylt, from Geiranger, May 1-September 30 at 7:40 and 10:15 am, 1 and 4 pm; departures from Hellesylt are 90 minutes later. Fjord round-trip tours, trips to Dalsnibba.

ÅNDALSNES

i Postboks, 6300 Åndalsnes, at the train station, tel. 71221622, open June 1-Aug 31, 9 am-8 pm, other times Mon-Sat 9 am-4 pm.

SS Grand Hotel Bellevue, Andalsgt. 5, tel. 71227500. **S Romsdal Gjestegård**, tel. 71221383.

Tinden museum, June-August 10 am-4 pm. **Rødven stave church**, 35 km north, June-August 10 am-4 pm.

Daily trains through Dombås to Oslo and Trondheim. Bus connections to Trollstig and Geiranger; for information call 70270600.

FROM OSLO TO TRONDHEIM

HAMAR
LILLEHAMMER
GUDBRANDSDAL
PEER GYNT WAY
DOVREFJELL
RØROS
TRONDHEIM

THE KING'S WAY TO ST. OLAV

The King's Way (*Kongsvegen*) from Oslo to Trondheim is the longest medieval land route in Norway and goes back over a thousand years. It acquired its almost mythical significance when Håkon V transferred the capital to Oslo. From then on, the royal road was the "umbilical cord" which connected the seat of government with the place of coronation and at the same time formed a connection with the "saintly," immortal King Olav.

The course of the present E6 corresponds only approximately to the King's Way. The modern road, for example, runs along the floor of the Gudbrandsdal right next to the river Lågen, whereas the old road ran halfway up the mountainside because of the risk of high water in the spring. The King's Way was also a route of pilgrimage and penitence. There were processions to petition Olav, the saint, to help achieve or accelerate the realization of specific goals; too, offences against ecclesiastical and social norms could be atoned for by a pilgrimage to Trondheim. In her 1922 novel *Kristin Lavransdatter,*

Preceding pages: Winter evening in the Olympic town of Lillehammer. Left: The stave church of Ringebu, a jewel of the Gudbrandsdal.

Sigrid Undset describes the pilgrimage of the unmarried, pregnant Kristin.

For the Olympic Games of 1994, almost the entire length of the E6 between Oslo and Lillehammer was expanded into a throughway, and it's been subject to a toll ever since. There's also a high-speed railway between the capital and the Olympic city: passengers can cover the whole route to Trondheim on the Nordland Railway, a very scenic ride in comfortable, modern carriages, which takes 5 to 6 hours.

After Gran and Kløfta the road passes **Gardermoen ❶**, site of Oslo's new airport. Nearby is **Raknehaugen ❷**, northern Europe's largest burial mound, dating from the large ethnic migrations around AD 500; 95 meters in diameter, it measures 15 meters high. The burial chamber was opened in 1870; interred here was King Rakne with his two horses, servants and guards.

Twenty kilometers further on is the **Eidsvollverk ❸**. In 1814, after the separation of Norway from Denmark, a delegation of 112 people gathered in the main building of this former iron foundry to draw up a constitution. This was ratified on May 17, now a national holiday; with this document, Norway declared itself an independent kingdom with a constitutional monarchy.

The assembly room has been left exactly as it was on this historic date; today, it serves as a museum. Oscar Wergeland's painting depicting the Eidsvoll Assembly today hangs in the Storting, or parliament building, in Oslo.

In **Eidsvoll ❹**, 8 kilometers away, there's a monument to the poet Henrik Wergeland, who was the first Norwegian to speak out against the clause of the Eidsvoll Constitution that refused Jews and Jesuits entry into the country. Six years after his death in 1845, this article was in fact abolished. During this poet's lifetime, Sweden's Jewish population erected a monument to him in expression of their gratitude; this stood in Stockholm until the border opened. It was subsequently transferred to Oslo. Every year on Constitution Day there is an hour of commemoration at this memorial; and this is also an occasion to remember and honor Norway's Jewish citizens who

Above: Fruit tree in blossom by Lake Mjøsa, Norway's largest lake.

were deported and murdered between 1940 and 1945.

In the summer the *Skiblander*, the oldest operative paddle-wheel steamer in the world, dating from 1856, crosses **Lake Mjøsa ❺** from Eidsvoll to Lillehammer. The E6 reaches the lake at Minnesund; roads and railway bridges cross its southern end. Lake Mjøsa, a good 100 kilometers long and 360 square kilometers in area, is Norway's largest inland lake. Together with the Oslofjord it forms the northern end of one of the large rift valley zones in Europe. On picturesque **Kosøgård Bay** is **Espa ❻**, a quiet, inviting place for a stop.

From here, the E6 leaves the lake's shores, not to rejoin them until Hamar. To stay closer to the lake, take the R22, which continues through **Tangen** to **Stange ❼**, which has one of the finest stone churches in the Hedmark. Dating from the 13th century, built on the site of an even earlier building, it includes both Romanesque and Gothic elements. Along the shore between Stange and Hamar there are many large old farmhouses; **Ringnes Farm ❽** was mentioned in the Olav saga, and its buildings are some 350 years old.

★HAMAR
Bishop's Residence on the Lake

Hamar ❾, which was originally located a little farther east, is Norway's largest inland town, with a population of 26,000. Its rise to prosperity began when it became the center of a diocese under Pope Hadrian IV. The cathedral, a basilica with three towers and three naves, was built outside the town on the peninsular of Storhamarodde, where the bishop's palace was also located. When the Kalmar Union collapsed, the Swedes attacked Hamar and almost completely destroyed it. Plague epidemics finished off the job, and towards the end of the 16th century the small market town that remained also lost its town charter. The population decreased and Hamar was forgotten. Not until a parliamentary edict was issued in 1848 was the rebuilding of the town commenced.

The four high arches forming the southern arcade of the **cathedral** are today the symbol of Hamar. These arches, the base stones of the three-part choir and parts of the transept are the remaining features of the once splendid cathedral; together with the ruins of the bishop's palace and farm they form the core of the **Hedmark Museum**, which also includes a collection of wooden houses from the area. The ruins have been thoroughly researched and are being preserved from further decay. Some of them have been integrated into the new museum building, and when conservation work on the southern arcade has been completed, the whole cathedral ruin will be encased in a giant glass cube to protect it from frost and rain. Another branch of the Hedmark museum is the **Museum of Emigration** by the town's little harbor; this features

From Oslo to Trondheim

early settlers' huts brought here from North America. En route to the cathedral ruins is Hamar's new symbol, the Olympic **Ice Rink** from the 1994 Games, built in the form of an upside-down Viking ship.

Furnes Church near **Dobloug ❿**, north of Hamar, was built in 1708 out of stones from the ruined cathedral.

Brumunddal ⓫ is the center of the district of **Ringsaker**. It also marks the end of the *Birkebeinerveien* from Sweden, the route taken by the *Birkebeinerne* when they marched on Oslo with Sverre Sigurdson to take the throne and the kingdom. At **Moelv**, the R213 cuts off from the main road; if you want to go on to Lillehammer, it's better to take this road, which is not only toll-free but affords a nicer view of the lake than the E6.

Some 3 kilometers south of Moelv, is **Ringsaker ⓬**, which boasts the most beautiful church in Hedmark. This stone basilica was built in the 12th century, but its Gothic choir and the transept date from the 13th century, and the 70-meter

Info pp. 160-161
141

boasts both downhill runs and cross-country ski trails that are illuminated at night. It came as a surprise to everyone when the town was selected for the Winter Olympics in 1994; before then, Lillehammer was known only as a tourist resort and as the location of Norway's largest **open-air museum**.

This museum, the *Sandvigske Samlinger* on the hill of **Maihaugen**, was founded by the dentist Anders Sandvic (1862-1950). As he went from farm to farm to treat his patients, he established that woodworking skills in the valley were gradually disappearing; wooden utensils were being replaced by articles of pottery and metal. He began collecting objects, often taking such articles in payment for his services, a fact that was very welcome to his patients, since as far as they were concerned these wooden dishes and spoons were only suitable for burning. When Sandvig also began collecting granaries, farm workers' huts and barns, people thought he had gone completely mad.

tower was added in 1694. Among the highlights of the interior are the old Flemish altarpieces, painted in 1520 in Antwerp. The fragments of wall painting in the nave show the arrival of St. Olav in Ringsaker.

South of Ringsaker, a car ferry runs across Lake Mjøsa between **Mengshol** and **Gjøvik** ⓭ (a 15-minute crossing, 5 times a day). Gjøvik is known as the "white town" because of its many light-colored wooden houses; it now has a new attraction in the form of an ice hockey stadium, which was built in 1994.

Soon his garden was no longer adequate for his rapidly growing collection, and in 1887 he persuaded the district authorities of Lillehammer to let him have Maihaugen Hill, which was eventually turned into a museum. Items were offered from all over the Gudbrandsdal, and today the museum has more than 100 houses and farms, some of which are fully furnished. The oldest exhibit is the **stave church of Garmo**, the oldest parts of which date from the 12th century.

*LILLEHAMMER

Lillehammer ⓮ ("Little Hamar"), population 23,000, has always been an important center for winter for the population of Oslo and the surrounding area; it

Other outstanding exhibits are the teacher's, clergyman's and bailiff's houses, a large farm built of massive tree trunks and the so-called **Peer Gynt Hut** dating from 1700, in which the hero of Ibsen's verse drama is said to have lived. There is also a new building containing a large number of workshops; among the trades represented are cloth-making, carpentry, gunsmithing and broom-making; and even Sandvig's dental practice is

Above: Enthusiastic supporters at the Olympic Games in Lillehammer in 1994. Right: School outing to the open-air museum in Maihaugen.

From Oslo to Trondheim

here. He himself is buried above the Garmo church, and there is a monument to him on Lillehammer's central **marketplace**.

One tangible consequence of the Olympic Games is that the best view of Lillehammer is now from the big ski jump a little north of the town: from the steps leading up to the top, there's a splendid panoramic view of town and valley. The Olympic Village has now been dismantled, but the hotels have remained, making Lillehammer a good place for an overnight stop.

Through the Østerdal to Ulsberg: An Alternative to the King's Way

If you have already traveled the road through the Gudbrandsdal, there is an alternative route from Hamar: the **Østerdal** between Elverum and **Tynset** is less-traveled and offers a full range of scenic highlights. From the E6, turn off onto the E3 or R25; at **Elverum** ⓯, you're in the valley of the **Glåma**, Norway's longest

river, which flows for a total of more than 600 kilometers. Until after the war, more than a million cubic meters of wood were floated down this waterway to the coast every year.

The fortress of **Christiansfjell** in Elverum, dating from 1630, was supposed to prevent the Swedish from invading the Glåma valley. The town, with 17,000 residents, has been the market town of the Østerdal since the 18th century; in 1877, it acquired a railway link to Oslo and Trondheim. In 1940, the place was almost completely destroyed, but the city has long since regained its position of economic and administrative prominence. It has a **Forestry Museum**, which also has exhibits relating to hunting and fishing. A bridge links it to the **Glåmsdal Museum**, which displays 80 restored houses from throughout the Østerdal.

Until Tynset the E3 follows the route of the Trondheim railway line through the Glåma valley; the R30, on the other hand, turns off eastward in Koppang, only to rejoin the E3 in Tynset. About halfway be-

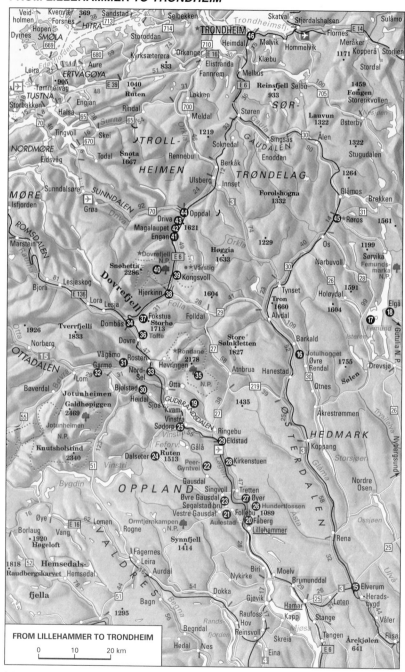

FROM LILLEHAMMER TO TRONDHEIM

0   10   20 km

tween them is the **Jutulhogget** ⑯, 150 meters deep and 2.5 kilometers long, the largest canyon in southern Norway.

In Åkrestrømmen, at the northern end of the long Storsjøen, the R217 branches off from the R30 and offers, via the R26, access to **Lake Femund** ⑰, and to two little-known, but very appealing, national parks, **Gutulia** (19 square kilometers) and ⋆**Femundsmarka** (390 square kilometers), both of which are adjacent to the Swedish nature preserve of Norddalarne on the other side of the border. In summer, a boat runs the length of the lake, with a stop in **Elgå** ⑱, a good point of departure for hikes into the quasi-primeval evergreen forest and along the lake. The hilly northern end, by contrast, is an expanse of barren rock.

From Sørvika, at the northern end of Lake Femund, it's only 22 kilometers along a little side road to Røros. There are plenty of other hiking trails, some with overnight huts, between Østerdal and Femundsmarka.

GUDBRANDSDAL: "Valley of Valleys"

Accorded this title by Henrik Wergeland in the 19th century, the ⋆**Gudbrandsdal** ⑲ is still the epitome of a Norwegian valley with rich farming establishments. Gudbrandsdal is also the name of the whole region, including not only the valley of the Lågen but also the side valleys of Gausa, Espe, Sjøa and Otta. The main valley was cut by the River Lågen in the extensive Norwegian high fjell complex; it is a wide, evenly-proportioned trough between Jotunheimen, Rondane and the Dovrefjell, with only 440 meters of vertical ascent in 200 kilometers.

The lakes formed along the Lågen have been supplemented by reservoirs created to produce hydroelectric power on the one hand, and to help regulate the water level when the snow melts on the other.

Most of the grass that grows on the valley floor is used for winter feed; on the hillsides, the locals grow potatoes and grain for their own use.

The valley's real wealth is higher up: the extensive, seemingly endless forests that spread across the gradually rising fjell. The large farmsteads are positioned halfway up the side of the valley, which gives them three advantages: the sun shines longer here than it does down at the bottom of the valley; the houses are safe from high water; and the farmers have an equal distance to go to get to the hayfields in the summer and the timbering areas in the winter. The small farms in less favorable locations were occupied either by small tenant farmers compelled to serve the local nobility, or younger sons of large farmers with no right of inheritance. The valley's villages are a later, 19th-century development.

Until well into the 19th century, the big landowners ruled over their domains like autocratic princes. They meted out legal rulings, held services and masses, and had to give their permission before a laborer and farm girl could marry – often enough, they claimed the right of the first night for themselves as well. Only first-born sons had the right of inheritance; the others had to stay and work on the farm as laborers, or simply leave. As many as 100 people lived permanently on each farm, but only the farmer's family lived in the main house. There was also a building for the old farmer and two separate communal houses for male and female laborers and servants; the men's and women's houses stood as far away from each other as possible. Married farmhands usually lived in cottages outside the farm complex: before they married, these couples had to sign a guarantee that their children would work on the farm.

In the long winter nights on these large farms, people would often while away the hours in story-telling. Some of these traditional tales have found their way into

From Oslo to Trondheim

world literature through the writings of Ibsen and Asbjørnsen and the subsequent Nobel Prize winners Bjørnson, Undset and Hamsun, all of whom had close ties to the Gudbrandsdal.

North of Lillehammer, a road running parallel to the E6 bears the name of the most famous legendary figure, Peer Gynt. This fictional hero is almost certainly based on historical figures. Although Asbjørnsen did not know Peer på Hågå personally, he was the first to write down the stories that were traditionally told about him.

Ibsen also knew these stories. With considerable poetic license, he composed his verse drama about the reckless adventurer who eventually returns, enlightened after his wanderings, to the love of his youth and finds peace. In addition to Hågå and the Jotunheimen mountain guide mentioned earlier, Ibsen indubitably worked other people into the figure of

Above: Gudbrandsdal, center of large-scale farming in Norway.

Gynt, since with this character he wanted to hold up a mirror to Norwegian society.

IN THE FOOTSTEPS OF PEER GYNT

The first stop on the E6 going north from Lillehammer is **Fåberg ⓴**, which has a wooden cruciform church dating from the 18th century. The building has been painstakingly restored, and the font and altarpieces are of particular interest. In Fåberg, the R255 branches off and runs along the Gausa valley to **Follebu**.

Past the stone church is **Aulestad ㉑**, the large farm Bjørnstjerne Bjørnson bought in 1874 as a meeting-place for his literary circle, as well as to fulfill his ambition to live like an *odelsbonde* (hereditary farmer) himself. He invested a great deal of money in the farm, and the agricultural business here is still in the hands of his family. The house itself was purchased after his death with the help of a public collection and has been turned into a **museum**.

Map p. 144, Info pp. 160-161

At **Segalstad bru**, take the R254 to **Svingvoll**. This marks the start of the **Peer Gyntvei ㉒**, a *bomvei* (toll road) to Brynsbakken near Vinstra. Because of the six high fjell hotels along this road catering to tourists in this splendid area, the route was once known as the *Hotellveien*. It is paved, has a maximum gradient of 10 percent and reaches its highest point at **Rauhøgda** (1,053 meters), with many panoramic views along the way.

The highest mountains near the road are the **Skeikampen** (1,123 meters) at **Gausdal**, which has a chair lift, the **Postkampen** and the **Gråkampen**, both 1,220 meters and the 1,400-meter Espedal range to the west. After Gausdal, there is a splendid view of the **Golåvatn**. Of the hotels, the **Peer-Gynt-Hotell** deserves special mention as a very comfortable establishment on the high fjell. In addition, this route passes a number of good restaurants, as well as some nice campgrounds.

At **Øvre Gausdal ㉓** is the parish farm of **Riddervolden**, the largest in the country. The house alone has 34 rooms, and the farm has 230 hectares of land, on which 17 *husmen*, small farmers, were obliged to work.

At **Vollsdammen** there is a road to **Lake Fefor** and **Dalseter ㉔**, where Scott trained for his unsuccessful Antarctic expedition.

From Vollsdammen, continue down onto the R256 and on to **Sødorp ㉕**. Here, in the old cemetery by the church, there is a tombstone with the inscription "Per Gynt, Per Olson Hågå 1732-1785." This is the so-called **Peer Gynt Grave**, where the farmer Peder Olson Hage from the Hågå farm in Nordgarden is buried. The farm itself is 2.5 kilometers east of **Vinstra** on the *Peer Gynt Setersvei*, and consists of 18 privately-owned houses. Two of the buildings have been sold: one is in Maihaugen, while the second serves as Vinstra's tourist office. The best time to enter "Peer Gynt territory" are the first

weeks of August, when the Peer Gynt festival is held at and around Lake Golå, which is itself a picturesque backdrop.

From Lillehammer to Dombås along the Lågen Valley

A few kilometers after Fåberg is **Hundertfossen ㉖**, a waterfall that has been tamed by a dam and a power plant. In **Øyer ㉗** is the "Temple of the Holy Trinity," a cruciform church dating from the 18th century that is a splendid example of rural Baroque. 500 meters above the church is the first royal establishment of the Gudbrandsdal, the **Vedumgård**, which goes back to the time of Håkon IV. **Tretten** was once the largest horse market in the valley.

In **Kirkestuen ㉘** stands **Fåvang Church**, a former stave church; the grooves for the staves on the north wall show that it was designed as a cruciform church even before it was rebuilt.

From **Elstad ㉙**, a road leads to the best-known stave church in the Gudbrandsdal, **Ringebu Church**, next to the old King's Way. In this early 13th-century building, its noticable that there are significantly fewer carvings of dragons and fabulous beasts in relation to the number of plant motifs. The church of Ringebu was rebuilt in the 16th century and restored in 1923. The carved altar has been here since the very beginning, but the other elements of the interior decoration were collected from other, abandoned churches. Inside, you can still see fragments of the original wall paintings, with dragon's heads and mythical beasts. The church often hosts organ concerts, and is also very popular as a wedding chapel.

Vinstra is the halfway mark between Oslo and Trondheim. A few kilometers northwest, in the valley of Sjøa (**Heidal**), more than 20 of the old farms are under landmark protection. Best-known of these is **Bjølstad ㉚**; it's been in the same family for 25 generations.

From Oslo to Trondheim

In **Otta**, the R15 branches off westward from the E6 toward the Geirangerfjord, Stryn and the Vestkapp. The idyllic old farmsteads of the Otta valley could be veritable sets for Norwegian fairy tales. In **Vågåmo ㉛**, visitors can inspect **Vågå Church**, the second-oldest in the country. **Garmo ㉜** offers the **Hamsunstugga** in commemoration of author Knut Hamsun, who was born here in 1859.

Nord-Sel ㉝, on the E6, has a wooden cruciform church faced with slate; the edifice incorporates elements of an older stave church. Off the road a bit are the farms of **Romundgård** and **Laurgård**, which figure in Sigrid Undset's novel *Kristin Lavransdatter.* For the film version of this novel, the crew reconstructed the **Jørundgård** farmhouse, which now transports tourists back into daily life on a medieval farm. From here to **Dovre**, the Gudbrandsdal becomes steadily narrower

and steeper; the river forms rapids and small waterfalls in several places. The transportation hub **Dombås ㉞**, population 1,500, subsists primarily from tourism. Here, the Nordland and Rauma trains split off from each other, as do the E6 and E136.

From the stretch of the E6 from Vinstra to Dombås, a number of small summer roads and hiking trails branch off east of the Gudbrandsdal, into an area that's very popular with skiers and hikers. At the center of this region, in the ***Rondane National Park ㉟** (572 square kilometers), is its highest mountain, **Rondslottet** (2,178 meters). Ice Age glaciers simply pulverized the quartz stone of Rondane, leaving scree and dead ice holes in their wake. This mountain realm is desolate and hostile to human settlement; long valleys indicate the courses of ancient glaciers.

Yet easily accessible (on the E6 to the west or the R27/R29 to the east), with reasonably easy and not-too-long hiking trails commanding views extending to the

Above: In Rondane National Park. Right: The Rondane Park huts are cozy and inviting.

highest peaks of the Jotunheimen, Rondane Park remains an attractive destination.

Near the south end of the narrow, 4-kilometer-long lake **Rondvatnet**, the DNT operates the large, comfortable "hut" of **Rondvassbu** (132 beds). There are a few other huts within the park, and a wide range of accommodation in the area, especially along or near the E6. Most of the hiking trails radiate out from Rondvassbu. Allow about a day for the ascent of Rondslottet; boats on the Rondvatnet shave some of the length off a few of the routes. A historic path runs across the southern end of the park between **Mysuseter** (10 kilometers west of Otta) and **Neset** in the east on the R27: *Rørosveien*, the old trade route to the mines of Røros. From **Høvringen**, too (near Nord-Sel), there's access to a number of hiking trails.

South of the park, a road 50 kilometers long leads drivers on the round trip from Vinstra to Kvam, through a varied landscape dotted with lakes and hills. The gravel road parallel to the E6 that runs between Dovre and Dombås (accessible to cars) offers better views of the Lågen Valley. It also passes the old **Royal Farm of Tofte ❸⓺**.

Owned by the same family since 1688, this complex physically dates, in its oldest parts, from the 17th century, but supposedly there really was a royal residence here in the 10th century. The story goes that Harald Hårfagra, here for the *Julmahl* (Christmas dinner), saw a Lapp woman whom he desired so intensely that he wanted to take possession of her on the spot. Her father, however, insisted on there being a proper engagement; the marriage was later legalized and there were four children. An 18th-century painting depicting this scene still hangs at the farm, which has been the setting for several films.

On a 15-kilometer hike from Dovre to **Fokstua ❸⓻** (on the E6), you can get to know the *Kongveien*, the historic **King's Way**, up close and personal. Marked with blue and yellow crowns, the trail leaves the Gudbrandsdal, passes the 200-year-old mountain farmstead of Budsjord and scrambles over the west flank of the **Hardbakken** (1,200 meters) onto the bare Dovrefjell itself.

ACROSS THE DOVREFJELL TO TRONDHEIM

Between Dombås and Hjerkinn, the E6 has not yet been modernized, so that the road is narrower and more winding than in the Gudbrandsdal; for the first few kilometers it climbs steeply. The Nordland railway, which runs alongside the road, negotiates the 400 meters of vertical ascent by means of helical tunnels.

It's not far to Fokstua, where the remains of so-called *Sælehuser* ("mercy huts") have been found. There were large numbers of these huts on the Dovrefjell, dating back to the days of King Øystein. From his reign on the inhabitants of the Gudbrandsdal were required to demonstrate their concern for others by building this type of accommodation for the hordes of pilgrims. Many of these huts went up in flames as a result of carelessness, but they were always rebuilt. However, the *Sælehuser* and the bridges on the pilgrim's route were sometimes deliberately destroyed to hinder the advance of the Swedish invaders.

The **Fokstumyra** is a high moor east of Fokstua that extends as far as the E6. This moor, Norway's first **nature reserve**, has a large population of rare birds, including merlins, cranes, moorland finches and redpolls. The peak breeding period is from May to July; walkers are strictly prohibited from leaving the marked trails, and all the vegetation is protected. **Dovregrubbens Hall** is an old *Kro* (inn or hostel) on the King's – and pilgrims' – Way; it is now a restaurant and hotel.

Right: In the Kongsvoll Hotell, the traditional accommodation for nature-lovers on the Dovrefjell.

The E6 continues to **Hjerkinn** ❸ (956 meters), Norway's "driest" town in the rain shadow of the Dovrefjell. Remains of the *fjellstua* which was mentioned in Snorri Sturluson's saga have been found west of the town. King Øystein, who is said to have financed the original building, may have ordered it to be rebuilt, since German coins and Irish gold jewelry from the 10th century were found during the excavations. This shows that the King's Way was an important trade route even before the time of Olav. At the junction of the R29 and the E6 there is a modern church built in memory of King Øystein and his "mercy huts"; it was consecrated in 1969. Over the entrance is a statue of the king, while a memorial stone commemorates the 41 Norwegian kings who passed this way.

West of the E6, the Norwegian army has a shooting range; this is military territory, so it is also off-limits to hikers! About 1 kilometer further on, the road reaches the highest point on this particular stretch (1,026 meters). In the west are Snøhetta and Svånåtindane (2,286 and 2,215 meters), at the foot of which large herds of wild reindeer still graze. 500 reindeer skeletons were found near the fjellstua, demonstrating that early pilgrims, too, used them as a source of food.

The E6 now follows the Nordland railway over the fjell. Wooden tunnels and snow fences protect the rails from snowdrifts, which pile up in the driving wind even in this area of low precipitation. The **Kongsvoll Fjellstua** ❸ is today a botanical and zoological research station, but continues to run as a restaurant and hotel, as well. The old **Kongsvoll Kro**, located nearby, is also a guest house.

Not far from here is a small botanical garden laid out by the Norwegian national railway company; for the region is famous for its flora, evidenced by the wealth of species in evidence in ***Dovrefjell National Park** ❹. Extending over 265 square kilometers, the

From Oslo to Trondheim

park is adjacent to a nature reserve of almost equal size on the opposite side of the road. Botanists believe that some of the rare plants here are survivors of the last Ice Age.

North of the Kongsvoll, a branch of the King's Way continues parallel to the E6 as the *Vårstig*, the **Spring Way**. This route was used in the spring when high water in the Driva made the narrow valley impassable. The road, which was already mentioned in a document in 1182, was feared by pilgrims because of its steep gradient and frequent rockfalls. In 1700 it was improved so that carriages and barouches could drive along it; today, still very steep and 2.2 meters across at its widest point, it is used as a hiking trail.

At **Engan ❹**, Oppdal slate is mined; in **Magalaupet ❷**, the valley forms a gorge through which the Driva foams. From the **Driva train station ❸** you can detour into the mountainous countryside centered around the **Loseter**. To the east is the peak of **Sisselhø** (1,621 meters), which takes 3 hours to climb.

Oppdal ❹ has a population of 6,000, is a well-known winter sports resort with five ski lifts, and has the only *vinmonopolet* (liquor store) for miles around. Near the town is one of the largest **burial fields** in the country, with more than 1,000 individual graves from the later Iron Age which were plundered in the 19th century. The wooden cruciform church dates from the 17th century and has a painted choir decorated with carvings.

From Oppdal the R70 branches off into the Sunndal; it's another 70 kilometers to Sunndalsøra. Countless minor access roads and hiking trails lead off this gorgeous scenic route into the popular walking region of Trollheimen.

It's 116 kilometers on the E6 from Oppdal to Trondheim. The road is in good condition and the scenery is attractive, but there are no special highlights along here, and you can easily cover the distance in two hours. One other option is to detour through Ulsberg and Tynset on the R3/R30 to the old mining town of

Røros, from where you can return to the E6 by way of **Støren**. This excursion is also possible by train from Støren or Trondheim.

*RØROS
Museum Town of the Mining Industry

This old mining town of **Røros** ㊺ is the fourth place in Norway on the UNESCO's World Heritage List. The town and the fate of its miners became well-known as a result of a trilogy of novels written by Johan Falkberget (1927-35). This is Norway's only fjell town; located at an altitude of 630 meters, it has a very harsh climate. Copper was found here quite by chance in 1644, and the first smelting works were opened in the same year.

Since Norway had no mining tradition, miners were engaged from all over Eu-

Above: The "museum town" of Røros is still full of life. Right: King Olav Tryggvasson gazes down at Trondheim.

rope to dig and work the mines in **Storvola**; either because of these foreigners' corruption of this place-name or as a nod to the name of the first engineer, the German Oskar Schwartz; the town was soon nicknamed "Storvarts." Over the 333 years in which active mining took place in Røros, a number of other mines were opened, including Hestkletten, Christianus Quintus, Nyberget and the **Olavsgruva** or Olav Mine, which is to-day open to the public.

The development of the mining industry was not continuous, since every time there was armed conflict with Sweden, Røros was burned to the ground. The town was characterized by small, shallow wooden houses, some of which are still standing in the shadow of the slag heaps. The buildings for the "higher-ups" – the directors, engineers and officials – were located at a suitable distance from these huts, further down in the town.

In those days, **Malmplass** (Ore Square) was the center of town; it was here that the ore was weighed and the bell was sounded to mark the beginning and end of the shifts. Towering above the town is the **octagonal church** built in 1784; construction material for this building was stored on its terraces, and in some places can still be seen there. Adorning the tower are images of the hammers and mallets that are the symbol of the miner's trade. Inside, the church has open and closed galleries and a royal box; its walls sport pictures of past pastors and mine directors; and it even boasts a Baroque organ.

Opposite the church is a **monument** commemorating the discovery of the first ore, and a little to the south of the Bergmannsgate is the **Copper Works Museum**. This museum contains mining tools and lamps as well as the flags and weapons of the miners' corps.

To the west of the church is the **Aasen Gård**, the oldest building in Røros. In 1644 Hans Aasen not only cleared the land and built his farm here, but also discovered the first copper ore, and he is therefore regarded as the "founding father" of the town. On the eastern edge of the built-up area are the **miners' rooms**, a block of accommodation for miners who were either unmarried or here without their families.

The Olavsgruva, today's **Mining Museum**, is 12 kilometers northeast of Røros on the R31; in summer, an hourly bus service runs here from the Røros tourist office.

Visitors pass through the 17th-century Nyberget mine to enter the Olav Mine, which was worked from 1936 until the mining company went bankrupt in 1971. The machinery is still intact, and audio tapes are meant to create the illusion that people are still working here. One of the large hollow spaces has been turned into a theater where, in summer, there are concerts and folk performances. The audience has to dress warmly, however, as 500 meters down inside the mountain the temperature averages a mere 5°C.

*TRONDHEIM
Old Cathedral, Young Residents

Nidaros, as **Trondheim** ❹ was called until the early 16th century, was the first capital of Norway and its first and only religious center. Olav Tryggvasson, who was later known as Olav I, founded the city in the year 997. The great-grandson of Harald Hårfagra, he was anxious not to repeat the latter's mistake of not naming one city as the country's central capital. For this purpose, he selected the strategic site within a curve of the Nidaroselv (Nidelva). Here he built his royal court, the **Nidarnes**, and the city's first church, dedicated to St. Clement. After his death at the battle of Svolder (AD 1000), governors appointed by the Danish kings ruled in Nidaros until Olav II took over the regency in 1015. During the 13 years he was in power, he implemented strict reforms and established Christianity as the state religion; neither move was calculated to win him sympathy from the aristocracy and the farmers, who feared for their influence. In fact, he was compelled to flee the country, and when he was on his way back from Gardarike to Norway to reclaim his throne, he encountered a popular army in Stiklestad, which dealt his own army a crushing defeat. Olav himself was killed and buried here in the sand. Ironically it was his death on the battlefield on July 30, 1030 that sparked Nidaros's development as the religious center of the country. After only five years, in 1035, this undesirable king was canonized and his body brought to St. Clement's Church. So many pilgrims journeyed to the shrine of the "new" Norwegian saint that St. Clement's soon became too small to accommodate them all. It was but a short step from here to the idea of building a new, larger church, construction of which began in the same century. At the same time, all of the amenities necessary to support the crowds of pilgrims, such as restaurants, inns and hostels, had to appear, and the town consequently began to grow. When in the 11th century Olav Kyrre withdrew the Norwegian church from the jurisdiction of the ecclesiastical authorities in Bremen who had hitherto held sway, and created the dioceses of Oslo, Bergen and Nidaros, Nidaros was the largest of the three. In 1153 it became an archbishopric with seven dioceses subordinated to it.

As a result of the pilgrims and the growing trade with Northern Norway and the Atlantic islands, Nidaros also embarked on its first period of prosperity. Until the beginning of the 14th century, it was also the capital of Norway. Even after Håkon IV transferred the capital south to Bergen, Nidaros remained the country's religious center: in addition to the cathedral, nine churches and five monasteries were built. Even the Kalmar Union, in which the Danes assumed a dominant role, was unable to weaken the town's religious authority.

However, trade did suffer as a result of Copenhagen's dominance and the privileges enjoyed by the Hanseatic League; furthermore, the outbreak of fires at what seemed like regular intervals thwarted attempts at continuous economic development. In addition, the Reformation in 1536 put an end to the streams of pilgrims, and the archbishop was forced to leave Nidaros. It was at this time that the name of the town was also changed to Trondhjem. When in 1931 there was a movement afoot to change the name back to Nidaros, a majority of the population voted against it, so that all that was changed was the spelling.

With the decline of the Hanseatic League and the recognition of Norway as an independent state under the Danish crown, Trondheim entered a new period of prosperity, developing a thriving export trade in herring, dried cod and copper from Røros. When in 1681 a devastating fire reduced the town to rubble yet again, Trondheim was redesigned. Until then, the houses had been rebuilt atop the original foundations, and the old street plan had remained intact; now, the streets were widened considerably, the first stone houses were built, and the chessboard grid still evident in Trondheim's city center was created. General de Cicignon, the town planner responsible for this, centered his designs around the monumental buildings that remained. He created one main boulevard from the cathedral toward Monk's Island, the Munkegate; and placed a second one at right angles to it past St. Mary's Church (now called the Church of Our Lady), the Kongensgate. He also designed Bakklandet, east of the Nidaroselv (Nidelva), the first municipal district outside the protected peninsula.

Although trade was soon in the hands of foreigners again, these too gradually took Norwegian citizenship. This period saw the construction of the large merchant homes such as Stiftsgården and Hornemansgården and the palaces of the Møllmann and Schøller families. In 1800

154

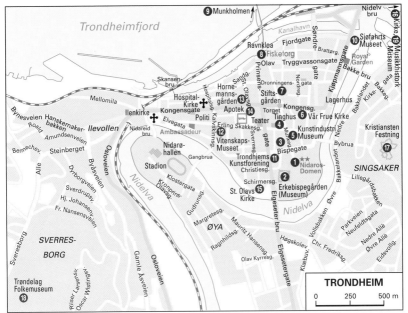

there were more people living in Trondheim than in Oslo, and in 1814 the Eidsvoll constitution named the cathedral of Trondheim as the official church for the coronation of Norway's kings.

Industrialization ushered in a new period of growth. The harbor was enlarged in 1880, and the new harbors built at the north end of town. At the same time the steamship line to Oslo was opened and the Røros railway completed, followed at a later date by the line over the Dovrefjell and the Meråker line to Sweden.

By 1914, the town already had a population of 55,000, and new districts were constantly springing up. Today Trondheim has spread far beyond the chain of hills that surround the city center, and its population is around 140,000. There is a broad economic base in a range of fields. In 1969, the pedagogical and technical colleges were combined to form a single university which today has a student body of around 10,000; Trondheim is very much a student town. This old young

town, as it likes to call itself, has a high standard of living; it has everything from historic sights to a wide range of activities and events that extend from concerts in pubs to the famous cathedral concerts during St. Olav's Week. And you can even fish for salmon right in the town center. Like Oslo and Bergen, Trondheim has introduced a toll which has to be paid every time you drive into the city.

The Cathedral of the North: **★★Nidaros**

Nidaros Cathedral ❶ is Norway's largest medieval building. Measuring 102 meters long and 50 meters wide, it is the largest Gothic church in the whole of Scandinavia. This church where Norway's kings are crowned has an eventful history that extends back more than a thousand years.

After Olav II's body, perfectly preserved, was brought back from Siklestad to Nidaros and buried in **St. Clement's Church**, a spring with healing properties

is said to have risen by the church, its waters able to cure all illnesses. When in 1066 Olav Kyrre came back to Nidaros with the body of his father, who had fallen in England, he was accompanied by members of the Anglo-Saxon nobility. Kyrre buried his father, Harald Hardråda, in St. Mary's Church, had St. Clement's pulled down, and gave orders for a new large church to be built for St. Olav, his uncle. This was probably designed by a member of his English retinue, as the extra-long nave suggests Anglo-Saxon influence. Kyrre's building was presumably not completed, since the foundations of the nave break off abruptly at their western end. In the 12th century the nave was redesigned and the transept was added, still in the Romanesque style.

It was Øystein Erlandson, second archbishop of Nidaros, who, after a journey to

Above: The facade of Nidaros Cathedral is adorned with saints, kings and martyrs. Right: The massive crossing tower dominates the cathedral building.

Rome, introduced a new architectural style, that of the Cistercians. This transitional style between Romanesque and Gothic is evident in the upper parts of the transept and St. Mary's Chapel, the present sacristy. After a dispute with King Sverre, Øystein was exiled to England for two years. In Canterbury he discovered the English Gothic style and conceived the idea of implementing it in the completion of the church over Olav's tomb. After his reconciliation with Sverre he began to build the choir. The **high choir** was designed in the shape of an octagon with an ambulatory in a delicate Gothic style that is not to be found anywhere else in the north. After Øystein's death in 1188, work was halted until 1210 by further disputes with the king. Only after this were the octagon and the vault over the ambulatory and long choir completed. Among the master builders there were probably architects from Lincoln who were experts in Gothic ribbed vaulting. The crossing tower, begun in 1100, was rebuilt in the Gothic style between 1235 and 1250; at the same time, the star-vaulting was added and the aisles parallel to the nave were built. The towers of the west facade had not yet been completed.

The first fire struck in the 14th century; there followed others which did a great deal of damage, and by the time of the Reformation the nave was a ruin. Although an attempt was made to restore the choir and transept as a Protestant parish church, the Danes transported the church treasure to Denmark and melted most of it down, including the silver shrine of St. Olav. The wooden inner shrine remained in Trondheim and was later buried in a walled grave, which the Danish king Frederick II ordered to be filled with earth so that the saint would be forgotten. Today, the exact burial place is unclear, but it is probably near the high altar, where nine chiseled crosses represent St. Olav and the eight other kings who are buried in the cathedral.

Restoration of the cathedral began in 1869. By 1906, the nave, the aisles and the long choir had been restored in the Gothic style; the main choir had remained undamaged. All that had remained of the facade were the ruins of the lower parts and five sculptures, so it had to be completely rebuilt, based on the model of a contemporary engraving from the 17th century.

Christian Christie, the first supervisor of the construction work, brought the sculptor Gustav Vigeland to Trondheim. Vigeland was not at all happy with the commission: although, as he wrote to a friend, he "was earning a lot of money," he was "selling his soul," and the whole cathedral had become altogether "too Protestant" for his liking. He nevertheless hung on for ten years before resigning. Later, in 1928, a competition was held, which was won by the 30-year-old Helge Thiis, who also became supervisor of the artistic side of construction work. The facade was not yet complete when the cathedral was consecrated on St. Olav's Day in 1930, but it was not too early to play the church's German-built organ.

Not until 1946 did artisans and artists finally tackle the **west facade**. Stinius Fredriksen was in charge of design and arranged the figures on the facade to create what is effectively a picture book of the Christian faith. From Adam and Eve and the prophets of the Old Testament through archangels and saints to the Virgin and Child and the resurrected Christ, the facade brings together all the important figures in the Bible and the legends of the saints. The figures, with the exception of the bronze archangel Michael on the northern tower of the facade, were all new; it's easy to see that they were made by a number of different artists. Several of the beautiful windows are by Gabriel Kielland. and there is an impressive **rose window** over the west portal.

Sights in the City Center

South of the cathedral is the **Archbishop's Palace** ❷, known to locals as

Erkebispegården. It is the oldest secular building in the north, dating back to the days of Bishop Øystein. The building's wings, connected with a gatehouse and facing the Nidaroselv, are in the early Gothic style, but they seem positively earthbound in comparision with the soaring Gothic of the cathedral. After the Reformation, the palace became the seat of a feudal lord and a military base. One well-preserved feature is the **Knights' Hall**, built in 1180. Today some of the buildings are being used as a **museum**. Displays of weapons, flags and equipment document Norway's military history from the peasant armies of the 16th century to the forces of the Norwegian resistance in World War II.

North of the cathedral complex is **Munkegate**. Here stands the brick building of the old **cathedral school** ❸, and, a little to the north of this, the **Thing House** ❹, an administrative building from the 1950s with bronze doors and ceramic reliefs depicting scenes from the town's history. Opposite this is the **Museum of Decorative Arts** ❺, with historic furniture, jewelry and national folk costumes, as well as designer objects from the 1950s and 1960s.

Munkegate continues to the large market, the **Torget**, featuring a 20-meter column topped with a statue of the town's founder, **Olav Tryggvasson**, which here also functions as the pointer of a sundial. This central square is the setting for a picturesque market on weekdays; at its southeast corner stands a statue of a cheerful, rotund market customer.

If you turn into **Kongensgate**, you'll come after a few paces to the **Church of Our Lady** ❻, which was built over the remains of the old St. Mary's Church. In the 18th century, this church was lengthened to the west, and its tower was also an addition from this period. The Baroque

Right: The old storehouses of Trondheim have been painstakingly restored.

altar in its interior once stood in the cathedral.

Further north on Munkegate, at the corner of **Dronningensgate**, is the **Stiftsgården** ❼. This palace, 13 meters wide and 58 meters long, and thus one of the largest wooden palaces in Scandinavia, was built in the Rococo style in 1770 for the Schøller family. Today, it's the residence of an even more eminent local family: that of the Norwegian king. Right at the end of Munkegate is the **Fish Market** ❽, purveying a huge variety of fresh and smoked fish.

In a straight line from the end of Munkegate, 2 kilometers out of town in the Trondheimsfjord, is **Munkholmen** ❾, Monks' Island. Boats to the island leave from **Ravnkloa quay** below the fish market. Before Benedictine monks were allowed to build a monastery here, Trondheim used this island as its place of execution. After the Reformation, the monastery was deserted, and in 1531 it was completely destroyed by fire. A fortress was built out of the ruins, but this was abandoned when it was established that the cannons could not even fire as far as the mainland. After this, Munkholmen functioned as a prison island. Now, however, a bathing beach and a restaurant attract visitors in fine weather.

From Ravnkloa, walk down the busy **Olav Tryggvassonsgate** to the Nidelva. At the northern end of **Kjøpmannsgate**, which runs alongside the river, is the old 19th-century prison, now the city **Shipping Museum** ❿. If you bear south, you'll find a row of attractive old ***storehouses** built on stilts, which have been painstakingly restored and are now under a preservation order. The best view of the city is from the old **Bybrua**, a drawbridge which was once the only access to the town. Here, you've come full circle and are back at the cathedral.

The **City Art Gallery** ⓫ (Bispegate 7) in the middle of town is worth a visit: it displays works by Norwegian artists, in-

cluding a Munch room with drawings by this artist, as well as a collection of European paintings from the 19th and 20th centuries. At Skakkesgate 47 is the **Museum of Natural History and Archeology** ⑫, with displays relating to everything from ornithology, mineralogy and zoology to church art. On Kongensgate, near the Torget, are the old **Hornemannsgården** ⑬ and the **Swan Pharmacy** ⑭, two beautiful wooden buildings dating from the 18th century.

In the cellar of the savings bank on the Torget are the remains of the **church of St. Gregory**, built in the 12th century. Of the nine churches which were built in Trondheim in this period, only two others remain: the ruins of **St. Olav's Church** ⑮ near the cathedral, and **Lade Church** ⑯, belonging to the manor of the same name in the eastern part of town.

Sights Beyond the City Center

On the eastern bank of the Nidelva is **Kristiansten Fortress** ⑰, dating from the 17th century. In the early morning the best view of the town is from here. A better view in the evening, however, is that from the **Trøndelag Folke Museum** ⑱, in the west part of town. Assembled here are 55 wooden buildings from Trøndelag, Sami (Lapp) tents, and the remains of the old **castle of King Sverre**.

Below the museum, where Sverdrupsveien curves to meet Byåsvei, there's another panoramic view of Trondheim. A third place with a good view is the **revolving restaurant** atop the 85-meter **television tower** on a hill in the eastern part of town.

Near the E6, on the road north out of town, is the old manor of ***Ringve Gård**. Surrounded by a new botanical garden, the house has been turned into a **Museum of Historic Musical Instruments** ⑲, based on the collection of a Russian émigré who settled here. Exhibits are presented in chronological order, with musical demonstrations for visitors. In summer, the Ringve Chamber Ensemble uses these instruments in their concerts.

EIDSVOLL

i Postboks 2080 Eidsvoll, tel. 63952530; June 1-Aug 31, 9 am-8 pm, other times Mon-Sat 9 am-6 pm.

$$ Feiring Hotel, 2093 Feiring, tel. 63966210.

Eidsvollverk, May 2-June 14 & Aug 16-Sept 30, 10 am-3 pm; June 15-Aug 15, 10 am-5 pm; Oct 1-Apr 30, noon-2 pm.

Skibladner paddlewheel steamer, Eidsvoll-Gjøvik-Lillehammer, mid-June to mid-August; contact Skibladner, Parkgt. 2, 2300 Hamar, tel. 62527085.

HAMAR

i Postboks, 2300 Hamar, by the cathedral, tel. 62521217; June 1-August 31, 9 am-8 pm, other times Mon-Sat 9 am-6 pm.

$$ Scandik Hotel Hamar, Vangsvn. 121, tel. 62527000. **Hotel Astoria**, Torggt. 23, tel. 62528222. **$** Seiersted Pensjonat, Holsetgt. 64, tel. 62521244. **Hedmark Museum** with cathedral, May 15-Sept 15, 10 am-4 pm. **Museum of Emigration**, same hours. **Ice Rink**, open only for events. **Ringsaker Church**, 20 km north, pick up key next door.

LILLEHAMMER

i Elvegt. 4, 2600 Lillehammer, tel. 61259299; June 1-Aug 31, 9 am-8 pm, other times Mon-Sat 9 am-6 pm.

$$$** Quality Hotel, Turisthotellvn. 7, tel. 6128-6600, lovely place with indoor pool, right by Maihaugen. **$$ Best Western Breiseth Hotell, 2600 Lillehammer, Jernbanegt. 1, tel. 61269500. **Norlandia Oppland Hotel**, Storgt. 2A, tel. 61258500. **Comfort Home Hotel Hammer**, Storgt. 108, tel. 61263500. **Bjørns Kro og Motell**, Vingnes, tel. 61258300. **$** Euro Birkebeineren Hotel, Motel og Apartments, Olympiaparken, Birkebeinerv. 24, tel. 61264700. **Lillehammer Camping**, Dampsagveien 47, tel. 61253333, some cabins, near "Skibladner" quay.

Maihaugen Open-Air Museum, middle to end of May and mid-August to end of September 10 am-5 pm, June-August 9 am-6 pm, other times Tue-Sun 11 am-4 pm, guided tours every hour, in several languages.

The hotels in the Lillehammer area are open year-round; there's downhill and cross-country skiing from late November to early April. Reservations are necessary, especially around Christmas.

ELVERUM

i Postboks, 2400 Elverum, tel. 62416060; June 1-Aug 31, 9 am-8 pm, other times Mon-Sat 9 am-6 pm.

$$ Central, Storgt. 22, tel. 62410155.

Christiansfjell Fortress, always open. **Glomdals Museum**, June 15-August 15, Mon-Fri 10 am-6 pm; other times 10 am-4 pm, closed Sat.

PEER GYNT WAY

$$$ Golden Tulip Rainbow Skeikampen Høifjellshotell & Apartements, 2622 Svingvoll, tel. 61228700, inexpensive apartments. **Dale Gudbrands Gard**, 2647 Hundorp, tel. 61297111, historic court with viking graves, etc. **$$** Fefor Høifjellshotell, 2640 Vinstra, tel. 61290099. **Peer Gynt Fjellstue**, 2640 Vinstra, tel. 61291930. **Wadahl Høifjellshotell**, 2645 Harpefoss (Gålå), tel. 61298300. **$** Fagerhøi Fjellskole og Aktivitetssenter, 2647 Hundorp, tel. 6129-7000, sports hostel. **Skei Fjellandsby**, 2622 Skei/Gausdal, cabins.

Churches of Fåberg and Follebu, open in July, otherwise keys next door. **Aulestad**, open May 18-31 and September, 11 am-2:30 pm, June and August, 10 am-3:30 pm, July 10 am-5:30 pm.

To book the **Senengårdtour**, a hike along the Peer Gynt Way (late June to early August) with luggage transfers from one hotel to the next, contact **Peer Gynt Hotels**, c/o Gausdal Turistkontor, 2622 Skei/Gausdal, tel. 61220066, fax. 61229330.

From November into May, the high fjells are certain to have snow, and there's a full range of winter sports. Make sure to book hotels well in advance.

GUDBRANDSDAL

i Øyer, 2636 Øyer, tel. 61277000. **Ringebu**, Postboks, 3630 Ringebu, tel. 61280533. **Vinstra**, Nedergt. 5A, 2640 Vinstra. **Dombås**, Postboks, 2660 Dombås, tel. 61241444, June 1-August 31, 9 am-8 pm, other times Mon-Sat, 9 am-6 pm. **Otta**, Otta Skysstation, 2670 Otta, tel. 61230244.

$$ Rondablikk Høyfjellhotell, 2650 Kvam, tel. 61294940, by Peer Gynt-Seter Way. **Ringebu Hotell**, Brugt. 27, tel. 61281250. **Feforkampen Fjellhotell**, Fefor, 2640 Vinstra, tel. 61291644. **Sødorp Gjestgivergård**, 2640 Vinstra, tel. 26291000. **Vinstra Hotell**, 2640 Vinstra, tel. 61290199. **Venabu Fjellhotell**, 2632 Venabygd (Ringebu), tel. 61284055. **Dovrefjell Hotel**, 2660 Dombås, tel. 61241005. **Rondane Høyfjellhotell**, 2670 Otta, tel. 61233933. **$** Øyer Fjellstue, 2636 Øyer, tel. 61278237, mountain pension. **Gaiastova-Hafjelltoppen**, 2636 Øyer, tel. 61275000, large cabin complex. **Rustberg Hytteutleie og Camping**, 2636 Øyer, tel. 61278184. **Rybakken Hytter og Camping**, 2636 Øyer, tel. 61278270, country farmhouse with cabins. **Skotten Seter Storhytte**, 2630 Ringebu, tel. 61282961, mountain pension. **Bøygen Camping**, 2640 Vinstra, tel. 61290137, camping cabins. **Fagerli Fjellstue**, 2640 Vinstra, tel. 61298566, mountain pension with cabins. **Otta Camping og Motell**, 2670 Otta, tel. 61230309, 12 cabins. **Otta Turistsenter**, 2670 Otta, tel. 61230323, cabins. **Killis**

Overnatting, Ola Dahls gt. 35, 2670 Otta, tel. 61230492, small pension, self-catering. **Toftemo Turiststasjon**, 2662 Dovre, tel. 61240045.

🏛 **Ringebu Stave Church**, open June 15-August 15, 10 am-6 pm. **Royal Farmstead of Tofte**, privately owned, can only be viewed from outside.

⛷ A range of winter sports are available between Ringebu (downhill skiing), Otta and Dombå, and in the Rondane massif. Make sure to reserve in advance.

RØROS

ℹ Bergmannsplassen, 7460 Røros, tel. 72411165; June 1-August 31, 9 am-8 pm, other times Mon-Sat 9 am-6 pm.

⬛ ⊛⊛⊛ **Quality Røros Hotel**, An-Magritts Vn., tel. 72411011. ⊛⊛ **Bergstadens Hotel**, Oslovn. 2, tel. 72411111. ⊛ **Vauldalen Fjellhotell**, 7470 Brekkebygd, tel. 72413100.

🏛 **Church**, open year-round. **Copper Mine Collection, Mining Museum**, open year-round; contact the tourist office for guided tours. **Olavsgruva (copper mine)**, 13 km north, daily departures from the tourist information office.

TRONDHEIM

ℹ Trondheim Aktivum, at the Torget, tel. 73929400. In summer, city tours at noon; bike rentals.

⬛ ⊛⊛⊛ **Royal Garden Hotel**, Kjøpmannsgt. 73, tel. 73521100, the ultimate luxury hotel; the lobby is a palace of glass, filled with plants; there's also an elegant nightclub (Opera). **Britannia Hotel**, Dronningensgt. 5, tel. 73535353, Trondheim's most traditional hotel in the style of centuries past, but fully renovated. **Radisson SAS Hotel**, Kjøpmannsgt. 48, tel. 73535310. ⊛⊛ **Ambassadeur Hotel**, Elvegt. 18, tel. 73527050. **Hotell Fru Schøller**, Dronningensgt. 26, tel. 73505080, nice comfortable hotel. **Quality Panorama**, Østre Rosten 38, tel. 72886522, nearly 10 km south. ⊛ **Singsaker Sommerhotell**, Rogertsgate 1, tel. 73520092. **Munkenhotel**, Kongensgt. 44, tel. 73534540, simple rooms, ample breakfast.

✗ **Galagsen / Palmehaven**, in the Hotel Britannia, tel. 73535353, first-rate, but very expensive. **Rødebriggen**, Backlandet 66, tel. 73518320, in an old warehouse on the river, with good fish and reindeer; often has live music. **Vertshuset Tavern**, Sverresborg, tel. 73520932, since 1739, traditional Norwegian cuisine. **Dickens**, Kjøpmannsgt. 57. **Egon**, Th. Angells gate 8, tel. 73517975, snacks, young crowd; extends over many stories. **Hos Magnus**, Kjøpmannsgate 63, tel. 73524110, known for its fish, especially the salmon.

🛍 **Artisans' Association**, Prinzengt. 34, especially good for Norwegian sweaters. **Artisans' Association**,

Munkegate 8, good for jewelry. **Arne Rønning**, Nordregate 10, good for wood crafts.

🏛 **Nidaros Cathedral**, May 15-September 15, Mon-Fri 10 am-3 pm, Sat 10 am-2 pm, Sun 1:30-4 pm; October 1- May 14, Mon-Fri noon-2:30 pm, Sat 11:30 am-2 pm, Sun 1:30-3 pm. **Crown Jewels**, June 15-August 20. **Archbishop's Palace and Museum**, south of the cathedral, June 1- August 20, Mon-Fri 9 am-3 pm, Sat 9 am-2 pm, Sun noon-3 pm. **Church of Our Lady**, on Kongsgt. East of the market, June-August Tue-Sat 10 am-2 pm. **Stiftsgården**, Munkegt. 23, June 1-August 31 weekdays 11 am-2 pm. **Fish Market**, weekdays 7 am-noon. **Munkholmen Island**, departures from Ravnkloa quay, June 1-August 31 every hour on the hour after 10 am; visits 10:30 am-5:30 pm; swimming is possible. **Shipping Museum**, Fjordgt. 6, weekdays 9 am-3 pm, Sun noon-3 pm. **City Art Gallery**, Bispegt. 7, Tue-Sun noon-4 pm. **Museum of Natural History and Archaeology**, Erling Skakkesgt. 47, daily 10 am-3 pm. **Ruins of the Gregorian Church**, visits during business hours in the cellar of Strindens Sparebank, Kongensgt. 4. **Kristiansten Fortress**, June 1-August 31, Mon-Sat 10 am-3 pm, Sun 10 am-2 pm. **Trøndelag Folk Museum**, May 20- August 31, 10 am-6 pm. **Television Tower**, weekdays 11:30 am-11:30 pm, Sun noon-6 pm. **Ringve Museum** (of music history), in Lade, guided tours in German and English daily at noon and 2 pm, May 20-September 30, also on Tue and Wed at 7:30 pm from June 20-August 19, at noon in October, and other times of year Sundays at 1 and 2 pm.

🎵 **Organ concerts in Nidaros Cathdral,** July 15-August 20 daily at 3 pm, other times Sat at 1 pm. **St. Olav's Week**, last week in July, choral concerts daily at 7 pm. **Golf Tournament** on June 19 and 20.

🏊 There's a heated salt-water swimming pool on Prinzengate.

🚢 Fjord trips, fishing tours, excursions to Dovrefjell and Røros available year-round from Midt-Norsk Reiseliv AS, Postboks 65, 7001 Trondheim, tel. 73929394

✈ AIR: Several direct flights a day to Oslo, Bergen and Tromsø. Trondheim is also a stop on the western coastal line, which flies from Stavanger to Tromsø. TRAIN: Daily express trains between Oslo and Trondheim, some of which also use the Røros route. The Norland Line runs north to Bodø; to the east, the Meråker Line links Trondheim to Sweden. BUS: Service via Røros to Oslo; links to Bergen and Tromsø. BOAT: Hurtigrute ships depart from Trondheim every day at 6 am traveling north; at 11 am traveling south. Between April and Sept, several other boats ply the coast every day between Trondheim and Kristiansund. For information, contact Kystekspressen, Pirterminalen, 7005 Trondheim, tel. 73525540 and 71219501.

From Oslo to Trondheim

THE LONG JOURNEY
TO THE NORTH CAPE

TRONDHEIM – MO I RANA

MO I RANA – NARVIK

NARVIK – TROMSØ

LAND OF THE SAMI

HAMMERFEST

NORDKAPP

Until the early Middle Ages, the Norwegians were not interested in the area north of Trondheim, which was known as "Lapp Hell." Not until resourceful merchants discovered that there was good business to be done with the Sami (Lapp) fur hunters was more attention paid to this region. For a while, trade flourished to mutual satisfaction and the Lapplanders also did well out of it. Then, inevitably, the Scandinavian kings also started to take an interest in the area, first sending in their tax collectors, and eventually, in the 16th century, starting to squabble over the territory. Russia also intervened in this dispute between the Danish-Norwegian side and the Finnish-Swedish side, securing its own claim to the Kola Peninsula in the process.

From the 17th century on more and more southern Norwegian farmers' sons migrated into the northern Norwegian valleys. They despised the Sami and deprived them of their rights; however, rather than allowing themselves to be exploited as cheap labor, the latter simply retreated north, away from the newcomers. Subsequent 20th-century attempts to integrate them into industrial society

Previous pages: Mother and daughter in Lapp festive costume. Left: Cotton grass is a protected plant and must not be picked.

have only succeeded in part. After World War II they were granted special rights as a national minority.

FROM TRONDHEIM TO
MO I RANA
On the E6 to Snåsavatn

There are two alternative routes out of Trondheim: the new toll road and the old road along the fjord. The latter passes though some attractive Trondheim suburbs and takes approximately an hour, whereas the 15 kilometers of toll road can be covered in 10 minutes. The two roads meet again at **Hell ❶**. Rock drawings from the Stone Age have been found very close to here; in fact, the whole inner Trondheimfjord has many such prehistoric sites.

Shortly before the tunnel which runs under Trondheim Airport is 13th-century **Værnes Church**. The ends of the beams in its open roof truss have been carved into imaginative animal and human heads. The church's splendid pulpit was carved in 1685, giving rise to the term for a whole artistic style, the "Værnes Style."

Shortly after the airport, the E14 branches off in the direction of Sweden. **Hegra ❷**, which has a fortress that was built to defend the area against Swedish attack, and Meråker are on this route.

The Long Journey to the North Cape

Meråker ❸ is an old mining town where copper and galena, or lead ore, were extracted, although the mines here were never as important as those of Røros. The town's church has an impressive Baroque altar. Meråker was the home of one Johan Fundtaunet, the church bell-ringer and a goldsmith who is said to have secretly run a silver mine, illegally pocketing the profits himself: officially, all mines of precious metals were property of the crown. The truth of this story is impossible to verify; Fundtaunet took his secret with him to the grave. However, his beautiful pieces of jewelry are still on display in Meråker's town museum.

Fifteen kilometers along the E6 is **Tiller ❹**, surrounded by fields running down to the fjord. A small road leads to the water's edge. At low tide, you can cross on foot to the **island of Steinvikholm**, otherwise the only means of crossing is the boat belonging to the island's groundskeeper. It was here in the year 1525 that Olav Engelbrektson, the last archbishop of Trondheim, built a fort. Whether he had already intended this to serve as a place of refuge is not known, but it is not unlikely, since he was trying to arm himself in every manner possible against the approaching Reformation: with, for example, the unsuccessful royal election of Bud. When the Reformation finally arrived in 1536, the authorities assumed that Engelbrektson would try to leave the country, and sealed off the whole Trondheimsfjord. The archbishop, who had probably foreseen this, went to Steinviksholm, taking St. Olav's shrine with him; he stayed there until 1537, when he was able to leave the country in secret.

Although there is no record actually stating that his escape was the result of his striking a deal that allowed Engelbrektson to go free in return for his leaving the shrine of St. Olav, which he did not take with him, this is quite a likely scenario.

In any case, the archbishop took his revenge on the northern Europeans from his exile in Rome by writing books in which he deprecatingly describes their meterlong shoes, the fish they ate, the size of their houses, and the endless days and nights when it got neither fully dark nor fully light.

One of the most unusual sea battles of World War II took place at **Langstein ❺** in 1942, when a fisherman with a torpedo hidden under his boat made an unsuccessful attempt to torpedo the German battleship *Tirpitz* which was anchored here. Eleven kilometers further on, at Åsen, the R753 turns off down the **Frosta Peninsula**. Located at **Logtun ❻** (23 kilometers) is one of the major Thing sites of the north; in 940 the so-called *Frostating Laws* were passed here. This was a legal code governing the whole Trøndelag area.

To see the rock drawings of **Holtesmoen ❼**, near **Holte**, leave the new E6 at **Ronglan** and take the old road. This leads right to these 3,500-year-old illustrations of animals and hunting.

Smoking in **Skogn ❽** are the chimneys of the largest newspaper factory in Norway, which produces half a million tons a year. At **Korsbakken** there is a small path to **Alstadhaug Church ❾**, a stone church dating from the 13th century. Visible here are unique medieval frescoes which were uncovered during restoration work in the 1950s.

Near the church hill, from which there is a good view, is the *Ammenstue* (Wet Nurse House), a two-story wooden building where mothers used to go and stay with their children until their christening. The *Ammenstue* is the oldest wooden house in Trøndelag and today houses a museum.

Close by is the **Ølivshaugen**, a burial mound 6 meters high and 20 meters across; this dates from the period of large-scale ethnic migration, around the 5th century AD.

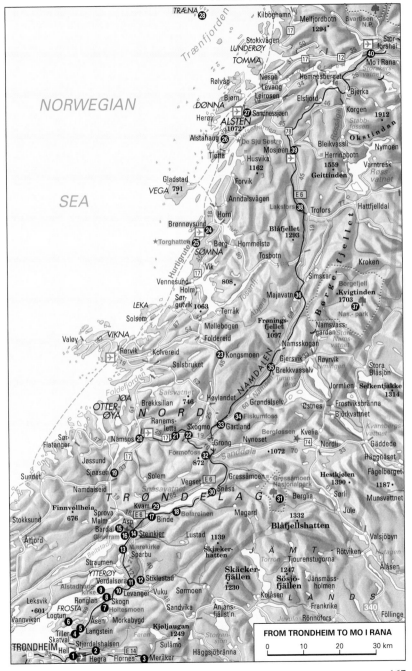

Near **Levanger** ⑩ is another, even older burial site: the **Geite Gård**, which dates from the Iron Age. At the beginning of the 20th century, the site was popular with Norwegian archaeologists, as the graves contained quantities of jewelry and other funerary objects. From the hill of **Geitehøgde** there is a good view of the fjord and the fertile agricultural countryside. Eight kilometers to the east are the ruins of **Munkeby Monastery**, which were restored in 1968.

Verdalsøra ⑪ (population 7,000) today lives almost exclusively from the construction of oil platforms, which are cast out of reinforced concrete in the deep waters of the fjord. From here, it is only 8 kilometers to **Stiklestad** ⑫ (R757), site of the battle in 1030 in which the "Missionary King" St. Olav lost his life. Every year on July 29, 300 performers reenact the *Spelet om heilag Olav* (St. Olav Play)

Above: An individual style – the Vaernes Style – was named after this 17th century pulpit in Vaernes. Right: Rock drawings at Bardal.

in the new **open-air theater**, attracting an audience of some 5,000 people. Also here is an **equestrian statue of St. Olav**, which towers over the theater.

In **Stiklestad Church**, built on the battlefield between 1150 and 1180, a mass is still said for the saint every year on the anniversary of his death. The wall paintings in the nave were uncovered during restoration work in 1930. The baptismal font and the choir with its ribbed vaulting date from the Middle Ages, but the frescoes in the choir with scenes from the famous battle were painted by Alf Rolfsen in 1930. In summer, the above-mentioned St. Olav Play is frequently presented in this church in the form of a slide show. There is also a **St. Olav Column** on the site of the shed where the body of the saint is said to have lain the first night after his death. The stone on which his head rested was supposedly later incorporated into the altar of the church; anyone who touched it was immediately cured of any and all illness.

Maere Church ⑬, 30 kilometers north on the E6, dates from the 12th century and was first rebuilt in 1277. This stone church has an open roof truss, and the ends of the supporting beams are carved into grotesque animal heads; its altar and pulpit are of later vintage, dating from the 17th century. It had already been suspected long ago from the prominent position of the church that this was on the site of an old thingstead, something that was confirmed by excavations carried out when the building was last restored.

Steinkjer ⑭ marks the innermost end of the Trondheimfjord. Today boasting 21,000 inhabitants, this town had to be almost completely rebuilt after the ravages of World War II. Numerous important postwar artists from the Trøndelag contributed to the church, which was completed in 1965. Apart from this, Steinkjer's sights include a small open-air museum on the hill of Flathaugen and, at Tingvold, a group of 38 *bautasteinen*

(memorial stones without an inscription) which have been set up again in an approximation of their original positions. In this area, with its wealth of prehistoric sites, it's worth taking the time to detour to **Bardal** ⓯ (some 11 kilometers to the northwest), where you can examine drawings from the Stone Age (depicting elk, reindeer and people) and the Bronze Age (of ships, horses and suns).

At **Helge Farmstead** near Byfoss, about 2 kilometers north of Steinkjer on the R763, there are burial mounds, 4-meter-high *bauta* stones, a stone circle and a stone wall which were originally also parts of this shrine. Near the Ice Age end moraine of **Eggevammen** is the **Gjævram Farmstead** ⓰, built over the remains of an old fortified farming settlement from the time of large-scale ethnic migration. Such settlements were legion in the area around Steinkjer; to date, nine of them have been found.

The E6 continues through Asp and Sem to **Snåsavatn**, a freshwater lake 36 kilometers long which is full of trout and eels; the road runs along its western shore.

An alternative is to take the R763 along the eastern shore of the lake, which is equally beautiful in terms of its scenery, and of even greater interest for anyone interested in cultural history. You have the best view of the Snåsvatn in the whole area from the look-out point at **Gusthaugen**, near **Binde** ⓱.

Around 30 kilometers north of Steinkjer, between the train stations of **Valøy** and **Vikran** (the Nordland railway line also runs along this eastern shore) is the most famous rock drawing in northern Norway: the 6,000-year-old **Reindeer of Bøla** ⓲ (*Bølareinen*) a life-sized representation scratched in the rock with a sure hand by a Stone Age artist.

**Away From the Main Road:
The R17 through Namsos to Mosjøen**

Between Steinkjer and Mosjøen or Mo i Rana, there is an alternative to the E6: the R17, which runs through Namsos,

Skogmo, Foldereid, Brønnøysund and Sandnessjøen. This route through the district of Namdal, along the fjords and over the islands, is very scenic; note, however, that it also takes much more time than driving along the E6, as it involves three or four ferries.

After Asp the road passes through several small farming villages before arriving, 40 kilometers further on, at **Sjøåsen** ❿ at the end of the shimmering blue **Lygnenfjord**, with 600-meter snow-capped mountains towering above it.

The road follows the fjord and crosses the Namsen shortly before **Namsos** ❷⓪ on a bridge 900 meters long. An observation point here commands a panoramic view of the town. Namsos has a population of 11,000 and is the only community apart from Steinkjer in the northern Trøndelag with a city charter. When Allied troops landed here in 1940, Hitler's army bombed the town and completely destroyed it. Reconstruction, however, began even before the war was over, financed by donations from Sweden; the district that was built then is still called *Svenskebyen* (Swedish Town).

In Namsos the **Namdal Museum**, by the road into town, is worth a visit; there is also a good view from the local hill, **Bjørumsklompen**, above Fredriksberg Park. The museum displays boats and household articles from Trøndelag, and has one section devoted to Sami (Lapp) settlements and culture. Namsos is a good center for tourists, who can choose from among fjord excursions, boat trips to the islands, express shipping connections to Trondheim, or long walks through the Namdal.

From here, the R17 accompanies the broad river Namsen, cutting across some of its curves, which gives drivers some great river views, on its way to **Ranemsletta** ❷①. Here, the old **Ranems Church**, close to the river, dates from the

Right: Island scene at Alstahaug.

13th century. According to a prophecy, one year, on the Protestant holiday of repentance and atonement, the church is supposed to fall into the water full of people. In order to prevent this it was protected by fascines, or bundles of sticks used as supports, on the river side as long ago as the 18th century. This measure seems to have proven to be effective, as the church is still standing on its original marble base.

At **Skogmo** ❷❷ the R17 leaves the Namsen and another road continues along the river as far as Grong, where it meets the E6. Skogmo is a fisherman's paradise, especially for salmon anglers.

The R17 now follows the Kongs-moelva to **Kongsmoen** ❷❸ on the **Indre Folda**, a narrow but long (70 kilometers) and deep arm of the Foldafjord. It is from Kongsmoen that the iron pyrite from Skorovass was shipped out after traveling the 45 kilometers here by cable car. Shortly before the little harbor town of **Foldereid** there is a bridge across the Indre Folda, and from **Trolldalen**, the hill immediately behind Foldereid, there is a splendid view of town and fjord.

The road continues along the **Kollfjord** and the **Sørfjord** and on through **Møllebogen** to **Holm**, where drivers have to take the first of this route's several ferries across to **Vennesund** (a 20-minute trip, 15 times a day). After **Vik** and **Berg** comes **Brønnøysund** ❷❹, which is already in the province of Nordland. The town's harbor is a regular stop on the *Hurtigrute* and an important trade center for the Helgeland coast.

This area has many prehistoric sites, natural grottos and caves; best-known of the latter is **Torghatten* ❷❺, 10 kilometers south of Brønnøysund on the island of Torget. Here, when the land was some 100 meters lower after the last Ice Age, the sea wore away a cave 160 meters long, 14 meters wide and 30 meters high in a granite rock. Visitors can reach the Torghatten either by road or by sea; in

good weather the *Hurtigrute* ships also detour around this hole in the rock.

After the ferry between **Horn** and **Anndalsvågen** (a 20-minute crossing, 8 times a day) it is only 17 kilometers to the next ferry from Forvik to **Tjøtta** (a 60-minute trip, 7 times a day) on the **island of Alsten**. The R17 runs along the west side of this island past ***De Sju Søstre** (The Seven Sisters), a chain of mountains with their seven peaks lined up like beads on a necklace. Between 800 and 1,100 meters high, these peaks are traversed by a hiking trail where a "race" is held; the tourist information office of Sandnessjøen takes applications.

The trail begins in the south at **Alstahaug ㉖**, where the pastor and popular poet Petter Dass (1647-1707), son of a Norwegian woman and a Scotsman, assumed his last pastorage in 1689. Dass's masterpiece, the epic *Nordland's Trumpet*, is a loving, detailed and accurate description of the hard lives of fishermen and farmers in contemporary Helgeland. Today, there's a Petter Dass Museum in the restored **parsonage**. The poet-pastor is interred in his 12th-century **church**, which is worth a visit in itself; here resided the first bishop of northern Norway. The **Royal Graves**, the largest in the north, are also worth a visit.

Sandnessjøen ㉗ is a trade and service center in the district of Alstahaug and has a population of 7,000. *Hurtigrute* boats also call in here, and there are a number of ferry and shipping connections to the offshore islands of the Helgeland coast, including a fast connection to **Træna ㉘**, an island group 40 kilometers offshore and right on the Arctic Circle, which takes 6 hours to reach. It consists of 5,000 islands, but only five of these are inhabited year-round. With a population of only about 100 people, the islands represent what is undoubtedly Norway's smallest community, and there is still something very special about them. From Træna you can go on by boat to Stokkvågen. Otherwise, continue from Sandnessjøen over the new **Helgeland Bridge** back to the mainland.

The Long Journey to the North Cape

From **Leirosen** you can either take the R78 to Mosjøen on the E6 or the ferry from **Levang** to **Nesna** (a 25-minute crossing, 11 times a day) and continue on the R17 and R12 directly to **Mo i Rana**. Another option is to continue on the R17 to Bodø; although this involves two more ferries and the road is not very good, the scenery is impressive and the ferry crosses the Arctic Circle in the middle of the **Melfjord**.

Through Nordland on the E6 from Snåsavatn to Mo i Rana

The E6 runs along the western shore of the Snåsavatn. Halfway along the length of the lake, at **Kvam ㉙**, there's a former schoolhouse which has been turned into a rest house; particularly inviting is its attractive lakefront terrace. At **Vegset** at the end of the lake, the R763 branches off to

Above: When the snow melts, the reindeer set off for the north. Right: June to August is the salmon-fishing season.

Snåsa ㉚. With its population of 1,000, this is today one of Norway's six Lapp centers and is responsible for the Sami population of northern Norway. There is a Sami boarding school here and the administrative centers responsible for local cottage industries and reindeer breeding, areas which once came under the aegis of the so-called Lapp Governor. 1979 saw the opening of the **Sami Culture House**, which includes a Lapp library and a permanent exhibition documenting the lifestyle of this minority group. Among the 300 exhibits displayed here is a collapsible organ which an early Lapp priest took with him on his missionary journeys.

The choir and sacristy of **Snåsa Church** are medieval, and the nave was restored in the 19th century. A more interesting building, however, is the **Sognestua**, a wooden house dating from the 16th century which is one of the oldest houses in the Trøndelag region. In addition, the area around Snåsa is known for its rare species of orchids; near the train stations of Snåsa and Jørstad there are protected areas where these striking plants can flourish.

In the area of the Snåsa community is **Gressåmoen National Park ③**, established in 1970. On this 171 square kilometers of protected land, fir trees grow in veritably primeval opulence, providing a habitat for lynx. The area is trackless except for a single path which generally follows the course of the **Luru**, a river that flows on an east-west axis; this is a historic trade route leading east to **Berglia**, outside the park's borders (where you rejoin the road). For the most part, however, this trackless expanse of moor and fjell is only to be recommended to very experienced hikers. You can reach the park (35 kilometers east of Snåsa) through the Luru valley.

For a long time the 30-meter **Formofoss ③** waterfall on the **Sanddøla** (back on the E6) represented an insurmountable obstacle to salmon. To enable the fish to follow their natural instincts to swim up river as far as possible to spawn in stiller waters, a tunnel salmon ladder was built which took ten years to complete.

At **Grong** you are back on the River Namsen, which the E6 follows for the next 100 kilometers.

In **Gartland ③**, where there is a new expressway leading off to the R17, is 17th-century **Gløshaug Church**. The supporting pillars in front of the choir are from a 13th-century stave church that was pulled down. The present church was also scheduled for demolition until it was bought by an Englishman and so rescued from this fate. So-called "Finnish Masses" were once held in this church. Originally it was the duty of the clergymen of Snåsa and Overhalle to visit the Lapplanders once a year, say Mass and christen their children; but later on the pastors were spared this obligation and the Sami were instead required by law to come to Gløshaug Church once a year

and attend Mass there. The Lapp Governor also came, using this as a convenient opportunity to collect taxes.

In the **Namdal**, which now narrows, numerous wooden galleries are placed in the river for anglers during the salmon season. At the time when the salmon are due to arrive, experienced anglers keep close watch so that they can make optimal use of the short season.

The **Fiskumfoss ④**, 7 kilometers north of Gartland, is a double waterfall 30 meters and 7 meters high, where power plants and artificial salmon ladders have been built. In **Grøndaselv** the R764 follows the route of the former Tau Railway, which transported pyrite from the Skorovas mine to Kongsmøen on the Indre Folda.

Brekkvasselv ⑤ is popular with salmon anglers. From here, the R773 leads off to **Røyrvik** and to the unspoilt lakes of **Tunnsjøen** and **Limingen**. This area is famous for its goat's cheese, which is, however, something of an acquired taste.

The Long Journey to the North Cape

The town of **Majavatn** ❸, on the east shore of the large lake of the same name and already within the boundaries of the Nordland region, was one of the Sami's favorite locations for making their winter camp, from which they journeyed north to find good pasturage. Several Sami families have now settled permanently on the east side of the lake and breed reindeer here.

In the past there was also a Sami mission, and there is still a so-called **Lapp Church** next to the road. The **Majavatn Vertshus** by the lake is an inviting place to stop off and tank up.

From Majavatn, as well as 6 kilometers to the north, there are trails to the 1,106 square kilometers of **Børgefjell National Park** ❸, which lures experienced outdoorsmen who have a taste for wilderness with its rapid rivers, lakes, and peaks (up to 1,703 meters high).

Above: Open-air theater in Mosjøen. Right: Just below the treeline – the Korgfjell between Mosjøen and Mo i Rana.

The E6 now rises to the watershed between Namsen and Vefsna at a height of 375 meters; there are a number of little streams both before and after this highest point in the road. Some 10 kilometers past Trofors is the **Laksfors** ❸, only two hundred meters or so from the road. The water falls a total of 16 meters in five steps, and the salmon use this natural ladder to reach the upper course of the river. Right next to the waterfall is a **cafeteria**, from the terrace of which diners can observe the fish fighting their way along. A little way from the old road is **Laksfors House**, best described as a clubhouse belonging to English anglers; the lounge, with its open fireplace, is hung with countless pictures of the many prize salmon they have caught.

Mosjøen ❸, (population 10,000), is centered on the **Skjerva** and the Vefsnfjord. Southwest of the river is **Sjøgata**, the largest contiguous inhabited settlement of wooden houses in northern Norway. All of the houses here are from the 18th and 19th centuries, and the octagonal **Dolstad Church** on the E6 going north out of town also dates from the 18th century; it is the oldest of its kind in the north of the country. Although completely restored, the church has retained items of its original decor, including the twelve pictures of the apostles grouped around the pulpit; and its roof and walls, which had been restored in the course of time, have been changed back into their original form. Next to the church is the **Vefsn Open-air Museum**.

Southwest of the town is the spectacular **Øyfjell Grotto**, which contains a small river, a waterfall and a lake. To visit it you need rubber boots, a waterproof jacket, rope and flashlight; you also have to join a guided tour.

The **Harevollen** on the Kjerringavei, Mosjøen's local hill, commands a panoramic view of the town, the Vefsnfjord and the Øyfjell. Kosjøen's main sources of revenue are the aluminum works and

the artificial fiber works in the northern part of the town. The **Salmon Co-operative** at the freight depot sells fresh and smoked salmon at reasonable prices.

For the next 55 kilometers, the E6 climbs as far as the **Korgfjellet**, at a height of 550 meters. The road passes four lakes which are so sheltered from the wind that they perfectly reflect the mountains that surround them. At the watershed, where there is a restaurant, the road also reaches the tree line; from here, it leads down to **Korgen**, where there was a camp for Yugoslavian prisoners of war during World War II. They were put to work building this stretch of road, and many of them died in the process; there is a memorial stone to them by the road. The remaining 37 kilometers to Mo i Rana follow the **Ranafjord**; in good weather, you can see all the way to the glacier area of Svartisen, north of Mo.

Today **Mo i Rana** �40 has a population of 10,000, most of whom didn't come here until after the war. Originally it was a trading place for Norwegians and Sami,

who bartered dried reindeer meat and hides for butter, flour and tobacco. In the 19th century, these market rights were transferred to the Meyer family, who by 1860 were rich enough to buy the whole place. Around the same time, mining of zinc, lead and iron ore began in the Mo area, and 1900 saw the opening of the mines of the Dunderdal, as well. The ore was shipped out until 1946, when the Norwegian parliament decided to build a steelworks in Mo; these became the largest in northern Europe. The industrial complex also includes a coking plant which processes coal brought in from Spitsbergen. Since there is an abundant supply of hydroelectric power, and as technology has been improved, more and more electrical energy has been used since the 1960s for the iron smelting process. The works still had 3,600 employees in the 1970s; but today, that figure has dropped to 200.

The **Rana Museum** in Mo is based on the collection of the Meyer family; its displays include crafts, geography, mining

and geology, as well as items from the collections of the National Gallery and the Munch Museum in Oslo. Mo i Rana is also the seat of the Norwegian National Library.

FROM MO I RANA TO NARVIK
Between Mo i Rana and Bodø

The road to **Svartisvatn** begins shortly after **Røssvoll** Airport. Halfway there (5 kilometers), near the **Grønli Farmstead**, is the ★**Grønli Grotto** ❹, which is approximately 1,200 meters long and has impressive stalactites. There are, in fact, more than 200 limestone caves in the area; you can also visit nearby **Seter Grotto** and other caves in the north, near **Beiarn** ❷.

The **Svartisen** glacier area is the largest glacial plateau in northern Norway; together with the **Saltfjellet** to the east, it

Above: 66°33'N – the Arctic Circle, where at the summer solstice the sun no longer sinks below the horizon.

forms a 2,105-square-kilometer **national park** ❸. The 370-square-kilometer plateau, divided by the Glomsdal into two parts, sends glacier tongues out in all directions; since the 1950s, however, these have been slowly but steadily shrinking. This is also the explanation for the formation of the Svartisenvatn, which is effectively the "puddle" left by the melting glacier. Even if experts are still arguing about whether the Svartisen really is a holdover from the last Ice Age or whether it was formed during the cold period 2,500 years ago, it is undisputed that the main cause of its melting is air pollution, which interferes with the reflecting properties of the ice; one source of this pollution is the steelworks at Mo.

From the **Svartisenhytta** ❹ you can depart on boat trips or hikes to the glacier tongue of Østerdalsisen at the end of the lake, and there are also guided walks on the glacier itself. Never venture onto the glacier on your own. From the information center *Porten til Svartisen* on Holandsfjord, on the R17, you can take boat tours to the Svartisen's west side.

The E6 and the Nordland Railway now follow the course of the **Rana**. **Storforshei** ❺ is a mining village, but few of its 1,000 inhabitants still work in the pits of the Dunderdal. However, in the open-cast mines you can still see the largest trucks in Europe, weighing some 245 tons, and capable of transporting 170 tons.

At **Krokstrand**, the **Silfoss** ❻ waterfall tumbles into the Rana. **Randalsvoll** marks the start of the old fjell route to Sweden. 10 kilometers to the east, already on Swedish soil, are the **Nasa silver mines**, which were closed down a long time ago. In the 17th century, during the war with Sweden, a feudal lord assembled his farmers, marched with them to the mine and destroyed it.

At 580 meters the road crosses the treeline and goes up onto the **Saltfjell**. Shortly before the watershed (692 meters) it crosses the **Arctic Circle**, a point marked by a **Polarsirkelensenter**  with souvenir shops, a multivision show and a cafeteria; standing in front of this is the much-photographed Artic Circle column.

The Arctic Circle (66°33'N) is a designation for the line at which the sun appears to reach the horizon on Midsummer's Eve, but no longer sinks below it – from the perspective of sea level. Atop the Saltfjell, this line is marked with a series of globes set on pyramids. Numerous tourists have also built their own cairns, following the old Sami tradition that dictates that you build such a cairn in a place to which you would like to return.

Next to the parking lot is a memorial to the Yugoslavian prisoners of war who were forced to build the road over the Saltfjell. At the time, this represented the only overland route to the north, since the Nordland railway only ran as far as Mo. Today this railway line, protected by snow fences and wooden tunnels, runs right across the Saltfjell, and the train always whistles loudly when it crosses the Arctic Circle.

In this barren area the vegetation is limited to stunted bushes, mosses and lichens. After the watershed the road follows the **Lønsdal**. About 3 kilometers to the north, at **Stødi** ⑱, are three old **Sami sacrificial stones** where the Lapps, who had no fixed places of worship but took advantage of natural conditions, sacrificed to their gods. When there was not much to eat, which was not at all unusual, a few bones also sufficed as an offering. Between Stødi and **Semska** there's a **nature reserve**; don't pick the cotton grass here, which is protected. To the west of this extends the hiking area of **Saltfjells**: trails here lead over the fjell and through long valleys, past lakes and moors, and along rivers with a wealth of avian life.

From **Hestbrinken** the R77 continues through the Junkerdal to Sweden; this route is also known as the **Silver Road**, as the Sami traveled along it with their pre-

The Long Journey to the North Cape

cious metals to Sweden, where the raw material was processed into jewelry. The Swedish silversmiths crafted it into typical "Lapp silver": thin, wide pieces of jewelry with many holes in them. In this way they didn't have to use much of the raw metal and made a considerable profit.

The hiking region of the **Junkerdal**, named after the "Junker" or local lord who destroyed the Nasa mines, is famous for its flora: in addition to Arctic plants it also has flowers which require warmer temperatures and are familiar in central Europe. As a result of this remarkable symbiosis, the valley became a protected area as long ago as 1928.

Located in **Storjord** are the headquarters of the state tree and forestry academy. **Russånes** marks the start of the Saltdal, which was settled in the early 19th century by farmers' sons. The E6 was completely rerouted through this wide, fertile

Above: In summer the marshy meadows of the north shimmer with cotton grass. Right: In the Aviation Museum of Bodø.

valley and now runs as an expressway, bypassing the villages. Passing **Røkland**, you come to **Rognan** ➍ at the southern end of the **Saltfjord**. The town boasts a modest degree of industry and, near its church, a cemetery for English soldiers; at **Botn** there is one for German soldiers and Russian P.O.W.s.

The E6 continues high above the Saltfjord, with panoramic views from the laybys. At **Straumnakken** ➎ the last Ice Age left unmistakeable "fingerprints" in the form of strangely-shaped moraines.

After a few kilometers, the E6 comes to **Fauske** ➎. Bombed in the war and rebuilt, this town was the terminus of the Nordland Railway until 1962, when the line was extended to Bodø. The northern bus lines to the North Cape and Kirkenes start here. Fauske (population 6,500) is famous for its marble quarries, which supplied the material for the facing of the UN building in New York.

From here it is worth making the detour to the town of Bodø. Follow the R80 to **Vågan** ➎, where there is a famous

4,000-year-old rock drawing, and turn off at Løding onto the R17 and the *Saltstraum (Salt Current). Here the tidal range is only 3 meters, but the water is forced through the narrow fjord like a jet, reaching speeds of up to 50 kilometers an hour. The new bridge across it is a good place from which to look at the fastest tidal current in the world.

Bodø ⑤⑨ (population 34,000) is an important ferry port; among the destinations served from here are the southern Lofoten Islands. Destroyed in World War II, it was rebuilt and then began to expand, and its colleges soon combined to form a university. Because of Bodø's location, it's a good place to observe the midnight sun, visible here from June 4 to July 18.

Bodø's **Nordland Fylkemuseum** on the Prinsensgate is one of the most important museums in the north. The fishing section documents the development of this branch of the economy from prehistoric times to modern deep-sea fishing. The oldest exhibits in the historic section are 20,000 years old, and the Viking section includes the Treasure of Røsvik, and Anglo-Saxon and Arabic coins found in 1919. There is also a folklore section and one about the town's history which includes memorabilia from Pietro Quirini, a Venetian merchant who attempted to sail from Crete to Flanders in 1431; however, once he got to the southernmost Lofoten island, Røst, he had to wait there for the three months of Arctic night to pass. The attractions of Bodø's new **Aviation Center** include a JU 52 rebuilt as a seaplane and a flight simulator. 40 kilometers north is **Kjerringøy ⑥⓪**, a popular open-air museum consisting of 15 wooden buildings. It was in Kjerringøy that the novelist Knut Hamsun completed his commercial apprenticeship. A fine finish to a day in Bodø is sunset from the panorama bar of the SAS hotel by the port.

Along the Fjords from Fauske to Narvik

The section of the E6 between Fauske and Narvik is one of the most beautiful stretches of road in Norway. The fjords are very deep, making the mountains, polished smooth by the Ice Age, look higher than they really are. Between Fauske and Bognes, where you take the last ferry along this route, there are 15 tunnels up to 2,700 meters long. The new route of the E6 passes through unspoiled countryside with no other traces of civilization.

From Fauske, the E6 continues to **Vargåsen** and then along the **Sørfolda**, crossing its side fjord over a bridge almost 200 meters long. Close by is one of the largest national park areas in Scandinavia: the area known as **Rago Park** 55 on the Norwegian side continues in Sweden with the parks of Padjelanta, Sarek and Stora Sjöfallets. A side road leads to **Lakshola** 56, the starting point of a hiking trail to the Storkogsvass- and **Rago-hytta**, and the point at which the park crosses the Swedish border. The rest of this region of lakes, rivers and fjells (up to 1,300 meters high) is trackless.

The E6 now follows the **Leirfjord** and crosses the **Blåfjell**, a stretch of completely unspoiled countryside. The toll levied for this section of the route, which has replaced the ferry from Sommarset to Bonåsjøen, will be permanently suspended in 2002.

The road continues past the **Mørsvikfjord** to the **Kråkmofjell** 57 (Crow Heath). Of the nine Kråkmo peaks, only the three highest have been given names; the others just have numbers. From **Kråkmo Gård** by **Tennvatn**, 390 meters in altitude, it is a hike of 2 hours to the top of **Kråkmotinde**, the third highest of the peaks (924 meters), from which there is a splendid view of the seven lakes of the **Sagvassdal**.

At the end of **Sandnesvatn**, which starts on the other side of Kråkmo, is the **Fjellstua** 58, an old inn which is today a

Right: One of Narvik's attractions is the cable car up Fagernesfjell.

hotel and campground. This part of the lake is said to be the domain of a water troll, and it's not hard to imagine his presence in windy weather when the waves beat against the rocks that stick up out of the water. Here begins the Salten region, where Knut Hamsun grew up and which he immortalized in his novels.

At the end of the narrow tongue of land between **Sagfjord** and **Kaldvågfjord** is **Innhavet** 59. A local road leads onto the **Reili Peninsula** between the fjords; the Sami have a winter camp here, and sell reindeer hides and other souvenirs even in the summer.

At **Sommerset** there is a new road to **Drag** and the 40-minute ferry crossing (7 times a day) to **Kjøpsvik**, an alternative to the busy ferry on the E6. Both ferries cross the **Tysfjord**, which, together with its continuation, the **Hellemofjord**, penetrates so far inland that from the end it is only 6.5 kilometers to the Swedish border.

As it approaches **Ulvsvåg** 60, the E6 descends in a steep series of double curves. Since there are no offshore islands or mountains to block the view, there is a fantastic panorama of the ★**Lofoten Wall** 30 kilometers away.

In Ulvsvåg, the R81 branches off to Skutvik and the ferry to Svolvær (Lofoten). Here, in **Hamsund** 61, is the **Hamarøy Farmstead** where Knut Hamsun grew up; his father, a man named Pedersen, bought it when Knut was three years old. Later in life, the poet changed his name to that of his childhood home. As an adult, he lived for a time in Kråkmo, where two of his works, including *The Growth of the Soil*, were written. His childhood home has been turned into a museum.

From **Bognes** there is ferry service to the Lofoten Islands. To continue north on the E6, however, take the ferry that shuttles the 25 minutes over to **Skarberget**. From the boat, you can see the **Eidet** to the east, an 846-meter natural obelisk

said to be the largest in the world. The road continues through **Skjellesviks-karet** and past bizarrely-shaped mountains such as the **Kugelhaugen** (979 meters) to **Sætran**. From here, three bridges lead over the bare islands in the **Efjord**. This part of the fjord is called the *Kjerringstraum* (Witches' Current) because, constricted by the islands, it flows extremely rapidly here.

Ankenes ❷ on the **Beisfjord** is already part of Narvik. If you take the cable car up to the ski center (255 meters) you have a splendid view of Narvik, the ore loading complex, the Ofotfjord and the mountain ranges stretching away into the distance. One of these mountains, which resembles a fat man in a reclining position, is known among the Sami as "The Old Man Around the Corner" and in 1945 was rechristened "Winston Churchill."

Shortly before Narvik, a bridge crosses the Beisfjord and a small road leads to the town of the same name, from where hiking trails run up to the glacier areas of **Blåsen** and the Storsteinfjell. The

Beisfjordglubben, in the middle of Narvik, is a natural stone formation resembling a troll and is perennially popular with passing photographers.

*Narvik

Narvik ❸ (population 14,000) is situated on a tongue of land between the Beisfjord and the Rombakfjord. This city owes its importance to the Gulf Stream on the one hand and its relative proximity to the Swedish ore mountains of Kiruna on the other: because Narvik's harbor is free of ice all year round, it was the only place from which ore could be shipped out at reasonable cost.

Narvik was an insignificant fishing port until 1883, when an English-Swedish company was given the concession to build the **ore railway**. When this firm proved unable to complete the task, the Norwegian national railway company took over the Norwegian section of the railway in 1887; the railway was opened in 1902.

The ore from Kiruna, with a 70 percent iron content, was in demand all over Europe and the town soon began to prosper. The **loading complex** (*Malmkaien*) where the ore is transferred to the ships has constantly been expanded. Today the freight cars of trains as much as 400 meters long are unloaded fully automatically, and the conveyor belts to the ships, themselves as much as 350,000 G.R.T., move 10,000 tons per hour. Only half the annual capacity of 30 million tons is however exploited, since ore of comparable quality from overseas is a cheaper alternative for European steel producers, given the decreasing costs of sea freight.

Narvik's ore port was one of the main reasons for the German invasion of Norway. The town was attacked and taken on September 4, 1940, shortly before the British could arrive, and the loading station, the harbor complex and 900 houses

Above: "Sunbathers" on deck aboard one of the Hurtigrute ships had better be warmly wrapped.

were destroyed in the process. In the northern part of the town there is a **military cemetery** for those who fell in this battle.

The ore loading complex divides Narvik into two parts; to the west is the residential area of **Frydenlund**; to the east, the business district of **Oscarsborg**. The **Brugate** links the city's two halves. From the bridge, there is a good view of the loading quay; guided tours are also available.

A ride on the ore railway to Bjørnfjell on the Swedish border is a fun excursion: the trip takes 45 minutes and the line follows the Rombakfjord, rising steeply until it is high above it. There are also through passenger trains to Kiruna and on into southern Sweden.

Another recommended trip is the 13-minute ride on the **Fjellheisen cable car** up onto the **Fagernesfjell**, 700 meters above sea level. The view from the restaurant, especially when the midnight sun is shining (June 10 to July 8), is Narvik's star attraction.

By the bridge to Frydenlund is the much-photographed **signpost** which gives the distances to places all over Europe. On the **Torget** (Large Square) is the **War Museum**, which concentrates particularly on the battles in the early summer of 1940.

On the **Sjøvei** in **Brennholt Park** is a 4,000-year-old life-sized rock drawing of an elk. From Narvik, you can also take fjord tours and excursions of several days to the Lofoten islands.

FROM NARVIK TO TROMSØ

"Calotte" is the word for the little skull-cap with which the Catholic priests protected their tonsure from the cold, and "North Calotte" is the usual name for the thinly-populated, barren area north of the Arctic Circle, which sits on top of Europe like this cap. Since, however, the Gulf Stream makes Norway's climate milder than that of the countries to the east, and the country's coasts are therefore populated beyond 68°N, in Norway the "North Calotte" begins north of the Arctic Circle, at Narvik.

Bjerkvik, which you can see from Narvik, is 40 kilometers away. The E6 crosses the Rombakfjord, and shortly after this the E10 branches off toward Sweden. For the short distance from Narvik to Bjerkvik, the E6 and E10 follow the same route; the E10 then runs west to the Vesterålen and the southern tip of the Lofoten. This major European road is generally known as the *Nordkalottenvei* because it crosses this area from east to west.

North of Bjerkvik, the road climbs to the top of **Ofoteidet** (350 meters) in a series of double bends to cross from Nordland into the province of **Troms**. **Kolbanskaret** marks the start of the **Salangsdal**, one of the many valleys with similarities to the Gudbrandsdal. This is doubtless one of the reasons why so many farming families from the south settled here; they also brought the names of their home villages in southern Norway with them.

By the **Lundamo Gård** **64** there are two museums: the **Bardu Bygdetun**, a collection of old houses, and the **Defense Museum** (by the Toftakerstua). The whole of the North Calotte is still covered with military installations, since Norway was the only NATO country that had a common border with Russia. Listening equipment, barracks and training grounds are to be found all along the road; here, as with all military installations in the world, there is a total ban on photography. **Kobberyggen** is the watershed between the Salangsdal and the **Bardudal**. Here there is a good view of both valleys and **Istinden** (Ice Peak, 1,490 meters) in the east.

Setermoen **65** is the center of the district of *Bardu*, a name of Sami origin meaning "Bear Valley." The church in this little town is a copy of the church of Tysnet near Røros, the original home of the first farmers who settled here. **Elverum** **66** was also founded by settlers from the Glåmadal.

From here there is an alternative to the E6, the R87 to **Øvergård**. This road follows the Målselv, a salmon river (there's a salmon ladder at the Målselvfoss), past lakes full of fish and many waterfalls; at Skjold, you can detour over to **★Øvre Dividal National Park** **67**, with its abundance of wildlife and hiking trails, huts, and trekking expeditions with packhorses.

The next stop on the E6 is **Anselv-Bardufoss** **68**, a double town dominated by the military, which has a large airport that prisoners built for the occupying powers during World War II. Since 1990, this has also been open to civil aircraft. From the large town square, lined with the town's shops, the post office and the bank, there is a road to the airport; by the side of this road is the waterfall from which the town takes its name. Bardufoss

The Long Journey to the North Cape

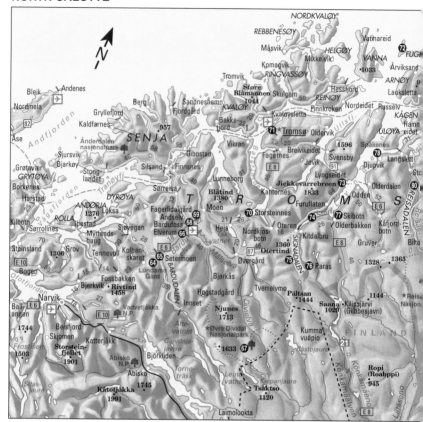

also has the only *vinmonopolet* between Narvik and Tromsø.

In the **Målsdal**, on the way to **Moen**, is the **Fagerlidalgård** ⑥⑨, a farm dating from 1789 which was built by the first settler from southern Norway; this is still a working, inhabited farm. Since the 1960s, musk-oxen from Greenland have been bred very successfully in this valley.

In Moen, the road crosses the end of the **Målselvfjord** and then follows the Takelv up to **Takvatn**, a lake in a splendid fjell setting with mountains of more than 1,400 meters high rising above it. The silhouette of the **Blåtind** (1,380 meters) bears a marked resemblance to the Matterhorn. At Heia is the watershed between the Malselvfjord and the Balsfjord.

On the other side of this divide is the **Sagelvvatn**. This is another large lake with an inn next to it. The marshy area around the lake has been turned into a nature reserve; it's a good place to observe waders and rare species of duck. If you are not pressed for time, take the old E6 along the east side of the lake to **Storsteinnes** ⑦⓪, a town with a population of 7,000 and the largest cheese dairy that produces *geitost* (brown goat's cheese) in Norway.

The E6 follows the **Balsfjord**, with snow-capped mountains 1,300 meters high on either side of it, and at **Nordkjostbotn** meets the E8 (coming from Finland), which continues on to Tromsø.

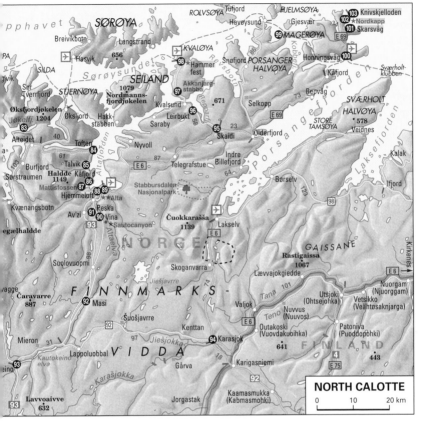

★Tromsø

The 73-kilometer stretch from Nordkjosbotn to Tromsø follows the Balsfjord to Laksvatn; an alternative route as far as this lake is the district road from **Seljelvenes** around the 1,219-meter **Lilletind**. The E8 continues through the narrow **Lavangsdal** to the **Ramfjord**, a side arm of the Balsfjord. At **Norberg** there is a splendid view of the **Balsfjord** and its islands, which is rightly considered to be one of the most beautiful fjords in Norway. 10 kilometers further on is **Tromsø ⓻**, located at 69°39' north on an island in the middle of the Balsfjord. Today, two bridges connect the town with the mainland on one side and with the islands of **Kvaløya** and **Ringvassøya** on the other.

Tromsø is a relatively young town with a population of 55,000, most of whom live on the fjord island of Tromsøya. In terms of the land it occupies, Tromsø is one of the largest towns in the world, covering an area of 2,400 square kilometers, but only 3 percent of this is actually built up. The climate is favorably influenced by the Gulf Stream, and in the summer, when the temperatures can be as high as 25°C, the gardens are full of flowers and the Tromsø palm, a type of fern which grows up to 2 meters high, puts out its pinnate leaves.

Tromsø was first mentioned in a document in 1250, when Håkon IV built a

Tromsø first became internationally known through the polar expeditions. From Carlsen, who went around Spitsbergen, to Nansen, Amundsen and Andree, who attempted a balloon flight to the North Pole, all the polar explorers either stopped off in Tromsø on their journeys or started from here. Amundsen also began his last journey from here when he set out to try and rescue his colleague Nobile.

Today, Tromsø lives mainly from its harbor, which is surrounded by a concentraiton of export-oriented industries. There are high expectations of the gas fields of Tromsøflakt, and the red supply ships already dominate the harbor. Tromsø is also a trade and service center, and since 1972 has been the location of the northernmost university in the world. The high proportion of students in the town has transformed its image: nowhere else in the north are there so many restaurants, bars and discos.

church here, which the Pope named the "Church of St. Mary with the Heathen." The town, which acquired town rights as long ago as 1794, had little chance of developing while trade in northern Norway was dominated by Bergen and Trondheim. It was not until the town engaged in barter with Russia that it saw some modest growth, which was then accelerated by shipping in the Arctic Ocean at the beginning of the 19th century. In addition, herring, whales and seals were caught in the Arctic waters, which commanded increasingly high prices. The population consequently grew from 18 in 1801 to around 5,000 in the year 1890. In 1814, the Eidsvoll Assembly made Tromsø an administrative center and diocese. For a short time, in 1940, it was also the seat of the government, which had fled from the German occupying powers and from here went into exile in England.

Above: Choir wall of the Arctic Ocean Cathedral of Tromsø (glass mosaic by Victor Sparre).

Arctic Cathedral and Northern Lights: The Sights of Tromsø

Just before the 1,300-meter **Tromsøbru**, the bridge leading into town, is modern ★**Tromsdalen Church** ❶, generally known as the "Arctic Cathedral" (*Ishavskatedralen*). The church, designed by Jan Inge Hovig, was consecrated in 1965 and is modeled on the frames used in the north for drying cod. The 140-square-meter choir wall of the church was designed by Victor Sparre, and depicts the Second Coming of Christ. For this he used the unusual Dalle technique developed in France in the 1930s: glass blocks – measuring 10 centimeters in thickness, they can hardly be called panes – are wrapped in reinforcing iron and cast into concrete. In this way he created a colored glass mosaic 23 meters high.

Once across Tromsø bridge, start your tour of the town from the **Dampskipskaie** ❷, where the *Hurtigrute* ships

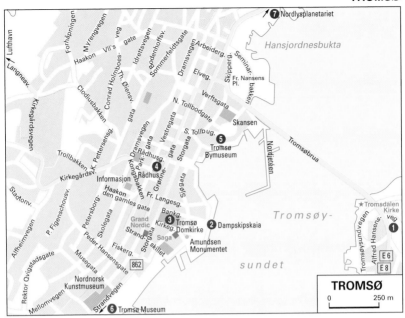

The Long Journey to the North Cape

still dock. On the large square behind the *kaie* is a **statue of Amundsen**, the polar explorer, who stands facing north. Nearby, on Kirkegate, is the wooden **Cathedral Church** ❸, one of the largest in the country, which seats 750. It was built in 1861.

Follow the **Storgate**, Tromsø's main road, to **Rådhusgate**. Here many of the old wooden houses are still standing, as Tromsø is the only large town in Norway that was not set on fire when the Germans retreated in 1944.

The area in front of the **town hall** ❹ has been turned into a large pedestrian zone, with a **whalers' memorial** at the bottom end. It is here that the morning **fish market** is held, an event not to be missed. In the middle of this complex is the little wooden Catholic **Church of St. Mary**, which, since Tromsø is a diocese, is actually a cathedral; the smallest in the world.

On the Tollbogate, a little to the north and almost under the Tromsøbru, is the **By Museum** ❺ with exhibits document-

ing the history of the town and the polar expeditions.

To visit the **Tromsø Museum** ❻, 5 kilometers away at the southern tip of the island, it is best to drive or take a bus. The decorations that frame the exhibits here were produced by the people of Tromsø themselves in the long winter nights. There are sections devoted to church art, flora, fauna, geology and the life of the Sami and the Lofoten fishermen. A marine biology station is also attached, with an **aquarium** that is open to the public.

Also worth visiting is the ***Nordlysplanetariet** ❼ (Northern Lights Observatory) on Breivik in the north of town. This institute, which conducts research into the light effects created by the solar wind, shows films of the phenomenon; the Northern Lights themselves, of course, cannot be seen on bright summer nights.

You can, however, see the midnight sun, which appears here from May 21 to July 23; a particularly good viewpoint is the **Storstein**, a 420-meter hill in

Tromsdalen on the mainland side. In good weather, the cable car runs until well after midnight, and the **Fjellstua Restaurant** is also open this long. Remember, however, that in Tromsø – at 19° east – the sun in fact reaches its lowest point at 11:18 p.m., or at 12:18 a.m. during summer (Daylight Savings) time. In winter, on the other hand, the sun remains utterly invisible from November onwards. When it at last reappears in January, the people of Tromsø celebrate with the *Nordlysfestival*.

In fine weather take a walk across the town bridge, Tromsøbru, which rests on 84 pillars, to the Storsteinen, from which you can ride a bus back into town.

You can also embark from Tromsø on a range of fjord excursions as well as and short cruises to the North Cape and Spitsbergen.

Above: As many as 300,000 puffins breed on the bird island north of Svensby. Right: Hikers in Lappland should know a few rudimentary cooking skills.

THROUGH THE LAND OF THE SAMI
From Tromsø to Alta

If you want to continue further north from Tromsø, either return to Nordkjosbotn and then follow the E6 or take the R91 from Fagernes, which does not meet up with the E6 until Olderdalen.

The latter alternative is 48 kilometers shorter than the route on the European ("E") roads (192 kilometers), but involves two ferry rides which take a total of 60 minutes. The R91 passes snow-covered mountains and small waterfalls on its way through Horn to **Breivikeidet**, where there is a ferry to **Svensby** (a 25-minute trip, 14 times a day). During the crossing, you can see the bird island of **Fugløya** 🔢 to the north; this is the largest puffin breeding colony in Norway. 40 different species of bird breed here and the island may have as many as 300,000 puffins nesting on it.

At **Lyngseidet** 🔢, the next ferry makes the 35-minute trip across the picturesque

Lyngenfjord to **Olderdalen** (14 times a day). Lyngseidet is an old trading center which received market rights as long ago as 1789. If you have to wait for the ferry, you'll have a chance to visit Lyngen Church, an 18th-century cruciform church which had to be completely renovated after the occupying forces misused it as a stable. From the ferry there is a good view of the glacier tongues on the eastern **Lyngenfjell**.

If, however, you choose to leave Tromsø on the E8, you'll join up with the E6 in Nordkjosbotn, and shortly afterwards comes to the **Storfjord** ⓻⓸, the southern end of the **Lygnenfjord**, considered the most beautiful fjord in northern Norway, which it then follows for 120 kilometers. There are numerous inviting picnic spots and panoramic views, and only a few towns of any size, between here and Alta.

At **Kitdal bru** a district road branches off into the **Signadal** ⓻⓹. The vegetation, unusually luxuriant for Norway, was already attracting farmers from the Østerand Gudbrandsdal in the 19th century. If you drive along this road via **Signalnes** to **Paras** ⓻⓺, you can start on a walk that will lead you through Norway, Sweden and Finland in a mere four hours.

The E6 continues to **Olderbakken**, where the E8 turns off to Finland and Sweden, following the old trade route the Sami used to get to the market at **Skibotn** ⓻⓻. Here, they exchanged hides and reindeer meat for flour, butter and tools – and, after the beginning of the 20 century, for tobacco and alcohol, as well. Finnish *kvænen* (emigrants) also entered northern Norway by way of the Skibotndal.

On the west side of the fjord, you can now see the peaks and glaciers of the **Lyngenhalvøya** (Lyngsal Alps). Although Olderdalen is visible from **Odden** and is only 3 kilometers away, it is necessary to go 33 kilometers around the **Kåfjord** to get to it; now, if not before, you will understand how it is that the length of the Norwegian coast can correspond to half the circumference of the earth.

The E6 follows the Lyngenfjord as far as **Djupvik**. Here, travelers should detour over to **Spåkenes** ⓲ (2 kilometers), where there is a splendid view from the natural platform that juts out into the Lyngenfjord. In **Langslett**, the R866 turns off to **Skjervøy** ⓳, which has the oldest church in the diocese of Troms.

Cross the fjell (227 meters) between Rotsund and Reisafjord to **Storslett**. Here, travelers can detour on the R865 into the mild climate of the **Reisadal** ⓼. 43 kilometers further on, in **Bilto**, boats can be hired to go along the river to the **Mollisfoss** ⓵, a waterfall with a straight drop of 270 meters, and one of the largest in the country. This is in the *****Reisa National Park** ⓶, traversed by a hiking trail to the RV896, 35 kilometers before Kautokeino.

Running along the **Straumfjord** and **Oksfjord**, the E6 climbs to an altitude of

Above: Dried cod is produced by exposing the fish to the wind on huge frames. Right: The rock drawings of Alta.

402 meters on the Kvænangsfjell. The **Gildetun Hotell**, in a splendid position on the fjell, is one of the finest hotels in northern Norway. The owner has gone to great trouble to make every room of the main house different, using only types of wood from the area for the various interiors. From the hotel, there's a magnificent view of the Kvænangenfjord and the **Øksfjordjøkul** opposite. Just below the hotel, Kautokeinen Sami have established a winter camp with the typical Sami earth-covered huts.

The road leads down to the Sørstraumen bridge over the end of the Kvænangenfjord, which saves going the 33 kilometers around the fjord. The road again ascends to a height of 270 meters, and from **Burfjord** the peaks of the Kvænangstindan (1,175 meters) are visible in the west. From **Alteidet** there is a road to the **Jøkelfjord** ⓼ and from here you can opt to take a boat trip to the **Øksfjordjøkul**, the only Norwegian glacier which calves in a fjord.

The watershed between Burfjord and Langfjord marks the border between the province of Troms and that of Finnmark, the northernmost and also the largest province in the country. For more than 40 kilometers the E6 now follows the beautiful **Langfjord**, with numerous frames for drying cod along the shore. The platform of **Toften** ⓼, where the Langfjord enters the **Altafjord**, was fortified by the German army; the fortifications do not, however, obstruct the view across the fjord to Alta, which seems near enough to touch but is 43 kilometers away on a narrow winding road.

In the 19th century there were several zinc and copper mines in the region around **Talvik** ⓼ and **Kåfjord** ⓼. An English mining company had the concession and enticed employees from all over the country, promising them the earth. Once they had moved to the mines with their families, the moving costs, monthly rent and the resulting interest were de-

ducted from their pay packets, so that they were virtually wage slaves. Also dating from this mining era are the English churches with their typical staggered choirs.

By the **Mattisfoss** ⑰, a salmon ladder 450 meters long and 45 meters high circumvents the waterfall.

In **Hjemmeluft** ⑱, settlements from the Neolithic period have been excavated together with a large collection of Sami silver dating from the 16th century. Here, right next to the road, is the largest surface area in the country covered by **rock drawings**. More than 2,000 individual drawings have been found on rocks worn smooth by the Ice Age, with the largest area measuring 20 meters by 26 meters. After these drawings were placed on the UN World Cultural Heritage List, a new museum was built together with wooden walkways leading visitors to the individual drawings. They are not easy to interpret, as they were created over a period of at least 3,000 years (5000 to 2000 BC), but they certainly had something to do

with a cult, and various game animals and fish can be identified, as well as sleds and boats. The people depicted are mysteriously simplified as stick figures while lines – continuous, dotted or resembling railway lines – seem to indicate some sort of territorial borders, even if there are similar figures on either side of them. The highly instructive ****Alta Museum** provides information not only about the rock art but also about Sami culture, mining and fishing.

The reason that the Altafjord was permanently settled from such an early date is its exceptionally mild climate. Nowhere else in the world does corn ripen at a latitude of more than 70°N. The houses are also surrounded by gardens full of flowers, as if the inhabitants were trying to live up to the southern Norwegians' teasing nickname for the area: "The Italy of Finnmark." You can see the midnight sun in Alta from May 16 to July 26.

In **Alta** ⑲ itself, which is, with 15,000 inhabitants, the largest town in Finnmark, it's easy to see that the town is comprised

of several villages that have been joined together (lining the E6 for 10 kilometers). Bossekop was the name of the place where the Sami held their markets; in spring and autumn, people came here from far and wide to exchange products. From the 19th century on these markets were dominated by fur traders from the south, who sold the Lapps guns in return for precious metals and paid for the furs with alcohol, which they were not allowed to drink themselves but which they were allowed to give to the Sami.

Today, the Sami in Alta again represent a minority. The military has had a hand in this: there's a large military base in Alta, and soldiers' families are encouraged to settle here. The military commander resides, appropriately enough, in the building that originally belonged to the **Arctic Mission** (*Missio Circuli Polaris Arctici*). This was the seat of the governor of

Above: The Sami Easter meeting in Kautokeino begins with a religious service. Right: This is followed by a reindeer sled race.

Finnmark until 1814, when it was transferred to Tromsø. When, in 1851, the Eidsvoll Assembly's ruling barring Jews and Jesuits from the country was abolished, the above-mentioned Catholic Mission was founded in Rome and Alta was chosen as its seat. The empty **Amtsgård** was then acquired and a bell tower added to it.

The Arctic Mission was, however, a rather unsuccessful undertaking; it was soon abandoned, and the building passed into the hands of the army. Burned down in the war, it has since been carefully restored, and even the bell tower has been rebuilt. This white manor is located in the northern part of town, near the airport and right on the E6; it's an impressive place with its neat white fence and militarily cropped lawn.

Alta's biggest attraction is the annual salmon season on the **Altaelv**, when thousands of fishermen fly in to take advantage of a river that has more salmon than any other river on northern Norway's Atlantic coast.

From Alta to Kautokeino: Capital of the Lapps

If there is any road which deserves to be called the "Road of the Sami," it is the R93 from Alta to Kautokeino. Only in the area around here, in the interior of Finnmark, do the Sami, or Lapps, represent a majority of the population. Having pushed the Sami out of the more attractive fertile valleys farther south, the Norwegians left them this landscape between tundra and taiga, where only mosses, lichens, stunted birches and cranberries grow. There are still 20,000 Sami living in northern Norway, out of a total of 35,000 throughout the country. Since two-thirds of the 70,000 inhabitants of Finnmark live on the coast where the climate is better, the Sami, statistically speaking, have at least 2 square kilometers per person at their disposal (shared with 7 reindeer). In spite of this, however, the area is overpopulated, since there is hardly any employment for the people and 150,000 reindeer are far too many for the tundra to support: although vast, this is a barren land.

The influence of the Gulf Stream is only moderate here, and the climate is continental and hence colder. Average annual temperatures in the minus range are normal and for seven months of the year the land is blanketed in a harsh, cold winter. The plants that make up the very thin layer of vegetation have adapted to it: they reproduce only every two years. After developing from their blossoms, the cranberries remain hard and unripe on their branches, and don't fully ripen until the following summer. A banana peel takes more than a year to rot here, and it takes ten years for vegetation to grow on new road embankments.

It is, therefore, hardly surprising that more and more Sami are giving up their traditional nomadic life and looking for "regular" day jobs. While the whole clan used to move north with the herds, today

only one or two herdsmen go, following the animals on sturdy motorbikes. Often, these herders are only employees of the actual owner of the reindeer, who may well have settled down permanently somewhere. In recent years, the herds have gotten larger and larger as a result of government subsidies paid per reindeer. The reactor catastrophe of Chernobyl accelerated this development: because of the risk of contamination, the demand for reindeer meat completely dried up for a time, and the highly subsidized meat was sold as feed to mink farms. It took a long time for the demand gradually to increase again, and this meant that prices stayed down, and larger herds were necessary to keep up the owners' base incomes. Since there are few other jobs, many breeders who would rather give up this line of work have no alternative but to carry on.

In **Tangen**, the R93 leaves the Altaelv; if, however, you continue along the river you come to a provincial road to **Vina** ⑨⓪, where the largest canyon in Norway begins, the 6-kilometer ***Sautso Canyon**.

The Long Journey to the North Cape

This was once a place of unspoiled beauty through which the reindeer herds moved north; today, however, part of the canyon has been dammed, and is flooded with water. Work was completed on this hydroelectric plant in spite of massive protests, and in spite of the fact that the potential consumers of the electricity have long since filed away their investment plans.

At **Peska** ⊕ are the Alta slate quarries, which for a long time were the most important source of income in the non-agrarian sector. **Av'zi** – in the Tangdal – marks the transition from the coastal strip to the interior. The water foams down through the narrow valley and the road rises alongside it onto the plateau. The **Suolovuopme** (Sami for "Wood Island") **Fjellstue** marks the highest point on this route (418 meters), and the old and new roads also intersect at this point.

Masi ⊕ is a small Sami settlement with a new chapel, which is already the fourth that has stood on this spot.

The road now follows the **Kautokeinoelv** to the Sami capital, which the Sami themselves call *Guovdageainnu*. Of the town's 2,000 residents, 80 percent are Lapps. Be warned, however, that ***Kautokeino** ⊕ is also the capital of midges, which descend on it by the billions every year. The **Sami Institute** in Kautokeino, built to look like a Sami tent, addresses problems of the Sami culture and lifestyle. Half the local population still lives from reindeer breeding. In the spring and autumn, this is where the so-called reindeer separation takes place: animals that look too weak to make the journey to the pastures or to survive the winter are winnowed out and slaughtered. During the spring separation at Easter, the new-born fawns are also branded; this period also sees the big reindeer sled race, which in-

Right: Not just for sport, but also an important means of transportation – a dog sled in Finnmark.

volves as many as 150 animals. Easter Week is also the time of weddings, when the Sami proudly sport their traditional costume.

An interesting feature of Kautokeino is **Juhls' Silvermiths**, a collection of curious houses built here by a Dane and a German, for which they would probably never have been given planning permission anywhere else in the world. With employees from all over Europe, they make modern jewelry in the traditional Sami silver style. As the founders have also collected many objects from the land of the Sami, the complex is at once a workshop for modern jewelry based on traditional Sami silverwork and a kind of unofficial museum.

Through Karasjok to the Arctic Ocean

From Kautokeino, it's 43 kilometers on the R93 to Finland, 35 kilometers on the R896 to the entrance to Reisa National Park (see p. 190), and 130 kilometers to Karasjok. This last route, the R92, begins 30 kilometers north of Kautokeino and follows an old Sami route to the pasturing grounds, leading through a bleak but definitely appealing tundra landscape of scrub forest in which the only variation comes from small lakes or reindeer herds.

Karasjok ⊕ has 2,500 inhabitants, 85 percent them Sami, and the oldest extant church in Finnmark, which was built in 1807. There is a Sami grammar school, in which some of the lessons are held in the Sami language; in the primary schools the curriculum even includes reindeer breeding. The library has a large collection of Sami literature; this is part of the **Samiske Samlinger** which also has sections documenting reindeer breeding and the life of the Sami, as well as examples of winter huts and tents on display.

From Karasjok, the E6 leads on north to Lakselv on the Porsangerfjord (75

kilometers) or east to Kirkenes (321 kilometers). After 14 kilometers, the R92 reaches Finland; from here, a route branches off to the south (running for part of the way laong the border river Anarjåkka) to ***Anarjåkka National Park**, which borders on Lemmenjoki National park in Finland. Together, these 4,400 square kilometers of tundra and moor, a wilderness without roads or even marked trails, are a veritable El Dorado to any experienced hiker who's weary of civilization and in very good physical shape.

From Alta to Hammerfest

From Alta, the E6 follows the Altafjord for 22 kilometers with panoramic views en route. At the end of the **Rafsbotnfjord** the road goes up onto the **Finnmarksvidda** and for a good 50 kilometers crosses this tundra landscape at an average elevation of 300 meters; the winds here are often very cold. A few individual small houses belonging to fjell

Sami and the **Lapp Church of Duodde Sion** are the only variations in the barren landscape. At **Telegrafstue**, the E6 reaches the **Repparfjordelva** and follows its deep valley. This river is full of fish and the stunted birch groves have an abundant crop of rough-stemmed boletus, which no one has really picked since Chernobyl.

Skaidi ⑨⑤ consists of a bridge, a gas station, two hotels and many weekend houses belonging to Hammerfest residents. There is a junction here with the R94.

*HAMMERFEST: The World's Northernmost City

Leirbukt ⑨⑥ marks the beginning of the reindeer breeding area of Hammerfest, and the animals are often to be found lying on the road, since the pavement retains heat and they like its warmth. There has been a bridge over the Kvalsund since 1976, and now the intelligent reindeer use this too instead of

swimming, as they used to, across the sound. There are parking lots before and after the bridge so that drivers can stop off and take photos. 10 kilometers after the bridge is the **Akkanjark Stabba** ⓐ, a Sami sacrificial altar from pre-Christian times. From here it is only 20 kilometers to **Hammerfest** ⓑ.

The northernmost town in the world has had a city charter since 1789. In spite of the favorable conditions here, such as an ice-free harbor, good fishing grounds and, for a long time, tax-exempt status, prosperity was slow to come. What finally brought change was the institution of "overseas trade" with Russia – Norwegian grain for Russian fish. This even became essential to the area's survival during the Napoleonic Wars, when the English blockade cut off all shipping connections to Finnmark and the population lived on the grain deliveries from

Above: If the sun doesn't rise for 60 days out of the year, street lights are no luxury – view of Hammerfest.

Murmansk. An English attempt to land in Hammerfest was also unsuccessful, and it was during this period that the town became the most important port in Finnmark. Its position was reinforced by the fur trade and several polar expeditions which started out from here; by 1840 Hammerfest already had 400 residents.

Destroyed several times by fire and storms, it was always rebuilt. In fact, Hammerfest became the first town in Norway to have electric street lighting, which was introduced in 1891: in a place where the sun does not rise from November 22 to January 21, this was undoubtedly a necessity. Hammerfest's worst catastrophe came when the German army retreated, setting fire to the town in several places as it left.

Today, the ctiy of Hammerfest lives only partly from the catching and processing of fish. North Atlantic oil has become an increasingly important source of revenue, and the many new houses are evidence of the prosperity of those who work on the oil rigs. Tourism, however, is also making a significant contribution to the economy.

Hammerfest Church, on the way into town, is not dissimilar to the Arctic Cathedral of Tromsø; it, too, has a triangular glass wall behind the choir with sides 8 meters long. There is no altar, so that the view of the abstract glass wall is not obstructed; instead, in the baptistry off to the side there is an old, naive altarpiece from the 17th century. In the summer organ concerts are held here every day. Opposite the new church is the old cemetery chapel, which survived the fires. In the center of the town, between the Strandveien and the harbor quay, is the **town hall**, which also houses the **Polar Bear Club**; the latter contains a small museum that includes exhibits from whaling history. The official, rather pompous name of this club is *The Royal and Ancient Society of Polar Bears*. Markets are often held on the town hall square and fjord tours, including a mini-cruise by catamaran to Honningsvåg, leave from the quay. On the mountain side of the Strandveien there is a **pavilion** with the insignia of the Polar Bear Club. A few yards further on is the Catholic **St. Michael's Church**, which many young Germans helped to rebuild. Its crucifix was carved by a German prisoner of war in Narvik who brought it in person to Hammerfest.

By the church there is also a road up to **Varden**, on the local hill of **Salen**, from which there is a good view of the surrounding area. A new cafeteria has been built here, a good place from which to observe the midnight sun between May 17 and July 28.

North of town, on the other side of the harbor bay, is the **Meridian Column**, which commemorates the joint Norwegian-Russian-Swedish surveying project. Begun in 1816, this task took 30 years, but the results were so precise that when at a later date satellite measurements were made there were only minimal variations from these old measurements.

*NORTH CAPE:
Goal of Many Arduous Undertakings

From Skaidi, the E6 rises onto the barren fjell and follows the Olderfjorddal to **Olderfjord** on the **Porsangerfjord**. This is one of Norway's largest Arctic fjords, extending 120 kilometers inland. The E69 to the North Cape island of **Magerøya** ⑨⑨ (Lean Island) begins here; today the ferry crossing between **Kåfjord** and Honnigsvåg is the only bottleneck, and there is sometimes a traffic jam several kilometers long on the approach to it. This too will soon be past history, as a tunnel to the island 10.7 kilometers long was begun some time ago. The stretch of road along the Porsangerfjord has fine views of the fjord and the mica schist cliffs in a landscape almost completely innocent of vegetation. From Kåfjord, ferries make the 40-minute crossing of the Magerøysundet to Honningsvåg up to 11 times a day.

Honningsvåg ⑩⓪ (population 3,5000) lives from fishing and tourism. *Hurtigrute* ships dock in the harbor and there are often cruise liners in the sound. In recent years new hotels have been built in response to growing demand, and they are always booked out in the summer season.

From Honningsvåg, the E69 continues across the island, with some dizzying double bends, but it is a wide road. There are some spectacular views, especially at night when the sun is low, and the reindeer also graze here at night.

Skarsvåg ⑩①, the only Arctic Ocean harbor on the island, is worth a detour. Especially in the late evening, when the sun is low, there is a magnificent view of the Arctic Ocean from the old quay. Here the sun sometimes still shines even after the North Cape has disappeared into the mist. Cruise liners often stop here when there are too many boats in the Magerøysund.

The **North Cape** ⑩② is a 307-meter schist rock which rises almost vertically

from the sea. It was given its name by Richard Chancellor, who was trying to find the Northeast Passage in 1553 and believed when he sighted this rock that he had been successful.

Tourism to the North Cape began a long time ago. The Italian Pietro Negri reported such a journey in the 17th century; Louis Philippe, the subsequent French bourgeois king, came here in 1795; and Oscar II also paid a visit. In those days it was still necessary to anchor in the Sandfjord and the royal personages, together with their consorts, had to be hauled up the rock face with ropes. After Oscar's visit, cruise ships began to sail round the rock, and once the road was built, tourism gradually grew to reach its present proportions. Today around 180,000 tourists visit the North Cape every year.

The old North Cape Hall was pulled down a long time ago and replaced with a

Above: Waiting for the midnight sun at the North Cape.

tourist center blasted out of the rock. Here are underground souvenir shops, stands selling certificates and stamps, a restaurant, bar, multivision cinema and an Arctic Ocean hall and balcony.

The midnight sun shines at the North Cape, at 71°10'21", from May 14 to July 29 – not that you can always see it: here, where the Gulf Stream meets the Arctic Ocean, there is often fog. However, if it is foggy in Honningsvåg, it may be sunny at the North Cape, and vice versa.

Statistically, no more than 10 percent of all visitors here actually see the red midnight sun, which reaches its lowest point at 11:21 p.m. (12:21 a.m. in summer). It is at its best in May and late July, when it almost touches the water and glows fiery red.

The actual northernmost tip of Europe is at 71°11'48", at **Knivskjellodden** ⑩. Hikers can reach it from the E69 in an 8-kilometer walk of about 2-3 hours, and are rewarded, with any luck, with a view of the North Cape illuminated by the midnight sun.

STIKLESTAD / VERDAL

i **National House of Culture, Stikelstad**, tel. 74073100, open June 1-August 14, also sells tickets for the St. Olav Play.

Saga Park Hotell, Jembangt. 11, 7650 Verdal, tel. 74072200. **Verdal Hotell**, Jembangt. 13, 7650 Verdal, tel. 74078800. **Nye Verdal Vertshus**, Magnus den Godecvei, 7650 Verdal, tel. 74076366, small hotel, good summer rates.

Værnes Church, 10 km past Trondheim, June 24-August 8, weekdays 11 am-6 pm, Sun 1-6 pm. **Steinvikholm**, 20 km north of Trondheim, for visits and trips to the island, contact island's caretaker. **Alstadhaug Church**, part of the Skogn Open-Air Museum, open June 1-August 31, 10 am-4 pm. **Stiklestad Church**, open June 20-August 8, weekdays 10 am-6 pm.

Last week of July: **St. Olav's Week**, Stiklestad, presentation of the St. Olav Play in the open-air theater, slide-show at the church.

STEINKJER

i Postboks 10, Steinkjer, tel. 74166700; open June 30-August 2, Mon-Fri 8 am-7 pm, Sat 10 am-3 pm, other times Mon-Fri 8 am-4 pm.

Quality Grand Hotel, Kongensgt. 37, tel. 74164700. **Tingvold Parkhotel**, Gamle Kongeveg 47, tel. 74161100. **Statskog**, Hødingv. 10, 7700 Steinkjer, tel. 74165877, cabins in Inherred and Namdal.

Mære Church, 5 km south of Steinkjer, pick up key next door. **Steinkjer Church**, open weekday afternoons. **Egge Museum**, Eggevammen, 1 km north, Tue-Sat 10 am-4 pm, Sun noon-6 pm.

NAMDAL

i Postboks, Namsos, tel. 74270988, June 1-August 31, 9 am-8 pm, other times 9 am-4 pm; fishing permits for salmon fishing (expensive).

Euro Central Hotel, Namsos, Kirkegt. 7-9, tel. 74271000. **Namsen Motorhotell**, Spillum, tel. 74276100. **Børstad Gjestgiveri**, Carl Gulbransons gt. 19, 7800 Namsos, tel. 74272131, small hotel (14 beds). **Sjøåsen Hotell**, Sjøåsen, 7733 Namdalseid, tel. 74278700, hiking, fishing, boat trips on the Lyngnenfjord.

Namdal Museum, June 1-Aug 1, 10 am-4 pm. **Ranemsletta Church**, 25 km northeast of Namsos, keys next door. Excursions with open sailboats, boat and bike rentals, tel. 74286944. Fjord trips, tel. 7427-3470, in summer.

Several flights a day to Oslo, Trondheim and Bodø. Rapid boats to Trondheim, tel. 74272433.

ISLAND ROUTE TO MOSJØEN

i Postboks 314, Brønnøysund, tel. 75011210. Postboks 414, Sandnessjøen, tel. 75044130, open June 1-August 31, 9 am-8 pm, at other times of the year 9 am-4 pm.

Torghatten Hotel, Brønnøysund, Valvn. 11, tel. 75020200. **Rica Hotel**, Sandnessjøen, Torolv Kveldulvsonsgt. 16, tel. 75040077. **Vegahotel**, Vega, tel. 75036400. **Sandnessjøen Kro & Motell**, Sandnessjøen, tel. 75044011.

Galeasen, Brønnøysund, Havnegt. 34-36, tel. 75021444; good and abundant Norwegian food.

Alstahaug Church, 20 km south of Sandnessjøen, open daily except Sun, noon-5 pm. **Alstahaug Parsonage**, same opening times.

From Brønnøysund, there are boat tours to the **Torghatten**; contact Torghatten Trafikkselskap, tel. 75018100. From Sandnessjøen, a boat leaves for Træna every Fri at 11:30 am. Daily departures from Stokkvågen. To go on to Bodø, change in Onøy. Information: in Træna, tel. 75064100; in Bodø, tel. 75501020. Book hiking tours of the "Seven Sisters" through the tourist office in Sandnessjøen.

SNÅSA / GRONG

i Postboks, 7870 Grong, on the marketplace, tel. 74331550, open June 1-August 31, 9 am-8 pm, other times 9 am-4 pm; permits for salmon fishing.

Snåsa Hotell, Snåsa, tel. 74151057. **Gronggård**, Grong, tel. 74331116.

Snåsa, 25 km south of Grong: **Church**, **Sami Library**, **Sognestua** and **Vinje Parsonage**, 10 am-1 pm, opened for visitors by the staff of the church's information booth. **Gløshaug Church**, 8 km north of Grong, keys in the sacristy.

MOSJØEN

i Postboks, Mosjøen, tel. 75176120, open June 1-August 31, 9 am-8 pm, other times 9 am-4 pm.

Fru Haugans Hotel, Strandgt. 39, 8650 Mosjøen, tel. 75170477, 200-year-old house, good summer rates. **Norlandia Lyngngården Hotell**, Vollanvn. 15, tel. 75174800. **Mosjøen Hotel**, Vollanvn. 35, tel. 75171155. **Karlsen's Hospits**, Vollanveien 23 (E&), 8650 Mosjøen, tel. 75177544, open March-November. **Mosjøen Camping**, Kippermoen, 8650 Mosjøen, tel. 75177900, open March to mid-December, cabins, camping, lots of activites including winter sports.

Dolstad Church, June 1-August 31, 8 am-4 pm. **Vefsn Open-Air Museum**, June-September, Mon-Fri 9 am-4 pm, Sun 11 am-6 pm. **Øyfjell Grotto**, register for tours at the tourist information office.

The Long Journey to the North Cape

MO I RANA

ℹ️ Postboks 225, 8601 Mo i Rana, tel. 75139200, June 1-August 31, 9 am-8 pm, other times 9 am-4 pm.

🛏️ 💲💲 **Meyergården Hotell**, Olsensgt. 24, tel. 75134000. **Best Western Homen Hotell**, Th. Von Westensgt. 2, 8600 Mo i Rana, tel. 75151444. 💲 **Bech's Hotel & Camping**, Hammerveien 10, 8600 Mo i Rana, tel. 75131577. **Fammy Hotell**, Ole Tobias Olsensgt. 4, 8600 Mo i Rana, tel. 75151999, also apartments. **Rana Gjestgiveri**, Hans Wølnersgt. 10, tel. 75152211.

🏛️ **Rana Museum**, 9 am-3:30 pm, summer only. **Natural History Department**, Mon-Fri 10 am-2 pm. **Mo Church**, open in summer Tue-Fri 9 am-3 pm.

🔷 To **Svartisen Glacier**, guided tours from Svartisen Hytta. Boat trips across the glacier lake, June 20-August 31, hourly 10 am-4 pm. Glacier hikes every Sat in July & August, 9 am, depart from the quay, tel. 7516-2379. Tours of **Grønli Grotto** from Grønli Farm, June 15-August 20 daily 10 am-7 pm, hourly; book through tourist information office in Mo. Excursions to the **Arctic Circle** (90 km), year-round, tel. 75093264.

FAUSKE

ℹ️ Postboks 224, Busstorget, Fauske, tel. 75643303.

🛏️ 💲💲 **Fauske Hotel**, Storgt. 82, tel. 75643833, 200 beds. **Brygga Best Western Hotell**, Sjøgatan 86, 8200 Fauske, tel. 75646345, medium-sized hotel.

🏛️ **Fauske Open-Air Museum**, open daily in summer 10 am-3 pm. **Fauske Marble Quarry**, open in summer Mon-Fri 10 am-3 pm.

🔷 **Deep-Sea Fishing Trips** from Fauske, year-round, tel. 75774329.

BODØ

ℹ️ Postboks 514, Bodø, tel. 75526000. June 1-August 31, 9 am-8 pm, other times Mon-Sat 9 am-4 pm.

🛏️ 💲💲💲 **Quality Diplomat Hotel**, Sjøgt. 23, tel. 75527000. **Radisson SAS Hotel**, Storgt. 2, tel. 75524100. **Skagen Hotel**, Nyholmsgt. 11, tel. 7552-2400. 💲💲 **Bodø Hotell**, Prof. Schyttesgt. 5, 8005 Bodø, tel. 75525778. **Comfort Home Hotel Grand**, Storgt. 3, 8006 Bodø, tel. 75520000, open April-December (both hotels offer good summer rates). 💲 **Norrøna Hotel**, Storgt. 4B, tel. 75525550.

❌ **Panorama Restaurant**, in the SAS Hotel, expensive, but fabulous view.

🏛️ **Nordland Open-Air Museum**, Mon-Fri 9 am-3 pm, Sat 10 am-3 pm, Sun noon-3 pm.

🔷 Summertime **concerts** in the church, Sat 1 pm.

🔷 Boat tours to the southern **Lofoten Island of Røst**, on the Bodø – Værøy – Røst – Moskenes ferry line, tel. 94803115, year-round.

🛬 SAS and Widerøe operate several flights a day from Bodø to Oslo, Tromsø, Trondheim, Kirkenes and the Lofotens. There are year-round ferry links to Sandnessjøen, the Lofotens and Stokmarknes (Vesterålen). Bodø is the terminus of the Nordland railway; there are two direct trains a day to Trondheim. From Bodø there are daily buses to Svolvaer (Lofotens), Harstad (Vesterålen) and Narvik, with connections to Tromsø, Alta, Hammerfest and Kirkenes.

HAMARØY

🛏️ 💲 **Gjestegård**, Oppeid, tel. 75770305. **Hamarøy Hotell**, Innhavet, tel. 75772560. **Tømmerneset Camping**, Innhavet, tel. 75772995.

🏛️ **Hammarøy Farmstead**, Hamsun Museum, June 1-August 31, Mon-Fri 10 am-8 pm.

🛬 Ferries from Bognes to Lødingen (Vesterålen) 12 times a day; the trip takes 1 hour.

NARVIK

ℹ️ Kongensgt. 66, Narvik, tel. 76943309, open June 1-Aug 31, 9 am-8 pm, other times Mon-Sat 9 am-4 pm.

🛏️ 💲💲 **Grand Royal Hotel**, Kongensgt. 64, tel. 96941500, nice view over the Ofotfjord. **Narvik Hotel A/S**, Kongensgt. 36, tel. 76947077. 💲 **Narvik Sportell**, Skistuavn. 8, tel. 76947500.

🔷 **Ore Loading Dock**, tours through the tourist office. **Funicular to the Fagerfjell**, June 10-July 8, until 2 am. **War Museum**, mid-June to September 1, Mon-Sat 10 am-10 pm, Sun 11 am-4 pm, other times 10 am-3 pm.

🔷 In summer, two-day **Lofoten Tours** depart every day from the tourist office. Ski season lasts from December to April (this is the northernmost World Cup venue); Narvik Ski Center, tel. 76942799.

TROMSØ

ℹ️ Storgt. 63, 9001 Tromsø, tel. 77610000, June 1-August 31, 9 am-8 pm, other times Mon-Sat 9 am-4 pm.

🛏️ 💲💲💲 **Grand Nordic Hotel**, Storgt. 44, tel. 77685500. 💲💲 **Rainbow Hotel**, Grønnegt. 50, tel. 77687520. **Saga Hotell**, Richard Withs Pl. 2, tel. 77681180, good view from the roof over the fjord. **Scandic Hotell**, Heilovn. 23, tel. 77673400. 💲 **Hotel Nord**, Parkgt. 4, tel. 77683159.

❌ **Peppermøllen**, Storgt. 42, tel. 77684165, oldest house on the square. **Panorama**, Sjøgt. 39, tel. 77688100, lovely view of the harbor. **Compagniet**, Sjøgt. 12, tel. 77655721, good, but terribly expensive. **Brankhos Mats og Vinhus**, Storgt. 57, tel. 77682673, reasonably priced.

🏛️ **Arctic Sea Cathedral**, June 1-August 15, weekdays 10 am-5 pm, Sun 1-5 pm. **Cathedral Church**, weekdays in summer 11 am-1 pm, sometimes 11 am-6 pm. **Fish Market**, weekdays 7-11 am. **By Museum**, daily in summer 11 am-3 pm. **Tromsø Museum**, daily in summer, 10 am-5 pm. **Polar Lights Observatory**, tours in summer, Mon-Fri 1:30, 6 and 7:50 pm, Sat & Sun 12:30, 2, 3:30, 5 and 6:30 pm, tel. 77676000. **Storsteinen Funicular**, in summer 7 am-5 pm, during the midnight sun, 9 pm-12:30 am.

Deep-Sea Fishing Trips several times a week. Freighter tours to **Svalbard** can be reserved through Tromsø Arrangement, Storgt. 61/63, tel. 77610000.

Flights to Oslo, Trondheim, Bodø and Kirkenes, Spitsbergen and to numerous small airports of the North Calotte. Regular boat links to Harstad and Honningsvåg; in Honningsvåg, tel. 78411000; in Harstad, tel. 73515120. *Hurtigrute* boats leave Tromsø at 3:30 pm (north) and 11:45 pm (south). Express bus service to Alta and Narvik several times a day.

KVÆNANGSFJELLET

Hotel, **Restaurant**, **Café Gildetun**, Sørstraumen, tel. 77769958, a somewhat dilapidated place with great views, open April to mid-October.

ALTA

Postboks 80, Alta, tel. 78437770, open year-round, 9 am-8 pm. **Destinasjon Alta AS**, Postboks 1327, 9501 Alta, tel. 78437999.

Rica Hotel Alta, Løkkevn. 61, tel. 78482700. **Parkhotel**, Sentrum, tel. 78436211. **Øytun Gjesteheim**, tel. 78435577.

Alta Rock Drawings, open in summer 8 am-10:30 pm. **Alta Museum**, mid-June to mid-August, daily 8 am-11 pm, May and September 9 am-6 pm, other times Mon-Fri 9 am-3 pm, Sat-Sun 11 am-4 pm. **Pæskatun**, quarry, tel. 78433345.

Boat Trips: Alta Friluftspark, Storelvdalen, 9500 Alta, tel. 78433378. **Dog Sled Trips**: Canyon Huskies and Sled Dog Safari, Stengelsen, 9500 Alta, tel. 78433306, 94134467.

KAUTOKEINO

Postboks 7848, Kautokeino, tel. 78486500, June 1-August 31, 9 am-8 pm, other times Mon-Sat 9 am-4 pm.

Norlandia Kautokeino Hotell, tel. 78486205. *CAMPING:* **Kautokeino Camping og Motell**, tel. 78485400.

Juhls' Silversmiths, western edge of town, 8:30 am-10 pm during tourist season. **Sami Cultural House**, Mon-Fri 9 am-4 pm, tours arranged through the tourist office.

In winter, reindeer and dog sled rides as well as snowmobiles from the Norlandia Hotell; in summer, boat trips on the Kautokeino River.

KARASJOK

Samelandssenteret, Postboks 192, 9370 Karasjok, tel. 78466900, open June 10-August 10, 9 am-6 pm, Sat 10 am-6 pm, other times of the year Mon-Sat 9 am-4 pm.

Rica Hotel Karasjok, tel. 78467400. **Annes Overnatting**, Tanavegen 40, tel. 78466432.

Sami Restaurant in the Sami Center – a real experience!

Old Church, keys can be picked up in the tourist office. **Sami Collection**, open 10 am-4 pm during the summer.

Guided **hiking tours** through the tundra to Kautokeino (several days). The tourist office also organizes boat tours on the **Jiesjokki**, on demand.

HAMMERFEST

Postboks 460, Hammerfest, tel. 78412185, open June 15-August 15, 9 am-7 pm, Sat-Sun 10 am-5 pm.

Rica Hotel, Sørøygt. 15, tel. 78411333. **Hammerfest Hotel**, Strandgt. 2-4, tel. 78411622, in the town center, on the harbor, renovated in 1992. **Håja Hotel**, Strogt. 9-11, tel. 78411988, small, but centrally located.

Pomoren Mat og Dansebar, Storgt. 27, tel. 78411893, the loach (*Steinbit*) is a specialty.

Hammerfest Church and **St. Michael's Church**, open mornings year-round, also afternoons in summer. **Polar Bear Club Collection** (Isbjørnklubben), in the town hall, Mon-Fri 8 am-7 pm, Sat-Sun 10 am-5 pm (in summer, otherwise by arrangement). On Saturdays there's a picturesque **market** on the large square in front of the town hall.

Deep-sea fishing and mini-cruises to the **North Cape** from June 10-August 19, tel. 78414344.

SKAIDI

Skaidi Hotell, tel. 78416120. **Skaidi Touristhotell**, tel. 78416121.

NORDKAPP

Honningsvåg, tel. 78472599.

Rica Hotel, Honningsvåg, tel. 78473388 (lots of groups). **Nordkapp Hotell**, Honningsvåg, Nordkappgt. 4, tel. 78472333 (no groups). **Nordkapp Turisthotell**, Skarsvåg, tel. 78475267. **Hotel Havly**, Honningsvåg, Storgt. 12, tel. 78472966.

North Cape Hall, with post office, bank, tourist information, North Cape certificates and overpriced souvenirs. **North Cape Museum** in Honningsvåg

Free multivision show in the North Cape Hall, daily every half-hour from 8 pm. Mid-July: **North Cape Festival** in Honningsvåg.

The Long Journey to the North Cape

FJORDS ON THE ARCTIC OCEAN

EASTERN FINNMARK
FROM THE NORTH CAPE
TO KIRKENES

EASTERN FINNMARK

If you like solitude, wide-open spaces and unspoiled natural beauty, the coast of the Arctic Ocean is the place for you. As soon as you leave the Porsangerfjord behind, you plunge into another world. Many things here look just as they did along Norway's Atlantic coast in the 1950s. Right after the war, local authorities began to create transportation links to the communities of eastern Finnmark. While boats were the main form of transportation in the prewar years, the war had seen construction of landing-strips and gravel roads; after 1945, these airports remained, and the gravel roads were leveled out and paved. Since 1983, the E6, which had thereto ended in Troms, has continued on to Kirkenes.

Fishing and mining in the Kirkenes area, as well as traditional reindeer breeding, remain the region's main sources of revenue. The Iron Curtain's fall sparked great hopes for the region's economic future; all along the border, which once bristled with weapons, there are now points of entry which allow a limited degree of trade and even tourist traffic.

Preceding pages: Salmon fishing on the Näätämjoki, eastern Finnmark. Left: White winter coats camouflage reindeer in the snow.

The landscape of the eastern Finnmark is flatter and far less scruffy than the Norwegian Atlantic coast. In the south, it extends into broad expanses of tundra. It's colder here than along the Atlantic, but the influence of the Gulf Stream, although dwindling, nonetheless makes itself felt all the way to Murmansk, keeping even this northern harbor free of ice. The coasts along the fjords here were settled as early as the Stone Age, but in more recent ages the only residents have been a few fishermen in villages along the Barents Sea and the Sami with their reindeer herds.

Trade with the settlements along the north coast of Russia led to an economic upswing in the 18th century; contributing to this were Finns and Swedes who had emigrated here a century before as a result of widespread famine in their home countries. In World War II, this area was bitterly contested. When, after the war, Finland was compelled to turn the Petsamo region over to the USSR, and the fronts hardened in the course of the Cold War over the ensuing years, there was suddenly a common, and soon utterly impenetrable, border. Fortunately, many of the restricted military zones have been opened up today, so that there are few remaining limitations to one's freedom of movement.

Fjords on the Artic Ocean

FROM THE NORTH CAPE TO KIRKENES

After the **Olderfjord**, the E6 follows the Porsangerfjord in a southerly direction. In **Kistrand** ❶, a finger of rock thrusts into the fjord; here, after a short walk, you have a magnificent view over the fjord, the island of **Store Tamsøy** and the Arctic Ocean. In the middle of the fjord is the island of **Reinøy** ❷, a popular breeding-ground for sea and coastal birds; for the whole southern end of the Porsangerfjord is a bird reserve. After 61 kilometers, you come to **Lakselv** ❸, on the gravel moraine by the river of the same name. With a population of 2,500, this town is the trade and service center for the entire Porsanger area, and a transportation hub for northern Norway's bus and airline companies. Lakselv is also an ideal base for sports fishermen: the area's

Above: A midnight mood on the Tufjord in northern Finnmark. Right: The church and old fishing harbor of Vardø.

numerous small rivers are as well-stocked with fish as the Lakselv is full of the fish – salmon – that gives it its name.

From Lakselv, travelers continuing on have two options: the R98 north to the Arctic Ocean or the route via Karasjok to Tanabru, where both routes join up again.

Quintessential Northland: Between Porsangerfjord and Tanafjord

On the eastern shore of the Porsangerfjord, the R98 turns off to the north. **Børselv** ❹ (42 kilometers) is one of the Finnish settlements from the wave of emigration in the 18th century; Finnish is still spoken in its schools. The main road ascends to the **Børselvfjell**, but a small gravel road also leads along the Porsangerfjord itself; this road later crosses the Sværholt Halvøya and ends in **Sandbakken** on the Laksefjord. This detour is particularly enjoyable for devotees of bird-watching.

A little ways past the highest elevation of the Børselvfjell (190 meters), right beside the R98, is a Sami chapel dating from 1962. This fjell has been the summer pastureland of the Kautokeino Sami for generations. Continuing on through the valley of the **Storelv**, the road then runs down to **Laksefjord**. A row of attractive lay-bys and lookout points runs along the southern end of this fjord; also worth a stop is the 37-meter **Adamsfoss 5** by **Adamsfjord**.

Twenty kilometers further on, you come to **Ifjord**, starting point of the R888 to the north. The road is unpaved in places, and closed in winter. It leads right through the **Nordkinnhalvøya** to the fishing villages of **Kjøllefjord 6**, **Mehamn 7** and **Gamvik 8** (122 kilometers), which were whaling stations until into the 1960s. Here, at the end of the European mainland, excavators have found rock drawings 4,000 to 5,000 years old, certainly the northernmost such in the world. These three fishing villages are ideal observation points for the midnight sun, which shines here from May 20 to July 20. Anyone who makes his way into the isolated reaches of the coast of the Arctic Ocean should bear in mind that he'll have to retrace his steps to Ifjord, for there are no ferries across the Tanafjord, nor does any road lead along its shores.

The R98 reaches the Tanafjord by way of the Ifjordfjell. The road ascends to 370 meters; after a few kilometers, drivers can spot another **Sami church 9**, right on the shore of a lake. Immediately next to it is a corral for reindeer and a few summer huts of the Karasjok Sami.

In **Rustelfjelbma 10** is the **Tana Church**. Consecrated in 1964, this edifice has an open bell tower; the slate in which the church is faced comes from Alta. A worthwhile detour is the little road that leads 10 kilometers north to **Gavesluft 11**, from where you have a great view out over the fjord. Compared with the greenery along the other Arctic Ocean fjords, the vegetation here seems positively lush.

From here, the R98 follows the Tanaelv upstream to the south, and after another 30 kilometers reaches **Tana bru 12**. This reconstructed bridge across the Tanaelv, 195 meters long, is the center of the town of the same name. Here, the E75 and E6 join to cross the Tana River, on the eastern bank of which the R890, the so-called **Arctic Ocean Road**, branches off at the northwest tip of the Varanger Peninsula.

The Varanger Peninsula

This detour, 135 kilometers long, is an eminently scenic route. The R890 follows the alluvial delta of the Tanaelv. By **Luoftjok 13**, you can see traps for wild reindeer, which are still captured and incorporated into the half-domesticated herds to freshen up the stock.

From **Austertana**, the road ascends to an altitude of some 300 meters so that it can gently descend again toward the sea. The ocean has formed this landscape, for most of this peninsula was underwater after the last Ice Age. Freed from the pres-

Fjords on the Artic Ocean

sure of ice plates as much as 3,000 meters thick, the land began gradually to rise, a process that has not yet ended, as you can see from the old high-water marks of ages past. In this region, free of human habitation, you may encounter a half-wild reindeer or two, but seldom will you see another vehicle.

In **Gednjehøgda**, the road forks: the R890 leads to **Kongsfjord** and on to **Berlevåg ⓮** (population 1,400), while the R891 goes to **Båtsfjord ⓯**. All three of these communities originally subsisted from whaling; today, however, it's mainly cod and *lodde*, a herring-like fish, that are caught and processed in the region.

Because of the difficulties of life during the long, hard winters here, the population tends to emigrate to warmer climes. For lack of local personnel, the job vacancies in the fish factories have been filled with Tamil refugees. When these new arrivals first got here, they feared that the snow might never melt and the sun might never appear – and indeed, their fears are justified, but only for part of the year.

Back in Tana bru, there's another detour worth taking in **Skipagurra** to **Polmak ⓰** (18 kilometers), a Sami settlement near the Finnish border with more than 6,000 reindeer. Halfway there, the isthmus of land between Tana and **Gollevarre Mountain** is studded with traps for wild reindeer; more than 500 traps have been counted here. Polmak's church was built in 1850; it's among the oldest in the Finnmark.

From Skipagurra, the E75/E6 leads up to the **Seidafjell**. In summer and autumn, thousands of reindeer move across this fjell, which is also an isthmus between the Tanafjord and the Varangerfjord.

In **Varangerbotn ⓱**, the little exhibit **Samiske Samlinger** presents a number of curios from the region, including some of the odd items that have washed up on its shores. The whole town evokes the spirit of the set of an old Western.

The Route East: Vadsø and Vardø

If you've made it this far, you might as well go all out and detour 165 kilometers to Vardø and Hamningberg. For the first 50 kilometers the route (E75) hugs the **Varangerfjord**, which, at 2,500 square kilometers, is the largest fjord in Norway. In **Nesseby ⓲**, on a peninsula, stands the only church in Varanger that wasn't destroyed in World War II. There are nice views from the road, especially at the **Klubben ⓳**, where the **Fugleåsen** (bird cliff) is easily accessible.

Vadsø ⓴, with 6,000 inhabitants, is now located on the mainland – but only because the inhabitants of the island of **Vadsøya** moved their settlement to the

mainland in the 17th century. The old church still stands on the island, as does the **mooring mast** where Amundsen and Nobile moored their dirigibles in 1926 and 1928 respectively. Vadsø was twice bombed in World War II, first by the Germans, then by the Russians. The city has some large fish factories, mainly involved in the production of fish meal and oil from local *lodde*. The **City Museum** (*Tuomainengården*), on the R75, documents 18th-century emigration and the influences which various ethnic groups have had on the region. The **Esbensengården**, directly opposite, is the only old patrician house that survived the wartime bombings; it dates from the early 19th century, and is today part of the museum.

The next stretch of road also hugs the Varangerfjord, which here is as much as 55 kilometers wide. In **Ekkerøy ㉑**, remains have been found of a woman's grave 900 yeas old, bearing striking similarities to southern Norwegian graves from the same period. In **Komagvær ㉒**, you can still see German fortifications from the last war. **Kiberg ㉓** is the easternmost point on mainland Norway.

★Vardø ㉔, with all of 4,000 residents, is located on an island; the present-day tunnel to the mainland wasn't completed until 1983. Relatively old, this town received its city charter in the same year as Hammerfest, 1789, but its history goes much farther back than that: in 1307, when the only way to reach this area was by boat, Bishop Jørve consecrated the first church here, and around the same time Håkon V had the **Vardøhus Fortress** built. This fortress was converted into a castle around 1377, after a treaty had put an end to the years of border disputes with the Russian tsars. The city, far beyond the reach of the trade monopoly of Bergen and Trondheim, developed nicely, and by the 19th century boasted Norway's largest concentration of fisheries. Some two-thirds of Vardø was destroyed in World War II, but today fishing and fish processing are once again the main sources of income; the city built a new fishing harbor on the mainland after the old one, between the islands of **Østøya** and **Vestøya**, grew too small. But it's across these islands, now linked by a narrow, man-made spit of land, that the present-day city extends.

On Østøya is the **star-shaped fortress** of 1732 that replaced Håkon's building. It was only operational for 67 years before it was retired, although it was briefly reactivated in the 19th century, when border disputes flared up once again. The fortress's cannon are fired off once a year at the moment when, after the long Arctic night, the sun first appears again above the horizon. This fortress also contains a small museum which displays the only beam that still exists from Håkon's original building. Since the 16th century, many rulers have left their signatures in this *Kongestokken* (King's Rafter), from Norwegians (Christian IV) to foreigners (such as Italy's Vittorio Emmanuele). In front of the **Commandant's Headquarters** stands the northernmost rowan tree in the world and the only tree in town; it has to be bundled up warmly every winter in order to spare it from the fate of its seven sisters, which all froze to death.

Excursions to the bird islands of **Reinøy** and **Hornøy** are also pleasant.

Right: You can catch salmon with a rod and reel, or you can simply net them.

Hornøya is the easternmost point in Norway, at the same longitude as Yalta on the Crimean Peninsula.

It's well worth your while to go on to **Hamningberg ㉕**, an old abandoned whaling and fishing village 40 kilometers northeast of Vardø. There's an element of fantasy to the drive along the twisted crags of the rocky coast with its little bays which collect veritable treasure troves of flotsam and jetsam. A number of films have been made in the dramatic setting of the half-ruined, yellowing houses here. The midnight sun shines here from May 20 to July 20. There are few places in northern Norway which afford a better view of this phenomenon; certainly none which allow you to see it in such privacy.

Between Fjell and Tundra: From Lakselv to Kirkenes

From the town of Lakselv, the E6 leads more than 75 kilometers through a landscape of fjell and tundra to Karasjok. For more than 30 kilometers of this stretch, it follows the Lakselv, a paradise for salmon fishermen. Nowhere in Norway do you find larger salmon; the national average weight of 4.4 kilograms is exceeded here by an average of 2.2 kilograms, and the record fish weighed in at an impressive 36 kilograms. In fact, all of Finnmark is known for its salmon; nearly a third of the 1,300 tons that are caught in Norway every year are landed here.

The farther south you go on the E6, the bleaker the landscape becomes. Only a few settlements cling to the side of the road, although this road is fairly heavily traveled, as this "course" connects the North Cape, Finland and Karasjok.

By **Porsangermoen ㉖**, the North Calotte Army maintains a large exercise ground. **Skoganvarre ㉗** is a settlement of 16 Sami families who own a total of more than 8,000 reindeer. In **Rivdnjisvadda**, you can climb a small hill by the road to discover the region's best view of

this broad fjell landscape. After 30 kilometers you reach **Karasjok** ㉘ (see p. 194). From here, the E6 follows the Karasjokki river to the Finnish border. There, the road veers off to the north and follows the Tanaelv for more than 180 kilometers through the tundra to Tana bru, the only bridge over the river. Most of this stretch of road is lined only with endless lengths of reindeer fencing. These are supposed to keep the Norwegian herds separate from the Finnish ones; the river, of course, is no obstacle at all for a reindeer.

Sirbma ㉙ is an old reindeer corral; you can still see the large pens. Passing through Tana bru and Varangerbotn, the E6 comes to the southern bank of the Varangerfjord. By **Karlebotn** ㉚, where the waterlines of bygone ages are clearly visible, archaeologists have discovered a number of Stone Age dwellings: in **Advik** ㉛, a whole settlement has been excavated; and dwellings have been found in **Grasbakken** ㉜ and **Nyelv** ㉝, as well. In **Brandsletta** ㉞, the old water line forms a veritable terrace, which is to-

day under preservation order. A 15-kilometer detour leads off to **Bugøynes** ㉟, the only fishing village that wasn't destroyed in World War II. Here, there are still a few houses from before the war, showing a distinct Russian influence. **Bugøyfjord** was home to the most famous Sami artist: Johan Savio (1902-1938); 7 of his woodcuts are in the National Museum in Oslo.

Until 1826 **Neiden** ㊱, the capital of the Neiden District, was part of Russia; but the whole district was subsequently handed over to Norway; the neighboring territory of Pasvik was divided between the two powers. A holdover from Russian days is **St. George's Chapel**, Norway's only Orthodox church. St. Trifon, a monk who came here as a missionary in the 16th century, supposedly built this tiny church with his own hands. **Neiden Church** (1902) echoes the stave church style; it's a strikingly colorful building.

*Kirkenes ㊲ (population 9,000), the end of the *Hurtigrute* line, sits on a point of land between the Langfjord and the

Fjords on the Artic Ocean

delta of the broad **Pasvikelv** river. 11 kilometers south of town is its erstwhile economic heart: the **mines of Bjørnevatn**. From 1906 to 1996, miners quarried magnetite, which was enriched to a 60 percent iron content here and then exported through Kirkenes. Mining in the area actually began much earlier: the "labyrinths" on the **Holmengrå** peninsula and the island **Kjøøy** are evidence of early mining, although it's unclear whether these shafts date from the Iron Age or the Middle Ages. During the fighting around Kirkenes in World War II, most of the townspeople took refuge in the mine shafts.

Since the fall of the Iron Curtain, travelers can visit the nearby Russian village of **Boris Gleb** ㊳, which once you could only gaze at across the river. There are also bus and boat excursions to Murmansk and the Kola Peninsula. The ex-

Above: Abandoned mine shaft of the Bjørnevatn Mine; visitors have to register in advance.

cursion north to the border town of **Jakobselv** ㊴ (41 kilometers) has lost some of its interest since the "curtain" opened; today, the main attraction here is the stone church, which dates from 1869.

For a kind of Siberian taiga in miniature, visit the ***Øvre Pasvik National Park** ㊵, established in 1970, which lies on the Finnish-Russian-Norwegian border. Especially noteworthy here are the protected, centuries-old stands of pines. To reach this "primeval forest," you have to drive 90 kilometers along the R885 through the Pasvik valley and then go on for another 25 kilometers through the forest. Brown bears are also indigenous to this border region. Along the R885, old sod houses alternate with new, spic-and-span cottages and long stretches of empty moorland with seemingly endless meadows of cotton grass. The few observation points, such as **Høyde** and **Gjøkåsen**, command extensive views over the vast Russian realm, but restricted military areas here and there represent a hindrance to photographers.

LAKSELV

🛈 Postboks, tel. 78462145, June 8-August 16, 10 am-6 pm, year-round. **Porsanger Arrangement**, Postboks 18, 9700 Lakselv, tel. 78462620.

🛏 ☺☺ Lakselv Hotell Best Western, Karasjokvn., tel. 78461066, relatively large, on the fjord. **☺ Banak Motell**, tel. 78461031. **Stabbursdalen, Camp og Fritidspark**, E6, 9710 Indre Billelfjord, tel. 78464760. **Russenes Kro, Motel og Camping**, E6/69, 9713 Russenes, tel. 78463711. **Skoganvarre Hytteutleie**, E6, 9722 Skoganvarre, tel. 78464846. *HOSTEL:* **Lakselv Vandrerhjem Karalaks**, tel. 78461476. *CAMPING:* **Solstad Camping**, tel. 78461404.

🎣 Salmon fishing in northern Norway's best-stocked river, late July to mid-August; fishing permits from tourist office. **Salmon safaris** are arranged by **Stabbursdalen Camp og Villmarkssenter**, tel. 78464760 (also hunting). **Rental rowboats** for fishermen available from **Russenes Camping**, tel. 78463711.

✈ Daily flights to Oslo and Tromsø, as well as to small local airports throughout the Finnmark; central bus station for eastern Finnmark.

BÅTSFJORD / BERLEVÅG

🛈 Boks 164, 9991 Båtsfjord, tel. 78983100, open June 1-September 1. Berlevåg Community, Kulturkontoret, 9980 Berlevåg, tel. 78982114.

🛏 ☺☺ Båtsfjord Nye Hotel, Båtsfjord, nice house, not often seen hereabouts, tel. 78983100. **☺ Berlevåg Camping & Apartement**, Rv 890, 9880 Berlevåg, tel. 78981610, camping June 1-September 30, apartments February 1-December 15.

IFJORD / KJØLLEFJORD

🛈 Ifjord, tel. 78499869, June 15-Aug 15, 10 am-6 pm. Kjøllefjord, tel. 78498364, June 24-Aug 24, 10 am-6 pm.

🛏 ☺☺ Nordkyn Vertshus, 9790 Køllefjord, tel. 78498333. **☺ Nilsens Gjestgiveri & Camping**, Rv 98, 9780 Lebesby (Ifjord), tel. 78499817, also cabins. *CAMPING:* **Friborg Gård Hytteutleie**, 9780 Lebesby, tel. 78499162.

VADSØ

🛈 Tel. 78954490, June 15-September 15, Mon-Fri 9 am-6 pm, Sat-Sun 10 am-3 pm.

🛏 ☺☺ Rica Hotel Vadsø, Oscarsgt. 4, tel. 78951681. **☺ Lailas Hotell**, Brugt. 2, tel. 78953335. *CAMPING:* **Vestre Jakobselv Camping**, tel. 78956064, 7 cabins.

🏛 Vadsø Museum, open daily in summer after 10 am, as long as people come. **Church** (new) open 10 am-2 pm in summer; the old church is closed.

🚤 Boat tours to the bird cliffs of **Klubben** should be booked 24 hours in advance, either through the tourist information office or from **Vestre Jakobselv Camping**, tel. 78956064.

🎣 Salmon fishing in the Jakobselv, 17 km west, in the Skallelv, 31 km west, and in the Kommagelv, 44 km east. Fishing permits available from the tourist office or Vestre Jakobselv Camping.

VARDØ

🛈 Postboks 45, tel. 78988270. Open June 15-August 31, 10 am-6 pm.

🛏 ☺☺ Vardø Hotel, Kaigt., tel. 78987761. **☺ Gjestegården Bed & Breakfast**, tel. 78987529.

🏛 Vardøhus Fortress, open June 10-August 31 daily 8 am-10 pm, guided tours twice a day. **Vardøhus Museum**, Mon-Fri 9 am-6 pm, Sat-Sun 10:30 am-6 pm.

🎣 Bird islands of Reinøya and **Hornøya**, Norway's easternmost point. Excursions to the abandoned settlement of **Hamningberg**; you can reserve a guide from the tourist office.

NEIDEN

🛈 Postboks, tel. 78992501, open June 15-August 31, 10 am-6 pm.

🛏 ☺☺ Neidenelven Fjellstue, tel. 78996141. **Neidenfoss Camping**, tel. 78996203, fishing permits also sold here.

🏛 St. George's Chapel, Neiden Church, arrange visits through the tourist office.

KIRKENES

🛈 AS Grenseland, Postboks 8, tel. 78992544 and 78992501, open year-round 8:30 am-4 pm, June 1-August 30, 8:30 am-6 pm.

🛏 ☺☺ Rica Arctic Hotel, Kongensgt. 1-3, tel. 78992929. **☺ Barents Frokosthotell**, E6, 9900 Kirkenes, tel. 78993299. *CAMPING:* **Kirkenes Camping**, Maggadalen, tel. 78998028.

🏛 Ore labyrinth, daily tours from the tourist office.

🎣 Daily trips to **Murmansk**, by bus with Sovjetreiser, Postboks 217, Kirkenes, tel. 78991981, from June 1-August 31 (visa required); by boat, from June 22-August 3, for reservations, call 78411000 (no visa required). Excursions to the **Grense Jakobselv** and **Pasvikdalen** are arranged by AS Grenseland, Postboks 8, Kirkenes, tel. 78992501. Pasvik Tourist, Pb 157, 9901 Kirkenes, tel. 78995080, arranges trips to the Kola Peninsula.

✈ Daily flights to Oslo. *Hurtigrute* boats arrive every morning at Kirkenes (last stop), and leave every afternoon. There are daily express buses to Lakselv and Alta, and local buses to eastern Finnmark.

Fjords on the Artic Ocean

THE LOFOTEN, VESTERÅLEN AND SVALBARD ISLANDS

LOFOTENS
VESTERÅLENS
SVALBARDS

THE **LOFOTEN ISLANDS
Cod and Cormorants

"The prettiest piece of Norway" was Knut Hamsun's term for the Lofoten, the southern section of the largest island chain in northern Norway. These islands, known collectively as Vesterålen in Norwegian, are better known in central Europe by the name of their southern extension, the **Lofotens**. The chain is 240 kilometers long, extending from Andenes at the northern tip of the Vesterålen to Renfsvik at the southern tip of the Lofoten island of Moskenesøy.

The coasts of the four main islands of the Lofoten group – **Austvågøy**, **Vestvågøy**, **Flakstadøy** and **Moskenesøy** – are craggy and creased with countless fjords and sounds. Inland, the mountains rise up in bizarre shapes to heights of as much as 1,000 meters. Planting crops is possible only in a few sheltered regions of Vestvågøy Island; apart from this, fishing is the dominant source of income, as well as the islands' signature occupation.

In the **Vestfjord**, which separates the Lofotens from the mainland, the cod population of the Arctic Ocean moves in to-

Preceding pages: Panorama of the wild Lofotens near Reine. Left: Dried cod is the Lofotens' principle export.

ward the end of winter to breed. The broad fjord narrows toward the north, so that the waters of the Gulf Stream build up, and the area stays warmer longer than the waters of the open sea. As cod prefer warmer temperatures when they're breeding, they flock here in huge schools. This period starts in January and culminates around the month of April.

As early as the 11th century, Viking chiefs from Trøndelag sent their vassals to fish off these islands; and in the 12th century King Øystein had so-called *rorbuer*, huts with sleeping quarters and storage areas for provisions and equipment, constructed for these fishermen. It was in this period that the first settlements and churches began to spring up. More and more, farmers and independent fishermen also started fishing for cod off the Lofotens, and fixed regulations were soon established to govern protocol for this fishing. According to these, landowners had to share the fishing grounds with the seasonal fishermen, and also rented them *rorbuer* at a rate of 20 to 30 fish per day. In addition, the tenants had to give 2 percent of their catch to the landowners, the same amount to the church, and 4 percent to the state.

The catch was dried or salted, packed up for shipment by assistants of the Hansa or the Bergen-Trondheim monop-

Lofoten, Vesterålen and Svalbard

oly, and sent throughout Europe. The price for these perishable goods were, of course, lowest at the height of the season – a state of affairs that persisted until J. Jppe in Molde began, in the 17th century, to pickle fish in brine and then dry them as a means of preserving them longer (*klippfisk*). With this step, preserving fish became the task of the fishermen, who started to stay on the Lofotens for longer and longer periods; some of them settling down here altogether. This, however, meant that they became dependent fishermen obliged to keep paying a portion of their catch to their superiors.

This remained true until the 19th century, when fishing was opened up to everyone; but this also meant that the area started to be overfished. The incredibly hard work of a Lofoten fisherman, exposed to the Arctic night, cold and wet, has given rise to countless stories and anecdotes, the most famous of which Johan

Above: A flood of evening color – summer skies over the Lofotens.

Boyer incorporated into his novel *The Lofoten Fishermen*.

Today, many fishermen have abandoned fishing altogether and have opened fish farms in which they breed salmon and trout. The state leases the necessary concessions for this industry, and also makes sure that none of these farms exceeds the regulated size, thereby preventing the development of large-scale businesses which would threaten the delicate balance of the economy.

Tourism has also created a number of jobs to replace fishing. Not a few *rorbuer* have been converted into vacation homes; hotels and restaurants have sprung up; and the whole infrastructure of the region has been markedly improved in the last few years. Today, the main islands of the Lofotens and Vesterålens are linked with bridges and tunnels; the Vesterålen island of Hinnøy is even connected to the mainland. Only between the Vesterålen island of Melbu and Fiskebøl in the northern Lofotens is the ferry still essential, and even this is supposed to be replaced with a new road from Lødingen to Fiskebøl in future.

Through the Lofoten Islands

Coming from the south, you can reach Moskenes on the island of Moskenesøy from Bodø in about 4 hours by ferry (3 times a day); from the east, the ferry crossing from Skutvik to Svolvær takes about 2 hours (8 times a day); and from the north, it's only a matter of the short ferry crossing to Fiskebøl (30 minutes, 10 times a day).

If you start your Lofoten tour on the island of **Austvågøy**, in **Fiskebøl ❶**, you take the E10 along the **Budalenfjord** for a few kilometers. Here, you quickly get a sense of the typical Lofoten vegetation: a few fjell birch groves in protected areas alternate with treeless, rocky slopes and cliffs overgrown with moss and lichen, shimmering in every conceivable shade of green. Past **Budalen**, the E10 crosses the isthmus on the island of Austvågøy and comes into view of the **Higravs-tinden**, the highest mountain on the Lofotens at 1,146 meters. At **Higrav**, you reach the Austnesfjord, and at **Vestpollen** a little road runs over to Austvågøy's west coast, where little settlements of *rorbuer* stand along the protected bays.

Past Helle, the airport, the road arrives at the town of **Svolvær ❷**, which, with its population of 4,000, assumed its current role as capital of the Lofotens thanks to its natural, deep harbor, taking over the function thereto filled by Kabelvåg when that town's harbor became too small. Downtown Solvær with its souvenir shops, banks and *vinmonopolet* is ranged around the harbor, which is where *Hurtigrute* boats dock. During the main cod season, from February to April, some 3,000 boats still wait here to see action.

The harbor, where the *Turistik* office is also located, is the point of departure for excursions to the offshore island of **Skrova**, along the Lofoten Wall, into the

Lofoten, Vesterålen and Svalbard

Austnesfjord and the magnificent **★Troll-fjord**, a small side fjord of the Raftsun-det. There, the rock walls rise to heights of nearly 1,000 meters, making this a popular place with rock climbers. A wide range of mountain tours, in fact, is of-fered from Svolvær, from simple hikes to more difficult climbs. There are, further-more, countless flat, sandy bays, in which the water temperature can rise to as high as 22° C on hot summer days.

The Lofotens' gorgeous landscapes at-tracted painters as early as the 19th cen-tury. For artists today, there's a guest house on the rocky island of **Svinøya**, where foreign and Scandinavian artists can live and work. Another attraction of the town is the **Svolværgeita**, a stone cliff shaped like a goat, of which you have the best view from the cemetery.

If you leave Svolvær traveling south, you reach **Vågan ❸** after 3 kilometers.

Above: After it's dried, the cod is sorted by hand. Right: Nusfjord – a whole village under landmark protection.

Located here is the largest wooden church on the Lofotens, dubbed **Lofoten Cathedral**. Dating from 1898, it has 1,200 seats. Hans Egede, the "Greenland Apostle," is among its former pastors. **Kabelvåg ❹**, the first fishing harbor on the Lofotens, takes its name from the cha-pel (*kappel*) which King Øystein once had built here, together with the first *rorbuer*. Lofoten's erstwhile main harbor leads something of a shadowy existence today; in fact, residents have blown up a mountain to fill in a part of the bay in order to create more farmland. An inter-esting stop in Kabelvåg is the **Lofoten Museum**, located in an old trading center 3 kilometers outside of town, and devoted to the history of life and fishing on these islands. Not far from this is the **Lofoten Aquarium**, whose pools are a stomping-ground for every sort of sea dweller that's indigenous to this region.

A pleasant detour leads to **Hennings-vær ❺**, a small, very photogenic fishing village on a bare, rocky skerry sur-rounded by huge drying racks for codfish.

On the smaller, outlying islands you can often see cormorants huddled, drying their feathers. Their numbers have been drastically reduced since they, together with the seals, were held responsible for the fact that the cod weren't coming back. In Henningsvær harbor you can see large warehouses filled with dried fish and fishheads waiting – aromatically, or pungently, depending on your view – to be shipped out.

Continuing on, the Lofoten road E10 passes the little island of **Gimsøy**, linked by bridges to the islands around it. This is held to be one of the oldest settlements in the Lofotens, based on archaeological finds from the Stone and Iron Ages. On **Vestvågøy** Island, the E10 passes through **Borge** to Leknes. Near Borge, excavations have established that the climate here must have been much milder 2,000 years ago, enabling farming and livestock breeding on a scale that would no longer be possible today. A more interesting route, however, leads through **Smorten** on the R815 and 817 to Leknes. This road

follows the eastern shore of Vestvågøy and leads through **Valberg 6** and **Stamsund 7**, the two largest fishing villages on the island. **Leknes 8**, with 1,500 residents, is the service and shopping center of the whole island, and, together with **Gravdal** and **Ballstad**, boasts the largest fish refinery in the area.

Running under the **Nappstraum**, which separates Vestvågøy from **Flakstadøy**, is a toll tunnel nearly 2 kilometers long (1,750 meters). If the weather's good, you might want to detour from Napp over to **Myrland 9**; there, you can often see spectacular sunsets or have great views of the midnight sun.

Just past **Kilan**, you can turn off to the *Nusfjord 10*. This fishing village, which looks like a toy town on the water, is facing an uncertain future, as the fish farmer who owns the whole place has gone bankrupt. However, the complex, which is under landmark protection, has not been altered, and the picturesque 19th-century *rorbuer* are still being rented out. A pretty hiking trail leads right along the Vestfjord

Lofoten, Vesterålen and Svalbard

across the fjell to the abandoned fishing village of **Nesland**.

In **Flakstad** ⓫ there's an old church from 1780, painted bright red, and generally held to be the prettiest in the whole archipelago. Originally, it was built entirely of driftwood. **Ramberg** ⓬, the main town on this island, has unusually long sand beaches which command fine views of the **Selfjord** and the **Fuglehug** (bird cliff) on the opposite shore.

A bridge 160 meters long leads to the island of **Moskenesøy**. The trading and fishing village **Sund** ⓭, the oldest on the island, boasts a small but interesting **Fishing Museum**. Administrative center of the island is the town of **Hamnøy** ⓮. Here, in **Kirkefjord**, there are a number of fish farms, while in the harbor you can see whaling vessels which still bring in some 1,600 dwarf whales every year. As whaling is forbidden by international treaties, this catch is officially chalked up to "interests of science."

Shortly before *Reine* ⓯, right by the road, there's a cliff with a large colony of kittiwakes. The town itself is accounted the artists' colony of the Lofotens; the mighty mountain backdrop of the Kirkefjord was already attracting artists aplenty in the 19th century. **Moskenes** is the ferry port for boats to the small southern Lofoten islands of **Værøy** and *Røst*, with their fishing villages and large bird colonies (especially puffins); the ferry to Bodø stops here, as well. South of Moskenes are the fishing villages of **Sørvågen** and **Å**; the last attracts tourists who want to be able to say they've visited the village with the shortest name in the world. The ocean current between Moskenesøy and Værøy, the **Moskenstraum**, is said to be one of the most dangerous in the world – Edgar Allen Poe and Jules Verne both immortalized it as the "great maelstrom."

Right: Nyksund, an abandoned whaling village on the Vesterålen.

THE *VESTERÅLEN ISLANDS: Wheat and Whales

The northern extension of the Lofoten chain is the island group of the Vesterålen. The main islands here, **Hadseløya**, **Langøya**, **Hinnøya** and **Andøya**, are linked by means of bridges, so you can reach all of the most important Vesterålens without recourse to a ferry.

Although the Vesterålens have the same geological composition as the Lofotens, they are quite different in terms of landscape. Broad, flat strips of coastal moorland alternate with gentle slopes blanketed with woods and meadows. In contrast to the barren Lofotens, agriculture is practiced intensively here, with livestock breeding and even the cultivation of summer wheat. Nonetheless, the main economic force here, too, is fishing, although, again in contrast to the Lofotens, it's herring that take the spotlight here, as they are especially easy to drive into and catch in the islands' long, narrow sounds and fjords. The narrow Raftsundet, 26 kilometers long, between the Lofotens and the Vesterålens was an arena for military altercations in the 19th century: in the so-called Trollfjord Battle of 1890, riled-up fishermen attacked the first steamship that had dared to venture into these waters in search of herring, and actually drove it away. Whaling, originally practiced from the northern tip of the Vesterålens, has practically come to a halt altogether. Today, the local population and the government place high hopes in oil and gas exploration, as well as in tourism, which has heretofore played a rather modest role on these islands.

On the Vesterålens

To reach the islands, travelers either go from Narvik via Bjerkvik on the E10 or take the Fiskebøl-Melbu ferry over from the Lofotens. **Melbu** ⓰, at the southern end of the little island of **Hadseløya**, is an

old Viking trading post which lives today from fishing and tourist exchange with the Lofotens. A small museum here evokes the original Viking settlement, which wasn't actually on the site of present-day Melbu, but rather stood farther north, in **Hadsel**. Near the church, you can still see the 35-meter **Hill of Skipsnausthaug**, an old Thing site which was connected to a chieftain's court. **Stokmarknes** ⑰ is the administrative center of modern Hadseløya. Numbering 3,500 citizens, the town has an airport, and is a port on the *Hurtigrute*.

A bridge 33 meters high and more than 1,000 meters long forms a link with the neighboring island, **Langøya**. Following the protected east coast of this craggy, indented island, the E10 leads to **Sortland** ⑱, center of the central Vesterålens; here, another bridge arcs over the **Sortlandssund** to Hinnøya. Here, visitors can opt to follow the R820 and 821 to the western part of this island, still undiscovered by tourists. Bird-watchers, especially, stand to benefit: in any of the small fjords here,

they can observe puffins, rare species of gull, cormorants, and sea eagles.

Extending over more than 20,000 square kilometers, **Hinnøya** is the second-largest island in Norway. Because of its size and the fact that only a very small sound separates it from the mainland, it's easy to forget that it's an island at all. Just past the bridge over the Sortlandssund, the R82 veers off toward **Andøya**, to the north. 99 kilometers long, this well-paved stretch of road leads through the moors and across a bridge to the neighboring island. The old whaling settlement of *★Andenes ⑲ has today gone over wholesale to whaling tourism. Weather permitting, boats depart every day on whaling safaris, on which passengers have excellent chances of spotting these huge sea mammals in their natural habitat. In addition, there's a **whale information center** in the harbor. Every July the town hosts a sea fisheries festival.

If you stay on the E10 on Hinnøya, you pass **Sigerfjord** ⑳, where there's a new chapel containing an old statue of St.

Lofoten, Vesterålen and Svalbard

Olav. Here, at the narrowest point of the island, the road runs across it past Gullesfjord to its eastern coast and the town of **Lødingen** on the **Tjeldsund**, which separates this island from the mainland. 50 kilometers farther north, there are parking lots at either side of the **Tjeldsund Bridge**, with great views out over the Vesterålen landscapes.

Visitors should also detour from here over to the capital of the Vesterålens, **Harstad ㉑**, which lies 25 kilometers further along on the R83. With its gentle light, this city of 22,000 has long attracted painters. It saw its first ascendancy in the so-called "herring years" of the early 19th century, when herring were so plentiful in the Vågafjord that you could scoop them up with a pitchfork; a herring festival in July commemorates this fishy past. Shipbuilding and the textile industry later joined fishing as significant economic factors, and since the end of World War II fishing has steadily declined in importance. Today, Harstad is an administrative center for northern Norway's oil and gas industry, which is the main reason for the town's considerable growth.

Most noteworthy sight in Harstad is the oldest Romanesque church in the north, **Trondenes Church**, located on a peninsula 3 kilometers north of town. This edifice dates back to an old wooden church which King Øystein had built in the 12th century. The stone church you see today was built around 1250 and has been renovated several times since. Inside, there are three altars from the Middle Ages. Both the mighty church wall and the remains of two fortified towers facing the sea indicate the building's original defensive character.

This church saw the baptisms of both Hans Egede, the "Greenland Apostle," and Olav Engelbrektson, Trondheim's last archbishop; both men were natives of Harstad. Crowning the remains of the fortification walls is a huge German canon from World War II.

Visitors can also take boat excursions over to the "down island" of **Bjarkøy ㉒**, which was once used as a breeding ground for eider ducks, so that the eider could be easily collected after the breeding season was over.

Returning from Harstad to the Tjeldsund, you can take the bridge over to the mainland, and continue on the E10 along the Ofotfjord to Bjerkvik and the E6.

THE *SVALBARDS:
Islands of the Cold Coasts

Svalbard was what the Vikings called the group of Arctic islands between 74° and 81°N, which they had discovered by the 12th century at the latest. Their name for the archipelago is indicative of their degree of interest in these territories, for even Vikings couldn't muster up much enthusiasm for "cold coasts," which is what the name means in translation.

Accordingly, the islands were again forgotten until the Dutchman Willem Barents came across them once again in 1596. Barents was looking for a sea route to China, so he didn't stay long; furthermore, he erroneously believed these islands to be part of Danish Greenland, and thus didn't even bother to claim them for his own nation. As he killed a bear on the southernmost island, he christened it "Bear Island," Bjørnøya, and he coined the name "Spitzbergen" for the main island with its pointed silhouette. Despite his lack of possessiveness, his visit sparked a lengthy confrontation between Danish Norway, Holland and England, the main bone of contention being whaling rights in these waters.

By the early 19th century, the whales were nearly extinct, which effectively ended these disputes; the only inhabitants remained a few Russian hermits who

Right: Icebergs show up all year round in the harbor of Longyearbyen on Spitsbergen.

eked out a living as fur-trappers. The arguments, however, flared up anew when large coal deposits were discovered on Spitsbergen at the beginning of the 20th century.

Not until the Treaty of Sèvres (1920) was Norway finally able to attain complete sovereignty over this island group in 1925, and even then it had to promise to tolerate economic activities of the treaty's 41 other cosignatory nations, and keep the archipelago free of any military installations. This resulted in Norway and the Soviet Union jointly mining coal and establishing settlements which are still home to 95 percent of the island's 3,500 inhabitants.

Although coal mining no longer makes any sense from an economic standpoint, the major powers in the Cold War continued the activity in order to justify their continued presence on the islands. Today, negotiations have begun to cease mining activity and turn the islands over to the native population: polar bears, seals, birds, polar foxes, and wild reindeer

herds. There are also plans to develop some form of ecological tourism.

Measuring some 63,000 square kilometers in area, the Svalbard archipelago has six main islands: **Spitsbergen**, representing more than half of the archipelago's land mass; **Nordaustland**, 15,000 square kilometers; **Edgeøya** and **Barenstøya** in the southeast, and **Bjørnøya** and **Hopen** all the way to the south. The islands are craggy, with mountains of as much as 1,700 meters high, and sprinkled with many fjords into which glaciers frequently calve.

For such an Arctic latitude, the climate is strikingly mild: although temperatures seldom get above 10°C in summer, they don't usually fall below about -16°C in winter, either. The flora and fauna are Arctic, but there are five indigenous species of mammal, legion birds, and nearly 200 different kinds of plant living and flourishing on the Svalbard islands.

Most of the tourists who make their way up here come on cruise ships which generally travel into those fjords where

Lofoten, Vesterålen and Svalbard

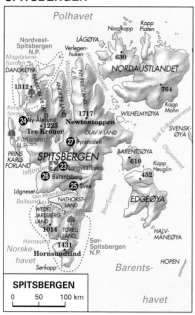

Polhavet

Kapp
Nordkapp Platen

Nordvest-
Spitsbergen LÅGØYA
N.P. Verlegen-
Magdalene- huken
fjorden
DANSKØYA NORDAUSTLANDET
1812 764

Kapp
Kongs- 1717 WILHELMYØYA Mohn
fjorden Ny-Ålesund
•1225 Newtontoppen
Tre Kroner OLAV V LAND SVENSK-
Forlandet ØYA
N.P. Pyramiden
PRINS BARENTSØYA
KARLS SPITSBERGEN 610
FORLAND Longyearbyen Kapp
Isfjorden Heuglin
Barentsburg •452
Svea
Lågneset
Van Mijenfjorden NATHORST-
Bellsund LAND EDGEØYA
WEDEL
JARLSBERG
LAND
1014 TORELL HALV-
LAND MÅNEØYA
Hornsund 1431 Sør-
Norske Hornsundtind Spitsbergen
havet N.P.
Sørkapp HOPEN
Barents-

SPITSBERGEN

0   50   100 km

havet

glaciers are in the process of calving or in which you can spot spectacular icebergs. That such excursions are not entirely undangerous was demonstrated by the *Maxim Gorky* accident a few years ago. Usually, however, a cruise ship is the most comfortable way to visit the Svalbards. In fact, there aren't any other regular boat links since the *Hurtigrute* stopped calling here. Anyone who wants to arrive by boat today has to arrange for passage on a freighter in a travel agency in Tromsø, and should allow at least a week for the whole enterprise.

It's easier, faster and cheaper to fly with SAS or Braathens to **Longyearbyen** **㉓**, a mining town and the Norwegian capital of Spitsbergen. From there, small planes provide irregular service, weather depending, to **Ny-Ålesund ㉔**, the polar research station at the northern end of Spitsbergen, or **Svea ㉕**, a Russian mining settlement at the end of the **Mijenfjord**.

In addition, there are boats between Longyearbyen and the Russian town of

Barentsburg ㉖ on *Isfjord, another port of call for cruise ships. Also available are smaller boat tours calling in at a number of Svalbard islands and including land excursions. These are neither regular nor cheap; but they can be booked in Tromsø.

Individualists could long warm their hearts on the fact that there was only one official facility for overnight accommodations on Spitsbergen: the tiny campground of Longyearbyen, where you had to be able to show that you had adequate clothing, provisions and an arctic-weight sleeping bag in order to be admitted, since you can't buy anything other than postcards and ammunition on the Svalbard Islands. In fact, bringing ammunition in is prohibited, and yet a loaded gun is a prerequisite for any expedition here, since polar bears can attack without warning.

For expeditions outside of Longyearbyen, you need a permit from the Sysselmann, the administrative head of the Svalbards, as well as accident insurance. The number of visitors is also restricted.

In 1995, the 60-bed **Svalbard Polar Hotell** opened its doors, making longer stays possible for the first time. Today, excursions are becoming more and more prevalent in Longyearbyen, as well as in the Russian mining town of **Pyramiden ㉗** on the northern shore of the Isfjord, which you can reach on Russian helicopters. In good weather, these also offer flights over Spitsbergen; the **Magdalenenfjord** in the northwest is a particularly impressive sight.

Also spectacular is the midnight sun, which is visible here from April 19 to August 24, twice as long as on the North Cape. The flip side of the coin is the fact that the Arctic night falls here on October 27, and lasts until February 15 – hence the "long year" in the name of the capital, founded in 1906 by an American coal tycoon.

SVOLVÆR (LOFOTEN)

Postboks 210, tel. 76073000, on the harbor; Jun 1-Aug 31, 9 am-8 pm, other times Mon-Fri 11 am-4 pm.

Best Western Svolvær Hotell, Austnesfjordgt. 12, 8300 Svolvær, tel. 76070909. **Euro Marina Hotel**, tel. 76070777, only open June 1-August 15, on the harbor. **Golden Tulip Rainbow Vestfjord Hotel**, Havna, tel. 76070870. **Havna Hotel**, O.J. Karbøesgt. 5, tel. 76072850. **Royal Hotel**, Siv Nilsengt. 21, tel. 76071200. **Hotel Havly**, Sjøgt., tel. 76070344. **Knutmarka Feriesenter**, Leirskolevn. 16, tel. 7607-2164, open March-October, cabins, camping. **Svinøya Rurbuer**, tel. 76070880.

Svolvær Church, June-August Mon-Sat 10 am-10 pm. **Lofoten Cathedral**, Vågar, 3 km south of Svolvær, Mon-Sat noon-3 pm. **Lofoten Aquarium Kabelvåg**, 21 km south, Mon-Fri 10 am-3 pm, Sat -Sun 11 am-3 pm.

Boat trips to the **Trollfjord**, the **Lofotenwand** and the artists' island of **Svinøya**; Lofotcruise, 48 seats, tel. 76070963; Svolværgult, 30 seats, tel. 76070336; Trollfjord, 35 seats, tel. 76071790. Year-round **climbing tours** are offered by Henningsvær Climbing School, tel. 760774911.

NUSFJORD (LOFOTEN)

Tel. 76060594, June 1-August 31, 9 am-8 pm, other times Mon-Fri 11 am-4 pm.

Dahl Nusfjord Rorbucamping, rents out historic *rorbuer* (fishermen's huts), contact the Leknes tourist office, tel. 76060594.

Nusfjord, pictursque fishing village on UNESCO's list of World Cultural Heritage Sites.

Flakstad, 15 km west of Nusfjord: **Driftwood Church**, can be opened by sacristan.

Summer concerts in the Flakstad Church.

Å (LOFOTEN)

Hamna Rorbuer, rentals through the Balestrand tourist office, tel. 57691255.

Fish Processing Museum (great for a rainy day), Mon-Fri 10 am-4 pm, June 20-Aug 20, 10 am-6 pm.

To cross the Moskenesstraum to **Værøy** and **Røst** (a very rough but worthwhile trip), the best option is the car ferry to Bodø, which stops at both islands and runs year-round.

STOKMARKNES (VESTERÅLEN)

Postboks, tel. 76152955, open June 1-August 31, 9 am-8 pm, other times Mon-Fri 11 am-4 pm.

Kinnarps Turistsenter, tel. 76152999.

Hurtigrute Museum on the quay, open when *Hurtigrute* ships dock, generally between 1:30 and 3:30 pm.

ANDESNES (VESTERÅLEN)

Postboks, tel. 76115600.

Norlandia Andrikken Hotell, Storgt. 53, tel. 76141222.

The **Lighthouse** is open in summer for tourists, even at night, providing fantastic views of the midnight sun. **Whaling Museum** and **Polar Museum**, June 20-August 20 daily, visits must be arranged through the hotel or the tourist office.

Whale safaris (sightings guaranteed), June through August, daily (in good weather); to reserve, call 76142611, 76141273.

HARSTAD (VESTERÅLEN)

Torvet 8, tel. 77063235, open June 1-August 31, 9 am-8 pm, other times Mon-Fri 11 am-4 pm.

Quality Arcticus Hotel, Havnegt. 3, tel. 77065000.

Grand Nordic Hotell, Strandgt. 9, tel. 77062170. **Viking Nordic Hotell**, Fjordgt. 2, tel. 77064060. **Centrum Hospits**, Magnusgt. 5, tel. 77062938. **Harstad Vandrerhjem Trondarnes**, Frilynte Folkehøgskole, tel. 77064154, open from June to mid-August.

Trondenes Church, open in summer Mon-Fri 9 am-2 pm, Sat 9 am-noon. **New Church**, Tue-Fri 9 am-2 pm, the pastor from next door gives tours.

Excursions to observe the **midnght sun** (May 23-July 22) and to the "down island" of **Bjarkøy**, information at the harbor.

Fishing and Herring Festival in June; **Northern Norway Festival** on Midsummer Night.

SPITSBERGEN (SVALBARDS)

Næringsbygget Postboks 323, Longyearbyen, tel. 79022303, June 1-August 31, 9 am-8 pm, other times Mon-Fri 11 am-4 pm.

Arrival: By plane or freighter; contact the Tromsø tourist office for information, tel. 77610000.

Funken Hotell Spitsbergen, Haugen, tel. 79022450. **Svalbard Kro Spitsbergen Travel Hotel**, Longyearbyen, tel. 79021300. **Svalbard Polar Hotel**, 9170 Longyearbyen, tel. 79023501, also arranges tours.

Nybyen Gjestehus Spitsbergen Travel Hotel, Nybyen, tel. 79021005, open March-September, tour arrangements from Longyearbyen.

Any activity outside the settlement must be discussed in advance with the Longyearbyen tourist office.

Ski, **sled** and **dog sled tours** (year-round): Spitsbergen Tours, Postboks 6, Longyearbyen, tel. 79021068.

Lofoten, Vesterålen and Svalbard

227

THE HURTIGRUTE:
Cruise without a Label

Forget the little black dress and the dinner jacket. Apart from normal, family-style meals, you won't have any social obligations on this most unusual cruise in the world – and yet it's often booked out months, even years, in advance.

Actually, the *Hurtigrute* is nothing more than a mail boat, which started out in the 19th century to link 70 ports along Norway's coast and provide a means of transportation for residents of the northern harbor towns and the hinterlands, as well as guaranteeing regular delivery of mail and other essentials.

After World War II, when the roads improved and the network of airports expanded throughout northern Norway, the

Preceding pages: Stave churches, Norway's contribution to ecclesiastical architecture in Europe. Above: Aboard the Hurtigrute ship "Harald Jarl." Right: "King Neptune" baptizes a new initiate to the Arctic Circle.

number of passengers on the *Hurtigrute* ships began to decline; although, growing numbers of tourists were quick to fill the vacuum. However, even though transporting tourists is in fact now the main source of revenue for this royal mail boat line, the official purpose of these ships remains providing regular, year-round service to the Norwegian ports between Bergen and Kirkenes. Even today, the ships take eleven days for the 2,500 nautical miles (4,630 kilometer) from Bergen to Kirkenes and back, and operate on a fixed schedule every day, even if they only call at 36 harbors on the present plan. Only the size of the ships has changed: where once small steamers of 2,500 G.R.T. plied these waters, today the *Hurtigrute* boats are diesel-powered vessels of as much as 20,000 G.R.T., able to transport cars as well as a range of goods, and offering cabins complete with private showers and toilets, a luxury that's reflected, of course, in the prices.

Even today, when much local mail comes in by plane, the postmaster hangs the red mailbox of the Royal Mail on the gangway in every harbor; and even today, local residents appear to pick up goods and check out the disembarking passengers, or see if anything's arrived for them as groceries and packages are unloaded on forklifts from the hold.

On board, the social life has remained refreshingly straightforward. The food is simple and good, with large buffets and sit-down dinners, and everything is available in ample portions. On the large, new ships such as the *Kong Harlad*, *Nordlys* or *Richard With*, digestifs are even available in the shipboard bars.

Boats leave Bergen in the evening and pass the Vestkapp the next morning. In the skerries by Ålesund, boats go right past the bird island of Runde. The first call at Trondheim is in the early morning, enabling passengers to visit the old city and Nidaros Cathedral. After a glimpse of the Svartisen Glacier near Mo i Rana, "Neptune" puts in an appearance among the passengers to "baptize" everyone who's crossing the Arctic Circle for the first time.

For much of the trip, the ship travels between islands and the mainland; but it crosses open sea north of Bodø, a sometimes rough trip with compensation in the form of the view of the majestic Lofoten Wall. A day later, the ship docks in front of the Arctic Cathedral of Tromsø, and then continues on through the islands of northern Norway to Hammerfest and Honningsvåg, where passengers can depart on an excursion to the North Cape. The rest of the trip to Kirkenes is broken by little fishing harbors, Norway's easternmost point by the island of Hornøya, and the best views of the midnight sun above the Arctic Ocean.

In most of the major harbors the boat docks long enough so that passengers can see the main sights; there are also a range of excursions to more distant highlights, timed to fit in with the ship's schedule. If you want to tarry longer or change ships,

it requires considerable advance planning, as every stop and every change of vessel has to be booked several months in advance; it's futile to gamble on a berth coming free at the last minute. Any trip through Norway, whether by plane, train or car, can be combined with a stretch on the *Hurtigrute*: port cities with airports offer transfer buses to the harbor; there are similar transfers to train stations, and plenty of parking spots available for cars.

Another perk is the friendly staff on board, who do their best to accommodate passengers who decide at the last minute that they do, after all, want to go along on a given excursion. In return, passengers are expected not to do anything to interfere with the loading and unloading of cargo, to return punctually from excursions, and to show up on time for meals. However comfortable they appear, these remain primarily cargo ships, which are happy to welcome passengers, but can't allow them to determine the course of the trip; for this depends on two things, the weather and the timetable.

Hurtigrute

STAVE CHURCHES

The wooden churches resting on long beams or rafters (staves) adorned with dragons' heads, known as stave churches, are Norway's only original contribution to the body of European ecclesiastical architecture. The Christianized Vikings who first developed the form basically turned their boats upside down in order to hold early masses in the shelter of the hold – this, at least, is a common description of the origin of this genre. While this description isn't actually inaccurate, it doesn't really do the churches justice, for it limits the story to the actual builders rather than placing it in the context of European architecture, which is what made such edifices possible in the first place.

Two things are important here: first, Christianity tended to take hold in Europe only when subtler methods replaced the traditional "fire-and-sword" brand of missionizing; and second, throughout Europe, churches were deliberately built in a style quite different from that of a community's residential houses, in order to emphasize the uniqueness of God in architectural terms. This was true in Norway, as well.

The spread of Christianity in Norway began with the arrival of Viking mercenaries in Normandy; these soldiers eventually settled down permanently and became Christians and vassals of the French king. Through family ties, which were inviolable, news of the new beliefs penetrated to the courts of the early Norwegian kings, who saw a chance to use this monotheistic religion as a way to reinforce their own claims to a single, unified kingdom – united, of course, under their own rule.

Attempts to harness Christianity to politics in this manner were doomed to failure as long as the new religion was spread by force, as it was under Olav Tryggvasson, for example. Not until Olav Kyrre traveled to England with his father did he learn that Christianity was fully able to incorporate and integrate "heathen" deities and customs. From then on, the rule in Norway was "as many heathen customs as possible, and as much Christianity as necessary," and once this policy was established, Christianity began its triumphal progression through the country.

As the Christian saints were presented as corollaries to the heathen deities, the average man in the street didn't have to worry much about changing tradition: the transition was so mild that it was easy to perceive the new religion as merely a continuation and development of the old. The populace, therefore, was fully prepared to erect new places of worship for the new gods, and adorn them with symbols taken over from the old creed. By 1250, when the country was completely Christianized, there were said to be between 700 and 1,000 stave churches throughout Norway.

Why, then, this particular type of church? Brought into play here were specifically Norwegian elements. The wealth of wood available, and people's long experience in working it, had created two completely different technologies: the construction of solid, insulated houses made of tree trunks, and the construction of light, portable ships. If the aim was to build the house of God in a style different from that of the solid log cabins of the secular population, the only other option was to take over the shipbuilders' techniques; for large stone buildings still lay far in the future.

Thus was born the idea of using ship's architecture in a church, simply turning the ship upside down. This is certainly easier said than done, for a ship standing on its head, especially on dry land, has all kinds of structural problems. The number of masts has to be increased in order to

Right: Vertical beams carry the weight of a stave church's roof (Umes).

support the heavy roof, but the masts can't stand alone; they have to be connected in such a way that the building doesn't resist the wind, but is able to bend with it.

With the bracketing technique, corresponding to ribbing in shipbuilding, and the newly-developed vaulted crosses which were soon known by the name of the martyr St. Andrew, this problem was soon under control.

It was more difficult to develop a method of preservation which would protect the weight-bearing masts from rotting: if they were simply buried in the earth, they would soon be rotten to the core in no time at all. To solve this problem, the church floor was outlined in stone slabs, upon which powerful beams were stood to create the outline of the completed building. The staves were fastened to these with wooden supports and held up temporarily until the roof was completed, which gave the building greater stability. The next step was to start linking up the staves, using only wooden

"nails" to prevent any cracks from forming. Last of all, the exterior walls were planked with vertical timbers and the roof covered in resinous larch bark, which, like the whole building, was impregnated and waterproofed with wood tar.

Due to considerations of stability as well as warmth, windows were generally not a feature of these unheated buildings, which were illuminated with candles and pine torches. The lack of heat, the plague, and the open flames of the candles are all reasons why only about 30 of the 1,000-odd stave churches have survived. Many of them burned down. In the plague years, three-quarters of the population died, and the wooden churches rotted; later, the communities built new stone churches, which could be heated.

In decorating the portals and roofs of their stave churches, the old architects drew on the magical ornaments, symbols and patterns which had long protected their boats from spirits, Norns and the wrath of the gods. Thus it is that Odin often stands in for the Christian God.

THE SAMI

The oldest traces of human habitation in Scandinavia are those of the Kromsa culture along the coast of present-day Finnmark. There's considerable evidence to indicate that these early settlers were Sami ("swamp people") who had emigrated from Siberia. Thus, one could describe them as the original Native Scandinavians. However, Sami settlement can only be continuously demonstrated since the Iron Age (800-300 BC), in a period in which the Germanic tribes were preparing to invade the north.

The Sami had little wherewithal with which to withstand the aggressive Germanic tribes. Their survival technique was withdrawal, rather than combat. So, at least, runs the description which Ottar of Hålgoland sent in a 9th-century report to King Alfred of England, which is the

Above: The four points on a Sami hat represent the four cardinal directions in which a Sami can travel. Right: Sami artisan work.

oldest written evidence we have of Sami life. Here, too, are demonstrated the Vikings' arrogance toward the peaceable, "cowardly" Sami, who were soon known by the derogatory name "Lapps." They were also seen as competitors for land and provisions, who could conveniently be driven out of their settlements and pastures without putting up any defense. In addition, you could do good business with them, for they had little idea of the actual value of the precious metals and furs they were trading away. As long as they retreated into regions of no economic significance, such as the barren expanses of the Finnmark, allowed themselves to be forcibly converted to Christianity, paid their taxes and didn't rock the boat, they were permitted to stagnate as a disdained but tolerated minority.

Yet it was exactly this trend of pushing the Sami into inhospitable regions where they were only able to survive as nomadic reindeer herdsmen that helped create the distinctive Sami culture as we know it and attempt to protect it today, complete with huts (*gammen*), tents, traditional clothing, reindeer sleds (*akja, pulka*) and skis. Before they commenced their herding life, the Sami were also farmers and fishermen, but they had to give this up when they were forced off of their fields and away from the coasts. They were therefore compelled to base their whole lifestyle, diet and rhythm on the single domestic animal that remained to them: the reindeer. Any part of these beasts that wasn't actually edible could be used to make clothing and equipment. Another source of raw materials was the barren forest tundra with its dwarf birches, mosses and stones. The only luxury was the few sheep which provided the wool the Sami used to weave their clothes, decorative bands and caps. The four points of this traditional headgear represent the four cardinal points and the Sami's freedom to move in any of these that they please.

The policy of pushing the Sami out of mainstream society didn't begin to lighten up until the beginning of the 20th century. With the best of intentions, but altogether misguidedly, the state began to heap its social benefits upon the tribes in an attempt to "civilize" them in the manner of good-natured colonial rulers.

Not until after World War II did people start to realize that the old Sami culture could only be preserved "from within" – especially the distinctive Finno-Ugric language – and that Sami traditions were an important element of Scandinavian life as a whole. It was then that people began setting up Sami schools and cultural centers, and the state began to provide supplementary incomes, grants and scholarships. Since 1990, there's been a "Sami Parliament" in Karasjok, which, however, has only an advisory function. Many Sami have given up their traditional lifestyles and reindeer herds to settle down and compete for the limited number of jobs available in the economically weak region of northern Norway. As a result, a number of new government-subsidized jobs have had to be created in agriculture and forestry in order to keep the Sami in the country. Whether or not this is a way to preserve their culture remains open to question; for their artisan traditions, their sagas and songs (*joik*) and their extensive family clans originally developed out of their nomadic lifestyle. But steady jobs require permanent living spaces; apartments which are usually designed for smaller family units. The problem lies in attempting to integrate a lifestyle which developed out of privation with the "blessings of civilization," which have made themselves felt even among the nomadic Sami in the form of mobile homes, televisions, snowmobiles and cross-country motorcycles.

Today, scarcely more than 2,000 of Norway's 20,000 Sami still practice a "modified" form of their traditional lifestyle, earning most of their income through selling weaving and souvenirs of birchbark, reindeer hide, horn or bone to tourists.

HIKING IN NORWAY

With nearly 20,000 kilometers of marked walking trails, Norway is a hiker's paradise. Some 300 huts, scattered throughout every region of the country, are available to passing hikers. Some of the huts have staff and are veritable mountain hotels; for the unstaffed ones, travelers can pick up the key from the DNT (see p. 245), and they'll also find a full range of provisions. This unique system places a great deal of trust in the strangers who are using the huts.

The Norwegian winter lasts for a long time; ski season lasts into May, and no one should plan on hiking before the end of June. Usually the huts open on the last weekend in June, when all the bridges are operational again. At the beginning of hiking season, however, the water may still be fairly high in the rivers. Depending on the altitude, you can find yourself walking across snow-covered meadows even in summer. The main season, when the huts are most crowded, is mid-July to mid-August. August is seen as an ideal time for walking tours: the rivers are at their lowest, the likelihood of snow is low, and the sun often shines for days on end. In early September, the fall foliage is particularly impressive; the huts close again by the middle of that month.

When planning a tour, Norwegian novices should note that the conditions at 1,000 meters in Norway correspond more or less to those at twice that height in the Alps. Furthermore, the weather is seldom stable in the west and around the fjords; walkers should always take rain gear along, including a good raincoat or poncho and sturdy hiking shoes. Be prepared for rocky paths that demand a good deal of attention; and even if the trails are

Right: The Hurrungane Mountains (between the Kossbu and Fannaråken huts) can be reached from the Sognefjell high road.

marked with red Ts or stick figures, you should never set out without a map and a compass.

A day's hike generally ranges from 4 to 7 hours of walking; so hikers should make sure that they're in adequate physical shape. The lighter your day pack, the easier the walk: women should aim to carry no more than 8 kilograms, men, 10-12 kilograms. This is only possible through careful planning and packing beforehand. Nearly all of the staffed huts have drying rooms, so that you can wash a few things as you go.

Jotunheimen: In this national park, in the center of southern Norway, are the highest mountains in the whole country: the very highest, the Galdhøpiggen, towers to 2,469 meters. This alpine region of Norway boasts more than 150 peaks of more than 2,300 meters, and a number of glaciers; glacier tours are even offered in some areas. The marked trails lead through green mountain valleys, often over scree and gravel, and command imposing views of the majestic peaks.

Hardangervidda: *Vidda* means "expanse," and this seems limitless in Hardangervidda. Europe's largest high plateau is relatively flat; only in the west is it more mountainous, reaching altitudes of up to 1,700 meters. In spite of the relatively low average altitude, however (1,100-1,300 meters), the demands on walkers are still considerable: the treeline is at 900 meters, and the vegetation here is already Arctic.

Time and again, you find yourself crossing small moors and countless streams and little rivers, and it therefore makes sense to don waterproof footwear. The level of precipitation increases markedly as you move from west to east. The Hardangervidda is rich in traces of old hunting cultures and old trading routes, the *Nordmannsslepa*.

Rondane: A popular area with local hikers, this region, located in the eastern part of the country, is blessed with a dry,

stable, sunny climate. Ten mountains here exceed altitudes of 2,000 meters, but they were rounded off in the Ice Age and are therefore relatively easy to ascend. The landscape can get a bit monotonous, with stony trough valleys and moraines, but the myriad lichens that grow here provide splashes of glowing color, especially in the fall. Rondane is a great hiking area for walkers without much experience in Norway.

Trollheimen: North of the Dovre mountains and south of Trondheim is the lovely hiking region of Trollheimen, where a many-faceted landscape provides continually new challenges to the walker, with its abrupt ascents and descents. Especially appealing is the Innerdalen, dominated by the Innerdaltaarnet. Here, climbers come into their own; the DNT also organizes climbing courses (see p. 245).

Setesdalheiene: This varied hiking region lies above the tree line in the extreme south of the country. Setesdalheiene, Sirdaheiene and Suldalsheiene are all names which can be lumped together under the umbrella designation of Rogaland Highlands. As a hiking region, Setesdalheiene is characterized by variety and by a lot of literal ups and downs. Open valleys with lush green meadows are juxtaposed against bare rock cliffs, craggy and sprinkled with many smaller stones. Here, too, are many rivers and lakes, some of them manmade. Hitherto little known beyond the country's borders, this hiking area is easy to reach from Hamburg via Kristiansand; it's also easy on the pocketbook, as most of its huts are "self-catering."

Femundsmarka: A rather quiet area, this region can also be accounted rather "neglected" by foreign walkers. Røros is the best point of entry to this countryside dominated by primeval forests of pine trees. There's regular boat traffic on the lake, so that you can vary the route by breaking up hikes with boat trips. The highest elevation here measures 1,305 meters, but most of the trails are around 800-900 meters high.

Hiking in Norway

237

MIDNIGHT SUN AND NORTHERN LIGHTS

You'll never believe it if you haven't experienced it for yourself. So it is no wonder that the descriptions of the phenomenon of the midnight sun, recounted by early travelers to Scandinavia, fell on skeptical ears when they returned home to central Europe.

And yet the phenomenon itself is easy enough to explain from an astronomical point of view. In the course of a year, the earth travels once around the sun, but the earth's axis isn't vertical in its journey; rather, the globe is tilted at an angle of 23°27'.

What this means is that when it's summer in the northern hemisphere, the "crooked" Earth's northern axis is tilted toward the sun, enabling the sun to shine over the North Pole and onto the side of

Above: Midnight sun over the Lofoten Islands. Right: Solar particles in the atmosphere create the northern lights.

the globe where it would normally be night.

At its peak – that is, on June 21, Midsummer's Eve – it can be seen even at "night" at a latitude as far south of the Pole as the earth's axis is tilted in relation to its orbit. As the North Pole is at 90° and the earth's axis is tilted by 23°27', this point is 66°33'N; this latitude is known as the Arctic Circle, and within it, the sun doesn't set on Midsummer's Eve.

The phenomenon of "white nights," when it remains relatively light all night, although the sun isn't actually visible, is evident south of the Arctic Circle up to 50.5°. At the North Pole itself, the 187-day long "Arctic Day" begins on March 21 and lasts until September 23. As the sun then "travels" farther south, it disappears from view as soon as it crosses the Equator, ushering in the 178 days of "Arctic Night."

When the sun finally reaches its southernmost point, it is no longer visible within the limits of the Arctic Circle; this is the winter equinox.

Another typical Arctic phenomenon is the red color of the sun; the lower it appears on the horizon at midnight, the redder it gets. The reason for this is that as the sunlight penetrates the atmosphere of both the "day" and "night" sides of the planet, the short-wave blue and ultraviolet rays are filtered out more strongly than is the case in normal atmospheric penetration.

Another fascinating heavenly manifestation in the polar regions, especially after particularly active sunspot activity, takes the form of colored "veils" of light: the aurora borealis, also known as the Northern Lights, which are evident only on the long, clear arctic nights. In Norway, you can sometimes see the Northern Lights even considerably to the south of the Arctic Circle.

This phenomenon is caused by "solar wind," a current of electrically charged particles that the sun constantly emits. The earth's magnetic field pulls in these particles, which are drawn to the two geomagnetic poles.

There, in the upper levels of the atmosphere, at altitudes of between 70 and 400 kilometers, these solar particles collide with the ionized, electrically charged particles of the earth's atmosphere. In the process, the solar particles' energy is transferred to atoms of the atmosphere, which results in this characteristic light. This light, which moves in continually changing patterns across the sky, ranges from blue-toned, transparent curtains to wavy green veils, sometimes sprinkled with threads of yellow and red; for anyone who has ever seem it, a memorable cosmic fireworks display.

Through the Northern Lights, scientists have also been able to learn more about the exact nature of the solar wind. As the composition of the earth's atmosphere is fairly well known, it's possible to determine, from the nature of the light, the composition of the particles that are colliding with it. Thus the Northern Lights are also a kind of messenger providing information about the inner workings of the sun.

Midnight Sun and Northern Lights

239

METRIC CONVERSION

Metric Unit	US Equivalent
Meter (m)	39.37 in.
Kilometer (km)	0.6241 mi.
Square Meter (sq m)	10.76 sq. ft.
Hectare (ha)	2.471 acres
Square Kilometer (sq km)	0.386 sq. mi.
Kilogram (kg)	2.2 lbs.
Liter (l)	1.05 qt.

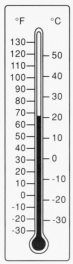

PREPARING FOR YOUR TRIP

Norway in Statistics

Area: 323,878 sq km (Svalbard 62,700 sq km).

Population: 4.3 million.

Population Density: Oslofjord: 118 per sq km; Finnmark: 1.6 per sq km.

Population of Cities: Oslo, 483,400; Bergen, 219,700; Trondheim, 142,900; Stavanger, 103,600; Kristiansand, 68,600; Tromsø, 55,700.

Highest Mountain: Galdhøpiggen (2489 meters).

Form of Government: Constitutional Monarchy.

Location: Western edge of the Scandinavian Peninsula.

Ethnic Makeup: More than 90 percent Norwegian. Large minorities are the Sami (Lapps) and Kvener.

Religion: Followers of the Lutheran State Church, among others.

Language: Norwegian and Finno-Ugric languages of the Sami.

Norwegian Tourist Offices

U.K.: Charles House, 5 Lower Regent St., London SW1Y4LR, tel. (0171) 8392650. **U.S. and Canada**: 655 3rd Avenue, Suite 1810, New York, NY 10017, tel. (212) 9492333.

Entering the Country

To enter Norway, residents of the European Union and affiliated countries only need a valid passport or identity card, which entitles them to entry for up to three months. Anyone traveling from another Scandinavian country doesn't even have to show a passport, since these countries all share a single passport. Children under 16 can be entered in one of their parents' passports, or can have their own passport. Bringing in pets is difficult and requires a six-month quarantine; the punishment for trying to sneak a pet in is stiff, and includes immediate expulsion from the country.

If driving in from another country in the European Union, make sure to have your vehicle registration papers, which are valid in Norway, as well. Inoculations are not generally necessary unless you're coming in from an at-risk area.

Money

Norway's currency is the *krone* (NOK), which is subdivided into 100 *øre*; the smallest coin denomination is the five-øre coin, so cashiers will round up or round down. One US dollar is worth about 7 krone; the pound sterling is worth about 12 krone.

You can bring in as much cash as you like, but taking more than 5,000 krone out of the country is prohibited. Cash machines that take Eurocards and other standard international ATM cards are plentiful. Banks will accept Eurochecks if you show your check card and passport, but they won't always change them into Norwegian krone without an additional commission, generally 25 krone a shot. Personal checks from non-EU countries will probably be more difficult to cash.

Banks will also exchange travelers' checks for a commission. Credit cards are common currency in Norway, especially MasterCard (Eurocard) and Visa; you can use these at any cash machine, even in the smallest villages, as well as at hotels, supermarkets, gas stations, ticket counters, airline offices and even in the hospital.

Health Precautions

Norway's health care system is extensive and extremely efficient. Generally, a sick person or an accident victim will be taken to the emergency room of a *sjukhus* (hospital), rather than to a private doctor. In an emergency, any Norwegian will be able to tell you where the next hospital is.

It's always a good idea to check with your health care provider about travel insurance and coverage abroad before you go. As the names of medicines generally vary from country to country, it's also wise to bring with you any medicines you think you're really going to need. Things like mosquito repellent, however, a necessary aid in Norway's humid forests and moors, are readily available throughout the country.

Climate / When to Go

Because of the Gulf Stream, Norway's average temperatures are 12-15°C higher than those at comparable latitudes in other regions of the globe. The climate, therefore, roughly corresponds to that of northern Germany, rather than Alaska; although there's considerably more precipitation here than in central Europe, thanks to the steady, humid west wind that blows in from the coast. As the country is more

than 1,700 kilometers long from north to south, it goes without saying that there are considerable climatic variations from one end to the other. The weather also changes frequently: a beautiful morning is by no means a promise of a beautiful afternoon, and vice versa.

Norway's peak season begins in May, when spring flowers begin to unfold along the fjords in the southern part of the country; although many roads in the mountains are still completely snowed over this early in the year. By the beginning of June all of the main roads are open; May and June, furthermore, are the driest months of the year. July and August mark the height of travel season, even though by mid-August the midnight sun is no longer visible from the North Cape. During this vacation period, of course, prices are higher, and the hotels tend to be full. It's relatively dry, and still comfortably warm, in September, which is a very nice month to travel if you don't want to venture up into the extreme north. In winter, the main season is between Christmas and the end of January; but since even in the south you're guaranteed snow in the ski areas from late November to April, canny vacationers can take advantage of the slower seasons on either side of this peak time, when prices are lower.

Clothing

In Norway, the most practical approach to dressing is based on the "onion principle," with several lighter layers of clothing that you can put on or peel off as necessary. Always bring a raincoat or anorak; umbrellas are useless in the strong winds along the coast. Outside the city, sturdy shoes are also essential. If you plan to overnight in hostels or simple huts, you should have towels and a sleeping bag. As far as dress codes go, Norwegians are fairly casual; people certainly don't change for lunch or even dinner, unless they're attending some sort of official ceremony or function.

Guidelines

241

TRAVELING TO NORWAY

By Air

SAS and a number of other carriers offer direct flights to Oslo from the rest of Europe. SAS is the only carrier with direct flights from North America; travelers from Australasia have to change in Europe or North America for Oslo service. In summer, there are a few charter connections to other major cities, such as Bergen or Tromsø.

By Train

If you're traveling from England or most other European destinations by train, you have to head for Copenhagen, Denmark and change there for service to Oslo. From Copenhagen, there's a night train with sleeping cars to Oslo that reaches the city in about ten hours.

By Boat

There are a few direct ferry links between Britain and Norway: **Color Line** operates from Newcastle to Stavanger and Bergen; while **P&O Scottish Ferries** offers service from Aberdeen, Scotland to Bergen, as well as from Lerwick, on the Shetland Islands. The Newcastle-Stavanger-Bergen route sometimes calls at Haugesund, as well: the trip to Stavanger takes 21 hours; to Bergen, 25 hours. The Aberdeen-Bergen line is 28.5 hours. Both these lines accommodate cars and motorbikes. If you're coming up from mainland Europe, there's the following service from Denmark: Copenhagen – Oslo (16 hours), Frederikshavn – Oslo (10 hours), Hirthals – Oslo (9 hours), Hansthold – Egersund (7 hours). Other options include Frederikshavn – Larvik (6 hours), Frederikshavn – Moss (9 hours) and Hirthals – Kristiansand (4 hours). Another popular option is the Stena Line ferry from Kiel, Germany, to Göteborg, Sweden, a 14-hour ride; from Göteborg, it's 170 kilometers to the Norwegian border at Svinesund.

By Bus

Bus service links many Europan cities with Oslo. The longest possible route is from Lisbon. For information in Germany, call Deutsche Touring Frankfurt, tel. +49 69/79030.

By Car

Drivers who want to bring their cars into Norway should check out the above ferry connections; all ferry services from the British Isles allow cars as well, but you have to make sure to reserve a place well in advance, particularly if you plan to travel in peak season. If you opt for a less direct route from Britain or are driving up from the Continent, there are a few other alternatives. Ferries run from Harwich to Hamburg and to Hoek van Holland. From Hamburg, the route to Svinesund involves two ferries, Puttgarten – Rødby und Helsingør – Helsingborg; 1 hour and 10 minute crossing.

If you want to start out on Norway's south or west coast, you can also go from Hamburg through Flensburg and Jutland to Frederikshavn, Skagen, Hirtshals or Hanstholm, from where you can catch ferries to Moss, Larvik, and Kristiansand or Egersund/Bergen. If you want to go to Oslo, this route is a good alternative, especially if you can't get confirmation on the more direct Hamburg-Oslo route.

Anyone traveling to Norway in their own vehicle from mid-June to mid-August should be sure to book their ferry passage well in advance!

TRAVELING IN NORWAY

By Car

In general, Norway's driving rules are identical with those throughout central Europe, with a few additional stipulations. Drivers always have to drive with parking lights on; when driving through a town, the driver is absolutely not allowed to smoke; and there are strict limits on permissible levels of alcohol in a driver's blood (0.5 ppm). Speed limits are to be observed at all times, even at night on well-paved expressways; these generally run at 60 kmh in towns, 80 kmh on country roads, and 110 kmh on expressways, unless posted otherwise.

Throughout the country, sheep, cows and reindeer have the absolute right of way. Norway's roads, especially the European or "E" roads, are in very good condition. Because of the scenic beauties the country has to offer, it's often well worth it to use the older, curving *riksveis*.

The emergency road service is called NAF, tel. 22341600. Emergency phones also stand at the ready along major routes.

Some new stretches of roads, especially those that have replaced ferries, and many private roads require tolls (*bompenger*). A toll is also required from everyone driving into the cities of Oslo, Bergen and Trondheim, although there are special tourist subscriptions good for anywhere between one day and one month.

By Train

There are actually only three railway lines in Norway, apart from the access lines from Göteborg and Stockholm to Oslo. There's the Sørland or Southern Line from Oslo to Stavanger, which runs along the south coast with a number of little detours; there's the Bergen Line over the Hardangervidda, with its connection to Flåm, the spectacular and justifiably famous Flåmbanen; and there are the Northern Line and Røros Line, which run through the Lagendal or through the Glåmadal to Trondheim. The trains along this stretch are particularly notable for their comfort and ease. Both lines end in Bodø (Fauske), from where the only way to continue further north is by bus.

Since passenger trains have started using the "ore train" line between Kiruna and Narvik, there's been an additional train connection to Narvik by way of Sweden.

By Bus

Towns that aren't near a railway line are all serviced by buses; the most famous of these is the Fauske – Kirkenes route (*Nord Norge Buss*, 1,260 kilometers). You can break up this trip as often as you like, something that's not true of every long-distance journey. There's also express service between Oslo and the North Cape, which leaves Oslo every day at noon and travels through Sweden and Finnland to reach the North Cape in 34 hours, nonstop. Buses to smaller towns may run only once a day, or even once a week. You can pick up timetables at local tourist offices. There are also special tourist tickets available from the individual bus companies. For information, contact Nor-Way Bussekspress, Karl Johansgate 2, 0154 Oslo 1, tel. 22330190.

By Ferry

Ferries within Norway are accounted a regular part of the road network. Local residents, transport vehicles and commercial buses, as well as taxis, have precedence over other travelers; the latter simply have to line up and wait their turn. You can't make advance reservations for state ferries; but reservations may be necessary for a few smaller, private ferry lines, such as the one that runs on the Lysefjord. The ferries operate on fixed schedules which are posted in every hotel, campground and tourist office and are printed in the NORTRA timetable brochure. Prices depend on the size of a vehicle and the number of passengers.

Fjord Excursions: There are countless boat excursions and tours offered in and around the fjords of Norway. Most of these offers involve points in the south and southwest, but there are certainly opportunities available all the way up to the North Cape. Many of these tours operate according to fixed schedules. You can find timetables with departure times and ticket prices at the Norwegian Tourist Office and individual local tourist offices.

Guidelines

Island-Hopping: There is some kind of boat connection to all 2,000 of Norway's inhabited islands, although frequency of service varies from daily to once a month. Car ferries run to the large islands; the smaller ones may be serviced by passenger ferries or even by private boats. For information, contact local tourist offices.

Telemark Canal: Norway's answer to Sweden's Göta Canal is the Telemark Canal between Skien and Dalen. In its 110 kilometers, the canal takes in 72 meters of vertical ascent over its 18 locks.

Between June 1 and Aug 31, the boat *Victoria* runs 3 times a week in each direction. The trip takes 10 hours; you can get bus transfers to the departure points. For information, contact the Norwegian Tourist Office.

Coastal Routes / *Hurtigrute*: Best-known of the coastal shipping routes, although far from the only one, is the *Hurtigrute*, which runs 2,315 kilometers between Bergen and Kirkenes. Ships depart from Bergen every day at 11 pm and return 11 days later at 2 pm, all year round. Passengers can reserve a place for any stretch between two harbors along the route.

The new, larger ships can also take up to 50 passenger cars. For the most part, you can still spontaneously decide for a day trip, but if you want to travel farther, it's absolutely essential to reserve ahead – as much as a year ahead, in fact, if you want to travel during the peak season .

In addition, there are regional coastal ships that run in summer: from Mosjøen and Sandnessjøen, for example, to the North Cape. These are not quite as comfortable as the *Hurtigrute* ships have become. The Norwegian Tourist Office can give you more detailed information.

Those in search of adventure can ask at the port authorities of individual harbors about the possibility of traveling aboard one of the freighters that travels these waters at irregular intervals.

By Plane

Norway's domestic air network links up more than 50 airports, from the "heart" of the transportation hub Oslo to the "capillaries" of smaller destinations, such as Svolvær on the Lofoten Islands. Service is frequent between the main airports, but decreases by the "capillaries" so that there may only be a single flight a week. The three airlines SAS, Braathens and Widerøe coordinate their timetables, and each accepts tickets from the other.

Rental Cars

The major international car rental companies have offices in the large airports and in all the major cities. You'll need a driver's license, passport and a credit card; without the latter, you'll have to pay a high deposit. The large international companies generally have no problem accommodating travelers who want to drop off the car in a different city than the one in which they picked it up. Because Norway's VAT is so high, prices are generally higher than those in some other parts of Europe. One agency which rents campers and has a large network throughout the country is Touring Norway, which has its central office in Gardermoen, near Oslo, tel. 63978850, fax. 63978822.

PRACTICAL TIPS FROM A - Z

Accommodation

Norway has a wide range of hotels to offer; the one thing they have in common is that they're all relatively expensive. The hotel categories in the *Info* sections of the travel chapters are: ⚫⚫⚫ (luxury; over 1,000 krone), ⚫⚫ (moderate; 350-1,000 krone) and ⚫ (budget; 200-350 krone). Many hotel chains offer check arrangements, which involve a traveler's paying for a certain number of nights before he even gets to Norway. "Summer hotels" tend to be student dormitories rented out during summer vacation; they are generally located somewhat out of town. Huts for hikers come in every permutation from simple "haylofts" to luxurious weekend homes. Cabins can often be rented at campgrounds. Hotels can be booked via the Internet at:

www.norway-booking.no

It is advisable to pre-book your first planned overnight stay, whether at a hotel, hostel, hut or campground, either directly or through a travel agency. The tourist office can provide you with a list of places to stay. Local tourist offices can also arrange accommodation (phone numbers are given in the Info sections).

Hut Rentals: **Den Norske Hyttevormidling**, Postboks 3404 Bjølsen, 0406 Oslo, tel. 22356710; **DNT (Norwegian Mountaineering Association)**, Storgt. 3, 0101 Oslo, tel. 22822822; Fjordhytter, Lille Markeveien 13, 5005 Bergen, tel. 55232028; **Narbo Ferie A/S**, 6410 Midsund, tel. 71278200. **Valdreshytteutleie**, 2900 Fagernes, tel. 61360400.

Alcohol

The only alcoholic beverages that can be sold without restriction in Norway are light beer (*lettøl*) and non-alcoholic wine. Anything stronger (*brennevin*) is subject to state control, and is sold only in *vinmonopolet* shops to people who are demonstrably over the age of 21. *Vinmonopolet* are open weekdays 10 am-5 pm and Saturdays 9 am-1 pm. Licensed restaurants and bars can only serve beer and wine before 3 pm; only after that can you order hard liquor. On Sundays, serving anything hard is prohibited altogether. Furthermore, only very simple drinks are served, although they tend to be twice as large as the European norm. They're also extremely expensive. It is strictly forbidden to sell any alcohol which has been brought into the country as duty-free goods, and the fines for doing so are very high.

One popular beverage is the local "Line Aquavit," a potato and caraway schnapps which is supposed to mature in "moving" sherry barrels, and therefore crosses the Equator (hence the "line" of its name) twice, on board ship.

Banks

There's a fairly high concentration of banks in Norway, but their hours of business in smaller villages can be rather brief: generally weekdays from 8:30 am to 3 pm, and sometimes until 5 pm on Thursdays. Today, there are ATMs or cash machines in virtually every town with a population of more than 200.

Camping

There are more than 1,400 campgrounds in Norway. NORTRA, the Norwegian Tourist Office, can send a listing free of charge on request; this contains details about quality standards and available services, and can also be helpful for non-campers, as it contains such information as the location of rental or full-service huts. Mobile homes and campers are obliged to park in campgrounds; the law of free use that used to govern Norway's countryside in "pre-tourist" days has been scaled down as a result of thoughtless behavior on the part of too many travelers. If you just want to pitch a tent, you can stay for one night on private property if you keep far enough away from any place of residence, don't behave intrusively, and take all your garbage with you when you leave. If you want to stay longer, you have to get permission from the owner. Take note that between April 15 and September 15 it is absolutely forbidden to build open fires outdoors.

Customs Duties

Visitors can only bring in 200 cigarettes or 250 grams of tobacco duty-free, and you have to be at least 16. People over 20 can bring in 1 liter of hard liquor, 1 liter of wine and 2 liters of beer duty-free, and an additional 4 liters of wine or spirits and 10 liters of beer for an additional charge.

There are no restrictions on camera equipment and film.

Bringing in hunting weapons can be rather complicated; the best route is to apply to the agency or person organizing the hunt, who will have to sign the entrance papers in any case. Bringing in any fresh agricultural products such as eggs, meat or vegetables is also prohibited.

Eating and Drinking

The assertion that Norway's main contribution to Europe's culinary culture to date has been the invention of stainless steel is just plain mean. Food in Norway is good, simple and abundant. The real specialty, of course, is fish – salmon, cod, herring, halibut, trout – which appears in many variations on the country's menus and buffet tables. Lamb is ubiquitous; other delicacies include roast reindeer (*rein*) and air-dried mutton (*spekkamat*). Salads are always part of the meal.

Fast-food imports such as pasta and pizza are making their presence increasingly felt in the country's restaurants. One popular dessert is *rømmegrot*, a compote of red fruits served with ice cream or whipped cream.

Geitost is the Norwegian goat cheese; another local cheese, *mysost* is brown, sweetish, and an acquired taste. Fresh water, free of charge, is always served, as is coffee afterwards. Cafeterias generally offer refillable cups of coffee; that is, once you've paid for a cup of coffee you can refill it two or three times. Often, dinner consists of a cold buffet, which is locally known as *kolbord*.

Hotel breakfast buffets consist of a wide range of cold and warm dishes, including cereals, dairy products and fruit. These are meant to be consumed in the dining room, rather than used to prepare lunch to take along with you for the day.

Electricity

Norway's electrical current is the European-standard 220 volts.

Emergencies

Emergency phone number for police: 112; ambulance: 113; fire: 110. These are posted in telephone booths and can be dialled free of charge. Often, a better option is to flag down a passing car, since nearly every Norwegian vehicle, and certainly every bus or truck, has a cell phone or a short-wave radio.

Festivals and Holidays

Church holidays in Norway are identical with Protestant holidays in other European countries; in addition, Norway celebrates Maundy Thursday and New Year's Eve. Secular holidays include May 1 and May 17, the national holiday commemorating the passing of the constitution, and June 23, Midsummer's Day, though not an official holiday.

Local festivals and cultural events have undergone a veritable renaissance in recent years. Each region now seems to have its own special festival, from folk festivals to ones devoted to jazz and rock. Most of these events are held between the end of May (the Bergen Festival) and mid-September (the Lillehammer Jazz Festival). The Norwegian Tourist Office has a calendar of these events which it distributes free of charge.

Fishing

Along the coasts and in the fjords, anyone can fish without a fishing license. For freshwater fishing, however, you will need a permit (*Fiskekort*); these are valid all over the country, and can be obtained at any post office. Fishing equipment has to be disinfected in Norway, and proof of this must be carried with you at all times. During salmon season (June 1-September 15), you need an additional regional fishing license; the tourist offices can give you more information.

Shopping

Opening hours of most large stores are generally from 9 or 10 am to 5 pm from

Monday to Wednesday, 8 pm on Thursday and Friday, and 3 pm on Saturday. Newspaper stands are open on Sundays, as well; these close at 10 pm on weeknights. Many 24-hour gas stations have mini-supermarkets with in-house video rental and souvenir shops.

In TAX FREE shops, foreigners are given a check for the sales tax on any purchase they make of more than 300 NOK; when you leave the country, you get the money back, as long as you have a passport and can demonstrate the object you purchased, still in its store packaging.

Smoking

In Norway, smoking is prohibited in all public buidings, such as train stations, airports, and the like. Some cafeterias in such places do have tables reserved for smokers. In most restaurants, there are separate areas for smokers and non-smokers, but smoking in a hotel dining room where there's a buffet is always prohibited. A pack of cigarettes costs about 40 krone.

Telephones

You can place international calls from all Norwegian telephone booths; sometimes, these are located in specially marked private homes. Card phones are now more common than coin phones; you can buy cards at any telegraph office (which isn't always in the same building as the post office) or, more simply, at gas stations or any other place that sells cigarettes.

Telephoning is relatively cheap; even international calls are cheaper than in many other countries of central Europe, as long as you don't place them from your hotel room. There are no area codes within Norway. Norway's country code is + 47.

Time

Daylight Savings Time in Norway lasts from late March to late October.

ADDRESSES

Camping

Lists of campgrounds are available from **Norges Automobil Forbund**, Storgaten 2-6, 0105 Oslo, tel.22341600.

Airline Offices

SAS Reservation Office, Oslo, tel. 67596050. **Braathens** SAFE, tel. 6759-7000. **Widerøe**, tel. 81001200. **Air Stord**, tel. 53403742.

Tourist Information

Oslo, Vestbahnepl., tel. 22830050. **Bergen**, Torgalmen., tel. 55321480. **Tromsø**, Storgt. 61/63, tel. 77610000. **Trondheim**, Munkegt. 19, tel. 73929400.

Norwegian Embassies

Australia: 17 Hunter St., Yarralumla, Canberra ACT 2600, tel. (06) 273-3444. **Canada**: Royal Bank Center, 90 Sparks St., Suite 532, Ottowa, Ontario, K1P 5B4, tel. (613) 238-6571. **UK**: 25 Belgrave Square, London SW1X 8QD, tel. (0171) 235-7151. **Ireland**: 34 Molesworth St., Dublin 2, tel. (01) 662-1800. **New Zealand**: 61 Molesworth St., Wellington, tel. (04) 4712503. **US**: 2720 34th St. NW, Washington, DC 20008, tel. (202) 333-6000.

GLOSSARY

thank you	*takk*
you're welcome	*vær så god*
good morning	*god morgen*
good day	*god dag*
goodbye	*farvel*
right	*til høyre*
left	*til venstre*
old	*gammel*
new	*ny*
how much does it cost?	*hva koster?*
expensive	*dyr*
today	*i dag*
yesterday	*i går*
doctor	*lege*

Guidelines

dentist . . . . *tannlege*
overnight . . . . *overnatting*

In the Restaurant

eat . . . . *spise*
drink . . . . *drikke*
bill. . . . . *regning*
pay . . . . *betale*
menu . . . . *spiseseddel*
meat . . . . *kjøtt*
beef. . . . . *okse*
pork. . . . . *svin*
lamb. . . . . *lam*
reindeer . . . . *rein*
sausage . . . . *pølse*
fish. . . . . *fisk*
cod . . . . *torsk/skrei*
trout . . . . *ørret*
herring. . . . . *sild*
shrimp . . . . *reke*
vegetables . . . . *grønsaker*
beans. . . . . *bønner*
peas . . . . *erter*
potato . . . . *potet*
lettuce. . . . . *hodesalat*
fruit. . . . . *frukt*
apple . . . . *eple*
pear . . . . *pære*
milk . . . . *melk*
cream. . . . . *fløte*
water . . . . *vann*
bread . . . . *brød*

Driving

slow . . . . *sakte*
prohibited . . . . *forbudt*
closed. . . . . *stengt*
open . . . . *åpen*
exit. . . . . *utkjørsel*
entrance . . . . *innkjørsel*
construction site . . . . . . *veiarbeide*
tow . . . . *ta på slep*
spare part. . . . . *reservedel*
driver's license. . . . . *sertifikat*
tires. . . . . *dekk*
repair shop. . . . . *bilverksted*
gas station . . . . *bensinstasjon*

Miscellaneous

letter . . . . *brev*
stamp. . . . . *frimerke*
post office . . . . *postkontor*
telephone book. . . . . *telefonkatalog*
telephone booth . . . . . *telefonkiosk*
frost. . . . . *frost*
thunderstorm. . . . . *uvær*

Numbers

1 . . . . *en*
2 . . . . *to*
3 . . . . *tre*
4 . . . . *fire*
5 . . . . *fem*
6 . . . . *seks*
7 . . . . *syv*
8 . . . . *åtte*
9 . . . . *ni*
10 . . . . *ti*
11 . . . . *elleve*
12 . . . . *tolv*
13. . . . . *tretten*
14 . . . . *fjorten*
15 . . . . *femten*
16 . . . . *seksten*
17 . . . . *sytten*
18 . . . . *atten*
19 . . . . *nitten*
20 . . . . *tjue*
25 . . . . *tjuefem*
30 . . . . *tretti*
40 . . . . *førti*
50 . . . . *femti*
60 . . . . *seksti*
70 . . . . *sytti*
80 . . . . *åtti*
90 . . . . *nitti*
100. . . . . *hundre*
150 . . . . *hundre og femti*
200 . . . . *to hundre*
1000 . . . . *tusen*

The Norwegian ø corresponds to the German ö: purse your lips to say "ooh," but say "ee" instead; å is sometimes transliterated as "aa"; it's a long, dark a; æ is like the German ä: purse your lips for an "a," and say "ee." Other vowels and consonants generally correspond to English.

AUTHORS

Gerhard Lemmer, Project Editor and main author of this book, is a tour guide. During and after his university studies (sociology, political science, history and art history) he led numerous trips to destinations around the world, until he turned his hobby into a profession in 1983. He visits the "northern perimeter" of Europe several times a year.

Elke Frey is a tour guide who studied geology and geography and turned her interest in exploring new countries and meeting new people into a profession. Her forte is traveling slowly through particularly stunning landscapes, which has made her an expert in regions as dissimilar as Sri Lanka and Norway. She wrote the chapters on "Geography" and "Southern Norway."

Helga Rahe organizes and leads hiking tours in Norway and is the German representative of the Norwegian mountain hiking association DNT. She wrote the feature on "Hiking in Norway."

The authors would like to thank **Michael Endter**, whose friendly and critical assistance was a great help in the preparation of this book.

PHOTOGRAPHERS

Guidelines